KT-593-034

William Collins
An imprint of HarperCollins*Publishers*
77-85 Fulham Palace Road
London W6 8JB

WilliamCollinsBooks.com

First published in Great Britain by William Collins in 2013

Illustrations by Nicolette Caven
Diagrams/plans by Martin Brown

19 18 17 16 15 14 13
11 10 9 8 7 6 5 4 3 2

ISBN 978 0 00 730140 9

A catalogue record for this book is available from the British Library.

Publishing Director: Myles Archibald
Senior Editor: Julia Koppitz
Copy-Editor: Mark Bolland
Picture research: Helen McFarland and Danielle Rhodes
Design and layout: Lucy Sykes-Thompson and Simeon Greenaway
Production Director: Anna Mitchelmore
Colour reproduction by FMG
Printed and bound in Spain by Graficas Estella

Contents

The Building of England

—*Introduction*

Building in England 410–1930

This book is a history of English buildings, although it is intended to be more than that. It is also about the beliefs, ideas and aspirations of the people who commissioned them, built them, lived in them and saw them while going about their daily business. It is about how people discovered new ways of building, both for improved structural performance and for enhanced aesthetic effect. It is about how buildings reflected changing economic circumstances, shifting tastes and fashions. It is about the architectural expression of power, of hierarchy, of influence. It is the history of a nation through what it built.

So this book aims to put building back into the history of England. For some this will be a questionable enterprise because much recent British history is written as the history of the British Isles.[1] Yet we should remember Britain was only created by an Act of Parliament in 1707, although the Crowns of England and Scotland had been united in 1603 and Wales had been incorporated in 1536. Thus, for 1,300 of the 1,520 years that this book spans, England and Scotland, at least, were separate political entities. Although now one country, before 1603 England and Scotland generally looked in different directions – and influences on building in each were markedly distinct. Even after the Act of Union, to take a single example, urban housing in Scotland was based on the tenement and in England on the terrace.[2]

Moreover, through the whole period covered by this book it was rarely if ever only England that was governed from London. If we are to take a wider perspective on the political and cultural context of English history it would be desirable not only to include Scotland, Wales and Ireland but also to include much of France, the Netherlands, Hanover and, latterly, a huge, worldwide empire. All these places brought influences to bear on English building but it is what happened in England that is the focus of this book.

Writing only about England, the danger is of claiming English exceptionalism. Exceptionalism – the assertion that England was and is fundamentally different from other countries – is a strong streak in English historical writing but will not find much of a place in these pages. Whilst I will argue, repeatedly, that English buildings looked different from those in other countries, this makes no stronger claim than suggesting that buildings in Spain, for instance, looked different, too. Perhaps England was, at certain times, more insular than some other countries, but it was always open to external ideas and influences. There is one period, however, in which I will argue for exceptionalism. After 1815 England moved into a position of world dominance that has had no parallel in history. The achievement was unquestionably a British one, but it was one directed from London. For a period that lasted from perhaps the 1830s to the 1920s England was home to building types and categories of places that were to have worldwide influence. This was exceptional and this book will make no apology for that.

(Above) St Pancras Station, London. The engine shed of 1866–8 by W. H. Barlow and R. M. Ordish. With a clear span of 240ft and a length of 690ft this was an unprecedented enterprise.

The Problem of English Architecture

Writing a history of English building is fraught with problems, many of which have been inadvertently caused by architectural historians. Architectural history is still too often divorced from mainstream historical research and, with some notable exceptions, has concentrated either on general popular accounts or on a series of questions interesting only to a small circle of people concerned with stylistic analysis.

This latter approach ultimately derives from the work of the Swiss art historian Heinrich Wölfflin, who became Professor of Art History at Berlin University and then at Munich in the first decades of the 20th century. His achievement was to establish a more empirical way of judging art and architecture, and his *Principles of Art History* set out how each artist's personal style existed both within a national style and a period style. The job of the art historian, he suggested, was to disentangle and explain these stylistic strata. From this time onwards the identification of personal, national and period styles in architecture – and naming them – has been among the primary activities of architectural historians. With most types of buildings thus categorised, architectural history turned in on itself, spending half a century arguing whether the stylistic categories were correct and whether various architects had been allotted to the most appropriate category.[3]

My late friend Giles Worsley, writing in his excellent book *Classical Architecture in Britain*, opens a chapter with two questions: 'Was Sir William Chambers a neo-Classical architect? Was Robert Adam a neo-Palladian architect? Convention,' he writes, 'would give a positive answer to the first question and a negative one to the second.'[4] This present book does not set out to address such questions. The problem, as I see it, is that almost every art-historical term has ended up being more of a subject for debate than what it attempts to describe. So, for instance, there is much disagreement about whether 'Norman architecture' or 'Palladian architecture' can really be said to exist.[5]

A closely related problem concerns the assumptions that flow from the identification of a particular style. After deciding when a style begins – an art-historical industry in itself – historians see it growing, maturing and then waning. This view of style has both Darwinian and moralistic overtones. But styles do not have a life cycle and so there is nothing particularly degenerate, late or waning about late Gothic architecture, any more than there is anything immature about early Gothic. Nor is there any reason to assume that things evolve from the simple to the complex or from the small to the large.

These ideas about stylistic development lead to a series of assumptions that have distorted much writing on English architecture. At its root is the problem of determinism; in other words, the temptation to tell the story of English building as if everything that happened was inevitably going to bring about the outcome we see. There are many examples that illustrate this, but here I present just two. The first concerns the search for the origins of the more faithful rendition of classical buildings seen increasingly in England after 1720 and commonly called Palladianism. Knowing how the story ends, historians have given huge weight to a small number of classically correct buildings built by Inigo Jones nearly a hundred years earlier. As a result, everything that was built between 1630 and 1720 is seen in the light of Jones's work. Compared with Jones's buildings, nearly a century of English architecture has been regarded as somehow backward or at least not living up to a standard set by him. The reality is different. Jones's buildings, at the time, were regarded as oddities outside the mainstream and had little impact on building in his lifetime. He did have his day as an influential architect, but only a century after he was dead.[6]

The search for the origins of English buildings designed in a style known as Modern has been even more distorting. Knowing that, after the Second World War, the Modern movement had a significant impact on English building, elements in buildings as early as the 1870s are seized upon as precursors. Although a very small number of mainly foreign architects built Modern buildings in England from the 1920s, these buildings have come to form part of the main

(Right) Somerset House, London. Neo-palladian or neo-Classical? A nicety or a fundamental question?

narrative of English architecture, and the overwhelming mass of other fine and important buildings from the inter-war period is either ignored or deprecated.[7]

The sensible solution is therefore to put to one side stylistic labels, most of which are relatively recent inventions and few of which would have been recognised by those contemporary to what is being labelled, and start again. But as historians need to label things, because that is how they communicate and make sense of the past, an alternative strategy is needed. An answer may lie in a different approach: periodisation.

This is, however, another minefield. Historical periods are, of course, an alternative way of characterising what happened in order to make sense of the past. At one level they are self-explanatory, so people will have an idea about the Iron Age, the Romans, the Saxons and the Normans simply on account of the name (although not everyone can remember in which order they came). British scholars, uniquely in Europe, use royal dynasties to describe periods in their history. Plantagenet, Tudor, Stuart, Georgian and Victorian reflect changes in dynasty but they tell us very little else in historical terms. The fact is that dynastic changes rarely represented moments of meaningful architectural change. Even the most famous and apparently absolute dynastic division in English history, the Norman Conquest of 1066, did not represent an architectural break. It would also be hard to argue that anything architecturally decisive took place in either 1485 or in 1603, two of the most frequently used dynastic-break dates in English history. This, of course, is not to say that changes of monarch might not run parallel to architectural changes. The death of the military-minded Conqueror and the accession of William Rufus; the Restoration of Charles II after the Commonwealth; the accession of Edward VII after the long late Victorian years – all of these led, to a lesser or greater extent, to an outbreak of architectural exuberance.

For the same reason that we have to reject dynastic change as a basis for periodising English building we must also reject a rigid calendrical method. Although the unit of a numbered century is easily comprehended, it makes

(Above) Castle Howard, the breathtaking Yorkshire country house chosen as both the television and film setting of Evelyn Waugh's 1945 novel *Brideshead Revisited*. Nostalgia, fiction and aesthetics combine to give undue architectural influence to such buildings.

even less sense as a basis for explaining things than the period of rule of a family of kings or queens. Nothing particularly significant happened in 1500, 1600 or 1700 – there is no reason why it should have. The challenge is to try and divide up the story of building in England in such a way that each chunk makes better sense of what was happening. Readers will decide whether my divisions have made understanding English building easier or whether they only confuse it. Obviously, I hope that my divisions help to shed light on why things happened.

But, alas, there is another pitfall. Architectural change does not take place evenly across time, geography or building type, so chronological divisions will only ever be a rough guide to what took place. This is particularly problematic in this book, which considers a much broader spectrum of building types than is usual. The study of buildings has long been divided up into the separate analysis of churches, castles, industrial archaeology, engineering, country houses, urban studies and vernacular architecture. Archaeology, of fundamental importance for understanding the built world, exists in an even more discrete enclave. Studying individual building types – or even sub-sets of them – as separate disciplines necessarily limits a discussion on the cross-currents between them; more seriously, it fragments the visual and spatial world in which our ancestors actually lived. Distinct disciplines are certainly important – we need people who have a deep understanding of lap joints in 12th-century timber buildings as much as we need those who can spot the derivation of a particular type of Corinthian capital. But we also need synthesis; someone who tries to link up James Wyatt and James Watt.

Much architectural history of the last thirty years has been preoccupied with the study of the country house, to the exclusion of other building types.

The country house has sometimes been portrayed as a national driver of innovation, and more pages of English architectural history have been devoted to the development of this single building type than to any other – indeed, it has sometimes been claimed as Britain's unique cultural contribution to European art. There are reasons for this, of course, not least the enormous success of the National Trust with, at the time of writing, its four million members. But it must be doubted whether the country house really deserves such lopsided attention. Most of the key developments, in fact, took place in an urban context, as this book will argue.

Another area to gain disproportionate attention is the careers of famous architects. Architectural history has too often been about the study of architects, while the role of patrons has consistently been underestimated. This is, in part, perhaps because architectural history was at first written by architects. Indeed, it was not until very recently – and only in specific cases – that the design and construction of a building were handed over to a design supremo who would relieve the patron of almost all input into the structure. Patrons from Benedict Biscop in the 7th century, through Archbishop Lanfranc in the 11th, Lord Burghley in the 16th to William Beckford in the 18th all exercised decisive design influence over their buildings. Innovation might be laid at the feet of a designer but it is just as likely to have originated from a patron who was better read, more widely travelled, and who had seen and experienced many more different types and styles of building.

Designers of buildings before the 1750s had either risen up through the building and craft trades or had come to design through gentlemanly curiosity. But into the 19th century the size and complexity of building construction demanded a spectrum of skills that these traditional routes did not permit. Three branches emerged – architect, engineer and contractor – and, of these, architects have dominated the history books.[8] Yet builders, engineers and, indeed, manufacturers can all claim credit for having formed the built environment of England after 1800. In fact, architects have rarely been the sole force in the design of a building; perhaps their only period of absolute ascendency was between the mid 1950s and the late 1970s, a period outside the scope of this book.[9]

Excessive interest in famous architects and their oeuvres prevents us from acquiring a rounded picture of what was built and what was important. A good instance of this is the way in which Sir Christopher Wren has come completely to eclipse his contemporaries by having designed palaces, public buildings, churches and cathedrals – the traditional diet of the art historian. Most people have never heard of Wren's brilliant and distinguished contemporaries Edmund Dummer and Michael Richards, both of whom were very considerable designers responsible for works of equal skill and novelty; unfortunately for their posthumous reputations, they built in naval dockyards and military enclaves, and most of their buildings do not survive.[10]

Essentially, no matter how hard we try, architectural history is determined by the accidents of survival; extant buildings will always have a primary claim over the historian's understanding. Archaeology can fill in the gaps and topographical sources can show what things once looked like, but there is no substitute for a surviving structure. In this book I have deliberately chosen as examples buildings that survive. This is to encourage people to go out and see places they perhaps would never otherwise have thought of visiting. But I have not shirked from mentioning, sometimes in depth, important buildings that are now lost. This is because, without them, we cannot understand what happened.

So the task I have set myself is a difficult one and I suspect I have not entirely succeeded. The fact is that writing architectural history, avoiding the pitfalls I have just set out, is complex and raises issues that do not arise in the evaluation of music, painting or literature.[11] The most important and obvious of these is the utility of architecture. A building cannot be understood in isolation from its function and it is not possible to separate its aesthetic effect – or its historical significance – from the function that it fulfils. Similarly, the location of a building cannot be separated from its effect and significance. Most art forms are mobile. Architecture is not, and it can only be comprehended in the context of its surroundings. Third, although new inventions are made in other art forms, such as acrylic paint in fine art or the electric guitar in music, architecture is fundamentally fashioned by developing technology. The invention of the sash window, of plate glass, structural cast iron or reinforced concrete all opened new chapters in architectural aesthetics, performance and functionality. For these reasons, function, locality and technology play a very large role in this book.

Some Big Ideas

Leaving behind some of the problems of this enterprise, I now want to turn to some overarching ideas that affect the whole story I have to tell. They will be covered in more detail in the following chapters, but a few moments' consideration here will, I think, help set the scene.

Let us start with England. It is small. France covers 212,209 square miles; England covers only 50,333. It is on an island but is not itself an island, accounting for 57 per cent of a landmass also occupied by Wales and Scotland. As an offshore island, on the edge of a continent, Britain has an extraordinarily rich geology. Pumped, pummelled and folded by tectonic activity for three billion years, it has a variety of underlying strata not found on a great landmass. A traveller across the United States might go for hundreds of miles before noting a change in scenery; in most parts of England changes come thick and fast, influenced by over seven hundred types of soil and their underlying geology. England is the most fertile and easily cultivated part of Britain: only 13 per cent of its land is upland (i.e. over 600ft); in Wales and in Scotland the figures are 42 per cent and 48 per cent respectively. Yet England itself is divided into lowlands and uplands by a line that runs between Teesmouth and Torquay. This is a fundamental determining factor in both agriculture and building. In general terms, in the lowlands farming is arable and in the uplands liveli-

(Above) The Customs House, King's Lynn, Norfolk – a building for merchants, built by merchants to advance sea trade.

hoods are maintained by grazing livestock. Upland or lowland, England is an extremely fertile country with a temperate climate, and the successful and innovative practice of agriculture, in a variety of guises, was a crucial factor in its early economic development.

What lay beneath the fertile meadows and ploughed soils later came, perhaps, to be even more important. From the early Middle Ages the presence of flint, slate, limestone, brickearth and millstone grit, to name a few, influenced the form and appearance of man-made structures; but, decisive in England's history, was the exploitation of clay, salt, metal ores and, particularly, huge amounts of coal. It was coal, extracted at first for the domestic needs of Londoners but later to power industrial production, that was first to transform Britain and then the world.

The geographic and geological distinctiveness of England, the individuality of its regional building traditions and the diversity of its economy make it hard to write a history of English building. Some recent books have acknowledged this, taking a regional approach and declining to paint a national picture.[12] This is welcome, as generalisations about change in any one period in any one place are almost certain to be compromised by examples taken from other parts of the country. Yet it is possible to paint a national picture and desirable to do so. This book relies on the fact that the diversity of building in England means that although national generalisations might not be quite right, they are equally likely not to be completely wrong.

The Roman historian Tacitus wrote of Britain that 'nowhere does the sea hold wider sway . . . in its ebb and flow, [it] is not held by the coast, but passes deep inland and winds about, pushing in among highlands and mountains, as if in its own domain.' It was up Britain's rivers that attackers came, from the Vikings to the Dutch, and down those same rivers developed the trade that gradually placed them at the centre of a worldwide network of waterways. The seas around Britain were, of course, a major deterrent to potential invaders; although there were waterborne assaults on England after 1066, none was successful in taking England in battle. This fact is fundamental to England's history as, unlike all of its European rivals, it was not continually overrun by adjacent states. Its boundaries, even those with Scotland, were fixed from an early date, giving it territorial stability and helping to establish itself as a nation state before 1066.

During the Middle Ages the sense of national identity grew strongly, but the Reformation significantly intensified nationalism, characterising Catholic Europe not only as hostile but as oppressed and poverty-stricken. Protestant England was increasingly seen by its inhabitants as a sort of chosen nation, blessed by God. The Civil War strengthened this underlying culture, and over the following century the idea of individual liberty safeguarded by parliament was added to it. Indeed, from the Viking raids to the First World War, national identity has been shaped by war. In particular, war with France: the Hundred Years' War, the wars after the Reformation, intermittent war through the 18th century, and then the Revolutionary and Napoleonic wars of 1793 to 1815. As well as building and bolstering national self-image, these

(Above left) Rievaulx Abbey, Yorkshire was suppressed in 1538 and sold to the Earl of Rutland. A series of detailed accounts chronicle its partial demolition by the Earl over the following two years.

wars also accelerated social, economic and architectural change. This is a theme that runs throughout this book, which sees 1815 as a decisive moment in the national story. A final victory over France, with the help of its allies, put Britain into an unassailable position of world power, hurtling it into a century of rapid and fundamental transformation.[13]

Trade was central to this. Being on an island, England had to use the seas in order to trade. It was not unique in being a seafaring nation, but, it was unique in that trade with countries other than Scotland had to be seaborne. If exports were bound for Calais, they might as well be bound for Bordeaux, too – or for that matter Bombay or Buenos Aires. In this way, once Britain had secured the freedom of the seas after its European wars it was in a position to build up a dominating global trading network.

So in terms of fundamentals, England, on a temperate and fertile island, with rich mineral resources, a powerful sense of national destiny and a strong maritime culture, was blessed with a number of advantages. These contributed in some measure to England being a populous country. Changes in its population have also had a fundamental impact on its history and architecture. In particular, relatively rapid population growth in the century before 1300, between the early 1500s and 1650, and then exponential growth after 1760 have had a wide range of important impacts, many of which have determined the narrative in this book.

A central feature of English social structure is the rights and privileges of the individual over the group or over the state. This leads to a particular view of property rights. Nowhere else in Western Europe could an owner dispose of his property with such freedom as in England; everywhere else the proportion that could be freely sold was limited by law and children had some claim over their parents' property. In England, even with primogeniture, which became the rule from the 16th century, it was possible to sell at any time, effectively disinheriting the following generation. So English land and buildings were commodities that could be easily transferred, and all property was purchasable. Individualistic property ownership lies at the heart of the history of English building.

On four occasions in English history property transfer took place on a national scale. The first was the plunder of Anglo-Saxon estates by the Normans, in which the majority of English land changed hands; soon after there was another, less traumatic, transfer – the granting of substantial estates to the Church from the Crown and the aristocracy. By 1200 this had created the skeleton of the medieval landscape, comprising a series of great estates owned by Crown, aristocracy, bishops and abbots, a situation that remained until the 1530s, when Henry VIII triggered a third great shift. The Dissolution of the Monasteries saw a reversal of the process started during the early Middle Ages, secularising the ownership of both rural and urban estates. Despite the disruption of the Civil War and Commonwealth, which saw an assault on the lands of the Crown and bishops, the Dissolution set the scene for the whole of the period up to the First World War. After 1918 came a fourth transfer. The great estates of the aristocracy, now no longer economically beneficial for their owners, were largely, but not completely, dispersed, with ownership transferring to smaller operators and being sold for urban expansion.

In tandem with these major changes in land ownership were cyclical management decisions by landlords. From the Conquest to the First World War, landlords chose either to manage their lands themselves or to rent them out to tenants, depending on which was more profitable. So, for instance, between about 1184 and 1215 landlords took their lands in hand, but after the Black Death – between around 1380 and 1410 – lands were rented out to tenant farmers.

The ordinary English people who were involved on a micro level in these changes in land tenure were, from at least the 13th century, individualists. They were socially and geographically mobile, market-oriented and acquisitive.[14] They exploited the opportunities presented by the redrawing of property ownership and in due course transformed the practice of agriculture, making England the most productive country in Europe per head.

How English Buildings Looked

Explaining how the look of English buildings changed lies at the heart of this book. But it opens up some big questions. Is changing architectural fashion down to individual whim or an expression of something deeper, a physical representation of contemporary society? Do, for instance, Georgian terraced houses, 15th-century parish churches and Victorian town halls in some way express the society in which they were produced? Is architectural innovation generated by craftsmen and designers or requested by kings, bishops, aristocrats or industrialists? Is the appearance of a building driven by its function or does a desire for it to look a certain way come first? Do engineering advances create new styles or do engineers devise ways of facilitating aesthetic effects? These questions will be addressed in the chapters that follow, but there are some general points that need to be made about how English buildings look.

Roman Catholicism was a globalising force, bringing remarkable stability across the whole of Europe from the 5th until the 16th century. There was a unity of ideas that engendered cultural conformity – and this applies to building, as to much else. English medieval building was in the mainstream of European Christian architecture, if distinctive and recognisable. The English monarchy played an important part in this, on a European scale. Starting, perhaps, with Alfred the Great's building of Winchester Cathedral, through Edward the Confessor's and Henry III's Westminster Abbey, and culminating in Henry VII's works of piety, the English monarchy was consistently among the greatest architectural patrons in medieval Christendom.

After the death of Henry VIII, who channelled much Church wealth into his own buildings, English royal building became overshadowed by the architectural efforts of courtiers and eclipsed by the buildings of foreign monarchs. It was only under George IV that the Crown started to build ambitiously again; and then it was the Crown, and not the monarch, for George's work at Windsor Castle and Buckingham Palace was paid for by parliament. Thus, after the Reformation, although architects who worked for the Crown are important in the story of English building, royal buildings themselves seldom are.

In the 16th century, better surviving documentation means that we can begin to understand what people actually thought about architecture. This has led many to see a fundamental change in people's attitudes to building during the Tudor period. However, as this book will argue, John of Gaunt was probably no less interested, or informed, about building in the 1370s than was Henry, Prince of Wales, in the 1610s. Only we know more about Prince Henry's interests as they have been written down. It is thus a fundamental premise of this book that people like to build and the rich, in particular, like to know about building, as it gives them pleasure and status. After all, only really rich people can build really big buildings.[15] Some of the wealthy people significant in the story of English architecture are known as individuals; many are not. One of the important characteristics of English building is the consistently growing class

(Above right) Burghley House, not some misunderstood attempt to imitate foreign buildings or styles but a native way of building.

of wealthy urban merchants, shopkeepers and professionals who demanded new types of building. Their rural counterparts were important, too, in certain periods driving innovation more urgently than the big landowners.

Some patrons travelled and wanted to imitate what they saw abroad; some even sent their architects to learn new foreign techniques. This does not mean that English architecture is just a poor imitation of designs developed elsewhere, neither properly understood nor executed. The old view of Gothic architecture was that it was copied from France, but imperfectly, and that as classical architecture came to be admired the Elizabethans muddled it up and 'got it wrong'. These views underestimate the insular traditions, as well as the inventiveness of English craftsmen and designers. New architectural languages were not simply copied – that was seldom, if ever, the intention. In reality, ideas, motifs and elements were absorbed and recast as new ways of building were being created.[16]

On a number of occasions new architectural languages were imported in a measured form that was then embellished and decorated. This reflects an underlying preference for ornamentation. The severity of Norman Winchester Cathedral (fig. 44), for instance, soon gives way to the exuberance of the nave at Durham Cathedral (fig. 51), something, perhaps, more florid and native, while the introduction of austere classical forms at Longleat House, Wiltshire (p. 212), turns into the encrustations of a house like Wollaton Hall, Nottinghamshire (fig. 195).

So there is a pendulum of taste swinging from austerity, simplicity and minimalism to ornament, colour and exuberance, and then back again. The Norman Conquest swept away the decorated buildings of the late Saxons, generating an architecture of military sobriety; but this gave way, in reaction, to the exuberant buildings of the 12th century. The way the English used Gothic from the 1170s was very austere, but this led to its elaboration and decoration from the 1250s. Simplicity of line and cleanness of form began to return in the 1340s, remaining the accepted language until the 1450s, when it became decorated and exuberant again. Towards the end of the reign of Henry VII and lasting until

(Left) Sudbury Hall, Derbyshire, built by George Vernon 1660–80. The staircase with remarkable carving and breathtaking plasterwork is at the exuberant end of English architectural taste.

around 1530, simplicity and austerity returned before being overwhelmed by the theatre of Henry VIII's court architecture. Then there was a short period of austere classical rigour from the 1550s to the 60s before a riot of Elizabethan and Jacobean decoration commenced. By the 1630s the mood swung back to minimalism, which remained to the Restoration until the richness and inventiveness of Wren, Hawksmoor and Vanbrugh become fashionable. Under the influence of Lord Burlington and his approved architects a more tempered and austere classical architecture then took over until the 1760s, when there was an explosion of decorative styles. The simplicity of the Grecian revival in the 1820s was transformed into the richness and colour of revived Renaissance styles in the 1830s. The purity of Gothic Revivalism in the 1840s then led to a riot of expressiveness of High Victorian Gothic in the 1860s, before a return to the simplification of forms of so-called 'Queen Anne' from the 1870s. This, in turn, gave way to a revival of interest in baroque forms, which itself stimulated a new breed of minimalist modern classicism.

Of course, moderation and excess are not opposites – they can coexist both within architecture and within the human spirit. They are different states of the same mind, not different states of mind. Yet their presence is certainly discernible to a greater or lesser extent through the building history of England. This observation is not a causal analysis nor an explanation of what happened. It is a description of a chain of events. The impulses that caused the pendulum to swing each time are complex and multi-causal – and different for each swing. The reasons that the geometric clarity of early Norman architecture was lost to Decoration are quite different from those that explain the transition from the minimalist classicism of the Restoration to the exuberance of Vanbrugh. Fashion, for that is what these changes are, can change quickly or slowly, but change it does.

'The history of architecture is the history of the world.'[17] It would be tempting to take this remark by the architect A. W. N. Pugin as a conclusion to this book. But what buildings of the past tell us is less important than the way they affect us now. We have today more of the physicality of the past around us than at any previous time. Depending on your point of view, our lives are either imprisoned by the buildings erected by our ancestors or ornamented by them. Thus, for me, it is a remark made by Sir Winston Churchill, in connection with the Houses of Parliament, that captures the significance of the story of English building: 'We shape our buildings and afterwards our buildings shape us.'[18]

The fact that the constructions of our ancestors are inescapable is a profoundly levelling fact. More than anything else, the story told in this book gives the lie to the notion of progress. No mason alive today could create the high vaults over the Henry VII chapel at Westminster Abbey or the spire of Salisbury Cathedral, and no brick maker could fashion the terracotta of the Natural History Museum, London. The computer-driven precision of the contemporary glass-and-steel tower cannot be said to be an absolute advance over the brilliant eye–hand–mind coordination of the pre-modern age.

Indeed, the very notion of progress was alien to the people of England for the first 1,400 years covered by this book. Progress, as an accepted phenomenon, dates from the 18th century. For most of English history people thought in terms of trying to return to a previous, more virtuous, age. Architecture thus also gazed to the past rather than being on some forward trajectory that represented, at each step, an improvement on the previous one. The belief that progress is taking place, that it is inevitable and that it makes people happier and therefore should be pursued is not, I think, borne out by the evidence. There have been good times and bad; some of the bad times were terrible, and some of the good inspiring. Buildings, likewise, have waxed and waned. This book attempts to tell that story.

1— Beginnings: The Collapse of Rome

—410-700

Splendid is this masonry – the fates destroyed it; the strong buildings crashed, the work of giants moulders away. The roofs have fallen, the towers are in ruins, the barred gate is broken.

The End of Rome

In 410, when the Roman army finally left Britain, neither England nor the English existed. The geographical area that is now England was part of the Roman province of Britannia and was occupied by British and Romano-British peoples. It took a long time for England to emerge from the ruins of Britannia. The first real king of England was Athelstan (924–39), who struck his coins with Rex totius Britanniae (King of all Britain). Athelstan inherited a rich, successful, populous kingdom ornamented with churches, cathedrals, monasteries and palaces. So, technically, the history of England's architecture begins in around 900, but to understand how England looked then, and why, we need to start in 410.

This is easier said than done. The evidence is wafer thin – few buildings, a few more manuscripts and a volume of archaeological excavation carried out, not systematically, but where opportunities arose. The result is that the period 410 to 1000 is an incredibly controversial one, with heated debate among archaeologists and historians not only about why things happened, but what happened, and when.

One of the difficulties is that England was at least two and sometimes three different places before 1000. Indeed, Roman Britain itself had culturally been two places: the south and east, which were more Romanised, and the north-west and west, which were less heavily Romanised. Similar distinctions remained in Saxon England, with the Anglo-Saxons and the Vikings making a bigger impact in the south and east than, for example, in Cornwall. The southern parts, particularly Kent, had closer ties with the continent, while Northumbria was more influenced by Ireland. As a result, it is very hard to generalise about England as a whole, but it will be necessary to make some generalisations if any sense is to be made of this complex period.

The Romans were in Britain for an extremely long time – if they had left in the year 2000 they would have arrived in the reign of Queen Elizabeth I. During the centuries of their occupation they built a very great deal: there were over 60 towns, places of administration, justice, manufacture, trade and latterly church administration. Some were large, with populations of 15,000 or more, at least as large as medieval towns such as Norwich. In some areas the countryside was littered with villas and the coast with a messy series of forts. Hadrian's Wall, with its forts and towns, protected the Empire's northern border. Internal

Fig. 1 (right) The Multangular Tower, York. The lower part of this fourteen-sided tower dates from the late 3rd or early 4th century and formed part of the Roman fortress of York. The upper stages were rebuilt and reused in the 13th century. Throughout the early Middle Ages large Roman structures such as this dominated many English towns.

fortifications, too, were mighty. Many towns were walled, and the largest of these, like York, was built almost impregnably in stone (fig. 1).

In 410, in the face of complex problems across the empire and a decline in the importance of Britannia, the Emperor Honorius ordered the remaining units of the Roman army to leave Britain and told the Romano-British to fend for themselves. With the exit of the army came the collapse of Roman state control and its economy. The legions had been responsible for maintaining centralised government with coinage and taxation, laws and the physical infrastructure of roads and fortifications. Their removal exposed what was to become England to the destructive forces of the barbarian world.[1]

The first wave of settlers that came to East Anglia in the first half of the 5th century was from northern Germany. They were farmers attracted by the agricultural potential of England who had little direct experience of the Roman way of life – and even less interest in it. These peoples kept contact with their homelands, moving backwards and forwards, bringing and transferring fashions in everything from weapons to jewellery and, of course, buildings. The newcomers were not especially numerous but were highly successful at establishing themselves, by force, as the landlords of the native British population. So much so that by 600, although the genetic make-up of what is now England was still heavily British, people spoke Anglo-Saxon, worshipped Germanic gods and shared Germanic fashions. A hundred years later there was a sense of emerging Englishness, but not politically, for the land that became England was still divided into a number of small kingdoms, each with its own kings, customs and ambitions (fig. 2).

Many towns had already been in decline before the legions left, but after their departure the collapse was sudden and fundamental. We know that people continued to live in some of them after the Roman administration

Fig. 2 (above) Early Anglo-Saxon England showing the Roman road network and, overlaid in a thicker line, the roads that remained in regular use in the Anglo-Saxon period.

ended – in Colchester, Cirencester, Wroxeter, Carlisle, St Albans. But this was not a continuation of urban life, with civic, social and economic structures. It was life in towns, not town life. This is fundamentally different to what happened in Gaul; there, Roman cities formed the building blocks of Frankish rule. From these places taxes were levied, in them administration was centred, and to them secular and ecclesiastical rulers were attracted. So why were the British Roman towns abandoned?[2]

The walled towns of Roman Britain were generally much larger than those in Gaul, where, in the late Roman period, only the central part was protected. The walls of Winchester or Canterbury, for instance, enclosed the entirety of the settlement and were thus much longer than their continental counterparts (most enclosed around forty hectares). Such places were difficult to defend and expensive to repair. A Roman legion could do both jobs, but after the collapse of Roman authority, mechanisms were simply not in place for this to happen. Towns in Gaul, smaller, and easier to maintain and defend, had a strong afterlife in a way that the English towns did not.

As a result, what happened in Britain after the Romans left was more radical and fundamental than what happened to its nearest Romanised neighbours. In the years after 410 new social and economic structures emerged in which towns played no part – England was now agrarian, localised and small-scale, elites were mobile and there was no market economy.

Yet importantly, the physicality of Rome had not been forgotten. The Northumbrian monk, Bede, England's first historian, writing in 731, tells us that Roman 'cities, forts, bridges and roads' were still visible, while an anonymous contemporary of his wrote a poem about the ruins of Aquae Sulis, modern-day Bath: 'Splendid is this masonry – the fates destroyed it; the strong buildings crashed, the work of giants moulders away. The roofs have fallen, the towers are in ruins, the barred gate is broken.'[3]

As we shall see, in many places the ruins of Roman towns and fortifications dominated the landscape well into the Middle Ages. Roman buildings were, after all, built with iron-hard hydraulic lime mortar; they did not fall down, they needed to be demolished. Parts of the Roman road network survived, too. The Anglo-Saxons appropriated the most important of these as 'royal roads': the former Roman Watling Street, Ermine Street and Foss Way, together with the prehistoric Icknield Way (fig. 2). In addition to these it is known that other roads, such as Dere Street north of Hadrian's Wall, remained in serviceable use.

Bridges were an essential component of the Roman network, too, and it seems some of the most important of these remained intact. Roman bridges at Rochester, Chester, London and Cambridge are likely to have been maintained by the Saxons, and several others were rebuilt in timber.[4] Roads and bridges were not only important factors in the growth of settlements; they helped the movement of building materials. The Roman stone from which the church at Brixworth, Northamptonshire, was built (p. 42), was brought down the Fosse Way and then Watling Street from Leicester 28 miles away.

Even more important than the physical remains of Rome was its intellectual and cultural legacy. With the fall of the political and military empire, Rome entered a new phase as the headquarters of world Christianity and, for educated Anglo-Saxons such as Bede, became the headquarters of the world. For the whole Anglo-Saxon period there was a real sense that the cultural and intellectual capital of England was Rome. The East Anglian king, Raedwald, who was buried in a great ship at Sutton Hoo, Suffolk, in around 624, was surrounded by objects identifying him as much as a Roman ruler as an Anglo-Saxon feast-giver. Julius Caesar was claimed by 8th-century Saxon kings as among their ancestors, and some East Anglian coins even included an image of Romulus and Remus.[5]

This fascination with Rome is a thread that runs through this book. There is a sense in which the history of English architecture until the late 18th century can be explained as a quest to re-create Roman buildings. King Alfred the Great at Winchester (p. 46), William the Conqueror at the White Tower (p. 69), Edward Seymour at Somerset House (p. 280) and Lord Burlington at Chiswick (p. 318) were all trying to achieve the same thing. And it was not just the 18th-century Grand Tourists who went to Rome in person; in Anglo-Saxon England kings, bishops, parish clergy and ordinary people all made the long and dangerous pilgrimage to Rome. In the Leonine City on the edge of Rome was the Schola Saxonum, a lodging house for English pilgrims supported by a tax raised by English kings. England was no provincial outpost; those who had the wealth to commission buildings were not ignorant of the great buildings of the ancients in Rome.[6]

How the Saxons Built

The early Anglo-Saxon world, unlike ours, was not primarily a built one. Special places were normally natural ones: rivers, hills, woods. Indeed, their language had words for circles and curves, but expressing straight lines and right angles was difficult. The natural world therefore played a large role in building. Most churches, for instance, were not aligned by compass point to the east, but were laid out by sighting the sun at sunrise and sunset either on saints' feast days, Easter, or on the spring or autumn equinoxes.[7]

Almost all secular buildings were built of timber; indeed, the Anglo-Saxon verb 'to build' is timbrian, and buildings were getimbro. Timber was not seen as a lower-status material than stone, nor was the skill to use it effectively lesser than that of the mason. Indeed, even in the early Saxon period, the achievements of leading English carpenters were considerable. That English building between the Romans and the Vikings was almost entirely of timber demonstrates that efficient woodland management must have continued after 410, albeit at a local level. This involved cyclically harvesting the underwood (coppicing) but allowing the oaks to grow in longer rotations (between twenty and seventy years). Coppicing provided fuel as well as all the non-structural building timber, including poles for scaffolding. Oaks were selected by carpenters, felled, their branches and bark removed, and then squared up and used for the structure of buildings. Oak was worked green (without being seasoned), the structure tightening up as the timber dried out. The most important woodworking tool was the axe used for cutting and smoothing, but hammers, adzes, boring-bits, chisels, gouges, planes and saws have been excavated from Anglo-Saxon sites. Nails were not used and fastening was by simple joints with timber pegs. The highest-status buildings might also include iron straps, hinges and catches, as ironworking and smithing continued after the Romans left.

Fig. 3 (right) St Peter's, Wearmouth, County Durham. The lowest stage of the tower was built in around 680 and was originally a single-storeyed porch; it was heightened *c.*700 and then again in the later Middle Ages. The remarkable porch, which never had doors, is flanked by cylindrical stone drums probably turned on a lathe like timber balusters. The Saxon nave lies behind the tower; the aisle to the left is 13th century.

Coppicing produced the wattles necessary for certain types of wall construction. Wattling involves a row of upright stakes, the spaces between which are filled by interweaving flexible branches, often rods of hazel, which are then covered with daub, either mud, clay or, in more sophisticated buildings, lime plaster. Roofs were not covered with slate, tile or stone, as was often the case in Roman times, but only with thatch or shingles. The best thatch was made of reed, but most often it was straw or even hay attached with string or hazel rods. Shingles were small, geometric slithers of oak pegged or nailed to the roof structure, more durable than thatch and less prone to catch fire.[8]

Stone building implied infrastructure and organisation. Quarrying, transport and construction require the mobilisation of significant expertise and labour. All this disappeared after 410, and by 600 there can have been few masons left in England. Masonry was re-introduced by Christian missionaries and relied entirely on robbing Roman buildings for a supply of cut stone. It was not only the expertise that was lacking to restart quarrying, but the motivation; the ruins of Rome were a plentiful quarry and most Saxon stone buildings were built close to or among the ruins of Roman sites.[9] Where stone was used in a decorative fashion by the Saxons it was often carved as wood. The right-hand jamb of the archway at the base of the tower at St Peter's, Wearmouth, County Durham, of *c.*680 is a perfect example of the woodcarvers' art translated into stone (fig. 3).

Fundamental to the reintroduction of masonry building was the rediscovery of mortar; without this, stones could only be laid dry on top of each other at a very low height. Excavations at Wearmouth have revealed the earliest example of a post-Roman mortar mixer, a pit for mixing lime mortar with large, rotating paddles. The expertise for constructing this came from Gaul and required limestone to be burnt in a kiln before being mixed with water to form lime mortar.[10]

Where People Lived

In the years after the collapse of Roman rule power did not reside in fixed places – capitals, if you like; it resided with individuals moving from place to place. Leaders principally expressed their status through portable wealth, through personal adornment, through individual prowess and the ability to provide their entourage with great feasts. Places were occupied for short periods so that rulers could receive food-rents from surrounding farmers, feast with their households and move on. Yet the rulers who emerged in England wanted, as much as their Roman predecessors, to create monumental expressions of their power. In the Saxon poem *Beowulf* the heroic struggle between Beowulf and the monster Grendel is set in a spectacular timber banqueting hall, with doors bound with ironwork, and a carved and gilded roof strengthened by iron braces. Quite a number of these halls have now been identified, either by aerial archaeology or by excavation.[11]

Fig. 4 (right) A reconstruction of the royal hall at Yeavering, Northumberland, based on excavations in the 1950s and 60s. Started by King Edwin in the 620s, this great hall and accompanying structures, including a grandstand looking like a Roman theatre, would have been used by the king when he visited the region to feast on food rents owed to him by his subjects.

The only one that can certainly be identified as being royal was the complex of the Northumbrian King Edwin at Yeavering, Northumberland, started in the 620s.[12] There the excavators found a number of halls built in succession after a series of fires. The important point is the size and sophistication of these structures. The hall christened A2, for instance, was 82ft long and 36ft wide, had an entrance in the centre of each long wall, and two internal cross-walls making separate rooms at either end. The main hall was aisled and so was interrupted by supporting posts. The walls were made of planks sunk into a trench, then plastered inside and out. It is very likely that these were painted, and that beams and posts were elaborately carved (fig. 4). This was a building that required craftsmanship, engineering and organised labour, and it is likely that it was built in a tradition that was uninterrupted since the Romans. Roman villas had great halls or barns that are archaeologically almost indistinguishable from Saxon halls such as the one at Yeavering. In fact it is possible that some large Roman timber halls might have remained in use well into the period covered by this chapter. However, although the techniques necessary for their construction were probably essentially Romano-British, their decoration might have owed more to the traditions of their Anglo-Saxon owners.[13]

It was not only kings who built great halls. With royal grants of land, leading nobles also built places as estate centres and for feasting. It is likely that the remains found at Cowdery's Down, Hampshire, are just such an aristocratic settlement dating from the 6th century. Fine timber halls, palisaded enclosures and more humble timber houses were found in a tight-knit plan, demonstrating that the building technology available to kings was also used by the richest landlords. Here, again, the halls and houses owed much to Romano-British building traditions, suggesting continuity of structural techniques.

The places that these individuals chose to make their base, whether as living kings or as corpses, were often ones that had been significant in the Iron Age or earlier. This is the start of a phenomenon that is very strong in England's architectural history, the desire of the powerful to emphasise their legitimacy through references to the past. The locations of both the royal palace at Yeavering and the royal mausoleum at Sutton Hoo were influenced by pre-existing prehistoric settlements and barrows.[14]

This continuity of place seems to have affected lower-status settlements, too. Through the extraordinary upheavals and changes of the period Britain's population had remained fairly static. From the late Roman period to about 700 most people continued to farm the same landscapes that they had farmed from the late Iron Age, in a similar manner, and living in similar buildings.

Fig. 5 (left) A reconstructed 6th-century house at West Stow, Suffolk, based on archaeological excavation. The village contained five such halls strung out along the ridge of the hill, forming the spine of the settlement. A fire would be lit in a hearth in the middle of the single internal room.

Early Anglo-Saxon settlements were not villages in the sense that we would understand today. They were places occupied over a long period by perhaps ten families at most; built structures, all of which were of timber, would be replaced many times. These settlements were very loose, unfenced and unstructured, without streets or apparent geometry. At West Stow, in Suffolk, just such a settlement of the 5th and 6th centuries was excavated in the 1960s. Its inhabitants lived and worked in houses of a type prosaically described by archaeologists as Sunken-Featured Buildings. These were made by digging a rectangular pit over which a timber floor was suspended. Walls were made of planks sunk into the ground, and uprights at each end supported a ridge pole (or poles) that supported a thatch roof. These buildings were ubiquitous in English settlements from the 5th to the 8th centuries and were an Anglo-Saxon import, direct copies of a type of structure found all over northern Europe. In addition to the Sunken-Featured Buildings at West Stow there were larger, sturdier halls, probably for communal use (fig. 5). These bore less resemblance to their continental equivalents and are much more similar to Romano-British houses dating back to the later 1st or 2nd centuries.[15]

The Church before the Vikings

Although, when Pope Gregory sent St Augustine and his missionaries to England in 596, he was sending them to a place he regarded as at 'the end of the world', it was to one that had a Roman heritage. He instructed that bishops be seated in the Roman towns of Canterbury and London; perhaps he thought England was still the urbanised, centralised Roman society that it had once been. It was not. But despite this, Augustine did in fact found a see based on Canterbury, where he built England's first cathedral, possibly on the site of an earlier Roman church. Outside the Roman town he also built a monastery, later to be given his name.

Further cathedrals were to be founded at Rochester and London and, in the 620s, at York. A cathedral is a church that contains the cathedra, or throne, of a bishop; this is, in fact, the only difference between a cathedral and any other sort of large church. In their dioceses bishops were responsible for ordaining priests, consecrating new churches, dealing with clergy discipline, and administering land and finances. As such they were crucial in the conversion of the Anglo-Saxons.

After several faltering starts England had become Christian again by the 680s, and in 664 the Synod of Whitby had settled that the English Church should be modelled on that of Rome rather than the Irish Church. Within a century England was populated by several hundred minsters, that is to say churches with a residential religious establishment, and was divided into seventeen dioceses. Not enough survives of any early Saxon cathedral to say much about it, but several minsters do, and from these we can paint a picture of the first Saxon churches.

Remarkably St Martin's, the very first church of St Augustine and his fellows, survives in Canterbury, incorporating the brick remains of a Roman tomb (fig. 6). This ancient church, possibly first used as a mortuary chapel, though mauled and altered by time, is a powerful and evocative place to visit and is typical of the first places of Christian worship in Saxon England, built in close proximity to prominent Roman sites and constructed out of re-used Roman materials.[16]

St Mary's, Reculver, Kent, now precariously perched on the edge of a cliff, is a more complete example (fig. 7). In 669 King Egbert of Kent founded this minster in the centre of the old Roman fort. Most of the fort has now fallen into the sea and the church is abandoned, but it has been excavated. In plan it has a stubby, rectangular nave with an apsidal (semicircular) chancel lying behind a screen of two columns. On the north and south there are subsidiary rooms, known as porticuses. The apse, which contained a semicircular bench with a separate seat or throne in the middle, was an area set aside for the clergy, who celebrated communion facing their congregation in the nave. It is doubtful that St Mary's could have been erected by Saxon craftsmen, whose architectural tradition, as we have seen, was entirely in timber. The strong likelihood is that St Augustine brought masons with him from Italy who designed and constructed these early Christian churches; a likelihood that is strengthened by their stylistic similarity to the churches of Ravenna in northern Italy and the Alps.[17]

Roman missionaries from Kent took the gospel to Northumbria, where, after the Synod of Whitby, more minsters were founded. The twin foundation of Wearmouth (today Monkwearmouth, 674) and Jarrow (681) is by far the most important of these. Like St Mary's, Reculver, these churches were not designed by native hands. Their founder, Benedict Biscop, who had travelled Europe for sixteen years absorbing the latest ideas for the organisation and construction of monasteries, enlisted Frankish stonemasons and glaziers to construct his monastery in Roman fashion. They took their carts and their

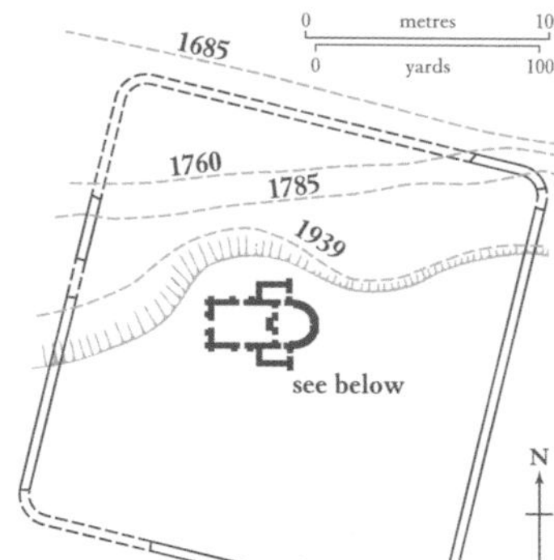

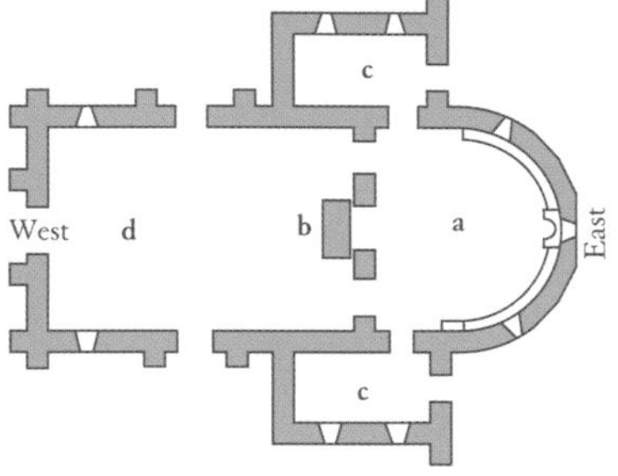

Fig. 6 (left) St Martin's, Canterbury, Kent. A reconstruction of the church of Bertha, Christian queen of King Ethelbert; St Augustine first worshipped here in the 590s. The walls of the present nave are partly Roman and may have originally been part of a tomb chamber. Though significantly altered, St Martin's remains the oldest standing church in England.

Fig. 7 (above) St Mary's, Reculver, Kent, of 669 from an excavation in 1927. The church was built in the middle of the Roman fort out of reclaimed materials. a) apse with bench and throne; b) altar framed by central arch; c) porticus; d) nave.

measuring rods to the Roman forts on Hadrian's Wall and returned with both building materials and construction techniques for the new minsters. Both were thus, in terms of fabric and technique, built in the Roman manner, and their dedications – to St Peter and St Paul, the patron saints of the Roman Church – confirmed that life there was to be based on Rome, too.

Wearmouth and Jarrow have been extensively investigated, and enough remains to demonstrate that the layout of Benedict's buildings was influenced by what he had seen in Gaul and elsewhere. In plan both sites were based on continental monastic models. The churches were long, narrow (their length three times their width) buildings with a western porch. Either side of the nave were lower porticuses or galleries, giving the buildings a basilican appearance (that is to say, a taller nave with lower aisles).

The church at Wearmouth had a narrow, 100ft-long, roofed gallery with glazed windows linking it with the domestic structures (fig. 8).

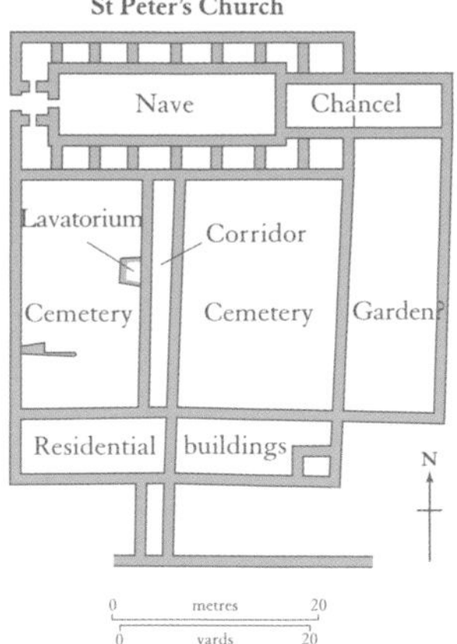

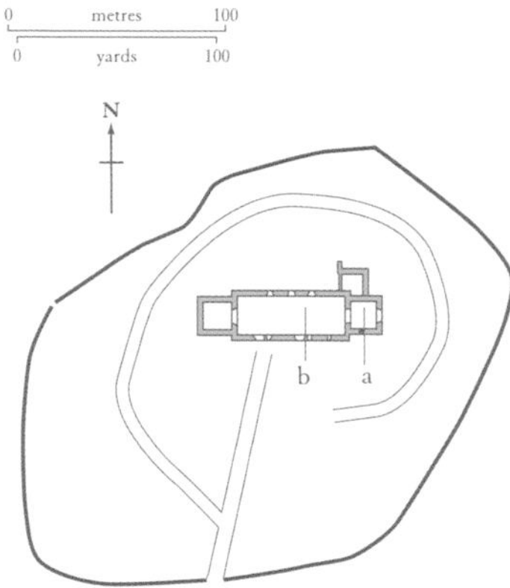

Fig. 8 (top) The Monastery of St Peter's, Wearmouth. Plan based on excavations showing the layout of the latest phase of the Saxon monastery. The church, with its skirting of porticuses, was linked by a corridor crossing the cemetery to the living quarters.

Figs 9 and *10* (above and right) St John the Evangelist, Escomb, County Durham; the most perfect Anglo-Saxon church in England. Massive Roman stones were used in its construction, including what is probably a re-set Roman arch in the chancel. Fragments of stained glass have been found and the windows have grooves for shutters. A patch of cobbled flooring in the nave is probably Saxon. The plan shows its original layout as revealed in excavation in 1968. The walled circular churchyard was a very early addition. a) chancel; b) nave.

This feature, a precursor of the monastic cloister, presumably used for reading, writing and exercise, is a feature Benedict could have seen on his travels. Yet despite all this novelty the church, and particularly the domestic buildings, refectory and dormitory, were very similar to large, secular, timber structures elsewhere in Saxon England. At the royal site of Yeavering, for instance, a timber church was excavated that was virtually identical in plan and size to the Wearmouth and Jarrow churches.[18]

Fig. 11 (above) St Andrew's, Greensted-juxta-Ongar, Essex. In Norway numbers of timber churches survive, but this is the sole early medieval survivor from thousands of such churches in England. While the walls are of the late 11th century, the brick sill on which they sit is of 1848 and the dormers and brick chancel are Tudor. The tower is later too.

Although conceived in a timber-built tradition, these Northumbri churches were among the first to be built in stone since the disappe ance of the Roman legions two hundred years earlier. This is import as stone building was associated by early Saxon Christians with Ror Christianity. When King Nechtan of the Picts accepted the Ron Easter he asked the Northumbrians for advice, not only on liturg issues, but in building churches in masonry 'after the Roman fashion'

A visit to the church of St John at Escomb, County Durham, still con a sense of what the churches at Wearmouth and Jarrow must have been like inside (figs 9–10). This is the best-preserved stone church of the early Saxon period in England, but its chiselled stone walls cannot do justice to what we know of the original interiors. Walls were plastered and painted white, carving was picked out in bright primary colours, the walls were hung with icons and the windows filled with stained glass.

Wearmouth and Jarrow are the only early Saxon monasteries about which anything is known architecturally. We do know, however, that as well as the monasteries of Northumberland and Kent there were many others in the Midlands, the Thames valley and the west. But before about 950 only the largest were of stone; most were still built of timber by people working in local building traditions.

At Greensted-juxta-Ongar, Essex, there is a remarkable survival: St Andrew's is the single surviving Anglo-Saxon timber church in England (fig. 11). Thanks to dendrochronology it is now known that most of its surviving timbers date between 1063 and 1100. Yet this building was constructed in the same way as hundreds of other much earlier examples, somenow revealed through archaeology. The walls were built of split oak logs with their rounded face on the outside and fixed together with concealed timber tongues. These are jointed into timber roof and base (sole) plates, making a rigid wall.[20]

As the Roman legions left the shores of Britain they took with them the know-how and infrastructure necessary to build in stone. For the next two hundred years rich and poor, strong and weak, pagan and Christian lived, worked and worshipped in timber buildings. Some of these were in a long tradition of native building stretching back to the Iron Age; others were introduced by Anglo-Saxon settlers; most were an eclectic blend of Romano-British and Germanic engineering and aesthetics. At the high end these were buildings of considerable sophistication and magnificence; at the lower end buildings of extreme functionality. It was the coming of Christianity that reconnected England with the stone-building traditions of Rome. As a result, English architecture acquired a distinct and vibrant character – a blend of native, timber-based building and stone-built Roman styles. This is what the Viking raiders of the 790s found when they started their systematic plunder of the kingdom of Northumbria. These attacks, and their political and economic effects, set English architecture in important new directions.

2— The Foundations of England

—700-1000

By 1000 it was not only England that existed but also a sense of Englishness among its inhabitants.

Introduction

Before the 10th century England was divided into numbers of small kingdoms that fluctuated in size and influence (fig. 12). Crudely speaking, in the years around 600, the kingdom of Kent was the most powerful of these; in the following century Northumbria was in the lead, and from about 700 Mercia was in the ascendant. Then from 865 until 954 everything was dominated by Scandinavian raiders – the Vikings who at first pillaged and then settled in the north and east. The problems caused by Viking aggression were only resolved by the royal dynasty of Wessex: King Alfred the Great (871–99), his son Edward the Elder (899–924) and his grandson Athelstan (924–39). In 927 Athelstan became the first true king of England, a position he secured with a series of decisive military victories and carefully planned treaties and alliances (fig. 12).

The success of the line of Alfred in uniting England owed much to the struggle against the Vikings. The imperative for defence and buying off the Vikings with cash payments stimulated the mobilisation of manpower on a large scale and the amassing of portable wealth by kings, both vital factors in the development of England and its architecture. Yet the Vikings themselves made little or no lasting contribution to England's architecture.[1] What foreign influences there were came from a much more powerful cultural source – the revival of the Roman Empire in Western Europe.

This revival was political, religious and, ultimately, architectural. Most important politically was the emergence, under Charlemagne (768–814), of a new empire that rivalled, in wealth, organisation and stability, the fallen empire of Rome. Its territories stretched from central Germany to northern Spain and into northern Italy. On Christmas Day 800, at the hands of Pope Leo III, Charlemagne took the title of Emperor of the Romans. This political revival was accompanied by a renewal of the authority and traditions of the Roman Church. In the 750s the Franks adopted the Roman liturgy to replace their Gallic forms; in 779 the payment of tithes to the church was enforced; in 789 all monastic orders were required to conform to the rules of St Benedict; and in 801 it was ordered that altars not containing relics should be demolished, stimulating a huge market in relics primarily from Rome. This represented not some generalised revival, but rather a self-conscious attempt to re-create the Emperor Constantine's heroic age of Christianity.

The political and religious revival of late Rome was accompanied by an architectural one. Under Charlemagne's influence his territories enjoyed one of the most important and creative periods of architectural development in European history. In his reign alone 16 cathedrals and 232 monasteries were

Fig. 12 (above right) Anglo-Saxon England, showing the approximate location of the kingdoms, towns, coastal trading settlements (wics), places mentioned in the text and places that were attacked by the Vikings before 865.

either founded or rebuilt, establishing most of the key components of medieval ecclesiastical design. The style in which these features developed was that of early Christian Rome, epitomised by the basilicas of St Peter and St Paul; a way of building known as the Romanesque. Romanesque is, in fact, not so much a style as an aesthetic programme, the name given to a variety of effects used by architects to re-create more closely and effectively the architecture of ancient Rome. It became possible to do this through advances in building technology, materials and engineering that were stimulated, in their turn, by the peace and prosperity of Carolingian rule. All these developments were important for England.[2]

The Mercian Kingdom

In the 8th century the kingdom of Mercia was dominated by two very powerful and successful kings who controlled most of England south of the River Humber. Ethelbald (716–57) and Offa (757–96) were the first kings able to organise huge labour forces to solve surveying, engineering and construction problems on a national scale. Ethelbald was probably responsible for starting a concerted programme of bridge and road building to improve communications. No Anglo-Saxon bridge now survives – most were probably of timber – but before 1000 a network of bridges carried roads on both local and national routes.[3]

Fig. 13 (above) Offa's Dyke, Clun, Shropshire, a massive piece of military engineering begun soon after 757. It stretched from sea to sea, and for 200 years kept the marauding Welsh out of Mercian England.

Offa is of particular importance as an international figure who corresponded with Charlemagne and was a friend of Pope Hadrian. He is also significant as the builder of Britain's largest monument: the 150-mile-long Offa's Dyke (fig. 13). The dyke was probably constructed to keep Welsh raiders out of Mercia and had 6ft-deep ditches with a 25ft bank behind; the rampart was topped by timber palisading and, in places, stone walls.

Fig. 14 (above) The corner of a tomb chest of *c.*800, probably from the shrine of St Chad, who died in 672. This fragment, found in 2003, shows that Mercian sculptors and architects, like their continental counterparts, were reviving late Roman styles.

Fig. 15 (right) St Wystan's, Repton, Derbyshire. The mausoleum of King Wiglaf of *c.*830. This compact but richly articulated space contained recesses to take the tombs of the Mercian royal family.

Offa was able to mobilise labour for this and for the fortification of towns, marking a major change in the way England's landscape was moulded by the power of the state. Offa's achievements in church building were no less impressive, if only fragments of his churches now survive. Much to the chagrin of Canterbury, Offa used his influence with the Pope to found a new archiepiscopal see at Lichfield. Nothing of Offa's cathedral remains except for a fragment of a contemporary shrine chest associated with the cult of St Chad (fig. 14). This carving, one of the most beautiful and moving to survive from Saxon England, reveals Mercian carvers following Carolingian fashions, reviving the sculptural style of the early Christian Church.[4]

An even more potent expression of Mercian interest in early Roman Christianity is their royal mausoleum at Repton, Derbyshire. The crypt here was first built as a freestanding burial chamber for the kings of Mercia. King Wiglaf, before his death in 839, transformed the chamber from a plain rectangular cellar into a spectacular mausoleum by incorporating it into the chancel of the church and building an internal vault supported by four twisted stone columns based on the most prestigious late Roman Christian monument in Rome: the tomb of St Peter. This daring allusion gave voice to the power of Mercian kings in the language of Carolingian Europe (fig. 15).

More substantial evidence of the Mercian revival of Rome is the church of All Saints', Brixworth, England's most exciting and impressive standing Anglo-Saxon building (fig. 16). The church is big, about 160ft in length, but is now shorn of its 'porticuses', five on each side, which originally flanked the open hall of the nave, rather like aisles in later churches, but subdivided into individual chambers. East of the nave was a separate space, a choir, enclosed by an apsidal sanctuary beneath which was a crypt encircled by an enclosed passageway.[5] The nave arcades are truly massive, their voussoirs made of reused Roman brick; whoever commissioned and designed this church was deliberately and successfully recreating a sense of Roman monumentality, and might have known contemporary Carolingian buildings.[6]

How many such churches existed in Mercia or elsewhere before the Vikings is quite unclear, but it is unlikely that Brixworth, and the major minster excavated at Cirencester, Gloucestershire, were the only two. These structures put architecture in England in the 8th and 9th centuries in the same bracket as some of the most avant-garde structures in Europe.

Fig. 16 (above) All Saints', Brixworth, Northamptonshire. This powerful church (the largest surviving Anglo-Saxon church in England) would have been even more massive before the demolition of its porticuses. The blocked-up ground floor arches along the nave would have originally led into these, just as at St Peter's, Wearmouth (as shown in fig. 8). The tower with its semi-circular staircase projection is probably 10th century.

The Anglo-Saxon Church

The importance of churches to Anglo-Saxon society cannot be overestimated. Whilst kings were mobile, their buildings only occasionally utilised, and their economic effects dispersed, churches were rooted to a single location and thus became centres of economic activity and often, in due course, the kernel of towns. Minster churches also needed land to support them, and Church land, unlike the land owned by aristocrats, was not transferable between generations but held in perpetuity. The amassing of land by the Church contributed to a shift in focus from movable wealth, a feature of Germanic societies, to the idea of permanent land holding, as in Roman times. Land transactions were thus increasingly recorded and legalised, and the landscape divided and packaged.

In addition to landed endowments, often provided by royal or aristocratic patrons, relics, pilgrimages and miracles were the trinity that underpinned the building economy and design of the medieval church. For Saxons, relics had supernatural power. They were placed inside altars, carried into battle, used for solemnising oaths; without them no church was able to function. The more famous the relic, the greater the chance of attracting pilgrims who would make gifts of money at the shrines they visited. But pilgrimage was not only a pious act; it was a visual education for the clergy, builders and the laity. It was the cause of mobility and design exchange, of competition and of rising architectural expectation.[7] Even modest numbers of pilgrims set architectural problems for church designers. People needed to be able to come close to relics in an orderly and controlled way that enabled suitable donations to be made, and satisfaction with the experience to spread by word of mouth.

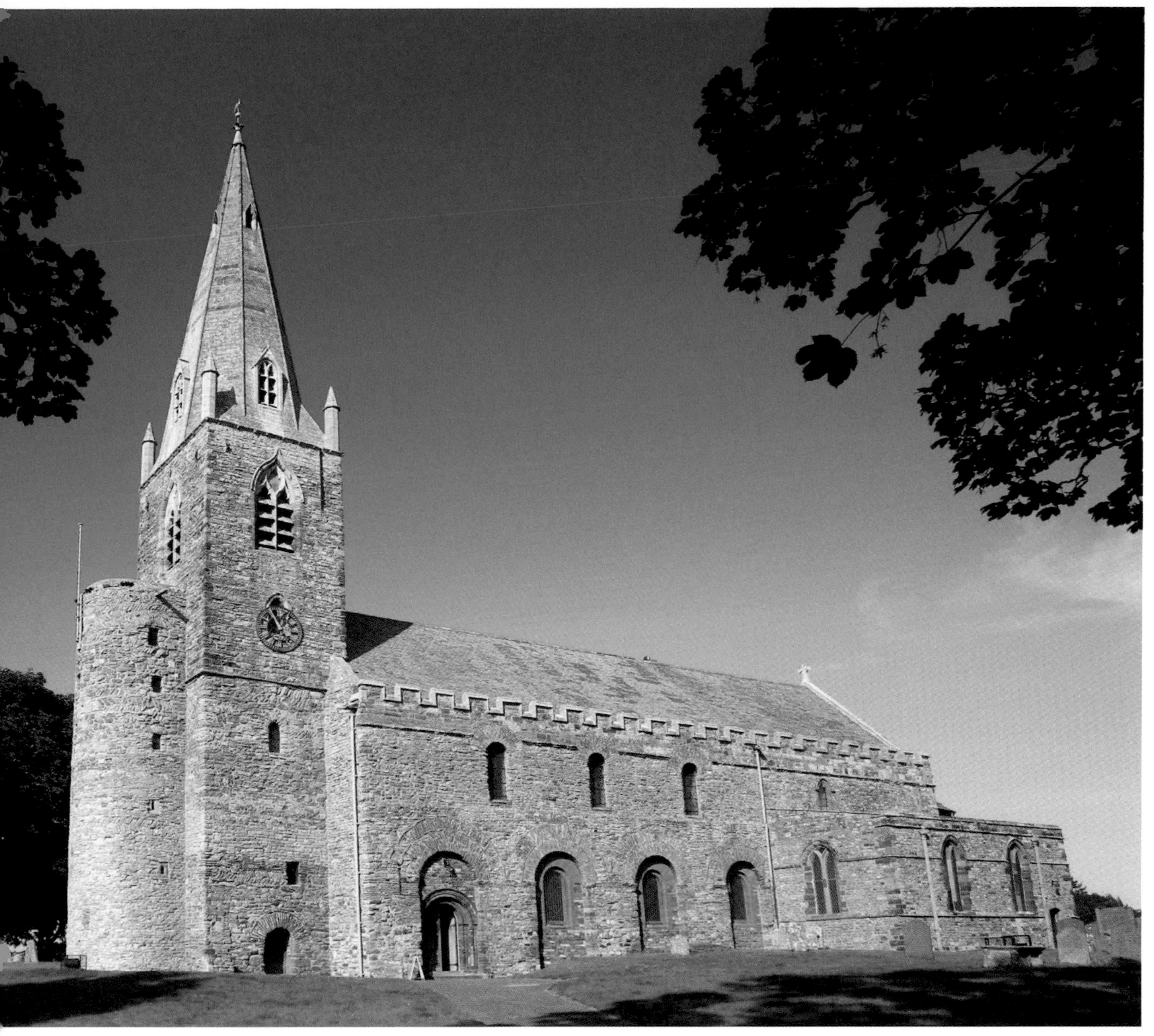

One of the most conspicuous innovations connected with pilgrimage was the crypt, a small underground chamber, normally under the high altar, designed to contain relics. It was the crypt at St Peter's, Rome, that established this feature as an aspiration for any late Saxon church. Brixworth (fig. 16) originally contained a ring crypt that allowed pilgrims to move round the apse, venerating relics, and the mausoleum at Repton was appropriated as a shrine to St Wystan, a royal prince murdered in 849. For this, a new acccss was cut, providing a proper circulation for pilgrims (fig. 15). Visitors to Repton and the surviving Anglo-Saxon crypts at St Andrew's, Hexham, and at Ripon Cathedral can still explore the mysterious and gloomy subterranean circulation designed to lubricate the flow of pilgrims.

If the need to provide access to relics above and below ground was a fundamental factor in the design of the Anglo-Saxon church, so was the Saxon view of the Eucharist. Whilst Christ was obviously the focus for worship, it was the consecrated bread – the host – itself, as a sort of super-relic, that was venerated. Inside chapels the host could be placed on an altar alongside other relics, forming an easily multiplied supernatural focus. Because the moment of consecration was less important than the veneration of the host, Saxon churches were not as focused as later medieval churches on a single altar at the east end. Rather they comprised an assemblage of compartments on several floors, each with its own ritual focus. The most common and flexible of these subdivisions was the porticus, which served as side chapel, tomb chamber, sacristy or viewing chamber. The most important and impressive was the westwork,[8] an enlargement of the west end of a church to provide a location for relics or shrines, a western choir, or occasionally a high-status viewing place (p. 46). These secondary spaces became progressively more important with a rise in the doctrine of purgatory and the appropriation of individual chapels by the rich for prayers to be said on their behalf. They also appealed to aristocratic aesthetic sense, which tended to the more ornamental, decorative and intricate than the big and bold.[9]

Before the 670s Christians did not expect to be buried in or near churches but were buried, like pagans, in cemeteries. By the late 7th century, however, the Church had wrested control of burial rites from friends and neighbours, and started to bury the dead close to Church buildings. Burial within churches themselves remained controversial and was made available only to individuals of the highest status. By 850, however, Christian cemeteries were serving large numbers of ordinary people, taking in land that was increasingly walled or fenced and populated by grave markers.

Monasteries

The Viking raids were devastating for early English monasticism. Whilst some monasteries survived, and some semblance of communal life might have remained, England's former glittering monastic tradition, with its learning, music and patronage of art, was effectively wiped out by the Vikings. The decisive moment in the re-foundation of English monasticism came in 939 when King Edmund (939–946) set up Dunstan as Abbot of Glastonbury Abbey. This was a decisive move because Dunstan's monastery, in line with those in the Carolingian empire, was founded according to the rule of St Benedict and Glastonbury went on to influence the foundation of thirty more Benedictine monasteries in southern England in as many years. At first each of these houses interpreted the rule as it wished, and it was not until King Edgar's monastic reform that a consistent version of the rule of St Benedict was imposed on all the largest and richest minsters by the Regularis Concordia of 973.

Fig. 17 (right) St Mary's, Deerhurst, Gloucestershire; view of the interior looking west. On the ground floor is the Saxon door leading into the tower. Originally above this was a timber gallery – the blocked door that gave access to it can be seen. The corbels in the corners would have supported the gallery. The two pointed windows above looked into the church from a large room in the tower on the other side.

The Concordia put English monasticism on a level with contemporary continental practice. There were, however, some important specifically English provisions. As a concession to English weather, during the winter monks were allowed to have a fire in a warming room and permitted to work inside rather than in the cloister. More overtly political and nationalistic was the fact that the king and queen were to be recognised as patrons and guardians of monasteries, and that they should be prayed for at each of the daily offices bar one.[10]

In the hundred years after the Regularis Concordia kings and aristocrats lavished gifts of land on the monasteries, so much so that by 1066 nearly a sixth of the income of England was held by monasteries in lands and rents. This not only made them a hugely significant economic force but created vast wealth for architectural display. So little remains of any of the thirty or so monasteries reformed in the 10th century that it is hard to generalise about them, but it does seem likely that most of the components of later medieval monasteries were already in place, such as the cloister, refectory, dormitory and warming house. The abbey churches, however, were very different from those that remain today.

Fig. 18 (left) St Andrew's, Nether Wallop, Hampshire. The paintings over the chancel arch are the best preserved Saxon murals in England. They show angels censing a lost figure of Christ. Such paintings would have been commissioned by wealthy patrons, in this case possibly the powerful Godwin family who held land in the area.

Fig. 19 (below and right) Winchester Cathedral, the layout of the Old Minster as recovered by excavation lies next to the later cathedral. Right, isometric diagram and cross section of the Old Minster at Winchester *c.*993–4, as reconstructed by the Winchester research unit based on excavations. The massive western towers – the westwork – probably contained the royal chapel or pew from which a view of the high altar was possible.

A single example of a Mercian minster church, begun in around 804 and re-ordered in around 970, survives at St Mary's, Deerhurst, Gloucestershire (fig. 17). This precious survival, before it was converted to a parish church, was a complex, multi-focused monastic church on a series of levels. At the west end was a four-storied porch containing three upper rooms, the room on the first floor housing a chapel with a deep gallery overlooking the nave. The taller and more impressive room above had two elegant windows giving clear views of the church interior; there was another balcony here, but this one was on the exterior of the west porch, allowing, perhaps, the display of relics to people outside the church. The porticuses to the north and south of the choir were two-storied, their first-floor rooms containing doors leading to an eastern gallery over the choir; the chancel was a polygonal apse also with a room above, with a balcony looking into the church.

St Mary's not only provides the best place to understand the complexity and ingenuity of Anglo-Saxon liturgical space, it also allows us to come closer to an appreciation of the way church interiors originally appeared. The interior of a church like St Mary's was richly painted, not only with figurative murals, but with carving and mouldings painted and decorated with organic patterns.

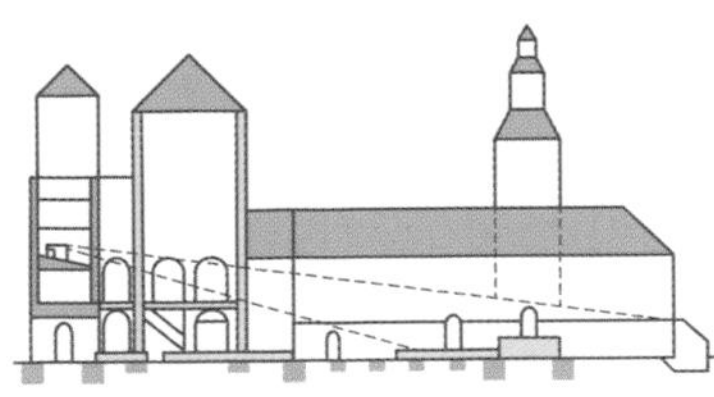

Whilst the surviving figure-work at Deerhurst is very faded, at St Andrew's, Nether Wallop, Hampshire, the lower part of an impressive mural of Christ in majesty survives from about 1000 (fig. 18). This decoration is painted in styles familiar to us from Anglo-Saxon manuscript illumination and decorative art. Whilst painting occasionally survives, very few Anglo-Saxon textiles do, but it is clear that prestigious monasteries and cathedrals, as well as richly endowed minsters and smaller foundations, were hung with textiles, often on the walls. These would have been a backdrop for rich metalwork in gold, silver and wrought iron. Aethelwig, Abbot of Evesham, adorned his church with 'a great many embellishments – chasubles, copes, precious textiles, a large cross and an altar most beautifully worked in gold and silver'. The overall effect of a great Saxon church interior would have been overwhelming. Anglo-Saxon taste was for richness, intricacy, detail and ornament, all of which added to the complexity and disorienting effect of liturgical space: balconies, side chapels, crypts, winding staircases, all painted and hung with textiles, dimly lit by lamps or windows filled with coloured glass, created a sense of mystery that it is impossible to gain from the whitewashed shells that remain.[11]

The residential parts of minsters have all vanished, but, from what we know, they were, like royal buildings, centred on great halls. It is likely that the stone hall, 120ft long, excavated in Northampton and dating from around 860, was part of a minster complex. This is where an abbot would have administered his estates, dispensed justice and entertained.[12]

Bishops and Kings

Early English dioceses were based on Anglo-Saxon kingdoms and, as power and territory ebbed and flowed between them, they were reorganised many times. The Viking incursions provided an opportunity to redraw the diocesan map, and after the 10th century dioceses more or less coincided with the new administrative shires of England (fig. 12). But there was no particular conformity of diocesan organisation; cathedrals were organised in different ways and many, uniquely for England, were also monasteries where the bishop lived his life in a monastic order.

Thanks to painstaking excavation, more is known about Winchester than any other Saxon cathedral. It was arguably the finest building standing in England at the Conquest. By 1066, however, Winchester had already had a cathedral for 418 years; this was the Old Minster, with a cruciform (cross-shaped) plan and a square end. Over the ensuing centuries the cathedral was enlarged and adapted so that by 1000, as well as the nave and high altar, it comprised four towers, three crypts, three apses, at least 24 smaller chapels and a baptistery (fig. 19). Despite strong English characteristics, the Old Minster was, by the time of the Normans, a church with a recognisably Carolingian plan. Most prominent was the westwork – the enormous, tower-like structure erected at

the west end of the cathedral in the 970s. Westworks developed in Carolingian churches in the 9th century and went on to form a component of many great churches in France and Germany built from the 10th to the 12th centuries. At Winchester the huge west towers performed a dual purpose, providing a focus for liturgy and an occasional grandstand for the kings of Wessex to view events in the main church below. Winchester, built next to the royal palace of Wessex and functioning as a dynastic church, might have been exceptional. More typical, perhaps, was the westwork of which fragments, surprisingly, survive at Sherborne Abbey in Dorset. The see of Sherborne was founded in 705 but came to prominence in the 9th century, when two of Alfred the Great's brothers were buried there. Bishop Aelfwold rebuilt and extended the cathedral between 1045 and 1058 in a form heavily influenced by developments in the Carolingian empire (fig. 20). The upper chamber in the west tower contained an apse in which the bishop's throne was positioned, opposite him; at the east end was a three-light window looking down into the main body of the church and before this stood the altar. This arrangement allowed Mass to be celebrated in public view in the upper chamber and distinguished members of the congregation to watch from chambers on either side.[13]

What we learn from Winchester and Sherborne, and from lesser investigations at Wells, Exeter and Rochester, is that Anglo-Saxon cathedrals at the turn of the 10th century were large, complex and sophisticated structures of European stature, but with an external form and internal organisation unique to England.

Bishops were men of considerable wealth, power and standing, and must have occupied magnificent palaces; of these nothing remains, but we do know about high-status royal residential buildings. Alfred the Great's biographer, Asser, writes of him having 'royal halls and chambers marvellously constructed

Fig. 20 (above) Sherborne Cathedral (now Abbey), Dorset. This reconstruction of the cathedral as it was rebuilt under Bishop Aelfwold between 1045 and 1058 shows the massive westwork with its own stubby transepts in which the bishop's throne was situated. The whole church is over 200ft long with an apsidal east end.

Fig. 21 (above right) Timbers from the Thames revetment at Vintner's Place excavated in 1989–91 came from the arcade of a 10th-century hall. Attempts to reconstruct its appearance by its excavators show: a) a cross section of the hall; b) a hypothetical elevation of the arcade (the lowest tier are the timbers that were found) and c) a perspective view of how the roof may have looked.

Fig. 22 (far right) The royal manor of Cheddar in the 9th and 10th centuries showing: a) King Alfred's hall; b) King Alfred's bower; c) unidentified buildings of King Alfred's time; d) 10th-century hall; e) 10th-century chapel; f) 10th-century bower.

a

b

c

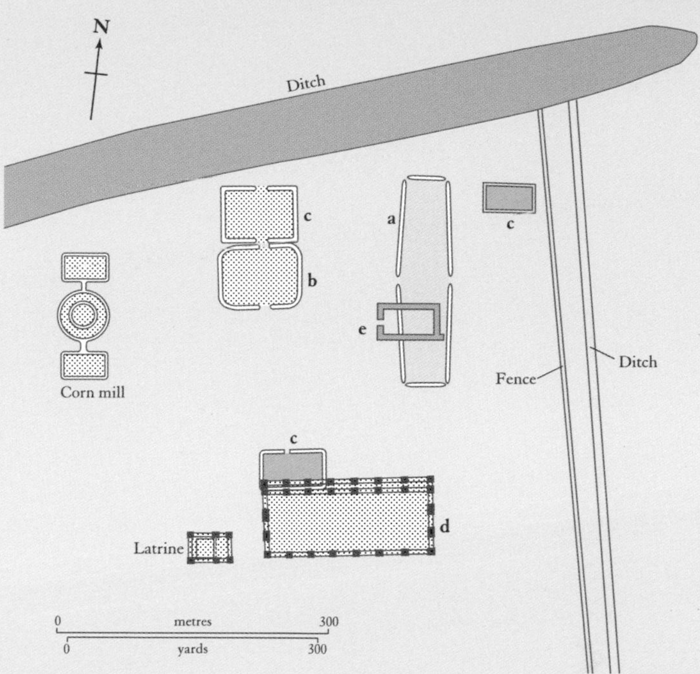

of stone and wood'. Of these, and of other late Saxon royal palaces, the remains of only one have been found. This is at Cheddar in Somerset, where Alfred the Great built a palace next to a large and prosperous minster (fig. 22). The buildings were his personal property and, later, became a favoured royal palace that continued to be used at least up till the time of Henry II.[14]

The buildings were undefended and, like all high-status secular buildings, of timber. The principal structure was a bow-sided hall 76ft long and 18ft wide, with the main room on the first floor; it was entered by doors on its north-east corner and in the middle of its long sides. There were porches immediately inside the doors and at least one staircase leading to the main hall, which was heated by a central hearth towards its south end. Nearby was a separate private building, known at the time as a bower. This was presumably a separate chamber for the king's personal use.

Alfred's sons further developed the site, replacing the original great hall and building a new one, rectangular, with a more regular timber frame and planked walls. On the site of the first hall a stone chapel was built, which was subsequently rebuilt.[15] These were without doubt high-status buildings, so it is particularly unfortunate that their upper parts cannot be recovered; presumably the timberwork would have been of the highest quality, painted and carved. Remarkably, however, the upper parts of a high-status timber arcade, contemporary with the later Saxon buildings at Cheddar, was excavated in London, where it had been reused in a river revetment. These timber components (fig. 21) make up an arcade with ogival arches – not necessary for structural stability but highly decorative. This single find confirms that the upper parts of high-status Saxon buildings were inventively and richly modelled and carved.[16]

Towns

Fig. 23 (above left) King Alfred's burghs as listed in *Burghal Hidage*, a document dating from around 911–14 that calculated the number of men required to defend the town based on its size.

In the two centuries after 700 towns once more emerged as an economic, social and political force. The first to be re-established were a number of coastal emporia that perhaps began as seasonally occupied trading and craft centres (fig. 12). Hamwic (Southampton), Eoforwic (York), Gippeswic (Ipswich) and Lundenwic (London) were not like Roman towns, walled and adorned with civic structures, but they were functional places with a regular layout and a defined economic purpose.

Hamwic was founded, probably by King Ine of Wessex, in about 690. It became the economic engine of his kingdom and covered 111 acres, with a population of about 4,500. Surrounded by a deep ditch, the town was laid out on a regular grid of metalled roads. Buildings lay at right angles to the streets 12ft to 15ft wide and up to 40ft deep, most containing metal, bone and glass workshops. Behind the houses, in yards, were wells and timber-lined pits. The Mercian kings, particularly Aethelbald, similarly developed Saxon London – Lundenwic – after they regained control of it in 733. Sixty Saxon buildings were excavated in Covent Garden, the site of Lundenwic, in the 1990s. They were of timber, with wattle and daub walls, beaten-earth floors and thatch roofs; very few nails were found, showing that these structures were still pegged and jointed. Inside, many had partitions and most had in-built timber benches along their long walls. Most houses had one or more rectangular hearths, some with wattle and daub enclosures.[17]

The Viking raids, which started in the 840s, brought to an end the age of the undefended coastal wics but led directly to a second type of urban settlement, the burghs – 'burgh' meaning 'defended place'. King Alfred's defeat and subsequent peace with the Vikings led to the division of England between the West Saxon kingdom and the Danelaw. In the 880s Alfred populated his kingdom with a network of strategically located fortified places containing craftsmen, tradesmen, markets, minster churches and sometimes royal palaces. A minority of these were re-used Roman sites such as Winchester, Bath and Exeter; a few were recycled Iron Age forts such as Hastings or Chisbury; most were fortified settlements set up around existing successful minsters or small trade centres such as Shaftesbury or Oxford (fig. 23). Alfred's burghs were laid out by highly capable surveyors and engineers expert in road building and the construction of earthwork defences. Some burghs, such as Winchester, had a grid layout, but many developed in a more organic way with winding lanes and alleys. The key feature of these places is that property boundaries were more rigidly defined than in the wics. This was necessary as these towns were owned by landlords in just the same way as the countryside, but with one important difference. In towns it would have been difficult and unnecessary for craftsmen and traders to provide labour services on the landlord's estate, so there was a special form of land holding known as burgage tenure, which allowed men to pay cash rents to their landlord instead. A 'burgage plot' is thus the term for the land owned by a townsman (burgher) for rent and, initially, the term 'borough' described a town in which burgage tenure took place. Saxon towns, such as Oxford and Winchester, would be divided into miniature estates, with an aristocratic house belonging to a rural landowner, burgage plots for his tenants and often a church.

Later Saxon boroughs had many distinctive buildings, whose construction techniques and building types suggest a melting pot of architectural influences. A slightly better class of dwelling developed on the street frontages, with suspended timber floors over a basement or cellar indicating, perhaps, a shop with storage below. On the land behind these were commercial buildings designed for storage or warehousing. These were windowless and sunk some feet into the ground. Higher still up the social scale were the houses of some landlords with substantial timber halls and, in some towns, the halls of craft guilds.[18]

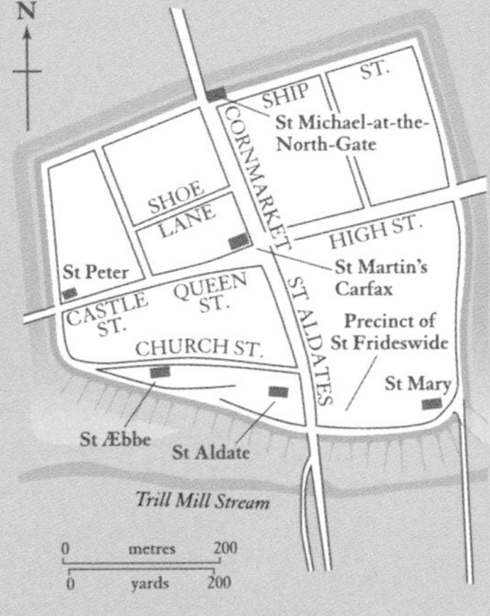

Fig. 24 (above) Anglo-Saxon Oxford showing the principal roads, churches and the area owned by Ealdorman Aethelmaer around the church of St Æbbe.

As well as existing minsters or cathedrals, in most towns new churches were founded by lay landlords for themselves and their burghers. Before 1100 it was relatively easy to found what we would now call a parish church, as church law put few restrictions on the rights and incomes that went with it. As a result three-quarters of all medieval urban parishes were in existence before 1100. So a town such as Stamford, Lincolnshire, which was urban before 925, had fourteen churches, whilst nearby Boston, which only came to prominence in around 1100, had only one. Churches were normally located at the junction of important streets, placing them at the heart of neighbourhood life; they were also frequently associated with marketplaces and, indeed, early churchyards were often used as markets, which were even held on Sundays.[19] Saxon Oxford illustrates these points nicely (fig. 24). In 727 the minster of St Frideswide was founded in what is now Oxford. A settlement and a market grew up around this foundation, and the Mercian kings seem to have built a fort. Alfred chose this place to be one of his burghs, surrounding the existing minster and settlement with earth ramparts. Initially these were supported by great timber posts and planks, but after 1000 they were faced with stone. At the north gate was an impressive five-storey stone tower, part lookout, part guard house, part church tower. In the 10th century Oxford was therefore a stone-walled citadel like its Roman predecessors. Inside the ring of defences a grid of metalled streets was laid out round a cross of main roads. The land was probably granted out to noblemen and part was reserved for a royal palace. One aristocratic owner was Ealdorman Aethelmaer, who had an estate in the south-west corner of the burgh. He had a residence, thirteen burgage plots and built a church – St Aebbe's.[20]

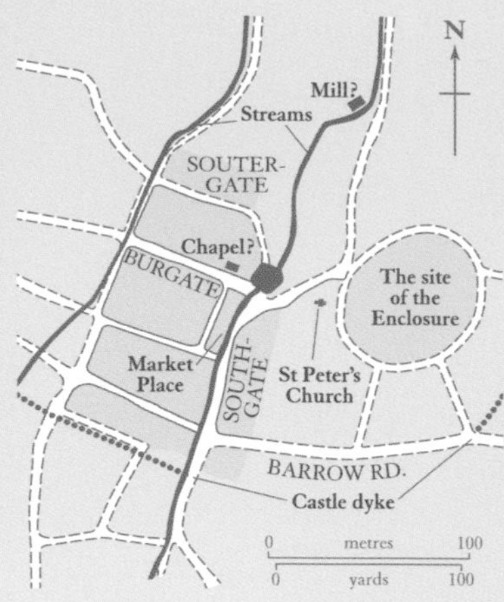

Fig. 25 (above) Anglo-Saxon Barton-upon-Humber, showing the landlord's fortified enclosure with the market place and church at its foot and the grid of streets and burgage plots to the left.

Oxford had several such landlords, with their halls and churches, whilst a small town in the Danelaw, such as Barton-upon-Humber, had only one. At the heart of Barton was the Saxon lord's residence, set in an enclosure fortified by an earth bank and presumably topped with timber ramparts. Located on the Humber estuary, he certainly needed a fortified house – this enclosure might have been the focus of a settlement that was fortified by the Vikings. In any event, next to the manor house the 10th-century occupant of the enclosure constructed St Peter's church. Subsequently, a street, Southgate, separated the church from the town market place; west of this were three blocks of burgage plots probably 35ft to 40ft wide on the street front and 150ft to 170ft deep (fig. 25). Up to a thousand people would have lived in Barton, engaged in agriculture (the town had three large common fields) and craft work. The market would have been at the heart of its economy.[21]

By 1066 there were about 100 towns in England, of which perhaps 17 had a population of more than 1,000. They were not evenly spread across the country, nor were they confined to the West Saxon kingdom, for the Danelaw also developed successful towns such as Norwich, Lincoln and York. These places represented a significant shift in economic activity. In a period of perhaps only a century many craft workers moved production from the countryside to towns; so weavers and potters, who had previously been based close to raw materials in the countryside, were working in tightly packed timber houses crowded into streets and alleys in order to be near their markets.[22] Yet the character of late Saxon towns, even one as important as Oxford, was distinct. Their social make-up and their links with the countryside made them aristocratic rather than mercantile in nature, very different from what they were to become in the following century.

The Countryside

The economic changes that accompanied the Romans' departure resulted in much less grain being grown. There were no legions to provision, no towns to feed and no villas to support. Agriculture slipped back to what it had been in the Iron Age, an activity based around livestock, with grain and other crops

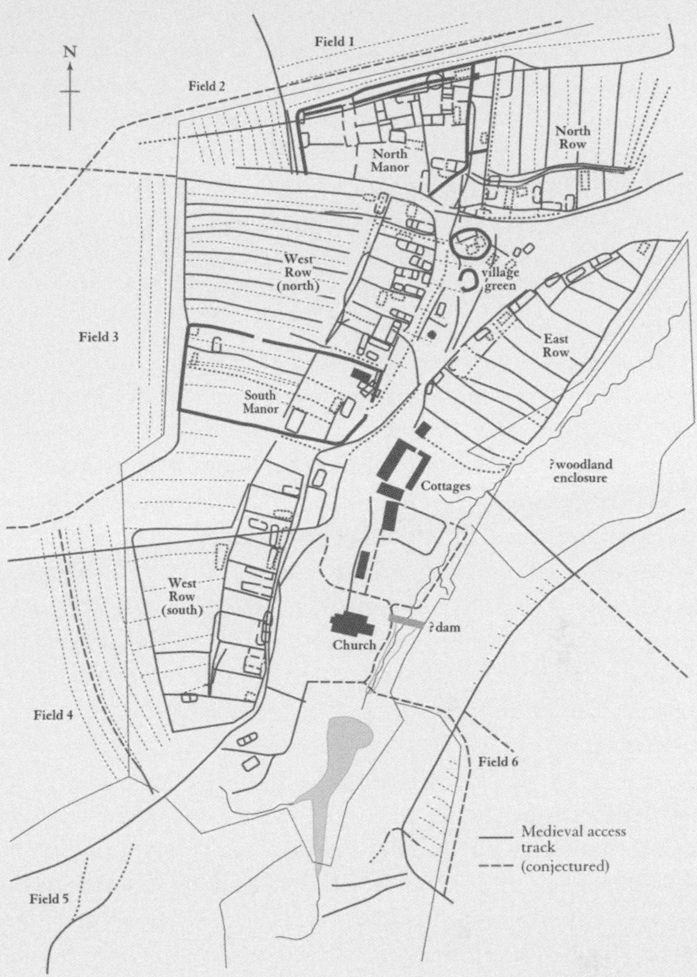

Fig. 26 (above right) Wharram Percy, Yorkshire. Layout of the 10th–11th-century settlement showing the main street with peasants' plots running back to the four big common fields behind. The two manors, church, mill and village green are all shown.

being grown largely for local consumption. The years either side of 700, however, saw a fundamental reorganisation and intensification of agriculture. A great number of settlements, such as West Stow (p. 31), were located on light, easily cultivated soil on river gravels. Around 700 of these settlements relocated to areas of heavier soil to intensify production and meet the demands of secular landlords, ecclesiastical communities in the monasteries and minsters, and the emerging towns. Settlements that had been occupied in the 5th and 6th centuries were almost all abandoned by this time; new settlements became more permanent and organised, with careful layouts and fenced areas for livestock and, importantly, large halls – the houses of the landlords.

Before the 10th century almost everyone lived in scattered settlements of no more than a score of people. But between the 10th and 12th centuries in the central arable areas of England peasant farmers abandoned their farmsteads and hamlets and moved to create villages. These normally had a church, a main street, and between 12 and 60 houses. Outside this central village belt, in the east, the south-east, the north-west and the far south-west, people lived in various types of hamlets or single farmsteads.

The now-deserted village at Wharram Percy, Yorkshire, was laid out in the 10th century by its landlords (fig. 26). The peasants lived in houses set on either side of a main street, at one end of which was a timber church and at the other was the village green with a common animal pound. Two manor houses sat hugger-mugger with the houses of their tenants. Each peasant family had a rectangular embanked enclosure or toft. The tofts normally contained a single peasant house. These houses were divided into two: the larger half with a hearth for the family and, on the other side of a cross passage, a byre for their livestock. The buildings were not materially different from earlier Saxon peasant structures.[23]

There is no single national factor that led to the formation of villages such as Wharram Percy in this period. For many villages the causes were different, even unique, yet there were strong, common centripetal forces. As the density of rural settlement increased and the intensity of farming became greater, the countryside became crowded and complicated to work in landholdings that were shared by a number of family members. At the same time landlords created a kernel around which to group by building themselves large houses and founding churches. At root these changes express a changed attitude to property and land ownership that saw a delineation on the ground – by banks, fences and hedges – to demonstrate who owned what.[24] The village belonged to landlords, and they would divide their land in two: the land worked by peasants, in exchange for cash rents and for labour, and the land farmed by the landlord himself – the demesne. At the centre of this stood the landlord's manor, which originally meant simply a house but later came to mean all the rights and property owned by the lord. Agricultural production in central England was eventually regulated by rules that seem to have developed concurrently with villages. Every household had its own landholding equally dispersed across the village in one or other of the large 'common' fields made up of strips of land (furlongs). Each year one of the two or three common fields would be left fallow and on this would be grazed sheep. The following year the fallow field, enriched by manure from livestock, would be turned over for sowing and one of the others used for grazing the sheep. The principle behind this was twofold: first, when the land was being cropped, it was in sole ownership, but when it lay fallow it was in common use. Second, to achieve common grazing the sheep had to be held communally in a single flock, although they were individually owned. Thus the system relied on close communal cooperation and mutual trust in order to obtain maximum economic benefit. The trust extended to landlords, too, as the demesne lands also benefited from communal flocks.[25]

This system was very successful and contributed to a doubling of England's population to 2.3 million between the time of Alfred and the Domesday survey of 1086. Agriculture yielded a surplus to feed the 10 per cent who now lived in towns, and peasants could pay cash rents to their lords. But, crucially, from the 8th century the common fields system was based on the folding of sheep. The development of breeds with fleeces better than those of the French or the Flemish created England's staple export – wool. Wool was to make England the richest country in Europe, with a strong and stable

Fig. 27 (below) Goltho, Lincolnshire, known to the Saxons as Bullington, where a substantial fortified lordly residence has been excavated with a hall, kitchen and bower (private retreat) as well as weaving sheds where wool from the lord's estates would be turned into cloth. Below, reconstructed section and elevation of the hall at Goltho built *c.*1000–1080.

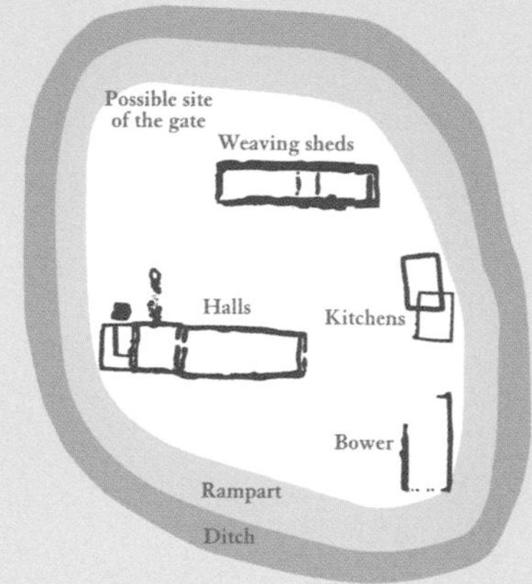

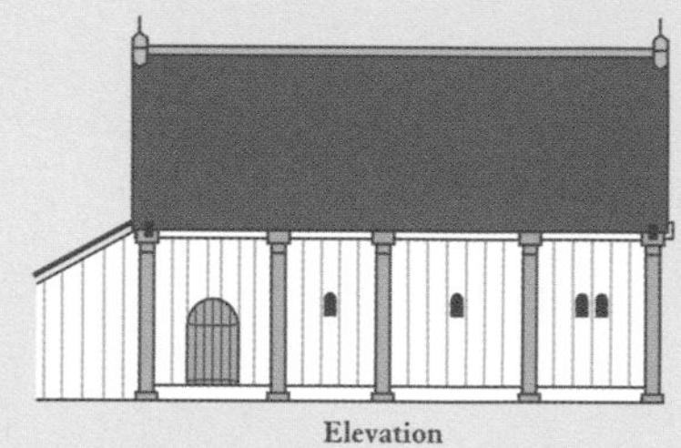

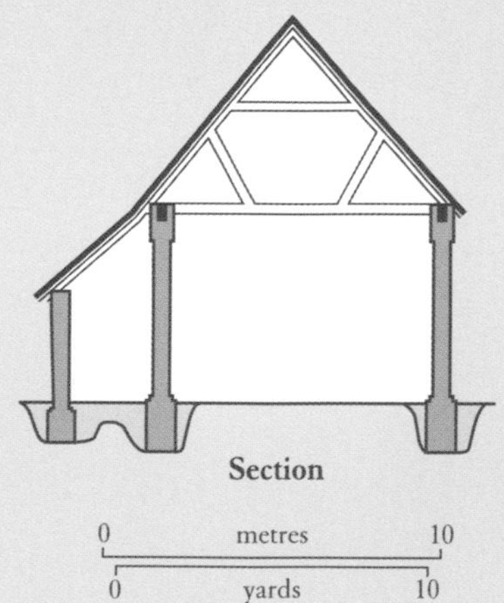

Fig. 28 (right) Portchester, Hampshire. The Roman coastal fort here had probably never been completely abandoned and some parts within the Roman walls had been ploughed and used for crops. During the 10th century a substantial house was built, partly of stone, the residence of a thegn – a man of knightly rank.

silver currency.[26] Much of this wealth flowed into the hands of the landlords, who invested it in building houses and churches for themselves. At Goltho, Lincolnshire, a Saxon lord's residence has been excavated between the church and the village. Goltho was occupied from about 900 until the middle of the 12th century. The excavators found, beneath a Norman castle, a whole series of Saxon buildings belonging to the landlords of Goltho, who knew the place as 'Bullington'. In the late Saxon period there was a great communal hall with a separate residential lodging house next door, a kitchen and several domestic buildings. The whole was surrounded by a deep ditch and a rampart topped with a timber palisade (fig. 27). The use of earthworks and timber palisading was increasingly adopted after 1000. The prehistoric mound at Silbury constructed in the third millennium BC was used in the 1010s and 20s as a fortified residence. Indeed it is possible that many so-called mottes, traditionally dated to the years following 1066, might in fact have been used as fortified residences by Saxon lords.[27]

A few residences were built of stone, as at Portchester Castle, Hampshire. Here, perhaps from the 980s, a lordly residence was constructed within the Roman walls, which stand to this day. A large timber-aisled hall and three smaller timber buildings, a well and a latrine building were arranged around a courtyard with a freestanding stone tower in the corner (fig. 28). Here, as at Goltho, the hall would have been for communal feasting and entertainment, and the smaller halls for the lord and his lady's more intimate use. In the construction of their great halls these fortified residences both used the same structural techniques that had been common since Roman times.[28] But, looking forward, these residences were part of a very important shift from the Saxon concept of communally defended places, such as King Alfred's burghs, to private fortified dwellings.

The great residences did not stand alone. They lay at the centre of agricultural estates and were accompanied by farm buildings, the most important of which was the watermill. This was a significant source of revenue, as tenants were obliged to use their lord's mill and pay a charge for the privilege. By 1086 there were 6,082 mills in England, many of which dated back to the 7th century. The technology was Roman, and it is likely that after 410 watermilling did not die out. The principle was simple: fast-flowing water powered a waterwheel that turned a mill stone on top of another stone. Corn was poured into a hole in the top stone and came out at the sides as meal. The waterwheel could either lie horizontally in the stream or, much more efficiently, be sited vertically. A large and ambitious mill, probably connected to a late 7th-century royal manor house, was excavated at Old Windsor in the 1950s. It had three enormous waterwheels set in a ditch (or leet) 20ft wide and 12ft deep. The leet was cut from a bend in the Thames three-quarters of a mile away. Many much smaller places, such as Wharram Percy (fig. 26), would have had less ambitious mills erected by landlords and used by the whole community.[29]

The Rise of Local Churches

For many Saxon landowners who were planning a village, building a manor house and founding a church would be inextricably entwined as these were all part of an economic, social and religious enterprise. Before the 10th century minsters had dominated the religious landscape, but by the 940s secular lords, with their coffers swelled by profits from their lands, increasingly began to commission their own churches. Many parish churches today have their origins as estate churches of an Anglo-Saxon landlord, which is why many parishes have boundaries that are the same as those of Saxon estates. The remarkably well-preserved church of St Peter, Barton-upon-Humber, Lincolnshire, is one such building. Built originally as an estate church next to a lordly fortified enclosure, it comprised a central tower flanked by a chancel in the east and a baptistery to the west (fig. 31). The chancel and baptistery were two-storeyed, and the tower had three storeys. This was not just a place of worship; it was a symbol of the lord's status, a place for his heir to be baptised.

Fig. 29 (above) All Saints', Earls Barton, Northamptonshire. Like St Peter's, Barton-upon-Humber, the tower of All Saints' is set with a pattern of long thin stones used by the masons both structurally and decoratively as if they were timber beams. As at St Peter's, the rest of the church is of a later date.

All Saints', Earls Barton, Northamptonshire (fig. 29), is another example of a magnificent church conceived and built by a Saxon noble. What is now a parish church originally had its nave on the ground floor of the tower and a small chancel to its east. The floors above the nave are referred to as a belfry; the term today is solely associated with bells but in Middle English it meant something like 'place of security'. This was perhaps where relics, vestments and plate presented to the church by its patron were stored.

Late Saxon stone-built church towers were not only status symbols and strong rooms for their patrons but were also linked to the evolving church liturgy. In the development of parish funeral rites the use of bells became increasingly important. Bells were rung as the body left the church as well as when it reached the graveside, drawing God's attention to the prayers of the faithful and sending the deceased's soul forth to heaven.[30] Some belfries, such as the one at St Peter's, Barton, were topped with timber spires. None of these survives today, but at St Mary's, Sompting, Sussex, the late Saxon spire was rebuilt in the 14th century to the same pattern (fig. 30). Typically, such spires

Fig. 30 (right) St Mary's, Sompting, Sussex. Although this church has a 14th-century spire, it captures the appearance of late Saxon examples. Like both St Peter's, Barton (which would have had such a spire) and All Saints', Earls Barton, stone is used on rubble walls like timber.

were supported by a central mast resting on a horizontal beam on the tower top; they were almost all shingled and had a characteristic shape known as a Rhenish helm. This type of pinnacle, and the central mast construction, link the design of these spires to those of Carolingian Europe.[31]

It is not known how many local churches were built by Saxon lords before the Conquest, but the majority of churches around which the parish system formed were in existence by around 1120. In total they numbered about 6,000 to 7,000 buildings. This was a major change to people's way of life and to the appearance of the countryside. Previously, people had travelled perhaps as far as ten miles to one of approximately 800 minster churches to worship. Now, for most, there was a church in their village or town.

Building Techniques and Materials

As this chapter has demonstrated, building in England begins to diversify and become more complex from the reign of Alfred the Great. This was a process that was driven by richer, better-informed and more powerful patrons.

According to King Alfred's contemporary biographer, the king 'did not cease . . . to instruct . . . all his craftsmen', and King Eadred (946–955) specially went to Abingdon Abbey 'to plan the structure of the buildings for himself. With his own hand he measured all the foundations of the monastery exactly where he decided to raise the walls.' A manuscript from about the 1030s shows Anglo-Saxon craftsmen at work on a complex building (fig. 32), with a spectrum of craftsmen and skills.

Fig. 31 (above) St Peter's, Barton-upon-Humber. The tower and baptistery to its left date from just before 1000. The nave and porch to the right are late 13th-century. The Saxon tower was heightened in the later 11th century; before this date the tower was probably crowned by a timber spire very similar to that at Sompting (fig. 30).

The most important phenomenon must have been the rise of the anonymous (to us) master builder or architect. The Anglo-Saxons used the Latin term *architectus*, not to describe an architect in the modern sense but to describe people with creative responsibility for a structure. Early buildings such as Wearmouth and Jarrow (pp 34–5) could be erected with minimum skill and engineering, but as buildings became more sophisticated masons, carvers and quarry owners became crucial and the designers had a much more onerous task. It would have been impossible to build great churches such as Winchester Cathedral, or even smaller ones such as St Mary's, Sompting, without drawings and small-scale timber models. Drawings might have been on parchment, but equally they might have been etched into large areas of plaster floor expressly laid for the purpose. In the 9th century masonry components began to be cut at the quarry, and so templates must have been made and passed to and fro. Late Saxon builders were still heavily reliant on salvaged Roman stone. St Peter's, Barton-upon-Humber (fig. 31), is typical in that its stone dressings were constructed using blocks of millstone grit possibly taken from the nearby Roman site at Winteringham or from further afield in York. The crypt at Hexham Abbey, Northumberland, contains carved Roman ashlars with inscriptions, and the nearby tower at St Andrew's, Corbridge, contains a reset Roman arch. In towns the ruins of Rome were upstanding and visible, and at Winchester, for instance, provided most of the materials necessary to construct the cathedral. In the late Saxon period it is likely that there were well-organised salvage contractors, perhaps acting under royal licence, deconstructing Roman ruins and selling on the materials for reuse.

Whilst masons were not numerous in early Saxon England, by 900 there must have been hundreds of craftsmen working in stone. The most skilled were re-cutting large Roman ashlars into window heads, balusters and quoins. Most, however, were little more than labourers. Given the relatively small number of stone buildings in Saxon England and the proximity of most to Roman ruins, the quarrying industry remained underdeveloped. Most Saxon quarries were merely shallow diggings producing huge quantities of rough rubble – the most common stone-walling material. Rubble walls could be built with a small number of technicians and a large number of unskilled labourers; such walls also relied on the skills of joiners rather than masons. Rubble was mixed with mortar and shovelled into timber shuttering; a third of the mix was mortar and this had to dry before another layer of rubble mix could be added on top. Sometimes levelling courses were put between layers of rubble, and these were often of Roman brick or tile, or perhaps herringbone masonry. Corners were now and then strengthened and straightened by stone quoins, this being known as long-and-short work. A church tower such as St Katherine's, Little Bardfield, Essex, was entirely built of rubble in diminishing stages. Here not even the window openings had stone dressings.[32]

Most rubble walls were originally plastered inside and out, concealing the original construction method. This provided a canvas for surface decoration as seen at towers such as All Saints', Earls Barton, or St Peter's, Barton-upon-Humber (figs 29 and 31). This decoration, whilst imitating Roman arcades and pilasters, was easily applied and constructed using the principles of joinery. Even the baluster window openings at All Saints' were conceived in the language of wood turning rather than masons' work.[33] Thus the role of carpenters in construction was crucial. They built the shuttering for wall construction and scaffolding as the building rose, in addition to the roofs (many of which were covered in timber shingles), doors, windows, balconies, staircases and other internal fittings. Moreover, the decoration of these structures was imagined in the mind of a carpenter not a mason. Finally, it is vital to acknowledge the increasingly important role of the smith in construction. Smiths were highly valued, largely through their role of arming men in a military society. Yet buildings increasingly demanded both decorative ironwork and more functional bars, cramps and hinges.

Fig. 32 (right) God witnessing the building of the tower of Babel; a manuscript from St Augustine's Monastery, Canterbury, Kent from the second quarter of the 11th century. This is a rare glimpse of Saxon workmen with their tools erecting a complex building (from *The Old English Illustrated Hexateuch*, *c.*1125–50, British Library. Shelfmark: Cotton Claudius B. IV, f. 19).

The Viking raids shook English society and stimulated the growth of the state. First the Mercians, then the West Saxons, mobilised labour and materials to reshape society and the very landscape of England. The country was divided into 32 shires, at least 20 of which took their names from burghs, which became centres of royal power and administration. Beneath these were smaller administrative units: hundreds in the south and west, and wapentakes in the north and east, the focus for justice and tax collection. The only exception was the north, which was only brought into the system after the Norman Conquest.

As the administrative matrix of England was created from above, so parishes formed from below. Instead of holding all the land themselves, kings granted it to their followers, who became the first generation of estate-owning English squires. These men built themselves fortified houses and founded churches and, across much of lowland England, this stimulated the move from dispersed settlements to villages. People's religious focus and loyalty also moved from the minsters to new parishes in both town and country. The sense of identity these changes created is of huge importance; by 1000 it was not only England that existed but also a sense of Englishness among its inhabitants. These were big changes and they were accompanied by important architectural developments. Alongside a timber-building tradition that was part Roman and part Saxon, a vigorous stone tradition developed. In this, before the 1040s, English buildings were eclectic combinations of strong insular traditions, themselves established through a mix of Romano-British and Saxon forms – with influences from Carolingian Europe – producing an architecture that was wholly English.[34]

There was, however, a strong underlying continuity. Although life had become more complex both economically and socially, rich and poor still lived in single-cell dwellings. Peasants, either in villages or in isolated houses or hamlets, lived in a single room in which they would cook, eat and sleep. Although their social and economic superiors had separate structures for communal entertainment, worship and cooking, they also lived in a single room, albeit constructed more robustly and decorated in the current fashion. This fact continued to be the foundation of everyday life for some centuries to come.

Propterea babiloniam contigit uocari ciuitatem. babel. id est hebrei confusionem uocant: de campo quo est sennaar in regione babilonis meminit sibilla dicens: Turris autem altitudo cuius causa diuise sunt lingue. duo milia centum septuaginta. iiii. tenere dicitur passuum: paulatim altitudinis angustior coartata erat. ut pondus imminens facilius sustentaret.

Hanc turrem. nembroth gigas construxit. Qui post confusionem linguarum migrauit inde ad persas. eosque ignem colere docuit.

3— England and Europe

—1000-1130

As the first generation of Normans died out, England's architecture was already looking very different to anything in their former homelands ... they might not have been able to express it in 1130, but the Normans and their architecture were becoming English.

Although King Alfred's dynasty succeeded in forging a single English state, it could not eliminate the threat from foreign predators. As a result, the kingdom was overthrown in the 1010s by the Danes, and from 1019 England became part of a Scandinavian empire ruled by King Cnut and his sons for 26 years. The house of Wessex was only restored in 1042 with the accession of Edward the Confessor. By this date England, as a unified kingdom, was one of the best-developed monarchies in Europe and probably the richest. It had a strong currency and efficient taxation, effective administration, laws and judicial system, more than 100 towns, and was home to some of the largest and most sophisticated buildings in northern Europe.

The conquest of the English state by the Danish kings prefigured the Norman Conquest by half a century. That William of Normandy's success lived on where Cnut's conquest was short-lived was a result of the stability, strength and close proximity of the Norman homeland. Yet for a quarter of a century the cultural orientation of England bent towards Scandinavia, opening the way for architectural and decorative influences. It is sometimes possible to detect these in sculpture and the decorative arts, but harder in architecture. It is likely, though, that the distinctive round towers of parish churches in Norfolk and Suffolk can be connected with missionaries coming from Saxony after the Danish invasions, but this is an isolated example, and the enduring architectural impact of the second Viking era was limited.[1]

Edward the Confessor

The same cannot be said for the reign of Edward the Confessor, who commissioned one of the most influential buildings in English architectural history. Edward's outlook was cosmopolitan. His mother was the daughter of the Count of Normandy and Edward had been brought up in the Norman court for 25 years. Out of a plethora of claimants for the English throne Edward was eventually crowned in 1043 and ruled, with some success, for 23 years. It was soon after his accession that he decided to build a new palace and abbey at Westminster. This was a break with tradition for, as a son of Wessex, Edward had been crowned at Winchester Cathedral, the burial place of his ancestors

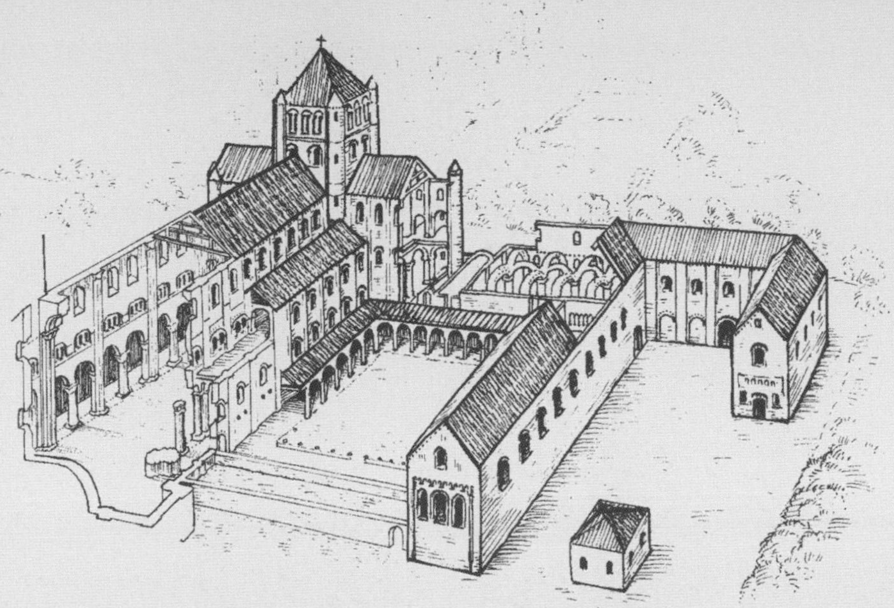

Fig. 33 (above right) Conjectural reconstruction of Edward the Confessor's Westminster Abbey showing in cut-a-way the nave arcades. This was a new way of building in England transforming the three-dimensional experience of internal space.

and his Danish predecessors. By the 1040s, however, London was the most important and populous city in England. It occupied a key defensive position, had the largest mint, was the biggest port, and contributed more in tax than anywhere else. Moreover, its citizens had taken a role in the acclamation of kings, choosing Edmund Ironside in 1016 and Edward himself in 1042. Edward was a realist and he saw that London, not Winchester, was now the key to the kingdom. His new palace and abbey, both built – presumably for security – outside the city, created a powerful royal enclave next to England's commercial and political capital. The thoroughness and scale of the enterprise were startling. The existing minster was entirely demolished, new quarries were opened up at Reigate and craftsmen were assembled from all over England. Building was underway before 1050, but whilst the east end was ready to receive the Confessor's body in 1065 the whole abbey was not completed until about 1080. The abbey church was enormous, about 322ft long, larger than anything built in England since the Romans, and larger than any church in northern Europe at the time. This reflected Edward's wealth and his desire to establish, in London, a royal dynastic centre to rival if not surpass Winchester.[2]

The Confessor's Westminster Abbey sent English architecture in a wholly new direction. The abbey had no direct precedent in England or Normandy, although, across the Channel, the Norman abbey of Jumièges was being constructed in a similar style almost simultaneously. Both the English and the Normans were in fact imitating a way of building invented in Burgundy, and developed there and in the Loire valley in the 1030s and 40s. The essential change was from interiors that relied for their effect on large areas of painted wall surface to spaces that were modelled in three dimensions, with arches, horizontal mouldings (string courses), semicircular shafts, stone vaults and ornamental mouldings. These ideas essentially came from Roman buildings, especially the large and prominent remains of amphitheatres with their tiers of arches and columns.[3]

So the interior of Westminster Abbey was conceived as a spatial whole rather than an agglomeration of small compartments as in Saxon churches (fig. 33). Its walls, which in an earlier Saxon church would have been a solid mass of masonry acting as a vast canvas for painting, now became an organised system of superimposed arches raised in tiers one above the other. The basic principle of the design was that each arch should be visibly supported by a column (or half-column) and a capital. This produced a clustering of vertical shafts round the piers that visually broke up the hard forms of the structure. The arches themselves no longer had simple square sections but displayed a range of shapes created by the addition of extra rolls and mouldings.

Equally, the plan of the church and abbey buildings at Westminster became the model for the layout of a monastery well into the Middle Ages (p. 98, figs 109, 175). The cross-shaped – or cruciform – church had a large eastern apse and smaller subsidiary apses on the short arms. There was a tower at the cross-

ing and smaller towers containing stair turrets. The conventual buildings (the abbey's domestic structures) were to the south, with the cloister in the corner between the south transept and the nave, and a chapter house with an apsidal end on the east side. There was a dormitory on the east side and a refectory on the south. Who conceived this new building for Edward will never be known, although the identity of the three most important figures is recorded: two had English names; the third appears, perhaps, to be German. In architecture stylistic change is normally more than a whim of the designer. In the case of Westminster Abbey, Church reform was an important factor (pp 73, 76); the new monastery, in common with its sister buildings in mainland Europe, was to be a model for reformed Benedictine monasticism. Edward's political and dynastic ambitions have already been mentioned, as has his wealth, but we should never discount the sheer fascination and enjoyment of building things in a new way – and late Saxon Westminster was new and shocking to anyone who saw it.[4]

In the 1050s local churches began to display similar architectural forms to Westminster and a much stronger spatial unity. At St Mary's, Stow-in-Lindsey, Lincolnshire, the transepts and crossing of a large minster church of *c.*1055 still dominate the small village. It is one of the first generation of buildings in which the Anglo-Saxon porticus had transformed itself into a fully fledged transept. The crossing tower at Stow would probably have been made of timber, but at St Mary in Castro, Dover, the masonry crossing tower survives (fig. 34), albeit much restored. A third church, Holy Trinity, Great Paxton, Cambridgeshire, not only has transepts and a crossing, but its nave has aisles with an arcade of compound piers (fig. 35). This small group of churches might once have been part of a larger family experimenting with new forms and spatial concepts, but it is likely that these architectural adventures were confined to the highest level of patronage; Great Paxton and Dover might have had been commissioned by the king, while Stow was founded by Earl Leofric and his wife Godgifu (Lady Godiva).

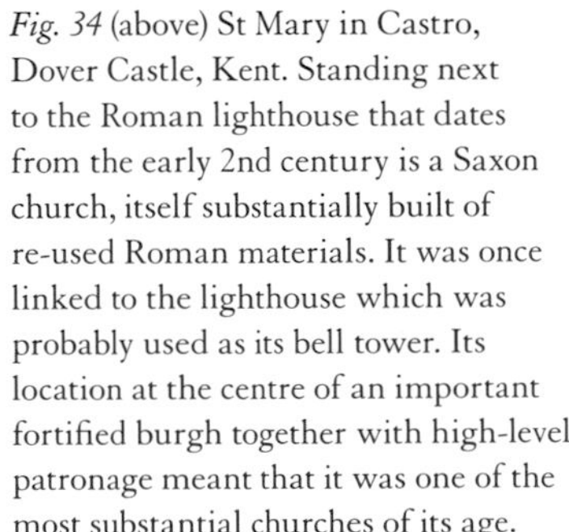

Fig. 34 (above) St Mary in Castro, Dover Castle, Kent. Standing next to the Roman lighthouse that dates from the early 2nd century is a Saxon church, itself substantially built of re-used Roman materials. It was once linked to the lighthouse which was probably used as its bell tower. Its location at the centre of an important fortified burgh together with high-level patronage meant that it was one of the most substantial churches of its age.

Fig. 35 (above right) Holy Trinity, Great Paxton, Cambridgeshire, the nave arcade; a mid-eleventh century example of compound piers with bulbous cushion capitals.

Patrons lower down the social scale, however, were also very active. After 1000 thousands of local churches, originally constructed in timber, were rebuilt in stone. This fashion was started by the rich landowners of commercially developed East Anglia, but soon spread to the nucleated villages of the Midlands and then eventually to western England. This was an important moment in English architectural history. On the one hand, it shows that there were now builders who could produce a sort of standard, ready-to-order stone church; on the other, it meant that more and more ordinary people started to experience complex and elaborate stone architecture on a daily basis.

There was a liturgical change, too. Most of the earlier timber churches were single spaces, but the separate chancels in the new stone churches meant that the priest was separated from his congregation. This created a different relationship between congregation and priest, who now had an elevated status. Meanwhile, the nave became a communal space in which people congregated to celebrate and to mourn. From the late 10th century local churches had their own burial grounds and from around 1050 permanent fonts.[5]

It will never be possible properly to judge the architecture of late Saxon England, as the vast majority of it was swept away after 1066. Yet what survives suggests that after 1000 a new aesthetic began to gain ground: a greater spatial harmony and a new architectural vocabulary. Much of this was promoted by a tiny super-rich elite, the structure of which was England's political Achilles heel: Saxon England was systemically weak, unable to settle the key question of succession. That weakness was exploited by Duke William of Normandy in 1066.

Conquest

The Norman Conquest looms large over English history, casting a shadow that obscures much of what came before and colouring what came after. It sounds obvious to say it, but in the year 1000 no one had heard of the Norman Conquest. In fact no one had heard of the Normans as such; to the English the people of Normandy were French. England and Normandy faced each other across the Channel, sharing a common cultural inheritance, both greatly influenced by Scandinavia. England was richer and bigger, and was experimenting with exactly the same types of architectural novelty as the Normans.

I have already suggested that the term 'Romanesque' is not very helpful in trying to characterise Anglo-Saxon architecture (p. 39), so this book does not use it. The same applies to what was built after 1066, which is normally categorised as Romanesque and commonly called Norman. Sadly, this too is simplistic and confusing, suggesting as it does that the buildings erected in England after 1066 were somehow in a style that was brought over by the Normans. They were not. What is normally called Norman architecture was developed in England after 1066, drawing on native traditions and absorbing

Fig. 37 (below) The White Tower, Tower of London; conjectural room uses as originally intended. Cut away reconstruction from the south west: a) basement level for storage; b) entrance level containing a hall, 'throne room' and private chamber; c) first floor hall, chamber and chapel. Cut away from the south east: d) first floor hall; e) chapel.

influences and ideas from across Europe, so it can more properly be called Anglo-Norman or Anglo-French. It was an inventive, eclectic, exotic and cosmopolitan style born of a unique coincidence of political, religious, social, cultural and economic events. English architecture for a period of fifty years was among the most original and influential in Europe.[6]

William and his immediate successors built on an imperial scale. The cathedral at Winchester (p. 47), the great towers at London and Colchester, and their own palace at Westminster (p. 79) were expressions of a parvenu dynasty at the helm of one of Europe's richest monarchies. William and his contemporaries expressed their power in the architectural language of ancient Rome. The blind arcading on the White Tower was a deliberate quotation from antiquity; the tower at Colchester was constructed on the podium of the Roman temple of Claudius, while the bishop's residence at Lincoln was framed as a triumphal arch (fig. 38). These buildings were not the busy, accretive structures of the Saxons; they set out to imitate the monumentality and spatial clarity of ancient Rome. The Normans had not built in this style or to this scale in Normandy; it was the Conquest that created a giddy mixture of excess, power and imperial triumphalism that was expressed in an outburst of architectural megalomania. Yet we should be clear, Anglo-French architecture was not a homogeneous style; it was one that varied significantly from region to region. Buildings in the west of England and in Yorkshire, for instance, looked very different. This account cannot describe the subtleties of these variations, nor does it attempt to do so.[7]

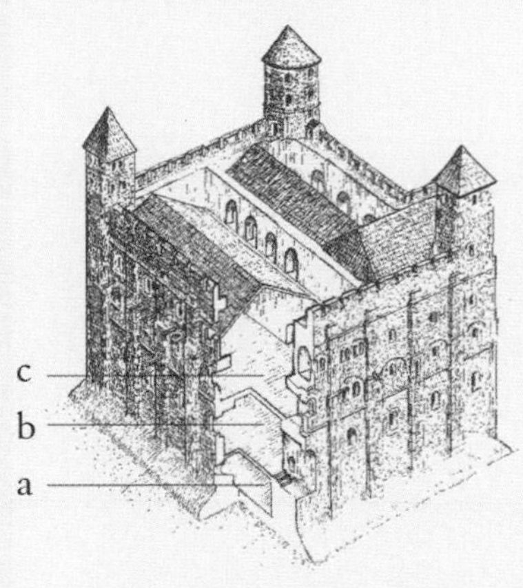

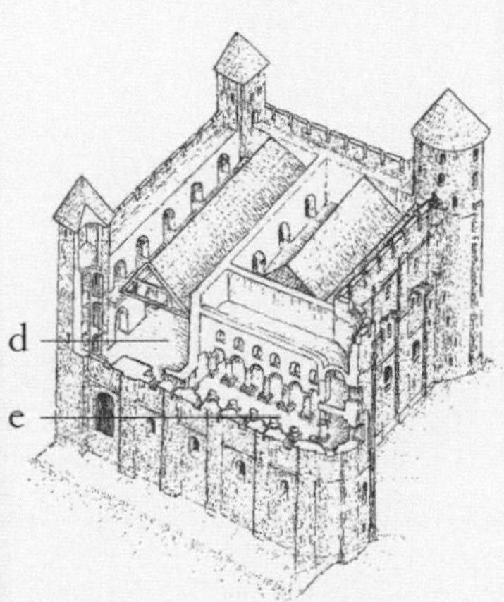

Fig. 38 (right) Lincoln Cathedral; a reconstruction of the west front as it may have appeared in the 1090s. Part monumental triumphal arch, part castle, part portal to a great church, it had an affinity to the westworks of Saxon cathedrals (compare figs 19–20) as well as reflecting the highly militarised nature of early Norman society.

The Norman Military Occupation

Anglo-Saxon England was no stranger to invasion or fortification; both Offa and Alfred had commissioned well-engineered and effective defences (pp 40 and 51). These royal enterprises, offering communal security, were matched by the individual fortification of aristocratic residences with ramparts, walls, towers and gatehouses (p. 55). The situation in Normandy was broadly similar. Few nobles lived in strongly defended residences, but in the years after 1000 a large number of fortified residences – or castles – were being developed. In England the word 'castle' is used for the first time in the reign of Edward the Confessor to describe fortified places on the Welsh border, but on the eve of the Norman Conquest castles were neither common nor well developed on either side of the Channel.[8]

This was soon to change. The military requirements of conquest caused a rapid development in military engineering and a proliferation of castles across the English countryside. The first ones were simple structures: either ringworks, that is to say an area enclosed by earth ramparts topped with a palisade, or mottes, which are mounds upon which a fortified structure was built. Ringworks were the most common form of castle in Normandy and similar to Anglo-Saxon fortified sites such as Goltho, Lincolnshire (p. 55). Mottes were less common, though it seems that prehistoric mounds in Wiltshire had been converted into forts from the 1010s (p. 55). The earthworks of both types of fort could be raised with unskilled forced labour, while timber structures could easily be built by expert native carpenters. The Bayeux Tapestry shows the motte of the Conqueror's castle at Hastings being built, under instruction, by Saxon slaves. Soon these mottes had a lower outer enclosure known as the bailey, which was used for stabling and accommodating any garrison.[9]

The most important of this first generation of castles were royal, a product of the systematic imposition of Norman sovereignty on England. They were erected in strategic locations to support field tactics and, crucially, in county towns (fig. 38). Many were built on the sites of former Saxon royal or aristocratic residences, most usually in a corner of the town walls (fig. 39). The novelty of these buildings was that they were not merely defensive residences; they were centres of administration, a symbol of new overlordship and a warning to the native inhabitants to submit.

As the Conqueror criss-crossed England he granted out land to his followers. The first grants were military commands intended to consolidate Norman power. A quarter of England was granted to the king's tenants-in-chief, some 170 or so of William's companions. Most of these men built castles, first as safe and secure places to live, but in due course as places from which to administer their lands and to enforce peace. While the tenants-in-chief kept about half of the land themselves, the rest they granted to some 6,200 vassals, knights and men-at-arms. Of these, the majority held lands valued at less than £1 a year, but a large elite, some 940, owned lands worth

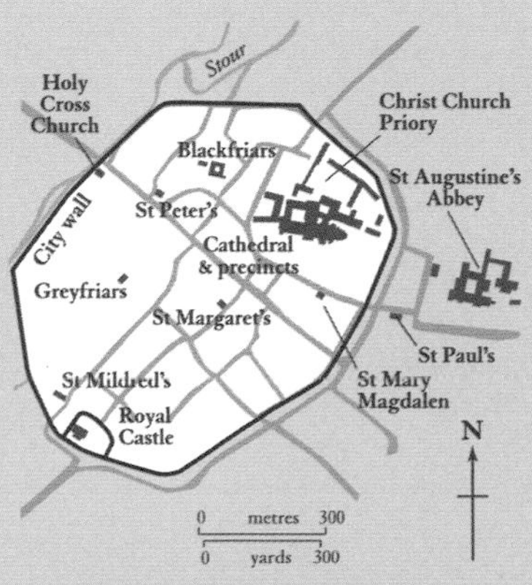

Fig. 38 (above right) Cathedrals and castles built 1050–1100. It is very noticeable that at this date there were few churches and abbeys in the west or north, and that the number of castles north of York is markedly less dense.

Fig. 39 (above) Canterbury, Kent, in the early Middle Ages. The cathedral lay in the north-eastern corner of the city – English cathedrals and abbeys are rarely placed in the middle. In the south, in its own enclosure, was the castle.

between £5 and £45 a year. A good number of these built small castles, too. Ultimately, this meant that in the period to 1130 there might have been as many as 500 castles in use, half of which were in private hands. This was a big change from the situation before the Conquest either in England or Normandy, where very few had had a fortified house.[10] Every one of this first generation of timber castles has been rebuilt, but there is no doubt that they were functional structures, primarily military buildings – a necessary and mechanistic part of the conquest and colonisation of England. In the autumn of 1066 just such a castle was built at Canterbury. A tower was raised up on a motte surrounded by a ditch, beyond which was a palisaded outer bailey, covering in all perhaps 5 per cent of the city. It overwhelmed the town and must have accommodated mounted knights as well as foot soldiers (fig. 39). At Abinger, Surrey, there was a castle belonging to an under-tenant at the other end of the social scale. The 35ft-diameter top of its motte has been excavated, revealing the plan of the original timber stockade and small tower. It is possible to visualise what these towers looked like by visiting the freestanding bell tower at St Mary's, Pembridge, Herefordshire, built between 1115 and 1150. Here, in the middle of this sleepy village, is a massive timber-built pylon with a weighty scissor-braced internal structure – about as close as we can come to envisaging the Conqueror's timber towers (fig. 40). They cannot have been comfortable or elegant places to live.[11]

Two buildings started by William, however, were – the White Tower, London, and its sister in Colchester. These colossal structures were palaces for the duke-made-king. They contained a suite of reception rooms and a large chapel in an overwhelming stone-built tower. Such towers had been built for rulers before in the Loire valley and, indeed, in Normandy itself, but not quite on this scale or to this level of sophistication. In fact, scale was integral to their purpose; the parapets of the White Tower were raised far above its roof line to create a more domineering silhouette (fig. 37). The population of London, as the largest and most important city, and that of Colchester, guarding the east flank of England from troublesome Scandinavia, would be in no doubt that their new king was a mighty and determined master. Yet these were sophisticated residences, too. They had fireplaces with chimneys, garderobes (latrines) and simple, bold architectural settings for thrones, tables and chairs. Furnished with rich textiles, brightly painted wooden furniture and sparkling with candlelit gold plate, these palatial towers were intended to be a pleasure to live in as well as a mighty image of royal power. The White Tower ranks as one of the most important buildings in English architectural history. Its direct influence was to be felt in the design of castles for more than a century and its effects on London continued for more than half a millennium.[12]

Fig. 40 (above left) Freestanding bell tower at St Mary's, Pembridge, Herefordshire. This late 14th-century tower is supported internally by eight mighty oak posts forming a square. They are braced diagonally and horizontally up to the pyramidal roof. Though this is a much later example, the footprints of such massive timber constructions have been excavated and dated to the 11th and 12th centuries.

Great Churches: The First Phase

In England and Normandy of the 11th century there was no hard distinction between Church and state. While the pope kept an eye on doctrine, lay rulers effectively governed their national Churches. Both William and Edward the Confessor were interested in Church welfare and reform, and welcomed a

Fig. 41 (above) English dioceses in 1100; several, such as Lincoln and York, were huge compared to their modern size.

series of reforming decrees starting in 1049 that slowly transformed canon law and liturgy in Western Europe. William had promoted reform in Normandy from about 1050 through his chief religious advisor, the Italian abbot Lanfranc, one of the greatest intellectuals of his day, and when William sailed from Normandy in 1066 he did so under the banner of the pope. Once in England, William used his power of appointment and patronage ruthlessly. He appointed Lanfranc as Archbishop of Canterbury in 1070 and, in a series of councils between 1072 and 1076, the structure, governance and morals of the English Church were reformed.[13] This was as much a political as a moral crusade; with William's support Lanfranc reorganised the boundaries of Saxon dioceses, moving cathedrals from the countryside to towns and ensuring that the diocese became, like the county, a unit of government control. So the Saxon cathedral at Dorchester-on-Thames moved to Lincoln, Selsey to Chichester and Elmham to Norwich, via Thetford. By the reign of Henry I there were 17 dioceses, with boundaries that remained nearly unchanged until the Reformation (fig. 41).

Within a period of less than 50 years each of these dioceses was to have an entirely new cathedral, perhaps the largest and most ambitious programme in English architectural history. It is easy to imagine that this meant the invention of a new type and shape of church, but there was no simple change from 'Saxon' cathedrals to 'Norman' ones. The sixteen cathedrals built between around 1070 and 1130 were not identikit structures; each mixed stylistic and liturgical influences in its own way according to the preferences of its bishop, the resources available and local traditions. This had probably not been Lanfranc's intention. He had hoped to abolish Anglo-Saxon forms and traditions, and bring the liturgical and architectural life of English cathedrals into line with the most advanced thinking on the continent. In this, Canterbury was to be the model. Lanfranc's Canterbury Cathedral was the most derivative of all the great churches built after the Conquest. Lanfranc had been the abbot of St Etienne at Caen and had overseen the reconstruction of the abbey church there; his cathedral at Canterbury was closely modelled on his old church, right down to the precise dimensions of the transepts and nave. But this was not just an architectural importation. The archbishop set down the liturgical practices he wanted performed in his new country: the Decreta Lanfranci was to replace the Saxon Regularis Concordia (pp 44–5) as the liturgical rule book for the English Church. In composing this, Lanfranc, who had trained as a lawyer and taught logical disputation (dialectic), turned away from the showy, flowery customs of the Saxons and set out a more austere, simpler and more disciplined liturgy. Lanfranc did not have the authority to impose this on everyone, but soon at least 15 monastic houses followed his rules.

Other than a few fragments, Lanfranc's cathedral at Canterbury has been completely rebuilt, but remarkably the liturgical arrangements implemented by him can still be appreciated by visiting the abbey church at St Albans, Hertfordshire, which was started in 1077 (fig. 42). Here there are three liturgical foci: the high altar at the east end; a choir altar for lay people facing the nave; and a huge crucifix (or rood) over the pulpitum (the screen that divided the choir from the nave). At St Albans, as at Lanfranc's Canterbury, relics remained hugely important and, just as in Saxon churches, the organisation of large numbers of pilgrims had a major impact on the design. The most important relics were either in a crypt below the east end where pilgrims would not interfere with the daily round of monastic services, or, as at St Albans, east of the high altar in a screened enclosure. This definitively divided the church into the part for the monks (the screened-off choir) and the parts for the laity (the nave for services, the shrine at the east end for pilgrims).[14]

Whilst a minority of churches followed the liturgical arrangements of Canterbury, most had a more sympathetic attitude to Saxon customs. Several new cathedrals preserved the idea of the westwork, providing a secondary focus at the west end. The most spectacular of these was at Lincoln, where the west end was a massy, semi-fortified bishop's hall, echoing a Roman triumphal arch (fig. 38). At Ely, too, a great central tower and part of a western transept survives. We know that at Winchester there was a western structure, now lost. These same cathedrals, like Saxon ones, had extensive areas of first-floor liturgical space for processions and altars. It was possible to do an entire circuit in the broad first-floor galleries at Winchester, and its upper altars were approached by spiral stairs just as in Saxon churches (fig. 43).[15]

At Winchester one can still gain a good impression of what the interior of the first generation of post-Conquest cathedrals looked like. In the 11th century there was no such thing as a capital city; Norman kings governed as they moved around the country. Yet Winchester, as the seat of the kings of Wessex, had a claim to be the traditional seat of the English monarchy (p. 48). William seems to have acknowledged Winchester's special status; he rebuilt the royal palace and constructed a castle. He was crowned at Winchester, too, for a second time, by two cardinals and a papal legate, and later his son Rufus was buried there. William also had a permanent treasury at Winchester, and at Easter time the cathedral was the location for one of the thrice-yearly royal crown wearings.

So it is not surprising that in 1070, when the Saxon Bishop of Winchester, Stigand, was deposed, the new bishop, Walkelin, resolved to rebuild the cathedral, emphasising the importance of the city and its royal associations.[16] Foundations were laid in 1079, and by the time it was finished it was the largest cathedral in Europe, its dimensions almost identical to those of St Peter's Basilica in Rome (fig. 43). The church was cruciform, with transepts as wide as the nave. There were towers at the west end, on the corners of the transepts and over the crossing. Today only the transepts survive from Walkelin's time (fig. 44), but here the essentials of the style of the new cathedral can be appreciated. Like the Confessor's Westminster Abbey, the elevations are three storeys high: a main ground-floor arcade, a gallery above and, crowning that, a clerestory. These levels are tied together by mast-like shafts that rise to the roof. Within this the individual parts of the elevation are subordinated to the whole. The arches at gallery level, for instance, are contained within a larger arch and the whole bay is bounded by piers running from floor to ceiling. The conglomeration of shafts, which visually fragment the piers, disguises the fact that they are, in fact, huge, thick sections of wall supporting the galleries and clerestory above.

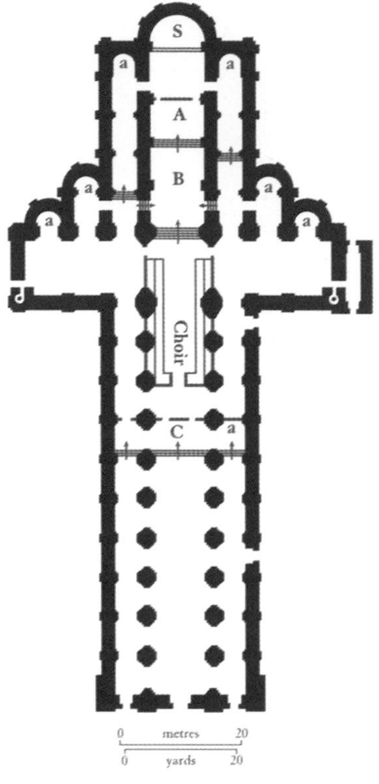

Fig. 42 (above) Abbey Church of St Alban, St Albans, Hertfordshire, reconstructed plan showing liturgical arrangements in around 1100: a) side altar; b) relic repository; A) high altar; B) matutinal altar; C) rood altar; S) shrine.

The Parishes

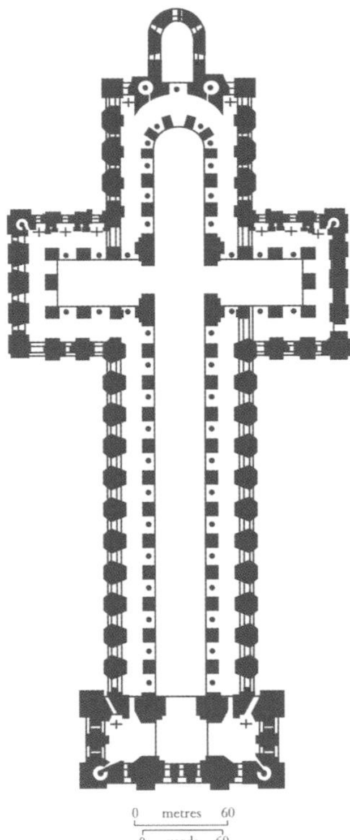

The period after the Conquest saw a huge shift in wealth from secular hands to the Church, a shift in landownership not equalled again until the reverse took place under King Henry VIII. Thus Norman landowners such as Robert and Beatrice, the landlords of Asheldham, Essex, endowed their church of St Lawrence by transferring its patronage to a local priory at Horkesley with sixty acres of land. Many such gifts were stimulated by the penitential ordinance of Easter 1067, which set out the penances owed by William's men who had killed and maimed on English battlefields. Those who were unclear how many English they had slain had a choice: they could either do penance one day a week for life or endow a church. If you were rich the choice was easy.[17]

This lent additional momentum to the rebuilding of timber churches in stone that had started around 1000 (p. 68). At Asheldham the timber church was replaced, the main street diverted and a burial ground formed. Asheldham church has now been rebuilt, but a small number of churches rebuilt soon after the Conquest have been preserved largely unaltered because of later depopulation. Such churches vividly capture the everyday experience of worship in the years immediately after the Conquest.

Fig. 43 (above) Winchester Cathedral, plan at tribune (first floor) level. The cathedral, begun in 1079, had many affinities with its Saxon forebears: there were altars in the galleries and a tribune or royal pew at the west end. Spiral stairs led up to the gallery at several points. + indicates a side altar.

Fig. 44 (right) Winchester Cathedral; the north transept. This precious surviving unaltered part of the cathedral shows the raw simplicity and power, almost crudeness, of the early Norman cathedral.

Fig. 45 (above left) St Margaret's, Hales, Norfolk. This lovely church has a Saxon round tower that was heightened in the 15th century, but its nave and apsidal chancel date from the early 12th century.

Fig. 46 (above) St Botolph's, Hardham, West Sussex. The wall paintings here, done in 1120–30, were covered up in the 13th century and only re-discovered in 1866.

Most of these are two-roomed (or, more correctly, two-celled), with rectangular naves separated from the chancel by an arch. Most chancels originally had an apse but almost all were later rebuilt square-ended. In east Norfolk a couple of remote churches still retain their original apse, and perhaps the best among these is St Margaret's, Hales. The round tower is later, but the apsidal chancel dates from before 1130 and retains some of its blank arcading (fig. 45).[18] Another group of well-preserved churches is in West Sussex. St James's, Selham, could be Anglo-Saxon; its masonry and carving are clearly by Anglo-Saxon hands, although the likelihood is that it was built just before 1100. St Botolph's, Hardham, miraculously retains its wall paintings of about 1120 that were whitewashed over and only rediscovered in 1866. The murals, painted in ochre and yellow, a typical Anglo-Norman bacon-and-egg palette, show St George slaying the dragon (the earliest such image in Britain), and wonderful figures of Adam and Eve (fig. 46). The halos are painted in green paint made by coating copper plates in urine and sealing them in a container for two weeks.[19]

Although these small Norman churches are sometimes almost indistinguishable from their Saxon predecessors, the difference was the discipline that the Normans sought to bring to parish life. Lanfranc's reforms subdivided dioceses into archdeaconries and deaneries to give greater supervision to individual parish priests. This was important, as most priests before 1000 were in minsters under close supervision; with the proliferation of local churches there were now hundreds of remote priests, poor, ill-educated (often illiterate), undisciplined and isolated. Some were drunkards, some said Mass armed, others had secular employment and many had wives. Almost all were English. Under the new regime more was demanded of them and greater discipline enforced. The life of the average clergyman was transformed in the century after 1066.[20]

The Towns

The impact of the Norman Conquest on English towns was enormous, physically, economically and socially. Saxon lords who had lost their country estates lost their urban lands (burgages) too. In the place of English burgesses Norman landlords settled, and in the place of English town houses new castles, cathedrals and priories rose. Many of these, such as those at York and Winchester, were instigated by royal command; others were the random and illegal acts of new landlords. Norwich was already one of the largest towns in England in 1066 and was to become even more important when the see was transferred there from Thetford. By the time of the Domesday Book in 1086 almost half of the Anglo-Saxon town had been cannibalised for the Norman castle, cathedral and new housing. One hundred and thirteen houses were demolished for the site of the castle alone, and 32 English burgesses – bankrupted by the seizure of property and royal tax – fled the town.[21]

As castles and cathedrals rose, existing towns were re-planned. At Richmond, Yorkshire, a vast castle covering 2 ½ acres was grafted on to a small, pre-existing settlement. Against the castle gate was laid out the market place, and on to this, in a D shape, the burgage plots of the townsmen (fig. 47). There is no doubt that Richmond was founded on the top of a cliff for

Fig. 47 (right) Richmond, Yorkshire: plan of the town based on a map of 1773. There are two centres to this town, the original village core round St Mary's Church on the east side and the semicircular castle borough to its west. Though the castle is perched on a dramatic cliff falling to the river Swale, the reasons for its location were as much economic as military.

military reasons, but the town was designed as an economic engine for Alan Rufus, who began the castle in 1070. Richmond was at the centre of a huge network of arable estates and soon became not only the principal market but also an industrial centre.[22]

New abbeys could have a similar impact. At Bury St Edmunds the colossal new abbey church (second only in size to Winchester) had a decisive influence on the town. The monumental abbey gatehouse provided the kingpin for the town grid (fig. 48).[23] Many of these extensions and remodellings were to be economically successful. At Bury the Domesday Book entry tells us that in 20 years the town had grown by 342 houses. Much of this was as a result of the economic stimulation of the construction industry, the effects of which in a town such as Bury or Norwich must have dominated the local economy for decades.

The Death of the Conqueror

William the Conqueror died in 1087 and the succession was split between his three surviving sons: Robert, William Rufus and Henry. Robert inherited Normandy but pawned it to his brother William when he went on crusade in 1096. William Rufus thus became king of England and, for a few years, controlled Normandy. In 1100 Henry succeeded Rufus as king and in 1106 seized Normandy from Robert, throwing him in prison. Henry died in 1135, the year after his brother. William Rufus's reign saw a reaction to the highly militarised nature of his father's time. There was an explosion of decorative excess. Rufus's court was known for its outlandish fashions: long hair, tight-fitting tunics, drooping cuffs, and shoes with long, pointed, curly toes. This sense of exuberance can still be felt in the fabric of his most important building, Westminster Great Hall. The ceremonial centrepiece of the Norman palace at Westminster, at 240ft long by 67.5ft wide it was the largest secular space in northern Europe. Outside, fearsomely tall stone walls were topped with a decorative band of chequered stone and crowned with a blind arcade. It was entered, not on one of its long sides as was normal for such halls, but at the north end, giving a much greater processional focus. Inside, at clerestory level, there were pairs of small arches set under larger ones as at Winchester Cathedral (fig. 44). The capitals of these were richly carved and brightly painted, and below, on the great blank wall, would have been paintings or hangings to give the hall a feeling of vitality and colour. The roof was probably carried by a series of vast timber trusses, themselves presumably painted and decorated, and the floor was probably of rammed earth, allowing for the entry of mounted knights. This was never a space for regular use. It was rather a ceremonial hall conceived as the setting for the great feasts that accompanied major religious festivals. In here William wore his crown in splendour and presided over his magnificent household as God's elected ruler.[24]

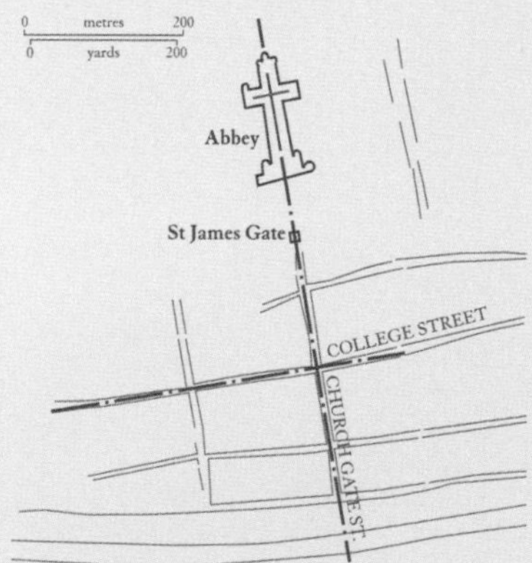

Fig. 48 (above) Bury St Edmunds in the 12th century. The Abbey church was built on axis with a gatehouse, St James's Tower and Churchgate Street as the central street of a grid. This matrix was laid out by Abbot Baldwin.

The Church after William's Death

Fig. 49 (bottom right) Westminster Hall, the largest structure in the palace of Westminster built 1097. A mistake in setting-out meant that the east and west walls were misaligned. The plan shows the hall at window level with its wall passage and arcades. Above the arcades are shown in elevation.

Archbishop Lanfranc died two years after William I and was succeeded in 1093 by Anselm, a figure more tolerant of Anglo-Saxon Church customs. This second generation of Anglo-Norman churchmen, perhaps, also lacked the sense of urgency and single-mindedness of Lanfranc and his contemporaries. They adopted a more florid architecture, closer to the ornamental taste of the Saxons. In achieving this they built on a generation of improving craftsmanship, the construction standards in the first Anglo-Norman cathedrals having been somewhat variable (fig. 44).

These changes can be seen as they take place at Durham Cathedral. The historic core of Durham, sitting high on a U-shaped bend in the river Wear, has the most dramatic site of any town in England. The scarp on which the cathedral and castle now stand was from ancient times a fortress, and here the Normans built the supreme English monuments of the Norman age. The castle, in timber, came first, but in 1093 the foundation stone for a new cathedral was laid – it took 40 years to build. In that period the austerity of the first generation of post-Conquest buildings was swept aside in an encrustation of decoration, indeed a resurgence of Anglo-Saxon aesthetics. Whilst the bones of the cathedral's design are familiar – the alternating compound and cylindrical piers are as in the Confessor's abbey – the first-floor gallery, at Westminster almost of equal height to the main arcade, has been reduced. The arcades at Durham are huge, and squeeze the gallery and clerestory up to the roof (fig. 51). This is an aesthetic change, in that the piers dominate the nave; but it is also a liturgical one, as the gallery was no longer considered to be a major liturgical space. Equally important was the invention, at Durham, of the rib vault. The naves of early cathedrals had been roofed in timber, with flat, painted-timber ceilings – the effect can now be seen at Peterborough (fig. 50) or Ely. At Durham a way was found of vaulting over a much wider space, with masonry highlighting the intersections of the vault with stone ribs (fig. 51).

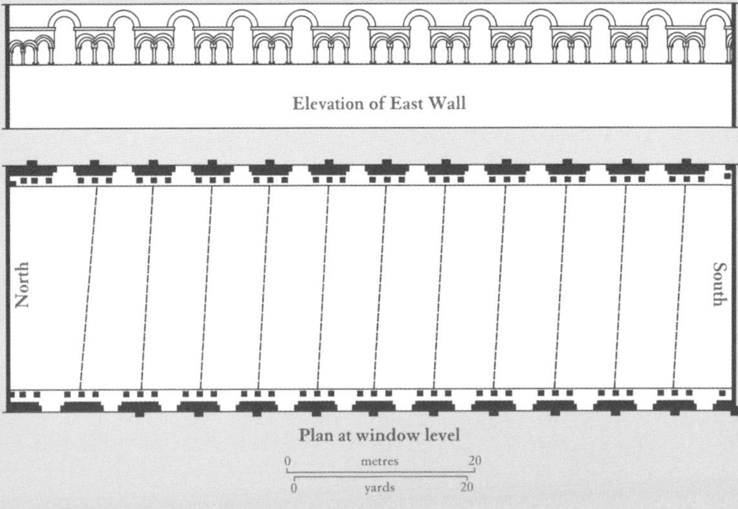

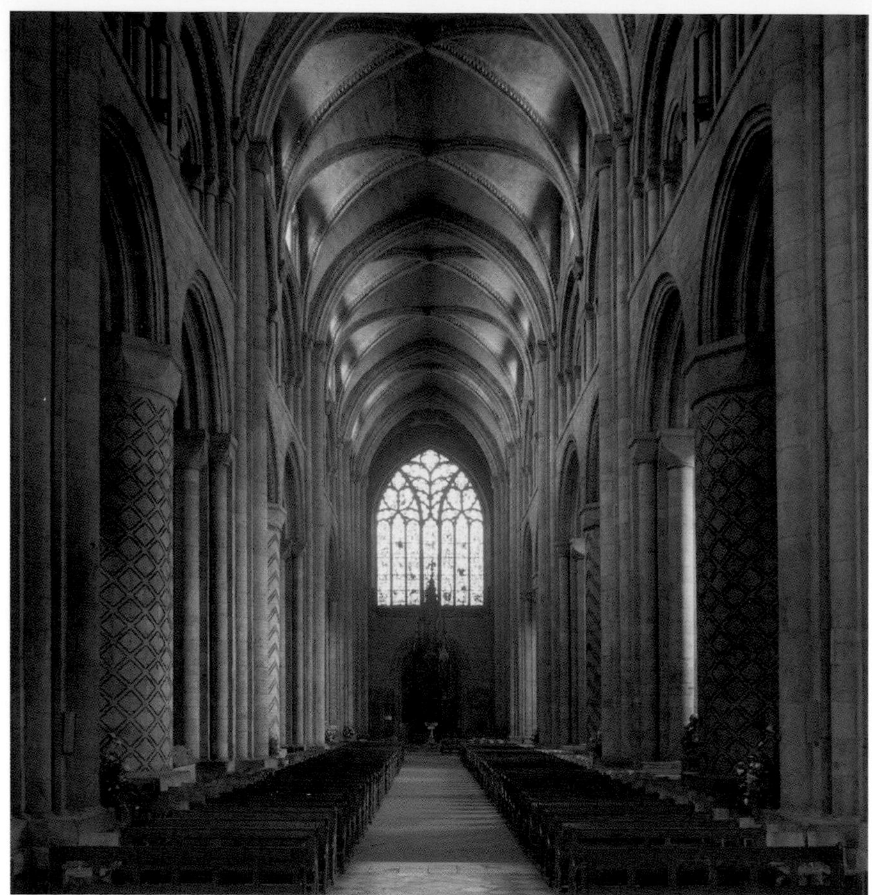

The vault was a crucial architectural development because a flat, timber roof broke up the unity of the space while a vault drew together all the elements into a coherent whole. Durham's novelty is not only in its structure; it also lies in its decoration. The eastern parts of the cathedral, which were built first, have little surface decoration, but the nave, built after 1104, gets progressively more showy towards the west. The piers are cut with lozenges and zigzags, the arches with chevrons, and the aisle walls are decorated with blank, intersecting arcading that looks as if it has fallen straight out of an Anglo-Saxon manuscript. This change from austerity to exuberance can be seen elsewhere: at Ely, for instance, where the decoration is external too, and at Norwich, where the tower is highly original, almost wacky, with bold roundels, lozenges and blind arcading (fig. 52).

The Anglo-Saxons had a rich tradition of carving in stone, but their sculptures were either freestanding or used as applied ornament, rather like a bejewelled clasp on a cloak. The new architectural forms developing in Normandy and England in the years around 1066 integrated sculptural decoration into architecture, and blended the roles of sculptor and mason. Architecture after 1066 introduced new opportunities for sculptural embellishment. Whilst Anglo-Saxon doorways were plain rectangular openings in plan, after the Conquest they were routinely recessed, with small columns and capitals supporting moulded arches. These often enclose a stone slab called a

Fig. 50 (above) Peterborough Cathedral nave; the flat wooden ceiling dates from *c.*1230 and is painted with images designed to be read from the nave far below. Colourful, expressive and a precious survival, it never succeeded in architecturally drawing together the great arcades of 1160–90.

Fig. 51 (above left) Durham Cathedral nave, unlike Peterborough, is visually united by its vault. We don't know who the designer was, but here force and splendour are coherently combined as nowhere else in medieval England. Rib vaults were first erected in the Durham choir in 1095 and were a ground-breaking advance of European importance. The ribs have their own structural integrity and the cells between are made of lighter material 12–18 inches thick.

Fig. 52 (right) Norwich Cathedral; the spectacular crossing tower was the last part of the cathedral to be completed in around 1140; it was erected only after the foundations of the crossing had been allowed to settle, thus avoiding the sort of collapse that had been experienced at Winchester or Ely. The turrets at the corners are part of the original conception – the spire was added in the 1480s.

tympanum, which provided an opportunity for a virtuoso display of carving (fig. 53). Likewise the capital, a ubiquitous and essential element of the new style, was a vehicle for carving. The vault of Archbishop Anselm's crypt at Canterbury rests on a forest of carved and decorated columns, each crowned with a sculpted capital; the best, such as the one showing a wyvern fighting a dog, are bursting with energy and motion (fig. 54). The style of these capitals is so close to the initial letters in manuscripts painted in the priory that they must have been designed by the same hands. These were exceptional; most capitals were of a type known as 'cushion', a squashed cube of stone that could be painted, carved or more usually left plain. These were rare in Normandy and, as used in England, were probably copied from Germany. They were easy to reproduce quickly in places where the skill, time or money was not available for anything more elaborate.

Sculptural traditions after the Conquest, as with architectural ones, were cosmopolitan, and masons working on the great cathedrals blended influences from Normandy, Burgundy, the Loire, Germany and Scandinavia to produce a rich variety of forms. The most expressive example of this is a group of churches in Herefordshire. One of these, St Mary and St David's, Kilpeck, displays 85 carved corbels, as well as carved door and window surrounds (fig. 53). Here a Scandinavian great beast with a snake-like body and a dragon's head winds its way through the stems of a plant of Anglo-Saxon decorative origin.[25]

Fig. 53 (left) St Mary and St David, Kilpeck, Herefordshire, one of the most perfect 12th-century churches in England. The richness of its decoration, done in the 1130s, is due to the patronage of Hugh of Kilpeck, the Lord of the Manor who also built a castle next door and founded a nearby priory. The south door has a tree of life in its tympanum and otherwise is a writhing mass of dragons, birds, lions, serpents, with the addition of angels and a phoenix.

Fig. 54 (above) Canterbury Cathedral, Kent. St Anselm's Crypt was unaffected by the fire of 1174 and perfectly preserves the exuberance of the Canterbury masons in around 1100. The subject of most capitals is fighting beasts which give them a restless, writhing quality.

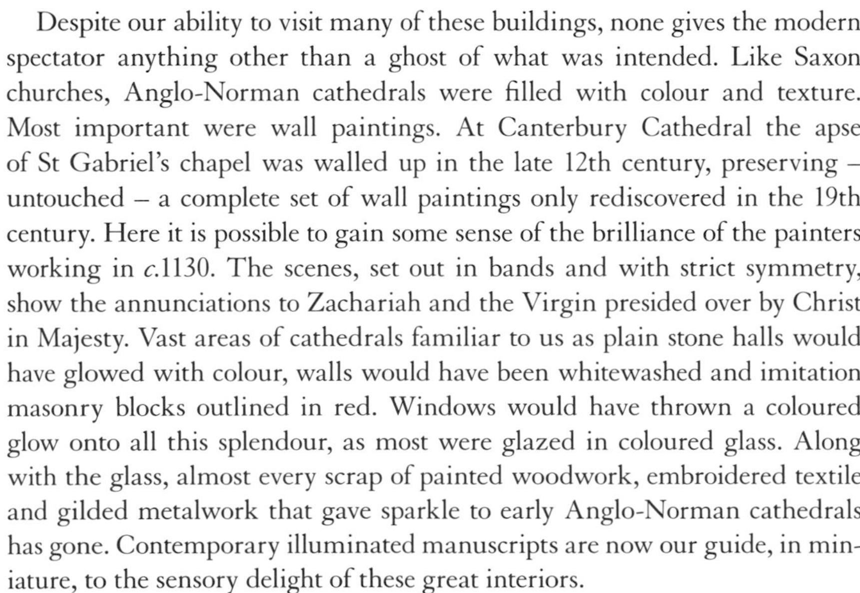

Despite our ability to visit many of these buildings, none gives the modern spectator anything other than a ghost of what was intended. Like Saxon churches, Anglo-Norman cathedrals were filled with colour and texture. Most important were wall paintings. At Canterbury Cathedral the apse of St Gabriel's chapel was walled up in the late 12th century, preserving – untouched – a complete set of wall paintings only rediscovered in the 19th century. Here it is possible to gain some sense of the brilliance of the painters working in *c.*1130. The scenes, set out in bands and with strict symmetry, show the annunciations to Zachariah and the Virgin presided over by Christ in Majesty. Vast areas of cathedrals familiar to us as plain stone halls would have glowed with colour, walls would have been whitewashed and imitation masonry blocks outlined in red. Windows would have thrown a coloured glow onto all this splendour, as most were glazed in coloured glass. Along with the glass, almost every scrap of painted woodwork, embroidered textile and gilded metalwork that gave sparkle to early Anglo-Norman cathedrals has gone. Contemporary illuminated manuscripts are now our guide, in miniature, to the sensory delight of these great interiors.

The Establishment of Castles

Fig. 55 (above) Norwich Castle Keep, though extensively repaired and restored by Anthony Salvin in 1835–9 its external elevations still exude the flamboyance and excess of the years around 1100.

William the Conqueror died knowing that the military conquest of England was complete and that a matrix of royal castles secured his power in its county towns. There were remarkably few new castles built during the following century; royal architectural attention had turned to Normandy, where the military imperative now lay. In England many castles, such as Canterbury, remained nominally in royal hands but in practice were under the control of constables or sheriffs. One still in royal hands was Norwich, newly elevated to the capital of a diocese.

Norwich, as we have seen, was England's second town (p. 77), and the construction of a palatial tower there by William Rufus is a parallel to the White Tower in London. But the Norwich tower was more audacious. It was sited on a high artificial mound or motte, linked to an outer bailey by a giant arched bridge. The same masons worked on the tower and on the cathedral, and the architectural exuberance of Rufus's reign is apparent in both. Although the tower has been refaced, a series of watercolours of 1796 shows a building without corner turrets, but with massive buttresses framing an intricately composed decorative façade. Inside, the plan centred on a great ceremonial hall lit by high windows.[26]

These towers were very much a feature of the first generation of Norman overlords. There is scant evidence that the White Tower was ever used as a regular residence, and many, such as Norwich, had long interruptions in their construction. Others, such as Colchester, remained unfinished. The vastness of these structures, conceived in a militarised society for feasting, security and image, was becoming unnecessary as quickly as they were built. But the image of power they were able to convey remained a desirable and fashionable accessory for more than a century to come (p. 102). Two of Henry I's courtiers demonstrate the allure of the great tower. In the 1120s Geoffrey de Clinton, chamberlain and treasurer to Henry I, was granted lands in Warwickshire, where he founded a castle and priory. The castle at Kenilworth was hugely ambitious and was bankrolled by the king, who wanted to establish it as a royal centre of power against the nearby Earl of Warwick, who was of doubtful loyalty. A great tower was erected and an inner courtyard enclosed around it by a wall. At Portchester, Hampshire, another Norman magnate, Hugh Pont de l'Arche, replaced the Saxon residential buildings inside the Roman walls in the 1130s with a square-plan great tower with a hall at first-floor level.[27]

Building Materials and Technology

The 11th century saw a revolution in English building. The reconstruction of thousands of local churches in stone and, after 1066, the rebuilding of the cathedrals meant a huge expansion in all branches of stone production. The quantity of stone required to sustain this boom was colossal, perhaps even greater than that quarried by the Egyptians for the building of the pyramids. We have already seen that Saxon quarries generally only produced rubble and small quantities of cut stone, but the effects that architects were trying to achieve from the 1050s onwards demanded much more cut ashlar (i.e. rectilinear blocks). These ashlar blocks formed the internal and external structural walls, with an internal core of rubble mixed with mortar. Much of the expense of stone building was the cost of bringing it to site, so great efforts were made to secure stone locally. At Battle, Sussex, William the Conqueror first contemplated importing stone from Normandy for the construction of his abbey but found that stone could, in fact, be quarried nearby. This was ideal; in many instances, however, the solution was not so straightforward. In Kent, where the local building stone is less suitable for ashlar, Archbishop Lanfranc turned to other sources of stone for Canterbury Cathedral. Whilst the rubble core work could be extracted locally, ashlar came by sea from Caen in Normandy, Quarr on the Isle of Wight and from Marquise near Boulogne.[28]

If stone had to be moved more than about 12 miles by land the cost of carriage exceeded the value of the stone and so it was better to bring it in by water, a slower but cheaper solution. Before the Conquest canals were cut to bring stone from the Peterborough area to Fenland abbeys. A sunken barge excavated at Whittlesey contained large blocks of Barnack stone perhaps destined for Ramsey. After 1066 many more waterways were dug and diverted to make the movement of stone easier. Much of the stone for Norwich Cathedral was brought by sea to Great Yarmouth and then put into barges that came right up to the cathedral by means of a new canal.[29] Whilst new sources of stone were found and old ones continued to be exploited, the plunder of Roman buildings continued. Lanfranc's Canterbury also made use of Roman brick and tile, and in 1077 the abbot at St Albans found stockpiles of already salvaged Roman materials. Meanwhile, a cathedral such as Winchester, which was largely built of relatively local Quarr stone, made use of the masonry of its Anglo-Saxon predecessor.

Quarries were key to the building industry. Stone was not only extracted there, it was cut and carved. Blocks of ashlar, columns, bases and capitals were mass produced and shipped directly to the site, thereby avoiding the transport of stone that would end up as chippings at their destination. Working at a distance was, in principle, familiar, as the components of timber buildings were often cut remotely, transported and erected on site; but the precision needed for stonework was much greater. The dimension of each course of stone, for instance, had to accord with any decorative or structural elements in it. So ashlars had to be cut to different dimensions in the correct quantity. These details had to be carefully calculated and communicated to the quarry by means of written instructions and templates. The quarries therefore also became training schools, producing masons and carvers who could move to the great building sites, where they could learn to set stone and undertake some of the more exacting work that was done on the bench in masons' lodges on site.[30]

In Normandy as much as in England the quality of masonry improved markedly in the hundred years after the Conquest; larger blocks, tighter joints, finer carving suggest more skilled design, increasing proficiency among masons and better tools. It enabled the shift from the austerity of Winchester to the exuberance of Durham. Yet architecture after 1066 was as experimental as the Saxon work that preceded it. From 1000, people increasingly became used to seeing and experiencing stone buildings, but this should not obscure the fact that even after 1066 timber remained the most important and common building material. Although most churches were now built in stone, the first generation of castles – and almost all domestic, agricultural and industrial buildings – remained of timber. Stone buildings, too, contained huge quantities of timber; the earliest timber roof to survive intact is at St Mary's, Kempley, Gloucestershire. It dates from soon after 1120 and comprises fifteen trusses, with sole-plates projecting into the church that were probably carved with animal heads.[31] Other fragments of early timberwork survive, including the unusual and handsome nine-bay balustrade of *c.*1180 at St Nicholas's, Compton, Surrey, and a door of *c.*1050 in Westminster Abbey.[32]

The construction of the great Norman cathedrals was overseen by masons who we would today call architects. After 1066 their names are increasingly known: Blithere at Canterbury, Robert at St Albans and Hugh at Winchester. These men understood the principles of engineering, not through the written word, but through observation and trial and error. They drew plans, sections and templates either on parchment, wood or on large plaster panels. The earliest English architectural drawing to survive (of *c.*1200) is at Byland Abbey, Yorkshire, where incised drawings on a floor slab and a wall are full-size sections of the west front rose window.[33] In addition to drawings, designers commissioned models and templates, either at reduced scale or sometimes full-size.

It has been said that by looking at buildings alone it would be impossible for a historian to guess that the Norman Conquest had taken place. In 1000 England's architecture had already reached a turning point and the changes that came rapidly after 1066 had been in embryo since the 1050s at the latest. Yet without doubt the Conquest hugely accelerated architectural change. The building and craft industries quickly developed and diversified, and by 1130 almost everyone could experience stone architecture in their own locality. The great Saxon estates had been broken up and, as well as the great magnates, there was now a large class of middling landowners who aspired to build themselves homes and churches.

The severe unsullied monumentality of early Norman buildings as seen in the transepts of Winchester or the elevations of the White Tower lasted merely a generation; they soon gave way to something more florid and playful. Likewise the reforming aspirations of the Norman churchmen were diluted and what remained was an English compromise. As the first generation of Normans died out, England's architecture was already looking very different to anything in their former homelands. Indeed, the men and their families were feeling different, too. They might not have been able to express it in 1130, but the Normans and their architecture were becoming English.

4— The Invention of English Architecture

—1130-1250

As the second generation of Normans felt more English, so the great cathedrals, abbeys, castles and houses then under construction became increasingly distinct from their counterparts in France.

The Normans and the English

Many thought the death of Henry I in 1135 a calamity. He was the Conqueror's last surviving son and was outlived by only one legitimate child, Matilda. Matilda was his agreed successor but his nephew Stephen darted across the Channel and was crowned before he could be stopped. This led to a period of disorder and uncertainty, often called the Anarchy, which was only resolved by Stephen's death and the accession of Matilda's son, Henry II, in 1153.

Henry II had huge strength of character, boundless energy, and a determination to re-establish order and the rule of law. His court was cosmopolitan and, through his marriage to Eleanor of Aquitaine, he presided over territories from Scotland to the Pyrenees. Henry was not a Norman king; he had Anglo-Saxon ancestry through his mother, and of his eight great-grandparents only William the Conqueror was Norman. But it was not only the monarchy that was no longer Norman. Families whose ancestors had arrived with the Conqueror had begun to see themselves as English; while the first generation of newcomers had usually been buried in Normandy, by the 1150s their children and grandchildren were buried in England.[1]

A sense of Englishness also becomes increasingly apparent in the work of a generation of historians writing between about 1120 and 1150. Henry of Huntingdon, for instance, set out to write the history of 'this, the most celebrated of islands, formerly called Albion, later Britain, and now England'. His *History of the English* continued up to his own time and explained that the past victories of the Normans, including the Conquest of 1066, were now English history. This was in many respects true. The Norman ruling elite had married English women, adopted English laws and customs, assimilated native administrative structures, appropriated English history as their own and made pilgrimages to the shrines of Anglo-Saxon saints. In fact, although they didn't speak English as their first language, the third generation of Normans were now Englishmen.[2]

Despite Henry II's strength and success, he, no more than William the Conqueror, could control events after his death, and his sons Richard and John frittered away the territories and powers amassed by their father. Yet in many senses the reigns of Henry's sons saw a further reinforcement of English identity: King Richard's absence in 1191; the loss of Normandy in 1204;

the interdict of 1208 (when the pope banned the administration of the sacraments in England) and the failed invasion of England by Prince Louis of France in 1216 – all these led to increasing insularity and even xenophobia.

This reinforcement was of great importance for the development of English architecture in the century or so after 1130. The growing wealth, self-confidence and identity of the English ruling class led to an energetic patronage of architecture. Magnates reorganised their estates, built themselves castles, and endowed churches and monasteries; bishops reconstructed their cathedrals and abbots built new abbeys. The style in which these buildings were constructed was ambitious, original and, with hindsight, English.[3]

Old Principles, New Fashions

The 1150s, 60s and 70s were a period of stylistic experimentation. New currents of design from France, mixed with native decorative and structural traditions, produced some of the most inventive and lively buildings ever constructed in England. Contemporaries recognised this but might have described what was happening in different terms to us. For them, architectural language was important as it expressed hierarchy. In the Middle Ages most high-status architecture was about the ritualised display of power: ceremony, ritual and liturgy were the driving forces behind the appearance of buildings. Their structure and decoration expressed social, economic and religious hierarchies, and so the architectural setting of an activity, whether it be dining or praying, had to match its importance – and the importance of the people who were doing it.[4] This could be achieved through progressive intensity of decoration, the least important places being plain and the most important richly decorated, or through association, either with past activities or people, or with Christian Rome. Various parts of buildings – and whole buildings themselves – were thus always accorded a status through their architecture. So, for instance, as the most important of all medieval secular spaces was the great hall, this was singled out for special treatment. The magnificence of the carving around the doorway to Bishop Puiset's Hall at Durham Castle, and the arcading in the room above (fig. 56), proclaim them to be of the highest importance. English great halls, unlike some of their continental contemporaries, were always roofed in timber rather than vaulted in stone, a sign of status and reflecting a tradition going back to Roman Britain.

In religious buildings presbyteries and shrines were the most important areas, and, even in the most humble parish churches, were given significance by their decoration. Antiquity conferred status, too. When the Lady Chapel at Glastonbury burnt in 1184 its replacement included Anglo-Norman (or earlier) stylistic elements to emphasise its importance and venerability. We have already seen that references to ancient Rome were a way of emphasising

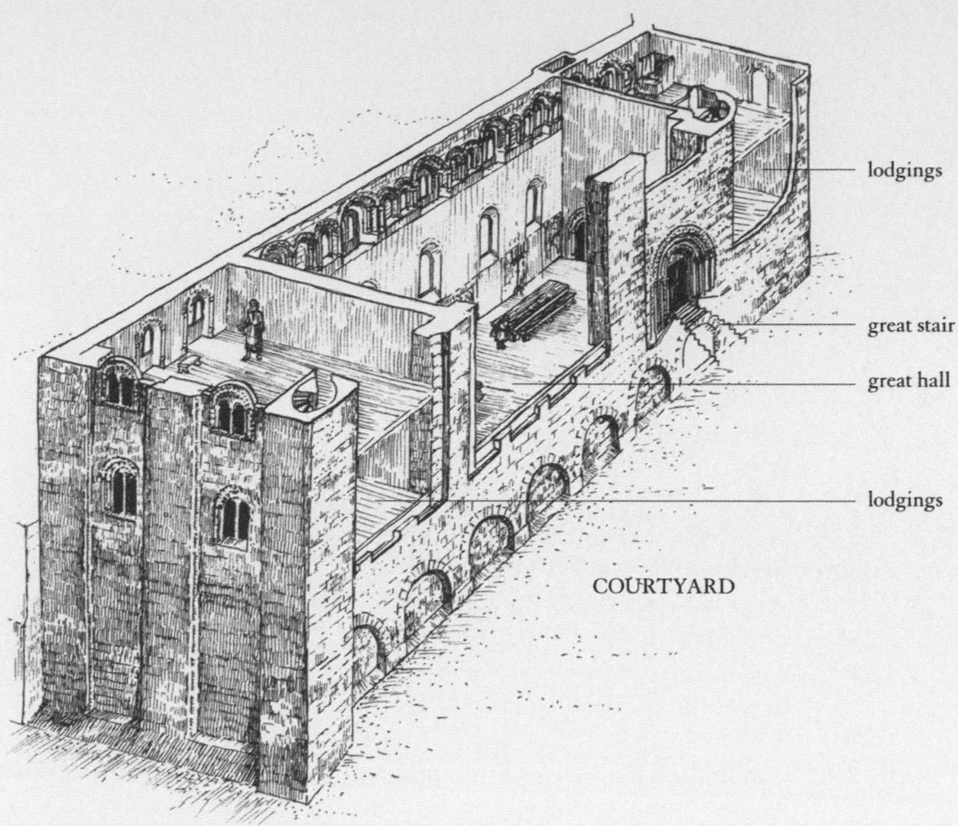

Fig. 56 (above left) Durham Castle; reconstruction of Bishop Le Puiset's lodgings, centred on his magnificent great hall with its spectacular doorcase originally entered directly from the courtyard. The upper part of the hall has a remarkable arcade with alternating windows and window seats, all encrusted with deep zig-zag friezes and bold scalloped capitals.

hierarchy (p. 69). When the east end of Canterbury Cathedral was rebuilt the great Purbeck piers were given Roman proportions, bases and capitals, echoing the early Christian basilicas of Rome (pp 94–5).[5]

So when we come to consider the architectural changes that swept across England from the 1150s onwards we have to bear in mind the importance of hierarchy and function, and the fact that new was not necessarily seen as better. The term later given to describe the new architectural language that came to dominate masonry buildings is 'Gothic', which in the minds of many has come to be associated with the pointed arch. But it is important to remember that pointed arches were reasonably common in Anglo-Norman buildings, such as those in the vaults of Durham Cathedral. Gothic architecture, as it developed in France in the 1130s, was about more than pointed arches; it was a manner of building that created stone vaults over tall, thin walls. The skeletal nature of the construction allowed the walls to be pierced by much larger windows and the vaults to be supported by thin piers and external buttresses. This was an engineering revolution. As a structural system it was more rational and economical than the Anglo-Norman one, concentrating supports only at points of real stress. This allowed the non-structural parts of walls to be cut away. The spatial effect was remarkable and apparently dissolved supporting walls into arches, shafts and spaces (fig. 57).

Fig. 57 (right) Part cross sections of a) Reims Cathedral, France, the nave; b) Durham Cathedral, the nave, illustrating the principles of Gothic architecture. At Reims the very tall thin nave walls are supported by two tiers of flying buttresses weighted down by heavy pinnacles. The structure is minimal and full of large openings. Durham is built in the English thick-wall technique, much squatter and heavier with passages cut into the wall thickness. The thrust of the vault is taken by a single buttress and most of the weight is converted into vertical thrusts in the massive wall thickness.

These new fashions started to have an impact in England after 1130. There is no simple political explanation for this, as the parts of modern France that were influential were not the lands in the west ruled over by Henry II and his sons. Inspiration in fact came from the Île-de-France, and from Picardy and north-eastern France, which English travellers crossed on their way to Paris. Innovations in style were transmitted by travellers, masons and, above all, churchmen. In the middle years of the 12th century some of the most important architectural commissions were in northern England, which had been slow to develop because of William the Conqueror's aggressive harrying of the north. The largest of these were the new houses of the Cistercians.

Gothic architecture

By the reign of King Stephen the Benedictine monasteries of England, with their elaborate liturgical life, were comfortable, secure, prosperous bodies integral to the economic and social infrastructure of the country. Yet across

Fig. 58 (above) Byland Abbey, Yorkshire; reconstruction of the nave as first built. The stalls for the lay brothers were integrated into the lower part of the nave arcade. The prominent rose window, 26ft across, was an architectural elaboration that the earliest Cistercians would have disapproved of.

Europe in the late 11th century and early years of the 12th century reformers increasingly regarded their way of life as a betrayal of the Rule of St Benedict, and groups of monks started to establish their own simpler reformed communities. One of these, later known as the Cistercians, was to create a new type of monasticism. Their success was largely due to their charismatic leader, St Bernard of Clairvaux. By his death in 1153 there were 340 Cistercian houses in Europe, 86 of which were in Britain.[6] The Cistercians set out to avoid wealth and ostentation, over-elaborate liturgy and complex intellectual pursuits; they wanted to be economically independent and their brethren were put to hard labour on their own estates. These convictions were at first expressed in architectural simplicity; the first Cistercian monasteries had plain, aisle-less churches. But as time went by they became less austere and more susceptible to international architectural influences. The exact chronology of the introduction of Gothic forms into their English monasteries is unclear but at least one church was built in a recognisably Gothic manner by the late 1150s.[7]

By 1170 work had started on Byland Abbey, the most ambitious Cistercian church of its age. This was no austere box. The walls were enlivened by three levels of pointed arches supporting a timber barrel vault; the west end was illuminated by a great rose or circular window. (fig. 58). But the architects of Byland

Fig. 59 (right) Canterbury Cathedral, Kent, looking east; the choir of 1175–84. Its principal architectural characteristic is the height of the main arcade, more than half the height of the whole elevation; above are clusters of polished black Purbeck marble shafts used for the first time in England. These lead the eye up to the high vaults, in six parts, with decorated ribs that complement the beautifully carved capitals of the arcade far below. Beyond is the presbytery (fig. 60).

were not using Gothic features as an alternative structural system like the French; they used them as an alternative form of decoration. This was the first manifestation of English Gothic, retaining the structural tradition of Anglo-Norman buildings but adopting the decorative vocabulary of Gothic architecture.

The adoption of Gothic detailing at Byland and then at York Minster was very influential in the north, but the repercussions of events at Canterbury between 1170 and 1175 were of much greater national impact. The most famous murder in English history took place on 29 December 1170 in Canterbury Cathedral; its victim was Archbishop Thomas Becket. Within days miracles were reported. The dead archbishop rapidly became a martyr and, within three years, a saint. This was a turning point in the history of Canterbury. Another took place eighteen months after Becket was canonised: the gutting of Archbishop Anselm's early 12th-century choir by fire. This gave the Canterbury monks the opportunity to create a spectacular new setting for their saint and his relics. After consulting a number of architects, the monks chose a Frenchman, William, who came from the French city of Sens, the location of a new cathedral built in the Gothic style. As the monks wanted to ensure continuity with their much-loved building, he decided to retain the crypt and the lower, undamaged, parts of the choir and construct inside it a new east end.

So what was new about William of Sens's choir (fig. 59)? Compared with the Anglo-Norman work of the nave the arcades were much taller, with gently pointed arches squeezing those of the gallery above. The vault springs from a low point and its ribs are decorated with dog-tooth motifs. The piers themselves were more slender and furnished with carved capitals. Polished limestone was used to enliven the elevations. William of Sens fell from his own scaffolding while supervising the construction of the highest vaults over the eastern crossing. He tried to carry on the work from his sick bed but had to return to France. His replacement was another William, known as 'the Englishman'. He not only completed the repair of the fire damage but was commissioned to build an enlarged chapel to the east of it to replace the Trinity Chapel, the crypt of which contained the relics of St Thomas. This was to have two parts: the Trinity Chapel itself and beyond that a circular shrine called the Corona, where the severed crown of the martyr's head was housed. The Englishman continued the main features of the choir through to the new chapel, which, being raised above a higher crypt, had shorter piers and much more satisfying proportions (fig. 60). The big windows were made possible by some of the earliest visible flying buttresses anywhere. The stained-glass scenes of the life of Christ and the miracles of St Thomas Becket are still largely intact, held in place by geometric iron frameworks (ferramenta). Their colours intensify the effect of the polished limestone columns, the use of which becomes progressively denser as the visitor moves eastwards. In the chapel the arcade piers are doubled-up and entirely made of Purbeck marble, while those nearest the shrine are of a hard pink-and-cream marble imported from abroad.

The experience of moving eastwards through Canterbury Cathedral towards the Corona is breathtaking. It is necessary to ascend steps over both Lanfranc's and William the Englishman's crypts to enter the extraordinary world of polished stone designed to evoke the heavenly Jerusalem in the Book of Revelation. A pilgrim would have felt as if he had been shrunk and placed inside an enamelled reliquary like the Becket casket in the Victoria and Albert Museum. Canterbury was to be influential, not so much through the details of its style or construction (although these were important), but for its lavishness. It was the mother church of England and set the standard for all that came after, particularly in its extravagant use of polished stones. Although Canterbury has more directly French features than any other English building of its age, its successors created a very different look, much more English and, in a sense, much more original. The rebuilding of Wells Cathedral was started soon after 1175 as a deliberate bid to replace Bath as the centre of the diocese of Somerset. It was sufficiently complete to be dedicated in 1239. Over a 60-year period it had at least three architects, all of whose genius must be recognised; for the building that they created was of huge originality and skill. It was the first building in England, if not in the whole of Europe, to be built with pointed arches throughout. But more important was the way the arches were handled. The overwhelming sensation gained by a visit to Wells is the horizontal effect of the nave created by three self-contained strata of arches (fig. 61). The lowest, the nave arcade, is supported by massive cross-shaped piers

Fig. 60 (right) Canterbury Cathedral, Kent. The presbytery was the culmination of the cathedral and the location of St Thomas's shrine from 1220 until its destruction in 1538. The use of polished limestone made a huge impact on both pilgrims and masons from elsewhere. The survival of the original glass is nothing short of miraculous.

Fig. 61 (above) Wells Cathedral, Somerset; the nave is now dominated by the scissor braces at the crossing added in the 14th century. Here the arcade and the clerestory are practically the same height and the triforium becomes a decorative band containing a denser rhythm of arches between the two. The effect of this was to abolish the rhythm of the bay structure and emphasise the great length of the cathedral, now, of course, interrupted by the scissor brace.

faced with 24 shafts bunched in groups of three. In Anglo-Norman cathedrals there was a substantial gallery above the nave arcades but at Wells there is the semblance of a triforium, which in French buildings is a much narrower passage in the thickness of the wall, fronted by an arcade. This arcade runs the entire length of the nave as a consistent band of decoration without vertical interruptions. Above is the clerestory, with the ribs of the vault supported on stubby shafts.[8]

Ideas from Canterbury and Wells fed into the greatest of early English Gothic churches: the cathedral at Lincoln. In 1185 a vault in the east end of the cathedral collapsed and the following year Henry II appointed Hugh of Avalon as the new bishop. These two events led to a rebuilding of the eastern parts, largely completed by the time of Hugh's death in 1200. This probably finished the original plan; but work continued and by about 1250 the whole cathedral, save the Norman west front, had been rebuilt. Lincoln was rebuilt in its own image. This was a cathedral that proclaimed its place at the top of the hierarchy, together with Canterbury and York. As a result nobody stinted on money, scale or decorative effect. Lincoln set out to dazzle – and dazzle it does.

Fig. 62 (above) Lincoln Cathedral; the vault of St Hugh's Choir of about 1200, the first instance anywhere of a rib that ran along the ridge of the vault. To this rib join ribs that have little structural necessity and do not define the bay structure – in other words, they are pure decoration.

The earliest part to be rebuilt was itself replaced in 1255 by the Angel Choir, but St Hugh's choir and eastern transepts remain. The first thing that strikes the visitor is the use of polished limestone in direct imitation of the work at Canterbury. The second thing is the form of the choir vault. The choir is still built with the thick walls, but the piers appear less massive than at Wells and the shafts from the vaults divide the elevation into bays. But the vaults do not reinforce the bay structure. For the first time there is a central rib running the length of the vault. Onto this, at seemingly random points, the transverse ribs join, creating a pattern that at first defies comprehension (fig. 62). This was not structural necessity, it was pure decoration. So at Lincoln ribs are used for the first time in an English way – as surface ornament. The nave vaults are slightly later and less idiosyncratic, but richer, denser, more complex and symmetrical. They succeed in making the vault as interesting and lively as the walls, bringing the whole together in a restless sea of ornament. The nave elevations below have extraordinary depth. This is not only achieved by passages in the clerestory and triforium but by the 27ft span of the arches, allowing a panorama of the aisle walls, which are deeply moulded with blind arcading. The effect is accentuated by the nave piers, each pair of which is subtly different.

The design of Lincoln, extraordinarily experimental and hungry for novelty, had a huge impact on the next two generations of English builders. In 1817 the Regency architect, Thomas Rickman, christened the style of Lincoln 'Early English', a term that nicely expresses the essential insularity of what was being built. The great churches described above, and the many others that followed them, were individualistic and original, taking French ideas and turning them into a decorative vocabulary unique to England. This concentration on elaboration and surface ornament was a development from the Anglo-Saxons through the late Anglo-Norman monuments into the first Gothic structures. There is a real sense in which, by 1220, a national style had been formed.[9]

Monasteries

Fig. 63 (above) Castle Acre Priory, Norfolk; the west front started in *c.*1130. Richly decorated with blind arcading; there were originally four tall windows in the middle, replaced by a single window in the 15th century.

The Norman Conquest did not lead to an immediate surge in the building of new monasteries. Patrons were too uncertain of their hold on England to invest in expensive new projects, preferring instead to donate English land to Norman monasteries. A small number of new monasteries were founded by the king and his richest followers. Of these perhaps the best preserved and most important is at Castle Acre, Norfolk. The small village of Castle Acre still retains the layout of an early Norman town. The house of its owners, the Warenne family, partly survives within the huge earthworks of the largely later castle, fragments of the town walls still stand, and just outside them within its own walled precinct lie the impressive remains of the priory. Land for the priory was given by William II de Warenne in 1090 but the church was only consecrated between 1146 and 1148, and the west front, the most famous and beautiful of all late Anglo-Norman façades, was not finished until the 1160s (fig. 63).

At its heart was the cloister, the great communal space of the priory. Here, between services, the monks could read, drawing books from a large cupboard on the east side. Regulated periods of Latin conversation were also permitted here, as were more mundane tasks such as hair cutting and washing clothes. Abutting the south transept was the chapter house, where the monks gathered each day to listen to the Rule of St Benedict being read and to attend to community business. This was the boardroom of a monastery and it was decorated to match its status. The walls at Castle Acre had interlaced blind arcading painted in bright colours.

The remainder of the east side of the cloister was occupied by a vast dormitory. This was raised up on a vaulted undercroft and at its south end had a remarkable two-storey latrine (or reredorter) with 24 seats. The monks slept fully clothed and descended by a stair to the church for the night-time offices. Below, in the day room, amidst the piers of the vaults, monks in winter could work and read. Detached from the dormitory, to the east was the infirmary, set aside for old or ill monks who received special care and rations.

The south side of the cloister contained the refectory, large enough to seat the whole community. This was a ground-floor room, which in secular buildings might be called a great hall. It had a dais for the prior and a pulpit from which lessons were read during meals. To its east was the warming house where, in deepest winter, a fire was lit on an open hearth in the middle of the room. To the west of the refectory was the kitchen; in the 12th century, monks cooked here in rotation. The vaulted ground floor west of the range next to the kitchen was used for storage of food and wine. Above was the priory guest house and a separate room for the prior. Next to this was the prior's chapel.[10]

Castle Acre was a Cluniac priory following the rites and rituals of the Benedictine Abbey of Cluny in Burgundy. Other orders varied the layout of their buildings and the structure of their governance, but, broadly speaking, from the early 12th century most full-size monastic houses of whichever order were governed and laid out much as at Castle Acre.

From the 1130s large numbers of new monastic houses were founded in England, 120 in the reign of Stephen and, by the end of Henry II's reign, a further 30 to 40. By Henry II's death in 1154 there were around 500. Most of these were new orders and numerically the largest group within them were the canons.[11] Unlike most monks, canons were ordained priests who spent some of their time outside the monastery working among local people. There were various groups of canons but the largest were the Augustinian (or Austin) Canons, who eventually had about 200 houses in England. Their buildings were usually modest – although they could be large – and often would share a parish church. Lilleshall Abbey, Shropshire, is still a parish church, but is fairly typical of one of the larger Augustinian priories, built in the 1190s and occupied by ten or eleven canons.

The most architecturally ambitious order was, however, the Cistercians. Their abbey at Rievaulx is now the most important, interesting and evocative ruined monastery in England. It was founded by Walter Espec, a rich and powerful baron at the court of Henry I who gave 1,000 acres to the new Cistercian order to build a house two miles from his castle at Helmsley,

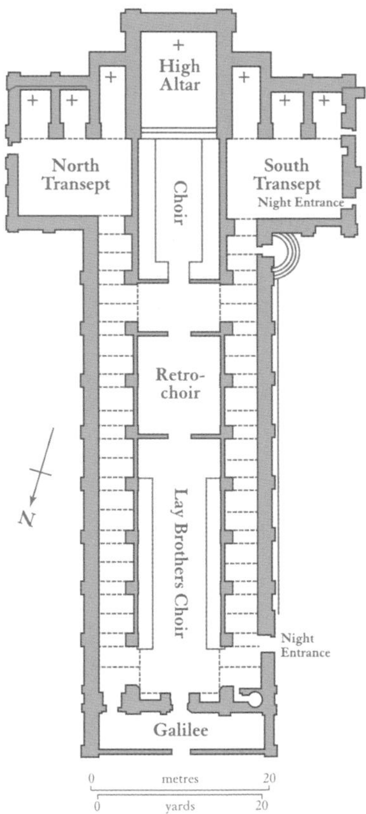

Fig. 64 (above) Rievaulx Abbey, Yorkshire: the east end of the abbey church as rebuilt in 1220–50. The early commitment of the Cistercians to simplicity in life, liturgy and architecture had given way to an intense commitment to the beauty of holiness. The original altar stone can be seen in the centre of the presbytery; behind this was Airled's shrine and behind this additional altars for the community.

Fig. 65 (below) The Abbey church at Rievaulx, Yorkshire as built 1147–67 showing the liturgical divisions. The monk's choir was effectively a church within a church.

Yorkshire. The first abbot, William, enlarged the community from 30 to 300 in a little over a decade, but its fame and success came through its third abbot, Aelred, probably England's greatest medieval churchman, who doubled the size of the community to 650 (most of whom were lay brothers and servants).

The abbey church lay at the heart of monastic life, the focus of the Opus Dei (the work of God), the eight daily services and the celebration of Mass. Early Cistercian churches were divided into three (fig. 64). The western part was reserved for the lay brothers, who were responsible for the heavy manual work of the abbey. They took simpler vows and attended fewer services. Then there was the retro-choir, divided from the lay brothers by a screen topped with a rood (crucifix); this was reserved for old and infirm monks unable to withstand punishing attendance in the choir day and night. At the east end and under the crossing was the monks' choir, the hub of the church. The presbytery was in a stubby east end flanked by altars. This arrangement served Rievaulx well for a century, but between 1220 and 1250 a huge new east end was built in the Gothic style. Cistercian churches began extending their east ends from the 1180s and, as we have seen, this was happening in many cathedrals too (p. 96). The work was done with great richness and expense, and reflected the incredibly successful exploitation of the abbey's estates by successive abbots. As at many cathedrals, Rievaulx's new east end was built to contain a shrine for their very own saint, Aered (fig. 65). This shrine, which was covered in silver and gold, explains the magnificence of the new architectural work that otherwise might have seemed too lavish for an order devoted to simplicity. The new east end cannot only be explained as an expression of architectural hierarchy, for by the 1220s other factors were involved. There were now few, if any, lay brothers, and so the nave was sealed from the choir by a huge stone pulpitum (screen) and used mainly for processions. Second, despite resisting it at first, the Cistercians were now prepared to offer Masses for the souls of donors (votive Masses), and this meant that more private chapels were required. As about one in three monks was ordained, there were probably 35 priests able to celebrate Mass, for whom five chapels against the east wall would have been a welcome addition.[12]

Where the Rich and Powerful Lived

Up to the 17th century kings and their households were constantly on the move. Organising the royal itinerary was a precise task as monarchs spent particular times of the year in specific places, above all during the great religious feasts of Christmas, Easter and Whitsun. They would also want to appear at provincial residences to reinforce their judicial, administrative and military policies and, crucially, to hunt in the royal forests. Royal houses and

castles formed the points around which the court gyrated (fig. 66). The king's preference dictated where they went, what was repaired, built or extended, and when. In each county the sheriff was responsible for organising royal construction work. However, just as bishops and deans employed architects to oversee big projects, so the king had ingeniatores (engineers or designers) in his household. The first of these about whom we know anything was an Englishman called Ailnoth in the 1150s; under him were the master craftsmen, the masons, carpenters and others – all highly paid technical experts, not just workmen. Ailnoth was responsible for Westminster, the most important royal house in England up until 1512, although the precise layout of the palace is unclear before the reign of Henry III (p. 144). The provincial civil residences of the Crown fell into two groups: those large manors that we can legitimately call palaces, such as Clarendon, Wiltshire, and Woodstock, Oxfordshire; and smaller houses situated in royal forests that were used as hunting lodges, such as Writtle, Essex, and Kinver, Staffordshire. Clarendon was the largest and most important royal house in the west. It was excavated in the 1930s, and it is possible to walk through the fields and see substantial chunks of masonry still standing in front of spectacular views of Salisbury.

Fig. 66 (above left) Royal castles and houses in the reign of King Henry III (1216–72).

Fig. 67 (above right) Clarendon Palace, Wiltshire; a reconstruction as it might have appeared in about 1275 looking north-east: a) great hall; b) kitchens; c) King's chambers; d) Queen's chambers; e) gatehouse; f) stables.

Clarendon was a complex of one- and two-storey buildings whose pitched and tiled roofs were arranged in a long line running approximately east–west. At its heart was Henry II's aisled great hall, with kitchens and larders to its west and the royal chambers to its east. The various parts of the building were arranged around cloisters containing gardens; these and other pentices linked the various parts. The house was largely built of stone, and contained rich carving and particularly spectacular tiled pavements, now in the British Museum.[13] The king's hunting lodges were similarly laid out; the one at Writtle, Essex, excavated between 1955 and 1957, was surrounded by a moat. Approached by a bridge and gatehouse, the buildings were again laid out in an axis, with a hall, a kitchen and a chamber (fig. 67). A house such as Writtle was not small; its great hall was about the same size as Clarendon's, but the accommodation was less extensive and built of timber, wattle and daub, not of stone.[14]

These houses, great and small, were not materially different in layout from their Saxon predecessors such as Yeavering or Goltho (pp 29 and 55). They were axially planned, with a large ground-floor hall and a more private chamber slightly detached from it. This continuity of plan suggests a continuity of function, with the royal households living much like their predecessors. At the heart of this was still the hall, a structure of fundamental importance to anyone of any means and pretension, not only to royalty. The hall was no mere structure; it signified its owner's social standing and was the centre of his public life. An example, although not a royal one, survives at Oakham, Rutland (fig. 68). It was built in around 1190 as part of a castle belonging to Walkelin de Ferrers, a sub-tenant of the Earl of Warwick. De Ferrers or his architect must have had close connections with Canterbury Cathedral, as the wonderfully crisp

and lively carving of corbels and capitals is closely related to contemporary work there. The room is of four bays with low aisles. The entrance door has been moved and originally would have been at the east end, with a dais for the owner at the west. With a fire in the middle of the floor, long tables and heavy drinking, the scene on a feast day can hardly have been much different from the time of Beowulf.

While the disrupted reign of King Stephen saw less permanent castle construction, in the reigns of Henry II, Richard I and John this was the largest single item of royal expenditure, consuming ten per cent of royal income. There was serious purpose behind this. First, it was necessary to modernise the forts of the south coast as a protection against invasion, but also as a springboard for continental expeditions and to protect communication routes to the continent. Then it was necessary to protect England's internal borders against the Scots and the Welsh. Perhaps most important of all was the lavishing of money on strategic royal castles inland. These had been established as the administrative, judicial and financial nodes of the kingdom, and many had become favoured royal residences too. All performed another crucial task, of emphasising royal lordship over both great and humble.

Few new castles were founded after 1130. As both prestige and warfare demanded buildings of stone, it was a period of rebuilding and reconstruction. For Henry II and his successors, the cultural and military value of a great tower was still unsurpassed and so, while many timber castles had their walls replaced in stone, the towers were in many cases a new addition. Newcastle-upon-Tyne, Orford, Peveril and Scarborough castles all acquired great towers, but the last, largest and most expensive was at Dover, where Henry II spent £7,000 between 1180 and 1190. To put this in some sort of

Fig. 68 (above left) Oakham Castle, Rutland; a very rare survival of a great hall of around 1190. It is built like a church with a central 'nave' and aisles, though without clerestory windows. The door was originally in the far right bay and the dormer windows are later additions.

Fig. 69 (above) Dover Castle, Kent. Henry II's Great Tower dominates the castle and is surrounded by a mighty curtain wall with 14 towers and two gates, one of which can be seen in this view. In the foreground are the 13th-century Norfolk Towers and the circular St John's Tower, while in the background can be seen St Mary in Castro (fig. 34).

context, the total receipts of the royal exchequer in 1130 were £24,500. Dover has a continuous history of fortification back into the Iron Age and perhaps beyond, but no securely dated remains exist before the reign of Henry II. Henry erected his great tower on the highest point of the site surrounded by an inner defensive wall, with 14 projecting rectangular towers and two gates protected by a defensive outwork or barbican. This inner wall was itself guarded by the Iron Age earthworks around it and a short section of wall to the north-east (fig. 69). The great tower was a colossus: nearly square, 83ft tall, with walls between 17ft and 21ft thick. Its silhouette was designed to be seen from France. Inside it does not disappoint. The great tower, like most post-Conquest castle towers, was approached by a fore-building with steps ascending to a second-floor entrance (fig. 70). Refinements in the Dover fore-building include a chapel on the stair, perhaps for giving thanks for a safe

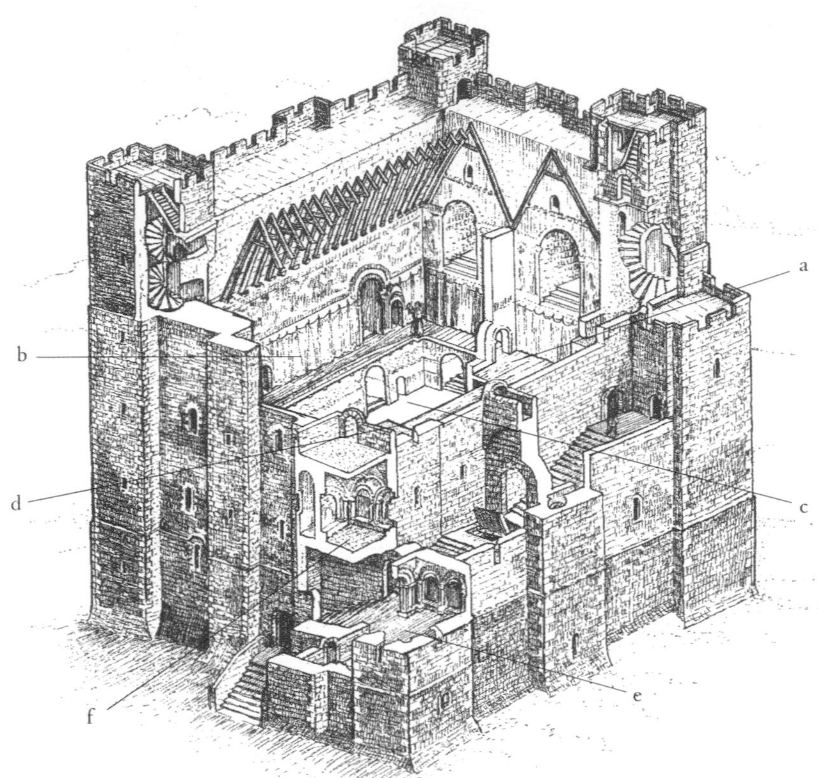

Fig. 70 (left) Dover Castle, Kent; the Great Tower: a) king's hall; b) king's chamber; c) guest chamber; d) guest hall; e) forebuilding, including chapel; f) chapel.

journey, a drawbridge, and a guard room by the entrance door. The main building was three storeys high. The ground floor was designed for kitchens and the two floors above contained two magnificent suites of rooms, one for the king on the second floor and another for guests below. Each had a hall and a chamber, and in the massive thickness of the walls were other subsidiary rooms, including garderobes. The king's floor also had a lavish chapel for his private use. The rooms were architecturally unadorned. Colour and decoration were provided by murals and portable furnishings: hangings, furniture and plate.[15] It is worth dwelling on the great tower at Dover as it was the last in the line of great towers built after the Conquest. Henry II constructed it at a time when military engineering had moved away from square and rectangular towers to cylindrical ones. But this was no ordinary castle; it was built in a deliberately retrospective style to emphasise royal gravitas and dynastic durability. It was also a gateway to England, a place where the king could receive important visitors, many of whom were on their way to the new shrine of St Thomas at Canterbury Cathedral. So while this was a military building, it was also a palace and guest house cast in the traditional language of dynastic triumphalism.

Dover was, of course, exceptional in both its scale and the thoroughness in which it was rebuilt. For many hundreds of other castles, rebuilding in stone took place piecemeal over a long period. In many instances timber palisades were replaced by stone walls, while the residential buildings inside remained

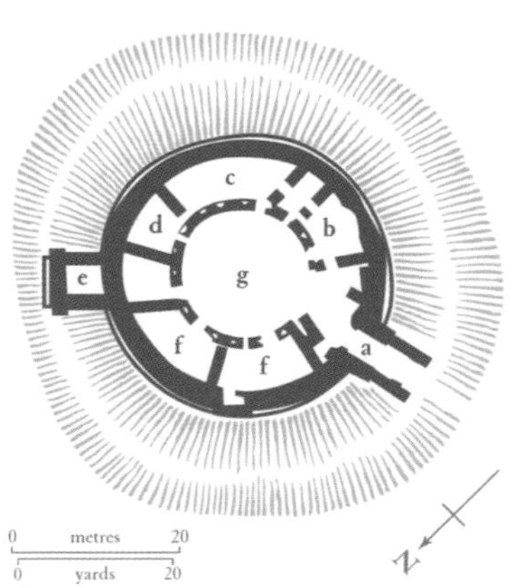

Fig. 71 (above right) Totnes Castle, Devon. The motte is what we see today, although there was a bailey with a great hall and other buildings in it. The circular curtain wall was topped with crenellations with arrow slits. Within the wall was at least one domestic building.

Fig. 72 (above) Restormel Castle, Cornwall was topped by a ring of buildings 130ft across: a) gate tower; b) kitchen; c) hall above; d) chambers above; e) chapel above; f) store; g) courtyard.

of wood. This can be seen at Totnes, Devon, an example of a motte and bailey castle dominating an important trading settlement (fig. 71). It was founded, together with a priory, by Judhael of Brittany, a commander in the Conqueror's south-west campaign. The timber palisades on top of the exceptionally large motte were rebuilt by his successors in around 1200. The arrangement of the domestic buildings inside cannot now be discerned, but at Restormel in Cornwall the whole plan can be read in a single visit. It is most impressive (fig. 72). The kitchen, hall, lord's chambers and guest rooms are all arranged inside the perfectly circular outer walls, with only the gatehouse and the chapel projecting outside the circuit. In the 12th century castles were never ordinary residences. Holding a castle proved that the owner was in royal favour with delegated authority to govern and dispense justice. The crown's ability to take and hold castles, to raise them and demolish them, to grant them out and to take them back was central to the exercise of power. Constructing a new castle required royal permission, and if the king were ever to need it he had the right to requisition it at will. From the 1150s to the 1210s the balance of castle power shifted markedly towards the Crown. At the end of the chaotic reign of Stephen there had been 225 baronial and 49 royal castles. By 1214 there were only 179 baronial castles and the number of royal castles had risen to 93; a shift in ratio from 5:1 to 2:1.

From the 12th century oxen began to replace horses for pulling ploughs and, soon, for pulling carts. Horses could be much faster than oxen but required better roads. By 1066 the Saxon kings had done much to improve the road system and build bridges (pp 25 and 40), but during the 13th century many hundreds of new bridges were built; indeed, of the rivers that were bridged before 1750 almost all had been crossed by 1250. This was certainly a transport revolution but also an engineering one. The technology to build stone bridges was developed by the architects of the great cathedrals, abbeys and castles. Before 1100 most bridges were of timber, such as the impressive bridge excavated over the river Trent in 1993, but during the following century techniques were developed for building foundations underwater, resulting in some impressive feats of engineering. An early surviving bridge, although now tragically marooned in a roundabout, is in Exeter (fig. 73). It was completed by about 1200 and originally had 17 spans of round-headed and pointed arches. The arches were built on wooden piles driven into the bed of the River Exe and protected by triangular cutwaters jutting into the stream. Exeter is typical of a lowland bridge; upland bridges had to withstand flash floods and fast-running waters, and thus had much higher and wider spans. The main arches of Elvet Bridge in Durham, which span over 30ft, were erected in 1228. The bridge, which originally had 14 arches, was commissioned by the bishop and built by his masons. It incorporated chapels at either end (fig. 74).[16]

It was the location of bridges that determined the course of roads and stimulated their growth. During the 13th century there was a change from the idea of a road that simply went to the local market to the idea of a network serving the whole kingdom. This was stimulated by increasing trade, new ports and the economic activities of castles, cathedrals and monasteries. However, most importantly, towns could not grow without bridges and roads. Horse transport and a road and bridge network supported the rapid

Fig. 73 (left) The medieval Exe Bridge, Exeter, Cornwall, built in 1200 through the efforts of Nicholas Gervaise, a wealthy merchant who was four times mayor of the city. Like many medieval bridges, it was endowed with property to provide an income for its upkeep.

Fig. 74 (above right) Thomas Hearne, view of Durham from the northeast *c.*1783. Elvet Bridge was rebuilt and extended in 1228 and incorporated St James's and St Andrew's Chapels, one at each end. In the background is the tower of the cathedral and, on a mound, the Castle Keep.

growth of towns such as London and Norwich that needed vast quantities of food, drink and firewood to survive. As a rough guide, a town of 3,000 people would need the produce of ten villages or over three square miles to support it, and all this had to be brought to town every day.[17] Finally, the growth of an effective road network made it easier to transport building materials. The reliance on cheap but slow water transport decreased as faster horse-drawn wagons took over as the principal means of moving material round the countryside.[18]

The Countryside

The Norman invaders came to exploit the English countryside. While they did not introduce a new system of social obligation on the population (Saxon lords had received all sorts of service from their dependants), the Conquest did result in the tightening and redefinition of the bonds of lordship. Norman landlords of the first generation were interested in labour obligations from their tenants, but later generations were more interested in cash from rents and fees, made possible by the fact that many tenants were generating a healthy cash surplus from agriculture by 1100. Villages were occupied by what we call peasants. The term is unfortunate as it gives the impression of poverty-stricken and down-trodden illiterates eking out a living from the soil. Villagers, who made up 80 per cent of the population, were in fact smallholders farming anything between 5 and 40 acres. Half held their land in villeinage; that is to say they owed their landlord payment, labour services and required permission to marry. The rest were freemen, who often had smaller landholdings. Villeins and freemen alike cooperated in the common-field system, where it existed (p. 54), but were also engaged in market activities: buying, selling and making money. By the 1180s the economic stability of the richer peasants started having an impact on the places in which they lived. This impact varied hugely across the country and even between adjacent villages. Dwellings were normally set in a banked or hedged toft of about a quarter acre within this (fig. 26). In some parts of the country – particularly the south-west – a single building or long house contained space at one end for people and at the other for animals. This arrangement was becoming less common by the 13th century; by then most tofts in the midlands and the south-east had a principal cottage grouped with a barn or granary and sometimes a byre. Richer peasants might also have a separate kitchen, a freestanding bake-house and even a dovecot or cart-house.

The crucial development in the period between about 1180 and 1320 was the introduction of various types of foundation, either for the full length of a building or just for its principal posts. The abandonment of earth-fast building (posts sunk in the ground) over most of England opened up the possibility for a variety of superstructures that in some parts of the country saw stone walls up to the eaves but more commonly saw a variety of timber structures resting on low or buried stone foundations. In the midlands, the west and north, most of these were crucks. A cruck is essentially an A-shaped truss made of large, slightly curving, timbers. A number of these could be erected on a timber base (or sole) plate and then be joined together at the top (ridge) and along their sloping side with beams called purlins (fig. 75a).

Alternatively, walls could be constructed with a box frame. Simple upright beams were jointed into a sole plate and capped by a top plate on which the roof trusses rested – this method was more common in the east and south (fig. 75c). A more sophisticated variation of this was the post-and-truss construction, essentially a timber-framed grid upon which the roof trusses rested, found in the west and south (fig. 75b). In all these cases the gaps were filled with wattle and daub – to make walls impervious to the elements – and the roof covered with thatch. Windows were small, glassless and furnished with shutters. Chimney stacks were rare, and fires would be lit in grates or boxes on the beaten-earth floors.

Most of these constructional systems resulted in framed units of about 15ft, making most houses either 30ft or 45ft by 15ft wide. So although peasant houses were dark and smoky, they were not smaller than workers' housing in Victorian cities.[19] They were also more private than might be imagined. Although the whole basis of village life was communal, especially where common-field systems predominated, the tofts – with their hedges and banks, which often rose to head height – and cottages with stout, locked doors, gave

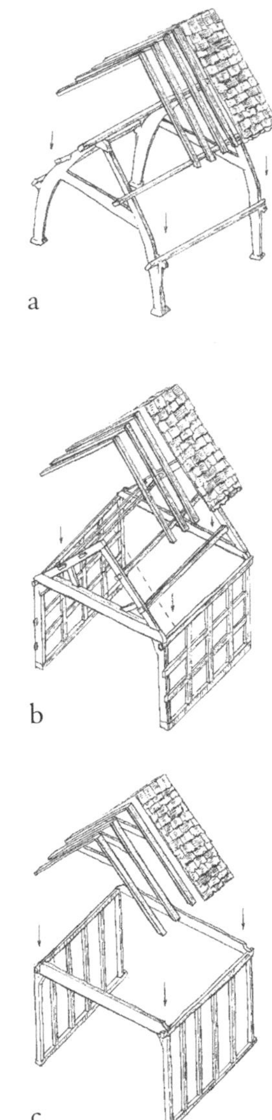

Fig. 75 (above) As with all issues to do with medieval construction, techniques were highly regionalised and are resistant to easy categorisation. Yet a) cruck; b) box frame and c) post and truss construction are the most common categories found in the Middle Ages in England.

Fig. 76 (top) The Psalter of which this is a page was commissioned by Geoffrey Luttrell, lord of the manor at Irnham in Lincolnshire in 1320–40. Uniquely, it shows scenes of everyday rural life, including this image of a typical 14th-century water mill. (from *The Luttrell Psalter*, c.1325–35, British Library. Shelfmark: Add. 42130, f.181)

Fig. 77 (above) An early 14th century stone frieze from the infirmary hall at Rievaulx Abbey, Yorkshire. A contemporary windmill is shown with steps up to the door and a pivot for the whole building to move to catch the wind.

Fig. 78 (right) Temple Cressing, Essex: a longitudinal section of the wheat barn of the 1290s. The barn is remarkably unaltered, and would have originally had wooden boarded walls.

peasant families individuality and privacy. At Steventon, Berkshire, there are a number of cruck-built cottages of about 1270 to 1280 associated with a medieval causeway, but surviving peasant houses of this date are rare and most of our knowledge comes from archaeology.[20]

These cottages could not have been built by unskilled labour. It was necessary to employ a carpenter and have access to properly cut timber showing that by the 13th century there were thousands of carpenters working in villages as well as for the aristocracy, Crown and the Church. Nor did a house come cheap. It is likely that a straightforward cottage would have cost a peasant a year's income, a sum that was probably borrowed and paid off like a modern mortgage.[21]

The aristocracy gained about 60 per cent of their income from rents and fees but they were much more interested in agriculture than their continental counterparts; between 1184 and 1214 almost all took their demesne land into direct management. This they did with some success, refining crop rotation and exploiting existing sources of income more efficiently. One of the most important of these was milling, which, as we have seen, was very profitable. After 1100 landlords were busy building new mills and refurbishing old ones, doubling their number to perhaps 12,000 by 1300. In this there was one really important invention: the windmill. It is likely that the first one was built in East Anglia not long before 1185, but they took some time to perfect and construction only boomed in the east in the 1240s, followed by other parts of the country where fast-running water was scarce. A new windmill cost about £10 but they tended to have greater repair costs than watermills, which were cheaper to run though expensive to build. The water engineering alone could cost £15 or more. Watermills were of the type shown in the Luttrell Psalter (fig. 76); the mill building was like any normal timber-framed building and had a thatched roof. The windmill was much more specialised as it had to turn and face the wind. This meant that it had to pivot on a central mast, which had to be sturdy enough to resist the huge stresses of wind drag (fig. 77).[22]

Technological advances in milling were matched by advances in the quality and construction of other agricultural buildings. Barns were pre-eminent in the farmyard, crucial for the safe and dry storage of crops. At Temple Cressing, Essex, are two barns that were once part of the large estate of the Knights Templar. The earlier is the barley barn, erected in the 1230s; the wheat barn is later, built in the 1290s (figs 78 and 79). The wheat barn shows some significant

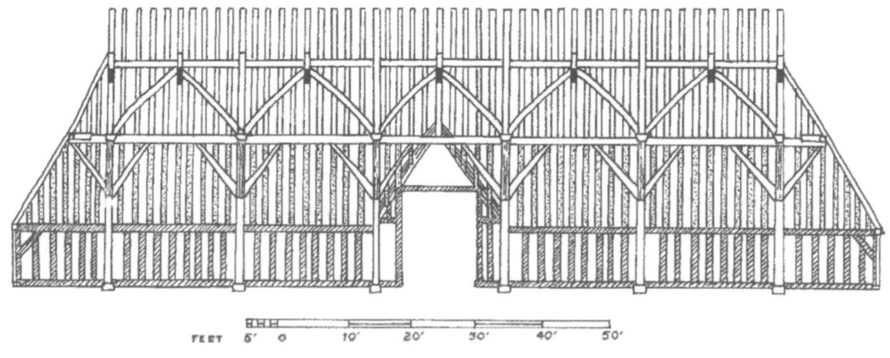

Fig. 79 (left) Temple Cressing, Essex, The Wheat Barn, interior. Squared timbers made more regular and integrated structures by the end of the thirteenth century.

technical improvements even though it was built only 60 years later than the barley barn. In timber building, structural capabilities are determined by the carpenter's ability to make strong joints. In early timber structures these were simple lap joints (one timber resting on another), but the Cressing barns show that during the late 13th century these simple joints were largely superseded by mortise-and-tenons and stronger types of lap joint. Moreover, the timbers were squared and more regular, and the structure was much better integrated, with all the elements soundly jointed together. These advances made possible the construction of very large barns for 1,000-acre estates such as Temple Cressing.[23]

Towns

Between 1100 and 1300 the percentage of the English population that lived in towns doubled to 20 per cent. In 1086 there were about 100 boroughs, almost all founded by royal will. By 1300 there were more than 500, many founded by the Church and the aristocracy. Towns were profitable business; rents from the burgesses were good, but landlords could also profit from market tolls and the borough court. The example of King's (originally Bishop's) Lynn, Nor-

Fig. 80 (below right) King's Lynn, Norfolk; maps showing the expansion of the town after 1150. As a consequence the town today, unusually, has two market places (Tuesday and Saturday) and two very large churches, the original parish church St Margaret's and a chapel of ease St Nicholas serving the town extension.

Fig. 81 (right) 28 Cornmarket St, Oxford is a three-storied 15th century house with cellars. All floors were originally jettied but the ground floor has been underbuilt. There is a handsome corner post.

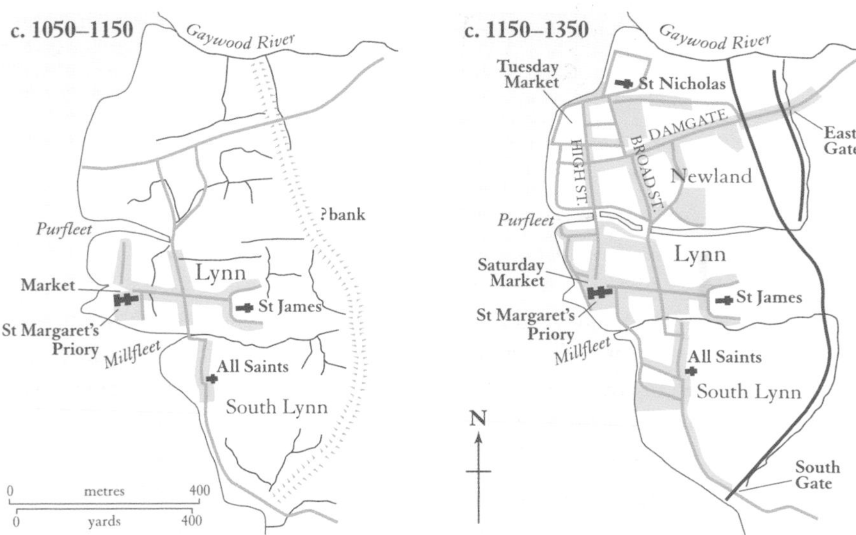

folk, demonstrates this nicely. In 1090 Herbert de Losinga, Bishop of Thetford, established a priory and market in the Anglo-Saxon settlement of Lynn. His intention was to capture a slice of the trade that would flow through the Wash and down the Great Ouse. The settlement was a success, and in about 1150 Bishop Turbe built an extension to the town, with a colossal new marketplace and a huge church. This was under the direct lordship of the bishop and was highly lucrative, so much so that the bishop bought back his rights over the original town and obtained a royal charter for the unified settlement in 1204 (fig. 80). A charter meant that the bishop could govern the town and collect taxes in exchange for a fixed fee paid to the Crown.[24] The excavation

Fig. 82 (left) Lady Row, York was a commercial development built in around 1316 in Holy Trinity Churchyard as an endowment for the chantry of the Blessed Virgin in the church. They are the earliest timber buildings in York and are a very early example of jettying.

of early medieval timber houses in Lynn, London and several other towns corroborates what the great barns at Cressing Temple tell us, which is that in the late 12th century timbers became squarer, cut by saw, mortise-and-tenon joints start to become common, frames were more stoutly constructed, with regularly spaced studding, and earth-fast posts were replaced by timber sole plates, often on foundations. This was all part of a process that led to fully self-supporting frames for domestic dwellings. The impetus for structural and technical advances, and the reasons for them, were not simple. On the one hand, they were driven by the need to solve intensely practical problems. For instance, the making of timber revetments that formed the London riverfront led to innovations in timber framing, their constructors having to battle against the intense forces of the tidal Thames. On the other hand, high-level patronage from bishops (as at Hereford), deans (as at Salisbury) or by the king himself (at Westminster) made stylistic and engineering demands that constantly pushed carpenters to the limit of their confidence. Technical improvement in the construction of timber town buildings was important as it changed the appearance of English towns. Earth-fast timber houses needed to be replaced or completely refurbished every 15 or 20 years as their foundations rotted. Timber-framed structures built on stone foundations lasted much longer – indeed, when well maintained, for centuries. Thus, owning a townhouse was now not merely the simple possession of a plot of land, it was a long-term investment. This meant that greater efforts were made in the building's appearance and decoration, its maintenance, and its visual and spatial relationship with other buildings. Houses got taller, too. Timber framing meant that they could be built three storeys high; the first medieval domestic skyscrapers were constructed by the 1190s, and soon after their upper floors began to be jettied out (fig. 81).[25]

Many townhouses were also shops. Trade was, of course, central to the purpose of towns; by 1234 Canterbury had 200 shops and by 1300 Chester had 270. But, as today, London was England's shopping Mecca. Its principal shopping street, Cheapside, was 450 yards long and 20 yards wide. The shops, 400 of them lined on either side, were occupied by goldsmiths, mercers, drapers, spicers, saddlers, girdlers, chandlers, wiredrawers, bucklemakers, pursemakers, buttonmakers and more. The shops themselves were very narrow, typically only 6ft to 7ft wide, and about 10ft to 12ft deep. Elsewhere in the city, where land was less valuable, shops were wider, their frontages measuring between 15ft and 20ft. The shops had a window opening and a narrow door, and window shutters were lifted during the day to reveal large, round-headed openings. Most shoppers would have been served standing in the street, rather like in an Arab souk today. Jetties overhead would have kept off the rain. Like a souk, too, the interiors were crammed with goods, and merchants' houses elsewhere in the city would have acted as warehouses to supply them. Most shops were of timber, but some party walls and some larger shops were of stone.[26]

No early medieval shops survive today unaltered and so we have to study later examples to get an understanding of how retail premises originally looked. Lady Row, Goodramgate, York, is a row of shops dating from 1316 that have lost their original windows (fig. 82). Lady Row is not untypical of what we know of commercial developments of shops built by single landlords and then rented to shopkeepers. The upper rooms may have been separately let as housing, or traders may have lived above their showrooms. A rare survival from *c.*1350 is 169 Spon Street, Coventry, a different type of shop, probably built by a merchant with a showroom on the street and a substantial house with a hall for the family behind (fig. 83).[27]

Fig. 83 (right) 169 Spon Street, Coventry. Although restored in 1970, this shop is a rare survivor from the 1350s in a district of Coventry devoted to the cloth and leather trades. No medieval shop in England survives with its original ground floor openings intact.

From the 13th century there were shops and houses built of stone; a remarkable surviving group can be found in the lower city at Lincoln, which, in the mid 13th century, was one of the largest and richest towns in England. Here two stone houses still stand and the remains of 30 more have been excavated. The Jews House, The Strait, of *c.*1190, was a prestigious structure probably containing three shops – two on one side of a central door and one on the other (fig. 84). The door led to a secure back range (now lost) for the storage of valuables, with a staircase to the first floor. The first floor contained two residential rooms, one with a fireplace. The external elevation was magnificent, with a fine zigzag-moulded door and heavily moulded two-light windows above. The chimney stack was incorporated into the front elevation as a badge of wealth and sophistication.

In contrast to Lincoln, stone houses in most other towns had undercrofts rather than rear strong-rooms. A complete, though restored, example is 58 French Street, Southampton, built for a merchant called John Fortin in the 1290s (fig. 85). It was one of about 60 stone and timber merchants' houses in one of England's most important ports. As at Lincoln there was a shop at the front, but behind was a hall and private chamber for the owner, and upstairs were two bedrooms. The whole was set upon an undercroft built for the secure storage of merchandise. This was typical of its type: a building that was a home, a showroom, a warehouse and an office all in one.[28] Towns were also home to the houses of the aristocracy, prelates and the Crown. Again, in Lincoln, one such high-status house survives, probably built for a visit of King Henry II in 1157. Like 1 The Strait, it presented its prestigious front to the street with not one but two large chimney stacks. The principal archway, which survives, was clearly the entrance to a very special house. On the first

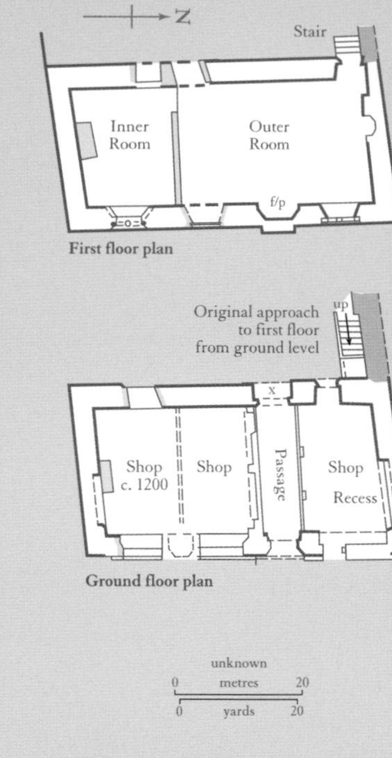

Fig. 84 (above) The Jews House, The Strait, Lincoln of around 1190. The plans show that, unusually, the fireplace was placed over the ground floor passageway, a way of emphasising on the street front that the house had such a luxurious facility.

Fig. 85 (below left) 58 French Street Southampton, though dating from the 1290s, was heavily restored after 1972. It is a rare survivor of a building type that was once very common in towns, the merchant's house-cum-emporium.

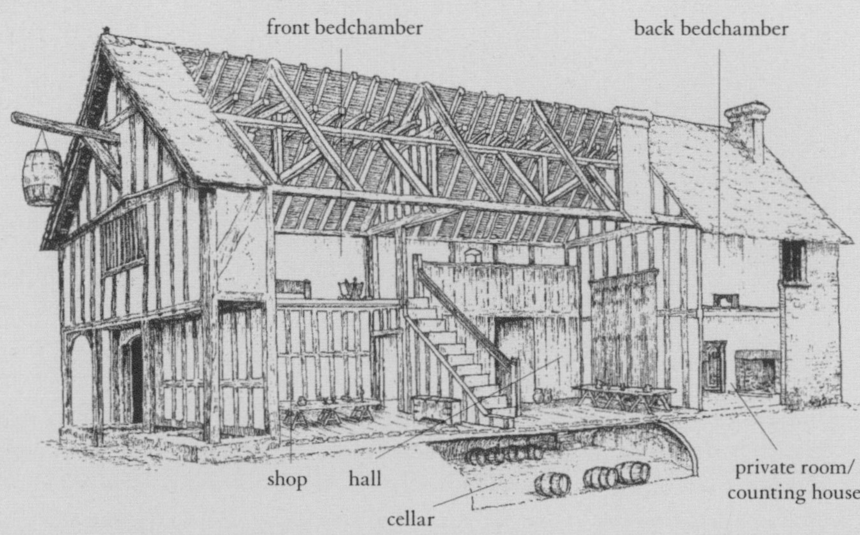

Fig. 86 (below) St Mary's Hospital Chichester of 1290–1300 looks like a church: its 'nave' was a ward for the patients who would lie on beds at right angles to the outer walls; they had a clear view of the 'chancel', a chapel at the east end separated from the ward by a fine screen.

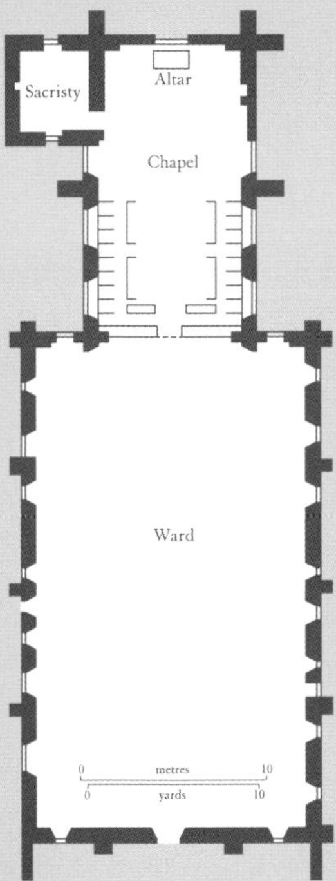

floor was a huge hall raised up above ground-floor vaults, and at right angles to it a withdrawing chamber for the king. This was a compact, but grandiloquent town house of the first order.[29]

As well as shops, many other trades were practised, particularly those concerned with food and drink, especially butchery and baking. Many of the larger towns such as Lincoln, York and Oxford specialised in the manufacture of woollen cloth and served an international clientele. Merchants were cosmopolitan; the best houses would have been comfortable, luxurious even, with goods from all over the world. The contents of a rubbish pit at one of the stone houses in Southampton not only contained pottery from France and Spain, but fig and grape seeds, and the skeleton of a pet monkey.

The picture painted above is of towns as engines of trade and prosperity, with robust, well-made houses, shops and churches. They were also chaotic. Everyone in a medieval town wanted to live in the centre, and rich and poor lived hugger-mugger in crowded, narrow streets, cohabiting with horses and scavenging pigs. Crafts and trades were practised in the centre of town, sometimes in the back of shops or in separate buildings in back yards. Many were noxious: tanning, brewing and smithing were all unpleasant to live close to. On the positive side, piped water supplies began to be developed, the removal of rubbish to out-of-town pits was encouraged, and early forms of building control enforced rules about the location and construction of privies. After 1200 towns started to acquire communal institutions such as hospitals, schools and colleges. Of all the institutions that were later to populate English towns, hospitals were, at first, most numerous. A single Latinised word 'xenodochium' embraced institutions that today we would separate out into hospital, almshouse and guest house, but in the early Middle Ages a single foundation was often a mixture of all three. Just as Norman kings and churchmen built castles and cathedrals, so they founded hospitals, most intensely between 1100 and 1220. Archbishop Lanfranc, for instance, founded three hospitals at Canterbury for ten paupers, 60 lepers and many elderly priests. St Mary's Hospital, Chichester, Sussex, although built between 1290 and 1300, is typical of these early foundations (fig. 86). The essential principle was that every inmate should have a clear view of Mass being celebrated in the hospital chapel. So the whole building was like a church, with the nave being a ward containing low wooden beds with straw mattresses, and the chancel being a complete chapel, separated from the rest by a screen. In such a hospital the sick would be cared for but passing travellers, especially pilgrims, would also be given beds.[30]

The Economics of Building

The sheer volume of building described in this chapter perhaps exceeded even the achievements of the first generation after the Conquest. Much was bankrolled by good economic conditions: the economy was swollen with silver and agricultural profits rose rapidly as a result of entrepreneurialism. The most successful cathedrals, such as Salisbury, enjoyed an increase in income of 168 per cent in a century. Towns grew, markets prospered, communications improved, and education produced a class of able and ambitious clerks and administrators.

But it was a different sort of building boom to the one stimulated by the Conquest. There were now proper quarries, better-skilled masons (and more of them), and few buildings were started anew. New monasteries were rare and, after the 1130s, no new dioceses were created until 1547 – only Salisbury Cathedral stands out as an entirely new structure. Most churches and castles were reconstructions, adaptations and extensions of existing buildings. Architectural leadership lay firmly with the cathedrals, whose golden age it was. These institutions were in cities, meaning that their influence in terms of architecture – as well as learning, ideas and education – was more profound than even the greatest of the rural monasteries. While most cathedrals were progressively rebuilt in new styles, many rural monastic churches remained Anglo-Norman.[31]

England's cathedrals are collectively one of the supreme architectural achievements of the whole Middle Ages. This is partly a result of the inventiveness of English masons and designers, but equally of the wealth of English sees. English dioceses were larger than those on the continent and correspondingly richer. The richest, such as Winchester (£3,000 a year), Durham (£2,700), Canterbury (£2,140) or Ely (£2,000), had incomes equivalent to the most prosperous earls. Indeed, by the end of the 13th century 12 out of Europe's 40 richest dioceses were in England. It was this wealth, carefully exploited by bishops and deans, that funded the extraordinary sumptuousness of cathedrals such as Lincoln and Salisbury. Salisbury, without its spire, cost around £28,000 over 50 years. A single bay at Lincoln (p. 96), because of the profusion of carving, probably cost twice as much as its French equivalent.[32]

Yet financing the construction of a cathedral was hugely expensive and it was unlikely that the normal revenues of a diocese, however rich, would suffice. At Lincoln, for instance, a fabric fund was created in around 1200, endowed by dividing the cathedral's income in two. This was supplemented by gifts from all over the diocese responding to the disastrous collapse of 1185. To encourage more giving, continual Masses were said for those who contributed to the work. Landowners might contribute half an acre of land and symbolically place a sod from it on the altar. A tax was also levied on every household in the diocese at the Whitsun procession.[33] While all these sources of income were important, financing the largest and most spectacular projects was substantially boosted by the financial muscle of a really famous saint. Although in many cathedrals Anglo-Saxon saints had been translated to Anglo-Norman buildings, their setting was now regarded as insufficiently magnificent. So through the 13th and 14th centuries the east ends of dozens of great churches were extended to provide suitably spectacular shrines for Anglo-Saxon and contemporary saints, as well as space for visiting pilgrims. This movement was given a huge boost by the new setting for the relics of St Thomas Becket at Canterbury. Thus between 1190 and 1220, for example, work started on building new eastern arms at Beverly, Ely, Hereford, Lichfield, Lincoln, Southwell, Winchester and Worcester.

As the English economy and infrastructure strengthened and towns grew, secular and ecclesiastical lords rebuilt their castles and cathedrals in new styles. Churches developed in response to changing liturgy, while the great secular residences remained much as they had done for generations, reflecting a more stable way of life for royalty and nobility. For richer ordinary people life also improved, and their houses became more sturdy, commodious and permanent.

As the second generation of Normans felt more English, so the great cathedrals, abbeys, castles and houses then under construction became increasingly distinct from their counterparts in France. Architecture had been through an intense period of experimentation from 1150 to 1170, but by about 1200 there was an increasingly uniform approach to large-scale building. Some of the excesses of late Anglo-Norman decoration were forgotten and the new Gothic style adopted simpler, but bold and deeply cut, pointed arches. Yet it was rooted in what had gone before: English cathedrals clung to the thick wall technique often with masonry 13ft thick. This not only characterised early English Gothic but influenced the proportions and scale of everything that came after. As cathedrals were rebuilt and extended they embodied the Anglo-Norman structural techniques. Thus from a European perspective early English Gothic was rich, insular and distinctive.

5— Extravaganza

—1250-1350

English architecture in the period from 1220 to 1350 displays the confidence that comes with wealth and independence.

Introduction

The hundred years after 1250 are among the most energetic, inventive and extravagant periods of building in English history, a time in which English architecture became as distinctive as its national character. The building boom that started in the 1220s continued strongly up to about 1300 (fig. 87). This almost precisely mirrored an extraordinary period of economic growth and national prosperity that was underpinned by rapid population growth (fig. 88).

Yet the period was not one of political stability. Politically it was characterised by a struggle between the Crown and the aristocracy. In 1215 King John had been forced to sign Magna Carta, a charter that protected barons, freemen and the Church against the arbitrary actions of the king, emphasising that royal power was held under the law. This, and the struggles to enforce it during subsequent reigns, are hugely important for England. Unlike France, where the king answered only to God, in England monarchs were not only below God but also subject to the law of the land.

John's reign descended into chaos and civil war. He died in 1216, to be succeeded by his son Henry III, who was only nine. Most of the country was in the hands of the nobility, who were in revolt against John, and in London resided their ally, Prince Louis, heir to the French throne, whom they wished to crown king. But after the Battle of Lincoln in 1217 Henry and his party soon regained control, and Henry was to go on to reign for 46 unstable and quarrelsome years. The crisis of 1216–17, Henry's subsequent favouritism towards foreign advisors, and the heavy-handed exercise of papal jurisdiction were important components in a strengthening sense of English identity during his reign. The process of national definition continued under Edward I, who came to the throne in 1272 at the age of 33. Edward was entirely different to his father; the first 20 years of his rule were characterised by decisiveness and determination, and saw the conquering of North Wales and almost continual war with Scotland. These years also saw persistent and heavy taxation, strengthening the role of parliament. Yet English national identity was also strengthened, partly in counterpoint to resurgent identities in Scotland and Wales.[1]

Edward II, who came to the throne on Edward's I death in 1307, was completely unsuited to kingship; weak, vindictive and directionless, he squandered the goodwill of the aristocracy, who had supported his father.

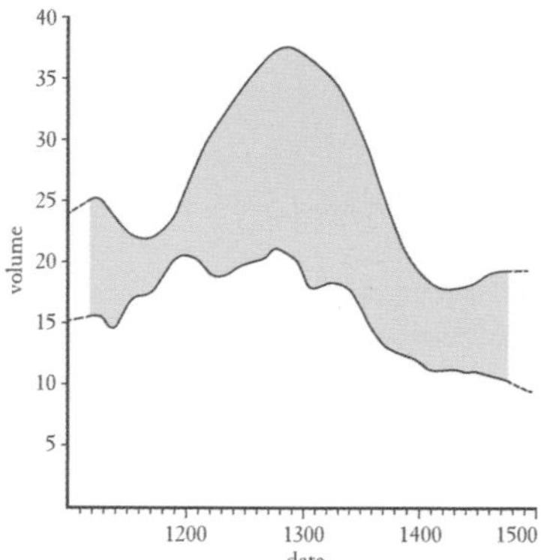

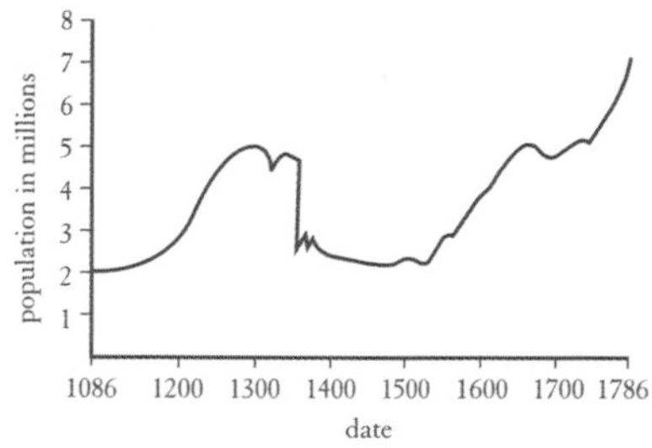

Fig. 87 (top) Graph showing volume of cathedral and abbey building in England 1100–1500. The upper curve represents the average trend of 40 major building campaigns in each decade; the lower curve the average trend of campaigns started by decade at 85 buildings.

Fig. 88 (above) The estimated population of England 1086–1786. The catastrophic effects of the Black Death in 1348 can be clearly seen.

He was deposed in 1327 and replaced by his son Edward III. On Edward III's accession the monarchy was ineffectual and unpopular, and the king was only fourteen. Yet Edward went on to forge a reputation as one of England's greatest warrior kings. John and Henry III had lost all the Crown's great continental possessions except Gascony, which Henry had agreed to hold from the French king. Tension over this, and Edward's claim to the French throne, led to the Anglo-French wars of 1337 to 1453, known as the Hundred Years' War.

Beliefs and Ideas

The way buildings look is governed by the way people think. During the 13th century there were some significant changes in the way people thought about God and about the relationship between the Church and society. These were European streams of thought and doctrine that had varying impacts on the appearance of buildings across Europe. In terms of English architecture, however, there were three particularly important theological developments.

The first came out of the Fourth Lateran Council held at the Lateran Basilica in Rome by Pope Innocent III in 1215 that promulgated the doctrine of transubstantiation – the transformation of bread and wine into Christ's body and blood during the Eucharist. Transubstantiation, which could only be effected by an ordained priest, further elevated priestly status above the congregation and put even greater weight on the significance of the chancel, the part of the church in which communion was celebrated. The statutes of the council made a direct contribution to a movement in England that saw, from around 1200, pressure to rebuild the chancels of churches to provide a suitable setting for the proper celebration of the Eucharist.

The second – another formal definition of an accepted belief – came out of the Council of Lyon in 1274. The council defined purgatory as the place where the soul rested between death and the Last Judgement while being refined by the prayers of the living. Prayers for the dead were now accepted as being as effective as prayers for the living – if not more so. This had a powerful influence on those rich enough to be able to guarantee prayers for themselves after they had died, and led, after 1300, to a huge upsurge in the foundation of perpetual chantries. At one end of the social and economic scale a chantry could simply be an endowment for a priest to say Mass for an individual's soul; at the other it could be the foundation of a large college, school or hospital with a dozen or more secular priests.

At the highest levels of society those with sufficient means founded a college of priests in their own residences. Henry III did this at Westminster (St Stephen's) and at Windsor (St George's). Thomas, Earl of Lancaster, did the same at his mighty castle at Kenilworth. These chantries and colleges did not replace the monasteries. Monasteries continued to be very important, especially to those who could not afford customised care of their souls in private institutions. Yet, as a result, few new enclosed monastic houses were founded after about 1300.

The third development was an increasing interest in the veneration of the Virgin Mary. Before the Conquest the English had shown a strong devotion to the Virgin, but in the 13th century this developed into a national obsession. The Virgin Mary was the universal saint – she could be worshipped anywhere, free from specific geographical or personal associations and, of course, she appealed to women. Lady chapels were increasingly built to honour Mary, and became major parts of monasteries and cathedrals.

To these theological developments we need to add a fourth, of a different and more amorphous nature – chivalry. From the time of the Norman Conquest the upper classes began developing a code of behaviour – manners, if you like – that centred on physical prowess, generosity, courtesy and loyalty. How these values, which are understandable in the context of the knightly hall or the tournament, applied to the gruesome world of medieval warfare is hard to comprehend. But this exotic aristocratic culture was the way that the Church rationalised the activities of a militaristic society. In this way the brutality of the Crusades, for instance, could be fitted into a Christian world.

Entry to the chivalric world demanded excellent horsemanship, and was therefore restricted to those with the means to equip their steeds and to perfect equestrian techniques. Mounted knights practised their art in peacetime at tournaments, initially to the death but later as a form of chivalric festival. In this the cult of King Arthur and his knights was an important component, with kings and knights modelling themselves on the legendary king and his companions.[2] Edward I ordered the construction of the 'Arthurian' round table that still hangs in Winchester Castle great hall; in 1344 his grandson, Edward III, outdid him when he constructed a building 200ft in diameter at Windsor to contain a great round table as the centrepiece of a festival at which he founded the Order of the Round Table. Arthurian legend and contemporary court life were inextricably connected.[3]

These romantic and militarised ideas were converted into architectural style. In this violent and warlike world castles were designed to defend their occupants from aggressors but their individual elements were often stylised. Turrets, battlements, machicolations, drawbridges and moats were as much elements of a chivalric style as functional components. Just as the 18th-century noble had a Corinthian portico, reflecting his self-image as an ancient Roman senator, so the 13th-century magnate had his machicolations, reflecting his as a heroic knight; thus from the reign of Edward I fortification was often as much a style as a form of defence.[4]

The most obvious external sign of the chivalric mind was heraldry. Heraldic badges and devices originated with the need for identification in battle, but a more coherent system began to develop from the 1140s, and English kings adopted the red shield with three gold leopards in 1198. By this stage broad rules for using heraldic devices were being developed and, as the 13th

Fig. 89 (above) Butley Priory, Suffolk. The early fourteenth century gatehouse is encrusted in heraldic shields representing the badges of donors and supporters.

century progressed, people further down the social scale began to use them too. In due course heraldic devices began to identity everything from vast buildings to miniature jewellery.

It was Henry III's use of his own arms and those of his royal connections at Westminster Abbey that set the fashion for using heraldry in architectural display. Once used as a decorative element in the 1260s, heraldry remained a dominant part of English architectural decoration into the 19th century. Butley Priory, Suffolk, is not the first, but is perhaps the most spectacular use of heraldic decoration in the early 14th century. The gatehouse is the sole surviving part of a priory founded by Ranulph de Glanville, justiciar of Henry II, and was built between 1320 and 1325. On the north front is a panel with 35 shields in five rows, including the arms of the builders and a litany of arms of the great and the good, ending with a list of East Anglian gentry (fig. 89).[5]

Landscapes of Power

By 1220 a traveller moving across England would have seen the hand of man everywhere. The whole landscape was managed to a greater or lesser degree and few places remained untamed. The most apparent unit of economic and social management was the estate. Estates, whether owned by the monarch, the Church, the great barons or the monasteries, organised the countryside for economic advantage. But the medieval landscape was not merely a money-making machine; the buildings and structures within it had meaning to the people who owned and looked at them.

Castles had a special meaning. In theory only the king could license the construction of a defendable fortress, as in the reign of King John a system had developed whereby magnates wishing to build a fortified residence applied for a royal licence to do so. The possession of a licence, whether it resulted in a building or not, was a sign of wealth and royal favour. It was also a sign of the times. All great houses in the 13th century were, to a greater or lesser extent, defendable. They had to be. It was not only residences on the south coast or the Welsh or Scottish borders that were vulnerable to raiders. Theft, vendetta and social unrest were all potential threats to the comfort and security of the well-off. High walls and towers were thus a sign of a man who could afford them, as well as an indication that he had something worth protecting.[6]

For those who could not afford to build a castle or obtain a licence there was the option of digging a moat. Moats had been dug from at least the 1150s, but during the period covered by this chapter as many as 3,500 moats were dug. Some of these were dug around manor houses, some around the houses of richer peasants. Not all parts of England were suitable for moats; they tended to be concentrated in Suffolk, Essex, Hertfordshire and in the central midlands, where there was a clay subsoil. Some moated houses were in the centre of villages, others were more isolated farmsteads.

The now deserted medieval hamlet of Winteringham, Cambridgeshire, had three moated houses, one of which was excavated between 1971 and 1972. The site of the excavated house had been occupied by two earlier houses before the moat was dug in around 1250. The former houses were simpler and humbler, and the increasing wealth of the family who owned them is apparent by their desire to build a larger, more modern house and surround it with a moat. The house itself consisted of a hall and residential cross-wing, with a detached kitchen, a bower, a storeroom and a circular dovecot (fig. 90). The buildings were connected by cobbled paths. This was not the house of the lord of the manor, but of a substantial and prosperous farmer who wanted to protect his possessions from ill-doers and demonstrate his wealth by sporting a moat.[7]

There was, of course, a huge gap between the aspirations of the owners of Winteringham and those of the great magnates. The magnates saw themselves as soldiers and their interests were in the governance of state and Church. Culturally their priorities were, loosely speaking, chivalric, expressed in mighty residences set in extensive and beautiful hunting parks. Hunting was fundamental to the life of the aristocracy. It was the activity, above all others, that defined aristocratic rank. It took great skill, it was dangerous, and it was run through with chivalric, religious and sexual symbolism.

All medieval residences of any pretensions were surrounded by hunting parks, 1,900 of which were created between 1200 and 1350. Most parks were between 100 and 200 acres in extent, the size of the park reflecting the wealth of its owner.[8] The largest park in 13th-century England was the royal park of Clarendon, Wiltshire, covering 4,292 acres. It was surrounded by an impressive earthwork 10 miles long and more than 10ft high, topped with oak paling. The park was divided into three areas: pasture to the north, woodland in a band

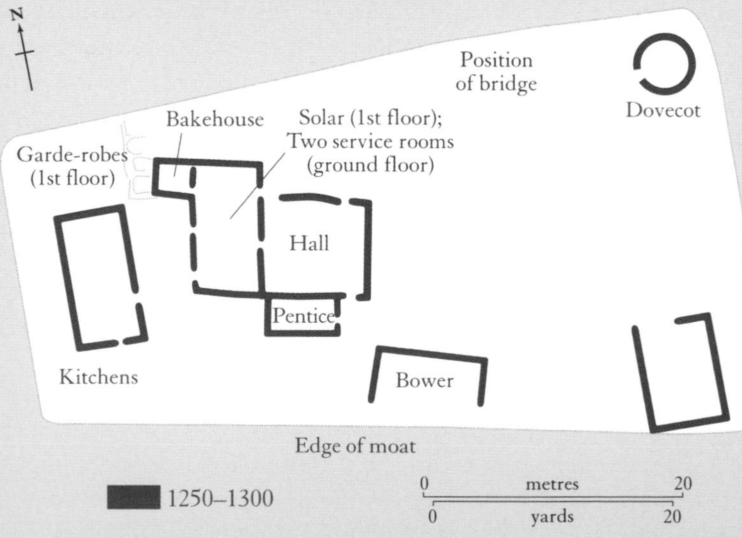

Fig. 90 (left) Winteringham, Cambridgeshire, moated house at *c.*1250–1300, excavated in 1971–2. This is the house of a prosperous farmer and his family, comfortable, convenient but in the tradition of residences built for at least two centuries.

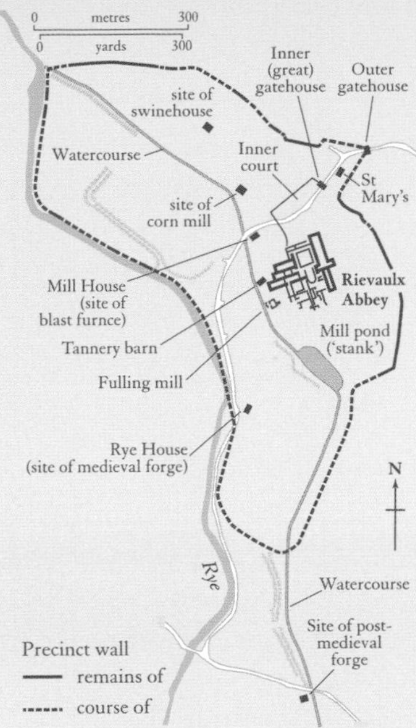

Fig. 91 (above) Rievaulx Abbey, Yorkshire, the precinct. A series of land deals enabled the monks of Rievaulx to acquire the land either side of the river Rye which allowed them to divert it for abbey use. The 92-acre precinct was exceptionally large; most Cistercian abbeys had precincts averaging 60 acres while Benedictines or Augustinian Canons tended to have much smaller precincts averaging around 30 acres.

across the middle and wood pasture to the south. In addition to the palace there were eight lodges – some guarded the gates, others provided special services, such as accommodating the royal kennels. Every part of the land was productive. The woods were bounded by banks, ditches and hedges to keep the deer out and allow coppicing. Slow-growing oaks were also cultivated as a crop, and oxen and cows would graze on the wooded pasture in the south. The northern pasture supported deer and included man-made ponds for drinking and wallowing, troughs for feeding and deer houses for winter shelter. Rabbits and hares were bred here on an industrial scale and provided continuous supplies of meat. Even the wild birds were hunted with hawks.

So the short periods during which kings hunted were interludes in a complex and lucrative agricultural industry. Henry I, Henry II, John, Edward I and Edward III all hunted at Clarendon in what was not only an economic and recreational landscape, but one designed and sculpted with aesthetics clearly in mind. The principal entrance to the park through Slaygate afforded a spectacular view of the whitewashed royal palace high up on the ridge, and views from the palace to the park were carefully contrived.[9]

It was not only kings who moulded and sculpted the landscape around their homes; almost every major residence had a wide-ranging impact on the landscape. The De Roos family owned Helmsley Castle, Yorkshire, and in the 1180s and 90s rebuilt and expanded the castle while purchasing more land for the creation of parks. There were three of these: the West and the East, each paled, and an inner park known as La Haye. The main residential parts of the castle looked out over La Haye and had a balcony from which the culling of deer could be watched.[10]

It was not only castles and great houses that remodelled their landscapes. Monasteries never stood alone but were linked to varying numbers of support buildings, normally in a walled precinct. At Rievaulx, for instance, within the precincts covering 92 acres there were 27 buildings (fig. 91). Some of these were for polite purposes, such as accommodating guests and abbey pensioners; others were for food preparation, such as baking and brewing. In the outer parts there were buildings that housed industrial processes including a fulling mill (for finishing woollen cloth), a corn mill, a water-powered forge and a tannery. Amidst these buildings were meadows, gardens and orchards.[11]

New Decorative Vocabulary

In the 1250s England's distinctive brand of Gothic architecture reigned supreme, but in 1245 Henry III's project to rebuild Westminster Abbey challenged the architectural consensus. The rebuilding of the royal abbey as a coronation church and shrine to the Confessor was the most lavish act of religious architectural patronage by any one individual in the entire Middle Ages. It was pursued with great energy until the latter parts of his reign and then more slowly till his death in 1272, by which time £45,000 had been laid out on the building.

Fig. 92 (above) Old St Paul's Cathedral; London: the chapter house, drawn by Wenceslaus Hollar in 1657. The chapter house and cloister were the masterpiece of the royal mason, William Ramsey. Note how the tracery of the windows continued over the walling below.

Fig. 93 (left) The construction of the nave of Westminster Abbey is one of the most remarkable stories in English building. Building began in the east in 1259–72, and subsequent abbots and masons continued the design from the 14th to the 16th century in exactly the same style. Though the inspiration was at first French, the details used over the long construction period are progressively more anglicised.

Westminster Abbey (fig. 93) was heavily influenced by French buildings and broke away from the style of recent work at Lincoln, for instance (p. 96). Its very proportions were French; at 102ft its nave is England's highest, supported by tiers of French-looking flying buttresses. Many other elements, from its polygonal east end to its northern triple portal, are direct quotes from French buildings. Henry III, who had travelled in France in the 1240s and 50s, was doubtless looking to the French coronation church of Reims and the jewel-like royal Sainte-Chapelle as models. Yet Westminster was no straightforward copy, and the general richness of carving and surface decoration of its interior was in long-established English taste. The influence of the abbey, rather like that of early Gothic Canterbury (pp 93–4), lay not in its composition but in its details: the richness of surface decoration, the use of tracery, the carved and painted heraldic shields, the large-scale sculpted figures and smaller-scale foliage sculpture.[12]

Nor was it alone, for England's largest and most important cathedral was independently following a similar path. From the 1250s the monks of Old St Paul's began to rebuild their east end with a massive extension that would make it the longest cathedral in England, whose exterior shared the richness and decoration of Westminster Abbey (fig. 92). A third London building encapsulated many of the new features displayed in the great churches. This was St Stephen's Chapel, the main royal chapel at Westminster Palace, which Edward I started to rebuild in 1292. Its building history is long and complicated, covering 56 years, only being finally completed by Edward III after 1348 (pp 157–8). Yet the chapel was the most prominent and architecturally magnificent royal commission of its age, and no self-respecting mason or patron was ignorant of its style.

To understand the appearance of buildings in the period from 1250 to 1350 it is best to look at the individual elements since the focus of architectural innovation was on decoration, not on the underlying architectural skeleton. It is hard to convey the importance of decoration in medieval architecture to the modern spectator, as so little survives. The Reformation and the Civil War dealt horrible blows to the greatest English medieval buildings, stripping most of them down to their bare bones. This has led to a loss of meaning, for the architectural bones were the skeleton for a programme of communication through sculpture and paint. Church buildings were designed to represent the kingdom of heaven, and were intended as a signpost and the gateway to paradise for mortals.[13]

The most important new decorative element was undoubtedly window tracery. It was possible, using lancets grouped together, to let in more light, but it was still obvious that these were individual windows with sections of wall between them. The invention of tracery allowed really big windows to be built without bits of wall in the middle. The adoption of bar tracery at Binham Priory, Norfolk, at Netley Abbey, Hampshire, and at Westminster Abbey and Palace immediately made anything built before the 1250s look old-fashioned (compare figs 58, 94). Windows were now not only a gap in the wall; they were transformed into one of the primary vehicles for decoration and elaboration. Part of this was the extraordinary variety of the tracery, but a great deal of the effect was achieved by advances in glazing technology.

From 1300 a much paler and more translucent type of yellow stain was introduced, thinner glass was being manufactured and the designs were being painted with better, finer brushes. All of these advances let more light into churches. The west window at York Minster, which was glazed in 1339 by Master Robert with the extensive use of yellow stain, can be contrasted with the much heavier, darker windows in the lancets of Canterbury Cathedral (figs 60 and 94). In the York window it is also apparent that stained-glass artists had mastered the use of perspective. Windows depict figures under canopies and vaults similar to, and fully integrated with, those in the architecture around them.[14]

The narrow lancet windows in early Gothic churches let in little light, creating a mystical and intimate effect. From the early 14th century larger windows and larger east ends made it easier to see the increasingly elaborate rituals that were being performed. These changes can be seen in churches such as St Denys's, Sleaford, Lincolnshire, with its wild, flowing tracery and west end covered in carving, or Holy Trinity, Hull, begun in around 1300 (fig. 95). Holy Trinity is one of England's biggest parish churches and the first to be largely built of brick. Its chancel and transepts have some

Fig. 94 (left) York Minster nave, looking west towards the great west window commissioned in 1339 – it is 55ft high and of eight lights. The whole nave makes the most of the possibilities of big windows, suppressing the visual impact of the triforium by linking it to the clerestory using continuous mullions.

Fig. 95 (right) Holy Trinity, Hull: the east end of the church of around 1300–20. The rich flowing tracery lights the retrochoir. The internal fittings of the choir were funded by the city corporation from a wool tax.

Fig. 96 (above) Eleanor Cross, Geddington , Northamptonshire, 1291–4. Edward I erected twelve crosses marking the nightly resting places of the coffin of his wife, Eleanor of Castile, as it travelled to London. The monument contains canopied niches for statues.

of the most inventive and beautiful traceried windows of their age, flooding the presbytery with light. Outside, the buttresses have canopied niches and parapets carved with wavy patterns.[15]

The second fundamental decorative element of the period was the niche. These miniature vaults with a triangular gable sheltering an arch can be found, in large scale, on the outside of churches, most prominently on the west front at Wells Cathedral in the 1220s, but from the 1260s they begin to shrink in scale and become a decorative component often coupled with pinnacles. Perhaps the most prominent use of this combination was in the series of monuments Edward I erected to his queen, Eleanor of Castile. Eleanor died in 1290, and within a year or so twelve crosses had been erected near the religious houses at which her body lay on its journey from Nottinghamshire to Westminster (fig. 96).[16] The crosses displayed a sort of micro-architecture of the type that can be found in contemporary metalwork and manuscripts and that was also well suited to tombs. The tomb in Westminster Abbey of Edmund, Earl of Lancaster, who died in 1296, captures the full possibili-

Fig. 97 (left) Gloucester Cathedral; the tomb of Edward II, *c.*1330–5. The effigy is of alabaster on a tomb chest clad in Purbeck marble, but it is the canopy that is a work of genius. It is a bewildering array of crockets, niches, pinnacles and buttresses, all originally painted as befitted a king.

ties of the niche and pinnacle. The astonishing tomb of King Edward II at Gloucester Cathedral of about 1330 is even more exotic, almost Moorish, with niches with S-shaped or ogee tops (fig. 97). The ogee arch had been used in Venice in about 1250, but from the 1290s it was taken up by English architects and designers like nowhere else in Europe. It first started to be used in tombs, then in niches, and then in prominent structures such as the great rose window of St Paul's Cathedral. The ogee arch gave an exotic, quasi-Eastern form to some of the greatest spaces of the era, such as the Lady Chapel at Ely. The most unforgettable of these is St Mary's, Redcliffe, Bristol, a parish church that aspires to the grandeur of a cathedral. The hexagonal porch, encrusted with niches with forward-thrusting ogee arches, contains a door that defies architectural description and looks to have escaped from a maharaja's palace.

One of the innovations introduced at Westminster Abbey was the idea of interior large-scale sculpted human figures integrated with the structure and the wider decorative programme. Big figures had been used to great effect externally, particularly at Wells on the west front, but their internal use was another idea taken from the Sainte-Chapelle. At Westminster these figures

Fig. 98 (above) Westminster Abbey, south transept, south wall; an angel, elegantly accommodated in a spandrel, wings spread and swinging a censer – a perfect marriage of sculpture and architecture.

Fig. 99 (right) Naturalistic foliage in the arches of the chapter house at Southwell Minster, Nottinghamshire, 1290s.

either told stories from the lives of saints or emphasised some important part of the building (fig. 98). Such large-scale sculptures were to be taken up with huge enthusiasm, bringing colour and ornament to interiors.

Medieval sculptors were not interested in accurately representing the human form, and figures – including those of people of great importance – were idealised. The statues of the queen on the Eleanor crosses do not capture the features of a real person; they represent an idealised Christian queen (fig. 96). Saints were instantly identifiable by how they stood or what they held; St Catherine had her wheel and St Peter always held the keys of heaven, while secular figures were identified by their badges or coats of arms. So Queen Eleanor's crosses were encrusted with the badges of León, England, Castile and Ponthieu.

Yet startling naturalism can also be found, such as the heads carved for the corbels at Salisbury Cathedral, some tomb effigies, but most of all the brilliantly naturalistic foliage in the arches of the chapter house at Southwell Minster, Nottinghamshire (fig. 99). Capitals were now less often carved with narrative schemes (fig. 54), but corbels became a sort of portrait gallery, with hugely expressive images of what were probably real people. Carving – and painting – reflected life, rather than commenting on it as today.

All these streams of embellishment are represented at Exeter. The Anglo-Norman cathedral there was rebuilt over a 60-year period beginning in 1275. Its new form was constrained by the decision to retain its 12th-century twin towers. Thus Exeter is characteristic of most Gothic cathedrals where bishops and deans grafted their new buildings onto older work. This meant that the Gothic parts normally followed the thick-wall technique of the Anglo-Normans, keeping cathedrals long and low with a stronghorizontal emphasis.

But that is where the conservatism ends, for a succession of bishops determinedly funded a rebuilding of the cathedral in the best modern style (fig. 100). Exeter is an extravaganza. Everything is multiplied: the piers are made up of 16 bunched

Fig. 100 (above left) Exeter Cathedral was the last to be rebuilt almost in its entirety, over a period of 60 years from 1275; the building work was funded by a voluntary tax on the bishop and the chapter's own income. A result of this is the perfect harmony of its interior, especially the nave, shown here, with its extraordinary high vaults 300ft above the floor.

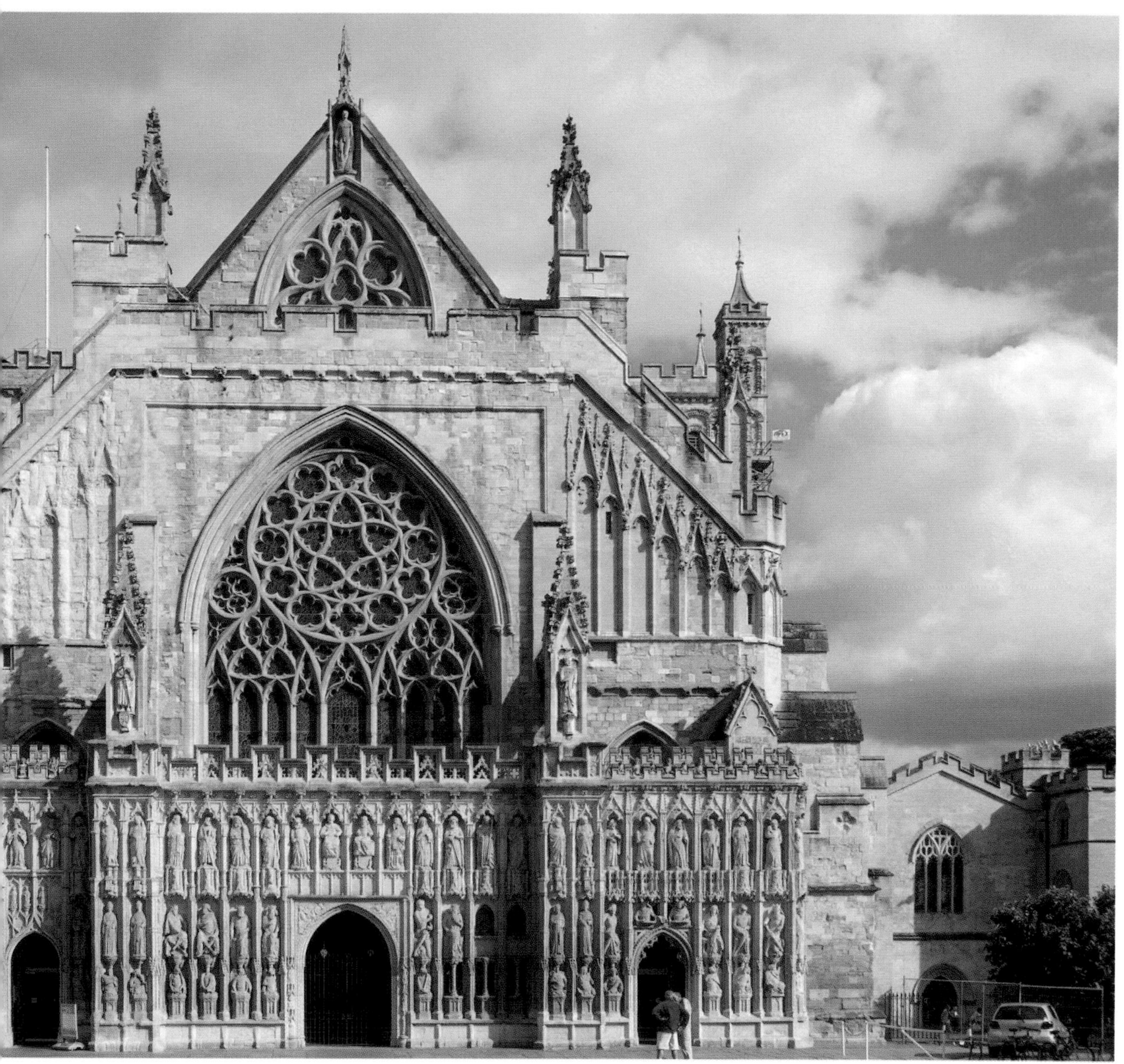

Fig. 101 (above) Exeter Cathedral; the west front. Originally (1320s–40s) the front had three great doorways, and the west window still remains from this period, but the image screen was added from the mid-1340s and figures were still being completed in the 15th century.

shafts, and the spectacular vault is a forest of 22 ribs in each bay, creating the longest single continuous Gothic vault in the world. Everything was patterned, from bosses, through corbels to tracery. The west front was started by Bishop Grandison in around 1346, and while it might not have the balance or harmony of the west front of Wells, here every decorative element in the designer's vocabulary is brought to bear as tiers of figures reside in canopied niches below, perhaps, the most fanciful window of its age (fig. 101). This frontage, like that at Wells, and elsewhere, was intended as a backdrop for the most important services of the year, particularly the processions of Palm Sunday. On this day a choir, hidden behind the façade, seemed to make the very statues, originally painted and gilded, sing.

How People Worshipped

We have seen that from the late Anglo-Saxon period local churches were founded and endowed by landowners as acts of piety (p. 56). These patrons – and their successors – retained the right to appoint the priest to their church or, if they chose, to give away the income to endow a monastery, with the condition that their church be provided for. 'Rector' is the term given to the priest or the monastery entitled to the parish church's income from tithes or other sources.

Many individual rectors took their responsibilities seriously and used the income for its proper purpose. However, when patrons decided to appoint members of their own family as rectors, the income was often simply treated as personal wealth. For instance, Bogo de Clare, the son of the Earl of Gloucester and Hereford, was rector of 24 parishes in 1291 with an income of over £2,000. This enabled him to live a life of considerable luxury while he neglected the parishes from which his income came. De Clare was an exceptional case, but a large minority of rectories were farmed for profit.

By 1300 only about half of all parishes had individual rectors; the incomes of the remainder had been transferred to monasteries, a small part of which was reserved for the employment of a vicar (which in Latin means 'substitute'). So the wealthy church of St Mary's, Whalley, Lancashire, with an income of over £200, had its income appropriated to the Cistercian monastery there. As parish costs were only £27, the abbey made an annual profit of £173. This system meant that the financial position of a medieval church varied not only with the size of its income but with who controlled it. The impact on churches themselves could be significant because – as we have seen above – responsibility for the fabric of the chancel fell to the priest. Non-resident rectors could ignore their responsibilities, as they did at St John the Baptist's, Yarkhill, Herefordshire, where water poured through the roof onto the altar when it rained; monastic owners could be equally neglectful of their duties, preferring to keep the income for their own institutions.[17]

Yet there were positive aspects, too. The earliest church-building contract to survive relates to the chancel of All Saints', Sandon, Hertfordshire, and dates from 1348. The church at Sandon was owned by the Dean and Chapter of St Paul's Cathedral. The Sandon estate was worth over £30 a year, and the Dean and Chapter decided to demolish the old chancel and replace it with a new one with fashionable windows, a sedilia, piscina and an Easter sepulchre (to receive the Easter effigy of Christ). The priest there was also well equipped; in 1297 he had three sets of vestments, two enamelled processional crosses, a censer and an incense boat.[18]

From the Saxon period individual experience of worship in local churches became progressively less intimate and more ceremonialised. At the same time churches became more complex and segregated. The increased focus on communion, following the doctrine of transubstantiation, led to the rebuilding of many chancels as a suitable setting for the celebration of the Mass. New chancels were longer with larger windows and had square ends, unlike

Fig. 102 (below) Much Wenlock Priory, Shropshire; the triple sedilia of the fine chancel added in the 1380s gives the church a beautiful and well-lit setting for its liturgy.

Fig. 103 (right) St Michael's, Stanton Harcourt, Oxfordshire; the mid-13th century chancel screen is a rare and early survival.

Fig. 104 (above) St Mary the Virgin, Stanwell, Surrey. A piscina with a ledge for vessels (a credence) and a cupboard (aumbry).

the Anglo-Norman ones. The chancel remained separated from thc nave by a wooden screen; few early screens survive, but there is a very rare *in situ* survival from about 1260 at St Michael's, Stanton Harcourt, Oxfordshire (fig. 103). This not only shows that views of the chancel were actually quite good, but that holes were cut at a lower level to provide a view of the elevated host for those kneeling. Many chancels were provided with a separate door for the clergy so they could come and go independently from the nave. Altars were now universally built against the east wall and the priest would celebrate communion with his back to the congregation. Since the 9th century priests in larger parishes had not celebrated Mass alone, but from the 13th century chantry priests, assistants and deacons were increasingly present. This was a reason for the increased size of chancels but it also explains the building of special seats for the clergy on the south wall. These sedilia (from the Latin for 'seat'), usually built in threes, were first seen in Anglo-Norman churches but became very popular in new chancels (fig. 102).

The emphasis on the proper celebration of Mass meant that a small wash-basin or piscina was now provided for water to be poured into after sacred vessels had been washed. Nearby was often a cupboard or aumbry for the storage of precious items. Sedilia, piscina and aumbries provided opportunities for decoration and often had carved, arched or canopied frames; sometimes two or three were combined in a single decorative unit (fig. 104).

Just as the chancel became more actively defined as the sphere of the clergy so, during the 13th century, legislation was enacted making the construction and upkeep of the nave the responsibility of parishioners. From early times there had been no permanent furniture in the nave and the congregation might have brought their own wooden stools to sit on. By the late 13th century pews were introduced, associated with a greater emphasis on preaching and sermons stimulated by the

Fourth Lateran Council. The earliest surviving pews are probably those at the beautiful St Mary and All Saints', Dunsfold, Surrey, of 1270 to 1290 (fig. 105).[19]

During the 13th century many naves were extended by the addition of an aisle. These first appeared in churches in the hands of rich men or institutions who wanted to bestow greater status on their church by giving it the form of a basilica; aisles also provided them with more space for private side altars and elaborate processions, and for burial inside the church. Less wealthy churches added aisles for more prosaic reasons: a rising population meant that for every churchgoer in 1100 there were three in 1300 and aisles simply fitted more people in.[20]

From the 1270s the practice of knights and lords being buried in their parish church became common. This was in contrast with the practice in France, for instance, where the rich wanted to be buried in cathedrals and abbeys. In England the strong tie between the lord and his land led to a desire for successive generations to be buried in the churches nearest to their homes. One such place is the manor of Aldworth, Buckinghamshire, where the de la Beche family lived. Sir Robert de la Beche was knighted by Edward I and on his death in around 1300 was buried in St. Mary's church with an effigy carved fully in the round, cross-legged with a hand on his sword. Eight other members of his family subsequently joined him. These figures of knights and their ladies are realistic and expressive but characteristically stiff (fig. 106). Although the effigies are now badly mutilated, the impact that such monuments could have on a church interior is obvious.[21] Less assertive, but no less magnificent or skilled, were the great memorial brasses of the period, in which England led the way.

As well as building outwards parishes were also building upwards. Although there had previously been periods of tower building, there was a rash of new towers from the 1270s, many capped with spires either of lead-covered timber or stone. Stone spires were concentrated in the wealthy, stone-rich midlands from south Lincolnshire across Leicestershire, Huntingdon and Northamptonshire, down through Warwickshire to Oxfordshire and Gloucestershire.

A spire was a luxury. It had no practical or liturgical function; it simply proclaimed the technical skills of its architect and the wealth of its patrons. It is for this reason that spires were often products of competition. Competitive imitation was one of the ways in which new styles and specific, sometimes quirky, features spread. The concentration of elaborate Easter sepulchres in Lincolnshire or the stone chancel screens of the West Country are examples of features popularised locally. But towers and spires were often not simply the product of imitation; they were built to exceed their neighbours in size and beauty. In neighbouring parishes in Huntingdonshire are the churches of All Saints', Buckworth, and St Peter and St Paul's, Alconbury (fig. 107). Their handsome, solid spires with windows (lucarnes) are both broach spires; in other words they rise directly from the tower without a parapet. Built around 1300, they were the result of two villages in fierce competition.[22]

The experience of worship in a cathedral was very different from that in a parish church. Although liturgical practices varied between cathedrals, a good idea of what they were like can be gained by considering Salisbury. Salisbury was the only cathedral during the Middle Ages to be built from scratch. This

Fig. 105 (top) St Mary and All Saints, Dunsfold, Surrey; remarkably early pews dating from 1270–90. Simple, robust, and just more comfortable than standing.

Fig. 106 (above) St Mary's Aldworth, Berkshire; one of the tombs to a member of the de la Beche family. The effigy lies under a canopy, defaced during the commonwealth, but still discernible as an extravagantly carved and cusped recess.

Fig. 107 (above right) St Peter and St Paul's, Alconbury, Cambridgeshire. The church has a fine broach spire of *c.*1300 built, competitively, at the same time as neighbouring All Saints Buckworth.

was down to Richard Poore, first as dean and then as bishop. Poore was also responsible for codifying its liturgical practices, introducing an orderly and regular framework for the feasts of the Christian year that set out how each ought to be celebrated. These liturgical instructions, which became known as the Use of Sarum, were applied to all churches in his diocese and by the 15th century were almost universally used as a sort of standard form of church worship.

Although it is not quite comparing like with like, it is useful to compare the plan of St Albans (pp 73–4 and fig. 42) with Salisbury (fig. 108) to show how things had changed since the 1080s.[23] The most important principle was that the clergy had their own enclosed area. This was located in the cathedral's east arm, which was itself of cruciform shape and thus a church within a church. The area was enclosed by screens and was six bays long, three for the choir and three for the presbytery (or chancel). The whole east arm was divided from the rest by a massive stone screen, the pulpitum, which had a central processional entrance.

Each bay of the main and eastern transepts held its own altars, and these, together with those at the east end, ensured that there were 17 altars available for the 50 cathedral canons to say Mass. The clergy had their own entrance to the cathedral through the north end of the eastern transept, while the laity entered through an elaborate north porch in the nave. The Use of Sarum specified that on major feast days the clergy and choir would process out of their part of the church, round the cloisters and, on the most important feasts, to the front of the cathedral and back in through the west doors. The west doors in cathedrals were generally reserved for ceremonial use only.[24]

At the east end of the cathedral was a large chapel dedicated to the Trinity. In practice this was used for the daily Mass dedicated to the Virgin Mary. As noted above, a daily Lady Mass was an innovation of the 12th century, the Feast of the Conception of the Virgin having been introduced in the 1120s. The cult of the Virgin had a major architectural impact, with Lady chapels being added to greater churches and cathedrals all over England. In cathedrals

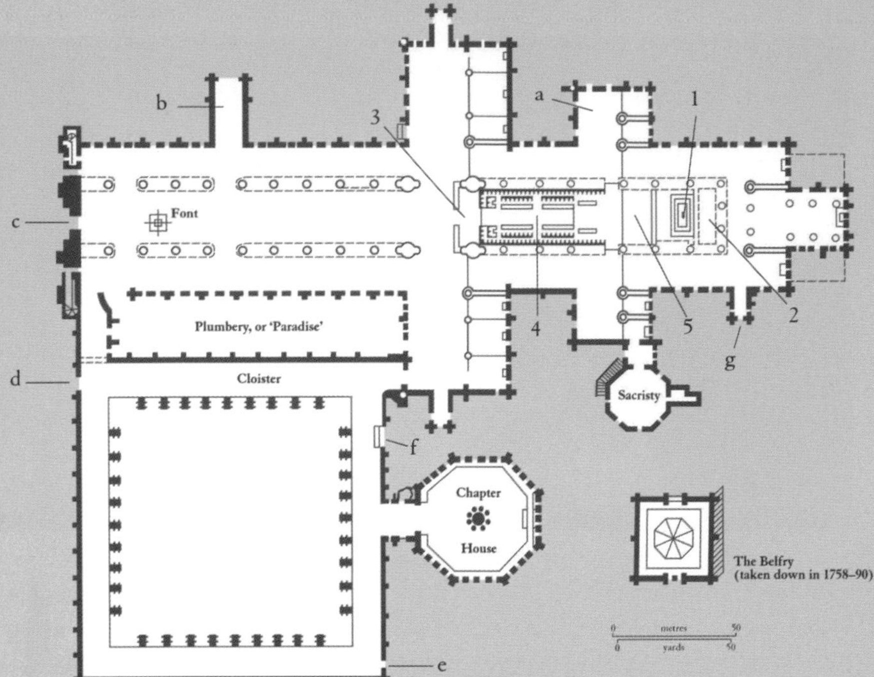

Fig. 108 (above left) Salisbury Cathedral, Wiltshire; plan of the cathedral showing liturgical arrangements. Liturgical features: 1) high altar; 2) Shrine of St Osmund; 3) pulpitum with rood above; 4) choir stalls; 5) presbytery. Doors: a) original entrance; b) entrance for laity; c) west entrance reserved for processional use; d) exit to cloisters for processional use; e) exit to Bishop's palace; f) exit to cemetery g) exit for funerals.

in which the east end was rebuilt, such as at Lincoln, the Lady chapel tended to be the easternmost part of the church, but other places were appropriated as Lady chapels, too, most famously at Ely, where the monks built a new chapel on the north side between 1335 and 1353. Here, although brutally mutilated during the Reformation, is a symphony in stone to the Virgin. Scenes from her life inspired by a sacred text encrust the lower walls and previously filled the vast windows.

These spaces were available to the laity, when not in use by the canons and monks, and strategically placed boxes would elicit donations from the curious and the pious. The cathedral's shrines would be regularly visited and at some times of the year mobbed. Pilgrims would leave objects at the shrine as either offerings of thanks or as requests; in 1307 papal commissioners listed 2,204 items next to St Thomas's shrine at Canterbury, including nightgowns, ships made of wax, wood and even of silver. On ordinary days people would congregate in the seat-less naves and genuflect at the Elevation of the Host. But many would come for the spectacle of the processions and for the music, both of which would have been infinitely more impressive than any parish church could achieve.[25]

New Urban Religious Institutions

Growing towns, filled with increasingly well-off and literate populations, began to present a challenge to the Church in the late 12th century. Its structures were organised to minister to populations in rural areas, where congregations were illiterate and priests barely above the intellectual level of their rustic parishioners. The rectors of churches in towns had either been appropriated by monasteries or were too poor to attract educated clergy. The church thus perceived a crisis in which educated townspeople would fall into heresy uninformed by the teachings and guidance of the Church. The solution was a radical new type of monasticism, that of the mendicant friars. The friars broke with the established principles of monasticism by refusing to own property and relying on charity for support, while at the same time abandoning the seclusion of the cloister to work among ordinary citizens. In 1221 the first of these orders, the Dominicans (Black Friars), came to England, followed in 1224 by the Franciscans (Grey Friars).[26]

By 1250 the two orders had established 70 convents in England, and 100 by 1300. Friaries of both sorts were found in 30 towns and, as other orders such as the Carmelites (White Friars) and Austin Friars joined them, many towns might have as many as four friaries. These were often built on the peripheries, as most of the central plots were already occupied by the mid 13th century. The new orders became very fashionable and almost immediately enjoyed generous patronage from bishops, the universities and, crucially, the Crown. Edward I, for instance, never visited a town without giving alms to the friars. As the friars were not allowed to own property their buildings were held in trust for them by corporations of citizens. Individual donors gave buildings or plots of land, but friars never held estates for investment like earlier orders.

At first friaries were very modest, even deliberately uncomfortable, but as their congregations grew the friars needed places in which to preach and work. The earliest surviving Dominican house is at Gloucester. Here there were also Grey and White Friars, but the first were the Black Friars, invited to found a house in 1239. Although later converted into a domestic house, here the essential features of an urban friary can be grasped. The church has a very wide nave designed to enable men from the town to hear sermons. The chancel is much narrower and was for the friars themselves, 40 in all. The rest of the buildings accorded to no set plan, as each friary organised its ancillary buildings itself. At Gloucester there was a simple cloister of timber and, on the south, its most important and rare survival, a library or scriptorium. This has ten or more carrels on each long side, divided by stubby stone screens and each lit by its own window.

The friars, like their predecessors, eventually acquired property and became rich, profiting from the desire of wealthy town dwellers to speed the passage of their souls through purgatory. The richest friaries, such as the London Blackfriars, which enjoyed consistent royal patronage, became palaces with luxurious lodgings and guest accommodation, as well as big, handsome churches.[27] Much of the Norwich Blackfriars survived the Reformation as a civic building and, even in its current state, gives a strong impression of a large and luxurious foundation (fig. 109). As with the friary at Gloucester the space inside the church was maximised, with narrow aisles and a wide nave lit by big windows and a slight clerestory. The junction between the nave and the chancel was occupied by an octagonal tower, a common feature of urban friaries. The passage beneath it gave access to the cloister, chapter house, dormitory and refectory. In due course the design of parish churches was influenced by rich and fashionable urban friaries such as Norwich; in addition, after 1350 they too began to have wide naves lit by big windows. Friaries were one aspect of increasingly sophisticated urban institutions stimulated by money and population growth. Another was the development of a new type of hospital. Burgesses in rapidly growing towns became ever more concerned about the underclass and people without family support who were too old, sick, disabled or deranged to work. Institutions were founded to support these people, combining charitable aims with a rigorous liturgical regime. Some were built, as earlier hospitals had been, by bishops or the aristocracy, but many were founded by the corporate efforts of rich townsmen. Most were sited on the outskirts of towns, partly to exclude the sick from the centre and to provide for the incoming wayfarer, but also because it was believed that the stress and noise of town centres discouraged recovery.[28]

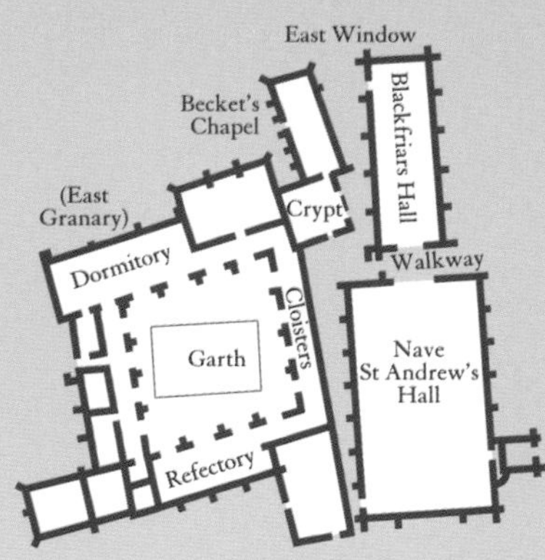

Fig. 109 (above) Norwich, Blackfriars, now known as St Andrew's Hall. The only complete surviving friars' church in England, it dates from 1440–70 – a rebuilding of the original foundation of 1307 after a fire. Yet the layout is entirely 14th-century.

Bishop Walter Suffield of Norwich founded the Hospital of St Giles just outside the precincts of his palace in 1245, and by the end of the century it was richly endowed with nearby rural estates, as well as a portfolio of urban properties. In 1270 it absorbed the nearby parish church of St Helen, adding parochial duties to its responsibilities. Its prime purpose was to care for the sick and aged priests of Norwich, but it also cared for a minimum of 30 others and fed – and in the winter, warmed – 13 others each day. Four sisters assisted by four lay brothers cared for the sick, while the master and four chaplains saw to their spiritual needs and prayed for the soul of the founder.[29] St Giles's Hospital was large and well endowed, one of the reasons for its survival to this day (p. 175). Many others were not. Hospitals that tended to the needs of wayfarers, especially pilgrims, were often overwhelmed and under-funded. The roads of medieval England were brimming with the ill, the disabled and the mentally disturbed making their way to nearby shrines, or sometimes on long pilgrimages in search of healing. Monasteries and other great houses had a duty of hospitality, but small hospitals played their part, too.

Life of the Rich and Powerful

The 13th century was a good time to be an English landed magnate. Throughout the century incomes rose and landlords had increasing disposable wealth. Six earls had an income of more than £3,000 a year and two of them grossed more than £6,000; at least half a dozen were on £400 to £3,000 a year and most barons earned between £200 and £500. To put these figures in context, a good annual wage for a labourer was £2 and the peacetime revenues of the Crown were only £30,000 a year. So there were a lot of rich people and in total their disposable income was probably in the region of £500,000 a year, more than ten times the income of the entire state. These people invested in building to a greater or lesser degree. Building maintenance probably absorbed about 5 per cent of a magnate's annual resources and there were also almost always capital investments, such as for barns and mills. In addition, a significant proportion of their disposable income was spent on new domestic architecture, in some cases up to 25 per cent.[30]

The general increase in the wealth and architectural capability of landlords contributed to social changes that were already underway. Communal feasting and hospitality remained at the heart of medieval life, and lords found ways of making their halls even larger and more spectacular. At the same time they increasingly wanted to spend time in more intimate spaces and withdrew from their halls to chambers in which they could spend time with their families and peers. This led to important changes in the design of high-status houses that become apparent from the 1180s.[31]

Up until the late 12th century the houses of the rich were generally an agglomeration of separate structures: hall, chamber and kitchen. But from the 1180s houses began to adopt a new arrangement that was to become the standard layout for all houses of pretension for the following 400 years. Essentially what happened was that kitchens began to be built on to one end of the great hall, forming a single unit; then, from the 1220s, chamber blocks were also constructed integrally with the great hall but at the other end from the kitchen. This gave the great hall an 'upper' end adjacent to the lord's private rooms and a 'lower' end adjacent to the kitchens. Whilst the hall was generally still on the ground floor the chambers at the upper end were stacked above it, so a stair led up from the lord's end of the hall to his rooms above. The kitchen, also on the ground floor, often had guest chambers above it, and a secondary stair would have led to these (fig. 110).

Access to the great hall was no longer from a door in the centre of one of its long walls but through a door at the lower end; this door led to a passage that was screened off from the rest of the hall by a timber partition. Doors from the kitchen, from the buttery (for beer) and pantry (for bread) would lead into

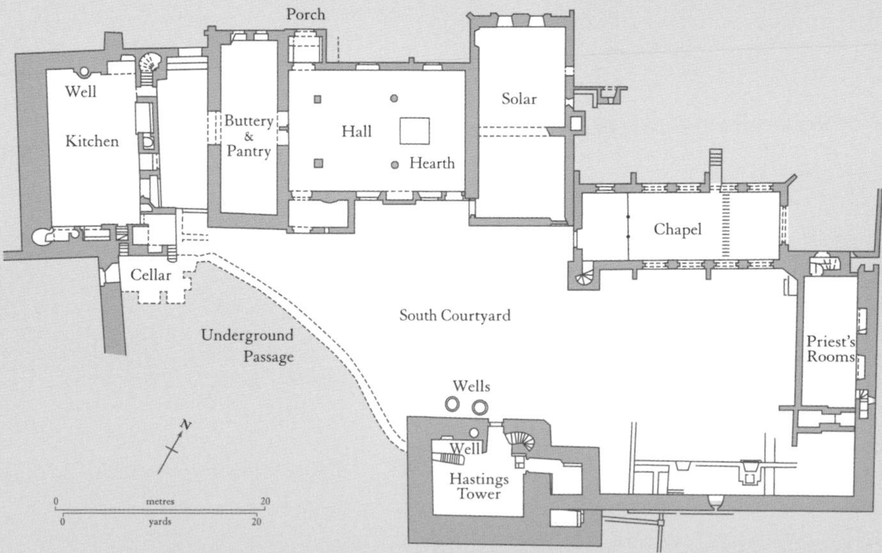

Fig. 110 (right) Ashby de la Zouch Castle, Leicestershire. Most of what is shown here was built by William, Lord Hastings in 1473–83. In its axial arrangement of kitchen, buttery and pantry, hall and great chamber, it displays a typical plan for a substantial medieval house.

Fig. 111 (above) Lincoln, Bishop's Palace: reconstructed as it would have been seen from the great courtyard of the palace. To the left is the great hall with its porch and bay window; on the right there is the kitchen linked to the hall by a passage. The palace was built on sloping ground and so the kitchen was raised up on a vault.

this enclosure, which became known as the screens passage. This more integrated arrangement allowed lords to spend more time in the comfort of their chambers while coming and going through their halls. This private space was a badge of rank, part of the charisma of greatness and wealth. To be inaccessible was to be important, as it enabled favour to be shown and intimacy to be conferred and withdrawn. More exclusive rooms that often included private chapels (or oratories) were further symbols of exclusivity.[32]

Many of these innovations in domestic planning were led by the bishops, who were single, rich and less conservative in outlook than the monarchy or the magnates. In the shadow of Lincoln Cathedral lies the now ruined bishop's palace, once among the most lavish buildings in the kingdom. Here modern-day visitors can see one of the earliest instances of a kitchen linked to the lower end of a hall, with three doors serving the buttery, pantry and kitchen (fig. 111). The hall was started in the 1220s and about 20 years later Bishop Grosseteste set out 23 rules for the smooth running of a household. In these he was careful to cover appropriate behaviour in the hall, and rules for the serving, seating and attire of dinner guests.[33] Such household regulations were increasingly enforced by chamberlains, the guardians of the lord's dignity and privacy. The chamberlain was not the only officer in a great household as, by 1100, most aristocrats were accompanied by men holding posts such as steward, butler, constable, marshal, clerk and huntsman. These people – and their more humble followers – were the human backdrop to aristocratic power: a household such as that of Bishop Grosseteste would have had as many as eighty attendants, that of a duke or an earl perhaps twice that.[34]

These structured and hierarchical households with their integrated kitchens, halls and chambers presented new architectural opportunities. Stokesay Castle, Shropshire, is a miraculously unaltered house of the 1280s built by the super-rich wool merchant Laurence of Ludlow, an early example of a man,

Fig. 112 (above) Penshurst Place, Kent; the great hall. A remarkable, perfectly preserved 14th-century great hall now only lacking its central louvre to let out the smoke. Originally there were large-scale murals depicting men-at-arms under gabled canopies.

Fig. 113 (above right) Stokesay Castle, Shropshire, the west elevation of the great hall and the north tower built 1285–1305. The hall windows were not glazed but closed with wooden shutters.

enriched by trade, who set himself up as a country squire. Laurence built himself a fine great hall with tall windows and a central hearth; at its south end was a block containing his own chambers, leading on to a tower with three large, well-lit rooms. At the lower end of the hall were more chambers, possibly for guests or perhaps his family (fig. 113).

One of the most innovative features of Stokesay is the great hall roof. It is one of the first to achieve an impressive span without aisle posts. A post-less hall was the holy grail of early medieval secular architects. Posts cluttered up the hall, reducing flexibility and visibility, and from the 1220s experiments had taken place to create wide spans without the need for posts. After about 1310 no hall had posts – all were clear, unsupported spans.[35]

Stokesay is a modest house; a more spectacular example, almost as well preserved, is Penshurst Place, Kent, begun by Sir John Pulteney between 1338 and 1349. Pulteney emerged as a financier in the 1320s and, thanks to a shrewd financial nose, became one of the richest men in England. At the heart of his house was a magnificent great hall, very much today as Pulteney left it. Entered by a two-storey porch and lit by tall windows with fine tracery, the hall is covered with a vast chestnut roof (fig. 112). The trusses are held together by collar-beams resting on richly moulded purlins. From the collars arched braces come down to another richly carved horizontal member, the wall plate. Each brace terminates in a life-size wooden figure originally standing on a stone corbel.

This was the social centre of Pulteney's universe. Here he sat at table on his tiled dais facing a wooden screen bearing a gallery for musicians. Between the windows were full-size paintings of men-at-arms. With a fanfare from above, his food would be brought from the kitchens, under the screen past a fire blazing

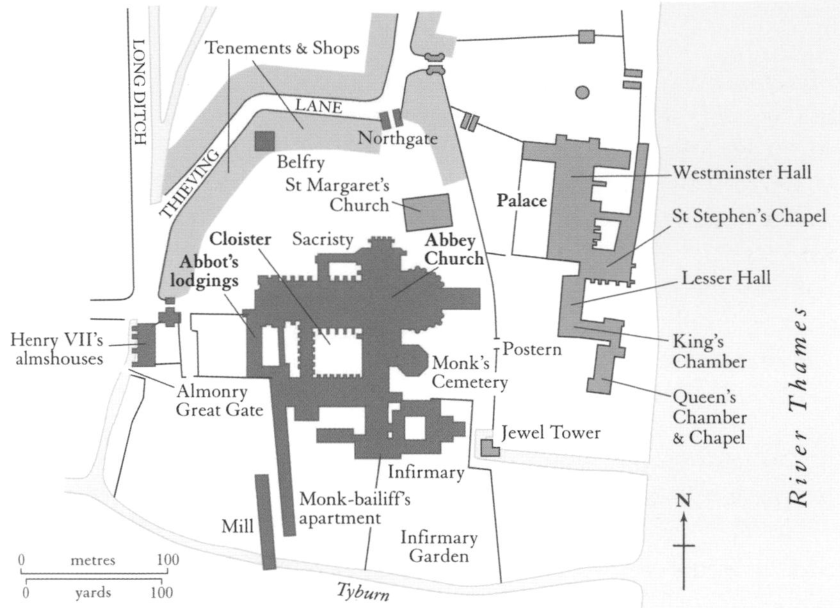

Fig. 114 (left) Map of Westminster in the later Middle Ages.

in the centre of the room and to his table. From his dais a spiral stair led up to a large chamber lit on three sides, heated by a fireplace and furnished with a latrine. Penshurst and Pulteney were as grand as it got, unless, that is, you were royalty.

The English word 'palace' comes from the Latin 'palatium', referring to the principal residence of the Roman emperors on the Palatine Hill in Rome. Westminster was the palace of the English kings and every medieval monarch contributed something to its adornment. By the time Henry III came to the throne William Rufus's great hall (p. 78) had already been joined by another hall to its south, smaller and more convenient for everyday use. There was a chamber at right angles to this chamber, its eastern windows overlooking the Thames (fig. 114). Henry III remodelled the chamber, giving it new windows, fireplace, roof and a small oratory. This room, soon to be known as the Painted Chamber after its extensive murals, was Henry's bedchamber, with his bed in a curtained enclosure and a small squint window providing a view of the altar in the oratory. To the south of the Painted Chamber was the queen's chamber and chapel, newly constructed by Henry III for Queen Eleanor between 1237 and 1238.[36]

Westminster Palace, with its conglomeration of fine chambers, did not stand alone. Part of Henry III's conception was for his palace and Westminster Abbey to be linked physically and institutionally, with the abbey serving as a private monastery to his principal residence. The chapter house, for instance, was always intended to act as a meeting place in which to discuss state business (and became a meeting place of parliament). This was typical of the intense personal interest that Henry took in the construction of the palace and the abbey that made both so influential.

Defence of the Realm

The crisis of 1216–17 (p. 120) and the continued tension between the Crown and the magnates caused some fundamental questions to be asked about the design of castles. It must be remembered that Dover, the most important and powerful castle in England, had been besieged in 1216 and nearly taken. At the start of Henry III's reign it was time to review how these powerhouses were built. Henry III spent the following 30 years completing the outer defensive walls at Dover, building outworks and what was probably the most impressive and complex gatehouse to any castle in England (fig. 115).[37]

Dover was key to the defence of the kingdom, as had been demonstrated in 1216–17. No less so was the Tower of London. Built to overawe Londoners, and by Henry III's reign the home of the royal treasury and arsenal, it was central to the power of the monarchy. Relations with the city had, however, been strained, and Henry felt it vital to bring this fortress up to standard, too.

At the Tower of London, in the 1220s and from the late 1230s, Henry III re-planned the defensive circuit around the Conqueror's White Tower, building a massive curtain wall protected by a series of circular and D-shaped towers and a 160ft-wide moat. A new gatehouse and barbican faced the City of London, and the White Tower assumed its current name thanks to its first all-over coat of whitewash. Henry's work, which increased the walled area of the Tower by at least an acre, probably remained unfinished; part of it certainly collapsed, and it was left to Edward I to complete the fortification of the Tower between 1275 and 1285. Edward threw a second wall around the one

Fig. 115 (right) Dover Castle, Kent; the Constable's Gate, probably the largest gatehouse ever built in England. Begun in 1217 as the new principal entrance to the fortress, but also to contain a residence for the castle's permanent chief, the Constable.

Fig. 116 (above) The Tower of London today. Although altered in the 18th and 19th centuries, the Tower is still recognisably a concentric fortress with rings of defences and, bottom right, an elaborate system of gatehouses, drawbridges and causeways that secured its entrance.

built by his predecessor, digging a new moat and creating a complex series of outworks and gatehouses as a new entrance. The Tower of London was now the first coherently planned concentric fortress in England (fig. 116).

To enter, it was now necessary to pass from Tower Hill on to the Lion Tower, a semicircular enclosure surrounded by a moat and guarded by two gates and a drawbridge. From here the would-be visitor had to pass through the twin-towered Middle Tower, a gateway defended by a drawbridge, gateway and two portcullises, before passing onto a parapeted causeway across the moat. Here visitors were confronted by a second twin-towered gatehouse, the Byward Tower, also defended by a gate, portcullises and a drawbridge. King Edward I is known, rightly, as one of the great builders in English history. As well as substantial work in England, over a 25-year period – and at the cost of £80,000 – he built a series of castles and fortified towns in North Wales as part of his campaign to conquer and subdue the Welsh. Caernarvon, Conway, Harlech and Beaumaris, for example, still stand witness to this remarkable chapter in royal patronage. As these buildings are in Wales they fall outside the scope of this book, yet it is necessary to ask what influence, if any, did this gargantuan building programme carried out for an English king with English labour and finance have on the development of English architecture?[38]

The first point to make is that the Welsh castles were exceptional, not only because of the incredibly impressive focus of men, materials and money, but because they were all built from scratch. Most English castles were a product of hundreds of years of piecemeal addition; very few new castles were built after 1150. Therefore, unusually, Edward had the opportunity to create a series

Fig. 117 (above) Brougham Castle, Cumbria, is a lesson in how to transform a severe Norman great tower into a compact but luxurious residence. The bottom three storeys date from around 1200 and contain a store, the castle's hall and above that the original lord's chamber. The storey above, with its fancy oratory and big fireplace, date from a century later and was added by Robert Clifford.

of brand-new ideal forts, building what were probably the greatest military achievements of their age in Western Europe. The design of the Welsh castles brought together ideas that had been tried and tested at Dover and the Tower. For instance, none of them has a great tower or keep. Their most prominent feature, and where the prime accommodation lay, was the gatehouse. It was the gatehouse that had proved decisive during the siege of Dover, and the new defences at Dover, particularly the Constable Tower, emphasised its importance. But there was perhaps more than military necessity in the prominence given to gatehouses. Since Saxon times the English had favoured the gatehouse as a sign of status (p. 52), and the Welsh castles of Edward I reinforced this as a major feature in English architectural design (p. 146).[39]

Finally, both Conway and Caernarvon castles effectively contained royal palaces.[40] This is an important point because neither Henry III's works nor those of Edward I were confined to defence. Henry III transformed his castles into major and comfortable residences for himself; his works at Dover and the Tower included new palaces, as did those at Windsor and Winchester. After his marriage in 1236, yet more building was commissioned to provide suitable accommodation for the queen. These royal works reflect a wider move by magnates who were making their castles more comfortable and spacious. The Cliffords at Brougham Castle, Cumbria, were typical in setting out to extend and modernise their Anglo-Norman great tower in 1300. They added an elaborate gatehouse to its face, raised it by a storey and added fine rooms, including a vaulted oratory (fig. 117). Brougham was no longer a cold northern fortress; it was a commodious and fashionable residence.

A Capital City

It was during the reign of Edward I that London became a capital city in the modern sense of the word, displacing Winchester as the seat of the state and the focal point for English identity, language and law. Its population was perhaps as large as 100,000, much smaller than Paris but four times the size of its nearest rival, Norwich. The years after 1300 saw London consolidate its position as the engine-house of England's economy. By 1306 it exported more wool than Boston, and by 1334, in terms of taxation, London was five times richer than Bristol, her nearest competitor.[41]

London was still surrounded by a wall with six gates, Roman in origin, and on a number of occasions during the Middle Ages these were manned to defend the City. Yet the population had already burst through the walls, especially in the west, where buildings lined the streets of the Strand and Holborn. Within the city most of the major buildings and structures that dominated its skyline to the Reformation had already been founded. The Tower and St Paul's Cathedral have already been mentioned, but London also had monasteries and 140 parish churches, as well as London Bridge, 906ft long with 19 arches.

The rich and powerful had houses in London from 1100, but from 1300 large numbers of bishops and abbots, and then lay nobles, built great houses or inns in London, seeking to be close to Westminster and the law courts, and to trade with each other. We have already met the pluralist Bogo de Clare (p. 134), who was typical of the very rich in having a house near Aldgate but only 950ft away also owning a substantial wardrobe – essentially an office where he could trade, entertain business contacts and conduct his financial affairs. His wardrobe had a courtyard with a well and a lawn, perhaps a chapel, too. Between 1285 and 1286 Bogo spent £375 on supplies through his wardrobe. This was big business for everyone concerned and demonstrated that aristocratic houses were crucial to the economy of the city. Their wealthy occupants spent heavily on supporting their households and equipping themselves with the latest luxuries. When Richard Swinfield, Bishop of Hereford, brought his household to London in 1291, his expenditure trebled from £1 to £3 a day.[42]

The houses of men such as Bogo were generally set back from the street in courtyards approached by a gatehouse. Their owners would often build and rent out shops on the street front, making their houses to an extent self-supporting. At the back of the courtyard was generally the great hall and an attached chamber built up over a vaulted undercroft. Many also had towers that lifted their owners above the noise, smell and confusion of the streets to daylight and spectacular views over the rooftops. No single 14th-century house or wardrobe survives, but in Southwark parts of the Bishop of Winchester's palace do, and these give us a glimpse of the magnificence of the richest of the residences (fig. 118).

Winchester Place was started in about 1200, and was extended and altered right up to the Reformation. The bishop had a separate chapel and, at right angles to this, was a suite of rooms built in the late 1350s containing a number of fine chambers, including a study and latrines. The new rooms overlooked gardens. The kitchen and domestic buildings lay to the west of the hall. The whole was bounded by walls and supplied by extensive stabling. This latter point is important as stabling was a huge problem, rather like car parking today. Pasture, fodder and a place to stable horses were crucial to the efficient existence of a nobleman, and good stables in central London were vitally important for a man of wealth.[43]

English architecture in the period from 1220 to 1350 displays the confidence that comes with wealth and independence. Architects had mastered both the structural capabilities of Gothic architecture and its decorative possibilities. Patrons wanted to translate their ambitions into stone, timber, glass and fired clay, and were not ashamed of extravagant display.

England was largely made up of the estates of the aristocracy, the Church and the Crown. All created landscapes that were in equal measure devoted to power, pleasure and production. Their economic lessers aped them, but also made their own distinctive contribution. The Crown did not exclusively set the way bishops, aristocrats and merchants created new forms of building. For everyone, however, architecture was, as always, about display, whether it was at Winteringham (p. 124), All Saints', Buckworth (p. 136), or Penshurst Place (p. 143).

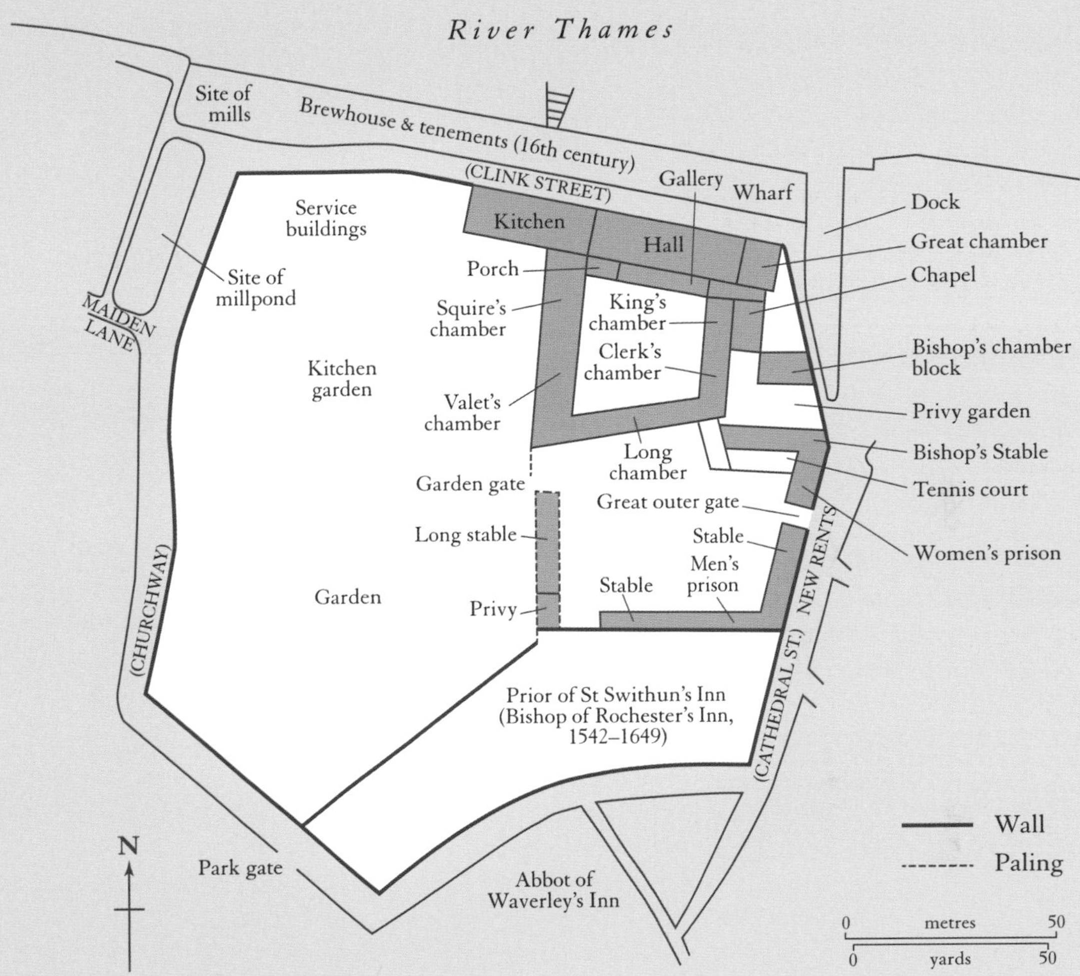

Fig. 118 (above) Winchester Place, Southwark in *c.*1400. This was a big London episcopal residence with a double courtyard and substantial garden. The bishop had his own private quarters and garden but they overlooked busy streets. The prisons related to the bishop's jurisdiction in a notoriously unruly suburb.

A strengthened sense of England emerged, as distinct from Wales, Scotland and the continental territories of the Angevin kings, and its architecture was equally distinct. What is normally described as Decorated architecture does not occur anywhere else, even in Scotland and Wales, yet it pervaded all parts of England. But architectural style in this period is a phenomenon not a homogeneous movement; local and regional variation produced thousands of one-off variations. (Architecture before the 1220s and after the 1350s tends to be less individualistic than the 130-odd years of exuberance in between.)[44] But boom leads to bust. The series of calamities that hit English society after 1300 came thick and fast: economic stagnation, climate change, famine and disease. All led to changes in the way that the English built.

6— From the Black Death to the Reformation

—1350-1530

The years between 1350 and 1530 produced a distinctive architectural language of considerable beauty and sophistication in England that was quite different from its continental counterparts. This individuality was to remain a hallmark of English building during the following century.

Introduction

Between the Black Death and the Reformation building in England entered a long period of architectural consensus. For nearly 200 years designers worked with an architectural language that, with relatively minor modulation and a greater or lesser degree of elaboration, retained its essential stylistic components. Through this long period new building types developed, new materials became fashionable and the way people lived, thought and worshipped changed. Yet, while the differences in buildings built between 1200 and 1300 are readily discernible, the same cannot be said of buildings built between 1400 and 1500. Precisely dating 15th-century buildings on stylistic grounds alone is a hazardous business, but the skills to do the same for 13th-century buildings can be readily developed.

Generations of scholars have made many attempts to explain this, each discrediting the views of the previous generation but each adding to the subtlety and complexity of our understanding.[1] Yet there are some important points that help. Gothic was an international architectural language, but after 1300 it acquired, if you like, many national dialects. Whilst Henry III's Westminster Abbey (p. 127) and St Stephen's Chapel, Westminster (p. 144), were consciously influenced by French models, this cannot be said of buildings after 1350. Architects looked to domestic models rather than to France, and so England, Spain, France, Flanders and elsewhere developed their own indigenous varieties of building. These varieties or dialects sometimes fed from one another; others acquired a particularly distinct tone. In England the dialect was very individualistic – and quite unlike those that developed elsewhere – and formed a national school of design that was strengthened by a close-knit network of masons and architects operating in a geographically defined nation state.[2]

This turning inwards of architectural design took place against a tumultuous background of international warfare, civil war, political instability, and economic and social disaster. It is this mix of apparent instability on the one hand with architectural consensus on the other that this chapter explores.

A Century of Crisis 1300–1408

Although 13th-century England was rich and populous, by 1300 both wealth and population growth had reached a temporary peak, with the century that followed bringing financial setbacks and a decline in population. Underlying many of the problems was a very modern concern – climate change. Between 1290 and 1375 the British climate became unstable and unpredictable; a series of wet summers prevented crops from ripening, rotted seed in the ground, and nurtured pests and disease, while coastal flooding inundated thousands of acres and torrential rain made thousands more unusable. Between 1315 and 1322 there was crop failure and widespread famine, killing perhaps half a million people. Starting in the 1330s the countryside began to contract, villages were abandoned, clay and sandy soils were left for more fertile areas.[3] During the 13th-century expansion in Dartmoor hamlets and farmsteads had been built on agriculturally marginal land. In 1300 in the southern hamlet at Hound Tor there were four longhouses and seven ancillary buildings. As the climate deteriorated the farmers who occupied these built stone walls to keep the moorland from eating up their fields. Initially they must have had success, but in the 1330s they built corn driers to combat the effect of wet summers. This cannot have been enough, for the whole settlement was abandoned less than twenty years later.[4]

A better-developed agricultural economy might have resisted the effects of climate change but climatic factors brought an immature system to its knees, particularly at the margins. A second global factor undermined 13th-century stability – a failure in the money supply. This was partly caused by a genuine shortage of silver; the mines simply couldn't produce enough to supply the mints as well as the luxury-goods market. But in part it was a result of taxation demands made by the Crown to pay for war, meaning that in the 1330s and 40s there was often no money available to buy goods.

For 40 of the 60 years between 1290 and 1350 England was at war. These wars were not skirmishes; they involved armies of 20,000 men or more, ships, horses, massive castles and extended supply lines. Paying for this was a burden levied on everyone, not just on those who were near to it. Sustained direct taxation, and the manipulation and exploitation of the wool trade, were bad for the economy.

All in all, the self-confidence and prosperity that had knitted society together in the 13th century was becoming unravelled. In 1348 it suddenly fell apart. Bubonic plague reached the south coast of England in the summer of 1348 and gradually spread northwards, bringing continued death in Scotland in 1350. Half the population was killed. Recurring bouts in 1361–2, 1369 and 1375 probably killed another 10 to 15 per cent (fig. 88).

It is remarkable, amidst such a catastrophe, that Edward III could still think of pursuing the Hundred Years' War (p. 168). But this he did. The first phase of Edward's war between 1346 and 1360 was a great success, culminating in the capture of the French king, John II, a £500,000 ransom, and a treaty giving Gascony, Poitou and Calais to Edward. This was good for everyone, especially the aristocrats, who fed off both the glory and spoils of war. But when war restarted in 1369 there was a more effective French king, Charles V, and Edward was verging on senility. England lost almost everything it had gained and, in the process, taxes were raised that alienated large parts of the population. National security was threatened by French raids along the south coast. Amidst all this, Edward died, leaving the throne to his ten-year-old son Richard.

Plunged back into a minority, English government was now in the hands of Richard II's uncle, John of Gaunt, Duke of Lancaster. John was unpopular and fed the simmering social discontent that was to boil over in 1381 in the Peasants' Revolt. This short but bloody uprising was a protest about tax and oppression by landlords and the government. Anti-clericalism was a strong strand, too, fed by the heresy known as Lollardy that had started in Oxford. But for the Crown a more formidable opponent than the pitchforks of peasants had grown up – parliament. Now filled with knights and JPs, wealthy landowners and burgesses, and emboldened by statutes that made their consent essential for taxation, parliament could be a powerful force if overruled or ignored.

Thus England in the 1380s and 90s was defeated and divided, and Richard II, like his great-grandfather Edward II, was not up to the job of kingship. John of Gaunt died in 1399, Richard was deposed and murdered at Pontefract Castle, and his cousin Henry Bolingbroke, heir to the Lancastrian line, came to the throne as Henry IV. Henry inherited a depopulated country, an empty treasury and an angry parliament, and suffered a series of aristocratic rebellions. Only in 1408 was he able to start to overcome these and re-establish some semblance of normality.

Effects on Building

Building is highly susceptible to economic fluctuation and recession is often heralded by a slowdown in construction. After 1300 fewer major building projects were started and during the whole of the 15th century there were few projects on the scale of, for instance, Salisbury Cathedral (p. 116). Equally significantly, where there was building – and the 15th century saw a lot of it – it was taking place in different places.

Between the 1330s and the 1520s the balance of wealth in England fundamentally shifted. Up to 1350, with a growing population, the importance of food production in the fertile central belt of England was crucial. The richest counties lay in a band running from Gloucestershire to Norfolk. During the 15th century, with fewer mouths to feed, the economic effect of the wool trade was much greater and the richest counties were Gloucestershire, Wiltshire and Somerset in the west; Kent, Surrey, Hertfordshire and Middlesex in the south; and Essex and Suffolk in the east. In these areas there was a further geographical shift. Because the cloth industry

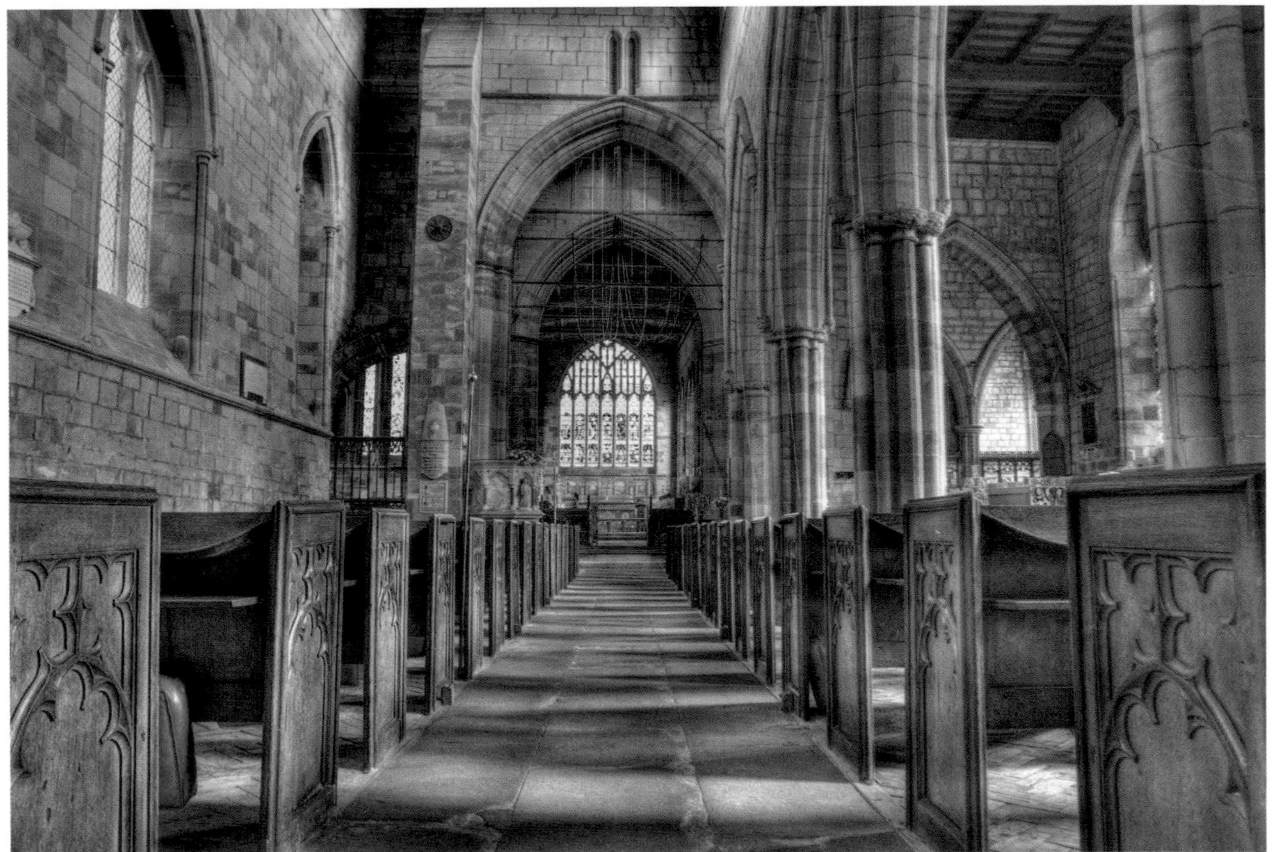

Fig. 119 (above) St Oswald's, Ashbourne, Derbyshire is a big and grand church. To the right can be seen the south aisle – the north aisle was never built. The big north-west buttress of the tower jutting out into the nave suggests that work was abandoned at the time of the Black Death and never resumed.

increasingly relied on fulling mills powered by fast-flowing water to beat and thicken the cloth, and because manufacturers were eager to avoid the monopolistic activities of the craft guilds, cloth production shifted from the larger towns into the countryside and to market towns. All this, of course, is vitally important in understanding who was building what and where. For instance, the great churches of the 15th century were in these rural, wool-rich, areas, not in the former agricultural heartlands where the monuments of the previous century had been.[5]

Many architects and masons were killed by the Black Death, many building projects were halted and many rich patrons died with cheques unsigned. In a few places this can be starkly illustrated. At St Oswald's, Ashbourne, Derbyshire, a very ambitious rebuilding that began in about 1300 suddenly stopped. In 1349 the tower, spire and aisled transepts were in place, as was the south aisle of the nave. But the north aisle was never built. Work stopped in 1350 and was never resumed, so a large buttress supporting the crossing now protrudes into the church (fig. 119). Elsewhere plague was a comma not a full stop. William de la Zouche became Archbishop of York in 1340 and, soon after, laid major plans for the completion of the nave and the construction of a new choir at his minster. Money was set aside and masons recruited. Then on 21 May 1348 the plague hit York. Canon Sampson, a major donor, died, as did the master mason Thomas

Pacenham. Archbishop de la Zouche fled to the countryside, leaving a suffragan in charge. Work eventually restarted, but only in the late 1360s.[6]

Plague and agricultural recession had a huge impact on the countryside. Between 1370 and 1520 as many as two thousand villages were deserted and many more shrank in size, leading to the abandonment of half a million buildings. Yet depopulation was, surprisingly, largely to the advantage of the people who remained behind. Basic foodstuffs were cheaper, and as more meat and fish was available people's diet markedly improved. Wages were higher, unemployment was lower, the choice of jobs was wider and women took on skilled jobs such as weaving. But the real change was the opportunity presented by a new economic model adopted by landowners.

Between 1184 and 1215 landlords had taken their own lands into direct management (p. 109); between 1380 and 1410 this process was reversed. Landlords realised that agriculture was now unpredictable and brought low profits; in contrast, renting their land would bring a guaranteed income. This change had a profound effect from 1400, bringing a new and powerful group of farmers to prominence. A farmer is simply one who pays a fixed rent or 'farm' for their land, and this new group acquired perhaps as much as a quarter of all agricultural land in England. Some were former employees of the lords, many were the richer peasants. A new class of people now shared landed wealth with the aristocracy, a group who created new social relationships and methods of production.[7]

Across large parts of England these men built themselves houses. Hundreds of timber-framed farmhouses from the period 1430 to 1530 survive today in the richer parts of the country, in Kent and Sussex as far west as Hampshire and north into Essex and southern East Anglia. They share a broadly similar plan, with a central hall open to the roof and two-storey blocks at each end containing chambers. The whole was contained under a single roof and in some parts the upper floors were jettied out over the lower ones (fig. 120). Watermill House, Benenden, Kent (fig. 121), for instance, is still much as its late 15th-century builder left it. In the midlands and western England similar types of building are found, although generally of a slightly humbler nature. What is really important about these houses is that they were detached from their farm buildings in such a way that there was nothing inherent in their design that revealed they were lived in by farmers. These families had their own halls, as did their social and economic superiors, and they had their separate bedroom, parlour and kitchen. Beams were carved, doors panelled and windows filled with glass. Decorative metalwork, drains and garderobes were all now commonplace.[8]

The owners of these buildings were active consumers of a wide range of household goods. Decorative ceramics, in particular, would have been ubiquitous, but furnishing textiles and furniture were also in great demand. To the English countryside was now added a type of housing below that of the gentry and above that of the peasant house, well built and tuned to the lives and aspirations of a new consumer class.

Fig. 120 (top) A Kentish Wealden house now in the Weald and Downland Museum, Sussex. The cut-away shows the central great hall with chambers at either end. To the north of the Thames such houses normally had gabled, not hipped, roofs.

Fig. 121 (above) Watermill House Benenden, Kent *c.*1500; a fine yeoman's farmhouse with bold exposed timber framing. The hall is in the centre and at either end of the rest of the accommodation; the upper floors jettied.

The Language of Architecture 1320–1400

If the death toll among architects, masons and sculptors was similar to that in the population at large, half would have died of plague. New men of a younger generation filled their shoes, with a different outlook and working in different styles. At Ely Cathedral, for instance, it seems as if almost all the carvers who had worked on the Lady Chapel were killed, as their particular style of figure carving does not appear again anywhere after 1350. In the diocese of Lichfield the death of large numbers of masons allowed their successors to build in a style markedly different to that before the plague. The shortage of skilled craftsmen stimulated competition between patrons that, in its turn, led to an escalation in wages and sometimes fierce competition for their services. The king, in fact, had to resort to his legal powers of impressment to force craftsmen to come and work at Windsor Castle (p. 164). The fact that many travelled so far to work must have contributed to the spread of stylistic ideas.[9]

Patrons were often new men, too, and an epidemic that left half of England dead must have had a huge effect on the way they felt. There was an emotion and movement in the architecture of the early 14th century that, as the century progressed, became less emotional and more static, less exuberant and florid, more controlled and less individualistic. This simplification began in the 1330s, unconnected with the tragedy of the mid-century, but after the Black Death it seems to have captured the mood, and stylistic change accelerated.

In understanding this it is essential to realise the importance of regional variations in style. Masons leant their craft in the great regional centres and looked to models nearby as well as to those in London. Thus buildings in Oxford, Warwick or Tewkesbury looked different from those in London and the Home Counties. Yet two metropolitan buildings do have an important role to play in the changes that took place in the middle of the 14th century: St Stephen's Chapel at Westminster Palace and the chapter house at St Paul's Cathedral (p. 127). These were the twin showpieces of London masons, incorporating ideas taken from French royal buildings. The specific innovation that was important was the use of tracery as wall decoration rather than simply as structural glazing bars.

In 1327 the lower chapel at St Stephen's was finished but the upper chapel was barely a shell (p. 127). Edward III's masons completed it by following closely, but not slavishly, designs laid down in the 1290s by one of the principal architects of Queen Eleanor's crosses, Michael of Canterbury (p. 129). The chapel was completed in 1248 but the upper chapel is now gone, which is tragic, as Edward III made it both one of the most lavish and, at the time, most admired spaces in England. At the outset it is important to realise that this was a building conceived in direct competition with Sainte-Chapelle, Paris, the principal chapel of French kings, designed as a glowing reliquary to contain their prized relic, the Crown of Thorns. In the completed St Stephen's Chapel every inch of the interior was carved, moulded, painted, gilded

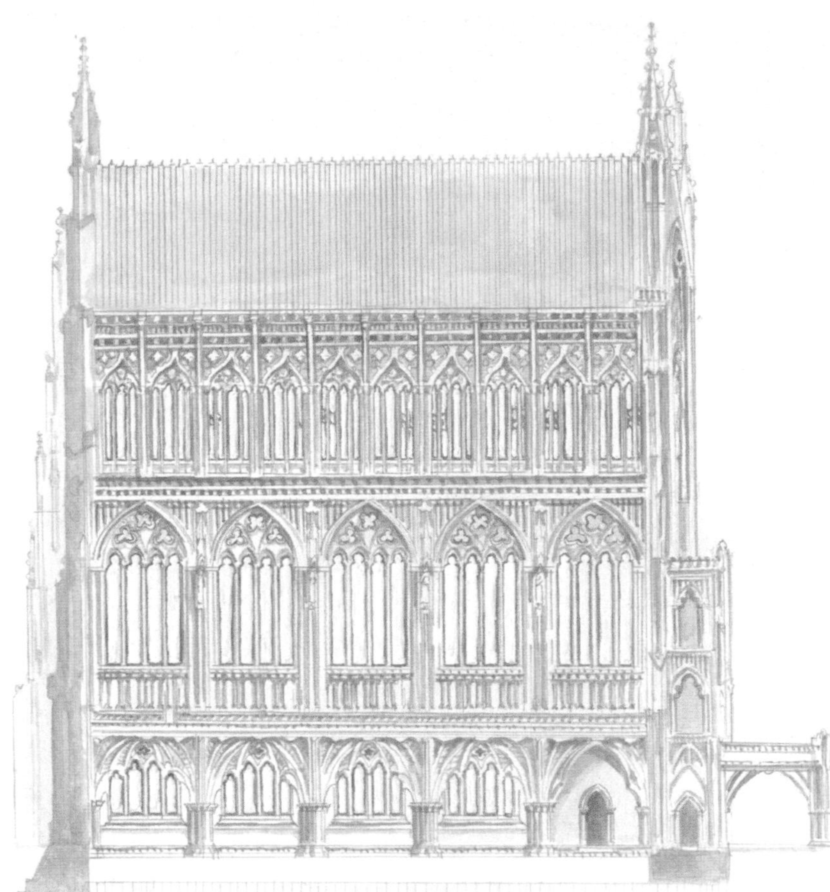

Fig. 122 (left) A longitudinal section of St Stephen's Chapel, Westminster Palace. Only the undercroft now survives. The chapel was hugely influential because it was the most important and glamorous architectural commission of its age, on which all the most ambitious masons and designers worked. As they turned to commissions elsewhere they took elements of St Stephen's with them.

or stencilled to create the richest possible effect. Architecturally, the chapel's extreme height compared with its length was its most notable feature, a characteristic emphasised by the cage-like grid of vertical tracery that covered its walls and windows (fig. 122). The tracery was detailed both on a decorative scale and on an architectural one, drawing the interior together into a visual whole. This was a novel effect that was to be widely imitated. Individual features were imitated too, such as the use of ogee arches (p. 130) and a new type of vault, the lierne, which had short ornamental ribs not connected to the springing points.

It is very likely that the architect of St Stephen's Chapel was Michael of Canterbury, and that, faced with the problem of modernising the interior of the south transept of Gloucester Abbey (now Cathedral), he covered the walls with a veneer of Gothic tracery (fig. 123) and built a south window in which a big central mullion splits and meets the outer arch, effectively creating two arches in one. These features were to become increasingly popular and, in due course, defining of a federation of stylistic components that was christened the Perpendicular style in 1817. The choir at Gloucester was built from *c.*1337 to *c.*1365 under another architect, who extended the stylistic experiment of the transept. It is an exciting place to be, lit by the single-largest window built in

Fig. 123 (right) Gloucester Cathedral; the east wall of the south transept is one of the most astonishing sights of medieval architecture. A raking internal flying buttress cuts across the highly innovative veneer of tracery built over the pre-existing Norman structure. The curtain of tracery was added in *c.*1335 for Abbot Wigmore, probably by his mason, Michael of Canterbury, and was one of the very earliest occasions when this decorative device was used.

medieval Europe (fig. 124). The effect is of a graph-paper-like grid of vertical panels covering the whole internal surface, window included. This was a new aesthetic, for everything was subjugated to the net of tracery and no individual element stood out, in contrast to earlier interiors in which statues and individualistic carving were everywhere. There is another aesthetic shift, too, in the way that the panels and shafts emphasise the verticality of the space rather than its horizontality. The vertical shafts sprout into a multitude of ribs that knit themselves into a bewildering but symmetrical geometric vault.

Fig. 124 (left) Gloucester Cathedral; east window. Because the edges of the window are canted out it is actually wider than the choir, giving the impression that it is not connected to it. This weightlessness combined with the grid of tracery were much admired and imitated.

Fig. 125 (above) Gloucester Cathedral; the cloister, one of the most exquisitely perfect spaces of the Middle Ages. Begun around 1360, but only completed in the 15th century, it has the earliest large-scale application of fan vaulting in England.

From about 1360 the architects of Gloucester took the design principles of the choir to their logical conclusion by applying the grid of panelling to the vaults. The east cloister has the first fan vault in England: a technological and aesthetic revolution (fig. 125). Previous vaults had relied on ribs for their strength. These fan vaults, shaped like upended half trumpets, were made of brilliantly jointed carved ashlar panels decorated with blind tracery that unified wall, window and ceiling in a single modular grid.

The components of this new style, seen best at Gloucester, soon started to make earlier buildings look old-fashioned. The most important of these was Canterbury Cathedral, where the monks started to rebuild their Norman nave in 1377. The architect they commissioned was Henry Yevele, the chief royal architect (p. 166), who took six years to complete one of England's greatest architectural masterpieces. The nave of Canterbury reversed the existing architectural canon, replacing the massive engineering of the arcades (fig. 59) with thin arches and virtually eliminating the clerestory and triforium (fig. 126). The original effect of extreme verticality has now been diluted by the insertion of later screens, but the clusters of vertical shafts sprouting into a vault 80ft above the floor set a model that was widely imitated.

There were few cathedrals and abbeys that were entirely rebuilt in this style and, as we shall see, it was high-status secular buildings and, above all, parish churches that applied and developed these new stylistic components.

Fig. 126 (left) Canterbury Cathedral, Kent; the nave, begun in 1377, was designed by the royal mason Henry Yevele and initially bankrolled by Archbishop Simon Sudbury. The vertical, slender elegance of this tremendous space is appropriate to its position as the nave of the prime church of England.

The attraction for many designers was the way that the system of tracery panels could be applied to many different circumstances, creating original effects within a standardised palette. The mason John Wastell was responsible for popularising the use of carved spandrels with a thick frieze above them on nave arcades, as at St Mary the Virgin's, Saffron Walden, Essex (1450–1525, fig. 127). An alternative treatment, seen most elegantly in the nave at St Mary's, Redcliffe, Bristol (1440–70), was for the verticals of the panelling to drop down and rest on the top of the arcade arches.[10]

Thanks to surviving documents such stylistic quirks can, in the late 14th and 15th centuries, be attributed more often to particular designers.

Fig. 127 (right) St Mary the Virgin, Saffron Walden, Essex was built between 1450 and 1525. The church was designed by John Wastell who used richly carved spandrels and a thick freize to separate the grid of the clerestory windows from the nave arcades.

Some of the biggest names, such as Henry Yevele, Hugh Herland and John Wastell, would have delegated work on site to deputies (called wardens) while they travelled between projects or spent time at their drawing boards. Drawings begin to survive from 1400, and these, for the first time, reveal what had been a feature of building projects for centuries – that English architects were accomplished draughtsmen. Also surviving in increasing quantity are original building contracts showing the complex arrangements that must have always existed between patron, architect and building contractor. They make the story of building in England richer, more accurate but harder to write concisely.[11]

Royal Builders and Buildings 1327–1400

As a builder, Edward III eclipsed his great predecessor Henry II (pp 88, 102–4) and became the greatest patron of English architecture in the Middle Ages. His influential work at St Stephen's Chapel has already been mentioned, but one other project must also be considered – his work at Windsor Castle.

At St Stephen's Chapel Edward was working within an inherited framework; at Windsor he was his own master. The reconstruction of Windsor Castle over a period of 18 years cost £51,000. The bulk of this, some £44,000, was spent between 1357 and 1368 on rebuilding the upper ward, a project masterminded by its 'chief keeper' and surveyor William of Wykeham. Here rose a massive residential block, partly subsuming the work of Henry II. On the north front there were Henry II's great towers, but on the inside, facing the inner ward of the castle, were the royal rooms laid out in a single range, the great hall, the chapel and the king's chamber (fig. 128). At the west end was the Rose Tower, a tall, slender tower containing private chambers. On the west and north were further chambers for the king and queen.

To the modern eye the great south elevation looks austere and monotonous, but to the contemporary observer it would have been radical and novel. Its sheer size, 389ft long, made it the longest secular façade in England. The absence of external sculpture would have set it apart from previous monumental structures, but most striking of all was the impression that individual elements were less important than the overall effect.

Because Edward III made Windsor his official summer residence, the plan of the royal lodgings was closely based on those at Westminster, the principal residence of the monarchy. The new great hall at Windsor was approached by a stair broad and shallow enough to ride a horse up; indeed the hall itself was used by Richard II for a tournament. But like Westminster Hall it was a ceremonial space and the king's great chamber would have been where he normally dined. Next to this was the stair to the Rose Tower, allowing Edward to retreat and enjoy sweetmeats in the luxury of his roof-top chamber after dinner. Beyond the dining chamber were two more large rooms that led to the royal bedchamber, which had an attached oratory. The extent and variety of private space at Windsor demonstrates that Edward spent much of his time segregated from his court; access to the royal person was a privilege and conferred status. This was part of a developing trend that will be noted throughout this chapter towards privacy and specialisation of rooms.[12]

Windsor and Westminster spawned another royal building – Kenilworth Castle, Warwickshire. John of Gaunt, Edward's fourth son, came to prominence when his older brothers died, leaving him the greatest aristocrat in the kingdom. Whilst Westminster and Windsor have either gone or been completely altered, at Kenilworth some of the bravura of Edwardian court architecture remains. Gaunt's great hall, approached by a massive stair, is England's grandest ruined domestic interior, its deep bays panelled with tracery, its cathedral-like windows overlooking the mere (fig. 129). The hall had

Fig. 128 (above) Windsor Castle, the royal lodgings in the upper ward 1357–68, masterminded by William of Wykeham. This was the most important building of its age, the sixteen bay façade containing a great hall and chapel back to back.

Fig. 129 (below) Kenilworth Castle: the great hall. It is not known what the roof was like, but the walls of this spectacular chamber remain, including the deep windows overlooking the mere. Four fireplaces show that this room was designed to be kept warm in deep winter. Below was a vaulted undercroft.

no fewer than six fireplaces, a far cry from the ineffective and smoky arrangements at Penshurst (p. 143). From the west the hall, flanked by the Strong and Saintlowe towers, echoes the monumentality of Windsor.

The medieval court was as much a military as a political institution. In all but its last years Edward III's court had been dominated by war and soldiers, but his son Richard II's was a civilian institution shaped by the fastidious, status-conscious and cultured Richard himself. Richard was concerned to elevate the status of the monarch and define the ranks of aristocracy.[13]

Henry III had made Westminster Hall into the principal throne room of the land, with a permanent marble throne set on the dais behind a massive marble table. Near this the courts of King's Bench, Chancery and Common Pleas met in the presence, as it were, of the king. In 1393 Richard II decided to rebuild Westminster Hall, a project that was completed by 1401. As in so many cathedrals the massive Norman walls were retained and Richard's masons inserted big new Gothic windows in them. Beneath was a cornice richly carved with Richard's heraldic beasts. The Norman roof was replaced by the largest and most important piece of carpentry in Western Europe. The challenge for Hugh Herland, Richard II's carpenter, was how to span spectacularly the 68ft width of the hall. To do this he used an emerging structural technique that was being successfully employed at Dartington Hall, Devon: the hammer-beam roof. This type of roof shortens the span that has to be covered by cutting the tie beam and leaving its stubs as projecting timbers or hammer beams. These are supported by curved braces from the wall. The hammer beams then reduce the span for the principal arches (fig. 130).

On each hammer beam was a massive angel holding the arms of England; the roof was thus a representation of the heavens spread over the earthly court of Richard II. This was not the only religious connotation of the hall, for on the south wall, behind the dais, were six rich niches containing figures of kings rather like a cathedral pulpitum, as at York Minster. The entrance façade was

Fig. 130 (right) Westminster Hall: though the walls of this vast hall were erected by William Rufus (fig. 49), as experienced today this is a space conceived for the court of Richard II. The roof, its most expressive architectural feature, has thirteen trusses and weighs 660 tons, carried by the great corbels anchored onto the Norman walls.

Fig. 131 (below) The entrance façade of Westminster Hall, now destroyed, with two towers clad with a screen of 27 niches containing statues of kings and queens. It was designed to look like a great abbey of the time, reinforcing the idea that the court was equivalent in status to the church.

Fig. 132 (left) St Wendreda's, March is perhaps the most elaborate expression of the angel roof, with three tiers of angels. Its origins lie with Westminster Hall.

also treated like a cathedral or great abbey, with two towers clad with a screen of 27 niches containing statues of kings and queens (fig. 131). In terms of architectural hierarchy Westminster Hall, uniquely in English medieval architecture, sought equivalence of status with the most important religious buildings, a comment on Richard II's conception of kingship.[14]

While this was never copied by lesser patrons, almost every other aspect of the hall was. The king's personal heraldic devices displayed on the cornice encouraged the fashion for the profuse display of personal heraldry in the interiors of secular buildings (p. 123). Timber roofs already had status in English building – unlike in France – but the hammer beam instantly became a special kind of roof that referred back to the principal throne chamber of the land. Edward IV and Henry VIII, for instance, chose them to cover their halls at Eltham (1475) and Hampton Court (1532), and the last was built at Burghley House, Lincolnshire, as late as 1561.[15] The religious connotations of the roof were taken up by parish churches, either as at St Wendreda's, March, Cambridgeshire, where there are three tiers of angels on a double hammer-beam roof (fig. 132), or at St Nicholas's, King's Lynn, Norfolk, where the angels sit tight against a boarded ceiling.

Richard II's reign saw one more important advance: the creation of a permanent office for royal building, the Office of Works. This was a change from the ad hoc recruitment of craftsmen and designers for particular projects to an established organisation with its own architects and artificers. The architects did not only work for the Crown, nor did the Crown exclusively use their services. Men such as Henry Yevele worked for other clients, including Canterbury Cathedral, while William Wynford also worked at Wells. Yet the

establishment of the office created an architectural establishment, recognisable in English architectural history well into the 18th century.[16]

Yet, for all this activity, the English Crown never created a recognisable court style, nor did it (with a small number of exceptions) consistently build bigger and better than its subjects. Windsor was a great feat but Arundel and Warwick castles were extraordinary achievements, too. In its size and ambition Windsor was also equalled by most of the monarchs of Europe, and the French kings built larger, stronger, more magnificent castles and palace-forts in greater numbers than the English monarchy ever did.[17]

Aristocratic Houses: the Wartime Generation 1350–1400

The Hundred Years' War was bad news for the French. On and off for 120 years armies viciously harried their country, causing destruction and misery. For the English the effects were costly but less destructive of property; indeed war for many signalled the rebuilding of nearby castles and churches in new and flamboyant styles. War was a speculative trade fought not for Crown and country but for cash. Wages, fees, booty, ransom, tax and protection money filled the purses of English soldiers. Those who were successful, particularly before 1380, returned home rich and eager to build. Thomas, Earl of Warwick, was lucky enough to capture the Archbishop of Sens, who was forced to pay £8,000 for his liberty, money that went towards a spectacular rebuilding of Warwick Castle. Edward III himself financed much of his work at Windsor from the spoils of war.[18]

Thus war and aristocratic architectural aspiration went hand in hand. Fighting in France could bring wealth and honour to nobles, which in turn could support the aggrandising of landed estates to pass on to their heirs. For these men war, honour and knighthood were in their blood. They wanted to build houses that reflected their martial success and would push themselves to their financial limit to do so.

Until after the Black Death England north of Yorkshire was thinly populated with great houses. There were royal castles at Carlisle and Berwick, for instance, and the castle-palace of Durham (figs 56, 74), but few noble houses of any size. During the reign of Richard II two families became the leading forces in the north, the Percys and the Nevilles; both were given wide-ranging powers of governance by the Crown. These families, and their followers, built a series of residences of extraordinary scale and magnificence over a period of about a century. The Nevilles were the greatest and most important builders in the north before the 18th century, starting at Brancepeth (*c.*1360–80), then at Raby (*c.*1367–1389), at Middleham and Sheriff Hutton. Supporters of the Nevilles built in imitation at Bolton and Lumley. The Percy family meanwhile redeveloped Alnwick Castle between 1310 and 1360, and the masterly Warkworth Castle in the 1390s.[19]

These mighty residences were palace-forts: massive, lavish and theatrical, and heavily influenced by Windsor and Kenilworth castles. They tended not to have a strong single visual focus provided by a keep, their silhouette being made up of instead of numbers of towers and walls. Crucially, they were planned around a central courtyard, a development that had begun just before 1300 and can be seen at Goodrich Castle, Herefordshire, where the Valence earls of Pembroke built an up-to-the-minute castle with a series of self-contained lodgings around a central court (fig. 133). The best surviving northern palace-fort is at Bolton, where in about 1378 John Lewyn, the most important architect in northern England, started a brand-new castle on a fresh site for Richard, Lord Scrope. Scrope was a soldier-turned-courtier who

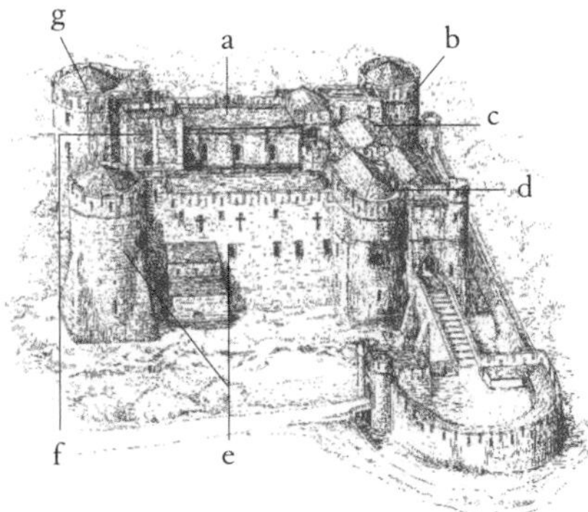

Fig. 133 (above) Goodrich Castle Herefordshire: a) great hall; b) lord's chambers; c) great chamber; d) gatehouse; e) household and guests; f) great tower (use uncertain); g) high-status guests.

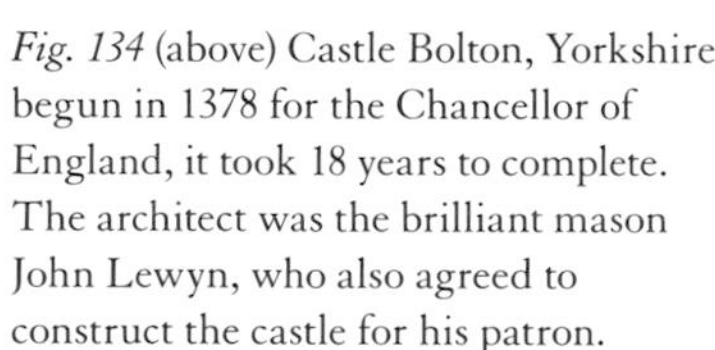

Fig. 134 (above) Castle Bolton, Yorkshire; begun in 1378 for the Chancellor of England, it took 18 years to complete. The architect was the brilliant mason John Lewyn, who also agreed to construct the castle for his patron.

Fig. 135 (above right) Castle Bolton, Yorkshire. The external appearance is utterly uncompromising, plain but overpowering in bulk. The internal plan is of extreme ingenuity with a large number of rooms for Scrope, his household, guests and servants.

rose to be Chancellor of England. Like Goodrich, his new house was built around a courtyard, with five strong towers at the corners (fig. 134). Its external appearance is utterly uncompromising, plain but overpowering in bulk. This austerity is all show, for it wraps around a plan of extreme ingenuity that created a large number of luxurious lodgings for Scrope, his household, guests and servants (fig. 135). Bolton represents the first generation of English aristocratic houses in which the complexity of a lavish civilian lifestyle is architecturally integrated with the visual communication of military power.[20]

A number of trends are discernible in these buildings, the first being their appearance. They were deliberately anachronistic in style, highlighting chivalric values, and emphasising and protecting the elite lifestyles of their owners. The second is their size. These palace-forts were designed to accommodate large households; big was beautiful, big was powerful and, as we shall see, big was practical, as the average household grew. Then there was an increasing elaboration of plan, already seen in royal buildings. This reflected a more complex and sophisticated lifestyle on the part of the lords and their

Fig. 136 (left) Warkworth Castle, Northumberland: the great tower, John Lewyn's masterpiece, was built in the 1390s. Unlike many such towers this is a work of great architecture, impressive in silhouette, ingenious in plan and commodious in function. This structure illustrates, better than any other, how a 14th-century magnate might appear powerful but live in considerable comfort – even luxury.

most important lieutenants. The master mason John Lewyn's masterpieces at Bolton and Warkworth (fig. 136) still dazzle today with the sheer technical complexity of plan and construction, expressing lifestyles to match.

Finally, over a period of about half a century, we see the growth of the individual lodging, for owners, their households and their guests. Generally speaking, lodgings for the lord and lady of the house developed at the upper end of the hall, normally in a wing built at right angles to it. Before 1400 most grand houses had a withdrawing chamber in this position, but increasingly this was only the first of a sequence of rooms that became progressively more private. We have already encountered Penshurst Place (p. 143), which was sold to Henry V's brother John, Duke of Bedford, in 1429. He built onto Sir John Pultney's withdrawing chamber a large three-storey block, containing household lodgings on the ground floor and two fine rooms above for himself, as well as a lobby and a private closet (fig. 137). To provide access to this suite the staircase from the hall was also rebuilt in a more stately fashion. On the ground floor of many of these cross-wings a parlour was positioned, although not at Penshurst. This could be used by the family for dining before ascending to the lodgings above. In the 15th century it also became common for high-status lodgings to be built over the kitchen end of the hall.[21]

Such lordly lodgings, which today are often gaunt and empty ruins, were furnished with extravagance. Key to a display of magnificence was plate and textiles. Textiles, particularly tapestry, often woven in the Low Countries, were hung in any room of status, and, in the most important rooms, sets of tapestries shot through with precious metals sparkled in the candlelight. Thomas Woodcock at Castle Pleshey in 1397 had a bed of cloth of gold valued at £180, equivalent to the annual income of a well-heeled knight. One of his tapestries, showing the history of Charlemagne, was 72ft long and was valued at over £48. Buffets covered in fine carpets or linen supported a dazzling display of plate: ewers, chargers, candlesticks and goblets. In his

Fig. 137 (right) Penshurst Place, Kent. The great hall (fig. 112) is to the right, the Duke of Bedford's chamber block of the 1430s to the left. The dormer windows are later. The Duke's new, and more impressive, staircase, can be seen butted up against the great hall, its battlements rising above it.

bedroom at Bolton Castle Lord Scrope had a bowl and ewer of silver, and in his great hall thirty-five gold and silver salt cellars.[22]

These houses also developed lodgings for the household and guests. Lodgings designed for occupation by a single person first make their appearance in colleges and religious communities. Mob Quad at Merton College, Oxford (1308–11, p. 189), is an example of communal lodgings that formed a model for similar suites in royal and aristocratic houses. At Dartington Hall, Devon, Richard II's half-brother, the Earl of Huntingdon, built two long two-storey ranges of lodgings in his outer court in the 1390s. The west range (fig. 138), which contained ten lodgings, retains the porches to the lower lodgings and external stairs to the upper ones. Each room measured around 20ft by 22ft and had its own entrance door, shuttered window, fireplace and garderobe. These rooms were for neither servants nor guests, but for knightly members of the earl's household who would stay in them with their attendants and squires. All the great palace-forts described above contained such facilities, either in ranges, as at Middleham (*c.*1400–30), or in towers, as at Bolton (*c.*1378–96).[23]

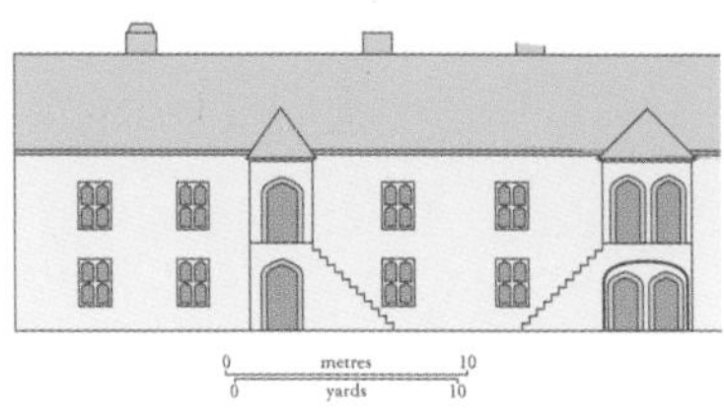

Fig. 138 (above) Dartington Hall, Devon: west range. Suggested original appearance showing external staircases that doubled as porches for the lodgings below.

The Parishes 1380–1530

Despite economic stagnation and depopulation, for many communities the period between 1380 and 1530 was one of active participation in architectural patronage. These 150 years saw the rebuilding of perhaps 50 per cent of all parish churches, a process quite different from previous waves of church building. First, there were few new foundations. New parishes more or less ceased to be formed after 1300, each church jealously protecting its existing rights and jurisdiction. The 15th century saw new naves, towers, porches, re-fenestration and internal reordering rather than new building on fresh sites. Second, this work was not funded by ecclesiastics or the aristocracy but by the gentry and merchants, and by middling or lesser men contributing to their local project. Lay patronage excluded the chancels, which remained the preserve of the rector, meaning that in some places, such as Somerset, small, old chancels were dominated by magnificent new western extensions. Third, rich and powerful guilds (or fraternities) were not confined to the immediate geographical area of the parish but bound like-minded people together for social, economic and, most importantly, religious mutual support (p. 178). Of the 2,000 or so guilds founded in the Middle Ages the great majority were founded after 1400. These organisations rebuilt parts of churches, endowed them with vestments and plate, and paid for huge numbers of clergy.[24]

Lay funding of parochial architecture was no amateur, part-time activity; it was sophisticated and effective. During the 13th century it had become the responsibility of elected lay representatives, the church wardens. They would hold lands, endowments, manage gifts and ensure donors' wishes were respected. While some parishes held land and could benefit from rental income, most did not. This meant the wardens had to budget carefully and run a programme of fundraising events and collections. Church ales, gatherings, revels, plays and dances held to raise money were part of the everyday diet of a medieval parish. Many churches were funded by bequests either of money or of goods and land that were later sold. This link with legacies was fundamental because the dynamo of late medieval parochial fundraising was death.[25]

The tragedies of the 14th century left a residual strain of morbidity in society. This is perhaps most starkly symbolised by a fashion among some rich ecclesiastics for double tombs. The upper tomb commemorated the patron in all his worldly glory and below lay his emaciated cadaver wrapped in a shroud. Sometimes worms creep from the belly, sometimes from eye sockets. In the tomb of John Wakeman, last abbot of Tewkesbury Abbey, Gloucestershire (*c.*1449), his putrefying corpse is being eaten not only by worms but frogs, mice and snails (fig. 139). More common expressions of morbidity were the terrifying murals that were painted above and around the chancel arch and behind the rood. Worshippers at St Thomas's, Salisbury, still stare at a huge doom painting made in around 1510 in which Christ in Majesty judges the world. On the left angels are raising the dead, some of whom are carried (with evident relief) heavenwards. On the other side is the Prince of Darkness watching a group of the damned, wrapped in chains, being dragged into the mouth of hell (fig. 140).

Fig. 139 (top) Tewkesbury Abbey; the Wakeman cenotaph commemorating the last abbot, who died in 1559 but whose tomb is a hundred years earlier. On top of the slab is a cadaver lying in an open shroud crawling with vermin. Unusually, the figure lay on the upper level, it being too large to be squeezed in below.

Fig. 140 (above) St Thomas of Canterbury, Salisbury has an early 16th-century doom painting that, although later heavily overpainted, shows vividly the horror conjured up by medieval painters. Here the damned are being dragged into the mouth of hell, depicted as a fierce and uncompromising red monster.

Such images heralded the transformation of late medieval parish churches into machines for memorial Masses and prayers for the dead (p. 121). While the fear of dying unprepared was universal, the responses to it varied according to wealth. St Peter and St Paul's, Salle, Norfolk, stands virtually isolated, with no settlement around it. Even at its peak Salle can have numbered no more than 500 people. Yet the church itself would not be out of place in a large town: a stout tower, a deep chancel and a nave with aisles, transepts and two porches of two storeys. Everything from the bold carving on the west front to the stained glass and the font is of the highest quality. This was a church paid for by a small group of local men and their families between 1410 and 1440. Death was on their minds, and with their fellows they founded no fewer than seven guilds with their chapels in the church.[26]

A super-rich merchant, such as John Greenway of Tiverton, Devon, could afford to build his own chantry chapel. At his parish church, St Peter's, he paid for a new porch and a chapel for himself and his family in 1517. It is ostentatiously carved with precise and lifelike images of the ships that brought him his wealth. In a class of its own is the private chantry chapel built between 1443 and 1449 for Richard Beauchamp, Earl of Warwick, at St Mary's, Warwick, at the phenomenal cost of £2,500. Vaulted and panelled, with an east window encrusted with angels, the building itself is only a vessel for the greatest and most beautiful of English medieval sculptures – a cast copper effigy of the earl, recording in super-realistic detail his physique and rare Milanese armour.[27]

Guilds also built their own chantry chapels in which Mass would be said for guild members, often by their own priest. These fraternities not only gave the poor an opportunity to be remembered after death, they gave people a stake in the fabric of their church. In Holy Trinity, Coventry, the tanners, the butchers and the mercers had their own chapels, and other guilds had chapels dedicated to the Holy Trinity, the Virgin and St Thomas. Many of these were not structural chapels but more cheaply formed areas divided off by a wooden screen. They became major features of church interiors in the 15th century, cluttering up naves and aisles, and returning them to the sort of compartmentalisation seen in the 10th century. Most timber screens are gone, but at St Peter's, Wolferton, Norfolk, two fine and delicate screens survive unmolested, showing how men of middling means could create a chantry without rebuilding the church.

Churches were a community of prayer and service, not only comprising the rector (or vicar), but several chantry priests working for individuals, families or guilds. The large parish of Stratford-upon-Avon had 1,500 communicants, far more than the parson alone could serve; luckily, he was assisted by five full-time priests employed by the Holy Cross guild. Parish activity not only multiplied inside the church but outside, too: rituals, feasts, ceremonies and processions significantly increased in popularity and number during the 15th century. What all this meant was that religion in all its expressions was knitted into the fabric of everyday life.[28]

The Poor, the Sick, the Pilgrim and the Wayfarer 1350–1500

Medieval society was surprisingly mobile. In the 19th century many people would not venture beyond the bounds of their town or village but it was quite normal in the Middle Ages to make fairly ambitious journeys. While war, disease, famine and economic change were incentives to get on the road, the most common motivation was pilgrimage (p. 42). Most pilgrimages were short, perhaps to the next town or village, but many pilgrims were drawn by the richer spiritual rewards of more distant monasteries and cathedrals with their famous saints and relics.

Offering hospitality to pilgrims was a Christian duty, one that fell most heavily on the monasteries, which had provided accommodation for guests since early times. At first this might have been a large hall where guests ate and slept, such as that excavated at Kirkstall Abbey, Yorkshire. From the 12th century the larger houses provided separate guest lodgings for different social groups. At Mount Grace Priory, Yorkshire, much of the guest wing built in the 1420s remains, albeit altered. Here there were four individual rooms on the ground floor, and above, entered by a staircase from the inner court, were the high-status suites, with an outer chamber on the first floor and a bedroom above. Guests would have dined in an adjacent hall with its own kitchen.[29]

As we have seen, many monasteries set up separate hospices for the accommodation of pilgrims, the sick and other wayfarers (p. 140), but these became less common and effective after 1350. One of the effects of the sequential crises of the late 14th century was a changing attitude to poverty. With an extreme shortage of labour after the plague, those who would not – or could not – work were regarded as idle troublemakers, a suspicion given weight by the Peasants' Revolt. During the 1380s legislation empowered mayors and sheriffs to incarcerate suspicious-looking vagrants, but essentially there was now a presumption that poverty and crime were bedfellows. As a consequence the thousand or so hospitals founded earlier in the Middle Ages were now often seen as supporting shirkers so, after the 1380s, hospitals began rapidly to redefine their activities.[30]

By 1400 the daily emphasis of a big and well-endowed hospital such as St Giles's, Norwich (p. 140), was as much on Masses said for its benefactors as for alleviating poverty and sickness. As a result, most of the 13th-century fabric of St Giles's has been replaced by the work of successive donors (fig. 141). It has an unusual plan for a hospital as, inserted between the western ward and the chancel, is the nave of the parish church of St Helen. The chapel, which acted as the chancel of the church, is spectacular: vaulted with a wagon roof of chestnut painted with 252 double-headed eagles. A cloister and a fine house for the master lay to the north, and on the south side of the nave stands a rich chantry chapel probably built by Master Smyth, who died in 1489.[31]

St Giles's survived under the patronage of the bishop of Norwich but many other hospitals were re-founded. These new foundations were more concerned

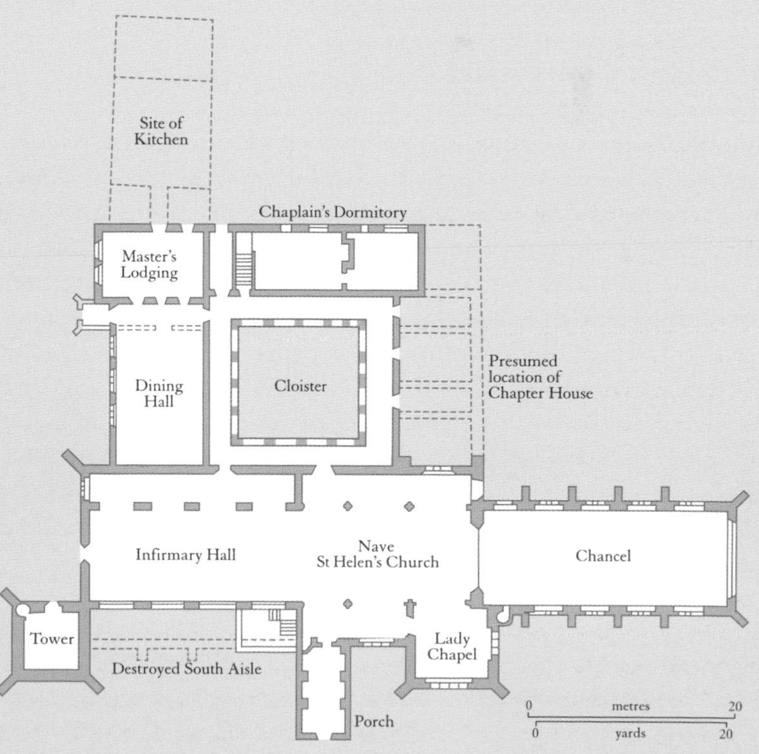

Fig. 141 (right) The Hospital of St Giles, Norwich (the Great Hospital), founded in 1249 and much extended and embellished since. The church is mainly late 15th century. Yet the medieval arrangement is still evident, and in use.

with providing long-term care for the elderly or disabled than with helping the 'undeserving' poor and sick. The almsmen so helped were expected to pray for the soul of the founder in exchange for board and lodging. The Hospital of St Cross, Winchester, is typical; Henry of Blois's original hospital of 1136 was re-founded in 1446 as an almshouse by the half-brother of Henry IV, Cardinal Beaufort. Beaufort did not envisage anything half-hearted. The almshouses and gatehouse are of the highest quality, providing originally for 35 retired brethren, three sisters and two priests. They each had their own private dwelling with heated rooms and garderobes, but they ate communally in hall (fig. 143). Crucially, their attendance at chapel was obligatory; missing prayers for the soul of the founder resulted in a fine. St Cross was planned more like a college and was among the first major English buildings of any sort to provide individual comfortable lodgings for its occupants.[32]

Such institutions were based on the principle of prayer – prayers for the founders, and prayers for the feeble and ailing inhabitants – with medicine playing a minor role. The first English hospital to employ full-time doctors was the Savoy Hospital, Westminster, begun in 1509. The Savoy was one of Henry VII's most important works of piety, one of three planned hospitals that would carry out works of charity and whose inmates would pray for his soul. The Savoy was not an almshouse but a hostel for the destitute of London, who would be received, washed, fed and given a bed with clean sheets for the night. If they were ill they would be seen by a doctor after the able-bodied had been sent out for the day. Their simple obligation was a prayer for the founder. The buildings constituted a radical break with tradition and were based closely on the Hospital of Santa Maria Nuova in Florence, to whose officials Henry VII's advisors wrote asking advice. The hospital was cruciform in plan and the inmates could witness Mass being said centrally under the crossing. Neither its unusual plan nor its medical provision was widely copied, and a hospital in the modern sense was still some centuries off (pp 276–8).

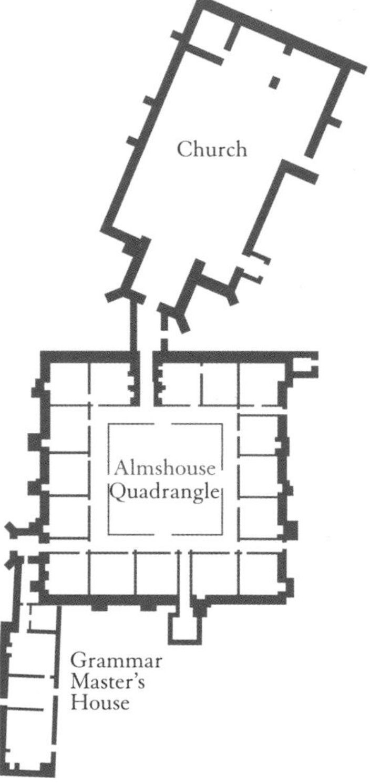

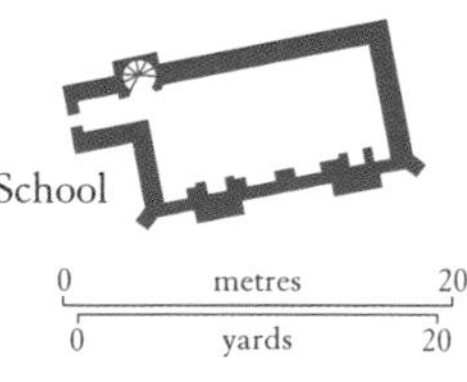

Fig. 142 (above) God's House, Ewelme, Oxfordshire, a similar early hospital to the Savoy Hospital. At the top is the church and chantry chapel, in the middle the quadrangle for the inmates and at the bottom the schoolhouse.

As charitable accommodation for wayfarers and pilgrims became scarcer, commercial options became more plentiful. From early times people had rented out space in their houses for travellers but by the 13th century inns became common in most towns of any size. The term 'inn' had several meanings in the Middle Ages: it was used to describe a large house belonging to a person of status (p. 148); a place where students lived, as in the Inns of Court (p. 188); or, as here, an establishment offering food, drink and accommodation for a fee. Inns in this sense were like hotels. Taverns, which provided good-quality food and drink, including wine, were more like restaurants. Alehouses were pubs providing basic food, ale and, on occasion, rooms. From the 16th century these distinctions were recognised in law, and defined licensing restrictions and the obligations of landlords. From a census taken in 1577 we can calculate that England had around 17,367 alehouses, 1,991 inns and 401 taverns.

Alehouses were often just people's ordinary residences, although larger houses with cellars were more successful venues. This is because before the 1450s, when more alcoholic beer fermented with hops became common, ale that contained only malt yeast and water needed to be kept cool if it was to last.

Fig. 143 (above) The Hospital of St Cross, Winchester, Hampshire. The hospital buildings date from 1446 and the gatehouse and hall can be seen on the right, while on the left are the brethren's lodgings; each house has four rooms served by one chimney; each lodging contained three rooms.

The larger houses, too, would have had attached brew houses in which ale, and later beer, were made. Taverns were also essentially houses, although larger and normally with cellarage for the storage of wine. Before the 15th century it was only the inn that had a distinctive architectural expression.[33]

Inns were commercial ventures constructed by landowners, often monasteries, to make money. The powerfully atmospheric George Inn, Norton St Philip, Somerset, was built in the late 14th century by the Carthusian priory of Hinton in order to provide accommodation for merchants visiting the market – and more generally to stimulate trade. It is typical of a type of inn that presents a fine stone façade to the street, with a hall, kitchen and rooms in a single range. The New Inn, Gloucester, is undoubtedly the most spectacular surviving example, but of a different type. Built by the abbey in 1450, it is a three-storey, timber-framed building constructed around a central courtyard. On the street front there are shops, and a passageway between them leads to the central court, surrounded by upper-floor galleries, leading in turn to over 20 rooms. These were large – 20ft by 12ft to 15ft – and would have contained several beds for up to half a dozen occupants so the whole inn could accommodate perhaps 200 people when full. There was a hall, a kitchen and a series of parlours for private dining (fig. 144).

Establishments such as the New Inn became worthwhile businesses partly because the rich now had fewer houses of their own and travelling from place to place required commercial lodging. The New Inn could accommodate the travelling household of an aristocrat with ease. The most important guests would dine in their own rooms, which were furnished with tables, chairs and benches. The less well-off dined in the hall, and shared beds with other travellers and a variety of bed bugs. A bed in a cheap inn would cost a penny a night, less than the cost of dinner; the swankier establishments would be more.[34]

Civic Pride 1350–1450

English towns peaked in size in about 1300 and from that time on population stagnated, before plummeting as a result of plague. Some towns, such as Lincoln and York, halved in size between 1377 and 1530. Yet in 1530 30 per cent of the population was living in towns, and some places such as Exeter and Worcester had grown in size and wealth.

English towns were run by wealthy traders, artisans and merchants, who would make key decisions, taking account of the views of common council, the representative body of small-scale operators. It was the merchants who sent burgesses to parliament, petitioned the Crown, fought law suits and courted favour with local aristocrats who could further their aspirations. During the 15th century these men attained social equivalence with the country gentry. Trade became respectable and the richest were knighted, bought country estates and formed dynasties. This new class, eager to express its wealth and sophistication in bricks and mortar, had a tremendous impact on the appearance of English towns.

Merchants were the leading members of religious fraternities or guilds (p. 172). These groups had existed before 1350 but thereafter became more numerous, prosperous and prestigious, and grew to occupy a key place in the local economy. Whilst at heart they were clubs investing in a collective chantry and employing priests to pray for their souls, their charitable activities were vital. They founded and funded schools, hospitals and almshouses, and paid for local infrastructure such as roads and bridges. Indeed, in some small towns most public buildings were funded by guilds.[35]

In King's Lynn, Norfolk, there were 59 guilds in 1389 and half a dozen of them had a huge impact on the town. Trinity Guild maintained the town walls and a public quay on the river, the guild of St Giles and St Julian built almshouses and three of the largest maintained their own guild halls.[36] In York, second only to London in wealth and population, two medieval guild halls remain: the Merchant Adventurers' hall of 1357–61 and the Merchant Taylors' of *c.*1400. Both are timber framed and the Adventurers' hall is one of the best surviving of the period (fig. 145). The guild was originally a social and religious one – the Guild of Our Lord Jesus and the Blessed Virgin Mary –

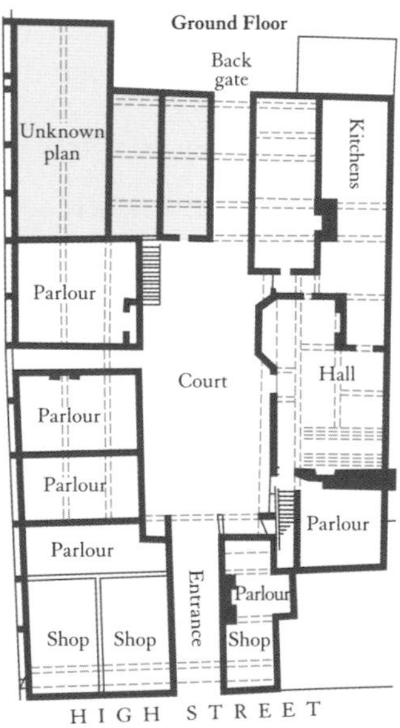

Fig. 144 (above) The New Inn, Gloucester. The street façade and archway now appear 18th-century and conceal the original medieval shops which fronted the inn on the high street. A nearly complete courtyard inn of *c.*1450 lies behind; in the courtyard are open galleries.

Fig. 145 (right) The Merchant Adventurers' hall, York is one of the few surviving medieval guild houses in England, and one of the very best. The undercroft, of 1358–9, is of brick and stone. Above is the timber-framed hall (89ft by 40ft) with later windows. The framing was originally concealed by whitewashed render. To the right is the guild chapel, rebuilt in the 15th century.

Fig. 146 (above) Reconstruction drawing of Thaxted guild hall, Essex. This compact and elegant multi-purpose building was built in the best position in the town, at the top end of the main street on a fork. It not only proclaimed the wealth of the cutlers but the sophistication and elegance of the town.

but it was later absorbed by a craft guild, the Guild of Mercers and Merchants. Their building combined spaces for trading, social events, religion and charity. The huge, aisled ground-floor space and stone chapel were a hospital for tending the sick, elderly and orphaned, as well as passing travellers and pilgrims. Above was the hall, the hub of the guild's trading and social activities.

There was often much overlap between membership of religious and craft guilds and, as we have just seen with the Merchant Adventurers, these sometimes combined. The craft guilds regulated and controlled the town's crafts and trades. From the 1260s these economic societies flourished; trade in London, for instance, had the guilds at its heart by 1330. The wealth of craft guilds was also expressed in magnificent halls; by 1475 London had 27 of them. The London halls, such as those for the Goldsmiths, Mercers, and Fishmongers, were generally the courtyard houses of rich merchants. All these halls perished in 1666.

It was not only in the largest towns that tradesmen formed guilds. In the rich Essex town of Thaxted the Cutlers formed a guild in 1390. Within 50 years they had built themselves a large hall, occupying the prime site in the town (fig. 146). Its open ground floor was rented out to stall holders, the first floor was a market hall for business transactions and the upper floor was probably reserved for the Cutlers' own social events. Although structurally and stylistically much like the timber-framed residences elsewhere in the town, this building was carefully designed by the guild for its specific purposes.

The fraternities, craft guilds and their buildings, together with the feasts and ceremonies that were an integral part of their purpose, gave a sense of character, history and pride to towns. In the richest towns this was expressed by the town government in its own civic structures. By 1300 the City of London had won self-government from the Crown. A mayor, 24 aldermen and two sheriffs were established, and they commissioned the mason John Croxtone to replace the old city guild hall in 1411. Over nearly 20 years he built the largest and most important building in the City after St Paul's. Most of it was hemmed in by other structures, so the entrance porch, facing Guildhall Yard, became the public face of England's wealthiest corporation. It certainly looked the part. The whole surface was covered by blank arcading and niches containing 4ft-high statues. At the top was Christ in Majesty; below, on the next level, figures representing law and learning; then, flanking the archway, four female figures representing the virtues of discipline, justice, fortitude and temperance trampling vice beneath their feet (fig. 147).

The porch led to the great hall, built in emulation of Westminster Hall and, in England, only second in size to it. It was probably originally intended to be vaulted in stone, a feat indeed considering its 46ft width. In the end it was given a hammer-beam roof with steeply pitched covering visible above the adjacent buildings. Inside, the entire wall surface was decorated with gigantic screens of tracery, the upper parts of which sailed over window openings on the same plane as the wall, giving the interior a remarkable harmony (fig. 148).

Inside there were daises at each end where courts could be held. On the north side was the entrance to the most important court, for the mayor; in a separate building at the back of this was a smaller court room for the alder-

Fig. 147 (left) The medieval guild hall of the City of London, the largest, grandest and most important civic building of the English Middle Ages. Eight bays long with massive octagonal corner turrets and emphatic buttresses, this building was about power – its porch carried not only decoration but more subtle messages about the Corporation.

Fig. 148 (above right) The medieval guild hall of the City of London; reconstructed section. Between the windows are large triple wall shafts with capitals, giving the room an emphatic rhythm. The stonework was originally painted in green and gold with red lining out.

men. Soon after these buildings were completed a chapel and college were constructed in which, each year, the Mass that preceded the mayoral election was celebrated. Next to it was a library, in theory open for the citizens of London but probably mainly used by the college.[37] This group of civic structures, hall, courts, chapel and library was the architectural expression of civic responsibility, good and godly government, and raw wealth.

Civic pride and responsibility were also expressed by the provision of a clean water supply. Following the lead of monasteries English towns started to lay on running water from the early 13th century. Bristol came first, followed by Salisbury, and then in 1237 London obtained its first piped supply, bringing spring water from Tyburn to a conduit head in Cheapside. During the 15th century other London conduits were erected, and in the early 16th century new pipelines were laid from Hampstead, Hackney and Marylebone.[38]

By 1300 around 200 of the 640 or so boroughs in England were fortified. Walls were nothing new. The Saxons had walled Oxford in masonry (pp 51–2), but from 1220 boroughs were able to obtain a murage grant – permission to levy a tax on goods brought into a town for the purpose of building or maintaining its defences. This contributed to much embellishment and rebuilding.

Whilst a walled circuit was without question primarily a security measure, town walls were much more than that. They conferred status on a place, giving it a presence and a dignity that un-walled settlements lacked. Walls regulated the town economy by controlling access: the corporation could impose curfews in times of unrest and manage the entrances in times of disease.

A surprising number of walls survive, not only in former Roman settlements such as York (p. 23), but in medieval towns such as Southampton, Ludlow and Bristol. Defences might be of masonry but equally could be earth banks, ditches or timber palisades. Walls were expensive but gates more so. These were not only the

Fig. 149 (left) Monk Bar, York. This gate is of the early 14th century with a top storey built in the 15th. A very large and tall arch with three shields under canopies is on the outer face. The wall below is pierced with four arrow slots; behind is the portcullis, still in working order. To the left the city wall has been breached to ease traffic flow.

valve through which the life of the town passed; they were the vehicle for the expression of civic pride. The great wall and gates of London are largely gone, but York retains the longest walls in England, almost three miles in circumference, with its original gates, bars and towers. Monk Bar (fig. 149), four storeys high, begun in the early 14th century with a 15th-century top storey, is in military terms sophisticated, each floor being independently defensible. The walls of York are stone. Further east, the favoured material was brick; the town walls of Hull, completed in

Fig. 150 (right) North Bar, Beverley, Yorkshire. England's earliest brick-built town gate was constructed in 1409–10 at a cost of £100. Like Monk Bar, York, the gate was closed by a portcullis. The cartouche over the arch is 17th century.

*c.*1409, contained 4.7 million bricks, making it the largest brick structure built in England since Roman times. At Beverley the brick-built North Bar of 1409–10 is one of the finest surviving brick civic gates (fig. 150). These gates could fulfil a number of roles: residences for the privileged, meeting places for town councils, lock-ups or gaols. They also had a symbolic value, displaying the severed heads of malefactors and functioning as assembly points for processions.[39]

Trade and Commerce 1350–1530

The most important aspect of urban life was a market held in the open air on certain authorised days of the week. Before 1350 the rising population and increased prosperity led to the establishment of more than 2,000 markets, many in villages selling basic goods to peasants and artisans. During the 15th century most of these ceased to function and trading activity became concentrated in around 600 market towns. These places acquired a particular character, with distinctive building types and town plans.[40]

Fig. 151 (left) The poultry cross, Salisbury is the sole survivor of four. Originally the town had the cheese cross, the wool cross and Barnwell's cross. The surviving cross is 15th century and has, at the apex of each of its arches, a statue niche topped with a pinnacle. The whole thing is crowned by big flying buttresses that carry a corona of six niches.

Fig. 152 (below) Shepton Mallet, Somerset; the 15th-century timber shambles is a unique fluke survival of a medieval market stall. In the background can be seen the market cross of 1500, but much rebuilt.

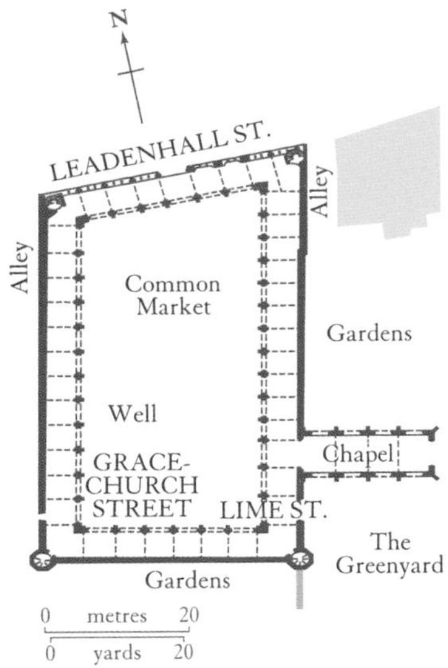

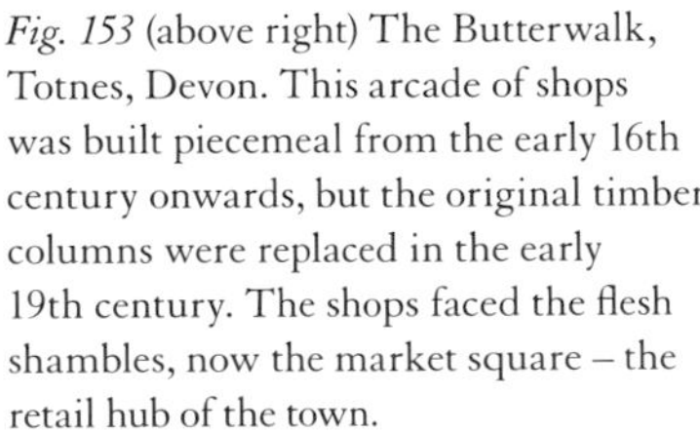

Fig. 153 (above right) The Butterwalk, Totnes, Devon. This arcade of shops was built piecemeal from the early 16th century onwards, but the original timber columns were replaced in the early 19th century. The shops faced the flesh shambles, now the market square – the retail hub of the town.

Fig. 154 (above) The Leadenhall Garner, City of London, completed in 1455, was, like many civic buildings, multi-purpose: this was a grain store, trading floor and chantry all in one. Its role in storing huge quantities of bagged grain was to guard against the effects of the periodic grain shortages that affected London.

By the 14th century markets had ceased to be held in the churchyard or even at the castle gate (pp 77–8), and most were held in a designated open space. At their centre was the market cross raised up on steps, acting as a focal point for the community and reminding people that their trade was being transacted in the sight of God. By the 15th century in richer, more aspirational, towns the cross had become a small, often octagonal, building, providing some modest shelter for the sale of goods such as butter, and much greater status for the market itself. The elaborate masonry cross at Salisbury (fig. 151), for instance, made the town market stand out from its competitors.

From the 1350s open market places increasingly became home to other permanent installations. The earliest types were fixed wooden stalls, such as the remarkable survival in Shepton Mallet that was originally for the display of meat (fig. 152). Stalls gave way to lightweight buildings and then eventually to shops.[41] Many would open their fronts and expand on to the square on market days, but others, such as those in Ludlow, Totnes (fig. 153) and Dartmouth, would be jettied, creating elegant arcades beneath. Most markets also had a market house for the collection of market tolls, for weighing produce and sometimes for the storage of grain. Often the lower parts would have an arcade, with offices above.

London, as always, was a special case. It had a vast and growing market, and a penchant for luxury goods. Keeping the metropolis supplied was a huge task and one that was successfully managed, save in the great famine between 1315 and 1317 when Londoners had to eat their pets. Cheapside remained the retail epicentre (p. 113) but activity had bled out west towards Newgate and east to Leadenhall. Fish was sold at Billingsgate and meat at Smithfield. Of only one market building do we know anything – this is the garner at Leadenhall, privately funded by Sir Simon Eyre, Lord Mayor, and completed in 1455 (fig. 154). The building was a quadrangle with an arcaded lower floor facing inwards. This was the venue for the sale of poultry, grain, eggs, butter

Fig. 155 (left) Clifton House, King's Lynn, one of the finest surviving medieval merchant's houses in England. To the right is the merchant's residence, refenestrated in the 18th century. The tower was probably built by the wine merchant and ship owner George Walden in 1570. The doorcase dates from after 1700. To the left are the warehouses belonging to the house with later dormer windows.

and cheese. The two floors above the arcades were devoted to the storage of grain, piled in sacks on strengthened floors; the windows were sealed with wooden shutters that could be opened for ventilation. On the east was a chapel and school, partly as a chantry for Sir Simon but also to provide divine service and education for the traders. On three sides there were no ground-floor windows. This was deliberate; the granary was fortified against civil unrest.[42]

Port towns have already featured in the story of England's building. By the 1520s half of the country's wealthiest towns were ports and among these London was pre-eminent, increasing its share of England's trade from 36 per cent in 1300 to 61 per cent by 1480; Southampton and Bristol came a distant second and third. The great losers in this process were the east-coast ports, whose wool trade was absorbed by London, causing places such as Boston and King's Lynn rapidly to decline.

From about 1300 the size of merchant ships began to increase. They rose from a maximum of around 200 tons to an average of 250–300 tons. This had a big impact on ports, as many of the smaller ones could not cater for ships of such size. As a consequence there was much rebuilding in the 14th

Fig. 156 (right) Dragon Hall, Norwich. On the first floor was the seven-bay hall that takes its name from a carved and painted dragon in the roof timbers. This is a rare survival of the sort of commercial premises erected by wealthy merchants in the late Middle Ages to eclipse their rivals in the sale of luxury goods.

century. Local people had to fund and construct breakwaters, revetments, stairs, quays, jetties, tide mills, cranes, weigh beams and more. At first this was achieved through the mutual actions of individuals, but after 1400 port towns took control of the essential commercial infrastructure, funding new works and maintenance through taxes.[43]

From the 13th century a distinctive type of building complex emerged in port towns. Merchants' premises – part dwelling, part showroom, part warehouse – occupied long, narrow plots running between the street and the waterfront. Most had an alley running down one side providing public access to the water. The street range might contain shops, but in larger and grander properties a residential hall faced the street. Behind were commercial and industrial buildings and, on the quayside, warehouses. At Clifton House, King's Lynn, Norfolk, a typical sequence of merchants' premises developed between 1250 and 1570. The great hall was on the street front, fine residential rooms were raised up on vaulted wine cellars and long warehouses stood at right angles to the waterfront. In the 16th century the owners built a five-storey brick tower, with precocious pedimented windows, in which to transact business and show off their wealth (fig. 155).[44]

Dragon Hall, Norwich, is a warehouse and showroom built on the river Wensum in the 1420s by the merchant Robert Toppes. Toppes, four times mayor of Norwich, was a leading cloth merchant, trading with the Low Countries and importing goods for resale in Norfolk. On the first floor, vaulted by a dazzling oak crown-post roof, was his trading hall. Three projecting full-height windows looked down to the street, pouring light onto tables displaying Toppes's wares. Below, on the ground floor and in the undercroft, would have been storage and administration space. Dragon Hall is the only survivor of scores of such buildings erected not as residences but as business premises in the larger trading centres (fig. 156).

Buildings for Education 1378–1450

Although in the Middle Ages people paid for education everyone whose parents or guardians could afford it was sent to school. Much elementary teaching was done by the parish priest or by a parish clerk who would assemble boys in the parish church, sometimes in a room above the porch but often merely on benches in the nave. The priest would teach basic grammar, music and the catechism.

Gradually, wealthy benefactors began to endow secular grammar schools in which children were taught to speak, read and write Latin fluently. Many were also taught administrative skills, such as writing contracts, and this required them also to learn French. Thus schools produced young men who would be bailiffs or stewards – or perhaps record-keeping trade apprentices. At first such schools were held in any building that was given for the purpose – a private house or a room above the city gate, as in Bristol. But in the late 14th century donors gave money for purpose-built classrooms, often with a master's house attached. Winchester and Eton are described below (p. 189 and p. 202) but were exceptional. Perhaps more typical was the school at Ewelme in Oxfordshire, founded in 1437, with a two-storey brick building with two chimneys and a house for the grammar master (fig. 142). Schoolrooms such as this were like secular great halls, the pupils sitting on numbered forms (first form, second form, etc.) and the master on a chair.[45]

As the English economy grew, the machinery of government developed and the Church prospered, the monarchy, Church and aristocracy competed for able administrators. Many of these aspired to a degree, the purpose of which was to equip them with the skills needed to run estates, go into law and fill posts in the Church. A degree in the Middle Ages covered grammar, rhetoric, logic and theology, and a fourteen-year-old would be a Master of Arts by the time he was 21. A doctorate would take another ten years.

Many sons of the aristocracy were interested in law and would gravitate to the specialised inns along the Strand. By about 1400 there were ten Inns of Chancery and four greater Inns of Court, with 700–800 lawyers and 200–300 students, whose life revolved round the hall, chapel and library. All the medieval buildings were rebuilt in the 16th century, unlike at Oxford and Cambridge.

Nobody founded a university in Oxford. It grew from the concentration of teachers who gathered there in the shadow of its monasteries. The word 'university' comes from the Latin 'universitas', which means those who are licensed to teach, and by the 1190s the town was well known for its teachers. In England students went to live in the town where they studied; they did not, as on the continent, go to a university in which they lived. So at first there was a big market for rented houses in Oxford, but from the 1240s academic halls began to be founded. These were essentially large houses, indistinguishable from private residences, normally belonging to a monastery but leased to graduates who would rent out rooms and provide meals for students. By the 1320s there were perhaps 100 of these in Oxford, catering for perhaps two thousand students.[46]

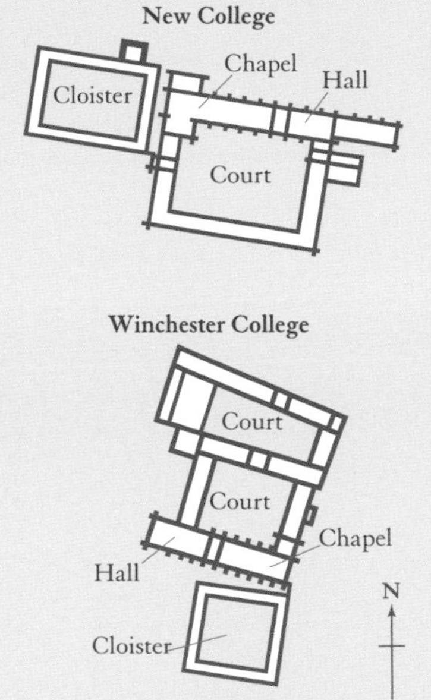

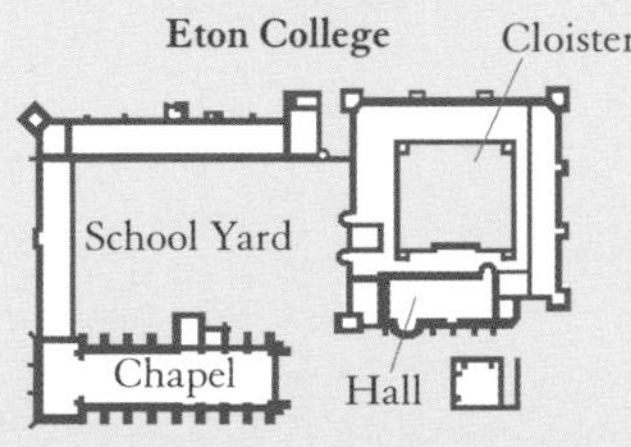

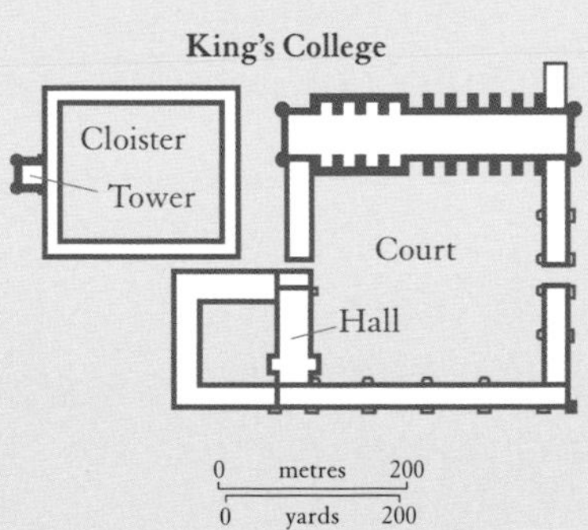

Fig. 157 (above) New College, Oxford, Winchester College, Eton College and King's College, Cambridge compared. The plans show the developing concept of a college with hall, chapel and cloister.

From the mid 13th century, academic halls began to give way to colleges that were founded both to educate scholars in a more disciplined way and also to act as chantries for their founders. They were endowed with land and other sources of revenue, and so acquired a wealth, independence and freedom that they retain to this day. One of the first was founded in 1264 by Walter de Merton, who had twice been Chancellor of England, and then Bishop of Rochester. His college was for 30 to 40 graduate fellows, who were to teach while pursuing higher degrees in law, medicine and, crucially, theology. Merton College, like other early colleges, was similar to a monastery in character but had a much looser and more informal plan. There was a first-floor hall on an undercroft for lectures and for dining, then there was a chapel, unfinished, but today still large and ambitious. Between 1304 and 1307 came the first residential buildings for the fellows; by 1378, with the addition of further chambers, these were to form the first quad in Oxford.

Life in Mob Quad (p. 172) would have been relatively basic and quite different from communal life in a monastery. The blocks of lodgings were one room deep, with the chambers lying either side of a lobby and staircase. Each chamber was for perhaps four fellows, who slept communally but had their own cubicle for study lit by a window. There was no glass in the windows (only shutters), no fireplace, and the ground-floor rooms had earth floors. On one side of the quad at first-floor level is Oxford's oldest library, arranged much like the scriptorium at Gloucester Blackfriars, with single-light windows illuminating the spaces between bookcases.

Oxford, like so many other towns, was hit hard by economic decline and plague, leading to depopulation in the 1340s and 50s. This presented an opportunity to found new colleges in vacant parts of the academic quarter. The most important of these was New College, founded by William of Wykeham in 1379. From the 1360s William's involvement with royal building projects rapidly scaled down (p. 164) and he became a close and powerful royal councillor, holding a series of high offices of state and, concurrently, a dozen ecclesiastical positions. His brilliant business sense allowed him to manipulate these positions to create huge wealth, most of which he directed to two educational foundations: Winchester College in his own cathedral city, and New College, Oxford. To design these he turned to the mason William Wynford, who had been a major influence in the royal lodgings at Windsor.

William of Wykeham possessed no formal education himself and was concerned at the lack of good clergy following the depredations of the plague; his institutions were to be a legacy that would stand the Church in good stead for the future. The buildings were conceived together, the school in Winchester to feed the Oxford college. From 1380 to 1402 New College took shape, its hall and chapel built as a single range, just like the royal lodgings at Windsor (fig. 157). These formed the north side of a quadrangle. Around the other three sides were chambers for seventy scholars and a gatehouse. To the west of the chapel was a cloister, added in 1389 and completed with a bell tower by 1400. Winchester College, which was built between 1387 and 1401, also for 70 scholars, had a plan very similar to New College, with a hall and chapel

Fig. 158 (above) The Divinity School, Oxford; perhaps the culmination of English medieval secular architecture. The intricately detailed stone vault appears to float above the floor as the walls are almost entirely of glass.

in a single range, and close by a semi-detached cloister.[47] These were educational establishments but they were also colleges of priests: New College, for instance, had ten chaplains, three clerks and sixteen choristers. It was their duty to observe the full rites of the Church, including processions in the cloisters.[48] The coherence of New College's design and the uniformity of its stylistic elements were equally important, setting a standard and a model for all subsequent Oxford colleges.

Whilst the colleges were leading patrons of architecture the universities generally were not. The Old Schools in Cambridge still contain medieval work but the Divinity School in Oxford ended up being one of the most spectacular architectural achievements of its age (fig. 158). It was conceived as a high-status lecture theatre befitting the status of the subject; work started in 1430 but ground to a halt, and when it started again in 1444 the design had changed to include an upper library for the books of Humfrey, Duke of Gloucester. The architect was to be the talented Oxford mason William Orchard. This long, low room has a vault of bewildering complexity and mouth-watering richness. The space is divided into five bays by low, four-centred arches; each bay has a pair of pendants, sprouting ribs that knit themselves into the ribs of the vault. Each intersecting rib is knotted together by carved bosses. The effect is electrifying as the pendants seem to support the vault, which they obviously do not.

Lancaster and York 1422–1485

The principles of government in 15th-century England were more straightforward than they might seem. The aristocracy had an interest in a strong monarchy with authority to lead and govern, to uphold justice, law and order. Because the hereditary principle was now universally accepted, these principles were undermined when there was a minority, and might be undermined further if genetics threw up a king who was incapable of effective rule. In these circumstances the aristocracy saw it as their right to show the king the way, remove bad influences and help re-establish order. In this way monarchy was intensely personal, relying on the character of the king, and his ability to command confidence and trust.

In 1413 Henry V was to come to the throne with the backing of a united political nation and went on to consolidate this with a series of brilliant military victories. But his son, Henry VI, was a nine-month-old baby when his father died of dysentery in August 1422. He grew up to be a weak and ineffective monarch, and English gains on the continent were lost, except Calais. Defeat abroad and ineffective government at home, coupled with high taxation, led directly to a series of bitterly fought conflicts that lasted some 35 years, the so-called Wars of the Roses. In these 'wars' a series of usurpers and claimants fought for, and sometimes gained, the throne. Edward IV, who seized the throne in 1461, might have succeeded in bringing an end to the uncertainty if he had not died young, leaving the way open for the murder of his children in the Tower of London. In 1485, when the army of the future Henry VII defeated and killed Richard III at the Battle of Bosworth, there was no indication that Henry would go on to found a dynasty that would rule England for more than a century. The reason that he did lay only partially in the effectiveness of his character. Equally important was the political and economic exhaustion of the aristocracy. This gave the monarchy the ability to centralise power in its own hands. When the vigorous and strong-willed Henry VIII succeeded his father as king in 1509, stability was assured.

That stability was built on foundations deeper than the character of individual monarchs, for during the 15th century the sense of Englishness that had been developing in the 13th century was consolidated. The shift in economic influence from the aristocracy towards the merchants and the gentry created a self-conscious and assertive political community that was represented in parliament. The Peasants' Revolt had ensured that this community would not, as for instance in France, make the common people entirely responsible for direct taxation, giving the upper classes fiscal immunity. That all classes shared the burden of taxation meant English society was far less stratified and much more mobile than in most northern European countries.

Englishmen now spoke a single language that was rapidly becoming the official language of administration and culture. The invention of printing meant that from the 1480s even relatively poor people could own a book in English and probably 30 per cent of the population could read it.[49] These points are important because they meant that England had a much more uniform culture than any other state in Europe, a fact that was expressed in its architecture. There is a much greater commonality of style in 15th-century buildings in England than in contemporary buildings in France, Germany or Italy, where centrifugal forces were much greater.[50]

Aristocratic Houses: The Second Generation 1470–1520

The most important development in the lives of the rich from around 1300 was a noticeable decrease in household mobility. Early medieval households were always on the move but during the 14th century they moved about less, some staying put for most of the year. This change in lifestyle had no single cause, but the fact that so much land was now tenanted meant that lords could not live off their own estates as they travelled and, at the same time, had less reason to visit their far-flung holdings. Much longer periods spent in one place affected the design and economy of the great houses. Far more storage space was needed for household goods and provisions, for instance, and permanent staff had to be accommodated in ranges of lodgings.[51]

Thus, as we have seen, great houses became larger, more complex and more richly appointed, and most lords chose one or at most two houses that could be brought up to the expected standards. So while Edward I had 20 houses Henry VI had only twelve. The Bishop of Hereford had 13 houses in 1300 but in 1356 decided to limit the number to just seven. There was a macro-economic dimension to this reduction, too. Most landlords saw their income reduced during the 15th century and so there was a financial imperative to retrench to core estates. The long period of decline for landlords slowed down in around 1470 and from then until the 1520s most saw an increase in revenue. This led to an upswing in aristocratic building.[52]

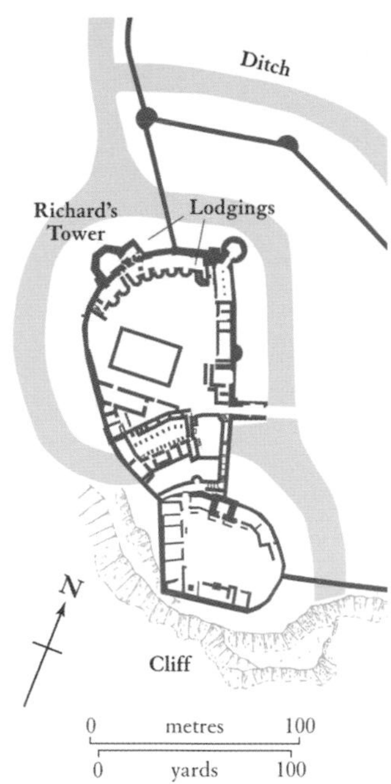

Fig. 159 (below left) Richmond Palace, Richmond-upon-Thames, Surrey. The palace is all but gone, but from the time of Henry V to the early 1530s was the principal royal residence to the west of London. To the right are the low galleries that enclose the gardens, behind the great hall rises, and to its left is the great donjon or tower that contained the royal lodgings.

Fig. 160 (top left) Ashby de la Zouch Castle, Leicestershire: the great tower. On the top floor was William, Lord Hastings's receiving room, hung with tapestry; below was his more private withdrawing chamber and below that was the vaulted kitchen. Part of the basement was for storage and part contained the entrance passage. To the right, at the lower levels, was his treasure chamber, only accessible by a ladder (for plan see fig. 110).

Fig. 161 (top) Nottingham Castle, from a 17th- century plan. Against the outer wall, adjacent to Richard's Tower, were new royal lodgings on the first floor. While they were within a massive fortress, their inner windows looked inwards and were an almost continuous wall of glazed bay windows. This was one of the first times such an elevation had been attempted.

In many senses the 15th century was a great age for the aristocrat. Their number had fallen from a peak of about 147 in 1350 to 73 a century later; in addition, there were 40 or so bishops and abbots who were involved in public life. Estates were concentrated in the hands of these family heads by the effects of common law inheritance, which meant that land generally descended to males as sole heirs. These estates were big business. The Neville family (p. 168), for instance, held lands in Yorkshire and south Durham focused on three residences: Raby, Middleham and Sheriff Hutton. These made Neville far and away the richest lord in those parts. Neville's household and residences were statements of his virtues as much as of his wealth. They expressed his liberality and largesse, important aristocratic qualities. Observers would judge him on how he balanced extravagance and magnificence, status and pride. In this, architecture was a vital ingredient.[53]

Towers, either free-standing or as gatehouses, had been at the core of English aristocratic building from late Saxon times. Although expensive to build, they were a dominating presence, conferring status on a place as well as being agreeable to live in and offering extensive views. English medieval architecture was always self-referencing and the great tower was continually re-invented to suit the lives of the rich and powerful. During the late 14th century a small group of aristocrats built a new sort of tower that was, in effect, a complete residence, integrating hall, chapel, lodgings and domestic offices. The best of these were at Warkworth Castle, Northumberland, dating from 1377 (fig. 136), and Old Wardour Castle, Wiltshire, started in 1393. These were precursors to the huge integrated tower started by Henry V and designed by the king's mason Stephen Lote at Shene (modern Richmond upon Thames) in 1414.[54]

It was probably Shene, nearing completion in the 1430s, that popularised great towers in a number of new aristocratic mansions (fig. 159). The men who built these were close to the royal family: Ralph, Lord Cromwell, Treasurer of England, built Tattershall between 1434 and 1446; the most powerful man in Wales, William Herbert, Earl of Pembroke, built at Raglan Castle, Gwent, from 1461; and William, Lord Hastings, Edward IV's chamberlain, constructed a tower at Ashby de la Zouche between 1474 and 1483 (fig. 160). Lesser men, too, followed, with towers at their houses, such as Lord Lovell at Minster Lovell and Sir Robert Harcourt at Stanton Harcourt, both in Oxfordshire.

By the end of the 15th century these towers became less independent structures and more integrated with the principal lodgings of the house. Two buildings are particularly important in this respect. The first is Edward IV's new lodgings at Nottingham Castle (fig. 161). There, inside the lower bailey, the king commissioned a massive new residential tower, integrated with a fine range of lodgings. Whilst these were built against the outer curtain wall, they faced inwards and presented a series of seven two-storey bay windows to the inner court. The king's private rooms were positioned in the tower but were approached by three magnificent chambers of state. At Greenwich, in about 1500, Henry VII's master mason Robert Vertue took this to the next stage. The royal palace there was not fortified in any way; it presented a long range to the river Thames, with bay windows looking out both ways. In the middle,

as part of the main range, a tower rose containing the king's privy rooms (fig. 162). Greenwich was to become a blueprint for houses of status and pretension for the following 20 years.[55]

The river front at Greenwich was only one range of a palace with two large courtyards. We have seen that at castles such as Goodrich the principal lodgings were built around a courtyard and that by the 1370s a residence such as Bolton succeeded in architecturally integrating the main rooms around a central court (p. 169). Across England this arrangement became popular; it can be seen most clearly today at Maxstoke Castle, Warwickshire, begun in 1345, or at Bodiam Castle, West Sussex, started in *c.*1385 (fig. 163).

For houses of the first order a single courtyard would not suffice. Most large castles were planned on the basis of two courtyards, wards or baileys; an outer one for the household, retainers and services, and an inner one for the lord's family. In the late 14th century the largest courtyard houses adopted a second courtyard (or even a third) for exactly the same reason. Thus a very large country house such as Dartington Hall (p. 172) or a big urban palace such as the Bishop of Winchester's in Southwark, London (fig. 118), would have had two courtyards. The most impressive survivals of this type are Wingfield Manor, Derbyshire (1440–56, fig. 164), which can be seen as the precursor to the next generation of top-end aristocratic houses: the Duke of Buckingham's Thornbury Castle, Bristol (*c.*1510–21), and Thomas, Cardinal Wolsey's Hampton Court (1514–28) (p. 216). In most of these double-courtyard houses the great hall was sited in the range between the two courts, acting as the vestibule to the more private inner courtyard and the lord's own lodgings beyond.[56]

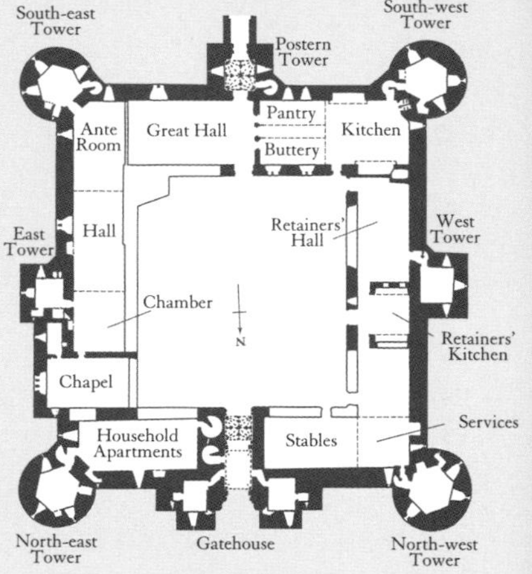

Fig. 162 (top) Greenwich Palace (sometimes called Placentia), Kent. The long low brick range had a chapel to the left, adjacent to a gatehouse providing ccess to the inner court. To the right on the first floor were the royal lodgings, culminating in a substantial brick tower where the most private and important rooms were.

Fig. 163 (above) Bodiam Castle, Sussex, built by Sir Edward Dallingridge from 1385. This was a commodious and comfortable courtyard house within a stout wall and surrounded by a wide wet moat. It might have not been the latest in defensive technology, but Dallingridge was a knight who wanted to have a house that looked like a castle.

Monasteries, the Final Phase

As we have seen (p. 139), in the 1240s and 50s English monasticism started losing ground to the friars, who set out to take the word of God to the people rather than studying it apart from the world. This loss of intellectual and spiritual leadership was compounded by economic crisis. During the first half of the 15th century the value of land and rents fell, and as a consequence many monasteries fell into debt. Some smaller houses merged or, in some

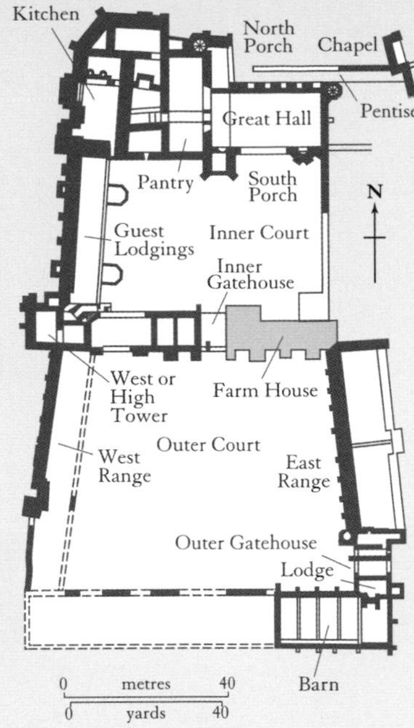

Fig. 164 (above) Wingfield Manor, Derbyshire, built by Ralph, Lord Cromwell, Treasurer of England in the 1440s around two courtyards: the precursor to the next generation of top-end double-courtyard houses.

Fig. 165 (below right) Engraving of the prior's lodging at Much Wenlock, Priory, Shropshire from the late 1420s. The west elevation, shown here, is faced by a double height gallery originally open to show the prior's handsome rooms.

cases, closed, and most communities, trying to economise, shrank in size. As a result, although there were a few abbeys in which significant programmes of innovative building were under way in the 15th century, this was not the great age of the monastery. Some abbey churches were modified; the great Cistercian churches at Rievaulx and Fountains, for instance, underwent reordering to take account of their smaller communities, to make room for burials and for nave altars. But most monastic architecture was now driven by a gradual dilution of community life in favour of individual privacy and comfort.[57]

This trend was given impetus by a Cistercian, Pope Benedict XII, who authorised half the brothers at a time to eat meat away from the communal refectory. This permanently undermined the sense of community, and encouraged individualism and independence. In 1421 Henry V accused senior Benedictines of a life of complacency, luxury and worldliness. To a degree he was right; the Rule, once so strictly observed, had been weakened and bent and, although few monasteries were vice-ridden, many were complacent and worldly. Monks had personal property, guest houses and holiday homes, and most abbots' lodgings were being rebuilt, giving them more privacy and luxury. Possibly the most magnificent, and certainly the best surviving, was the lodging range built by Prior Singer at Wenlock Priory, Shropshire, in the 1420s (fig. 165). Here the east side of the infirmary courtyard was occupied by a colossal range, faced with a grid of windows and buttresses forming the front of a long corridor that gave access to the main rooms. The prior's hall, with an elaborate carved wooden roof, dais, fireplace, wall paintings and other luxurious fittings, was served by its own private kitchen below. Next door was his private chamber, complete with its own garderobe.[58]

It was not only abbots whose lives became more comfortable; the lives of many individual monks were transformed, too. At Durham a new kitchen of great splendour and technical virtuosity was built between 1366 and 1370 to supply the monks with roasted meats, which they ate in an agreeable dining room called the Loft, where each monk had his own silver cup. The austerity of communal life was relieved by a spectacular new dormitory built between 1398 and 1404. This contained individual cubicles, each lit by its own low-level window, while the main room was lit by larger windows above. The seats in the reredorter were partitioned off to give privacy as the monks relieved themselves, and in the new cloister openings were glazed and the walks fur-

Fig. 166 (left) St Osyth's Priory, Essex. The gatehouse, built in the late 15th century, was highly ostentatious, covered in finely executed flushwork (knapped flint set in stone) with figures of St Michael and the dragon in the spandrels of the archway. Visitors entered beneath an elaborate vault with carved bosses.

nished with individual panelled carrals for study. If they should tire of all this, Durham owned a rest-house, Finchale Priory, sited in a pretty spot by the river Wear. Here, in groups of four, the brothers of Durham could rest, enjoy themselves and go for country walks.[59]

These changes, and others, were accelerated by an improvement in economic conditions in the 1470s so that by the 1520s almost all estates had seen a noticeable rise in income.[60] This boost led to a new wave of monastic construction, most directed not to the liturgical or economic needs of the monastery but to display. Church towers were very popular, as were showy gatehouses, guest lodgings and priors' quarters. Abbot Marmaduke Hoby of Fountains Abbey constructed a colossal 160ft-high bell tower, with statue niches in the massive corner buttresses. He was not the only one; similar towers were built at other northern abbeys, such as Shap and Furness. The tower at Bolton Abbey, begun in 1520, bore an inscription celebrating the abbot who began it. At St Osyth's Priory, Essex, Abbot Vintoner built a flashy new gatehouse faced with beautifully ornamented flushwork and containing richly carved niches (fig. 166). This was designed to be seen from without as the other elevation, facing the conventual buildings, was much plainer.

The Coming of the Tudors 1485–1530

Between 1415 and 1530 English kings were again among the greatest patrons of church architecture in Europe. Henry V planned three monasteries next to his royal palace at Shene (p. 193), where he had completed a large charterhouse; Henry VI founded chapels at Eton and King's College, Cambridge; Edward IV started a chapel at Windsor and a friary at Greenwich; and Henry VII commissioned a Lady Chapel at Westminster and a friary at Richmond. Most of these works only came to completion under Henry VIII.[61]

The royal monasteries are no more, but at Windsor, Westminster and Cambridge three remarkable buildings remain. All enjoy an increased rich-

Fig. 167 (above) The nave of St. George's, Windsor Castle; originally designed by Henry Janyns, it was completed by William Vertue after his death.

Fig. 168 (top) Westminster Abbey: Henry VII's chapel of 1503–10 replaced an earlier Lady chapel. This was overblown in every way: Henry VII ordered that 10,000 masses should be said in it for his soul. Stylistically the chapel gave birth to the new Palace of Westminster next door (fig. 399), making it one of the most influential buildings of its age.

ness or busyness of ornament and decoration that had already become discernible in buildings such as the Divinity School in Oxford (fig. 158). This style was practised most proficiently by a small group of families from Oxford: the Orchards, the Janynses and the Vertues. These designers produced architecture that was the product of a hundred years of English practice and experiment, at the heart of which remained the romance of chivalry. This was further reinforced in 1485 when William Caxton printed Sir Thomas Malory's *The Whole Book of King Arthur and his Noble Knights of the Round Table*, an immediate bestseller.

In 1471 Edward IV commissioned the new chapel of St George at Windsor Castle. This was to form an even more splendid setting for the services of the Order of the Garter in which the king took a special interest, but it was also to glorify the Yorkist line, and provide a mausoleum and chantry for Edward himself. The architect was Henry Janyns, who had worked at Eton College for Henry VI (p. 202); his work was completed, after his death, by William Vertue. Many of the elements of its remarkable interior will be familiar from Gloucester Abbey choir (fig. 124) and Canterbury Cathedral nave (fig. 126), but the combination creates quite a different effect, not at all vertical, indeed the nave seems wider than it is tall (fig. 167). This is because the extensive use of four-centred arches (which have arcs of very low pitch) makes the ceiling more like a cove than a vault. These arches became increasingly popular from around 1400 and almost ubiquitous after 1500, creating wide openings that allow light to flood in. The chapel in plan is more like a parish church than a royal chapel as it has transepts and a crossing, and was to have a central lantern.[62]

St George's was finished during the reigns of Henry VII and VIII, by which time another royal commission, conceived in a spirit of rivalry with Windsor, had been started. Henry VII commissioned a new Lady Chapel for Westminster Abbey that was to triple as a shrine to his pious uncle Henry VI and a chantry for himself and his family. This was the most ostentatious addition to the abbey since Henry III and was the triumphal statement of a nouveau riche king striving to create something more lavish in every way than the chapel at Windsor. So, rather than blank arcading between the arcade and the clerestory as at St George's and elsewhere (figs 127 and 167), there is a band of niches, each containing wonderfully expressive and lifelike statues. The designer was probably Robert Janyns and the chapel was completed by William Vertue after his death.

In the middle of the chapel was to be Henry VII's chantry behind a gilt-bronze screen containing a monument to the king and queen, and an altar and reredos with gold-covered figures, all topped by 100 9ft-long burning tapers. Above this rode the fantastical fan vault, with stalactite-like pendants falling from the conical fans. The weight of the vault is taken by hidden transverse arches and external piers fashioned as octagonal turrets crowned by ogee domes. But these are not recognisable as piers since they share the same grid of tracery as a series of tall bay windows squeezed between them, creating a continuous cage of tracery around the lower part of the chapel (fig. 168).[63]

King's College, Cambridge, had been begun by Henry VI in 1448 but in 1499 was still less than half completed. Henry VI had engaged Reginald Ely to design the chapel, but when Henry VII was persuaded to restart work there in 1507 William Vertue and John Lee were in charge, and John Wastell was eventually to complete the west end and some of the high vaults. The finishing touches were only finally installed in the 1540s under the patronage of Henry VIII. The chapel combines more brilliantly than any other building the principles of design begun at Gloucester in the

Fig. 169 (above left) King's College chapel, Cambridge. More refined and restrained than the Divinity School, Oxford (fig. 158), the chapel vies with it as the most spectacular culmination of English architecture of the later Middle Ages. Henry VIII's large oak screen, which divides the space, is embossed with his initials and those of Anne Boleyn.

Fig. 170 (above) King's College chapel, Cambridge. Few would now agree with the novelist and hater of Cambridge D. H. Lawrence, who said the chapel reminded him of a sow on its back without the piglets. Its regularity and symmetry are somehow not monotonous, but close to inspiring, lifting the eyes heavenward.

1340s and 50s (pp 158–61). The vaults, windows and panelling are perfectly integrated into a single cage of tracery, yet the detail is not what you see, for it combines to create a truly monumental space. The walls seem to be entirely of glass and the vault seems to confound gravity (fig. 169). Externally, it is clear how this illusion was achieved, as the elevation is broken up by the rhythmic verticality of massive buttresses. But even these are concealedby low-level chapels that hide the full depth of the buttresses at ground level (fig. 170).[64]

The Romans had used brick extensively and their buildings were ruthlessly plundered for nearly 1,000 years (p. 32). But it was not until the 14th century that brick started to be manufactured again on any scale. At first it was popular in counties in which there was no ready supply of building stone, particularly Norfolk, Suffolk and Kent. It was also convenient in towns such as London and Hull, where the demand for building materials was particularly high. In these cases, however, it was normally concealed by rendering or used internally under plaster. It was also often used in vaults, where the ribs were of stone, and for the hearths and chimneys of fireplaces, where its fire resistance was understood. In the 15th century brick moved from being a material that met special constructional needs to one of choice.

This was mainly due to improvements in manufacture introduced from northern Europe. Brick makers, many of whom were Flemish, German or Dutch, began to produce bricks of a uniform size and colour – and could do so in huge quantities relatively cheaply. These craftsmen also knew how to vary the brick colour in the firing, and how to make moulded and shaped bricks for decorative effect. These possibilities re-launched brick as a high-class building material capable of achieving quite complex architectural effects. In 1414 Henry V agreed to its extensive use at his new palace of Sheen and its associated monasteries, and not long afterwards his courtiers followed suit. Some of these men would have seen the extensive use of brick in France, particularly in Calais, and it may have been this that introduced them to its possibilities.

One of the significant benefits of brick was that it could be made anywhere that had good brick earth. Ideally, this would be directly adjacent to the building site, thus removing transport costs, one of the most expensive elements in any project. An expert overseer was necessary to identify the earth, particularly to ascertain whether there were suitable iron compounds to achieve a fashionable red colour. After that, cheap labour could be used to knead the clay, mould it into bricks, dry them and stack them in either a kiln or a clamp (a pile of dried bricks under which a fire could be stoked). Kilns were permanent and could be re-used, but were smaller. A clamp such as the one built at Kirby Muxloe Castle, Leicestershire in 1483 fired 100,000 bricks, not an unusually large number. By the early 16th century there were hundreds of brick makers in England; some were small operators, others contractors working on an industrial scale producing many millions of bricks for a building such as Hampton Court Palace.[65]

Whilst Roman bricks had been more like tiles (only 1½ inches thick and a foot long by 6 inches wide), medieval bricks were smaller, on average 9 inches long by 4½ inches wide and 2 inches deep (thinner and longer than modern bricks). Sometimes they were fired to special shapes, but this was complex as shrinkage had to be allowed for to get real accuracy of jointing. As a result they were more often carved with axes. This allowed

Fig. 171 (above) Farnham Castle, Surrey, the tower, 1470–5. Built for Bishop Waynflete, the tower uses newly fashionable brick in a virtuoso way. The windows are now eighteenth century but the diaper patterning and fine-cut brick machicolations and other mouldings show the capabilities of brick as a decorative material.

the production of runs of repetitive decorative corbels or machicolations seen on a building such as Faulkbourne Hall, Essex, of *c.*1439 or Farnham Castle, Surrey, of 1473 (fig. 171).

An important part of the effect of brickwork is the pointing, whether joints are wide or narrow, the mortar in them recessed, flush or proud; carved or moulded brickwork tends to have thinner concealed joints. Bright lime mortar was used as part of the decorative effect, and sometimes individual elements, such as windows, were rendered and painted to make them look like stone. Bonding (the way the bricks are laid) is another way that special effects could be achieved. By the 15th century a more or less standard bond had been developed, known as English Bond, identified by alternate rows of stretchers (bricks side-on) and headers (bricks end-on). It was possible in this method to introduce bricks that were more heavily fired – and thus darker – to produce surface patterns known as diapering (figs 171, 172).[66]

Fig. 172 (left) Eton College, Buckinghamshire, the eastern side of the east range of Cloister Court, 1441–4. 1.5 million bricks were delivered at the college in this period. It was the first large high status building to adopt red brick and stone with diaper patterning – a formula that soon became very widespread.

At first it was not only the manufactures who came from the continent; the designers and bricklayers were also foreigners. But soon English masons became proficient in designing and building brick structures, and adapting them to English ways of building. All the earliest major brick buildings are associated with the court of Henry VI and include the Manor of the More, Hertfordshire, built in striking yellowish brick by the king's uncle Cardinal Beaufort from 1426, and the great castle at Herstmonceux, Sussex, begun in *c.*1441 by Henry's treasurer Sir Roger Fiennes. The streams of design that these early brick buildings contain came together in Henry VI's great work of piety at Eton.

Eton College was one of the largest and most important religious foundations of the late Middle Ages, established by Henry VI in 1440 to offer prayers for his dynasty and to provide education, ultimately, for 70 scholars. The vision, as it emerged, was on a staggering scale and was never completed, but enough survives of Henry VI's work to understand what was new about it. This was a college much like William of Wykeham's New College, Oxford (p. 189), although the vast scale of the chapel proclaimed its primary purpose as a royal chantry. What was new was the comprehensive approach to the use of brick as a high-status decorative material, including extensive diapering on the principal elevations (fig. 172). Also new was the careful mixture of brick and stone; stone was used for the windows, arches and doorways, and as a material for string courses and buttresses. A new type of window was extensively used. These were much simpler openings in square heads without any cusping. Such windows appear at this time in a number of prominent brick buildings.

So what was happening at Eton? We know that a large number of the brickmen (as they were called) were foreign and were perhaps employed to create the ambitious diaper patterns. We also know that the king impressed many native brickmen, too, a number of them from prominent patrons who were themselves constructing large brick houses. Eton College thus became a building in which all the latest ideas about brick construction were used, and from which ideas were taken and spread to buildings elsewhere. In some senses Eton became the seminal Tudor structure, the father of a generation of buildings from Hampton Court to The Vyne, Hampshire.[67]

This chapter started by explaining that a new architectural language developed in England from the 1320s that came to dominate the way people built in the 15th century. The story of its development and use, as we have seen, is not a simple one, but it does contain some threads that can be brought together here.

The first is that the architectural hierarchy that defined the differences between buildings – and within them – from the early Middle Ages began to break down. By 1500 polite architecture encompassed a much wider spectrum of building types, and elaborate design was now not only found in churches and palaces, but in schools, colleges, hospitals, in castles, in the town houses of merchants and the houses of the gentry. So, for the first time, there was a much greater equivalence between secular and ecclesiastical architecture. After all, the same masons and joiners who built cathedrals and churches also constructed castles, barns and colleges.

Architecture was also now for more people, not just for the parson and the squire. People lower down the social scale had disposable income. They spent it in alehouses and taverns, in shops and on supporting their local church, chantry and perhaps other charities. This was a decisive shift in the way religious and charitable buildings were funded away from aristocratic patrons and monasteries to merchants and corporate groups. Participation brought a stronger sense of ownership. A sense of local identity was strengthened and by the fifteenth century people's focus was their guild and their parish and its institutions rather than the cathedral and the monastery.

The years between 1350 and 1530 produced a distinctive architectural language of considerable beauty and sophistication in England that was quite different from its continental counterparts. As we shall see, this individuality was to remain a hallmark of English building during the following hundred years but for very different reasons. But there was an underlying process that was more important: what had begun to change was the numbers of people who participated and experienced architectural design. It is too early to speak of a democratisation of architecture, but the audience was widening and, after 1530, was decisively and exponentially to widen again.

7— From the Reformation to the Civil War: A Century of Growth

— 1530-1630

In many spheres the architecture of 1530 to 1630 was one of exuberance and extravagance, a period of voracious conspicuous consumption and spendthrift patrons.

In around 1510, after a long period of stagnation, England's population started to grow again. Largely because of a reduction in plague mortality it expanded from two million in 1500, past four million in 1600 and by the 1630s had peaked at five million (fig. 173). This swift increase in population was a key factor in a century of rapid and fundamental architectural changes, which started in the 1530s. One of the consequences of population growth was inflation, a major economic factor throughout the century, whose influence on building will be considered below (p. 236). Two other such factors deserve note here: economic diversification and increasing urbanisation.

Between 1560 and 1630 the English economy rapidly diversified, with new industries and new crops being developed. These changes were at first driven by the Crown, starting with Henry VIII's encouragement of the iron industry in the Kentish Weald, but continued with a drive by his successors, especially James I, to make England more self-sufficient. The tool used was grants of monopolies – an idea copied from the continent by William Cecil – the first of which was a patent for making window glass in 1567. It was followed by dozens of others, most of which relied on expertise brought by foreign refugees fleeing religious persecution. These entrepreneurs and their domestic counterparts found an expanding pool of English labour to man their manufactories, bringing new materials and techniques to architecture, and at the same time stimulating a consumer revolution. The range of goods found in the house of a husbandman in 1600 was infinitely wider than a century before. Iron, brass, copper and pewter would be set off by a wide range of new textiles and ceramics. The larder would equally have been filled with a much greater choice of produce: sixty varieties of apple and twenty of pear. Local market towns became the places where these goods were sold, and shops became more numerous and specialised. By the reign of James I there was a new economic outlook; instead of England's prosperity being reliant on exports there was now an equally lucrative internal market.[1]

From the 1530s England's towns began to grow and the national proportion of town-dwellers increased from around 6 per cent in 1530 to 22 per cent in the 1670s. In this, London had a special place. In 1550 the population of London was around 70,000 but largely as a result of huge inward migration it had reached half a million by the end of the 17th century. From being the sixth largest city in Europe in the reign of Henry VIII it had become the biggest. It was not only size that mattered. London was a unique place, combining the country's principal port and trading centre with the political

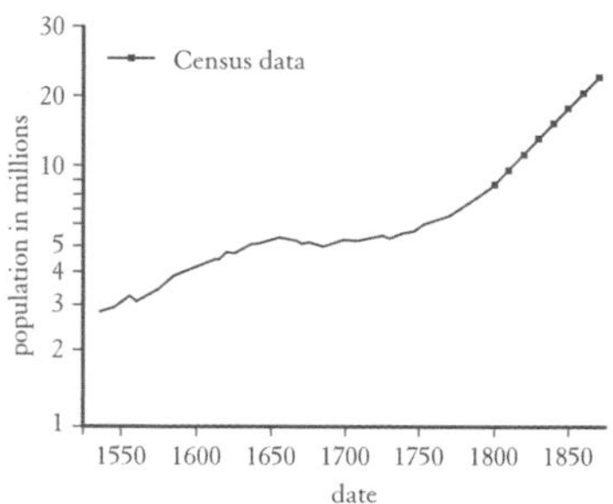

Fig. 173 (above) English population growth, 1550–1850. For population from 1086–1550 see fig. 88.

capital, legal centre and social hub. Urban expansion could not have been sustained had it not been for increasing productivity in English agriculture for, despite the huge population growth, England was still able to feed itself in 1650. Economic growth and agricultural productivity were sustained by political and social stability. Henry VII was able to pass the throne to his teenage son and in his turn Henry VIII passed it to a minor. From this point on (with the exception of William and Mary) the English throne has passed uncontested to the nearest in blood line. This stability was established by the strong rule of the Tudor monarchs combined with a deliberate policy to reduce the wealth, influence and size of the nobility, thereby rebalancing power between the Crown and the aristocracy.

But it was not just economics and politics that drove changes to English building in this period. Ideology was of fundamental importance, too. There was a new interest in classical learning – the Renaissance – and, from 1532, there was the reform of the English church – the Reformation. 'Renaissance' is neither a good nor a helpful term for understanding architecture in England. The terms 'Renaissance' and 'Middle Ages' were both invented by Italian humanists protesting against the narrowness of medieval university education. They disguise the appreciation and knowledge that existed before the 14th century of ancient civilisations, and the interest in and importance before the 18th century of ideas of chivalry. The difference that the Renaissance brought is that whilst a medieval scholar might have a good awareness of ancient texts, mythological figures or even architectural forms, there was little awareness of classical civilisation as a whole. Thus the intellectual movement known as the Renaissance was about a revival of classical thinking, of Roman literary style, of artistic techniques and, of course, eventually of the correct use of the architectural orders. It was a revolution in learning, and in England it established itself in the universities and was displayed most dynamically in letters.[2] In this sense there was no 'architectural Renaissance' in England in the period covered by this chapter. Whilst elements of classical architecture were absorbed, adapted and applied, only in a minuscule number of cases was an attempt made to create a building based on the rules of classical architectural grammar. For this to happen the Civil War was to come and go, a century had to turn and the pageantry of romantic chivalry so beloved of the Tudors and Stuarts had to fall from fashion.

The Reformation was much more important as a force for architectural change. In this, Henry VIII's quarrel was not with traditional religion but with the pope. In order to secure his divorce from Katharine of Aragon, which the Church would not grant him, he pursued the idea that he was the supreme head of the Church in his own dominions. This led to the assertion that England was, in fact, an empire, a realm without any superior on earth, a notion enshrined in the Act of Supremacy of 1534 and given muscle by a new minister or vicegerent, Thomas Cromwell. It was through the evangelically leaning Cromwell that the break with Rome began to lead to theological reform, and it was under a clique of Protestant politicians in the reign of Edward VI that England's Reformation became whole-heartedly Protestant.

When Queen Mary – a Catholic – was crowned queen in 1553 the beacon for religious reform that had shone across Europe from London was extinguished and under the Heresy Acts nearly three hundred people were executed for their Protestant beliefs. So when the Protestant Elizabeth I acceded to the throne in 1558 at the age of twenty-five she inherited one of the most bitterly divided kingdoms in Europe. Elizabeth swiftly set up a Protestant regime that was unique in its preservation of the traditional ministry of bishop, priest and deacon with the devotional life and endowments of the cathedrals.

Suppression and Iconoclasm

In the mid 1530s there were around eight hundred and forty monasteries, friaries and nunneries in England and perhaps four thousand chantries and guilds owning between 25 and 30 per cent of English land stock. After 1536 the vast majority of this was transferred to secular hands, most of it in a matter of twenty years. Closure of the smaller monastic houses was ordered in 1536, followed in 1538 by the shutting down of the friaries and, one by one, the closure of the greater houses. In 1545 royal attention had turned to the chantries, religious guilds and the whole edifice of intercession for the dead. Originally this was not on doctrinal but on financial grounds; however, under Edward VI's more Protestant reforms, a second Chantry Act finally abolished all chantries, free chapels, hospitals, fraternities and guilds.[3]

In May 1539 a bill was rushed through authorising Henry to establish a number of new bishoprics, cathedrals and collegiate churches. As a result seven of the monastic cathedrals were reconstituted under canons and two (Bath and Coventry) were abolished, as they came under existing secular cathedrals (Wells and Lichfield). Six former abbeys were then promoted to become cathedrals: Bristol, Chester, Gloucester, Oxford, Peterborough and Westminster.

At the start of the Dissolution of the Monasteries, the Court of Augmentations had been set up in 1536 at Westminster to receive the receipts of the sale of Church lands. Most of these sales were to relatively few established families. There was no huge expansion of the landowning class, indeed the biggest impact was on the tenant classes in both town and countryside, who suddenly obtained new and often more commercially savvy landlords. Most monastic land was bought as a safe, income-yielding investment at carefully calculated prices. The rewards for the Crown were huge. While monarchs for centuries had enjoyed a 2 per cent share of the national income in peacetime (3 to 4 per cent in war time), as a result of the dissolution Henry VIII enjoyed, for a brief number of years, 9 to 10 per cent of the national wealth – a fact that explains the extent of royal architectural patronage in the 1530s and 40s.

Whilst the destruction of the monasteries was the most well-known effect of the Dissolution, the most immediately obvious effects of the Reformation for the average person were in their parish church. Changes took place in fits

Fig. 174 (right) St Margaret's, Tivetshall, Norfolk. Under the fine 15th-century panelled nave roof is a gigantic painted royal coat of arms with the inscription 'God Save our Queene Elizabeth', as well as the Ten Commandments and the names of parishioners who 'caused this for to be done' in 1587.

and starts – and at varying speeds and intensity – across the country, but by 1580 a combination of royal asset stripping, judicious conformity and popular iconoclasm had transformed the interiors of almost every church. At the heart of the issue was idolatry, the visual context of worship, which, in broad terms, moved from the pictorial depiction of faith to its transmission by words. Literacy and liturgy entwined as church interiors were filled with painted texts and books. Thus the widespread destruction of stained glass served a dual purpose: ridding the building of idolatry and flooding it with light to enable people to read. Murals were over-painted with whitewash, figures were defaced or decapitated, and altars were demolished and wooden tables put in their place. Most prominent was the destruction of rood screens and their replacement by the royal coat of arms. A gigantic example, incorporating the Ten Commandments, was erected at St Margaret's, Tivetshall, Norfolk, in 1587 (fig. 174). The royal arms symbolised the changing nature of the parish church; instead of churches being integral to the social and economic fabric of the places in which they were built, they were henceforth much more narrowly defined as religious spaces.[4]

Yet the effects of the Reformation on the built world of the 16th century were deeper and more traumatic than the loss and alteration of institutional buildings. The assault on the Church was a transformation in the spatial context of everyday life. The early Tudor landscape was suffused at every level with the concrete symbols of Christianity. From the early Middle Ages England was littered with tens of thousands of crosses, within and outside churchyards, in market places, at road junctions and in prominent spots in the landscape; these kept man's mortal soul in the mind's eye and marked the progress of religious processions. There were also holy wells, pilgrimage and wayside chapels, bridge chapels and hermitages. All these daily reminders of the place of God in men's lives were, in a course of a few years, swept away.[5]

Fig. 175 (left) The west aspect of Newstead Abbey, Nottinghamshire, painted by Peter Tillemans *c.*1730. On the right-hand side are the principal rooms on the first floor and a new great stair with a porch at its head can be seen leading up to the great hall in the former prior's lodging. This is lit by large bay windows. On the left is the standing west end of the canons' church of the late 13th century.

Earlier chapters of this book stressed the huge influence that the ruins of Rome had on the mentality of people living in the following centuries. The Reformation had a similar effect. Few buildings were entirely erased; many were converted, some were dismantled, most were simply too expensive and complicated to level and, once timber, glass, lead and accessible cut stone had been carted away (and the work of local filchers was over), great hulks of masonry, especially core work, remained. Many former monastic buildings were active building sites for years; London in the 1550s and Canterbury in the 1570s were still scarred like London after the Blitz.

What men thought of the rapid and fundamental collapse of the architecture of the Roman Church can only be hinted at. But texts that tell the anguish of a few must have represented the dismay of millions. Some who bought the larger sites incorporated the finest parts into their new houses. The west front of the abbey church at Newstead Abbey, Nottinghamshire (fig. 175), or Castle Acre Priory, Norfolk (fig. 63), must have been deliberately kept as an ornament. Within a generation antiquarian tourists would seek out the sites of ruined abbeys and in 1655 William Dugdale published the first volume of his *Monasticon Anglicanum*, a scholarly elegy to a lost world. The Dissolution of the Monasteries was in architectural terms a barbarous holocaust, but it etched itself into the English imagination and fertilised the creativity of architects for centuries (pp 333–4).

Influences from Abroad

In the 15th century the commercial hub of northern Europe was Antwerp. Although its fortunes waned during the mid 16th century and it had lost its economic crown by 1600, the cultural influence it exercised over England remained undimmed. From the 1460s sculptors and stained-glass designers came from the Low Countries in significant numbers, bringing new ideas on ornament and design. These can be seen in the Henry VII Chapel in Westminster Abbey, an entirely English composition but integrated with the work of Flemish carvers (p. 197).[6] By the 1530s there was a small community of foreign craftsmen in the suburbs of London mainly working for Henry VIII and leading courtiers. The productions of this group were small-scale and isolated, but exploited new decorative fashions and experimental materials.

It was one of these media – terracotta – that reintroduced into England the four architectural orders of the ancient world. An order is a component of the colonnade of a Greek or Roman temple. It comprises a column with its base and a superstructure or entablature made up of various elements: architrave, frieze and cornice (fig. 176). The correct application of one or more of these orders was the principal means of creating harmony in ancient architecture – the quality which, it was believed, had been so brilliantly achieved. The use of the orders characterises what we call 'classical architecture'. But this term would not have been understood in the 16th century. Before the 18th century architects did not understand what Greek and Roman buildings actually looked like; they used the words 'Roman' or 'Antique' to explain decorative or architectural elements that we might call classical, and knowledge of these, for the vast majority of people, came exclusively through books and prints.[7]

Printing, of course, revolutionised the spread of knowledge, and this was particularly important in architecture as it was possible, for the first time, to distribute thousands of copies of line drawings cheaply and quickly. Single-sheet designs of ornament were inspiring designs by English craftsmen from the 1460s; the choir stalls at Ripon Cathedral, carved by William Bromfelt and his assistants, contain scenes copied from woodcuts printed in Brussels, and the misericords in the Henry VII Chapel, Westminster, were copied from prints by Dürer. Much of the decorative skin of Henry VIII's palaces – the stained glass, painting and furniture – was either directly copied from, or inspired by, imported prints. This was not a symptom of impoverished imagination. Even the great Hans Holbein the Younger in his most important English commission, the mural at Whitehall Palace, used Italian engravings for inspiration.

Fig. 176 (above) The five orders of architecture as interpreted by the French architect Claude Perrault in 1676. From left to right: Tuscan, Doric, Ionic, Corinthian and Composite. Each order had a matching base and pedestal, and entablature made up of architrave, frieze and cornice.

Generally, these prints came from Flanders or Germany, as indeed did many of the best craftsmen, and the few sheets that did come from Italy dried up in the wake of the Reformation. Yet, despite this, the single most influential printed source for 16th-century English architecture was, in fact, Italian: Sebastiano Serlio's *Regole Generali Architettura*. This was a new concept in architectural writing, moving beyond the text-based treatise *Ten Books on Architecture* by Vitruvius, written in the 1st century BC. Serlio's third and fourth books, published in 1540 and 1537 respectively, were profusely illustrated and used not for their text but for their pictures. Crucially, Serlio illustrated five orders of architecture: Tuscan, Doric, Ionic, Corinthian and Composite, and these became the canon of classical architecture from his time on. In 1611 Robert Peake published an English edition of Serlio and this, together with thousands of reprints, copies and plagiarisms, ensured that it was widely available right down the social scale. In 1563 the first illustrated architectural book in English was published. John Shute's *The First and Chief Grounds of Architecture* pandered to Elizabethan taste by accompanying each order with exotically and richly engraved human figures or caryatids to embody the spirit of each order, such as masculine strength or feminine grace.

Individual features and designs from these books were copied in detail. An early instance of Serlio's influence was a ceiling design pattern used on the chimneys of Somerset House, London, whilst the pilaster decorations at Kirby Hall, Northamptonshire, derive from Shute's title page. These are examples of the magpie attitude to the language of the orders; they were effortlessly incorporated into the existing vocabulary of English architecture.[8] In a less specific sense a great deal more was derived from these books. A traditional bay window at Broughton Castle, Oxfordshire, was recast with columns and pilasters in 1555, and a traditional cloistered walk at Dingley Hall, Northamptonshire, was transformed in *c.*1560 into a loggia by the application of columns (fig. 177). Porches were often the object of more correctly applied orders, such as at Wilton House and Longleat, both in Wiltshire, or at Gorhambury House, Hertfordshire (fig. 178). The latter was designed by William Cure, who had worked at both Henry VIII's Nonsuch Palace, Surrey (fig. 183), and Somerset House. He went on, with his sons, to have a practice that produced some of the most elegant and well-proportioned tombs, fountains and chimney pieces of the 16th century.

As well as adopting the four orders as a new decorative element there were occasional attempts to use them in a more correct manner. As far as we know the first of these was the Strand elevation of Somerset House, the great town palace begun by King Edward VI's uncle, Edward Seymour, Duke of Somerset and Lord Protector of England. Somerset presided over a socially and religiously radical government and was himself interested in the avant garde. Most of all he was a soldier and the classical elements were symbolic of his military status: the centrepiece of the Strand façade was a great triumphal arch fitting for a military hero (fig. 179). From this point on, and well into the 1610s, both houses and institutional buildings were entered by gatehouses or porches sporting a tower of orders (figs 189, 195, 202, 215).[9]

In the design of Somerset House, Somerset's collaborator was Sir John Thynne, who went on to design Longleat, one of the most correctly classical houses of his age. Longleat was unfinished at his death in 1580 but was completed by his son. The external work was carried out by a team of masons led by the Frenchman Alan Maynard and an Englishman, Robert Smythson. The bay windows from Somerset House make a reappearance, but there are more of them, and they are bigger and more sophisticated. They set the design of the whole building, bearing three tiers of columns with full entablatures. Longleat was a one-off and never imitated, partly because the patrons who displayed an interest in the Italian manner of composing with classical orders – and who were responsible for a small group of buildings – were part of a politically close-knit circle that was spectacularly destroyed at the accession of Mary I. It was also because travel to Italy and southern Europe had became more dangerous and difficult, meaning that direct contact with – and indeed interest in – Italian art and architecture declined.[10]

Fig. 177 (top) Dingley Hall, Northamptonshire, adapted in 1558–60 for Sir Edward Griffin, Attorney General to Edward VI and Queen Mary I. An otherwise traditional cloister walk with four-centred arches is transformed into something much more fashionable by the imposition of columns on pedestals of a made-up Ionic order.

Fig. 178 (above) Old Gorhambury House, Hertfordshire; the surviving fragment is the showy porch. Doric columns flank the arch and Ionic columns and niches flank the window above. The arms of Queen Elizabeth – a suitable adornment for a house owned by Nicholas Bacon, keeper of the Great Seal – are on the frieze above. It is dated 1568.

Fig. 179 (above right) Somerset House, The Strand, London, as depicted in a drawing by John Thorpe of *c.*1610–11. Additions to the original façade of *c.*1552 include the cresting on the roofline. The designer of the original façade is uncertain, but it certainly expressed the architectural interests of its patron Edward Seymour, Duke of Somerset. The window treatment at either end of the façade and the great centrepiece were to be influential motifs.

Fig. 180 (above) Red Lodge, Bristol; the great oak room fireplace, built for Sir John Young between 1585 and 1595 and attributed to the Bristol mason Thomas Collins. Above the fireplace are alabaster panels of hope, faith, justice and prudence and, in the middle, Young's arms.

Thus until the 1640s the underlying principles of English architectural design were, for want of a better word, Gothic. The architecture of the orders played only a minor role and, even then, one that principally fed the English passion for surface decoration. This passion was boosted from 1510 by the importation of other new ornamental ideas. In the 1490s Italian painters discovered the buried remains of the Golden House of Nero in Rome, whose painted domestic interiors were remarkably complete. These designs had an impact in England from the 1510s and continued to be popular for the rest of the century, although they ceased to be the height of fashion by 1560. By this date another craze gripped designers: strapwork, most prominently first seen in the galerie François 1er at Fontainebleau, France. These were borders of writhing and twisting leather belts or straps that developed faces, animals, buckles and studs to become a bizarre and comic world similar to that created by Bosch and Brueghel in painting.

Of the various designers who worked in this idiom, by far the most influential in England was the extremely prolific and talented Jan Vredeman de Vries. The hall screen at Montacute House, Somerset, is entirely made up of elements from de Vries's books, and in the mind-boggling overmantel in the great chamber of the Red Lodge, Bristol (*c.*1585–95), both the cartouche and the atlases are direct copies from his prints (fig. 180).

All these new sources of design were complementary to the existing decorative vocabulary of English architecture, especially that of heraldry. This was hugely important in a society in which the newly rich wanted to acquire the patina of age and distinction. From the 15th century heralds became increasingly strict about the use of arms, descending on parts of the country and inspecting people's use of titles. These so-called visitations were important events that occurred by county at least every twenty years. This strict policing of the use of heraldic titles and badges vastly increased the value of having them.[11] Genealogical gymnastics were performed to trace families back through Roman emperors to the first man, Adam: Lord Burghley's house, Theobalds (pp 228–9), was a heraldic shrine to his ancestry, the peerage of England and the monarchies of Europe. In around 1610 the Zouche family encrusted the hall screen of their house at Bramshill, Hampshire, with forty-nine painted heraldic shields and, in anticipation of their continuing dynasty, a further twelve blank ones. Heraldry should not be seen in opposition to the classical orders for the orders were, in effect, an extension of the heraldic mindset. Both heraldry and the orders were based on strict rules, governed by geometry, symmetry and balance, and, of course, both were emblematic, speaking of the place of the owner in society.[12]

Heraldry, and the four orders, mixed effortlessly with another class of emblems that combined images derived from the Bible, ancient history and mythology with texts designed to encourage the viewer to reflect on a concept or moral lesson. These emblems, normally known to contemporaries as devices, are found everywhere on Elizabethan and Jacobean buildings. Publishing collections of emblems became popular from the 1530s, and around fifty English emblem books, in over 130 printings, were produced before 1700. Henry Peacham's *Minerva Britanna*, for instance, provided the emblematic panels for the remarkable plaster ceiling in the long gallery at Blickling Hall, Norfolk, designed by Robert Lyminge for Lord Chief Justice Sir Henry Hobart in 1620 (fig. 181). Schemes such as these were sometimes composed with an overriding intellectual programme but equally often, one suspects, they were chosen for reasons of personal preference or ease of execution.

Sometimes the device was taken to extremes in whole buildings that adopted bizarre and stylised plans and forms embodying a moral or a message. Some, such as the Triangular Lodge at Rushton, Northamptonshire, built for Sir Thomas Tresham between 1594 and 1595, had complex and deep meanings; others, such as the pentagonal Chilham Castle, Kent, built by Sir Dudley Digges in 1618 around a hexagonal courtyard, are merely fanciful.[13]

Fig. 181 (above) Blickling Hall, Norfolk; an allegorical plaster panel in the long gallery ceiling based on Henry Peacham's *Minerva Britanna or a garden of heroical devises furnished and adorned with emblems and impresas of sundry natures newly devised, moralised and published*. The panel depicts a naked virgin seated on a dragon and carrying a mirror and a dart. The moral is that beauty is only skin deep.

Royal Palaces, Forts and Dockyards

Before 1530 Henry VIII had little interest in architecture and England's greatest builder – Thomas, Cardinal Wolsey – was also its first minister. Wolsey was the last in a long line of Church statesmen, low-born men who were catapulted to great power and wealth by personal talent and royal favour. These men built to match their status, which in Wolsey's case was not only that of archbishop and cardinal but also papal legate. Wolsey, and before him Cardinal Moreton and Cardinal Beaufort, maintained houses and households appropriate to their wealth and status. Such men were expected to live on a regal scale; their lifestyles were a matter of national pride as much as personal vanity. Princely consumption was thus a virtue not a vice, and was part of the proper order of society. This was a view held throughout the period covered by this chapter. Lord Burghley, for instance, in building his three colossal houses under Elizabeth and James I was fulfilling his duty as chief minister as much as his ambition for his family.

Wolsey had half a dozen houses, including a substantial town house, York Place, Westminster, and two country houses: Hampton Court and The More, Hertfordshire. These houses reflected the requirement of a great medieval statesman prelate who had to live his life in public, attending mass in his own chapel, receiving petitioners, ambassadors and even foreign monarchs in his

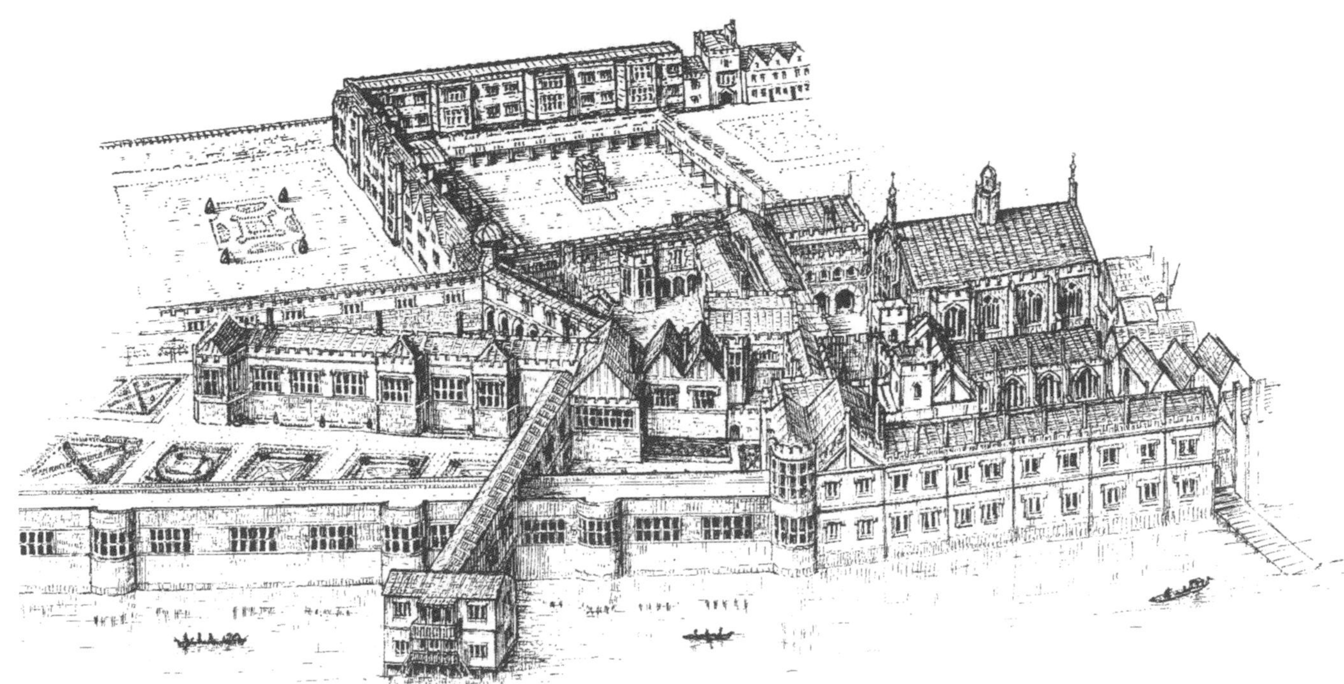

Fig. 182 (above) Whitehall Palace; conjectural reconstruction from the river in the reign of Elizabeth I. At the top is the temporary banqueting house of 1581. Far right, with a louvre, the great hall, and, in front of it, the chapel. The monarch's lodgings were in the gallery running vertically in the middle of the picture.

lodgings and processing everywhere, pompously, in state. The last of a generation to live like this, his successors as first ministers were secular men born into a world in which public figures did not need to prove their legitimacy on a permanent public platform. Thus Hampton Court and York Place were the final examples of a line of courtier houses built for personal public display and the culmination of a tradition that started in the 1450s at houses such as South Wingfield, Derbyshire.

By the late 1520s Henry VIII's interests had started to shift from the outdoor pursuits of his early adulthood to the more intellectual preoccupations of middle age. He was in love with a cultured and vivacious younger woman, and in 1529 began to acquire the houses of his fallen minister Wolsey. Soon his coffers were to be swelled with the wealth of the monasteries. England was set to see one of the greatest periods of royal building for two centuries. Between 1529 and 1530 the king began to adapt York Place and Hampton Court to be the two most important royal houses of the 16th century. York Place became Whitehall Palace (fig. 182) and its initial conception was highly original. Laid out in two halves on either side of a highway, King Street, the east side was a recreation centre that included a cockpit, tennis courts and bowling alleys, whilst the west side was the residential part, linked to the rest by a gallery and gatehouse. The royal lodgings were a mix of tradition and innovation. Traditionally centred on a great hall and great chamber, this palace had a long, narrow wing containing a privy – or private – gallery and a sequence of privy lodgings. It was the first royal palace to be built on a single level rather than incorporating a tower, and the first to have such extensive privy lodgings. The queen, too, had a suite of rooms and her own gallery. Over a period of fifteen years Henry VIII expanded the palace to provide lodgings for his children and subsequent queens.

Meanwhile, Hampton Court was developed to become the king's principal suburban palace. Here Wolsey had built an outer court for guests and a huge three-storey block of royal rooms on one side of a second court. Beyond this was a long gallery jutting out into the garden, and a substantial chapel. Henry VIII developed a third courtyard to contain suites of rooms for himself and his queen, as at Whitehall, on a level served by galleries. Both palaces represented decisive moves by the king at an architectural separation of his public persona from his private life.

These buildings were built in an eclectic style underpinned by chivalry. With their turrets, gilded vanes, brightly painted walls, coats of arms, badges and heads of Roman emperors, Henry's palaces were visions of the court of chivalry with a knightly king at their head. Henry had been obsessed with knighthood since adolescence, much of which he spent jousting, and his palaces can be seen as a chivalric stage set hurriedly thrown up for the tournament that was his life. Stylistically, the culmination of this was the palace of Nonsuch, begun for his son and heir Edward in 1538. The house was of two courtyards entered by gatehouses, just like Hampton Court, but its inner court was panelled outside and in with slabs of moulded stucco featuring scenes from mythology and classical history. The stuccos melded with a typically gaudy Henrician mix of brightly coloured turrets, gables, flags and bays (fig. 183).[14]

In 1538 Henry became convinced that a Catholic crusade to invade England was inevitable and commissioned a refortification of the English coast from Lowestoft in the east to Milford Haven in the west. Henry took control of the design himself, supported by a small group of military-minded courtiers. The executing architects were from the Office of Works, the same men who had just completed Hampton Court and started on Nonsuch. By the end of 1540 the extraordinary number of twenty-four new fortifications had been completed and garrisoned.

Fig. 183 (below) Nonsuch Palace; watercolour by Joris Hoefnagel prepared as a presentation drawing for Lord Arundel in 1568. Here seen from the park, the lower storey is obscured by a wall. Above can be seen the royal lodgings of the timber-framed palace with its panels of stucco depicting classical scenes. The great towers provided a prospect over park and gardens.

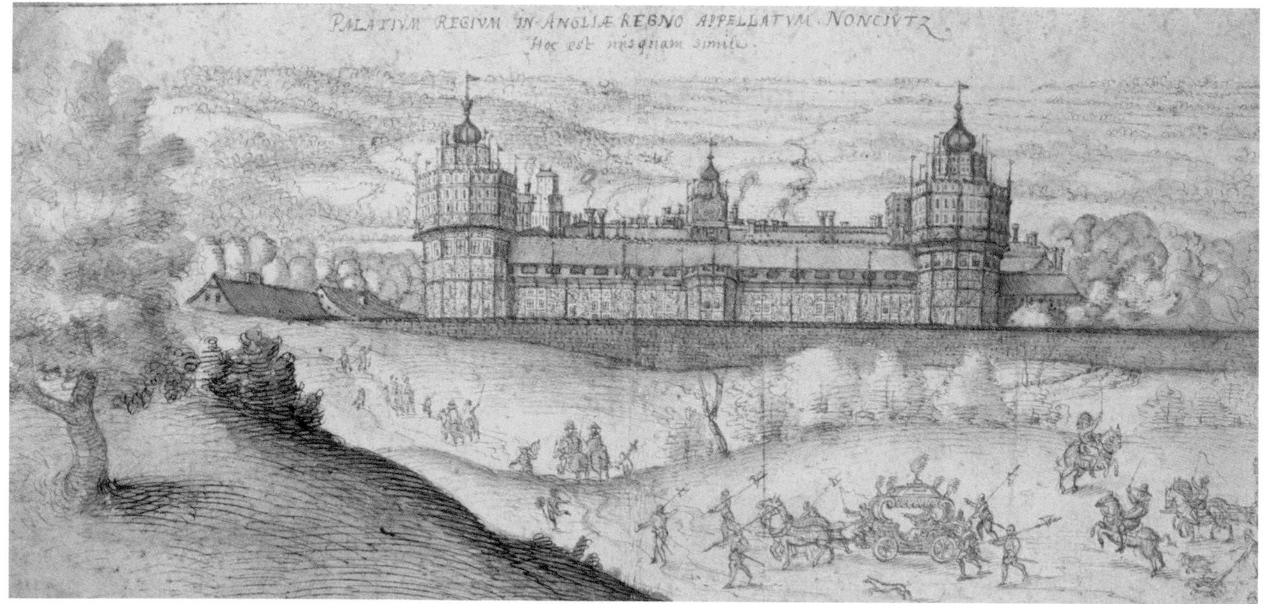

Fig. 184 (right) Berwick-upon-Tweed from the north. The town walls were begun by Edward I in 1296 but what we see today is almost entirely down to Sir Richard Lee, who brought the Italian system of bastions to the north of England from Portsmouth. The low-angled bastions face the attacker and are joined to the main curtain wall by a neck, narrower than the bastion, which allowed guns to be trained along the wall flanks.

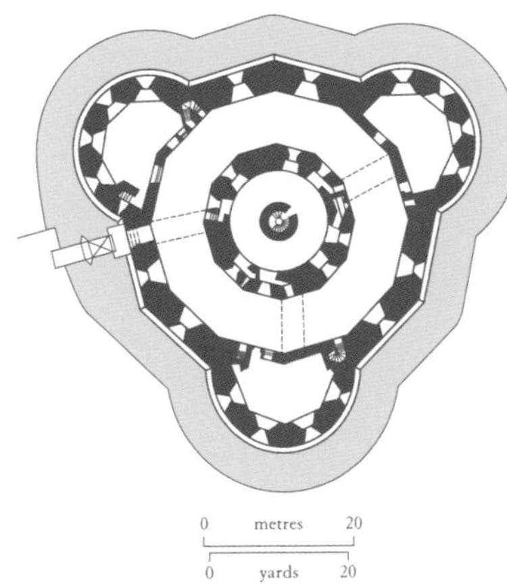

Fig. 185 (below) Hurst Castle, Hampshire, begun in 1541, protected the entry to the Solent through the Needles Passage. Though its design was sublime, like so much military hardware it became obsolete in a very short time as new Italian principles of fortification were adopted.

Henry's coastal fortresses were artillery forts, magnificent killing machines designed to emit the maximum number of cannon and musket balls to prevent an enemy gaining an anchorage for invasion. They were not designed to withstand a land-based siege nor heavy bombardment from the sea. So each had a tall, cylindrical keep surrounded by tiers of roofed, rounded, hollow bastions. The last to be completed was Hurst Castle on the Solent, facing the Isle of Wight. The geometry of the fort is exquisite – a twelve-sided keep echoed by a surrounding curtain, with three projecting semi-circular bastions (fig. 185). Rising up in three levels, it had six tiers of armament with seventy-one gun ports; the heaviest guns could be fired from at least three levels, including the top of the keep. This was terrifying firepower. Henry's forts, although never pressed into significant active service were continually maintained and modified, and formed the backbone of England's costal defences throughout Elizabeth's reign, during which the Spanish Armada threatened. But in the first half of the 16th century there was a threat closer at hand: Scotland.

In 1550 a survey was undertaken of border defences and, in particular, of the most vulnerable English town, Berwick-upon-Tweed. As a result of its findings a new citadel was constructed utilising Italian technology tested by Henry VIII's engineers on the Isles of Scilly. This was the use of low, acute-angle bastions with thick earth banks faced with masonry, a form ubiquitous in continental fortification, originally coming from Italy. The new citadel was never completed because in 1557 Sir Richard Lee, the Queen's engineer, was commissioned to undertake a complete refortification of the town. This he did, creating the most impressive work of English fortification of the whole 16th century. Lee's walls might not have been entirely up-to-the-minute in European terms but they were a fearsome deterrent to the Scots. The 20ft-high masonry-faced bastions, with provision for flanking fire, remain a hugely impressive sight (fig. 184).[15]

The Royal Navy can trace a continuous history from the reign of Henry VIII. This is partly a result of the mortal dangers that England faced from invasion, but equally because Henry established an infrastructure to support it. Storehouses were built at Deptford, Woolwich and Erith, and in 1517 Deptford Pond was dug as a sort of wet dock for the storage of battleships. Thanks to the sustained attention of Lord Burghley, by the 1560s the Navy Board, with its offices at Deptford, was responsible for a substantial infrastructure, including a shipbuilding industry at Woolwich under a master shipwright. At that point there were around six hundred and twenty people employed in the royal dockyards – by far and away the largest single industrial operation in the country.

In 1578 the engineers at Deptford invented a dry dock with water-tight gates that allowed ships to be repaired and refitted in the dry before the dock was flooded, the gates opened and the ship floated out into the Thames. This was an invention that put the Royal Navy in a position in advance of any of its rivals. The French, for instance, only built their first dry dock in 1666. In the 1570s Chatham became a major dockyard and during the reign of James I rapidly developed, with three double and three single dry docks, officers' houses, stores and a rope house.

We should have no doubt that ships built in the royal dockyards from the 1560s were architecture in their own right, and that their technology, engineering, carving, painting and design was transferable to building on land and vice-versa. The most remarkable ship of the period in this context was the *Sovereign of the Seas*, built in 1637. In terms of firepower this ship was easily the most powerful in the world at the time. It was entirely painted in black and gold, and covered with an elaborate programme of carving that mixed the usual antique, mythological and historical themes, all emphasising Charles I's mastery of the seas. She cost £65,586, far more than the £40,000 that it cost Lord Burghley to build the magnificent Hatfield House.

Urban Building

The Dissolution of the Monasteries triggered a revolution in tenure in English towns. In York, for instance, as many as two-thirds of the citizens found themselves with new landlords, mostly merchants, who had formerly invested their surplus wealth in country estates but now became energetic rentiers keen to invest in urban housing. These men were to benefit from the rising rental income that was a result of population pressure.[16]

The profits from renting were reinvested in more new buildings, accelerating a process that had begun in the late 15th century, when, in many towns, buildings for rental had already begun to be constructed more sturdily. After the 1540s stone-walling and tiled roofs became much more common; most new houses were of two storeys or more, with masonry chimney stacks, stone hearths, newel stairs and attached brick cesspits. Merchants rebuilt and modernised their own houses between the 1530s and the 1570s. Many open halls with central fires were replaced by rooms on two floors with fireplaces serviced by chimneys; new suites of smaller rooms were constructed and the larger rooms had impressive fireplaces and plastered and beamed ceilings.

From the 1580s into the 1620s changes continued to be made in urban housing, although there was more adaptation than rebuilding. Particularly common was the creation of attic rooms, resulting in the addition of dormer windows. Another common change was the re-facing of street frontages with brick to remove the overhang of jettied upper floors; both these changes affected houses of all sizes. Many of the middling sort of houses had rear extensions built at right angles, providing more specialised rooms. Though some of these, such as separate kitchens and parlours, were for domestic use, there was often still a mixture of residential, industrial and craft activity. However, first-floor rooms, in particular, allowed families to have respectable reception rooms. A dedicated dining room was increasingly popular, containing oak chairs and tables, and furnished with candlesticks and a variety of pottery and pewter.[17]

The men who had bought into towns from the late 1530s wanted greater control of local administration to secure their investments from disorder and crime, and to ensure their economic performance. An aspect of this was obtaining self-governing freedoms from the Crown, known as incorporation: two hundred boroughs were incorporated or had their incorporation confirmed in the century before 1640. The new corporations, led by a mayor, became the reigning oligarchy and centred their activities on a town hall. As a result around half the towns in England either built or rebuilt their town halls between 1540 and 1640.[18]

Some places had long had their own town halls, like the City of London or Bury St Edmunds (built 1179), whilst others had used the halls of guilds.

Fig. 186 (right) Much Wenlock guildhall, erected in *c.*1540 by a carpenter, Richard Dawley. In 1577 a prison was added to the north. The bay on the far right is a Victorian addition.

Fig. 187 (left) Leicester guildhall, originally constructed for the Corpus Christi Guild in 1343 but used as a meeting place for the Corporation by 1494–5 and transferred to them in 1563. The mayor's parlour is from this date and was re-fitted in 1637 to contain magnificent panelling, pilasters, frieze and fireplace. One of England's earliest public libraries was installed in the building in the 1580s.

There was a great upswing in town hall building in the 1560s and 70s, many utilising former monastic buildings, and then there was another surge in the 1610s. Some of the new town halls were like merchants' houses, with a hall, cellars and chamber, and were usually sited on a street front in the centre of town; others, like the fine surviving example at Much Wenlock, Shropshire, were raised up on pillars to create a ground-floor space for trading, and were sited in or on the marketplace (fig. 186).

Although town halls were not built to improve the economic performance of a town they had a crucial role in regulating economic activity. Prominent in this respect was the provision of a clock. The introduction of clocks onto the faces of town halls signified a more urgent attitude to the conduct of civic and economic affairs. In Shrewsbury, for instance, the town hall clock had three faces: one inside, one on the high street for inhabitants and a third to the corn market for traders. Punctuality, previously the preserve of religion, now came to bear on trade and civic governance, and soon affected travel, leisure and more.[19]

Inside, town halls were generally of three rooms. The largest was the council chamber, used for the meeting of the town government, for civic ceremonial and, on occasion, the staging of plays or entertainments. Usually at an angle to it was the court room, where more private and judicial functions were undertaken, and the parlour, in which the mayor and other dignitaries could speak (parley) privately. There were, of course, many variations to this pattern, the most common of which was the addition of a cell or even a prison for holding malefactors on their way to the court room. Many town halls began modestly but became larger and grander. At Leicester the mayor's parlour, built in 1563 and extended in 1637, still contains elaborate woodwork boasting of civic pride (fig. 187).

London's wealth rapidly outstripped that of all other towns in England. Its money first came from trade in cloth; by 1530 it had 85 per cent of the country's overseas trade, and by 1543 London's tax contribution was as large as all

Fig. 188 (above) Sir Thomas Gresham's Royal Exchange, City of London: the inner courtyard as depicted by Wenceslaus Hollar in 1647. Together with St Paul's Cathedral and the Guildhall, the Exchange was one of the three great buildings of the city. Royal patronage was proclaimed not only in its name but in the series of statues of monarchs in niches round the central court added after Gresham's death. In the background can be seen the great tower with its clock added in 1599.

the other towns in England combined. After 1600 London's exports dramatically changed as it started exporting lighter, finer cloth to the Mediterranean and began to be a European centre for the re-export of tobacco, sugar, pepper and silks. But perhaps most importantly, a huge domestic trade grew up in feeding, clothing and fuelling its inhabitants, and exporting goods to the rest of the country.

In the 15th century the main trading place for London's merchants was out in the open on Lombard Street. In 1531 Antwerp, northern Europe's commercial hub (p. 210), rebuilt its bourse, demonstrating the huge benefits of a purpose-built indoor trading centre. Although Henry VIII wanted London to follow suit, it was not until 1564 that Sir Thomas Gresham, London's wealthiest merchant and royal agent in the Netherlands to Queen Elizabeth, offered to build a bourse or exchange at his own expense. It was constructed between 1566 and 1567 under the supervision of Henry van Paesschen, possibly to designs by Cornelius Floris. The concept was a 15th-century one, an arcaded courtyard similar to the Leadenhall Garner (fig. 154), but in style the arcades, where the merchants conducted their business, were round-headed and rested directly on columns without any entablature (fig. 188). These were highly influential, and were copied at Burghley House (fig. 194) and elsewhere well into the 17th century. A sturdy tower rose over the complex, as at many a Netherlandish town hall, in which a clock with four faces was installed in 1599. This, together with a bell, marked the end of daily trading.[20]

Fig. 189 (above) Northampton (later Northumberland) House, The Strand, London, painted by Canaletto in *c.*1752 after the façade had been partially remodelled and the original windows removed or replaced. The great tower of the orders remains, however, as do the end turrets.

During the last quarter of Elizabeth I's reign London had become the engine of the national economy and one fuel that drove it was shopping. Gresham's Royal Exchange included two floors of kiosks above the arcades that sold luxury goods, shoes, watches, silks, gloves and more. These were only 5ft by 7.5ft but could generate huge profits for their tenants. In 1609 Robert Cecil, Earl of Salisbury, commissioned a rival emporium on the Strand amidst the houses of the aristocracy, designed with a view to being eye-catching. Like the Royal Exchange it had a street-side arcade and one hundred shops on two levels, but these were around twice the size of its predecessor's kiosks. Such buildings were an entirely new concept in shopping; their elite customers were not forced to walk the dirty streets but could browse in comfort and relative privacy. The upper floors of the New Exchange recreated a long gallery and fashionable shoppers were now on parade.[21]

Salisbury's venture was carefully located as large numbers of aristocrats began to build houses in London in the early 1600s, mostly along the Strand. This was another consequence of the Dissolution – the Strand had been the area in which bishops and abbots settled, and during the later 16th century their houses passed one by one to courtiers. In 1600 there were perhaps twelve major London houses owned by peers, mostly located in the City, but by 1640 there were twenty-six, nearly half of which were along the river. Northampton House (later renamed Northumberland House) was perhaps the most spectacular. Built between c. 1608 and 1611, the house had a large courtyard, with a great hall opposite a gatehouse and gardens that ran down to the river. Its huge street façade was dominated by the gatehouse, whose tower of orders was awash with strapwork and grotesques; the big oriel windows were inspired by the royal buildings of Henry VII and Henry VIII. Northampton House balanced fashionable decorative designs with deeply traditional forms (fig. 189).[22]

In terms of function, however, this was a new sort of house. Between 1590 and 1620 the London Season was established, and families would move to London during the winter. The court at Whitehall, rejuvenated by James I, was a magnet for any aspiring person who could afford to attend. Between 1603 and 1641 James I and Charles I gave the peerage gifts and favours worth around £3 million, reason enough to be at court in winter. But the less exalted, too, were searching for favours, pensions, licences or, perhaps, just fun. The simple fact was that fortune did not now lie in the provincial households of the great magnates; it lay in Westminster at the king's court.[23]

Although goods in London were dearer, living in the city was quite a lot cheaper for aristocrats than it was in the country; there was no need to keep open house, to entertain or to retain scores of servants. Thus the tenor of metropolitan existence was more private and convenient, and families had, on their doorstep, the pleasures of the city. One of these, increasingly popular, was the theatre. Dramatic performances had a long history in England but purpose-built structures for plays were an English innovation of the 16th century. Whilst plays continued to be performed in the galleried courtyards of inns and in the great halls of houses, palaces and colleges, dedicated playhouses were built on the city fringes or south of the river in Southwark from the 1560s and 70s, as they had been banned in the city. Of the half a dozen or more playhouses, The Rose (1587) is the only one about which hard-edged information exists and, although each theatre varied in its components and layout (and was adapted over time), it can be taken as illustrative of the type. The Rose was at first a fourteen-sided, timber-framed polygon about 71ft across, whose three storeys of balconies surrounded an open yard, with a floor that sloped towards

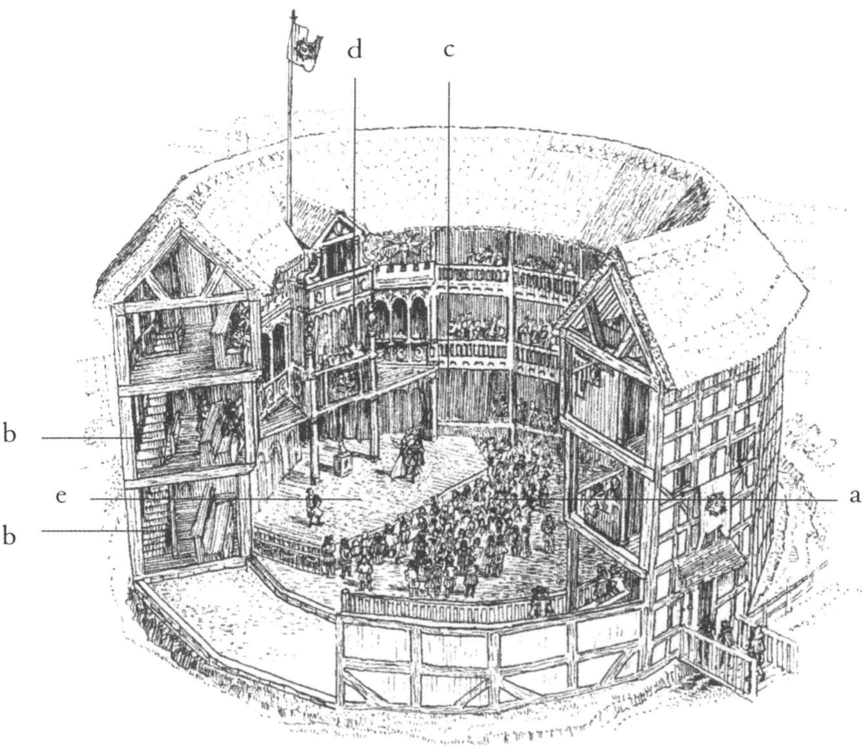

Fig. 190 (right) The Rose Theatre, Southwark, as reconstructed by its excavators: a) the yard for 'groundlings' (the standing audience); b) stairs to upper floors; c) public galleries; d) upper stage area with balcony; e) lower stage area in front of doors to tiring house.

a projecting stage (fig. 190). Behind this was a building for the actors known as the tiring (i.e. retiring) house. It could have housed around two thousand people, perhaps seven hundred of whom would be packed into the yard. The entrance was through a gateway, which led to the yard and galleries; the price of admission was a penny, with a further penny (or two) paid for a seat in the gallery. Men, women and children from a wide social spectrum were in the audience, making the theatres and their vicinities a rich social melting pot.[24]

Whilst, of course, ancient Roman amphitheatres were round or oval, English theatres were probably not based on them but were a native invention that grew out of traditional joinery skills and the geometry of medieval building. In any case, a specific model was much closer to home: the circular auditorium of the Cockpit at Whitehall Palace, built in the 1530s and used for a variety of performances. Cut-throat competition between theatres and their resident companies led to rapid architectural development in theatre design between the erection of the short-lived Red Lion in Stepney in 1567 and the destruction of London theatres after they were banned in 1642.[25]

From the early Middle Ages anyone with any means travelled around London by river, but in the 1550s a social revolution with very far-reaching consequences accompanied the introduction of the coach. For centuries people had been trying to devise a horse-drawn vehicle that could move at a trot without pulverising its occupants, and in the 1550s a new type of carriage appeared in England, originating from Hungary. Instead of the passenger compartment resting directly on the axles, the coach was slung on leather braces and by the 1620s, on occasion, on steel springs. This gave a much smoother and more comfortable ride. The first coaches arrived in London in around 1555, by 1600 their use was no less than a craze, and by 1620 coach making was one of the most lucrative industries in the capital. The finely carpentered carcasses were upholstered with luxurious silks and velvets that cost perhaps twice as much as the £50 cost of the bodywork. Whilst this was clearly out of reach for most people, it was a sound investment for the very rich as a single coach could carry a lady, her maid and four children with only two horses and a coachman.

Before the introduction of these carriages there were few horses stabled in London, but from the 1560s for every carriage there had to be at least two horses. As a result, separate entrances and yards for their stables were created for the aristocratic houses along the Strand, such as Somerset House, but providing stabling for thousands of lesser houses was challenging. What was to become the standard solution for the next two hundred and fifty years was invented by Inigo Jones. In Covent Garden (p. 268) a service road was built behind the terraces. Between this and the backs of the mansions were a garden and a stable – a mews, in fact. These mews buildings had coach houses with big double doors and stables for two to four horses. Above was space for a hayloft and accommodation for the grooms.[26]

Carriages also affected the orientation of the great town houses. From the early Middle Ages royal, episcopal and aristocratic residences were sited on the river and had landing stages or bridges linked to the royal lodgings by galleries. The water gates at the Tower of London, Whitehall Palace (fig. 182) and Hampton Court were prestigious structures at which the royal barge could moor and the sovereign disembark. With the advent of the coach there was a decline in water carriage, fury from the watermen and a reorientation of the great houses from the river to the street. Whilst households might retain barges for occasional formal use the fashionable way to move about town was now by road, and houses had forecourts and gatehouses specifically designed for carriages – and the newer ones had no formal access to the river.

The proliferation of coaches led to a drastic improvement in the road network round London; for twenty to thirty miles outside the capital the roads were now good. A coachman might make 12 miles per hour on a good stretch although a more realistic average was half that speed. A town coach could not safely travel beyond London and a much sturdier country coach, with big wheels and four or even six horses, was developed for long-distance journeys. These lumbering vehicles would only average around 3.5 miles per hour, or around thirty miles a day. This was faster than a wagon carrying goods but slower than riding.

The effects of the coach on the environs of London were huge. It was now possible to go out to Richmond or Greenwich for dinner and return the same evening and, of course, it was also possible to stay outside Westminster or the City in the calm and clean air of a suburban village, whilst having all the attractions of the capital within easy reach. Indeed by the 1630s most aristocrats lived in the suburbs rather than the city.[27]

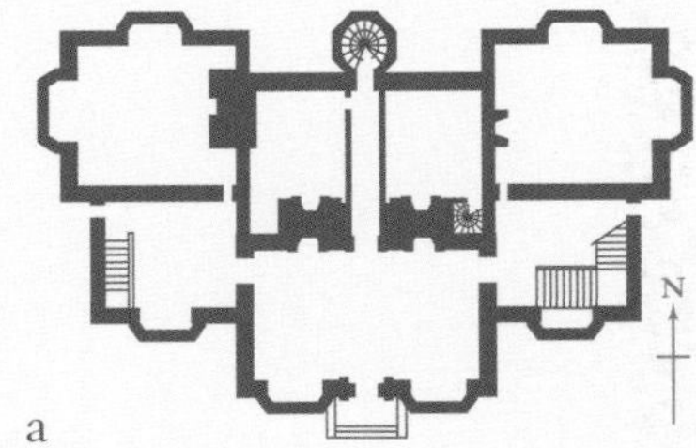

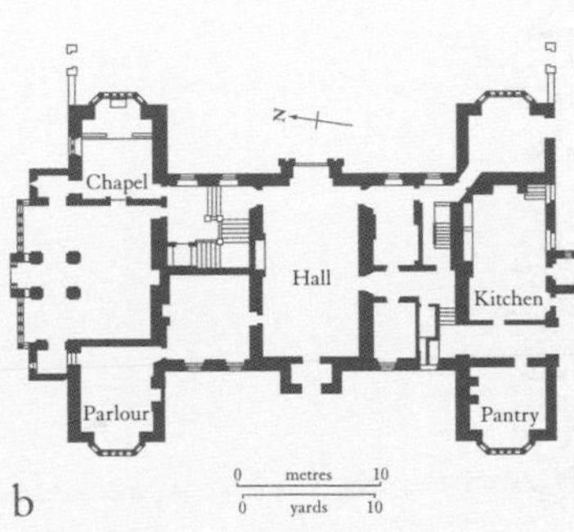

Fig. 191 (above) (a) Holland House, Kensington 1606–7, one of the first of a generation of double-pile villas, later extended then largely destroyed in 1941. (b) Charlton House, Greenwich, conceivably designed by John Thorpe. It is ruthlessly symmetrical and the great hall has no external architectural expression. The rooms of state are above, on the first floor; as the great hall is single-storeyed the great chamber is above it.

The aristocratic suburban house was a hugely significant development, enabling landowners to exchange the territorial obligations of the countryside for the social allure of the city within an affordable budget. At first these houses were not architecturally distinct. A surviving example is Sutton House, Hackney, built for the rising Tudor statesman Sir Ralph Sadleir in *c.*1535; it is barely distinguishable from any contemporary merchant's house or a small country mansion.[28] But from the 1580s a new type of plan known as the double pile was developed for these houses. This simply means that instead of being only one room deep there were two ranges of building back to back. Triple-pile houses were three rooms deep. These houses were much more compact, replacing the linear planning of earlier houses with something spatially and socially more complex.

The plan of these villas – for this is what they began to be called in the 1610s – derived ultimately from towns where all but the largest houses were built on deep and narrow burgage plots. The obvious solution to this constraint was to construct a lateral spine wall containing chimney flues and to erect ranges of building in front and behind. A big merchant's dwelling such as Clifton House in King's Lynn, Norfolk, was effectively already a double pile by 1400. One of the earliest and most radical villas was Holland House, Kensington, built by Sir Walter Cope, one of James I's courtiers, between 1606 and 1607 and enlarged by him in around 1613. It was double pile, with chimney flues in the central wall in the urban manner. There was no external architectural distinction between the high and low end of the hall: its façade was absolutely symmetrical, with bay windows flanking a central door, and the kitchens were in a basement (fig. 191a). Cope's hall was a polite reception room, not a place to entertain estate workers and tenants in the medieval mode. The design must have seemed revolutionary to people who visited this prominent house. Holland House was bombed-out in 1941 but Charlton House, Greenwich, built between 1607 and 1612, is a remarkable survival of this type of building (fig. 191b). Its builder was Adam Newton, tutor and secretary to the Prince of Wales. It, too, has a remarkable plan, for the great hall runs from front to back rather than from side to side, with double-pile blocks either side. These urban and suburban mansions were important because they pioneered a new way of living, with different relationships between servants and masters, landlords and tenants. It was a cheaper, more private and practical way to live, with warmer, more manageable rooms disposed in such a way that the family and guests could move about independently from the servants. These new ways of living were also reflected in the much larger and more magnificent houses of the super-rich.

Houses of the Nouveau Very Riche

The old nobility did not generally build country houses as they already had them. Their stately piles were admired for the weight and status they conferred on their owners. Equipped with their palace-forts the established aristocracy might add a fashionable bay window or two, or they might construct a banqueting house or garden, but history and romance sufficed as symbols of established status. For any aspiring man the acquisition of one of these great historic residences was the ultimate prize. The greatest sign of royal favour of Elizabeth's whole reign was the gift of two of England's greatest castles to Robert Dudley and his brother Ambrose. Kenilworth and Warwick, both in Warwickshire, were palace-forts drenched in history, famed for their antiquity, size and beauty.

It was thus the new men who built, generally those enriched by royal service, the law or trade. In Henry VIII's reign the best opportunities were through the purchase and adaptation of former monastic buildings, around thirty of which were converted into residences, mainly by courtiers. There was no standard treatment for these conversions. Some, as at Leez, Essex, were centred around the former monastic cloister; others, as at Mottisfont, Hampshire, simply divided up the church. The claustral buildings were used for a variety of purposes and sometimes the frater served as a great hall, as at Titchfield, Hampshire (fig. 192). At others, such as Much Wenlock, the abbot's lodging was taken over in its entirety as a house. These buildings continued to be adapted and converted well into the 18th century, and houses that now superficially appear later, such as Woburn Abbey, Bedfordshire, are at their core monastic conversions.[29]

Fig. 192 (above) Tichfield Abbey, Hampshire, was converted into a fine mansion by Thomas Wriothesley, Earl of Southampton in the late 1530s. The back of Wriothesley's massive stone-faced gatehouse, built into the nave of the church, can be seen. The range to the back, partly in Wriothesley's brick, incorporates part of the monastic church.

Sir William Compton, a courtier who held a mass of royal offices under Henry VIII, built an entirely new house at Compton Wynyates, Warwickshire, in 1523. It had a neat courtyard with an integrated gatehouse and great hall, and its principal rooms were ranged compactly on the first floor around the court. There was no attempt at symmetry in its external aspect, which was composed for the benefit of a romantic and lively silhouette; the internal courtyard, however, had uniform and symmetrical elevations. Little differentiated courtier Compton's house from a near-contemporary mansion built by a merchant at Hengrave, Suffolk, from 1525. Sir Thomas Kitson, a hugely wealthy London trader, also built his new house around a courtyard with asymmetrical façades and a regular courtyard interior (fig. 193).[30]

During Henry VIII's lifetime architectural leadership rested firmly with the Crown. With sixty royal houses to his name, as well as a string of royal castles and fortresses, Henry, backed by the wealth of the monasteries, was one of England's greatest builders. His children, however, were less prolific, partly because of their father's extravagance, partly because architectural initiative had shifted from the Crown to the nouveau riche ministers in its service. These men's wealth came not though salaries – which were negligible – but through the profits of office and gifts from the crown. The greatest Elizabethan builder was William Cecil, Lord Burghley, raised to the peerage in 1572, and the following year made Knight of the Garter and Lord Treasurer. With the treasurership came unimaginable wealth and part of this Burghley invested in three important houses, one in Westminster and two in the country: Burghley, Lincolnshire, and Theobalds, Hertfordshire.

The west front of Burghley House, designed by Henry Hawthorne, one of the leading architects from the Royal Office of Works, emphasised traditional architectural and social values, with gatehouse, towers, turrets and bay window; inside, the great hall has a hammer-beam roof. The courtyard, however, is a masterly assemblage of classical elements focused on an extraordinary tower of the orders (fig. 194). Whilst more correct in its deployment of the orders than most later Elizabethan buildings, Burghley is still a mélange of classical elements rather than a house that could have been built in contemporary France, where adherence to classical rules was de rigueur.

Theobalds was no normal house. It was to Elizabeth and Burghley what Hampton Court had been to Henry VIII and Wolsey, the architectural embodiment of their joint enterprise in running the country. Ownership was not the point; what was significant was the ability of minister and monarch to share in the fruits of office. It was not the exterior that impressed visitors but the extraordinary series of interiors, in which curiosity, delight and spectacle

Fig. 193 (top left) Hengrave Hall, Suffolk, completed by 1538. Built of yellow brick with an incredibly showy bay window over the main door, possibly by the mason William Ponyard. The façade was originally symmetrical; the right-hand side was refenestrated and heightened in around 1775.

Fig. 194 (above left) Burghley House, Lincolnshire, the courtyard from a drawing by John Haynes in 1755 before it was altered. The original design was by Henry Hawthorne from the royal works *c.*1573–88. The court is dominated by a tower of the orders and a fine loggia, on either side of which were centrepieces with viewing platforms or balconies.

Fig. 195 (above) Wollaton House, Nottinghamshire. Perhaps externally the most important surviving Elizabethan house in England, capturing the full decorative force of high Elizabethan taste. The whole house had wrap-around windows and the raised banqueting-hall-cum-prospect-room that tops the house has big windows on all four sides.

created a theatre for the court. At the entrance was a huge bunch of grapes that gushed red and white wine. In the great chamber was a grotto with precious stones and figures of men, women and wild beasts creeping through the bushes, whilst the ceiling was constructed as the sky at night, with a mechanical sun that moved across it.[31]

Theobalds has been entirely demolished, but Elizabethan England's most exciting house survives at Wollaton, Nottinghamshire (fig. 195). It was built by Sir Francis Willoughby, a coal-mining magnate who employed Robert Smythson, the most fashionable and experienced country-house architect, to design it (p. 212). Built between 1580 and 1588 it embodies the excess and exuberance of the architecture of the age. Like the vast house built by Thomas Howard, Earl of Suffolk, at Audley End, Essex, between *c.*1604 and 1616, Wollaton demonstrates the fundamental discomfort felt by the English super-rich for the austerity of pure classical forms, as the influence of Vredeman de Vries and his contemporaries is seen everywhere.

Fig. 196 (left) Montacute House, Somerset, completed in *c.*1601, is amongst the first of a generation to have a hall of a single storey. But it is still recognisably a traditional great hall, with porch, screen, bay window and stair off the high end.

So what are the trends discernible in the century of country-house building from the Reformation?[32] First is an increasing preference for symmetry. There were many houses from the 14th century onwards that were essentially symmetrical in appearance; entrance façades in particular were conceived symmetrically, but symmetry was principally admired within central courtyards. External elevations were designed, first of all, to express the form and hierarchy of rooms inside and, second, to make an exciting silhouette. From the 1580s houses that had looked symmetrical inwards now projected their symmetrical façades outside. This had the effect of making it impossible from the outside to discern the layout or function of rooms in the house.

A consequence of this was that it was now less necessary or fashionable to have an internal courtyard. As in the suburban villas round London, this led to the adoption of the double or triple pile. Before the 1540s ranges of building were almost always one room deep with a single pitched roof. Double ranges needed double pitches (M-shaped) and a valley gutter between them, complicated to get right and easy to get wrong. Later Elizabethan houses had broad lead roofs that could cover a double or triple pile, with gently stepped flats leading to perimeter gutters.

During the Dissolution the lead market was flooded with reclaimed roofing and the English lead industry was all but destroyed. In the 1560s, with the increasing adoption of the lead-hungry double pile, together with its use in the manufacture of pewter and munitions, demand soared. This could not have been met were it not for technological advances pioneered in the Mendips and then adopted in the main lead fields of Derbyshire. Originally, lead had been smelted in what were little more than bonfires fanned by westerly winds, but the invention of smelting mills with waterwheel-powered bellows and tall chimneys transformed the industry. In Derbyshire production increased from 300 fothers* a year in 1570 to over 3,000 by 1600.[33] This huge increase in productivity facilitated architectural ambition and the double pile opened up a whole new array of possibilities in planning, which will be explored in the rest of this section.

*1 fother = 22cwt or c. 1,118kg

It is important to remember that despite the increasing popularity of double-pile houses most continued to be planned round a hall, with the polite rooms opening off one end and the service rooms off the other. But the nature and position of the great hall was changing. Halls were now rooms of parade for their owners, symbols of their feudal duty to their tenants. They were never used as polite dining rooms, although in some houses the servants might eat there. The great hall at Burghley, built in 1578, was the last to have an open timberwork roof, ending an English tradition that had lasted unbroken since the Romans. Increasingly halls had flat-plastered ceilings, such as the one at Audley End; after 1600 most were built, as at Montacute, Somerset (*c.*1590), of only one storey rather than double-height (fig. 196). The double or triple pile allowed another innovation, which was to turn the great hall through ninety degrees and place it in the middle of the house running from front to back. This is what Robert Smythson built at Hardwick Hall in 1590 (fig. 198) and what was built at Charlton House between 1606 and 1612 (fig. 191b). These new halls were more practical, warmer and, with wall fireplaces, less smoky. Single-storey halls opened up new possibilities in planning the upper stages of the house as there was no longer a major interruption on the first floor. This enabled first floors to be more efficiently planned, and approached by elegant staircases that often led to the great chamber directly above the hall.

Bay windows had at first been commonly used in great halls but during the later 15th century had become popular in other domestic rooms. In the 1470s Edward IV made bay windows the principal feature of his royal lodgings at Nottingham Castle, triggering a fashion for their more emphatic architectural use from 1500 onwards. Wolsey and Henry VIII's houses popularised them as major features, enlivening façades and providing internal spaces for intimate or private conversation. At Hampton Court, for instance, they had

Fig. 197 (below) New Hall, Boreham, Essex. This tremendous façade was once the south front of the principal lodgings in the inner courtyard and not a freestanding range as today. It gained its impressive articulation at the hands of the Earl of Sussex after 1573. The parapet was added after the Restoration, but the doorway with its royal coat of arms and elegy to Elizabeth I is original.

formed the major feature in the queen's gallery and in both inner courtyards. During the 16th century and into the 17th century they were made into every imaginable shape and size, defining the plan and silhouette of most great buildings. At New Hall, Essex, a regiment of bays ended up composing the entire entrance façade, with the main door punched through the middle of the central one (fig. 197).

The possibilities afforded by very large windows had been amply demonstrated by church builders from the late 15th century. It was only in the early 16th century that these began to be exploited in domestic buildings. An early densely fenestrated elevation was the queen's gallery at Hampton Court, constructed in 1537, in which there was more window than wall. The gallery had fine views over the park and particularly the killing ground for the home park hunt. But one of the things that held back the adoption of big windows outside an elite circle was the cost and availability of glass.

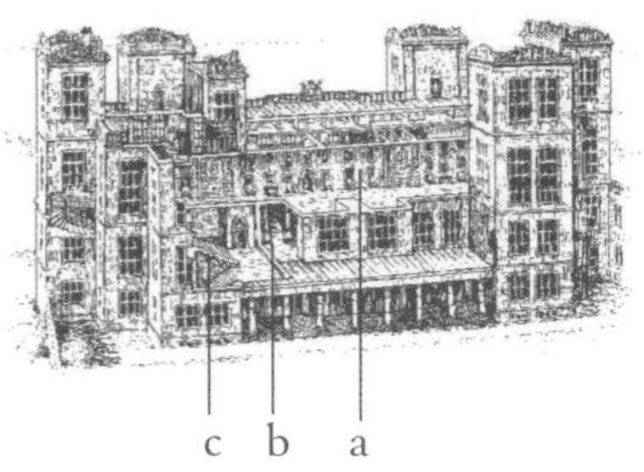

Fig. 198 (above) Hardwick Hall, Derbyshire, a highly compact house with strong vertical emphasis designed by Robert Smythson from 1590. The gallery (a) was on the top floor, reached from the great hall (b) by an impressive stone stair (c).

Before the reign of Elizabeth glassmaking in England was almost extinct, and the vast quantities of glass needed for churches, cathedrals and high-status houses were imported. In 1567 a royal patent to make window glass was granted to Jean Carré and Anthony Becku, both natives of the Netherlands. Carré went on to recruit a team of Calvinist Frenchmen to assist him. From this the window-glass industry expanded to meet demand from the 1570s onwards, when people went mad for big windows. In the late 1560s around nine hundred cases of glass were being imported into England annually but by 1590 there were at least three thousand cases made domestically, entirely wiping out the need for imports. Prices fell, and by 1600 it was not only the houses of the great that were glazed; houses of artisans would regularly be fully glazed throughout.[34]

The big-windowed buildings of the 1570s to the 1610s were remarkable and not paralleled again in their use of glass until the late 19th century (p. 00). They are an English phenomenon, too, the bay and the big window being mere architectural footnotes in continental Europe. Big windows at houses such as Wollaton (fig. 195) on south-facing façades made rooms very bright and warm, even in spring and autumn; but, of course, in winter they made them unbelievably cold. Few had shutters, and curtains were a feeble barrier to the icy winds – another reason, perhaps, why families wintered in London and why, by the 1620s, there was a reaction against big windows. Charlton House, for example, had much more modestly sized windows (fig. 191b).

Another new direction in the planning of large houses and palaces was the growing popularity of the long gallery. The first gallery to be built in England was constructed for Edward IV at Eltham Palace, Kent. It was a long, narrow building ranging out from the end of his lodgings and looking down over the Thames valley to London. Soon a generation of houses were provided with galleries that were attached at one end to the principal lodgings, often supported on arcades or loggias, enabling the occupants to view the surrounding landscape. These galleries became integrated into a courtyard at Hampton Court during the mid 1530s. This idea took some time to catch on, however, and Sir Nicholas Bacon's gallery at Gorhambury, Hertfordshire,

Fig. 199 (right) Knole House, Kent; the great staircase. The breakthrough of a cantilevered staircase was perhaps made by the joiner of this stair, William Portington, in around 1605. A screen of Doric columns supporting the upper landing acts as the introduction to the ascent, which is made bewitching by florid carving and scenic paintwork.

built in around 1571, was still free-standing. But the next generation of galleries at Burghley, for instance, were integrated into the courtyard plan and not discernible from outside. Many, as at Hardwick Hall, Derbyshire (fig. 198), were positioned on the top floor of the house, sometimes taking up the entire floorplate. Between around 1570 until the end of the 1620s every house of any pretension had a gallery at least 100ft long.

These galleries in the sky retained their primary purpose of providing a masterly view of the geometrically laid out gardens below, but this increasingly became combined with displaying art works. Dynastic paintings were particularly popular, as were tapestries and sometimes sculpture. Incredibly, the gallery at Hardwick Hall retains many of the paintings and tapestries hung there in around 1600.

The increasing tendency to locate the most prestigious rooms at the top of a house was boosted by a revolution in engineering. Before the 1580s stairs that were not a single straight flight had been built around a solid central newel. Very large versions were constructed by Henry VIII, such as the surviving haunted-gallery stairs at Hampton Court. In the 1580s it was realised that it would be possible to dispense with the newel and replace it with a timber framework. This created exciting possibilities for decoration and spatial effect, but not as exciting as the next development. This was to omit the central framework altogether and cantilever the steps out from the wall, creating an open well. One of the first was installed at Knole, Kent, between 1605 and 1607, but they were ubiquitous after 1620 and became the most important internal status symbol in a house. The stair at Knole, for instance, is decorated with scenes from classical mythology and figures, grotesques and strapwork taken from Netherlandish engravings (fig. 199).

Hunting rather than horticulture was fundamental to the setting of most medieval houses (pp 124–5). Cultivated gardens, however, were a feature of many castles, houses and monasteries, as well as colleges at Oxford and Cambridge. They were normally hard by the residential parts in walled enclosures, sometimes in courts or cloisters, and often contained aviaries or shady bowers covered in vines. Many were combined with fishponds, streams or artificial lakes, and adjacent areas were often planted as orchards. From the 15th century, with the decline in purposeful fortification in domestic residences and the ploughing-up of parks for agricultural production–, patrons increasingly wanted to have more substantial gardens close to their lodgings for relaxation. From this time gardens were laid out in square 'quarters' surrounded by low fences, and by the 1590s the area devoted to horticulture round high-status houses was very substantial.[35]

After 1500 some of these compartmented gardens, particularly at royal palaces, were extremely large indeed: Henry VII's garden at Richmond Palace, Surrey, and Henry VIII's gardens at Hampton Court were both huge compartmentalised landscapes with pavilions, banqueting houses and, in between,

Fig. 200 (right) Blickling Hall, Norfolk, 1618–29. One of the most important buildings of its age, Blickling Hall was designed by Robert Lyminge, who employed some of the country's best craftsmen, many from the royal works. The south façade is framed by two long service wings of great impact and importance, built in 1624. The ranges have been remodelled but originally contained stables and service accommodation. The Dutch gables are amongst the earliest in England and the east range is the earliest documented use of Flemish Bond in the country.

Fig. 201 (below right) Audley End House, Essex: the stables. First built to accommodate members of the Royal Court in *c.*1603–15 it was converted into stables permanently soon after.

Fig. 202 (left) Tixall gatehouse, Staffordshire built in the 1570s is dominated by three storeys of orders, Doric, Ionic and Corinthian under a ballustrade. In the spandrels are well-carved victories and warriors.

planted beds, fences, extravagant topiary and – at Hampton Court – heraldic beasts on poles. The compartments of the gardens of Edward Stafford, 3rd Duke of Buckingham, at Thornbury Castle, Gloucestershire, survive. An enclosed garden measuring 150ft x 100ft was created in c. 1520 on the south side of the duke's lodging; east of this is another of 200ft x 105ft, and beyond that was an orchard, in all covering perhaps three acres.[36]

With the widespread development of more extensive cultivated gardens the wide range of ancillary buildings that was scattered around medieval great houses was moved further afield, the entrance front normally being enclosed in a walled forecourt with a gatehouse and perhaps lodges. Gatehouses were a showy foretaste of the main house and often became vehicles for magnificent architectural display, as at Tixall Manor, Staffordshire (fig. 202). They also performed a function; like their medieval predecessors they allowed a porter to welcome guests by day and secure the house at night. At larger houses a gatehouse might be combined with other lesser pavilions or lodges, either integrated with the forecourt and gardens, or sited further afield as heralds for the main house and gardens.[37]

The stables alone remained near the house, for reasons of practicality and prestige. It had only been in Henry VIII's reign that these had become architecturally distinct buildings and they were normally arranged in a quadrangle, like the surviving ones built at Hampton Court Palace, Surrey, between

1537 and 1538. By the beginning of the following century stables began to become architecturally more pretentious. The grandest surviving early stable block, constructed in 1603 in a single range, is at Audley End (fig. 201). The stables at Blickling Hall, Norfolk, were built twenty years later, creating an impressive and symmetrical forecourt (fig. 200).

Underlying this extraordinary outlay of money, energy and creativity were some hard facts about Tudor and Stuart government and administration. Aristocrats of the 16th and 17th centuries, like their medieval forebears, essentially ran the provinces, and their honour and reputation were signified, above all, by good lordship; that is to say an appearance of liberality, and holding a hospitable and open household. The motivations behind building, over and above fashion and the pleasure of construction, were thus not any different from those in the 14th century.

Houses for Everyone Else

From 1400 to 1540 England had been dogged by its low population; people were scarce but land was plentiful. Villages shrank, landholdings increased in size, rents were lower and tenure was more secure. Indeed most villages were smaller in 1520 than they had been in 1320. This trend was reversed in the early 1500s. Population growth resulted in agricultural prices rising six-fold. Such inflation was catastrophic for people at the bottom of society but for others it was a boon. Arable farmers producing wheat with fixed outgoings were in a particularly good position and it gave the opportunity to landowners more generally to increase rents. Agricultural profits were poured into building, villages started to grow once more, and houses across the social spectrum were rebuilt and enlarged.[38]

In the Middle Ages, as we have seen, the major landowners were the Church, the Crown and the aristocracy. Few villages had a resident squire or landlord but by the 1650s around three-quarters of all villages had one or two resident gentlemen. Indeed, whilst in 1500 there may have been around four to five hundred knights and around eight hundred esquires, by the 1650s these numbers had risen to one thousand knights and baronets and perhaps one and a half thousand squires. These people owned approximately half of the country and were the Justices of the Peace, MPs and other office holders.

The mix of social responsibility and social aspiration that underpinned the construction of England's great houses was also that which underpinned those of the gentry. The gentry built houses in widely varying sizes, styles and materials, based on who owned them and where they were. Other than a few aspirational houses of the richer families nearer London they were generally built by local craftsmen in established traditions. This makes it impossible to generalise about plan form or style. Two examples, however, will illustrate the sort of houses that were being built. The first is Leigh, Winsham, Somerset, of 1617, which has a typical E-plan common to the houses of the gentry all over England, although Leigh had a hall to

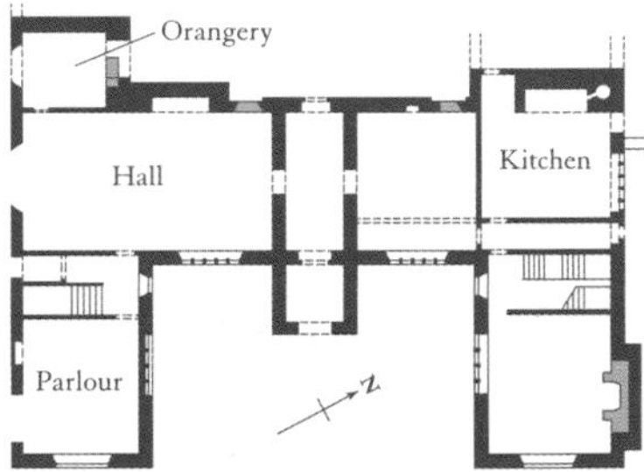

Fig. 203 (above) Fleming's Hall, Bedingfield, Suffolk is an impressive single long timber-framed range with big gables of about 1600; the ground floor was faced in brick in *c.*1700. The bold porch, off centre, leads into the great hall.

Fig. 204 (above) Red Hall, Bourne, Lincolnshire, an extremely elegant yeoman's residence with four rooms per floor. The two windows in the middle of the rear façade lit the staircase. On the top floor was a room for the maid and the 'high gallery' which, while aping galleries in larger houses, contained, in Fisher's time, cheeses and spare beds

Fig. 205 (top) Glebe Farm, Wilmcote, Warwickshire, showing its timber-framed structure: a) ground floor bedroom with room above; b) hall open to the roof without a chimney; c) kitchen and workshop.

Fig. 206 (above left) Leigh, Winsham, Somerset, 1617. The 'E' Plan was a very popular plan with various ways of disposing accommodation. Here the great hall, screens passage and kitchen occupied the long arm and more private rooms the two end wings.

one end of the house, a local feature popular in Devon and Somerset (fig. 206). The second is Flemings Hall, Bedingfield, Suffolk, of *c.*1550 and *c.*1620. This house is a single range, with four rooms and a stair in a compartment between the hall and the parlour, a feature common in parts of East Anglia (fig. 203). Although different in appearance and layout, they both provided comfortable and commodious accommodation for men of secure and growing means.[39]

Beneath the gentry came the 'yeomen', a term in common use by 1500 to describe those who held land to the value of £2 a year; it also embraced a large number who owned substantial farms that would be farmed by employees, although they worked a little themselves. Every village would have a few yeomen farmers with houses well built out of local materials with regional quirks of style and plan. At the lower end of the scale they were often single ranges, one room deep, and two, three or four rooms long, with at least one chimney stack and probably some upper floors. So Robert Arden, a carpenter of Wilmcote, Warwickshire, who died in 1556, lived in a timber-framed house, now Glebe Farm, built between 1513 and 1514. It had three rooms: a hall without a chimney in which there was a table, chairs and benches; a bedchamber containing a bed, linen and coffers; and a well-equipped kitchen with stone walls, which doubled as his carpenter's shop (fig. 205). At the other end of the scale was the fashionable Red Hall, Bourne, Lincolnshire, built in *c.*1620 for Gilbert Fisher, an aspiring yeoman. This was a double-pile-plan house with a staircase opposite the front door and, on either side of the passage leading to it, a hall and dining parlour. Fisher's kitchen was at the back, and over it, in the warmest spot, was his bedroom (fig. 204).

Further still down the economic scale were the husbandmen, the most numerous of the country dwellers, who rented land for their farms and were less well educated. Below them were the cottagers, labourers and servants who made up a quarter of the population and principally earned a living by working for others. For these people the nature of rural housing also changed radically between 1570 and 1630.

The most important advance was the control of smoke, first by the introduction of smoke hoods, then by the construction of chimneys and fireplaces. It is surprising that the Romans, with all their sophistication and invention, did not invent a fireplace with a flue and chimney. It is not known when the first fireplaces were built in England, although it is likely that Anglo-Saxon royalty would have had them, but the earliest surviving examples are in the White Tower and Colchester Castle. Chimneys become increasingly common from the 1130s and, other than in great halls, they were universal in polite buildings by 1500. Moreover, being a source of heat and light in often dark and cold rooms they quickly became vehicles for elaborate decoration.

By the early 16th century chimneys had been added to all but the humblest dwellings and built as part of every new one. This, together with the widespread adoption of window glass, enabled even quite humble houses to be decorated with wall paintings or hanging cloths. More importantly, by the 1630s houses and cottages – now not needing to be open to the rafters – could have upper floors. These changes led to the development of two dominant house plans. In the uplands a preference for the retention of a symbolic hall led to a plan centred on a cross passage, on one side of which was a kitchen and on the other two rooms, one heated by a chimney stack (fig. 207b). Much more popular, however, was the lobby-entry plan, which was a two-roomed rectangular house with a central chimney stack, on one side of which would be the entrance door in a lobby and on the other the stairs (fig. 207a). Although originally popular in areas of timber framing (utilising brick for the chimney), in due course it became the most common sort of small house in much of England and was the precursor the two-up, two-down that continued into the 20th century.

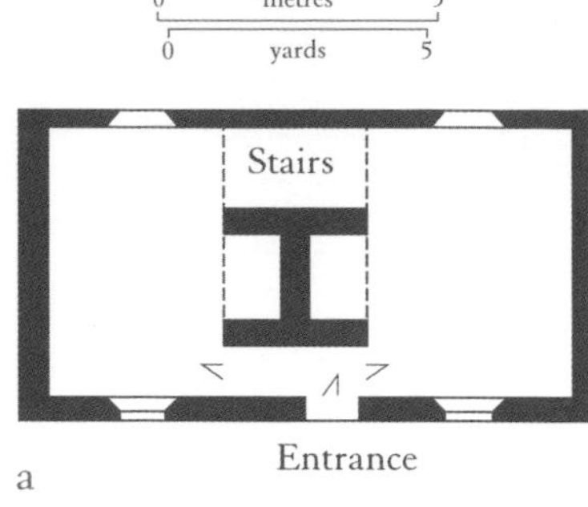

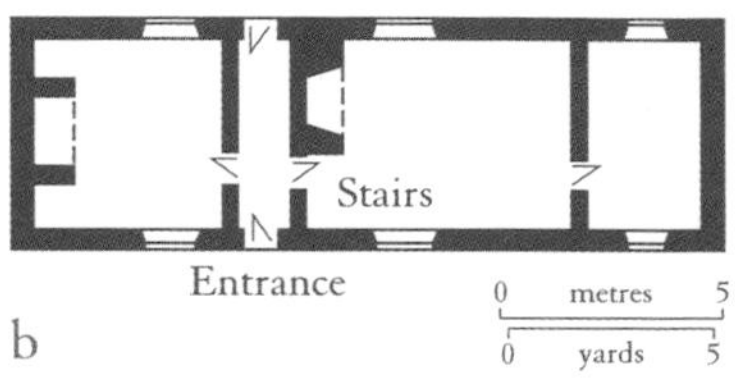

Fig. 207 (above) (a) A typical house built on the lobby plan. The central stack had the advantage of warming the whole house. A variation of this common house type, particularly in the west of England, was for the chimney stack to be placed on an outside wall – an advertisement for the comforts within. (b) A typical house built on the cross passage plan with two chimneys, one on the left in the kitchen.

Keeping Clean and Warm

The developing technology of fireplaces became crucially important in English social and economic development. Keeping warm had always been a preoccupation, especially from the mid 16th century when Britain suffered from the Little Ice Age. The problem was most acute in towns, particularly London, where vast quantities of firewood were needed to supply thousands of fireplaces. The price of firewood rocketed as London grew and increasingly ways were found to burn coal instead. Coal was at first used for industrial processes such as ironworking and brewing but not for domestic use. It was first used domestically on the east coast, where it could be easily delivered by water from Tyneside and Wearside; in Henry VIII's reign Hengrave Hall, Suffolk (fig. 193), had coal delivered by river from King's Lynn. But it was London – to which coal was brought by coastal shipping – that drove expanding coal consumption. In 1574 no coal was burnt at Westminster College but by the 1630s it was consuming around 75 tonnes a year. Indeed, by the reign of Charles I coal had become the principal fuel of London and by 1650 it was supplying half the nation's fuel needs.

Fig. 208 (top) London Charterhouse. The great hall fireplace was added to the room in 1614 by the mason Edmund Kinsman. The arms of Thomas Sutton are prominent and miniature canons refer to his Mastership of the Ordnance. The fine early grate, which also bears Sutton's arms, was originally in the great chamber and was relocated here in the 1950s.

Fig. 209 (above) Hobson's Conduit, Cambridge. The new river Cambridge was dug in *c.*1610 and brought water from south of Cambridge. Drinking water was piped to this handsome new fountain in Market Hill in 1614. It was removed to its present location in 1856.

To burn effectively coal needs to be contained and raised up from the ground to allow a good supply of oxygen, and because its smoke is much heavier than wood smoke it needs a powerfully drawing chimney. In the early 14th century grates were already in use, although only by the rich; most people who used coal were nearly suffocated by the smoke. So the spread of coal involved improved technology; fireplaces became smaller, their flues tighter and taller, and the smartest ones had integrally designed wrought-iron fire baskets. A high-quality example of an early coal-burning grate was installed in the great hall at the old London Charterhouse in 1614 (fig. 208). But the crucial development was the conversion of wood-burning chimneys to coal, which started apace in parts of the country with access to coal in the 1570s. In London the issue was forced after the Great Fire, when it was assumed that all new buildings would burn coal. The consequences of this were far reaching. Between 1560 and 1800 England's coal output increased 66-fold, making it by far the largest coal producer in the world. This, as we shall see, was one of the most important factors in English industrialisation.[40]

Water supply had always been a preoccupation for builders, fundamentally affecting the location of both residences and industrial processes. The earliest still-functioning wells are found in castles such as the Tower of London, and systems were soon developed for the capture and storage of rainwater, as can still be seen, for instance, at Warkworth Castle, Northumberland. Large building complexes like the priory of Christchurch Canterbury and Hampton Court Palace developed supplies that combined wells, springs and rainwater piped all over the complex in lead and pottery pipes. The growth of towns saw new conduit systems installed in the period from 1610 to 1625, many laid by entrepreneurs. A fine surviving example is Hobson's Conduit in Cambridge, jointly funded by town and gown and constructed between 1610 and 1614. Water was piped to various parts of the town and to a number of colleges. The original conduit head, now relocated, still stands, and with its niches, strapwork and cupola tells something of the civic and personal pride behind the project (fig. 209). A second wave of new conduits, mostly built by municipalities, came immediately after the Restoration.[41]

The removal of human excrement was one of the greatest challenges of urban life. Much was simply jettisoned into nearby watercourses, either from overhanging privies or from the emptying of chamber pots. For those who lived away from water, cesspits lined with boards or wattle were used. From the 13th century these were being built of stone in the richest houses, but it was only in the early 14th century that masonry pits became widespread. Above a pit were one or more seats supported by joists, rough and ready in the poorest houses, but finely carpentered in richer ones. In densely packed areas a pit might be shared by more than one dwelling, and seats on upper floors were connected to subterranean pits by shafts either built into wall thicknesses or against them. By the mid 16th century chimney stacks and garderobe shafts were often combined on the exterior walls of buildings, creating a characteristic rhythm and providing a degree of warmth (fig. 210).

Fig. 210 (left) Chenies Manor, Buckinghamshire; range built by Sir John Russell, Henry VIII's Lord Privy Seal from 1542. The range, of 1525–6, was for guests. A galley led to guest rooms which had fireplaces and in the projections garderobes and hiding places, as Russell was a Catholic.

The key to the cesspit system was regular emptying, a task undertaken by specialist contractors. Eventually this took place every night in better-off houses, but for the poor the stench was part of daily life. Royalty and aristocracy were exempt from such anxieties and used close stools with integral basins emptied after each use, but the invention of a fixed stool flushed with water was eventually to replace these. From the early 17th century royal palaces and the grandest aristocratic residences had fixed plumbing that allowed pewter basins to be flushed by the turn of a cock.[42]

Bathrooms were for the very rich. Edward III had a bath at Westminster Palace with taps supplying hot and cold water, and successive medieval kings had bathrooms at their principal residences. Henry VIII had bathrooms at all of his main palaces, often en-suite with his bedroom; several of these show the influence of the Ottoman court and contain sunken plunge baths, ceramic stoves and beds. It is likely that in the later 16th century the largest courtier houses were similarly served, but for the gentry and merchants a tub set up in front of the fire would have been the norm.[43]

Architecture for Learning

The Reformation had enormous implications for education, overthrowing the Church's monopoly on public life and creating a huge demand for lay administrators and professional men. Vast transfers of land required legal literacy amongst landowners; aspiring new men wanted their children to be literate and numerate; the gentry and aristocracy sought to master classical knowledge as a gentlemanly attribute; and the Protestant godly believed that education would guard against ignorance, profanity and idleness. The effect of all of these was a huge increase in formal education at both a local level and at the universities. By 1640 half of the population of London and a third of rural men could read, and at least 2.5 per cent of seventeen-year-old males were going to university, a proportion higher than at any time before the Second World War.[44]

In the early 1530s monasteries, hospitals, chantries and collegiate churches provided formal education for perhaps as many as five thousand children under the age of fifteen. As education had never been a state responsibility, providing an alternative to this arrangement was not a government priority, but pressure after the dissolution of the chantries – and corresponding royal pragmatism – led Edward VI from 1550 to create a number of new 'free' grammar schools with endowments from former chantry lands. In all there were twenty-six of these, half of which had originally been chantry schools. The movement continued under Elizabeth but only with royal approval, not with royal cash. Elizabethan schools were set up by civic action, much like the chantries that they replaced; indeed perhaps as much as a quarter of all Elizabethan charitable giving went towards school foundation.[45]

The model for these new schools was probably the school built by Dean Colet of St Paul's Cathedral, London, in 1512. This building no longer exists but comprised school rooms, chapel and attached houses for the teaching staff. Thus the children and their masters formed a distinct community within a single complex. The school at Ashbourne, Derbyshire, founded by charter in 1585, was financed by wealthy London merchants. It is a handsome gabled structure with a central school room and a dormitory above, with houses for the master and usher at either end (fig. 211). On a more pretentious scale is Guildford Grammar School, built between 1557 and 1586 (fig. 212). This comprises a small courtyard, with the main school room on the south side; the houses for the master and usher are attached on the east and west, and on the north side there is a small library. The children were taught in the ground-floor room on the north, sitting on forms, with their master at the end of the room on a shallow dais. The room above has a series of splendid fireplaces and was most likely used by the townsfolk as a civic space. Borders may have been lodged in the attics.

Both these examples were substantial buildings, richly endowed, but much more common was the single-room schoolhouse paid for by local people.

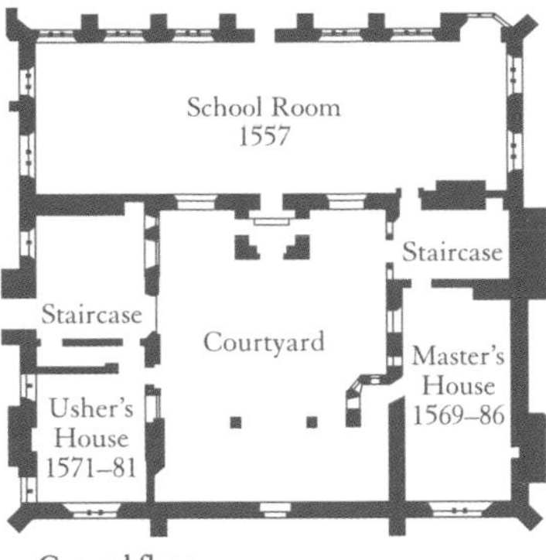

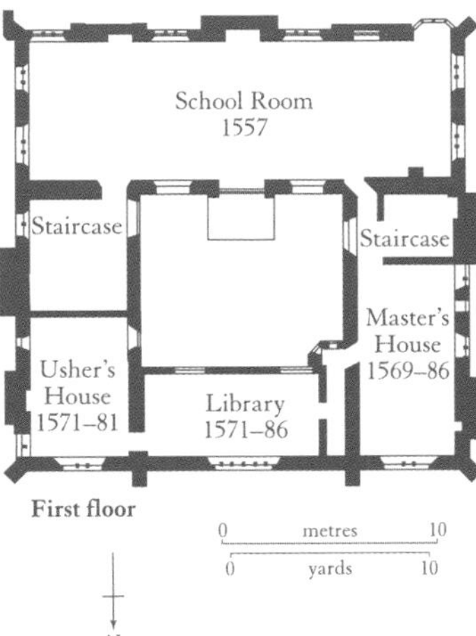

Fig. 211 (right) Ashbourne Grammar School, Derbyshire 1585–1603. An ambitious building for a school making a big splash in a small town.

Fig. 212 (above) Guildford Grammar School, Surrey. It was built in phases between 1557 and 1586. The upper school room has a fine queen post roof and its original fireplaces. The lower school room has lost its fireplace, replaced by a rear door. The street façade is adorned with the arms of King Edward VI, who granted a charter in 1553.

Fig. 213 (above) Uppingham Grammar School, Rutland. A plain rectangle dated 1584. The west front shown here has a tablet with inscriptions in Hebrew, Greek and Latin.

Fig. 214 (left) Middle Temple Hall, The Temple, City of London, completed in *c.*1570. Its ceiling and timberwork were designed by John Lewis, the carpenter from Longleat, Wiltshire. The screen is simply spectacular, with much figure carving, and the hall walls are panelled to sill level.

From around 1600 these became more and more common, partly because, with a greater sense of the dignity of ecclesiastical space, it was felt that church was not a suitable place in which to educate children. Education was also seen as an investment, and paying for proper facilities was part of that. So, although some churches continued to double as schoolrooms until the 19th century, hundreds of villages and towns clubbed together to build their own schools. Many of these buildings were in churchyards or in close proximity to the parish church, such as the simple rectangular schoolhouse at Uppingham, Rutland, of *c.*1584 (fig. 213). Such schools were built of local materials and designed by local artisans, but did not conform to a standardised plan or appearance. They did, however, reflect the much deeper penetration of education into society, with an emphasis not only on learning Latin but on what we today would call the three Rs.[46]

Fig. 215 (above) Gonville and Caius College, Cambridge; the Gate of Honour. Dr Caius was made Master of the college in 1559 and was personally responsible for the design of this gate, although it was completed after his death. It is one of the most charming buildings of its age – although small (the gate is 5ft wide), the structure includes just about every classical motif Dr Caius could throw at it. The result is not easy to categorise, but emphatically suggests the application of classical knowledge and taste.

The early 17th-century educational boom equally affected higher education and benefited not only the aristocracy, nor even just merchants and gentry, as university places were taken in large numbers up by the sons of the humble and poor. Money poured into collegiate education, the rich funding no fewer than five hundred new scholarships, as well as lavish new buildings and endowments to maintain dons in style and comfort.[47] Whilst the basic framework of college life remained centred on hall and chapel, standards of accommodation rose for students, dons and masters. In Oxford and Cambridge the halls and hostels of the Middle Ages were abandoned and college rooms began to acquire floors, fireplaces and window glass. New quadrangles were built three storeys high, significantly increasing available accommodation.[48]

Individual colleges, and the Inns of Court, vied with each other for students, especially fee-paying ones. New colleges were founded, old ones rebuilt and most were at the very least extended. These institutions were part of the establishment, inherently conservative and devoted to producing men who would go on to run the country. The country was Anglican, and Gothic forms were strongly associated with the Church, its history and authority. Middle Temple Hall, London's finest surviving Elizabethan interior, is a case in point. The vast space is slightly shorter than the hall at Hampton Court though no less wide, and is vaulted by a great double hammer-beam roof, symbolic of the ancient origins and authority of the inn (fig. 214). In Oxford the 15th-century Bodleian Library was extended in 1610. Inside it had the first bookcases in England to be ranged against its outer walls (the upper ones approached by a gallery), but its external elevations were panelled in blind tracery as they might have been a hundred years before. Thirty years later a new staircase to the great hall at Christ Church was covered with a fan vault as perfect as any built in the preceding century.

This does not mean that these institutions were either ignorant of classical forms of architecture or indifferent to them. It was about fitness. Traditional buildings suited the functional needs of the occupants and were seen as reflecting their intellectual outlook. That was precisely why there were specific references to fashionable classical or 'humanist' studies. The frontispiece at Merton College was the first in Oxford to have a stack of classical orders melded with blank tracery, pinnacles and battlements. In Cambridge John Caius, a physician who had studied in Padua and knew Greek, Latin and Hebrew, commissioned a series of emblematic gates at Gonville and Caius, the college he helped re-found. The Gate of Honour, built in 1573, was the one students passed though to claim their degree and contained a sophisticated mélange of classical elements mixed in with traditional forms (fig. 215). The screen in Middle Temple Hall, also from the 1570s, had Doric columns, figures of Hercules and caryatids mixed with strapwork (fig. 214), and the otherwise austere exterior of the Old Schools Quadrangle at Oxford is perked-up by a pinnacled tower faced with a five-storey frontispiece.[49]

Of all these creations the most important and ambitious was the new quadrangle built at St John's College, Oxford, by Archbishop Laud (fig. 216). The man who is credited with its design is Adam Browne, Laud's architect joiner,

but he may have been relying on drawings from Antwerp as the design of the frontispiece has close links with contemporary buildings there. The Canterbury Quad has defied attempts at stylistic categorisation on account of its easy mix of fan vaults, battlements and hood mouldings with Tuscan arcades, pediments and an aediculed niche. But Laud, his architects and contemporaries admired this rich and harmonious composition. The east and west courtyard elevations were deliberately emblematic; the busts of the Virtues and Arts proclaim Laud's belief in Oxford's medieval curriculum, and the frontispiece, based on Counter-Reformation church façades in Paris, combines the arms of the archbishop and images of the king and queen. Here was the ultimate statement of belief in the Anglican Church, a belief for which both Laud and his king were to perish.[50]

Fig. 216 (above) St John's College, Oxford; Canterbury Quad, 1631–6. No building better captures the age of Charles I. In the centre of the facade, in a niche, is Leseur's elegant bronze of the king, flanked by Ionic columns; below, the archway is flanked by Roman Doric, and the arcade has Tuscan columns. On top of the big segmental pediment perches a crown.

Patrons, Architects and Contractors

Because more correspondence survives and more books were printed from the 1520s, it is easy to believe that patrons were suddenly more interested in and informed about architecture, and that building was newly a matter of aristocratic education and polite debate. In fact what we have, from the 1520s onwards, is concrete evidence for an aspect of aristocratic life that was deeply engrained. Edward III's courtiers were no less immersed in the artistry and technology of their residences than the courtiers of Henry VIII; John of Gaunt can have taken no less interest and pride in his new buildings at Kenilworth (1373–80) than the Duke of Buckingham would have done at Thornbury Castle (1511–21).

The fact is that architectural design was a three-way partnership between the patron, who had a clear idea of what he wanted, those with technical knowledge and decorative skills, and the building contractor. The patron, rather than some individual design chief, was in charge. Many were active in drawing plans and elevations; we know that men such as Lord Burghley and Sir Thomas Smith could draw. Others such as Edward Seymour, Duke of Somerset, knew and worked very closely with engineers, designers, master craftsmen and other interested aristocrats on a range of architectural projects.

The word 'architect' was used for the first time in English in 1563 by John Shute in his book *The First and Chief Grounds of Architecture*. The term came to mean someone who designed a whole building but was not necessarily responsible for actually building it, but before 1640 the term embraced patrons, designers, craftsmen and surveyors. In reality it meant someone who could do architectural drawings.[51]

Quite a lot has been said about patrons and about decoration, but it is important to recognise changes taking place in the building trades. Building was still largely undertaken by individual master workmen, bricklayers, masons, paviors, carpenters, joiners, plumbers, glaziers, smiths and painters. Each had his own workshop or yard and, after serving an apprenticeship, was self-employed, supplying his services to patrons who often would provide many of the materials themselves.

Since the 14th century masons, carpenters and later bricklayers could only realistically make a lot of money by contracting rather than charging a day-rate for their services. From as early as the 1380s craftsmen were increasingly contracting for really big jobs, such as the completion of King's College Chapel, Cambridge (p. 198), or the completion of a big country house such as Longleat. Some masons achieved success by being retained by a patron as chief overseer, as Richard Kirby did for Sir Thomas Smith at Hill Hall; Smith even called Kirby his architect. Others bought or leased quarries where ready-made components would be fashioned and then transported to site. But very few craftsmen ever became gentlemen. Whilst the most entrepreneurial became rich, manual work was always perceived as low-status unless, that is, you worked for the Crown, where status came ready-made and complete with gowns, chains of office and a handsome salary.[52]

Churches from Elizabeth to the Civil War

The Elizabethan Act of Uniformity of 1559 and the Thirty-Nine Articles of 1563 put an end to thirty years of doctrinal uncertainty. The Church in England was to be a reformed one but was to keep some of the outward symbols of traditional religion, a sort-of third way between radical evangelicalism and Roman Catholicism. For most people there were two inescapable facts: attending church was a legal requirement and once there the use of the Book of Common Prayer was compulsory.

The physical manifestation of this was the division of church interiors into two liturgically distinct spaces. The rood screen still separated the chancel, where the monthly celebration of Communion took place, from the nave, which was the place for weekly preaching. In the nave were provided a seat or desk for the reading of the service, one for the parish clerk, who would lead the congregation in their responses, and a pulpit. Frequently these desks were combined into a triple-decker arrangement as at St Peter and St Paul's, Kedington, Suffolk, a church with unusually well-preserved Jacobean woodwork (fig. 217). Elsewhere as at St Peter and St Paul's, Salle, Norfolk (p. 173), the desks were just added to a medieval pulpit.

Fixed seating for the congregation became much more common from 1600. Whilst the poorer parishioners might still bring their own stools to sit

Fig. 217 (above) St Peter and St Paul, Kedington, Suffolk, has outstanding surviving Jacobean and earlier woodwork. The rood screen is dated 1619 and the triple-decker pulpit is likely to be of the same date. Opposite is a lovely pew belonging to the Barnardistons, patrons of the church. It was built in 1610 and is made up of sections of the late 15th-century rood screen.

Fig. 218 (above left) St Mary's, Whitby, Yorkshire; one of the most perfect and beguiling church interiors in England, miraculously saved from Victorian and Edwardian restorers. A rough-and-tumble of galleries, columns, screens and box pews illustrate the pains taken to accommodate the population of the little port efficiently, economically and with due regard to rank.

on, wealthier individuals or corporations would have their own seats constructed. Increasingly these were box pews – high-backed enclosures with benches entered by a door. These can be best seen at St Mary's, Whitby, Yorkshire, where a deliciously labyrinthine collection of box pews crowds around a triple-decker pulpit (fig. 253). Such pews were not only comfortable and draught-free; they also provided social and sometimes sexual segregation. Landowners, especially the gentry and aristocracy, could have large and imposing pews built for themselves, sometimes with roofs and windows. So the Shirley family pew at St Mary and St Hardulph's, Breedon, Leicestershire, built in 1627, looks like a Jacobean country house in miniature, hemmed in by robustly fenced family tombs (fig. 219).[53]

But it was not the nave that provided the liturgical battleground of the 17th century, it was the chancel. Here was the Communion table, moveable, but normally placed against the east end. Seating could be arranged on three sides but was sometimes ranged right around the table so that communicants would sit, as if sharing a meal. An amazingly complete survival of such an arrangement survives at Langley Chapel, Shropshire (fig. 220). These arrangements were favoured by the so-called 'godly'.

Fig. 219 (above) St Mary and St Hardulph, Breedon, Leicestershire; the Shirley family pew of 1627. With a vast coat of arms and towering obelisks laced with vigorous carving, it could be a screen from a country house, or a house itself!

Fig. 220 (below right) Langley Chapel, Shropshire, with liturgical arrangements dating to soon after 1601. Communion benches with kneelers and bookrests surround the communion table used for the monthly Eucharist.

Among the younger generation of Protestant clergy and gentry emerging from the universities in the 1560s were men who were frustrated at the bishops' unwillingness to take reform further. These people are now usually called Puritans but were known at the time as the godly. For many of the godly the bishops were the problem, not the solution, to a reformed church, and they wanted to see a Presbyterian system in England. For others there was a dislike of the Book of Common Prayer and a belief that in preaching men would find salvation. The godly would sit for Communion rather than kneel as required by the Prayer Book. To a generation of bishops emerging during the 1620s this was an abomination.

These men, represented perhaps most clearly by Lancelot Andrewes, Bishop of Winchester, started to emphasise the importance of Communion, rejecting it as a commemorative act and stressing the actual presence of Christ in the consecrated elements. This had significant consequences both in the performance of the sacrament and in its architectural setting that can be most accurately described as a more ceremonialised approach, emphasising greater dignity of action by the priest, reverence by the congregation and an enhancement of the chancel.[54]

The leading ceremonialist bishop from 1633 was Archbishop William Laud, who with his fellows drove through a ceremonialising agenda in parish churches. At Holy Trinity and St Mary's, Abbey Dore, Herefordshire, the 1st Viscount Scudmore restored the church and employed the capable carpenter and architect John Abel of Sarnesfield to refit the interior in 1633. Scudmore was a ceremonialising friend of Archbishop Laud, and Abel's new screen incorporated not only the royal arms but those of his patron and the archbishop. The 17th-century congregation sat outside the screen, and the altar – a slab of stone – was surrounded by a vigorous rail. Many churches saw the beautification of their chancels, such as St Nicholas's, Abbotsbury, Dorset, which was given a new plaster tunnel vault over the chancel decorated with angels, stars and the arms and motto of its donor, Sir John Strangways (fig. 221).

From 1600 many new churches were built and considerably more were re-ordered – sixty-three in London alone. This was not only in response to decaying fabric and changing liturgical taste; in London it was to service the rapidly growing population. Perhaps the most important new ceremonialised parish church was St Katharine's, Cree, in Leadenhall Street, London, consecrated in 1631. It combines arcades with Corinthian columns and a flat ceiling decorated with Gothic ribs, as well as a complex east window full of tracery and stained glass (fig. 222). The church was consecrated by Laud himself and perhaps exemplified his vision of the beauty of holiness.

But there were alternatives to the Laudian ideal. John Williams, concurrently Dean of Westminster and Bishop of Lincoln, represented a Calvinist middle way and sponsored not only a fine chapel at Lincoln College, Oxford, but a large chapel of ease in Westminster. The Broadway Chapel, Westminster (1635–42) (fig. 223), was a different sort of church to St Katharine's. It had a central plan without structural chancel, doors at the either end of each long wall and maintained a central axis to the altar. But it was undeniably a rectangular preaching box. Like St Katharine's it mixed classical orders (Tuscan in the arcade) with Gothic tracery in the windows. The Broadway Chapel type went on to inform a group of similarly planned churches in the godly East End.[55]

Stylistically, church architecture to the 1640s essentially remained Gothic, but classical elements sat with this, creating a distinctive episode in English church architecture. But the ceremonialised forms became associated with Laud's political stance, leading not only to his downfall but also to the end – for the time being – of the attempt to revive the ceremonial life of Anglicanism.

Fig. 221 (above) St Nicholas's, Abbotsbury, Dorset: the charming plaster ceiling added to the chancel in 1638. Chirpy, camp angels hold banners with mottos over the two bays of the chancel, with the donor's arms prominent below.

Fig. 222 (right) St Katharine's, Cree, City of London, 1629–31. St Katharine's was probably designed by the leading mason Edmund Kinsman, who had an extensive secular and ecclesiastical practice around London. Like the Canterbury Quad at St John's College, Oxford (fig. 25), the church interior comfortably, and without apology, blended classical and Gothic elements.

Fig. 223 (bottom right) The Broadway Chapel, Westminster, 1635–42; plan based on a survey of 1711. The altar is railed, but not in a chancel, or even a niche. The triple-decker pulpit is in front of it, approached by a staircase. Stairs on either side lead up to galleries. This church was an auditory above all else.

In the hundred years from the Dissolution of the Monasteries to the Civil War there were profound changes in the lives of Englishmen. Most important was the Reformation, a fundamental turning point in English history. In terms of building it altered the balance of architectural enterprise for three hundred years. Only in the second half of the 19th century would church building be a decisive building type again. The energies previously channelled into ecclesiastical building were redirected into secular construction. This was not just a quantitative change; it was qualitative, for secular buildings, built for an increasingly broad range of purposes, could draw on an architectural language no longer restricted by religious niceties and hierarchies.

Whilst pre-Reformation religious buildings ceased to be a primary reference point for designers after the mid 1530s, the same cannot be said for military structures. Chivalry, knighthood and their associative powers dominated building in England. Added to this was a new stream of ornament from abroad. Just as Gothic architecture, in its early phases, was a mode of decoration rather than a philosophy of design, so early classical forms appearing from the 1520s were an addition to an already rich palette of motifs and forms to be applied to traditional buildings as surface decoration.

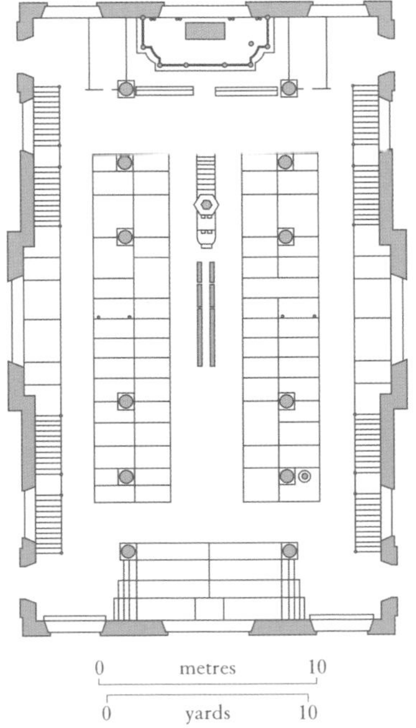

In many spheres the architecture of 1530 to 1630 was one of exuberance and extravagance, a period of voracious conspicuous consumption and spendthrift patrons. Yet this public show concealed a more private way of living. Upper-class life, in particular, became less public, households became smaller and the number of rooms and the complexity of their arrangement increased. For people further down the social scale, in town or country, this, in a lesser way, was reflected in their houses too.

And in all this London was becoming hugely significant, a force that drove so many changes and, as this book will show, continued to exert an often dominating influence over the physical development of England until the present day.

8— Protestantism, Power and Prosperity

—1630-1720

The elegant stripped architecture developed before the Civil War that matured at the Restoration was, from the 1680s, transformed into one of England's most original and exciting architectural periods.

Introduction

In 1642 England plunged into bloody civil war, a conflict that, to the horror and disbelief of the whole of Europe, culminated in the execution of King Charles I in 1649. During the following years Oliver Cromwell gradually established a military-backed dictatorship, but his regime was unsustainable and Charles II was called to the throne from exile in 1660. Charles's Catholic brother succeeded in 1685, but not for long, as his inept handling of the issue of his religious belief led to his flight and replacement by William and Mary in 1688 – the so-called Glorious Revolution. William died in 1701 without issue, and Mary's sister Anne, James II's other Protestant daughter, came to the throne and ruled until 1714. On her death, again childless, the crown was offered to George of Hanover, a prince who it was felt would secure the Protestant succession.

Out of breathless monarchical change came a new relationship between Crown and Parliament. Parliament now had the sole right to initiate financial bills, levy taxes, and control the army and the navy. Yet its primary concerns were peace, prosperity and stability, as the political class was a landowning one and wanted to protect property against arbitrary power and disorder.

Alongside these constitutional changes England's economy was transformed, and by 1700, the country had become a great power in a way it had never previously been. England's success was underpinned by a series of complex, interlinked changes: increased agricultural productivity, intensifying urbanisation, expanding overseas trade, a credit revolution and war.

Before the 18th century England's population could not rise above around five and a half million, a ceiling imposed by the limitations of agricultural production. English farm workers were only averagely productive in European terms in 1600 but by 1750, per head, they were the most productive in Europe. This huge leap in English agricultural efficiency enabled the population barrier to be broken and by the 1750s a minority of the workforce worked the land. Urban centres thus grew rapidly, and by 1750 people living in cities and small towns comprised 54 per cent of the population. Meanwhile, London became the largest city in Europe. England's growing towns were stimulated by developing trade and manufacture. Wool exports to traditional partners in northern Europe became far less important and the volume of trade with the

New World increased enormously. A re-export trade developed, expanding English ports, especially London, but also Bristol and Liverpool. In all, the value of English overseas trade increased from perhaps £8.5 million in the 1660s to £20.1 million a century later.

In 1694 the Bank of England was founded as a way of professionally managing the government's debts. War with France from 1689 resulted in a massive expansion of the Royal Navy (p. 338) and the Bank was a device to allow government to finance this on credit. By the end of the War of the Spanish Succession in 1714 government debt stood at £48 million. Government expenditure on war vastly exceeded any private investment in the economy and stimulated innovation, agriculture, manufacture and trade. Yet the Bank, founded on parliamentary guarantee, also made a huge contribution to private commerce, becoming the most powerful financial institution in the land, and facilitating transactions and dispensing credit to merchants and entrepreneurs.

The social changes that accompanied all this were no less far-reaching. The growth of the London money markets started to draw power and influence from the landed interest. Although England remained a hierarchical society the distribution of economic activity became much more balanced, and the middle ranks enjoyed huge advances in wealth and quality of life. These included merchants, doctors, lawyers, clothiers, engineers, builders and innkeepers; indeed, all self-employed men who employed people themselves. Their businesses relied on financial, educational and social capital, the acquisition of which was their priority. For the many thousands of successful families the amassing of material things was the result; new types of houses were filled with modern furniture and fittings, such as marble fireplaces, brass locks, mirrors, and mahogany doors and staircases. Carpets, books, paintings, furnishing fabrics, and more exotic goods such as porcelain clocks and coffee pots, were everywhere. These people were not necessarily aping their social superiors for, by the mid 18th century, the commercial and professional classes were all too often the pacemakers of change themselves.

Change also came through the way people thought. From the 1640s a group of natural philosophers had started to meet to discuss how they could promote the analysis of the world through experiment and observation – what today we would call science. This loose group formed a society for the promotion of 'physico-mathematical experimental learning' in 1660, which, three years later, with a royal charter, became the Royal Society. Restoration London was consumed by science; Charles II himself had a laboratory at Whitehall Palace, whilst all around telescopes and microscopes were opening up new worlds. As they did, old notions of astronomy, cosmography, biology and physics began to be demolished, and the earth-centred and man-centred cosmos inhabited by Englishmen since the Middle Ages began to be undermined.

Yet, whilst in scientific terms the knowledge of the ancients had been superseded, the cultural values that they were believed to represent were cherished. Classical literature, poetry and history were still the staples of a good education, and the ruling elite felt an increasing affinity with the Rome of

Emperor Augustus, with whose expansive mercantile culture they associated. This is why Rome became the ultimate destination of the Grand Tour, a rite of passage for most aristocratic young men (and some women). In the company of a knowledgeable tutor they learned the languages, history, customs and arts of Europe. Travelling to Rome via Paris, Venice and Florence the milords became acquainted, in particular, with the art and architecture of ancient Rome. The rich bought voraciously – Lord Burlington returned from his first trip to Europe in 1714–15 with eight hundred and seventy-eight trunks and crates – and the less well-off would return with prints and souvenirs.[1] These young men also returned with an increased belief in the superiority of England, of constitutional monarchy, of Protestantism and the defining idea of liberty.

Civil War

Architecturally the English Civil War was one of the most devastating episodes in English history. Between 1648 and 1650 parliament enacted a programme of castle demolition, to punish royalist owners and deny them future strongholds, and also to erase one of the primary expressions of the old social, religious and political order. Amongst many others the great tower at Kenilworth was mined (p. 164), as was the much smaller tower at Helmsley (p. 99).[2] Most castles were never rebuilt, some on grounds of expense but many because, by 1660, great fortified piles were no longer thought fashionable or practical. The Bankes family, for instance, decided not to return to Corfe Castle and built a fine new mansion at Kingston Lacy between 1663 and 1665, whilst the Hastings family built anew at Donington rather than rebuild Ashby-de-la-Zouche. In this way the Civil War marked a decisive shift from the ancient ancestral seats of many aristocrats to more modern and convenient houses.

All the royal palaces except those in central London were put up for sale, and although Hampton Court was reprieved so it could be used by Oliver Cromwell, most of them were demolished and their building materials sold. Like royal palaces, cathedrals, episcopal residences and their estates were ideological targets as much as military ones. At its most extreme in Norwich and Ely there were cries for the cathedral to be completely demolished; elsewhere hostility was more closely directed against fixtures and fittings regarded as idolatrous.[3]

Twenty-four bishops' palaces were destroyed or badly damaged, and just as aristocrats took the opportunity to start afresh in the 1670s and 80s, so did many bishops, abandoning their medieval seats and creating something new. In Winchester Wolvesey Palace was set aside for a new house built next door but many other long-standing houses, such as Bishop's Waltham, were simply abandoned.

At least one hundred and fifty towns and fifty villages were damaged – many had suffered sieges, suburbs had been cleared to prevent hostile troops using them for cover, and large houses on the outskirts had been demolished to stop them being garrisoned. Rebuilding and repair was not instant but came slowly in the 1650s and 60s. In some towns it took much longer and York had still not recovered in the 1730s. In the reconstruction public buildings were generally given priority. At Bridgnorth, Shropshire, a town that had been largely destroyed, a new town hall was built in 1652; the church of St Thomas's, Exeter, which had been burnt down, was rebuilt in 1657. Some churches were never repaired: St Botolph's, Colchester, is still a ruin, and most haunting of all is All Saints', Pontefract, where an extensive medieval ruin plays host to a quirky Victorian church tucked into its belly.

Polite Taste

As so often, war accelerated architectural change. Already in the 1630s the exotic cocktail of traditional forms – blended with ornament derived from prints – that had dominated English architecture began to seem stale and plainer buildings, a reaction against the excesses of the first thirty years of the century, began to be built. The Civil War accelerated this change, turning men against the whole notion of chivalric display. The bloodshed of the battlefields was anything but chivalrous; musket balls and cannon shot were not like jousting lances. Chivalry was dead both in reality and imagination, and the architectural effects of this were felt for a generation.

From the 1620s the craftsmen and designers of a series of houses in the environs of London, mainly built by rich city merchants, experimented with a new look. We have seen that from around 1610 suburban retreats encircling London began to be built as double-pile villas (pp 225–6). From the 1620s these began to shed their busy, decorated elevations, crammed with columns, and adopt a more compact and stripped-down external form. One of the first was Danvers House, built in *c.*1622 by the Parliamentary politician Sir John Danvers, who had travelled extensively in France and Italy in his youth. Here, on the banks of the Thames, he built, possibly to his own design, a villa and garden in the Italian style (fig. 224). It was a compact house with a sub-basement and a raised ground floor approached by a stair. Its first-floor windows were taller than those on the ground-floor, signifying a piano nobile (principal first floor), and the centrepiece was a tripartite – or Venetian – window, with a circular window – or oculus – above it. The details, assembled in a self-consciously Italian manner, all came from Serlio's books.[4]

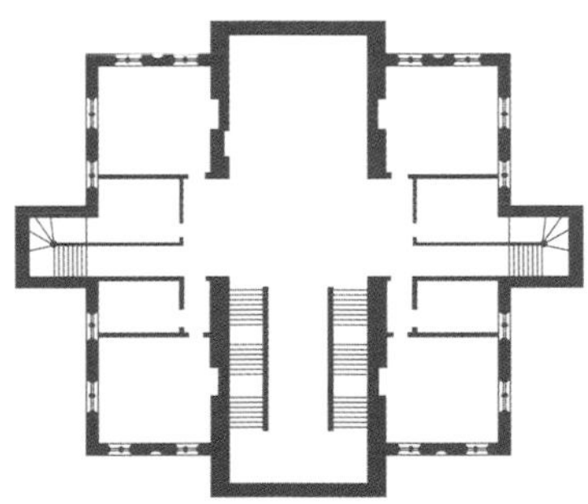

Fig. 224 (above) Danvers House, Chelsea, London *c.*1622; demolished in 1716. Ground-floor plan showing the main staircase accommodated in the hall, freeing the four corners for symmetrical apartments serviced by back stairs in turrets.

At almost exactly the same time Lady Mary Reade's compact new house – Boston Manor, Middlesex – was being built. It sported window surrounds with triple keystones, triangular and segmental pediments over the ground-floor windows, and an Ionic cornice above the first floor. Both this and Danvers House had traditional rooflines, but at Forty Hall, Enfield, completed in 1629 for Sir Nicholas Rainton, a rich merchant and Lord Mayor of London, there is a hipped roof – in other words a roof that has no gables and all of

Fig. 225 (left) Forty Hall, Enfield, 1629. Whilst the exterior of this house was a decisive break with the past, its internal decoration was much more conservative, including a traditional great hall. The hipped roof is the first in England. The sash windows are a later alteration.

whose sides slope down to the wall tops (fig. 225). This new type of roof was an important development as it enabled the double-pile house to be roofed efficiently and impressively. The elevations are very simple, only enlivened by corner quoins, two string courses and a simple modillion cornice. Forty Hall is recognisably a different sort of house to those being built just thirty years earlier; the emphasis is on the relationship of window to wall, not on decoration or on the use of classical orders.

It is likely that this style of house was developed by the master builders of the City of London, who designed for constricted building plots, but at the same time that these villas were rising so were a number of country mansions that shared the same aesthetic: West Woodhay House, Berkshire (*c.*1635); Chevening House, Kent (*c.*1630, possibly by Inigo Jones); Thorpe Hall, Cambridgeshire (1653, by Peter Mills); and on to the supremely accomplished Coleshill House, Berkshire (*c.*1651, by Sir Roger Pratt), now demolished (fig. 226).[5]

This minimalist approach to design cannot simply be seen as a reflection of a bloody civil war that led to a military dictatorship; nor is it easily identifiable with a less ceremonialised type of religion, although both these factors were its background. These buildings should rather be seen in counterpoint to the excesses of Jacobean ornament and satisfying a thirst for a plainer, more simplified, manner of building that relied much more on proportion.

In the development of these buildings the traditional master craftsmen continued to play the central role but to their ranks were added a new type of designer, men who had not come through the traditional apprenticeship route but through more gentlemanly pursuits. The first of these was Inigo Jones; he was followed during the 17th century by men such as Captain William Winde, Henry Bell, William Samwell, Hugh May, Roger Pratt, Sir Christopher Wren and Sir John Vanbrugh. These people were, in modern terms, more recognisably architects, but they closely collaborated with master

Fig. 226 (right) Coleshill House, Berkshire, designed for Sir George Pratt by his cousin Sir Roger Pratt in the early 1650s. This is a large country house and its garden front, here, comprises ten spacious bays, making it more expansive than its suburban contemporaries. It was amongst the first houses to have a ballustraded roof platform and cupola.

craftsmen. William Winde, the designer of Hampstead Marshall (from 1663), Combe Abbey (1682–5) and Castle Bromwich (1685–90), received drawings of pediments, plaster ceilings and gateways from the master craftsmen and, once approved, the craftsmen would execute these themselves.[6] In short, until at least the 1720s (and longer for less polite buildings) the master craftsman had as much to contribute to the appearance of a building as the chief designer. It is for this reason that the period covered in this chapter was a golden age of English architectural craftsmanship. The buildings described here had an originality and distinctiveness that could only be achieved by the freedom of the master craftsmen to contribute their own, often quirky, ideas.

Drawings are central to understanding this. Sometimes the gentlemen designers could produce technical drawings, sometimes not; Vanbrugh, for instance, sketched badly and relied on others for detailed drawings, whereas Jones and Wren were brilliant draftsmen. From the 1630s many more drawings survive and by 1700 drawings by all sorts of people are commonly found. Many of those that survive bear little relation to what was built, as they tended to be preliminary, presentation and experimental designs. Agreed schemes, often signed by the client, were used on site and survived less well. But looking at drawings, even by someone as established as Wren, it is clear that many hands participated. Both Wren and his master carver, Grinling Gibbons, might contribute to a single drawing, one the architectural framework, the other the carved embellishments. Many elements of a building would be conveyed either through a full-size drawing: possibly on parchment, or by a model, mould or template.

It is in the work of Inigo Jones that these features can be properly observed for the first time. Jones, an artist of exceptional talent, was born in 1573 and spent much of his youth travelling in Europe. He knew Denmark and Italy well by the time he became employed by James I's wife, the Danish Queen

Anne, as a stage designer and decorator in 1604. Soon Jones began to dabble in architecture, working for Robert Cecil, Earl of Salisbury, in London and at Hatfield House. In 1610 he was appointed Surveyor to Henry, Prince of Wales, and five years later, high in royal favour, he won the top architectural job, becoming Surveyor of Works to James I.

The Surveyor's work was onerous, with a heavy administrative burden, but Jones had been employed not primarily for his administrative skills but because he was recognised as the most talented designer at court. The men in the Office of Works at his side were much more experienced in building; many could draw plans and elevations, and all had overseen major building projects. But Jones had travelled more widely than any of them and had studied Roman buildings at first hand. He admired Venetian architects, especially Andrea Palladio and Vincenzo Scamozzi. In 1570 Palladio had published *I quattro libri dell'architettura*, a mixture of studies of ancient Roman buildings

Fig. 227 (above left) The Banqueting House, Whitehall Palace, London. Originally all but the end windows on either side were blind, providing walls for hanging tapestry that obscured the lower pilasters. The original niche, sited where the canopy now hangs, lasted only two years before being replaced.

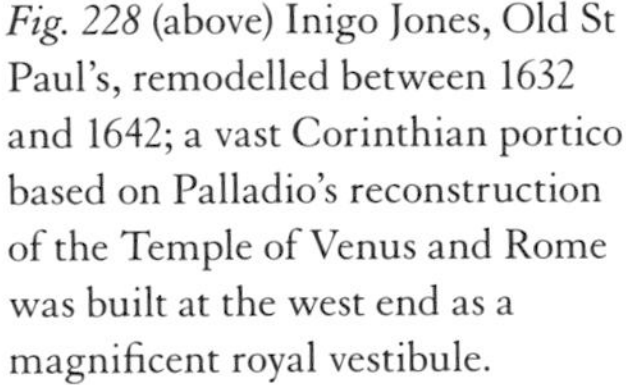

Fig. 228 (above) Inigo Jones, Old St Paul's, remodelled between 1632 and 1642; a vast Corinthian portico based on Palladio's reconstruction of the Temple of Venus and Rome was built at the west end as a magnificent royal vestibule.

Fig. 229 (above right) The Banqueting House, Whitehall, Inigo Jones, 1621. The facade is decorated all over with rustication and this brings out the plain pilasters in particular. At either end the design is given a conclusion by double pilasters. The façade was entirely re-faced in 1829, destroying the subtlety of the original contrasting stone types.

and designs by the author of town houses, villas and public buildings. Jones's copy is full of marginal notes, showing that he was determined to master the system behind the four orders and not just their use as ornament.[7]

Most of Jones's work was in the repair of existing medieval and Tudor structures, and the erection of relatively minor ancillary buildings. Yet three important new commissions did come his way: the Banqueting House at Whitehall Palace, Old St Paul's Cathedral and the piazza at Covent Garden (fig. 242). The only one that survives in any meaningful sense – although much altered – is the Banqueting House (fig. 227), envisaged as a great presence chamber to celebrate the Stuart dynasty. Completed in 1621, on one of London's main thoroughfares, it was based on Venetian villa designs and used classical orders in an archaeologically correct manner (fig. 229). The elevations were rich, rusticated from basement to cornice and constructed of stone of contrasting colours. Though the internal space was tapestry-hung with high clerestory windows like a traditional great hall, its architectural realisation, which came to include Rubens's great ceiling paintings, was radical. It was conceived as the nave of a classical basilica focused on a great niche, under which James I was intended to sit like a Roman emperor.

This scholarly use of classical precedent, skilfully blended with traditional forms and enriched for English taste, also applied to Jones's remodelling of Old St Paul's between 1632 and 1642. Here he was responsible for re-casing the transepts and nave in Portland stone, refenestrating them with round-headed and circular windows, and using the Romanesque buttresses to create a sort of Tuscan order. A vast Corinthian portico based on Palladio's reconstruction of the Temple of Venus and Rome was built at the west end as a magnificent royal vestibule (fig. 228). Had Jones gone on to re-case the tower, and had the cathedral been spared the Great Fire and the Blitz, it would have been a remarkable and influential building. But history was not kind to Jones's work there, which was obscured after only a couple of years and demolished after 1668.[8]

Despite their prominence, neither St Paul's nor the Banqueting House became widely imitated models, and Jones's other royal commissions were either in the private precincts of royal palaces, such as the Queen's House, Greenwich (completed in 1635), or at a distance from London, such as the Prince of Wales's house at Newmarket (1621, now demolished).[9] Most contemporaries failed to understand the subtleties of Jones's work and certainly did not perceive his buildings as inherently superior to others. As a result, his influence was extremely limited during his lifetime. More typical of the interest shown in classical precedent was the book written by Sir Henry Wotton, a former English ambassador to Venice. *The Elements of Architecture*, published in 1624, was a small, practical and un-illustrated manual of architectural design. Quite unlike Jones, Wotton was almost deliberately non-technical and anti-intellectual, providing simple rules for using the orders correctly.

Through the disrupted and unsettled years of the Interregnum building sporadically continued,[10] but the Restoration stimulated an explosion of cultural activity in painting, sculpture, literature, music and architecture – and the new king was interested in it all. Charles II had spent his exile in France and the Low Countries with those who now made up the cream of the court. Most gentlemen architects active in the 1660s had lived in the Netherlands and others had travelled further afield. The most important of these was Sir Roger Pratt, who had matriculated from Oxford in 1637 and gone on extended travels in France, Italy and Holland during the Civil War. On his return in 1649 he amassed an important architectural library and devoted himself to its study. Pratt became the leading designer of the 1660s, inventing, with a small group of others, a distinctive new architectural style for the Restoration. His most important house by far was the now demolished Clarendon House, Piccadilly, built between 1664 and 1667 for Edward Hyde, Earl of Clarendon, Charles II's Lord Chancellor and chief minister. Although it was in the tradition of the great aristocratic town mansions such as Northumberland House (fig. 189), this was a radical building, as new in look as Jones's Banqueting House had been but much more influential.

Fig. 230 (above) Clarendon House, Piccadilly, London, Sir Roger Pratt, 1664–7. This was unquestionably the most important house in Restoration England. Built for Charles II's Prime Minister in a highly prominent location, it showed a new way of building that was widely imitated.

Fig. 231 (left) Eltham Lodge, Eltham, London, 1664, designed by Hugh May for Sir John Shaw, a banker and favourite of Charles II. The novelty here was the use of pilasters and a pediment, possibly an idea that May became interested in during his exile in the Netherlands in the late 1650s.

Fig. 232 (right) Horseguards as seen from St James's Park, by Canaletto, 1749. This was the most important and prominent public building of the Restoration, symbolic of both a new order in government and architecture. Its designer is unknown but this was the first military barracks to be built in central London and became the HQ of the army.

The U-shaped house was raised up on a sub-basement and given a steeply pitched roof with dormers, capped with a balustraded platform and a lantern (fig. 230). There was little in this composition that had not been tried before in the suburbs of London in the 1620s and 30s, but Clarendon House was different in its proportions. It had no columns, pilasters or rustication. The addition of a pediment allowed the façade to be broken up, making it less monotonous than his earlier house at Coleshill (fig. 226), and the horizontal divisions of two storeys and big-hipped roof above a sub-basement made the house seem less vertical. This was a new, austere architecture escaping from the popular and almost indiscriminate use of details from Serlio intended to make buildings look more classical.[11]

An alternative type of house incorporating orders was designed for Sir John Shaw by Pratt's friend Hugh May – who had also been in exile – at Eltham Lodge, Greenwich, in 1665. Again much is familiar from before the Civil War, but the façade is adorned with four Ionic pilasters and a pediment containing a coat of arms supported by swags (fig. 231). The sense of proportion is also seen here, although the façade is much plainer, without quoins or string courses. In plan Pratt's and May's houses were double pile, with a great central room on axis like that at Charlton House, Greenwich (fig. 191b); they contained a principal stair and service stairs, and rooms disposed either side.[12]

Public buildings adopted Restoration austerity, too. It is uncertain how many people would have been aware of the new Ordnance storehouse at the Tower of London (fig. 260) but the new Horse Guards building in Whitehall occupied one of the capital's most prominent locations (fig. 232). After the Restoration a regiment of Foot Guards and two regiments of Horse Guards were created for royal protection. Between 1663 and 1664 a large new building, part barracks, part offices, was erected in St James's Park on the site of the old tiltyard. Its centrepiece was a pedimented pavilion squeezed between two taller blocks that were capped with little pediments on the street side. On the park side a steep roof with dormers supported a balustraded platform with a tower and cupola. It is not known who the designer was but this was a public building of a new form in the latest style.[13]

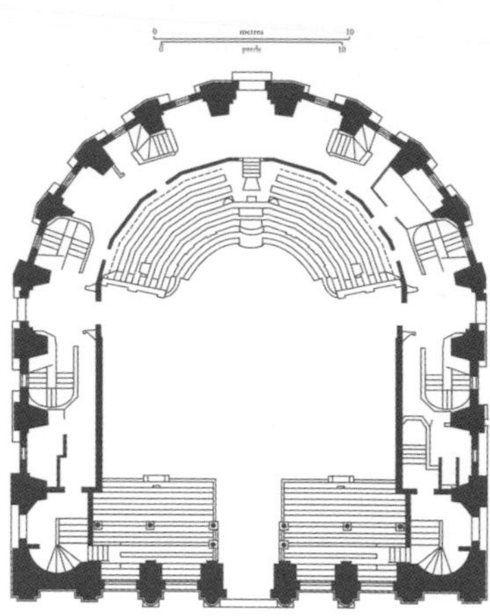

Fig. 233 (above) The Sheldonian Theatre, Oxford, Sir Christopher Wren, 1664–7. It was designed to be the ceremonial hub of the university and was one of the first buildings in England to be modelled on a Roman building – in this case the Theatre of Marcellus in Rome. The focus was, however, on the seat of the chancellor in the middle of its curved north end, not on a stage.

Fig. 234 (above left) The King Charles Block, Greenwich, 1664–9, started in a burst of enthusiasm but left unfinished and without a use after 1670. Webb created an assertive and distinctive image for the Restoration monarchy but one that had little traction with the reality of the time. The King Charles block is great architecture, but with little later influence.

All these buildings were probably subtly influenced by places seen by Pratt, May and their contemporaries on the continent, but in essence they grew out of the native tradition. They captured the mood of the Restoration, becoming the dominant models for English town and country houses for the next sixty years.

The most important of the gentlemen architects who emerged after the Restoration was Christopher Wren, a brilliant young Oxford scientist appointed Savilian Professor of Astronomy in 1661. He soon became interested in architecture and engineering, and was invited to design a new ceremonial hall for his university. This, the Sheldonian Theatre, built between 1664 and 1667, was a landmark in English architecture because here a university academic and architectural amateur who solved engineering problems that would have probably defeated the most seasoned master craftsmen (fig. 233). Wren's laminated roof trusses, which spanned a colossal 70ft and enabled uninterrupted views internally, were a technical marvel, launching him on a course that was eventually to see him named by Charles II as Surveyor of the Works in 1669.

After 1660 at court there was initially a return to the grand manner of the early Stuarts. John Webb, Jones's pupil, succeeded in winning Charles II's most important domestic commission, a new palace at Greenwich. The old one had been all but destroyed during the Republic and Charles II wanted to re-establish a palace in the east for the reception of ambassadors. The King Charles Block, built between 1664 and 1669, was a magnificent composition in Portland stone (fig. 234). Heavily rusticated like the Banqueting House at Whitehall, it featured assertive key stones and giant orders but was politically, economically and stylistically out of kilter with the times. This building, however, was not without influence and architects would turn to it again in the 1690s as a source of inspiration for a new, more assertive type of classicism. It is hard to keep down the English love of surface decoration, so powerfully seen in the work of Wren, especially at St Paul's (p. 276), and this combined with a reaction against the suave minimalism of the Restoration to produce something altogether more spirited. Just as Jacobean excess led, in counterpoint, to the elegant proportions of Pratt and May, so their architectural austerity led to a mannered classicism that deliberately flouted the rules to create a sense of drama and excitement.

Fig. 235 (above) Royal Naval Hospital Greenwich; the Painted Hall. This great hall was designed by Sir Christopher Wren in 1698–1705 and painted by Sir James Thornhill from 1707. It is his best piece of work. The oval in the main hall features William and Mary attended by the four cardinal virtues. Within the upper alcove Thornhill later painted Queen Anne and George of Denmark, while his collaborator Dietrich André painted the family of George I.

The origins of this revival of interest in the pictorial qualities of architecture came with Charles II's commission to Hugh May for the rebuilding of Windsor Castle between 1675 and 1684. From the outside the new apartments were austere, but inside there was an explosion of illusionistic wall painting undertaken by Antonio Verrio, who had worked at Versailles under Charles Le Brun, where Verrio had helped create a rich setting for the court of Louis XIV. These were spectacular interiors on the cheap, as the rooms themselves were plastered boxes; but they were incredibly effective and soon had imitators at Chatsworth, Derbyshire (1687–96), Burghley House, Cambridgeshire (1688–98), and most impressively in Sir James Thornhill's masterpiece, the Painted Hall at Greenwich Hospital of 1707–14. Of these, it was only at Greenwich that the external architecture began to match the internal décor. Unlike public buildings of the previous generation, such as the Bethlem Hospital (fig. 250), which were designed to be seen from a single perspective, Greenwich was much more three-dimensional. Here Wren and his assistant Nicholas Hawksmoor played with light and scale. Visitors entered by way of a circular vestibule with giant pilasters and a jutting entablature, flooded by light from a dome. From here the main vessel of the hall, lined with more giant pilasters and lit from both sides, opened out. At its end the high table was enclosed in another smaller space via a proscenium-like arch (fig. 235).

Fig. 236 (left) The Radcliffe Camera, Oxford. Not a very practical shape for a library, but one that James Gibbs turned into the most accomplished and exciting classical building of its age. It is anchored to the ground by a heavy rusticated basement. Above, three-quarter columns alternately frame windows and niches. The buttresses in the attic visually unite the drum and the lead-covered timber dome.

Thanks to Hawksmoor, Oxford became a centre for public buildings in this new, grand manner. Between 1712 and 1713 he designed the new university printing house – the Clarendon Building – as a giant Doric gateway. This set the pace for twenty years of building in Oxford, culminating in the most remarkable building of its generation, the Radcliffe Camera, built between 1737 and 1748 (fig. 236). The genesis of this library lay in the mind of Hawksmoor, who had first suggested a circular building in the middle of a *forum universitatis* – a public square at the centre of the university. But in the end it was the Scottish architect James Gibbs who was to design it. Raised up on what was originally an open rusticated basement is the domed library, circled by an arcade with massive piers faced with Ionic pilasters. It is a masterly space, perhaps the finest 18th-century classical interior in England, theatrically lit and invigorated by superb plasterwork, rich but not overdone. Outside, above the basement, pairs of giant three-quarter Corinthian columns support a cornice and balustrade. Above rise the massive internal buttresses crowned with urns, behind which sits the dome.[14]

Fig. 237 (above) Castle Howard, Yorkshire, Sir John Vanbrugh and Nicholas Hawksmoor from 1699. The great hall was the largest and most palatial room yet built in a private house. Square fluted giant piers support a dome far above.

At Castle Howard, Yorkshire, Hawksmoor and Sir John Vanbrugh had succeeded in introducing such theatrical effects into a country house. Here, in 1702, they started a great central hall, covered with a dome supported on four arches, each opening to a corridor or a staircase. This, the lavish centrepiece of an enormous house, would have not been out of place in a cathedral or a palace (fig. 237). Strange though it may seem, this ebullient style was easily transmitted from colossal commissions to domestic structures and was popular in the houses of the gentry. Francis Smith of Warwick, who built Chicheley Hall for Sir John Chester between 1719 and 1724 (fig. 238), was one of the most accomplished provincial designers. With giant pilasters, a big door case, heavily lidded windows, florid frieze and a sweeping centrepiece, Chicheley is typical of a very popular type of smaller house whose architects used engravings of Italian buildings by Bernini, Borromini and others to create a sense of theatre and exuberance. Lesser landowners, merchants and well-to-do artisans of provincial towns were also keen to adopt this theatrical language. As well as Thomas Bastard, who worked in and around Blandford Forum, Dorset, and John Etty, who worked around York, there were dozens of other anonymous architects and builders designing town and country houses in this style.

Whilst the Civil War had seen an assault on some of England's most important and impressive medieval buildings, the Restoration saw a return to affection and care for them. The half-century after 1660 saw a huge amount of new building, in which the restoration and reconstruction of medieval

Fig. 238 (left) Chicheley Hall, Buckinghamshire; the south front. The façade is illusionistic, like Thornhill's Greenwich paintings (fig. 235). The curving cornice gives the impression that the side bays curve out to a projecting three-bay centre, yet they are flat and the centre only projects a matter of a foot or so.

structures occupied much energy and resource. Many of those who were to take a leading role in the restoration of ecclesiastical buildings were members of the Society of Antiquaries of London, founded in 1707. Although the Royal Society, founded in 1662, had taken an interest in old buildings, the Antiquaries provided a forum for the study of history and antiquities, and was given its own royal charter in 1751. Its early members were actively engaged with the repair and embellishment of medieval buildings, and promoted the publication of surveys, histories and topographical views of medieval buildings. Some of these were produced locally; others more systematically by the Society of Antiquaries in the series titled *Vetusta Monumenta*.

Most architects worked in Gothic as well as classical styles, and major work at almost every cathedral, parish church and the universities of Oxford and Cambridge exposed the building trade to the principles and practice of medieval architecture. Most importantly, the Office of Works, the cradle of the English architectural establishment, continued to develop the stylistic possibilities of Gothic in a series of major commissions. Wren was appointed surveyor of Westminster Abbey in 1699 and under his supervision in 1719 the great northern entrance was effectively redesigned by William Dickinson. This was intended to be a faithful rendition of the original; but when Hawksmoor designed the Abbey's sublime west towers in 1734, he did so in a sparky and original late-Gothic idiom of his own (fig. 239). In Oxford members of the Office of Works were also busy developing Gothic styles. Wren turned away from executing a traditional Tudor gatehouse at Tom Tower, Christ Church, in 1681, designing instead a distinct new Gothic creation crowned by an early Tudor ogee dome. Meanwhile, in 1715 Hawksmoor designed the quadrangle and towers at All Souls College, not a serious essay in Gothic architecture, but a brilliant contribution to the cityscape, intended to enhance and set off nearby historic structures.[15]

Fig. 239 (right) Westminster Abbey; the west front towers, built in 1735–45. A sublime concoction, mixing a sophisticated use of Gothic panelling and the odd classical flourish. Particularly note the curly open pediments over the clock faces. Hawksmoor had been responsible for the repair of the west towers at Beverley Minster, Yorkshire, and the new work at Westminster bears a noticeable resemblance to these.

Although there were some who believed in the inherent superiority of classical over Gothic styles and who ridiculed buildings that drew on both traditions, most saw no inherent aesthetic objection to buildings conceived in either style or to those that incorporated features from both. As a result, right through the period covered by this chapter the pointed arch led a vigorous life, particularly in college and ecclesiastical buildings.

London

Elizabeth I, James I and Charles I disliked the growth of London but could do little about it. They saw the influx of the poor bringing problems of security, hygiene and sanitation, and the influx of the rich undermining the responsibilities of the aristocracy and gentry in the countryside. Each tried to restrict the growth of the metropolis, a process that was ultimately unsuccessful, as by

1700 it was the largest city in Europe, with a population of 575,000. Yet their efforts had important side effects on the appearance of the capital.

James I was determined to improve the appearance of London as a matter of national prestige and established a commission to oversee the enforcement of his building proclamations. It was revived by Charles I, who encouraged Inigo Jones to take an active role; indeed, during the 1630s, through the commission and its technical advisor, Jones, Charles effectively nationalised London's planning.[16]

Of the pre-Civil War developments the most coherent architecturally was Covent Garden. This was part of the land between the City and Westminster that had been acquired by the Crown after the Dissolution (p. 222) and had subsequently become the property of an aristocrat. Although it was superficially developed by Francis Russell, Earl of Bedford, the centrepiece – the piazza – was the outcome of a complex financial and legal deal that created a royal square to rival the Place Royal (later the Place des Vosges) in Paris. The king and his personal architect, Jones, took responsibility for the design, and the hapless earl had to conform to their expensive tastes. Work began in 1629 and the first houses were let in 1631.

The piazza was a long rectangle with houses on its north and east sides, whilst the south side was bounded by the garden of Bedford House (fig. 242). The whole of the west side was taken up by St Paul's Church and its associated buildings. The houses, designed by Jones, were modelled on designs from Book I of Serlio's work and raised up on a rusticated arcade. Doric pilasters aligned on the piers separated windows on two upper floors. There was no parapet nor gables, but a hipped roof with dormer windows. The whole thing was stuccoed to give the impression of stone. The front doors to the houses were under the arcade, each with a parlour and study on the ground floor, a dining room and drawing room on the first floor, and bedrooms above. Gardens at the rear led to coach houses and stables. So much of this was novel that the development must have been very striking, and it is not surprising that the earl could command £160 a year in rent. The development quickly became a magnet for the rich and titled, setting an entirely new standard for West End housing. In this sense, at least, one of Charles I's objectives was fully realised.[17]

What is important to note is that the Bedford estate outside the confined precincts of the piazza was not architecturally homogenous; indeed, much was illegally built in timber and even the brick buildings did not conform to regulations. Proclamations had already banned bay windows and jetties, specifying that windows must be taller than they were broad, and eventually introduced a standardised brick type (which remains the standard to this day). What the Bedford estate and many others did have in common with the piazza, however, was the emerging adoption of the terrace as a standard housing form, although at the time it was known as a row house.

Houses built in a row had a long pedigree in England; Lady Row in York of *c.*1316 has already been mentioned (p. 112 & fig. 82), and by the 14th century rows of shops with rooms above were a common sight in London and other large towns. Rows that were predominantly residential were known as rents, a term that persisted until the 19th century. A large speculative development

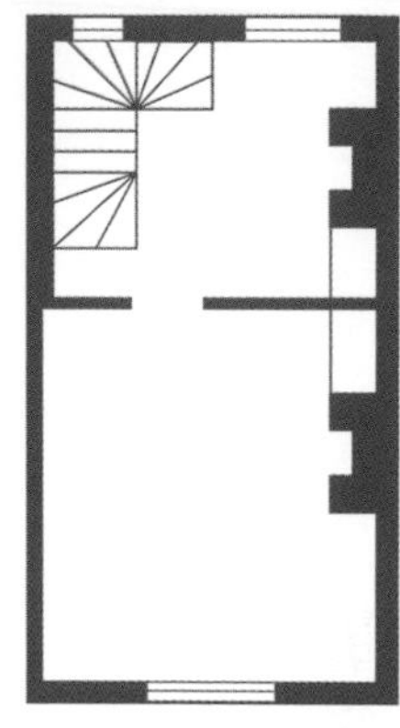

Fig. 240 (top) 74 Long Lane Smithfield, London. First floor plan *c.*1598.

Fig. 241 (above) 52–5 Newington Green, London, a speculative row built in 1658. The houses were only two bays wide with front and back rooms on each floor, a staircase squished between them. Yet the pilasters create a much greater sense of architectural presence.

Fig. 242 (above) Covent Garden Piazza, 1771–80 by John Collet. On the right are some of Jones's houses raised up on rusticated arcades. At the end of the market is St Paul's Church, flanked by rusticated gateways. See fig. 376 for later developments.

promoted by the Rich family at St Bartholomew's Fairground, London, from 1597 to 1616 resulted in the construction of one hundred and seventy-five row houses built by a variety of speculators. Most of these were one room to a floor, and of four storeys plus a garret and a cellar. One of these houses survives at 74 Long Lane, dating from soon after 1598. Its principal elevation to the street is jettied, but at the back, approached by a narrow alley, is the entrance to the rooms above via a staircase (fig. 240).

No. 74 Long Lane is timber framed, like most rows before 1600, but after that it became less normal in London to jetty out every floor and some houses began to be built in brick. In fact, the later parts of the St Bartholomew's development dating from 1616 were entirely in brick, probably London's first such development to date. Fire prevention aside, the motivation for this was commercial, as brick houses could be let for more, and whole streets of brick were admired as being more elegant and modern.[18]

The change to brick opened up new architectural possibilities. Heavily carved and moulded oak and plaster façades gave way to a version of this in brick. Cromwell House, a detached building on Highgate Hill of 1637–8 that is richly moulded and delineated in brick, gives a strong flavour of what was once common; a four-house group from twenty years later on Newington Green (fig. 241) is similar to the brick rows built on Henrietta Street and King Street in the West End in the early 1630s, with giant pilasters, gables and balconies. In the 1630s it became popular to incorporate a giant pilaster or two on the façade, as can still be seen on Lindsey House on the west side of Lincoln's Inn Fields, dating from 1639–41.

Fig. 243 (above) Amen Court, London; three houses of 1671–3, probably by Edward Woodroffe. They are five bays wide on low basements with two stories and an attic: rare surviving examples of the second class of house specified by the 1667 Act.

Fig. 244 (left) King's Bench Walk, Temple, London, looking south. Despite infills of 1814, this row of houses is a remarkable survival from 1677–8 and represents the third class of house specified in 1667.

From the 1610s London's westward growth accelerated, at first around Covent Garden, Long Acre and St Martin's Lane, and then, after the Restoration, north of Westminster in St James's, Soho and St Giles's. The rate of development was astonishing and, for many, disturbing, as green fields were weekly consumed by brick, stone and cobble. Long-cherished rights of way were blocked, communal lands were privatised, new boundaries, roads and districts were made. London became a conglomerate of districts impossible to hold in the eye. Yet its heart was the timber-built medieval City in which proclamations and regulations had made little difference. It was for this reason that when a fire started in 1666 it proved catastrophic.

Town fires were common in the 17th century. Northampton, Warwick and Tiverton were just three places to be destroyed, but London's fire of 1666 was the worst England had ever seen. The sheer scale of destruction was vast: over thirteen thousand houses, eighty-seven parish churches, fifty-two company

Fig. 245 (right) St Paul's Deanery (now Dean's Court), City of London, 1672, by Edward Woodroffe. This fine mansion, built for Dean Sancroft, is the best survivor of the fourth and largest class of post-fire buildings. Big windows make more glass than wall.

halls, the Guildhall, Royal Exchange, Customs House and Sessions House, and the Cathedral. The value of property destroyed was perhaps £10 million at a time when the city's annual income was around £12,000. Whilst such destruction was of course disastrous, particularly for those who lived through it, it placed London in a uniquely advantageous position. Five-sixths of the City had to be rebuilt anew and thus, by 1700, London had become a modern metropolis with an up-to-date infrastructure. Fire had, in fact, achieved what the monarchy had failed to do in the preceding sixty-five years.

Just as after the Blitz, London could be rebuilt only with state aid and control. A coal tax enacted in 1670 was to pay for St Paul's, parish churches and street improvements. Roads were to be laid out with greater breadth, noxious industries relocated and domestic building was to be heavily regulated. The 1667 Act for rebuilding the city specified four classes of house, all of which were to be of brick and stone. The most humble was a two-storey house of the sort that might face a lane. The second class was three-storey houses facing larger lanes and the river Thames; some of these survive in Amen Court behind St Paul's (fig. 243). A third class faced principal streets; these were permitted to be of four storeys, such as some surviving houses in King's Bench Walk in the Temple (fig. 244). These are big, with string courses and cornices, and the richer ones have decorated door cases. The fourth class was detached aristocratic residences, which were allowed to be larger; the Old Deanery by St Paul's is the sole surviving example (fig. 245). However, a marked effect of the fire was the drastic reduction in the number of large mansions in the City. After 1666 the rich favoured residences in the new West End (p. 268).

The regulations essentially codified what was happening in London before the Great Fire; they didn't invent a new type of building, yet they did reinforce a vocabulary that was to dominate London well into the 19th century. Streets were now lined with more or less regular, flat, narrow, brick-built fronts with a rhythm of upright windows. In plan they continued traditions established before 1666; most had pairs of chambers placed symmetrically about a central staircase. There was often a shop or workshop on the ground floor, a basement below and a yard at the back. The first floor contained the kitchen and dining room, and above was either one or two floors of bedrooms and a garret. For those who needed no shop the front room might be a counting house and the kitchen might be in the basement. Nearly two-thirds of houses had between five and eight rooms, and many were in shared occupancy.

Virtually all middle-class houses, even the poorest, had female domestic servants and larger ones might also have resident male apprentices or clerks. Servants were essential for status as they relieved the wife of the need to perform chores. Servants slept in the garrets, and toiled in the basement and kitchen, whilst also serving politely at table. London houses were vertically arranged – unlike most continental capitals – and all but the best had only a single staircase; thus servants lived lives closely entwined with their employers.[19]

The rapid construction of new houses was facilitated by three important changes in the building industry. First was the rise of a new breed of developer and contractor working within a system of contracts, leases and mortgages. Nicholas Barbon was one of the first and certainly the most prominent of these speculators dealing in both land and building. He would purchase or lease land financed by mortgages, and then sell leases to other developers or contractors. The purchasers, the building undertakers, constructed the houses and, once complete, agreed a ground rent payable to the landlord for the duration of the lease. When the leases fell in, the houses were the property of the landlord. Like Barbon, most developers were self-made men relying on capital borrowed from consortia of wealthy backers and legal agreements forged in the Inns of Court. Beneath them were men from both inside and outside the building trades, all with disposable income and hoping to make a return on their investment.

Alongside the speculators there were building contractors of a type more recognisable today. Particularly successful were the Fitch brothers: John, a bricklayer, and his elder brother Sir Thomas, a master carpenter. Between them they worked for Bernard de Gomme at Portsmouth, for Robert Hooke at the Bethlem Hospital (fig. 250) and for the bishop at his new palace in Winchester. It is possible that they also designed some of the buildings they built; they certainly constructed the great storehouse at the Tower of London (p. 286) and may have produced the design.[20]

The second change was the relaxation of trade restrictions imposed by the medieval craft guilds allowing, for the first time, non-freemen to work in the City. Third was a revolution in the production of building materials. Brick was the most standardised. Brick pits and kilns ringed late 17th-century London, exuding plumes of smoke day and night, although timber was still the most important material. For at least a century timber components had been fabricated in timber yards, but from the 1660s prefabrication increased to include windows, doors, balusters and cornices, and standardisation in size and mouldings increased. All these were of softwood (normally pine, known at the time as deal). Before the Great Fire structural and decorative timberwork in houses was generally of oak.

One invention of the period transformed the appearance of English buildings in the space of fifty years – the sash window. Although the term 'sash' is a corruption of the French word 'chassis' or frame, the invention was home-grown. In 1660 most windows were set in stone, brick or timber transoms and mullions containing a matrix of quarries (window panes) held together by a lattice of lead (cames) and supported by thin iron stay bars.

Panes of glass had become bigger since the 16th century, when they were invariably small and diamond-shaped, yet the proportion of structure to glass remained high. Sash windows transformed this situation as they allowed larger panes and smaller structural members.

The first sashes were probably installed by the architect William Samwell in Charles II's Newmarket Palace in around 1670, and they rapidly replaced casements in royal palaces and fashionable new buildings such as the Duke of Lauderdale's Ham House. Early sashes had two vertically sliding frames, each three panes wide and high, with square panes of glass and one-and-a-half inch-thick glazing bars. Brass pulleys, cords and lead counterweights in the frames allowed them to open easily (fig. 246). By the 1730s it was becoming more common to have larger panes and thinner glazing bars, and most windows were six over six. By the 1790s the slimmest and most elegant glazing bars were only five-eighths of an inch thick. Thinner glazing bars were desirable to reduce the weight of the frames and let in more light, but also for producing a more striking external effect, as sashes made a huge impact on façades. Glazing bars were far less visible than transoms and mullions, and so windows became voids contrasted against solid walls. It was this rhythm that became the principal proportional effect desired by architects from the late 17th century.[21] Perversely, the generation of houses built after the Great Fire, hastily thrown up by speculative builders in relatively standardised materials, were more ephemeral than the stout, bespoke, timber-framed buildings they replaced. The new London might have been less vulnerable to a repeat of the Fire, but almost all of its houses were replaced in less than a century. Indeed, the leasehold system triggered a perpetual process of construction and renewal that continues, in the City of London at least, to the present day.

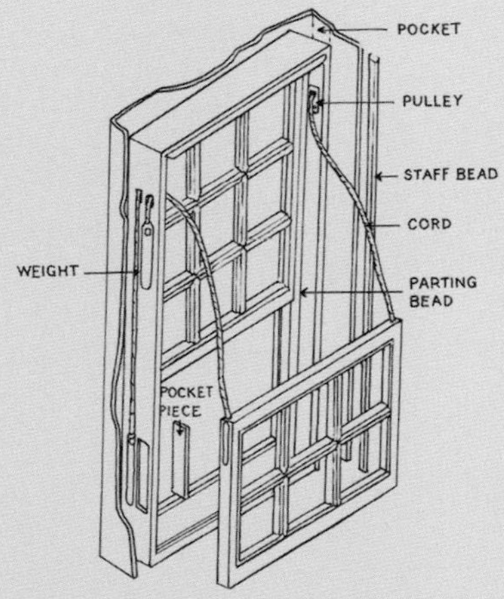

Fig. 246 (above) The sash window was a fundamentally important invention for the future of English building. A system of concealed lead weights in the box-like window frames counterbalanced the heavy sashes and made it possible to easily raise and lower them.

However, enough survives to understand the effect of the streets of row houses. They varied considerably in decoration and proportion. At 55 to 57 Great Ormond Street is a development begun by Barbon in the 1690s; the elevations are extremely plain, only perked-up by brick string courses, and the windows are all the same size, prettily framed with rubbed brick (originally these were casements, now replaced by sashes). Other developments were more elaborate. The surviving houses in Denmark Street, from the mid-1680s, have keystones above the windows, and the second-floor windows are smaller than those below. Fancier still are the houses of 1704 in Queen Anne's Gate; in addition to keystones and string courses there are cornices and carved door cases. Internally, clients often opted to choose their own panelling layouts and staircase turnings and, in the largest houses, carved chimney pieces and moulded plaster ceilings; the less well-off or less interested got a standardised fit-out.[22]

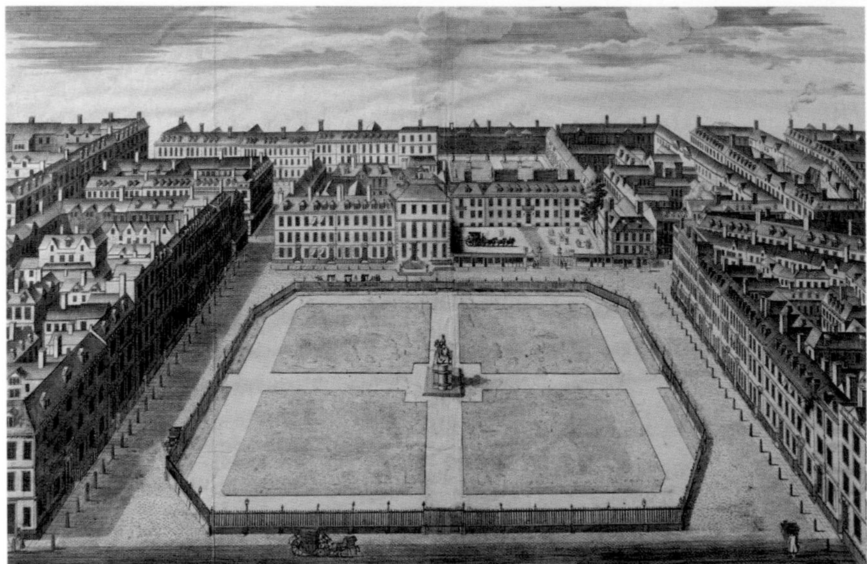

Fig. 247 (left) Leicester Square, by Sutton Nichols, 1727. On the far side of the square is Leicester House, with a forecourt containing a coach. The depiction of the house might not be wholly accurate, but the image of the great house set in a residential square is.

One of the most important developments after 1660 was the rage for squares. Moorfield's, Covent Garden and Lincoln's Inn Fields were great enclosed urban spaces, but none was quite like the city squares that developed after the Restoration. Many of the first new squares of Charles II's reign were conceived, like the piazza in Covent Garden, in relation to aristocratic mansions. Thus Southampton (later Bloomsbury) Square and Leicester Square (fig. 247) were forecourts and vistas in front of great houses, dignifying a mansion with an urban setting and creating rental value in the rows through social aspiration. Others, the most prominent of which was St James's Square, contained numbers of very large houses sufficient in themselves to bring prestige to the development.[23]

From the 1680s squares became a fundamental component of the smartest areas, and speculators with capital and political connections would develop a square hoping for big profits. One such person was the seventy-year-old retired military hero John Lumley. On retirement he put his cash into property speculation, purchasing in 1713 a large area of land between Conduit Street and Oxford Street. Thomas Barlow, the carpenter-turned-surveyor whom he appointed as his designer, came up with a dynamic design – a new square, approached by a funnel-like street on which Lumley proposed to build a church. The shape and width of the street would enable his spectacular church to be appreciated, and it would also provide a vista for his handsome new square. In 1714 Lumley declared that his development would be called Hanover Square (fig. 248), that the church would be dedicated to St George and that a huge statue of the monarch would adorn its portico. As the houses began to rise around the square between 1717 and 1719, wealthy and powerful aristocrats eagerly took leases. Many of the first inhabitants were, like Lumley, military men recently retired from the European wars; the Lord Chancellor, the Duke of Roxburghe and Lord Cadogan also lived there. Uniformity was not important in Hanover Square, nor was the way the streets

Fig. 248 (above right) Hanover Square, London, by Edward Dayes, 1787. The houses around the square were broadly speaking of a piece but each owner was left to execute their buildings as they wished. The elegant funnelling effect of the approach road with St George's Church prominently placed on the east side can be clearly seen.

entered the square. But from the 1720s squares become more uniform and standardised, their internal space more enclosed and restricted, and in due course the central space became an ornamental garden with decorative features such as statues or summer houses.

The rebuilding of the City after the Great Fire, coupled with the development of the West End, had a huge impact on provincial towns. Provincial practitioners in the building trades were sucked in to the capital, where ideas and techniques were exchanged and later exported to the provinces. The regular streets of new row houses were quickly copied in places such as Nottingham and Liverpool; London squares also exercised a huge influence. Bristol, England's second town, was the first to have its own square – Queen Square – begun in 1699. Five others were completed by 1784.

At the centre of the City of London was its cathedral, St Paul's. Unlike all others it was named after its dedicatee, not its city. It was the theatre of the monarchy, the social nexus of the populace, the symbol of the City's economic virility and only afterwards the cathedral of the capital. This is why monarchs had such concern for its fabric and why after its spire was destroyed by lightning in 1561 both Elizabeth and James made great efforts to rebuild it. In the end, frustrated at the lack of progress, Charles I nationalised the project, appointing his own architect Inigo Jones to reclad it and build a colossal portico crowned with royal statues and slogans. The portico was in court taste and expressed the aspirations of the Crown rather than the Church.

In 1666 everyone hoped that the cathedral – or at least parts of it – would be saved, but it was clear that the damage was too great. There were several tensions to be resolved in a new design, including the conflicting ambitions of the City, the Crown and the Church. Wren's preferred solution was for a centrally planned scheme based on a Greek cross but liturgically this was impractical, so the new cathedral rose, like its predecessor, as a Roman cross with a long nave. Wren and his team of draughtsmen and craftsmen were forced to resolve the details as the church rose; the dome was not finalised until 1697 nor the west towers until 1704. In this way the design of St Paul's was an empirical experiment, Wren modifying the elements as he went along until he achieved the desired effect. The cathedral reveals Wren's strengths and

Fig. 249 (left) St Paul's Cathedral, London; the west front from Ludgate Hill. Designed by Sir Christopher Wren and built 1675–1720, the details were constantly revised as the building rose. The west towers seen here were only completed in 1708. The west front was designed to be revealed from Ludgate Hill as people moved up it and round the curving street.

limitations as a designer. Close to, the elevations are busy, fussy and crowded; at a distance, the dome sits disconnected from the bulk of building below. But Wren was at his best when he worked on the grand scale, bringing poetry to engineering. The west front is a composition of genius, conceived to be revealed as the spectator ascends Ludgate Hill, and the dome, still one of the most moving structures in London, electrified the horizontal 17th-century skyline (fig. 249). St Paul's, as a carefully cut jewel in the city landscape, succeeded in restoring a sense of pride in the City after the Great Fire.

Palaces for the Sick, Injured and Mad

Seen through a foreigner's eyes, London in 1700 was topsy-turvy. William III lived at Kensington and St James's, the two most unassuming palaces in Europe, whilst his sick and injured soldiers and seamen lived at the great royal hospitals of Chelsea and Greenwich. Even the lunatics lived at the splendid Bethlem Hospital in Moorfields.[24] The Bethlem Hospital for the insane, designed by Robert Hooke, was built between 1674 and 1676. Hooke had been appointed Curator of Experiments at the newly founded Royal Society in 1662 and, like his close friend Christopher Wren, turned to architecture. He was an interesting choice of architect for this important public building, representing the triumph of a more scientific approach to medical care than that found in medieval hospitals, in which a good death and salvation were more important than a cure. As with the largest medieval examples, however, Bethlem had substantial architectural pretension, still necessary for attracting private donors.

The new hospital was a palatial composition, 600ft long and only one range deep, so that through-ventilation, thought to be medically essential, could be easily achieved (fig. 250). At each end were stone pavilions; in the centre a festive block containing a hall adorned with the names of benefactors, above which was the governor's room. Iron grilles in the hall allowed a view of the hugely

Fig. 250 (right) Bethlem Hospital, Moorfields, London, Robert Hooke, 1674–6. Prominently located and splendedly designed, this was one of the most influential public buildings of its age exerting huge influence over a generation of designers.

long galleries, off which lay the cells. The pavilions were in the latest style – hipped roofs supported balustraded flats, in the centre of which was a cupola. In elevation the pavilions had a strong Netherlandish feel, with pilasters supporting a pediment and swags beneath the windows, as at Jacob van Campen's Mauritshuis in The Hague. The long flanking wings owed more to London street architecture, although they were enlivened by a central pediment. This was a building that combined cutting-edge medical practice with the fashionable magnificence required to attract donations. It was also of considerable influence as one of the first and most flamboyant public buildings of the Restoration.

Bethlem was somewhat ahead of at least two of the three great London hospitals, St Thomas's and Guy's, which were built on constricted sites with courtyard plans. These were soon to be frowned upon for their lack of good and proper air circulation. The new generation of hospitals were expansive, like Bethlem, with wards stretched out in long ranges. St George's Hospital was set up in Lanesborough House at Hyde Park Corner, a building considered airy and in an airy position. Isaac Ware converted it into a hospital by the addition of wings between 1733 and 1736. St George's, and its provincial contemporaries at Winchester (1736), Bristol (1737) and elsewhere, were modelled on great houses, recognisable and acceptable models for their landed donors.[25]

Oliver Cromwell was the first to become interested in the idea of a military hospital, and the idea was taken up by John Evelyn in 1666, at which time sick and injured soldiers and sailors were still billeted at inns rather than sent to an institution. Charles II was determined to rectify this and was fascinated by Louis XIV's hospital in Paris, Les Invalides, started in 1670. The building that Sir Christopher Wren designed for him in Chelsea between 1682 and 1689 was, however, very English. Chelsea Hospital looks down towards the river Thames and what were once extensive water gardens at the river's edge; its 300ft-long sides contain the wards and terminate in houses for the hospital's officers, whilst the 230ft cross-wing houses the chapel and hall (fig. 251). The wings have a spine wall, with the pensioners' timber cabins on either side. The elevations, like Hooke's at Bethlem, are a version of post-Fire London street architecture but on a gigantic scale, made magnificent by the central Portland stone Doric frontispiece and crowning cupola. Chelsea was to become a model for hospitals and colleges for a century or more.[26]

Chelsea was monastic in its severity but its twin, the hospital for seamen at Greenwich, started in 1696 and not completed for 56 years, was considerably

Fig. 251 (left) The Royal Hospital, Chelsea, designed by Sir Christopher Wren in 1682–91. The central section of twenty-seven bays contains the hall and chapel, and the projecting wings the wards for the pensioners. The windows in the wings were originally casement, not sashes. This was monumental architecture, but severe, functional and unadorned, much like many 18th-century streetscapes.

more flamboyant. Its kernel was John Webb's abandoned royal palace, upon which work had ceased in 1670, and it was probably the incorporation of this showy wing that led to the hospital being conceived as a glorification and celebration of the navy for the many thousands who made their way up river to the City. But the hospital not only proclaimed English supremacy of the seas; in its demonstration of the seriousness with which the state took their welfare it was an advertisement encouraging potential sailors to join up (fig. 252).

Greenwich Hospital would have been built in a U-shape like Chelsea, had it not been for Queen Mary's desire to preserve views to the river from the Queen's House, a building – like the Banqueting House at Whitehall – that had become a Stuart architectural icon. Wren, who was appointed surveyor, solved the problem by leaving the vista open and enclosing it by four blocks. One of the two nearest the river was Webb's building, which was matched. Further south were two new symmetrical blocks containing a hall and chapel, with hugely long colonnades to enable convalescent men to walk under cover. The corners of the southern blocks were crowned with cupolas. The ensemble, despite its lack of a proper centrepiece, is one of the most picturesque compositions ever built in England. The contrast between the military and naval hospitals encapsulates the change in English architectural styles between the Restoration and the turn of the century.

These public buildings in the capital – designed to welcome travellers, spectators and particularly benefactors – set the tone for public building in England for a generation, being reflected close at hand in London and as far away as York, Worcester, King's Lynn and Portsmouth.

Royal and Aristocratic Palaces

In England there was no academy of architecture as there was in France; instead there was the Office of Works (p. 266). For major buildings the Office was the architectural focus of the nation and for three decades it was led by Christopher Wren. Wren came from a family with impeccable royalist credentials, fiercely loyal to the Stuart dynasty. Whilst he was obviously a man of talent and intellect, it was his royalism that gained him the Surveyorship of the King's Works in 1689 rather than architectural experience. Wren remained in office over five reigns before being dismissed in 1718.

Wren's office was at Whitehall and from there he not only managed royal domestic building projects but oversaw the rebuilding of the City parish churches, St Paul's Cathedral, two royal hospitals, and work at Westminster Abbey and at the universities of Oxford and Cambridge, as well as miscellaneous private commissions. His office was a mix of medieval and modern: part mason's lodge, part architect's studio. Over thirty years he employed a large number of assistants to help draw and design details, but he took overall responsibility – and credit – for the output himself. The men who assisted him both as draughtsmen and as master craftsmen were mostly employed by the Office, and had their own architectural careers, spreading ideas much more widely. From the 1680s Wren undertook less of the detailed design work himself, providing sketches to the most brilliant of his protégés, Nicholas Hawksmoor.[27]

Fig. 252 (above) The Royal Hospital for Seamen, Greenwich. Begun in 1696 by Sir Christopher Wren, Nicholas Hawksmoor played a significant rolein developing the design. It incorporated the King Charles block on the right (fig. 234) and the Queen's House centre. After Wren's death in 1723 work continued until 1751 under various Office of Works architects.

Most of the work of the Office was in the repair and maintenance of existing buildings, but there were new commissions, some of which were of great importance. Wren's pragmatic and empirical approach to design form was a reflection of functional demands rather than aesthetic dogma. The engineering of complex and challenging buildings such as the Sheldonian Theatre or St Paul's Cathedral drove aesthetics, rather than the other way round. He absorbed influences from the Netherlands, France and Italy, and, of course, from ancient buildings; but his work was deeply rooted in native tradition, serving a monarchy that was conservative and old fashioned.[28] As Royal Surveyor, not one of the great schemes he designed for the monarchy was fully realised, with either the death of his patron or the drying-up of financing preventing his vision from being realised.

Two buildings came close to completion: a massive new palace for Charles II at Winchester, which was roofed but never fitted out, and the new royal apartments at Hampton Court. It is at Hampton Court alone that Wren's attempt to give the British monarchy a new architectural face can still be seen. Several hands may be present in the design, and it is possible that Wren's preference for more animated and busy elevations was overruled and a much more austere building eventually constructed. From the gardens the apartments look long, low and a bit unyielding, but closer to, the enlivening Portland stone dressings against the finely jointed brick give a pleasing effect. This was a palace in the grand manner, the lodgings of Henry VIII re-cast for the late 17th century. As such, they were in many ways the end of a tradition rather than the start of a new one. Wren's Hampton Court didn't really find favour, and the court abandoned it after 1737.[29]

Up until the Civil War most royal palaces dated back to the reign of Henry VIII and, although their interior decoration had been modernised, their plans reflected court etiquette prevailing in the 1530s. The exception was Somerset House, which had been assigned to the Stuart queens. Here, removed from the stuffy formality of the monarch's residence, Charles I's French queen, Henrietta Maria, began to introduce French fashions and customs into her household. At the Restoration the dowager queen returned to Somerset House and commissioned John Webb to remodel her principal lodgings on the south front (fig. 253). These rooms were designed to facilitate an occasion called the circle, a social gathering in which the queen mother, the king and Duke of York could mingle more informally with their courtiers. The circle became, in the early part of Charles II's reign, the principal court event of the week.

After the death of Henrietta Maria and during the reigns of Charles II and James II the circle was held in the queen's drawing room and became known simply as 'a drawing room'. This social gathering was the most important court event of the 18th century. As a consequence, when Wren designed the new Hampton Court for William and Mary the queen's drawing room was the largest room of state in the palace. It occupied a central position on the east front, with a huge stone frontispiece emphasising its significance. Just as the Restoration saw the architectural formalisation of the circle as a dominant drawing room, so it saw the introduction – by Charles II – of formal French bedroom etiquette. The Tudor royal bedroom had been the most private of rooms, quite unlike the French royal bedchamber, which was the principal formal room of reception. Charles II, in exile, was familiar

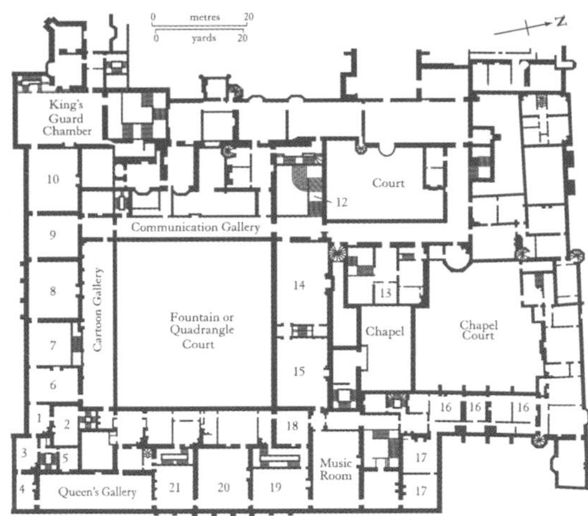

Fig. 253 (above) Somerset House, the Strand, London, from the river, by Leonard Knyff and Jan Kipp, 1707. This view shows the block built in 1660–2 by Henrietta Maria in the centre of the front, raised up on great arches. This contained her new presence and privy chambers, approached by a magnificent great stair.

Fig. 254 (above right) Plan of first floor of Hampton Court in the early 18th century. (1) King's little bedchamber (2) King's gentlemen of the bedchamber (3) closet (4) closet (Queen Mary) (5) King's back stair (6) King's Great bedchamber (7) King's withdrawing room (8) King's privy chamber (9) King's eating room (10) King's presence chamber (11) King's great stair (12) Queen's stair (13) Royal pew (14) Prince's guard chamber (15) Prince's presence chamber (16) Rooms occupied by the young princesses (17) Rooms occupied by the Prince of Wales (18) Oratory (19) Prince's privy chamber (20) Prince's drawing room (21) Prince's bedchamber.

with French bedroom usage and decoration, and immediately on his return rebuilt the Whitehall bedchamber with a deep bed alcove, a rail and French decorations to enable him to adopt a formal *levée* (waking-up ceremony) and *coucher* (bedtime ceremony) at court.

The plan of the first floor of Hampton Court reflects these developments (fig. 254). On the king's side the guard and presence chambers were essentially antechambers to the withdrawing room, which became the most accessible of the rooms of state. The great bedchamber beyond was a formal reception room and next to it was a lesser bedchamber in which the king could sleep in comfort. Beyond that was the closet – the king's study – which was originally intended to interlink with the queen's closet next door.[30]

These changes to the layout and decoration of the royal palaces influenced the social behaviour of the aristocracy, and eventually that of the gentry. In the grandest houses bedchambers became rooms of state; as at Hampton Court, they were approached by anterooms, with a closet at the other end. This triumvirate became known, in due course, as the state apartment, French terminology replacing the age-old English term 'lodging'. An early and surviving example of such apartments is at Ham House, Surrey, adapted for Charles II's friend and Secretary of State for Scotland, the Duke of Lauderdale, between 1672 and 1674. Here on the ground floor were symmetrical apartments for the duke and duchess on either side of a central and shared dining room (fig. 255). On the first floor another tripartite apartment was reserved for the queen.[31] Ham was a relatively modest suburban villa but in country palaces the arrangement could be extended. In *c.*1678 Robert Hooke designed Ragley Hall, Warwickshire, for Charles II's Secretary of State Lord Conway; there, on the ground floor, were four separate apartments entered from the hall or dining room. Gargantuan in scale, larger even than most royal palaces, was Blenheim Palace, Oxfordshire, designed by Vanbrugh for the Duke of Marlborough between 1705 and 1716. Here, off a central dining room, or 'saloon', as it was known, were astonishingly grand apartments fit for a national hero. This formal way of planning remained at the heart of country-house design until the 1720s.

The interiors of both royal and aristocratic palaces were created by upholsterers, who were essentially interior decorators and had – by 1600, at least – gained a distinct role in the decoration of grand houses. Long before then matching sets of furniture and hangings had been deployed in important rooms, especially bedchambers, but the 17th century saw a significant widening in the influence and control of upholsterers. Their rise coincided with the increasing use of easel paintings in interiors, coming to replace tapestry as the principal portable decoration in some rooms. Paintings were placed on silk wall hangings that were hung loose like a tapestry (fig. 256). The choice of material and colour was carefully considered to set off the paintings chosen. Matching curtains, covers to seat furniture and beds created a rich and harmonious appearance – and an expensive one. The damasks and velvets used were very valuable, always more expensive than the furniture, and often more than paintings. As in previous centuries plate retained its key role; silver and silver-gilt wall sconces, mirrors, chandeliers, candlesticks, wine coolers, toilet services and even furniture were put in the important rooms. Furniture was still of secondary importance, although after the Restoration new types appeared and walnut replaced oak as the most desirable timber. The biggest advance was the abandonment of the cushion and the integration of padding onto the wooden frame itself. This led to more comfortable pieces being made, such as day beds, easy chairs with wings and eventually, around 1700, sofas.[32]

As in royal palaces, apartments in aristocratic houses were serviced by back stairs that allowed servants to make fires and empty chamber pots without using the principal staircase. This was part of a general reduction in the visibility of servants within aristocratic houses; they no longer dined in the hall but had their own dining hall out of sight, normally in the basement (fig. 257). Kitchens were increasingly banished from the main house and sometimes located in a linked pavilion. Whilst this reflected an increased desire for privacy, it also denoted a structural change in society. Lower servants were no longer quasi-military retainers and upper ones no longer sought protection and social advancement. The bond between master and servant had loosened and changed; indeed, the household as an integrated social unit was being replaced as the key institution in society by a plethora of other bodies: grammar schools, law courts, universities, the army and the navy. The socially ambitious could now find their way in the world independently of the great houses of the aristocracy, and domestic servants became straightforward employees.

We have seen that hunting rather than horticulture dominated the setting of medieval houses and that cultivated gardens were disposed in walled compartments close by. This broadly remained the case through the 17th century, although the style of gardening changed. Whilst gardens were influenced by fashions from France and Italy there was a marked preference for fine turf in English designs. The royal gardens at Somerset House and Hampton Court in Charles I's reign comprised grass plots containing statues raised up on pedestals. Bowling greens with the finest turf were laid out close to houses for sport and aesthetic effect.

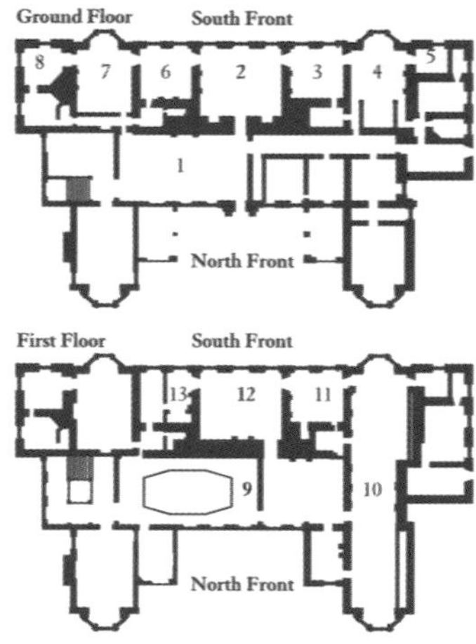

Fig. 255 (above) Ham House, Petersham; the most perfect surviving courtier house of the late 17th century. On the ground floor neatly symmetrical suites, or apartments, to give them their new name, lay on either side of a dining room. Above, approached by a fine gallery, was a suite reserved for the queen. (1) Great hall (2) Marble dining room (3) Duke's dressing room (4) Duchess's bedchamber (5) Duke's closet (6) Withdrawing room (7) The Volury (Duchess's former bedchamber) (8) Closet (9) Round gallery (10) Long gallery (11) Queen's antechamber (12) Queen's bedchamber (13) Queen's closet.

Fig. 256 (left) Ham House, Petersham; the queen's closet. Superb woodwork and an early example of scagliola (stucco painted to look like marble) on the fireplace make this room one of the best interiors of its date in England, especially as it has its original furniture, including two fashionable upholstered chairs.

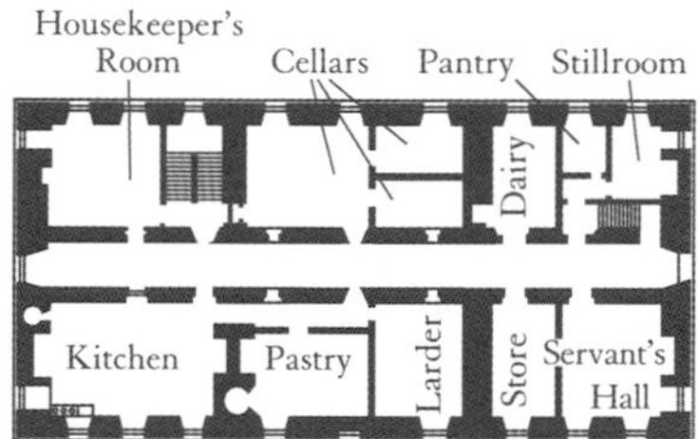

Fig. 257 (above) Coleshill House, Berkshire (fig. 226); plan of the basement in the 1660s. This was one of the first houses in England to have a separate servants' hall in the basement, freeing the room above to become a polite reception space. All the other rooms necessary to service the house were ingeniously planned and linked to the upper floors by back staircases.

Fig. 258 (above) Chatsworth House and gardens, Derbyshire, by Leonard Knyff and Jan Kipp, 1707. This was the most ambitious and perfect geometrical garden of its age. Started in 1688, the landscape blended grass, hedging, trees, beds, paths, statuary, ironwork and above all water into a tight and controlled whole centring on the house.

The Restoration brought, however, an admiration for aspects of French garden design, especially the gardens at Versailles, so Charles II employed André Le Nôtre, Louis XIV's garden designer, to lay out St James's Park with great formal avenues and a long canal. French garden features, particularly the avenue, were assimilated into English gardens throughout Charles II's reign. For instance, when Anthony Grey, Earl of Kent, had his house at Wrest Park, Bedfordshire, remodelled in 1672, a huge canal was dug, aligned on the south front. At Chatsworth the architect William Talman and his gardener George London created the most remarkable garden of the age. Largely inspired by French practice, jets of water, a cascade, a canal and parterres combine with statuary and great iron screens in a grid of paths and compartments around the house (fig. 258).[33]

When they came to the throne in 1688 William and Mary were already the great gardeners of Europe and were to build, at Hampton Court, England's largest formal landscape. It is not possible to simply categorise this garden as French, Dutch or English, for it drew on native preferences and combined them with ideas from Holland and France to create a distinctive English rendering of a formal landscape. Its formality and geometry, however, fundamentally derived from France, setting Hampton Court in a matrix of avenues and compartments in the same way as Versailles.[34]

William and Mary's gardens were not only about geometrical frameworks; they also showcased plantsmanship. The parterres of Chatsworth and Hampton Court were planted out so that people could appreciate individual specimens. At Hampton Court William and Mary gathered together a remarkable collection of rare and exotic plants, some from the East Indies. These were propagated and grown in glasshouses designed by their Dutch carpenter. In addition there were two orangeries, one integrated into the ground floor of the south front and separated from the king's bedroom by only one room. In *c.*1700 a second orangery, by William Talman, was erected to house orange trees over the winter.[35]

During the period up to the 1750s the vogue for formal gardens remained, although changes from around 1700 softened their impact, simplifying layouts and making them more English. The invention of the ha-ha (a sunken ditch with a steep retaining wall) in 1708 enabled walls to be removed whilst still keeping beasts out. This meant that compartments could be broken down; the north gardens at Chiswick House (pp 321–2), for example, were unwalled in 1718. Parterres were hugely simplified, the clipped evergreens of William and Mary's time were abandoned, and there was a return to English grass plots. The most important development, however, was the creation of woodland gardens and plantations disposed between gravel paths. These woods contained rooms or cabinets, and spaces of a variety of shapes. Henry Grey, Duke of Kent, created a huge woodland garden on either side of the canal that his father had dug at Wrest Park. As first built, long, straight rides gave access to hedged clearings, each of a different shape, many of which contained buildings, creating surprise and variety. The greatest was a stone pavilion of 1709–11 with alternating concave and straight sides, designed by Thomas Archer and sited at the end on the long canal. Wrest Park today shows, like nowhere else, this last phase of formal gardening (fig. 259).[36]

Fig. 259 (above) Wrest Park, Bedfordshire; the pavilion by Thomas Archer, 1709–11. A rigidly geometrical composition perfectly reflected in the long water, the pavilion pre-dates the Radcliffe Camera (fig. 236), and has some affinities with it. Designed for lunch and supper parties, the main room is painted in a rich Roman style by Louis Hauduroy.

The Army and Navy

The Restoration was an important turning point for the army and the navy. For the first time since the Romans England had a standing army, and for the first time ever parliament invested meaningfully in the navy between wars, and not just during them. These facts had some significant architectural consequences.

After the Restoration there were three departments of state responsible for building: the Office of Works, the Navy Board and the Board of Ordnance. Between 1640 and 1760 they commissioned more major individual buildings than all of England's private owners put together; the Office of Works built and maintained royal residences, the Board of Ordnance fortresses and barracks, and the Navy Board royal dockyards. The designers who worked for the Ordnance and Navy Boards are often anonymous, although men such as Sir Bernard de Gomme, Edmund Dummer and Andrew Jelfe were clearly men of talent on a par with their more famous contemporaries in the Office of Works.

The Board of Ordnance was responsible for supplying guns and ammunition to the navy from its operational headquarters in the Tower of London, which remained England's principal arsenal. As arms and munitions were given up after the republic a large new storehouse was constructed on the east side of the Tower to accommodate them. This imposing red-brick structure, completed in 1664, was a radical building in both function and form (fig. 260). Of two storeys, with attics lit by dormers, this U-shaped building with hipped roofs was completed the year Clarendon House was begun (p. 260). It demonstrates that Pratt had no monopoly on the new style and that at the Restoration this was the universal language of architectural prestige.[37]

The Restoration monarchy, however, was principally concerned with coastal fortification, as commercial rivalry with the Dutch had sparked a series of naval wars of varying intensity. The utterly humiliating Dutch raid on the Medway in 1667 resulted in the sacking of the fort at Sheerness, leaving Chatham completely exposed. This miserable event reinforced Charles II's determination to modernise England's outdated coastal fortifications. England was no stranger to the bastion system of fortification developed during the 16th century. This had been developed and perfected by the French and the Dutch through long-drawn-out continental wars, and was used by both sides in the English Civil War. Prince Rupert had brought to England Bernard de Gomme, a talented military engineer who masterminded the defences at Oxford, amongst other places. At the Restoration de Gomme became the king's favoured engineer and eventually the Surveyor General of the Ordnance.

Fortifying Plymouth during the Second Dutch War was de Gomme's first task, the most important component of which was rebuilding the citadel, creating an enceinte – or ring – of bastions and a ditch. The work was expensive, over £20,000 in all, and was as much about prestige as power. De Gomme's main gate, decorated by the mason Nicholas Abraham, speaks of Charles II's military ambitions for the place (fig. 261). But de Gomme's masterpiece was Tilbury Fort, Essex, begun in 1670 as the first line of defence for London at the point where the Thames narrows to only 800 yards. Based on an irregular pentagon, the fort protected and serviced fourteen revetted gun positions overlooking the river; seen from the air the mathematical and geometrical principles that underlay 17th-century fortification are revealed, every face being protected by another (fig. 262).[38]

Fig. 260 (right) The New Storehouse (New Armouries), Tower of London, 1664. Built at the same time as Clarendon House (fig. 230), this building was a radical new look. The sash windows are later.

Fig. 261 (above) The Citadel, Plymouth, Devon; the portal, 1670. This was designed as a triumphant entrance to Charles II's fortress. Ionic pilasters support an attic carved by a segmented pediment enclosing the royal arms. Much of the carving was originally gilded.

Fig. 262 (above left) Tilbury Fort, Essex, designed by Sir Bernard De Gomme, 1670–6. The original entrance is in the north (foreground) across a series of causeways, bridges and moats. The ring of moats were controlled by sluices so that in winter they could be emptied to prevent attackers crossing over ice.

After William III's accession in 1688 England aligned with the Dutch and other northern powers against France, a policy that was effectively to last for a century and a half. Two wars (the Grand Alliance of 1689–97 and the Spanish Succession of 1702–13) concentrated military efforts on the continent. The need for ordnance grew and in 1688 work commenced on a second storehouse at the Tower. This, the Grand Storehouse, was destroyed by fire in 1841. A colossal 360ft long and 60ft wide, and of three storeys, it was built of brick with stone dressings. The windows were big and round-headed, and there was a stone portico and a richly sculpted pediment crowned by a spindly cupola.[39] The Grand Storehouse was the first of a series of large military buildings designed by – or for – naval or Ordnance engineers, who looked for inspiration to public buildings such as the Bethlem and Chelsea hospitals. Indeed, the storehouse was a public building. Visitors were encouraged to come and admire the architecture and its contents – display was as important as storage.

After 1714 the Board of Ordnance underwent fundamental change, moving away from fortification in favour of garrison and industrial buildings. This was largely a result of the failed Jacobite rebellion of 1715, which gave rise to fears of civil war, and of the appointment of the Duke of Marlborough as Master-General of the Ordnance, who used his powerful reputation and contacts to ensure that the Board properly supported the army. He appointed Michael Richards as Surveyor-General of the Ordnance, responsible for the design of new buildings. Richards was a talented engineer who had become Chief Engineer of Great Britain in 1711, and who found himself in the hot seat after 1715 as the Board embarked on nearly a decade of building on a grand scale. Like the Office of Works under Wren, the Ordnance Board had a drawing office; here, at the Tower of London, they had a drawing master, John Fayrem, who presumably was responsible for the very high standards of draughtsmanship they achieved. Between 1718 and 1719 Andrew Jelfe was appointed architect to the Board, taking responsibility for one of the busiest periods in the Board's history, particularly as under the reforms of 1717–18 the Ordnance also had responsibility for the design and construction of garrison buildings.[40]

The standing army, established in 1660, grew rapidly. By 1685 it numbered 8,820 men, but with the outbreak of war with France numbers soared – in 1689 there were over 93,000 in arms. In 1689 the Bill of Rights effectively removed the monarch from a position of control and placed the army under parliament, transforming it from a royal tool into a national institution. But it was an institution with a problem because although troops could be mostly housed in the great manned fortresses such as Portsmouth or Dover, in wartime the majority of infantry had to be billeted in towns and villages. The Mutiny Act of 1689 made it illegal to quarter any soldier on a private citizen and so there was a great urgency to provide accommodation.[41]

The first permanent barracks were built at Horseguards between 1663 and 1664 (p. 261), but the term 'barracks' was not used to describe a building until 1667, when it was applied to timber-framed military houses at the Tower of London. By the time barracks were built at Tilbury Fort in *c.*1680, the building type had acquired a fixed pattern. The Tilbury barracks were designed for two companies of foot soldiers (one hundred and twenty men) and are a long, double-depth range of ten bays. Each room slept four in two beds and had a fireplace, a door to the outside and a window.[42] The accession of William and Mary created the Jacobite threat, especially in Scotland, and in response the most extensive and impressive set of English barracks of the early 18th century were built at Berwick-upon-Tweed in 1717. Nicholas Hawksmoor seems to have provided an initial design but the supervising architect was the Board's engineer, Captain Thomas Phillips. The language was similar to that used at Chatham and the Tower, with round-headed windows giving a military air.[43]

The most important task undertaken by the Board in the early 18th century was the creation of Woolwich Arsenal. Although the Office of the Ordnance had been active there for many years, after 1716 it became the home of a state-owned bronze-gun manufactory of great architectural presence and significance. The first building was the Royal Brass Foundry of 1716–17, designed by Michael Richards for the manufacture of guns. He had few models to follow for a large factory and so the building was essentially a timber-framed aisled barn with a brick front, containing a horse-powered machine for perfecting gun barrels. From the outside there was no doubt that this was a new type of building; the square central pavilion, with a hipped roof crowned by a lantern, was fronted by a colossal rusticated doorway of brick and stone surmounted with a huge coat of arms. Out of this came the cannons for the army and the navy.

Nearby Richards built the Great Pile, an evocatively named store yard containing warehouses for naval and army gun carriages. The Great Pile was entered through a low screen of buildings and a massive gateway, flanked by brick pylons, topped with mock machicolations and crowned with piles of shot. Looming up behind was the great warehouse, with a high ground floor and attic. The ends were given emphasis by framing the last two bays with pilasters; the centre broke through the roofline with a giant order and pediment enclosing a mighty arch, within which the central door was set. The third important building was not an industrial site but an administrative centre, containing a board room and training academy for artillery and engineer officers. Once more with a bold centrepiece, it was flanked with round-headed windows and the upper parts with circular windows that helped light double-height spaces within (fig. 263). This group of buildings, although

Fig. 263 (above) The Royal Military Academy, Woolwich, Michael Richards, 1718–23. The building contained a board room and a large school room for training young officers. The design is bold and powerful and confidently handles classical elements rendered in homogenous brown brick, creating a stone-like monumentality.

within a secure military compound, was a showpiece of military technology, engineering and design, and would have an impact on the growing language of industrial design over the following hundred years.[44]

From the 1650s the job that the navy was required to do had started to change. Rather than simply being used for seasonal operations, the fleet was increasingly kept at sea all year round and the navy was gradually to acquire bases all over the world to make this possible. In England extensive on-shore facilities were constructed, including ordnance yards, gunpowder magazines and victualling yards, as well as docks and facilities for construction and repair. The first naval bases were on the Thames and the Medway but during the 18th century Britain's commercial – and therefore strategic – interests moved westwards. Thus Portsmouth and Plymouth rose in importance, becoming the principal bases for the fleet. This fleet was vital to the economy, security and mentality of the English nation.[45]

From the Restoration the navy came to symbolise English political and religious liberty, although it was not for another half-century that William Pitt the Elder translated image into reality. This reality, whilst relying on fine ships and modern tactics, was founded on the excellence of naval administration. In this its naval bases were the key. The Navy and Ordnance boards had their own surveyors who were responsible for design but much of the building work was contracted out to big building firms, often from London.

The outbreak of war in 1689 led to a massive shipbuilding programme. In twenty-five years the royal dockyards built one hundred and fifty-nine ships of the line and one hundred and thirteen cruisers and this, together with the need to keep them at sea, led to the construction of a new base at Plymouth. Responsibility for this fell to Edmund Dummer, Surveyor of the Navy from 1692 to 1699. Work began on a grand scale and was to cost £67,000 by 1700. The yard was laid out with an eye to efficiency of operation and aesthetic impact, with a magnificent residential terrace at the highest point. In its centre was a residence for the Commissioner of the Dockyard and at either end blocks with pediments. Dummer was no isolated figure – he knew Wren and Hook – and his design was strongly influenced by both the Chelsea and Bethlem hospitals, but translated into a domestic form. A stone dry dock, also designed by Dummer, was the technological centrepiece of the yard. All previous dry docks had been made of timber, but Dummer's new dock had stone-stepped sides, providing better access, and twin gates angled outwards that were better able to resist water pressure.[46]

The royal dockyards were major centres of manufacture, importing raw materials from across the nation and the globe. Many activities were undertaken in straightforward buildings with timber frames and clapboard walls, but the scale of the structures needed for making full-size templates – or moulds – of ship components, sails and masts was huge. A surviving mould loft at Chatham with a mast house beneath was built in 1753, providing a space 55ft by 120ft that was used to lay out, amongst others, the lines of HMS Victory. Below, shipwrights worked on masts up to 100ft long that had been kept supple in nearby mast ponds.

The engine house of the navy was the roperies. The rigging of a third-rate ship of the line at the time of Trafalgar used some 70,000ft of rope, which needed regular replacement. For ropes to be really useful they had to be unspliced and twisted in a single length from bales of imported hemp. The first rope house was built in Woolwich in 1612, and brick roperies were subsequently established at Portsmouth and Plymouth, where a new pair of spinning and laying houses 1,200ft long was integrated into the plan in 1763.

By 1700 the older dockyards were cramped and chaotic, their storehouses old-fashioned and inconvenient with small staircases and narrow doors. In 1717 the Navy Board commissioned a new type of storehouse in Chatham. This was the three-storey cordage house, 194ft long and 35ft wide, built on a brick fire-proof vault. Like the 1664 Ordnance store at the Tower, it had wide doors, integral cranes and an undivided internal space. This provided a model for others to follow, although improvements continued to be made: the Ordnance Board's Morice Yard storehouse at Plymouth contained, in 1724, wooden railways for ease of moving goods.[47]

The contribution to English building made by the Navy and Ordnance boards should not be underestimated. During the early 18th century the boards developed a series of standardised designs for military buildings which, though they varied in decoration and size, were, in terms of planning and construction, alike. These supported huge, highly organised, industrial processes employing tens of thousands of men. Architecturally, designers were breaking new ground by inventing new types of building for new processes. They also were creating an architectural language for industry, one that would prove influential as the century progressed.

Even before the future Charles II went into exile in France and the Low Countries, French design had been highly fashionable in England. From the mid 1640s the magnetic power of Louis XIV's court exercised a fascination on English architects and designers. As part of a wider programme to stimulate and control the arts and the sciences Louis founded the Académie royale d'architecture in 1671, under the direction of the mathematician and engineer François Blondel. This helped establish France as the leading architectural force in Europe. England was a far less centralised state, and although the reign of Charles II did see the establishment of a number of royal academies – or societies – there was never one for architecture.

Yet after the Civil War the institutions of state devoted to architectural design were hugely strengthened. The Navy, Ordnance and Works boards wrought an enormous change in English architecture. Under men such as Michael Richards, Sir Bernard de Gomme, Edmund Dummer and Sir Christopher Wren England effectively obtained its royal academy of architecture; it was in the service (or the orbit) of the Crown that all the most important designers worked. In the drawing offices of the three boards two generations of engineers and architects were trained by these great masters. Architects, engineers, master craftsmen and contractors working on state-funded schemes became the most important agents of stylistic and technical dissemination, a situation that persisted well into the 1730s.

In terms of architectural style the Civil War was a dislocation, not a fracture, and much of what emerged as distinctive at the Restoration had roots that can be traced back to the 1620s and 30s. Stylistically, the century after 1630 saw another of England's pendulum-like swings from austerity to exuberance. The elegant stripped architecture developed before the Civil War that matured at the Restoration was, from the 1680s, transformed into one of England's most original and exciting architectural periods. Vanbrugh, Hawksmoor, Richards and a dozen lesser architects gave vent to dazzling invention, playing – often with great confidence and wit – with the elements of classical design.

On another front the Civil War accelerated some profound changes. The household began to disintegrate as the backbone of society, and although the great country houses lived on, if anything increasing in their formality and size, many fewer were built. Public buildings became much more important and the growth of the organs of central government, especially the army and the navy, created new building types. Meanwhile, the Great Fire made a huge contribution to the development of domestic building, establishing in its rows and squares a vernacular urban language that would dominate English towns and cities for two centuries.

9— Property, Commerce and Consensus

—1720-1760

More than a thousand years after the capital of Saxon England could be seen as Rome, in the reign of George I the cultural centre of the nation was visibly and intellectually once again the same place.

Introduction

Between 1714 and 1760 Britain was ruled by two monarchs whom nobody much loved and by an oligarchical system of government that, for a short time, was perfectly suited to its needs. The reigns of George I and George II were politically dominated by the Whigs, aristocratic property owners whose political beliefs rested on the assumption that property qualified men for full citizenship. It was a period of relative stability compared with the turmoil that had prevailed, to a greater or lesser degree, from the 1630s. Despite the threat of Jacobite insurrection, by the mid 1720s a sense of consensus had developed in politics, foreign policy, religion, literature and architecture. As political differences were resolved and economic interests converged, England acquired a governing elite who shared values of common sense, restraint, enterprise and a belief in progress that co-existed with a sort of insular self-satisfaction.[1]

Both houses of parliament were dominated by landowners, even if it were not for a property-owing qualification for all MPs, at least a fifth of them were the younger sons of peers. Property was king. Yet it was not a great age for country-house building, though some were built; it was the age of the towns, particularly London, where phenomenal numbers of houses were built, many for the well-off.[2] By 1715 parliament sat every year from mid January to May, bringing the political classes and the cream of society to the capital; London's importance in the nation grew and the influence of what happened there became more pronounced.

Commercial activity expanded; between 1714 and 1760 the tonnage of shipping increased by around a third, the value of exports increased by 80 per cent and the value of re-exports doubled. Mercantile wealth significantly increased, not only in London but also in provincial ports. When wars were fought they were thus over trade, for a share of the world's raw materials, markets and trade routes; in peacetime these rivalries continued but by economic means. Through these offices, and others, Britain pursued wealth, creating an increasingly consumerised society. The producers and consumers of much of this prosperity were the middle strata of society: merchants, shopkeepers, lawyers, farmers and small-scale manufacturers. These people were the most dynamic elements in English society, and many lived in towns.

Some clergy denounced the materialism of such people but the consumers were perfectly able to live with a notion of a godly society. Out of the 17th century came the strong conviction that England was a Protestant nation favoured by God, a uniquely free and favoured state, unlike the oppressed and downtrodden Catholic nations of Europe. This Protestantism embraced all the varieties of Anglicanism, as well as Nonconformism.[3]

Polite Taste

In the years around 1714 the sense of drama, richness of silhouette and surface decoration that had been so admired at the turn of the century started to become less fashionable, and designers began to give greater emphasis to a faithful and precedent-based rendition of classical architecture, based on printed sources. This mood was reinforced by the preferences of the new ruler George I, who, in his native Hanover, had promoted a style of architecture inspired by the buildings of the Veneto.

In the same years three books were published that, between them, provided inspiration for architects for nearly a century. Their genesis lay in an intense cut-throat rivalry between print sellers and architects promoting their own wares. Giacomo Leoni produced, with George's approval, the first English version of Andrea Palladio's *I quattro libri dell'architettura* (1715–20). This book was not a facsimile; indeed, Leoni considered it as an original work of his own. It abandoned the crude woodcuts of the original and reproduced the designs – with Leoni's enhancements – as engravings. Palladio's orders and almost all his villa designs were modified to suit English tastes, with Leoni adding pediments and domes, making buildings grander and richer than the originals.

Leoni's book was announced in April 1715 just as another ambitious architectural publishing project was gaining momentum. This was a compendium of views of the most important country houses in England to be published under the title *Vitruvius Britannicus*. Conceived by a group of print sellers in the swell of national confidence following the Treaty of Utrecht, the book is a celebration of English architecture and architects in the manner of earlier French publications. The man commissioned to undertake the draughtsmanship was Colen Campbell, an ambitious young Scottish architect newly arrived in London. The announcement of Leoni's Palladio alarmed the backers of *Vitruvius Britannicus*. In order to ensure that their book was not made to look old-fashioned they commissioned Campbell to write an introduction condemning modern Italian architecture (and thus Leoni), and eulogising Palladio and his English admirer, Inigo Jones. Campbell was also asked to add a number of new designs in his own hand demonstrating the principles of the Palladian style.

The one contemporary architect whose work was not included in *Vitruvius Britannicus* was another rival, James Gibbs. A Catholic Tory from Aberdeen, Gibbs had actually travelled to Rome, unlike Campbell, and had learnt the art of architecture from Carlo Fontana, one of the Italian architects condemned in Campbell's introduction. Gibbs had briefly been on the Commission for Building New Churches (pp 304–5) and had designed St Mary le Strand, a highly visible and much-admired public building. This led to Gibbs becoming the most successful and sought-after country-house architect in the 1720s and early 30s. The direct effect of Gibbs's exclusion from the three volumes of *Vitruvius Britannicus* was the publication of his own book of designs, *A Book of Architecture*, in 1728. This was the most influential and important English book on architecture of the whole 18th century, and the first by a living Briton of his own designs. The book was intended to provide inspiration for those who had not access to the leading architects of London, and as well as engravings of his completed works contained un-built designs for whole buildings, as well as details. It was expensive, at four guineas, and soon thirty-three of his designs were plagiarised by Batty Langley at the price of a shilling. Gibbs followed up his success with *Rules for Drawing the Several Parts of Architecture* in 1732, a practical manual designed to help people who wanted to use the four orders correctly. In practice, scaling up the correct proportions from Palladio's four books, or even Leoni's version of them, was difficult. Gibbs's idea was to invent a simple proportional system that avoided the use of fractions. It was instantly successful and instantly plagiarised. Langley and others incorporated his system into their manuals, disseminating it all over the country.[4] The direct influence of these publications can easily be seen during a perambulation around any mid-Georgian town (fig. 264). Door cases, in particular, were often exactly copied from pattern books, as were the more adventurous window configurations.[5]

The proportional, rational and text-based nature of the new classicism meant that it was possible to master the system and produce a building that was fashionable and handsome without complex training. It also meant that patrons could unmask charlatans who couldn't get it right. As will become clear, these facts opened the practice of building to a wide number of lesser and provincial practitioners and speculative developers. At the same time, however, it inhibited the freedom of craftsmen to make a distinctive contribution to the design. Inventiveness and individualism were replaced by l oyalty to the canon. By the end of the century English craftsmen were subservient to architects and designers dependent on them for moulds and drawings of each detail.

In addition to new streams of printed inspiration there were fundamental changes in the Office of Works. In 1712 Wren turned eighty and the office over which he presided was seen as inefficient and corrupt. It was doubted that the old man was really capable of managing expenditure of some £40,000 a year in addition to all of his other duties. In 1718 Wren was eventually dismissed and replaced by William Benson, a gentleman architect who had worked for George I in Hanover. Inspired by the work of Jones, Benson had designed Wilbury House, Wiltshire, for himself in 1710 and was an enthusiastic proponent of a more rigorous use of the orders. But Benson had neither the diplomatic nor the technical skills to perform the onerous job of Surveyor of Works, and his reign ended in disgrace in July 1719. His Surveyorship was, however,

Fig. 264 (above) Example of a Georgian Doric door case, copied from a pattern book, possibly William Palin's *Practical House Carpenter*, 1789.

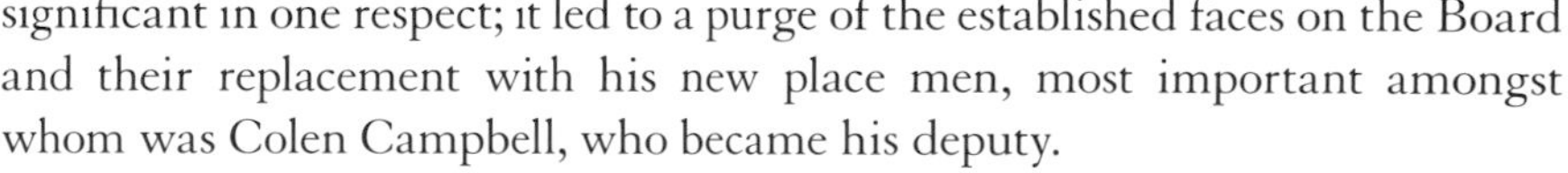

Fig. 265 (above) Christ Church College, Oxford; the Peckwater Quad, designed by Dean Aldrich in 1707–14. The elevations were modelled on Italian palazzo style and repeated three times round the quadrangle. The effect was extremely grand, and anticipated developments in urban housing in Bath (fig. 288) by more than a decade.

Fig. 266 (below) Wanstead House, Essex, 1714–20; the house was demolished in 1822 but was by far the most influential country house of its age. The façade was 260ft long and was divided into three, with a large central portico. This was no ornamental addition – the roof behind the pediment ran across the depth of the house and inside was a great Corinthian hall. Wanstead was the most Roman house yet built in England.

significant in one respect; it led to a purge of the established faces on the Board and their replacement with his new place men, most important amongst whom was Colen Campbell, who became his deputy.

Campbell was not the first architect to experiment with a stricter interpretation of classical architecture. Vanbrugh and Hawksmoor had both shown a strong interest (fig. 275), and so too had Dean Aldrich at Christ Church College, Oxford. Between 1707 and 1714 Aldrich had designed a new quadrangle to appeal to the young aristocratic men then coming up to Oxford. The influence of Jones was again strongly felt, and with its rusticated basement pedimented windows and Ionic pilasters, it was a serious and academic essay in classicism (fig. 265).

The Peckwater Quad was in Oxford, but Campbell's first commissions were in and around London. Through his position in the Office of Works he found powerful patrons at court, the first of whom was Richard Boyle, Earl of Burlington, whose town house on Piccadilly he remodelled (p. 315). Campbell went on to design a series of country houses, the first and largest of which was for Sir Richard Child at Wanstead, Essex (*c.*1714–20). The house comprised a central block, with a giant Corinthian portico approached by stairs that doubled back on themselves. Either side were austere ranges given rhythm and proportion by their windows (fig. 266). Wanstead was to exert an influence on a number of country houses built later in the century.

Campbell's early influence was eclipsed by that of his first patron, Lord Burlington. One can hardly call a super-rich aristocrat such as Burlington a gentlemen architect yet that is exactly what he became. His first mentor was Campbell, but very quickly Burlington's superior intellect, wealth and social position put him in advance of his tutor. His architectural views were refined by serious-minded study of ancient buildings first hand, and the purchase of a

cache of drawings by Palladio and Jones. From the start Burlington's buildings show a determination to be as faithful to Roman precedents as possible and his sources were by no means restricted to the works of Palladio. Indeed, his villa at Chiswick, built in around 1726, was designed with barely a reference to him, the majority of details being gleaned directly from ancient buildings or from Scamozzi (fig. 267). This was Burlington's attempt to visualise the sort of house that a Roman general or senator might have lived in outside Rome.[6]

Fig. 267 (above left) Chiswick House, London now stands as an isolated jewel, but as first built it was linked (on the right hand side) to Lord Burlington's adjoining Jacobean mansion. This was an architectural laboratory; a place where Burlington developed his ideas on Roman architecture. It was like an apprentice's model, miniature in size and details but perfect in execution.

Burlington became almost evangelical about changing architectural taste towards a much purer interpretation of Roman architecture. After the dismissal of Benson he was able to enlist the Office of Works in this mission by exercising his patronage through the Surveyor, his friend Richard Arundel. Between them they packed the Office with Burlington's approved designers: Thomas Ripley, William Kent, Henry Flitcroft, Isaac Ware, John Vardy, Roger Morris and others. Burlington's style developed in and around London, and for fifteen years was best seen in suburban villas, such as the exquisite Marble Hill House, Twickenham, built for Henrietta Howard, mistress to George II, between 1724 and 1729. Its north façade is divided into three parts, the central portion raised on a rusticated basement supporting a giant Ionic order. This was designed by Roger Morris, perhaps with advice from Campbell (fig. 268). Its great room on the first floor is the most beautiful of the 18th century in suburban London.[7]

From the 1730s a consensus began to emerge and public buildings soon followed. The York Assembly Rooms of 1731–2 were one of the first to be designed by Burlington himself, but in London over fifteen years buildings in the Palladian style included St George's Hospital (1733, p. 277), the Treasury (1733, p. 306), the Bank of England (1731–4, p. 305), the Mansion House (1739, p. 306) and Horseguards (1748, p. 307).

Burlington was a purist but those who followed him were not. He, Campbell and William Kent triggered a more intense interest in the work of a number of Italian architects, specifically Andrea Palladio, bringing a more general return to an austere use of wall surfaces, an increased use of the detached portico and an interest in the villa plan, particularly ones with

Fig. 268 (above right) Marble Hill House, Twickenham, 1724–9. Restrained and understated, the façade is carefully divided to produce harmony and balance. Inside, it is a different aesthetic; richness and depth of mouldings create a magnificence scarcely imaginable from the outside.

quadrants leading to ancillary buildings, such as the Trissino and Mocenigo villas in the Veneto. Palladio was an obvious source; he was the architect who best showed how ancient models could be adapted and incorporated into modern architecture. But his designs were mediated by Leoni's modifications and by Gibbs's simplified systems, and added to by favoured English motifs from Wren, Vanbrugh, Hawksmoor and by reference back to Jones and John Webb. In all, the period from around 1715 to 1760 was characterised by a search for a purer classical style though printed sources, and by 1760 those who wished to build in classical style followed a broad consensus. This was not a narrow replication of the work of Palladio or any other single authority, but the adoption of a broad-based classicism drawing on a kit of parts found in published works and first-hand experience of antiquity.

Whilst there was a general consensus in favour of constructing new buildings in a classical style this was never to the exclusion of the Gothic. Most architects retained the ability to design Gothic buildings when the occasion called and a small number, such as Henry Keene, Surveyor to Westminster Abbey, even specialised in it.[8] For colleges, churches, royal palaces, bishops' houses, castles and even some private residences the language of Gothic was often seen to be appropriate. These buildings tended to belong to institutions or families for whom demonstrable pedigree was important. Gothic details had strong associational power and emphasised tradition, continuity, antiquity and, in some cases, established religion.

For the monarchy the impulse to build in Gothic continued. As we have seen, Hugh May designed the external façades of his enormous extension to Windsor Castle (p. 263) in a neo-Norman style in 1675. The huge star on its front proclaimed the chivalric link with the Order of the Garter. In 1732 William Kent was commissioned by George II to rebuild part of Hampton Court for his son William Augustus. On Sir Robert Walpole's explicit instruction these rooms were to be in the Gothic style.[9] Private individuals, especially those who possessed ancient seats, chose Gothic, too. Henrietta Howard, Countess of Oxford, retired to Welbeck Abbey, Nottinghamshire, after her

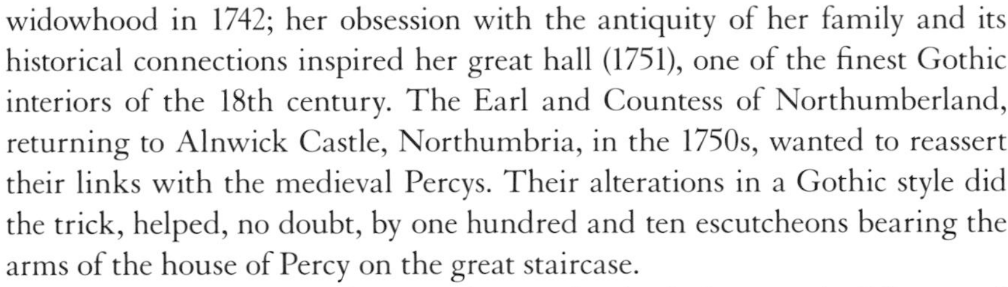

widowhood in 1742; her obsession with the antiquity of her family and its historical connections inspired her great hall (1751), one of the finest Gothic interiors of the 18th century. The Earl and Countess of Northumberland, returning to Alnwick Castle, Northumbria, in the 1750s, wanted to reassert their links with the medieval Percys. Their alterations in a Gothic style did the trick, helped, no doubt, by one hundred and ten escutcheons bearing the arms of the house of Percy on the great staircase.

The Church continued to employ Gothic both for new buildings and for alterations, as in many ways Gothic was now above all associated with Anglicanism. The polymathic William Kent was probably the designer of the utterly charming church of St John the Evangelist, Shobdon, Herefordshire (1748–56; fig. 269), showing him to be a major figure in the continuing Gothic tradition. His Gothic designs were published in 1744. Shobdon was not typical but it represents the boxy Gothic of the early 18th century that led, in due course, to the more assured use of the style at the church of St John the Baptist, King's Norton, Leicestershire, undertaken by a local architect, John Wing senior, between 1757 and 1761 (fig. 270).

There is a sense in which the collegiate buildings of Oxford were also built in Gothic styles to reflect Anglican traditions. Oxford was still the centre of high Anglicanism in the 18th century and conservative dons elected to emphasise this through continued use of Gothic. Thus the Oxford mason-architect John Townesend rebuilt the vault of the Convocation House in stone between 1758 and 1759, whilst Henry Keene gave the great hall at University College fan vaults and a chimney piece based on a Westminster abbey tomb (fig. 271).

Fig. 269 (above left) St John the Evangelist, Shobdon, Herefordshire. The pew ends have been altered but the wedding-cake Gothic of the original structure captures the spirit of the decorative Gothic of the early 1750s.

Fig. 270 (top) St John the Baptist, King's Norton, Leicestershire, is a lovely church built in 1760–1. The fantasy of Shobdon is nowhere to be seen; St John's is a building in which Gothic has been used properly, though inside it is clearly a church of the 18th century, with gallery and no chancel.

Fig. 271 (above) University College, Oxford; the hall, as remodelled by Henry Keene in 1766 (work removed in 1904). His fan vaults concealed the 17th-century roof beams and the fireplace was modelled on a tomb in Westminster Abbey, where he was surveyor.

Religious Building

The reformed Church in England had taken a decisively different direction to its sister Churches abroad. Indeed the body that became known as the Anglican Church often saw itself offering a more authentic Catholicism than that of Rome. Central to this was the view that God had intended bishops to be part of the structure of the Church. It was this belief that had been, in some ways, the trigger for the Civil War, and the abolition of episcopacy in 1646 was an important achievement for the Parliamentary regime. With the abolition of the central structures of the Church, parishes across England became a federation; nearly three thousand clergy lost their livings and each parish became free, within reason, to go its own way. In 1660 the House of Commons successfully re-established the Anglican Church under the bishops as a state-controlled monopoly. Legislation made holding public office dependant on taking Anglican Communion – the so-called Test Acts – and the Act of Uniformity required clergy to subscribe to the Thirty-nine Articles. In the early 1660s, with astonishingly little resistance, the bishops and cathedral chapters were able to regain their lands, and embarked on financial and architectural reconstruction.[10]

The bishops had long ceased to be the great landed magnates that they had been in Middle Ages. Royal appropriation and sale at the Reformation had reduced estates of most bishoprics to a kernel and the sale of all their lands in 1646 removed the rest. Only nine former bishops survived the Civil War, so at the Restoration most were new appointments and all had to confront the issue of reassembling their estates. Most, but not all, rebuilt their palaces in castellated or Gothic styles. Archbishop Juxon rebuilt the great hall at Lambeth Palace in 1660 with traceried windows and a hammer-beam roof at a cost of over £10,000, and it was described by Samuel Pepys as 'a new old-fashioned hall' (fig. 272); Bishop Cosin of Durham reconstructed Durham Castle, carefully blending his new facades into the medieval work but rebuilding the interiors in the latest style. At Hartlebury, the Bishop of Worcester's country palace, Henry Keene rebuilt the chapel based on the Henry VII Chapel at Westminster. There were some new buildings, too, most notably the Bishop of Winchester's fine new palace erected at a cost of £10,640.[11]

Fig. 272 (above) Lambeth Palace, London; the great hall, one of the most appealing and unusual buildings of the Restoration in England. It is medieval in concept and execution but effortlessly incorporates a cornice and frieze, pediments, ball finials and some elegant classical detailing on the lantern.

The shaping of parish architecture at the Restoration was profoundly influenced by the Great Fire of London. This rendered eighty-seven of the City's one hundred and seven churches unusable. It was agreed that fifty-one should be rebuilt, financed by the Coal Tax (pp 270–1), an extraordinary commission the likes of which had never been seen in England. Christopher Wren was appointed to preside and was assisted by the architect Robert Hooke and the Surveyor of Westminster Abbey, Edward Woodroffe. Later three of Wren's colleagues from the Office of Works, Nicholas Hawksmoor, William Dickinson and John Oliver, were recruited. England's most talented living designers worked together as if in a modern architect's office; Wren presided and set the parameters, but the design work was shared out between the various hands.

The overriding liturgical concern was the audibility and visibility of the preacher. The need to have clear lines of sight meant that obstructions such as pillars were not favoured – large, undivided spaces being the goal. Such churches had been built before the Fire; Inigo Jones's St Paul's, Covent Garden, was the first new church in London since before the reign of Elizabeth and had to grapple with the issue of a new type of space for the Anglican tradition. It was a single room, with its pulpit being the single most expensive fitting. The Broadway Chapel (pp 248–9), too, was a model that steered a course between tradition and moderate Calvinism.

The architectural challenge was thus how to span the roof width. The Sheldonian Theatre, Oxford (fig. 233), had been roofed by 70ft trusses, but this was technically complex and most of the unsupported roofs in the City churches were no wider than 40ft. For the larger churches either a single aisle (as at St Vedast's) or, more traditionally, two aisles (as at St Bride's) were introduced to support the weight of the roof (fig. 273a). These were all traditional forms, although plaster barrel vaults made the interiors look modern. More unusual were five of the churches (including St Mary's, Abchurch) that were centrally planned like the Broadway Chapel (fig. 273b). This was obviously a very good solution to audibility, and several other churches, such as St James's, Garlickhithe, combined a centralised focus with a longitudinal plan (fig. 273c). In all of these churches the altar was placed against the east wall, and was railed and furnished in a beautiful and dignified setting. In many churches galleries were built, as had often been the case since the 1620s, and a peal of bells hung in their tower.

Fig. 273 (below) Three churches designed by Sir Christopher Wren: a) St Bride's, Fleet Street, 1671–8 (as originally designed without galleries and the western vestibules): a traditional plan with two aisles; b) St Mary's, Abchurch, 1681–6: a centrally planned church under a dome supported on eight arches; c) St James's, Garlickhithe, 1676–82: with very narrow aisles, a clever melding of central and longitudinal planning, without a dome.

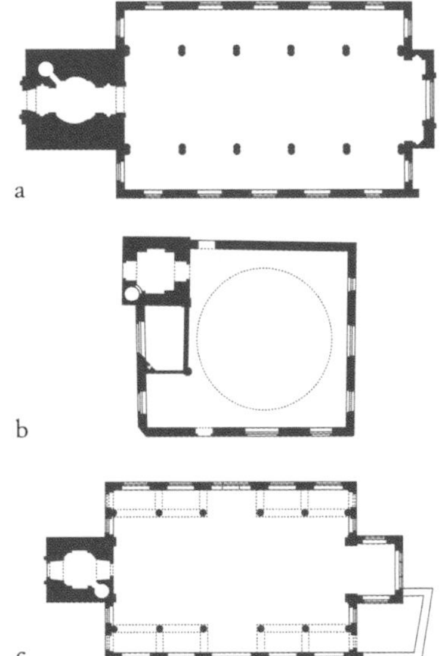

Many were built quickly and cheaply in the context of an extreme shortage of building materials. Wren took a pragmatic approach, treating each church, its site, its surviving walls and the preferences of the church wardens differently; no stylistic dogma dominated. Each church was composed using a mix of Gothic and classical elements, largely drawing on native traditions. As they were built on cramped sites the churches were designed to be appreciated from the inside; externally they were plain, with a single show front. Their greatest architectural expression was their towers and steeples, which were built over an extended period. Not one was the same; indeed, neighbouring churches were given deliberately contrasting treatments to create a varied skyline (fig. 274). The regularisation of the rooflines of domestic buildings meant that the steeples and eventually the dome of the cathedral punctured this horizon, creating London's remarkable skyline, the most remarked-upon feature of the city by contemporary tourists.[12]

In 1689 the Act of Toleration effectively abolished the official Anglican monopoly on English Christianity by granting dissenters freedom, on certain conditions, to worship alongside Anglicans. This presented particular problems for leading Anglicans in London because, as the city grew, Nonconformist meeting houses could be set up with relative ease but new Anglican parishes were difficult to create. The result would be, they thought, a huge increase in Nonconformists, who were, in their eyes, dangerously disconnected from the state. The new Tory administration of 1710, determined

Fig. 274 (above) St Mary le Bow, City of London, Sir Christopher Wren, 1670–80. Wren's best and most exciting city steeple, 224ft high, built 1678–80, was the first true steeple erected after the fire. It cost almost as much as the entire church. A rotunda of Corinthian columns bears a round of volutes that carry Composite colonnettes and then an obelisk.

Fig. 275 (above right) St Alfege, Greenwich, Nicholas Hawksmoor, 1711–14; the steeple is a replacement of 1730 by John James. Everything about the original design was big and Roman; this view shows the giant Doric pilasters and frieze around the long elevations.

to solve this problem and provide enough Anglican churches for London's growing population, passed an Act to build fifty new churches at the cost of £10,000 each, financed by an extension of the Coal Tax. The number of churches and their locations were scientifically targeted at areas of growing Nonconformity, particularly in the East End. In September 1711 fifty commissioners were appointed to regulate the project, and design and construction were entrusted to two co-surveyors, Nicholas Hawksmoor and William Dickinson, the most experienced church builders of the age.[13]

Twice in a generation the opportunity arose to embark on a huge church-building project under unified direction. But the 1711 Act did not possess the same imperative to rebuild that the Great Fire had created, nor could it avoid the complexity of purchasing new sites, a problem not faced in the City. By the time operations ceased in 1734 only eleven churches had been built, but they were the grandest and most spectacular built since the Reformation. This is partly because the churches were, in the end, lavishly funded. St Andrew's, Holborn, part of the post-Fire programme, had cost £9,530 between 1684 and 1686, and so a £10,000 budget per church in 1711 might have seemed reasonable, but the big City churches, such as St Bride's, Fleet Street and St Mary-le-Bow, had cost around £15,000 each. In the end the cheapest church built under the Act was St Mary's, Woolnoth, at just over £18,000, but St Mary le Strand cost £22,000 and Christ Church, Spitalfields, nearly £41,000. There was more to it than money, however, for the buildings were to be built of stone and seen as public edifices, adornments to the capital, not tucked away like the City churches. Indeed, they shared with St Paul's the no-expense-spared ambition of becoming national monuments.

Hawksmoor served on the commission for the full twenty-two years and personally designed eight of the churches, each combining in a unique and curious way the body of a Roman temple with a Gothic steeple. Norman churches and their Gothic successors had been modelled on Roman basilicas, but at St Alfege's, Greenwich (1712–14), the first of the churches started under the Act and the first by Hawksmoor, he created in plan a Roman temple with an attached portico and attached steeple, crowned with a version of the octagon at Ely Cathedral (fig. 275). This, and Hawksmoor's subsequent churches, attempted to connect with early Christian practice, a subject that interested both Anglican theologians and Hawksmoor himself. Remarkable as they are, none of the Queen Anne churches – as they are known – successfully integrated the body of a Roman temple with a Gothic steeple. Even Hawksmoor's masterpiece, Christ Church, Spitalfields (1714–29), crowned with a genuine broach spire, was two structures pushed together (fig. 276).

It was James Gibbs at St Martin-in-the-Fields, Westminster (1721–6), who brought Wren's church work – rapidly and cheaply conceived in the aftermath of the Great Fire – to something of a logical conclusion. He created the model for urban Anglican churches all over the world by integrating steeple and portico into a single composition (fig. 277). St Martin's was not one of the churches built under the 1711 Act but under a separate piece of legislation; it was therefore well funded (£33,661) and lavish, like its contemporaries. Gibbs, a Roman Catholic, had trained in Rome and brought to all his buildings a mix of English and Roman motifs and sources. Thus St Martin's owed much to Wren's churches, especially St James's, Piccadilly, but took a more vigorous approach to the orders. He banished the Anglican galleries behind a giant Corinthian arcade in which each column supported its own square of entablature, these supporting arches that intersect with a great barrel vault. The ceiling is decorated with rich plasterwork by the stuccadores Giovanni Bagutti and Chrysostom Wilkins (fig. 278).

The 18th century was a Christian century dominated by intense religiosity and a strengthened compact between the Anglican Church and the state. More books were published on religion than on any other subject and the single-most important literary form was the sermon. Religious debate was a key element of intellectual life, underpinning cultural activity from music to architecture.[14] The volume of church building reflected this; over the century there were ninety places of worship built anew in London and, in the rest of the country, some four hundred and forty-one. Adding in Nonconformist buildings, a grand total of six hundred and twenty-nine new buildings is reached.

Fig. 276 (top) Christ Church, Spitalfields; odd but overpowering. Hawksmoor takes a Venetian window with its arched central opening and turns it into a portico on which sits another Venetian motif and a Gothic spire. Originally the spire had a classical finial, crockets and small dormer windows, all of which added to the novelty and confusion of this remarkable confection.

Fig. 277 (bottom) St Martin-in-the-Fields. James Gibbs perfected all previous attempts to create a classical church with a steeple. It is 192ft high, topped with a concave-sided spire in the shape of an obelisk punched through with circular openings.

Fig. 278 (bottom left) St Martin-in-the-Fields, Westminster, James Gibbs, 1721–6. The nave is covered with a big barrel vault decorated with plasterwork by GiovanniBagutti and Chrysotom Wilkins. Each column has its own piece of entablature, a very correct interpretation of the language of the orders. The chancel is narrower than the nave, unusually for its date.

The Commission for Building Fifty New Churches had hoped that work in the metropolis would inspire builders across the nation. They had some success as the London churches of Gibbs, Wren, Hawksmoor and, before them, Jones provided the material architects needed to sustain a strong tradition of classical church architecture. Amongst the best provincial buildings was St Philip's, Birmingham (now a cathedral), built by Thomas Archer between 1709 and 1725, which uses a giant order inside and out. Archer, like Gibbs, had been to Italy and combined Roman baroque with English influences. At Blandford Forum, Dorset, John and William Bastard built a handsome stone church, St Peter and St Paul's (1733–9), drawing from both Wren's churches and elements of the Queen Anne churches.[15]

At the same time few medieval churches were not repaired, improved or enlarged by the Georgians; these modification touched galleries, pews, altars, reredoses, fonts and pulpits all across the country, and cathedrals underwent repair and alteration as well.

Public Buildings in London

Whilst the rebuilding of St Paul's Cathedral proceeded at a leisurely pace, the rebuilding of the Royal Exchange was a top priority, the new structure being completed in 1671 in just over two years and at the vast cost of £58,122. It was designed by the City Carpenter Edward Jerman and, although preserving the broad outlines of its predecessor (p. 221), presented a richly carved and decorated triumphal arch to the street.[16] The Exchange was important but in the 1720s and 30s a number of public and commercial buildings were erected in the capital that expressed fundamental changes in the basis of London's power, and were expressions of the Roman architecture with which the British state and its ruling oligarchy associated. These sought to gain financial credibility and express commercial superiority through their impressive façades.

Fig. 279 (below) The Bank of England, George Sampson, 1731–4. This was a new type of public and commercial building in the City of London and set the tone for all that was to come after.

By far the most important was the Bank of England (1731–4), designed by George Sampson, who had been brought into the Office of Works in 1719 by William Benson. The plan for the Bank was highly sophisticated, separating public and administrative functions, and segregating the Bank's technical activities. It was grouped around a succession of courts in the traditional manner, something that its clients would have found reassuringly familiar (fig. 279). Less familiar would have been its austere classical elevations; to the street it projected a palace façade that paid homage to the garden front at Somerset House (fig. 253), where Sampson had been Clerk of Works. The Bank, with its statues of Britannia and its founder William III, set out to establish itself as the heart of the Establishment. Its stone façades contrasted strongly with the City's customary brick architecture and established a monumentality in commercial structures that prevails today.

Fig. 280 (above left) The Mansion House, City of London, designed by George Dance the Elder on a site in the heart of the City. Originally it had two vast attics, giving spectacular height to the main state rooms and an internal courtyard to throw light into the heart of the building.

Fig. 281 (above) Mansion House, George Dance the Elder's Egyptian Hall which occupied the whole southern part of the house. The barrel vault was added in 1795 instead of the overblown clerestoried third storey originally designed.

Opposite the Bank, in 1737, rose the Portland stone Mansion House. Until this date mayors of London had resided in their own houses but, following the example of other cities such as York, the Corporation of London decided to build a house for their mayor that would combine residential and judicial functions, whilst providing a suitably magnificent setting for civic occasions. The design was by George Dance, recently appointed the City's Clerk of Works and a man who understood the requirements of the mayoralty. Externally, the building presented a huge six-columned portico to the street, approached, like Canons House, Wanstead (fig. 280), by a double flight of stairs. Carving in the pediment shows the City receiving the plenty brought to it by the river Thames. The mayor had the principal two floors, servants were on the ground floor and bedrooms were in the attic. The building was planned around a central courtyard on the far side of which was the banqueting hall, massive and imposing, inspired by Vitruvius' Egyptian Hall, a version of which had been already constructed by Lord Burlington in York (fig. 281). Nobody could be in any doubt that the Mayor of London was amongst the most powerful men in the land.[17] Financial advances in the City were mirrored by developments in the Treasury, which had to respond to the rapid growth of financial markets and the embryonic stock market dealing in government bonds. Proper financial controls were necessary to inspire confidence in the national debt and a new bureaucracy grew up to provide this. By the 1730s the Treasury had far outgrown its makeshift home in the converted tennis courts of Whitehall Palace and between 1733 and 1737 William Kent created a new building for the Treasury Lords next to the Tudor remains. Rusticated all over and raised up high on a round-arched basement, it has a four-column Ionic portico on the second floor. Although it looked like an aristocratic town house this was actually a specialised office block with a complex plan, tailored to the working needs of the Treasury Lords and their clerks.[18]

Next to the New Treasury was Horseguards (p. 261), which had been an experimental building in 1663 and had developed serious structural problems by the 1740s. It was known that rebuilding would be expensive and this created a decade of disagreement before work finally started in 1750. By this time William Kent, who had presented preliminary designs, was dead, and his successors on the Board of Works under Stephen Wright finessed them to perfection (fig. 282). The completed building was more than a barracks; it was no less than the War Office, with all its associated bureaucracy. The St James's Park elevation was the setting for a vast parade ground. Drill had become central to infantry training and Cromwell had included parade grounds in his Scottish barracks. Horse Guards Parade was the national parade ground, a show place for the British Army. The buildings associated with it were full of historical and militaristic references. Its street elevation in particular pays profound homage to its predecessor, Britain's first purpose-built barracks. On the park side the wide, heavily rusticated façade is almost a summation of early 18th-century architectural references.[19]

A third new building in Whitehall was of equal importance, the rebuilding of the Royal Mews. The sprawling Mews occupied most of what is now Trafalgar Square and part of the site of the National Gallery. Ever since the Restoration there had been schemes for rebuilding it but it was not until 1731 that there was money and will plentiful enough to see progress. Of a grandiose master plan, the new Great Stable was the only part to be built (fig. 283). Under the scrutiny of Lord Burlington, William Kent invented a new architectural language suitable for a more vernacular purpose. But the stables hardly looked vernacular. Although the long flank walls with blank arcading and Diocletian windows were severe, the centrepiece, perhaps influenced by the street gate to Burlington House, Piccadilly (p. 315), and the intermediate doors crowned with cupolas were decidedly regal. This building, in particular its use of Diocletian windows, became a model for industrial buildings in the following decades.[20]

Fig. 282 (bottom) Westminster. On the far right is the new Treasury by William Kent of 1733–7; it was joined by Horse Guards in 1750–9, also built to designs by Kent, but modified after his death in 1748. Together they are one of the most interesting, varied and successful compositions of their age in England. This was not austere, restrained classicism; it was lively, articulated and confident townscape.

Fig. 283 (below) The Royal Mews, Charing Cross, Westminster, William Kent, 1731–33 (demolished 1830). The mews were a seminal building inventing an architecture for utilitarian buildings within the classical language. The Diocletian window, in particular, became a favourite for stables and, later, for industrial buildings.

These public buildings were of stone. It was partly James I's desire to see London made a city of brick and stone rather than timber that reignited royal interest in the stone quarries on the Isle of Portland. Inigo Jones had recognised the stone's excellent properties and its ability to take the crisp details demanded by classical forms, and had roads, cranes and a pier built to extract the stone and ship it to London. He used Portland stone at the Banqueting House, Whitehall, and then to reface the exterior of St Paul's Cathedral. The sudden appearance of Portland stone in London is probably his greatest influence on 17th-century English architecture, leading to Wren's adoption of it as the main stone for the new St Paul's. But Portland stone is not easy to quarry and is hard to extract in very large blocks. For this reason commissions such as Hampton Court used Portland sparingly and for decorative details only. Nevertheless, Portland remained the stone of choice for public and commercial buildings well into the 20th century.

Polite Society in Provincial Towns

Fig. 284 (above) The Mansion House, Doncaster; the assembly room (today the banqueting room). Doncaster grew wealthy as an important coaching intersection. Opened in 1749, the Mansion House cost £8,000. The great assembly room was a double cube with a musicians' gallery over the door. The chandeliers are original to the room.

Whilst London remained the centre of polite society provincial towns became social hubs for their rural hinterlands. In these hubs a much wider range of people mixed than in earlier periods. The social distance of previous centuries was eroded, and polite society included anyone who could afford to dress well, converse easily and behave appropriately. This required property and education, commodities available to a growing sector of society. The phenomenon that expresses this change most clearly is the rage for assemblies that gripped provincial England for a century after 1720. Assemblies started as gatherings for conversation, cards and tea, but quickly expanded to include dancing of both delicate minuets and more rumbustious country dances. Ultimately, their success was the winning combination of sex and gambling; they were a marriage mart for the young and gambling dens for the established.

Assemblies were initially held in any suitable large communal space, but soon purpose-built halls were being built; the earliest to survive is at Stamford, Lincolnshire, dated 1726. By the 1770s all but the smallest towns had assembly rooms attached to inns, raised by local subscription, or sponsored by a local landowner or magnate. An early, architecturally pretentious example is York's Assembly Rooms, built by subscription between 1728 and 30, and designed by Lord Burlington (now, sadly, a pasta joint). But his experiment to recreate Vitruvius' Egyptian Hall failed to catch on and, in the end, as with so much architectural fashion, it was the Lindsey's rooms at Bath of 1728 that created a model. Here John Wood the Elder managed to blend a drawing room with a great hall to create a space that could accommodate the musicians in a gallery and a main floor glittering with mirrors, arched over by a great coved ceiling from which hung chandeliers. Ancillary to the ballroom was a card room and a tea room. This tripartite formula worked equally well

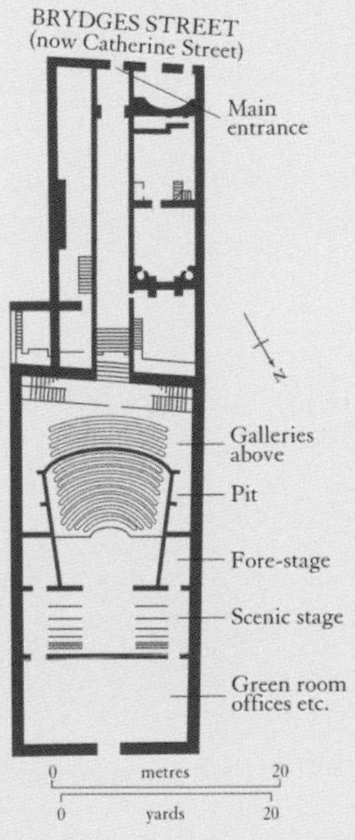

Fig. 285 (top) The Theatre Royal, Drury Lane; longitudinal cross section. The ancillary rooms and stage are to the right, the staircases and lobbies to the left. The stage was exceedingly deep in order to enhance the perspective effect of the scenery.

Fig. 286 (above) The Theatre Royal Drury Lane, plan. The Theatre was tightly hedged in and could be approached only by a narrow passageway.

in provincial King's Lynn, as well as in the aspirational ballroom designed by James Paine in Doncaster in 1745 (fig. 284).[21]

In 1660 Charles II granted the sole right to stage theatrical productions to two royal favourites, William Davenant and Thomas Killigrew. They both initially opted to convert tennis courts into theatres but Killigrew soon made plans to build a new one at Drury Lane. His first building burnt down in 1672 and in 1674 Killigrew turned to Christopher Wren to design a modern theatre for him (fig. 285). In this both architect and patron must have looked to Louis XIV's new theatre of 1659 in the Tuileries, Paris, which was designed along Italian lines. On the west were stairs and entrance lobbies on three floors, giving entrance to the pit (stalls) and galleries above. The seats here and in the pit were just benches, without backs and covered in green baize. A giant order of Corinthian pilasters reducing in size towards the stage framed the boxes. The main performance took place on the fore stage, which projected out some 20ft into the audience in front of the proscenium arch. Behind this, in the area that we would today normally call the stage, was the area devoted to scenery – the scenic stage, 45ft deep (fig. 286).

The opening of the Theatre Royal in Drury Lane in 1674 heralded a new era in London theatre-going. The new theatre was smaller, it was indoors and the seats were considerably more expensive. Going to the theatre became part of the leisure circuit for rich and fashionable society; they went frequently, and they were happy to see the same play time and again. A seat in the pit cost 2s 6d and a seat in one of the boxes 4s. Although the season did not continue into the summer months, when polite society decamped from London, there were still around 200 performances a year.

Despite a Theatre Licensing Act of 1737 theatres rapidly multiplied in provincial centres and the template for them was the Theatre Royal. Bristol's Theatre Royal, begun in 1764, was closely based on drawings of Drury Lane

Fig. 287 (above) The Theatre Royal, Richmond, Yorkshire; the oldest surviving theatre in England, complete with original stage, dressing rooms and staircases.

Fig. 288 (above left) Queen Square, Bath, 1728–36, one of the first successful attempts to portray a row of houses as a single great palace giving a sense of grandeur that no individual tenant could have afforded. For a precursor see fig. 265.

and Liverpool's theatre was actually named after it. But most provincial theatres were less pretentious. The Playhouse in Richmond, Yorkshire, built by the actor-manager Samuel Butler in 1788, is a rectangular space seating over two hundred, with a sunken pit, boxes on three sides and a gallery above (fig. 287). Other than turned Doric columns supporting the gallery, all of the architectural detail was painted. Travelling companies played at theatres each summer, moving from town to town; in the largest venues, such as Bath, productions would come from London.[22]

Social display did not only take place indoors. In 1660 the London Mall was laid out by Charles II and by the 1720s it had become perhaps the most popular promenade in London, crowded by people watching and being watched. Other towns created promenades or walks, either in existing spaces or on new land. Around 1710 a tree-lined pavement was laid out in Epsom and christened The Parade, and it was available for those who wanted to walk after taking the waters. In the 1730s and 40s there was a flood of walks in towns such as York, Norwich and Liverpool. Leicester's Queen's Walk was laid out in 1785 and remains a semi-rural, pedestrianised parade.[23]

In all, this one town set the pace – Bath. The medicinal properties of Bath's spa waters had been recognised for centuries but from 1700 the attractions of the cure became entangled with a new sort of town, a place entirely devoted to the leisure pursuits of the rich. In Bath the English invented the holiday, a period spent away from home and everyday cares. Beau Nash became Master of Ceremonies in 1704 and single-mindedly set out to transform the social scene. His achievement was to get different social groups to mix and interact politely. Rules for dress and behaviour, and routines for where to congregate, turned Bath into a remarkable social blender. Bathing became a secondary and then tertiary activity as assemblies, concerts, balls, promenades and gambling all became established parts of the daily round. The Bath playhouse was

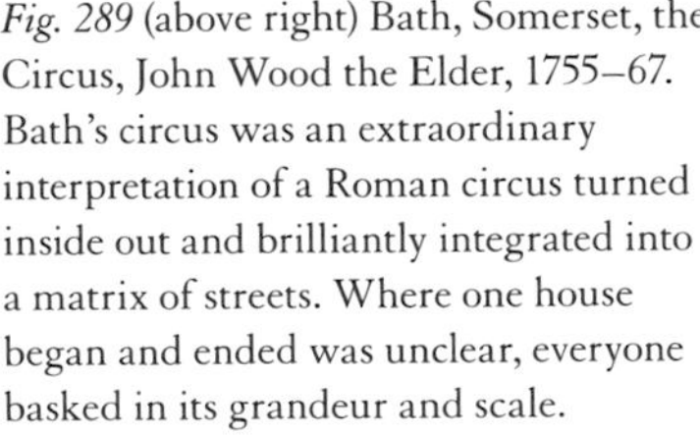

Fig. 289 (above right) Bath, Somerset, the Circus, John Wood the Elder, 1755–67. Bath's circus was an extraordinary interpretation of a Roman circus turned inside out and brilliantly integrated into a matrix of streets. Where one house began and ended was unclear, everyone basked in its grandeur and scale.

Fig. 290 (above) Central Bath from the air, showing the circus, crescent and their surrounding streets. The view from the crescent was deliberately rural.

built in 1705, a pump room in 1706, assembly rooms in 1708 and a ballroom in 1720. Churches were not left out: by 1800 Bath had eleven Anglican churches and nine Nonconformist ones.

From around 1725 Bath also began to set the fashion in town building. This was largely down to John Wood, a builder and surveyor who, after working on speculative developments in London, returned to Bath in 1727. By the time he started developing a new quarter for the town he had already been involved with the improvement of navigation on the river Avon and saw that this, and better roads, would bring a great rise in Bath's fortunes. From 1729 he applied his London experiences, especially his knowledge of Cavendish and Grosvenor squares, to the development of Queen Square, Bath (fig. 288). The square was the first successful realisation of a speculative development of eight individual houses that at first glance looked like a vast town palace. Residents could bask in an aura of grandeur that their individual dwellings could never convey. All the components of the Queen Square elevation had been executed before, and many published in *Vitruvius Britannicus*, but Wood's mastery of them was his own.

Wood was unusual in that he mixed architectural talent and commercial nous with antiquarian obsession. Even before work started on Queen Square he had conceived a megalomaniac scheme for Bath that would include a 'Royal Forum', a 'Grand Circus' and an 'Imperial Gymnasium'. His inspiration was Roman Bath and its invented – by him – predecessor built by the druids. In hands other than Wood's, and in an environment other than that which prevailed in mid 18th-century Bath, this scheme would have been categorised as the slightly loony dream of an otherwise sane businessman. But Wood and his son (who succeeded to his business) completed it all by the mid 1770s.

Most remarkable was a circus of thirty-three houses, built between 1755 and 1767, and entered by three streets, none of which aligned with another across the Circus (figs 289 and 290). This was important because by closing off vistas he made the internal circle feel private and enclosed. The sense of enclosure was strengthened by the regularity of the encircling façades, with paired Doric, Ionic and Corinthian orders separated by vigorous bands of base and entablature, and crowned with a parapet studded with giant acorn finials. This was the Coliseum in Rome turned outside in, grand but intimate, private but public. It was an instantaneous success. The Royal Crescent, built between 1767 and 1775, linked to the circus by one of the radial streets, was half the Circus but in elliptical form (fig. 290). It was brilliantly sited at the top of a rise, with its long, open frontage looking out on to fields receding into the distance, giving the lucky residents the feeling that they actually resided in a country house. Its elevations were derived less directly from antique sources and more closely linked to London house fronts.

Bath was an entirely different sort of place from the aristocratic towns of France or Germany. There was no princely or aristocratic palace around which the town was planned, no great vistas turning on fountains or obelisks, just an ebb and flow of streets and terraces that linked the various social hubs. This was all given additional harmony and beauty by the use of local Bath stone, and the town became hugely admired and widely imitated. Circuses were built in Exeter, Greenwich and in numerous locations in London, whilst crescents sprang up in towns from the 1790s – Buxton (the best), Brighton, and several in and around London. They remained a popular feature in town planning until the break-up of terraces into the houses of suburbia (p. 434).

Government, Justice and Commerce in Provincial Towns

The basis of county government was the Justices of the Peace, the JPs, appointed by the Crown on the recommendation of the Lord Lieutenant, who was invariably a major aristocratic landowner. These men, normally gentry and wealthy merchants, met at petty sessions to deal with minor offences and at quarter sessions for more serious ones. The quarter sessions were also administrative councils ruling on county infrastructure, such as roads, bridges, county buildings and various licences. Twice a year judges would come from London for the assizes, the crown court, which dealt with the gravest cases. The assizes were amongst the most important social and ceremonial occasions in the provincial calendar, accompanied by processions, dinners, balls and a church service. The sheriff presided over the system and in addition was responsible for coordinating the return of Members of Parliament.

In many county towns these administrative functions were still exercised from the great medieval fortresses erected in the early Middle Ages for that very purpose. The town corporation had no power over these, which still represented national authority and remained independent enclaves till 1888. Justice was dispensed in the great hall, the same space that would double for the assize feast and other social events, and its great towers frequently served as the county prison, as at Lancaster. In York, uniquely, the prison was rebuilt between 1701 and 1705. York Castle had gradually been subsumed into the plan of the city – the slopes of Clifford's Tower becoming a leafy promenade

Fig. 291 (above) York Castle; the county gaol, a monumental central block and two projecting wings. In the middle, below a clock turret and cupola, are two pairs of giant rusticated Doric pilasters. The wings are dominated by massive plain segmental pediments.

Fig. 292 (above right) Worcester Guildhall, 1721–4; England's finest 18th-century town hall. Its three-bay centrepiece is lavish; two giant Corinthian pilasters support a segmental pediment overladen with trophies: below, in a niche, Queen Anne; above, perching on the skyline, Justice, Peace and Plenty.

– and it was decided to embellish the area with a handsome new building to replace the old prison. It was probably designed by the talented gentleman architect William Wakefield and shows how up-to-the-minute architectural fashions could be transmitted across the country (fig. 291). His building was strongly influenced by Hooke's Bethlem Hospital and the King William Block at Greenwich. But Wakefield did his own thing, and York Castle Gaol is the most impressive and successful provincial public building of its age.

Towns that did not possess castles began to build themselves new county halls. Amongst the earliest is the remarkably vigorous hall at Derby built between 1657 and 1659, essentially a great hall with two processional entrances. Much grander and more sophisticated was Worcester Guildhall (fig. 292). This was a building raised by public subscription in 1721 to contain the town's assembly rooms, and the combined courtrooms of the town and county. There was a central door wide enough for two judges to process in side by side. The ground floor was a big U-shaped space with a long central hall off which were the civil and criminal courts, the latter with a counsel room for lawyers. On axis with the entrance was the grand stair that led to a large and handsome assembly room, now much remodelled. Externally, the influence of the Bethlem Hospital is again seen. We do not know for certain who designed the busy and swaggering façade, with lots of appropriate iconography, including statues of the Stuart monarchs, but it amply conveyed royal and civic dignity.

Sometimes judicial and commercial functions were combined in civic structures, as at Abingdon County Hall, built between 1678 and 1682 as the county hall for Berkshire (fig. 293). Christopher Kempster, one of Wren's London masons, was the designer. There was a basement for storage, an arcaded ground floor for trading and an upper sessions hall for the county assizes. With its cupola, balustraded roof and dormers it drew on the most prominent London models: Jerman's Royal Exchange (p. 305), Horseguards (p. 307) and, inevitably, the Bethlem Hospital (p. 250).[24] The Norfolk port of King's Lynn acquired two of the most architecturally sophisticated commercial buildings in England. The Exchange, today the Custom House, was erected by

Sir John Turner in 1683 and presented to the town corporation as a meeting place for its merchants (fig. 294). The ground floor was originally an open trading floor and the upper floors were soon occupied by the customs office. Its architect, Henry Bell, a local gentleman who had been on the Grand Tour as far as Italy, again drew on Dutch models and London's most prominent public buildings, thus thrusting King's Lynn into the mainstream of fashionable national design. In 1708 the town corporation decided to demolish the old market cross and shambles in the Tuesday Market Place and build anew. Bell was again the architect (fig. 295). There were three quadrant colonnaded shambles for meat and fish, and at their centre an octagonal, domed market hall. This was a truly remarkable building for a provincial town; stone built and 70ft high, it was domed with a cupola and encircled by an Ionic arcade supporting a balcony. It was built before Thomas Archer's remarkable domed pavilion at Wrest Park (fig. 259) and had few English parallels.[25]

Fig. 293 (above left) Abingdon County Hall, Berkshire, by Christopher Kempster, 1678–82. Most such halls were raised up to allow markets to meet beneath in the dry. The great arched windows have unusual mullions which link into an arch above the transom. This impressive building successfully secured the county assizes for the town.

Fig. 294 (above) The Exchange (now the Custom House), King's Lynn, Norfolk. As in Abingdon, the ground floor of this exquisite little building was originally open. The upper rooms were for merchants to transact their business.

Aristocratic Life in Town and Country

From the 1680s the West End of London had been built by Whig aristocrats: the Bedfords in Russell and Tavistock squares, the Cavendishes in Cavendish and Manchester squares, the Grosvenors in Belgravia. For them the West End was not only a financial investment, it was a social one, the very basis of their lives. The richest aristocrats still maintained at least three houses – a principal country house, a town house and a suburban villa. Thus Philip Yorke and his wife, the Marchioness Grey, owned Wrest Park, Bedfordshire, a house in

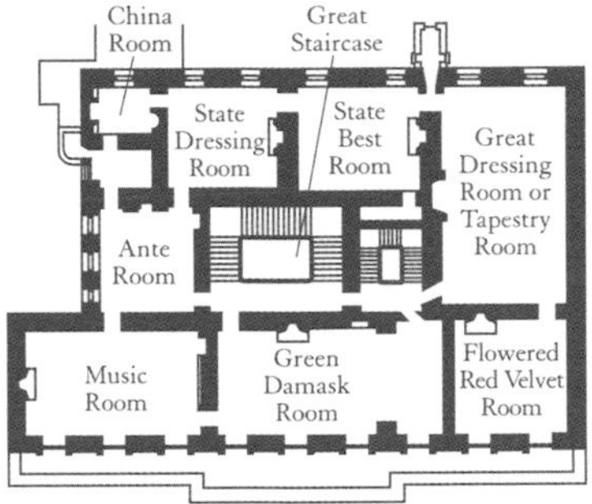

Fig. 295 (above right) King's Lynn, the Market Cross, Henry Bell, 1708–10 (demolished 1831). King's Lynn's merchants were ambitious and wanted a market cross that set them apart. As the second town of Norfolk they got Bell to design them a shambles with no previous parallel and a very striking modern appearance.

Fig. 296 (top) The street gate at Burlington House, designed in 1718 as part of the remodelling of the Earl's town house on Piccadilly.

Fig. 297 (above) Norfolk House, St James's Square, London, was nine bays wide, its breadth allowing a parade of grand rooms encircling a top-lit staircase. Lavish inside, the external elevations were plain – almost boring.

St James's Square and a villa in Richmond. They moved around the country in a fixed annual routine, coming to London in January and February, and staying for the season until August, when they would leave for the country. London was thus the home of the aristocracy for most of the year, and their town and suburban houses were of the utmost importance and splendour.

As we have seen, the Earl of Burlington commissioned Colen Campbell to remodel his town house on Piccadilly. Burlington designed a new façade in 1717 and a street gate in 1718 (fig. 296). This was a house of new austerity, rejecting the architecture found at, for instance, Marlborough House, designed by Sir Christopher Wren less than ten years before. The façade of the main block was executed in stone, with a rusticated basement, Ionic columns and pilasters, and the two projecting end wings had tripartite Diocletian windows. Behind his house he laid out an estate of fashionable houses in this new style, two of which he designed himself. These designs played an important part in ushering a much more serious-minded classicism into aristocratic town houses.[26]

This new generation of houses were normally of brick with stone dressings, relatively plain outside, drawing on the new, purer classicism. Inside there was a sequence of rooms leading one to another in a formal manner. However, in the 1750s this was to radically change as a novel and more informal layout was increasingly adopted. Norfolk House was designed for Edward Howard, Duke of Norfolk, by Matthew Brettingham in 1750. The novelty of the house lay not in its external appearance, which was very plain, but in its disposition round a central, top-lit staircase, about which the principal rooms were arranged. This allowed guests to ascend to the piano nobile, perambulate around a series of splendid interiors, each decorated differently, and leave after their circuit was complete without doubling back (fig. 297). The arrangement found instant favour and was imitated in almost all subsequent mansions. The finest remaining of these is Spencer House designed by John Vardy for John, Earl Spencer, and completed in around 1756. It is firmly in the Burlington/Kent tradition, with a rusticated ground floor and a piano nobile containing seven windows framed by engaged Doric columns. A rich frieze supports a pediment and balustrade, crowned by urns and statues.

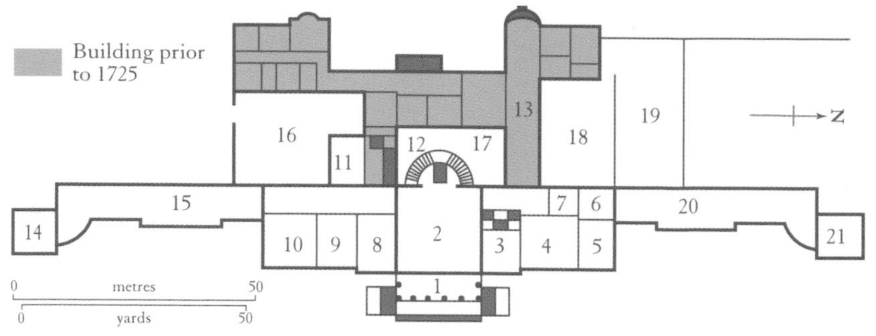

Fig. 298 (left and above) Wentworth Woodhouse, Yorkshire, by Henry Flitcroft, 1734–40. Many houses had their suites of reception rooms doubled-up or folded round a core. At Wentworth Woodhouse they were spread across the landscape to make the biggest possible splash. Suites were centred on a vast hall or saloon and ran off north and south.(1) Portico (2) Saloon or hall (3) Sculpure room (4) Dining room (5) First library (6) Second library (7) Third library (8) Ante-room (9) Van Dyck room (10) Whistle-jacket room (11) Chapel (12) Staircases (13) Gallery (14) South tower (15) South wing (16) South court (17) Middle court (18) North court (19) Offices (20) North wing (21) North wing.

The cost of Spencer House was colossal. The acquisition of the site alone was £14,000 and the house without its furnishings cost a further £35,000.

Spencer House, rather than the Spencer country seat, Althorp, Northamptonshire, contained the best artworks. Similarly, a 1798 inventory of the contents of Devonshire House, built between 1733 and 1734 by William Cavendish, Duke of Devonshire, and designed by William Kent, shows that its contents were worth £29,286 compared with the contents of Devonshire's infinitely larger Chatsworth at £17,560. Yet although the Devonshire and Spencer houses were like private museums, they were also family homes. Devonshire House had a ground storey with a lower, pillared entrance hall and modest rooms for daily living; above these was the piano nobile with an astonishing eleven state rooms, and on the second floor and in the attics were the bedrooms. Spencer House was occupied by the earl and countess together with their three surviving children, who were confined to the attic nursery on the second floor. To help them out there was a household staff of forty or fifty, some of whom, such as the valets and maids, would have travelled with the family, but a skeleton staff would have always remained in London.[27]

The suburban villas were no less important. Not for entertaining, but as a refuge from the pressures and constraints of the city. Like the previous generations of suburban retreats, they were also architectural forcing houses. Chiswick House (pp 298 and 318), White Lodge, Richmond, Canons House, Wanstead (p. 297), Syon House and Moor Park were all at the cutting edge of design and became places of pilgrimage for the fashionable, aspirational or simply the plain curious.

With such a strong metropolitan focus most aristocrats were too busy to spend time in the country but had to go there because they, with the gentry, ran the localities. In 1760 four hundred people owned a quarter of England and most of them sat in the House of Lords. These peers held most cabinet posts and almost all of the great offices of state, as well as most of the high-ranking military jobs. Meanwhile, their sons, sons-in-law and tenants-in-chief made up a substantial proportion of the House of Commons, elections to which they influenced by every manner possible. Through their positions as Lord Lieutenant they recommended Justices of the Peace and appointed officers of the local militia.[28]

Fig. 299 (right) Holkham Hall, Norfolk, 1734–65, comprises a central block linked to four satellite wings by one-bay links. The wings are for the chapel, the kitchen, guests and the family. Though it looks as if it is built from stone it is, in fact, finely made yellow brick.

This meant that the aristocracy still needed to build mega-houses, a trend that went back through the great Jacobean mansions to the aristocratic houses of the 15th century and earlier. Fewer were built from new but those that were compared well to their predecessors. Castle Howard cost £35,000, and its grounds and park buildings at least another £43,000; building there went on for fourteen years and even then the house remained unfinished. Thomas Watson-Wentworth, from 1746 Marquess of Rockingham, built Wentworth Woodhouse, South Yorkshire, from *c.*1735 (fig. 298). One of the largest private houses in the world, this leviathan was the anchor for Watson-Wentworth's power. Yorkshire was England's largest county and apart from a few towns, which could be easily controlled politically, its two MPs had to control a huge rural area and the discerning inhabitants of Leeds, Sheffield and Wakefield. Wentworth Woodhouse played host to entertainments with a thousand guests, so many that tickets had to be issued to direct people to one of the twenty-five state rooms.[29]

The most ambitious of all the great Whig houses was Holkham Hall, Norfolk (1734–65), where a combination of the talents of Burlington, Kent, Brettingham and Thomas Coke, Earl of Leicester, attempted to create the sort of country house that an ancient Roman aristocrat would have enjoyed (fig. 299). Serious consideration was given to ancient sources, the rooms were filled with

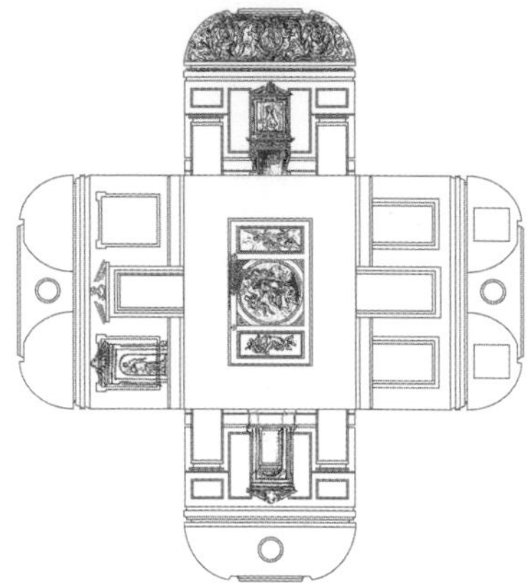

antique sculpture and its remarkable hard yellow brick was a careful match of Roman bricks sent from Rome to be copied in Norfolk. To finish the job off, Leicester had himself portrayed as a Roman patrician in a bust by Roubiliac.

Interiors were carefully designed to evoke those in Roman houses, first using Vitruvius' descriptions. Inigo Jones provided important models, as he had used details from ancient Roman buildings and combined them with features designed by 16th-century Italian architects. His ceilings at the Queen's House, Greenwich, and the Banqueting House, for instance, derived from Renaissance Italy and were widely copied.

Crucial in the development of a new type of interior were Lord Burlington, Colen Campbell and William Kent. Burlington House and Chiswick House both strove to create such authentically Roman interiors. The ceiling of the octagonal saloon at the centre of Chiswick House was modelled on one of the most famous buildings in Rome, the Basilica of Maxentius, whilst the apses in the gallery were modelled on the Temple of Venus and Rome. This makes the point that the models being followed were found in Roman public buildings rather than domestic ones.[30] At Kensington Palace (1722–7) and Houghton Hall, Norfolk, William Kent took control of interior decoration in a novel way. As we have seen, before around 1720 architects designed the rooms and, in close collaboration, upholsterers designed the interiors. Kent was probably the first Englishman to design rooms in their entirety on the drawing board, creating an exploded plan of floor, ceiling, wall paintings and all (fig. 300). Kent had spent ten years, mainly in Italy, examining Roman decoration and he made full use of this knowledge when composing interiors.

Oak panelling and dark paint were no longer favoured for the grandest rooms, which were now stuccoed and painted white in imitation of stone,

Fig. 300 (above) Drawing of William Kent's exploded or, as it was known at the time, laid-out, design for the North Hall at Stowe House, Buckinghamshire for Viscount Cobham, *c.*1730.

Fig. 301 (above left) The King's Gallery, Kensington Palace, London as decorated by William Kent. Chimney, doorcases and ceiling were all replaced for his own designs in 1725–7 and the room was hung with big Italian paintings in specially designed frames.

Fig. 302 (above) Dunham Massey, Manchester; the library: a room not for parade, but for scholarship, business and lots of books.

often with a touch of gilding. Less grand rooms might still be panelled but in these oak gave way to light-painted softwood. The gallery at Kensington Palace, redecorated by William Kent, still contained the oak dado from William III's time; this was painted white and gilded between 1725 and 1727 (fig. 301). There were advances in paint manufacture in the 1730s, and ready-mixed paint could be purchased rather than having to be made on site. This helped the spread of more standardised colours.[31]

Hangings were no longer loosely hung and, where wanted, were stretched tightly and hung permanently. Silk damask and velvet were still used, but only in smaller closets or in ladies' rooms. From the 1730s wallpaper was often the replacement, flocked in the state rooms and printed in the bedrooms. Another new material that became popular at the same time was papier mâché, which made possible, at a reasonable cost, ceilings that would have been impossibly expensive executed in plaster by stuccadores. It was also used instead of gilded wood in picture frames, fireplaces and architectural mouldings. Architectural components such as swags, drops and indeed whole ceilings could be bought in kit form in London and sent to the country to be glued on. Printing on textile also advanced, and in the 1750s printed-cotton fabrics began to be mass produced and were used for bed and curtain hangings.

The reign of the upholsterer was waning and cabinet makers were now as important. Indeed the word 'furniture' changed its meaning, shifting from what we today would call upholstery to mean wooden frames or carcasses that might or might not include upholstery. Advances in furniture making, especially in the use of the recently introduced mahogany, brought new types of furniture into interiors, made by craftsmen such as John Linnell and Thomas Chippendale. But, above all, the great houses were now a vehicle for displaying sculpture and paintings bought on the Grand Tour. At a house such as Holkham, which had an astonishing collection of classical sculpture displayed in the gallery, paintings were not randomly dispersed, and nor were they arranged in a modern way by school; they were conceived as part of the architecture and set in frames designed by the architect.[32] The iconography of the paintings was much more easily read in this period than today and subjects were grouped to create themes; at Holkham the saloon was hung with Roman subjects that could be interpreted as paying homage to Lady Leicester, and to her husband as a defender of female virtue. By the 1720s every new house of status had a library. In the 17th century books had generally been kept in the owner's closet, although examples do exist of libraries such as that at Ham House, where the bibliophile Sir John Maitland, Duke of Lauderdale, created a new library between 1672 and 1674. When Dunham Massey was rebuilt during the 1720s and 30s George Booth, Earl of Warrington, built himself a library with floor-to-ceiling shelving holding some two thousand volumes (fig. 302). The library was in the private part of the house, not intermingled with the state rooms. It was a business resource containing books of practical use rather than rare specimens collected for display. At Holkham the largest room in the family wing was the library designed by William Kent to contain rare books, but also to be a room of private resort.[33]

When in residence, aristocrats in these mega-houses worked hard at entertaining, seeing to the poor, attending the races and gracing the assembly rooms. But this was work, because Whig aristocratic attitudes were urban and they really wanted to bring the West End to the countryside with London pastimes, timetables, morals and company. Holkham Hall attempted to combine a great house of parade with a more intimate type of villa for comfortable life. The four pavilions provided the opportunity for a London lifestyle adjacent to the state rooms necessary for country life. Indeed, the Holkham pavilions might have formed the model for Norfolk House in St James's Square, London (fig. 297).

Living in the Country

As the population rose from around two and half million in the 1550s to six million in 1760, agricultural production expanded to feed it. New land was brought into cultivation or use by livestock – the totality of arable, pasture and meadow increased by as much as 38 per cent; there were new inventions – the swing plough and the seed drill; crop rotation and other means of boosting soil fertility were developed and became more widespread; and there was a greater use of horse power, improved animal husbandry and a huge decrease in communal farming in favour of individualistic enterprise. As a result regional specialisation was reinforced. In the uplands sheep and cattle were raised and dairy farming predominated, whilst in the lowlands there was a more mixed economy.[34]

In the central lowland belt the biggest effect, by far, was the result of enclosure. Although this had started in the 16th century and had hugely accelerated in the 17th, it continued under thousands of individual Acts of Parliament into the 18th century. Whilst it mainly affected areas of open-field farming it also

Fig. 303 (below) Village of Healaugh underneath Calver fell in Swaledale, originally surrounded by open countryside that was then broken up by enclosure.

Fig. 304 (above) Chiswick House, London; the Ionic temple, one of Lord Burlington's garden pavilions designed to evoke the landscapes of the ancient world.

brought areas of former waste into enclosed cultivation. Some new owners of enclosed fields sold their land, resulting in the amalgamation of smaller holdings into larger ones. The consequence was an increase in average farm size from sixty-five acres in 1700 to one hundred and fifty acres a century later. By the 1820s only 10 per cent of the countryside belonged to smallholders. By Queen Victoria's reign most farms were owned by substantial landowners and rented to tenant farmers. In parts of England, however, some small, owner-occupied farms persisted, especially in areas of dispersed settlement such as the south-west and the Home Counties.[35]

Enclosure fundamentally changed the appearance of the countryside. Land that used to be open was now lined out with hedges, walls and fences, and open views were broken up into a series of compartments (fig. 303). Enclosure also reversed two centuries of woodland depletion as landlords took up forestry as a long-term investment. Whilst many deplored this patchwork of new shapes, these quickly came to define the English countryside and attract admirers. In the course of the century it could even be said to have come to define Englishness. This was an irony, given that never before had so many been disconnected from the land, but as society became more urban so it defined itself in terms of nature – a nature that was, in fact, every bit as man-made as the urban spaces against which people reacted.[36]

The passion for the countryside affected all classes of society but exercised a particular hold on landowners, who were determined that future generations would manage, inhabit and enjoy the same lands as their forebears. This was a realistic aspiration in the century of political stability that followed 1688. Increasing numbers of landowners adopted the strict settlement whereby estates were held in trust for future generations and the landowner for the time being was essentially a tenant on his own estate. This encouraged long-term aggrandisement of estates. The Dukes of Bedford expanded Woburn, Bedfordshire, by purchase and transfer with neighbouring landowners, and by the late 18th century they had succeeded in consolidating their lands in a single bloc containing six villages and a series of tenant farms, some of which were as big as eight hundred acres. The rental from their estate rose from about £15,000 in 1692 to more than £37,000 in 1739 and over £51,000 in 1771. Of course, not all estates were as successful – but many were.[37]

This process of estate consolidation normally involved the creation of new field boundaries, access roads, bridges, plantations and estate cottages, much of which was funded by loans. Thanks to the expansion of money markets mortgages became a form of long-term borrowing rather than a short-term expedient. As a result landowners had less need to sell land to fund capital developments or raise marriage dowries for their daughters. In the longer term it allowed families such as the Temples of Stowe to carry colossal debts that would have simply ruined their forebears.[38]

From the mid 1720s the same questions about Roman authenticity that had been asked of buildings were asked of landscape. Lord Burlington, at his villa in Chiswick, began to experiment with ways of making his grounds suitable for the Roman house he had built. There was little hard evidence of how the gardens of Roman villas were disposed and so inspiration came from literature – writers such as Virgil and Horace praised rural life – and from painting – particularly views of Italian landscapes and Italian Renaissance gardens such as the Boboli in Florence. Over twenty years Burlington, with the involvement of William Kent, moved away from the fussy compartmentalised formal gardens of the turn of the century to a more unified landscape of groves, woods and vistas, interspersed with classical buildings and monuments. The latter was a novel idea, perhaps influenced by theatre designs, and each building was carefully placed for visual effect and moral purpose. One of the most delightful is Chiswick's circular Ionic temple inspired by the Pantheon in Rome, overlooking a grass amphitheatre and pool containing an obelisk (fig. 304).[39]

But Chiswick was a villa on a small scale; it was designers such as William Kent and Charles Bridgeman who were to develop the idea of an English Roman landscape on a grand scale. The largest and most remarked-upon garden of its age was at Stowe by Richard Temple, created Viscount Cobham in 1718. A new house was built on top of a hill between 1675 and 1683, commanding a fine prospect over at least twenty-five miles. Temple first employed Charles Bridgeman, the royal gardener, and Sir John Vanbrugh to lay out his gardens but subsequently involved William Kent, James Gibbs and Lancelot 'Capability' Brown. By 1732 Vanbrugh had already designed nine buildings at Stowe, including the surviving rotondo with a statue of Venus, patroness of the gardens. The landscape was criss-crossed by avenues, pockmarked by water features and studded by concealed monuments. Wood, park and farmland beyond were made to form part of the composition by ridings stretching deep into the estate (fig. 305).

Nearer by, to the south-east of the house, lie the remarkable Elysian Fields, a valley running down to a lake laid out by Kent in 1735. This was the setting for the Temples of Ancient Virtue, Modern Virtue and British Worthies. The latter encapsulates the conceptual programme at Stowe – the linkage between the classical and the contemporary world, English history past and English politics present. The monument is a curved screen with sixteen niches containing, on one side, men of action (including King Alfred, Francis Drake and William III) and, on the other, men of contemplation (including Shakespeare, Inigo Jones and John Locke). Over all of them in a niche set in a central pyramid was a bust of Mercury, the god responsible for leading souls to Elysium.[40] For Viscount Cobham Stowe was a canvas on which he could design a landscape expressing his understanding of philosophy, painting, architecture and classical mythology. It also expressed his patriotism, political allegiances and his knowledge of the world acquired on the Grand Tour.

The great houses set in vast, complex, designed landscapes became completely disconnected from the agricultural buildings that supported them. From the 1710s even walled orchards and kitchen gardens were located away from the house. The exception to this was the stables. These had previously been disposed as part of the forecourt of houses, and frequently mixed up with barns and other ancillary buildings (p. 235). From the 1730s stables were increasingly set up in quadrangles detached from the house. At Houghton

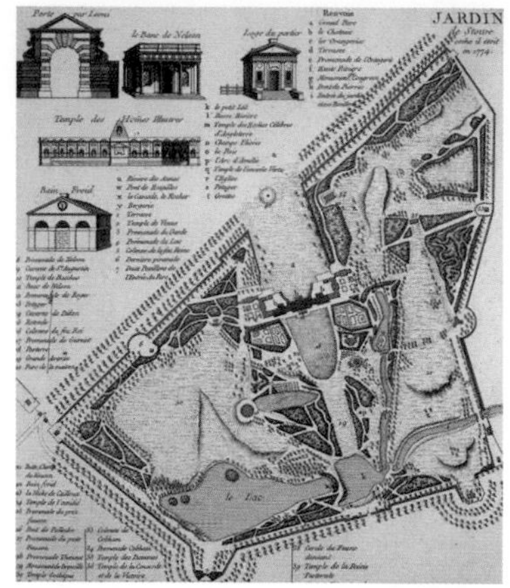

Fig. 305 (top) Stowe, Buckinghamshire, the gardens as shown in Les Nouveaux Jardins a la Mode, 1774. The Stowe landscape strewn with carefully designed and sited buildings was an allegorical as much as an aesthetic scheme.

Fig. 306 (above) Houghton Hall, Norfolk, the Stables, William Kent, 1732. These were the first stables to be given some sort of parity with the house; large, architecturally pretentious and carefully sited in relation to the mansion, the bloodstock they contained was given equivalence with works of art within the house.

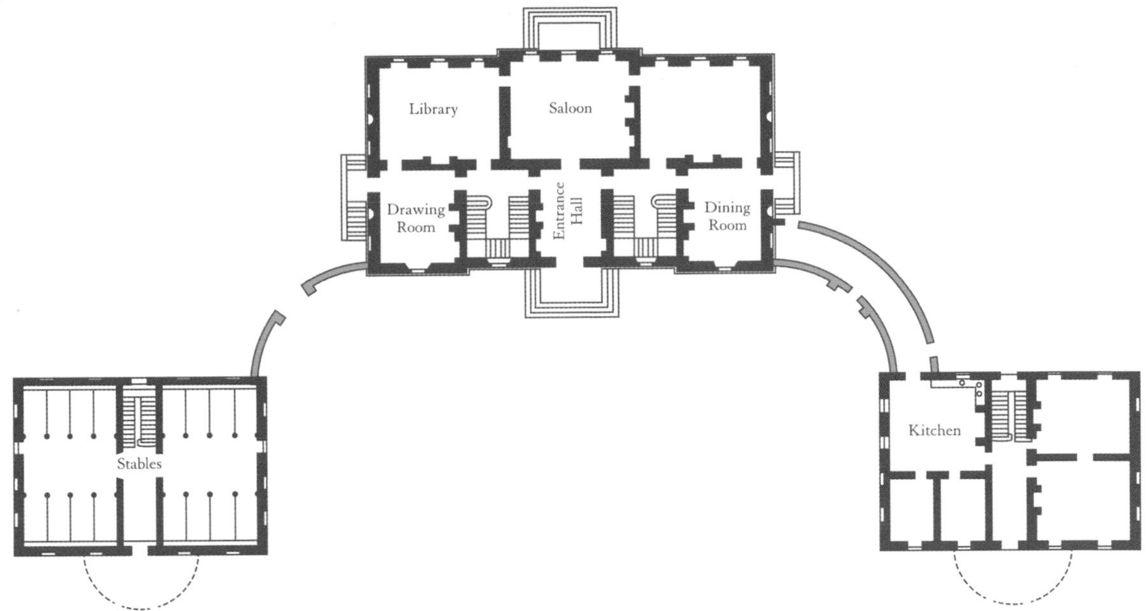

Fig. 307 (above right) Kelmarsh Hall, Northamptonshire; plan of the principal floor from James Gibbs's *Book of Architecture*. The hall and saloon formed an axis through the house, which stands on the top of a rise. The park elevation is restrained; simple, but elegant and ordered.

Hall, Norfolk, one of the greatest houses of its day, built by the Prime Minister Sir Robert Walpole, the stables were designed by William Kent in 1732. They were in a quadrangle to one side of the house in a block containing stabling for both hunters and coach horses, tack rooms, hay lofts, coach houses and lodgings for the grooms (fig. 306). The first country-house stables to complement the house in the landscape, Kent's design relied on his earlier stables at the Royal Mews (fig. 283), and the Houghton Hall stables were lit, again, by Diocletian windows tucked under the brick vaults. The stalls had giant Doric columns topped with balls. Detached quadrangular stable blocks were soon to be built at almost every country residence of any size or pretention. The largest were by James Paine at Chatsworth House, Derbyshire (1756–63) and Sir William Chambers at Goodwood House, Sussex (1757).[41]

Standing on rising ground overlooking a natural lake is Kelmarsh Hall, Northamptonshire, a large gentry house set in one thousand acres of good farmland (fig. 307). It was built between 1727 and 1732 by a Whig supporter, William Hanbury, the son of a lawyer who had married an heiress. His architect was James Gibbs, who created an austere and refined red-brick house of seven bays and two storeys, with a central pediment and flanking two-storeyed pavilions linked by quadrants. This is a quintessential gentry residence of the sort found all over southern England, typical in its symmetry, reticence and quiet confidence. It also has a typical plan. The ground floor is divided into eight compartments (fig. 307). The central two, on axis, are the entrance hall and the saloon, which looks out over the park. Either side are staircases and four subsidiary rooms. With many variations this double-pile plan, born at the Restoration, formed the basis of any house of aspiration.[42]

Men such as William Hanbury, and other lesser landowners, were more closely engaged with agriculture and country pursuits than the aristocracy. Although Kelmarsh was carefully set aside from any evidence of farming, houses only slightly further down the social scale were hugger-mugger with

Fig. 308 (left) Court of Noke, Pembridge, Herefordshire, a fine gentry house of *c.*1700; to its left are the buildings and outhouses that serviced its farmland.

Fig. 309 (below) Farm Hall, Godmanchester, Cambridgeshire 1746. This large but plain mansion was on the edge of a village but set in a landscape that was a great park in miniature.

their barns, dovecots and stable yards, and care was taken to make all of these part of an ensemble. George Mason, Doctor of Physic, from Monmouth, built Court of Noke, Pembridge, Herefordshire, in around 1700. His handsome seven-bay brick house sat beside his stables, mill, barns and dovecote, with a miniature park at the front. A fashionable element was an ornamental watercourse overlooked by statues in front of the house (fig. 308), but the farm buildings did not detract from this as they were a deliberate indicator that the owner was engaged in agriculture.[43]

Hanbury, Mason and other such successful professional men were architecturally aspirational. They wanted houses and landscapes that demonstrated their good taste and judgement, and many took up residence in country towns and villages. The successful lawyer, Charles Clarke, remodelled his family farmhouse in Godmanchester, Cambridgeshire, in 1746. By enclosing common land to the rear he created a mini park that he planted with a lime avenue centred on a small lake, adorned, on axis, by a cottage with Gothic windows and door. Facing the restrained red-brick entrance front there was a second avenue, framing a long canal running down to the river Ouse (fig. 309). The same village contains a second mansion, Island Hall, built by a merchant, one of Godmanchester's two bailiffs and later Receiver-General for Huntingdonshire. Finished in 1749, Island Hall was a miniature country house, with six hundred acres in the parish, and an ornamental park and

Fig. 310 (above) Island Hall Godmanchester, Cambridgeshire. At the other end of the village from Farm Hall this house, built in 1749, was much grander than Farm Hall, but was similarly set in impressive grounds including a Chinese bridge linking the gardens to an island in the river.

Fig. 311 (above) Island Hall, Godmanchester, Cambridgeshire, the entrance hall. The point about Island Hall is its magnificent first floor saloon, a room normally found in a much larger house. As a consequence much of the ground floor was given over to an impressive hallway and stair to approach it.

gardens (fig. 310). The elegant red-brick street façade led to a capacious hall and a very fine staircase (fig. 311); this entrance flourish is so sweeping that the ground-floor rooms either side have the proportions of dainty matchboxes. But the impressive stairs lead up to a large saloon, the point of which was to look out over the family parkland in front.[44]

The architects of Court of Noke, Farm Hall and Island Hall are unknown; all three were built by artistic and sophisticated local builders driven to make a splash for their status-conscious patrons. All emulated in architecture and landscape the estates of the gentry and aristocracy, and built in a national style not within a local vernacular tradition. The proprietors of all three owned and farmed their own land. During the 18th century the gap between these men and their economic inferiors grew. The effects of changing agricultural practices and tenures solidified the division of country dwellers into three classes: landlords, tenant and small farmers, and landless labourers. We have dwelt at length on the improving condition of the larger landowners but much more ordinary houses improved, too.

Ordinary farmhouses in the east and south of England had more rooms (between six and ten) almost all had first floors and most had more ancillary buildings. Houses in the north and the south-west developed less quickly, and for many their conditions remained much as they had been before the Civil War. By 1760 perhaps the most significant change in places that lacked local stone was the widespread adoption of brick and the virtual disappearance of timber framing. Ten years later England had become almost entirely a land of brick and tile.[45]

The aristocracy and gentry of England saw their world as a reflection of republican ancient Rome. Thus, more than a thousand years after the capital of Saxon England could be seen as Rome, in the reign of George I the cultural centre of the nation was visibly and intellectually once again the same place. Burlington, Hawksmoor, Gibbs and many lesser-known designers all strove to understand and recreate Rome in England. Their attempts embraced urban and rural landscapes as much as individual buildings.

Their sources were essentially text-based, and the rapid growth of printing and literacy after 1700 meant that models could be rapidly circulated across geographical and economic divides. After 1720 a much larger slice of the population, in distant parts of the country, was participating in choices about polite architecture and many new practitioners emerged. In the new buildings and landscapes the stern, ordered, public values espoused by the ruling oligarchy were reflected. Yet traditional ways of building were never forgotten and propriety was always observed. Gothic and vernacular forms were still deployed as a living architectural language wherever appropriate.

The dominance of classical forms was brief. Most of the leading architects had been trained in the Office of Works and by 1760 change was coming; one generation was dying and another came to take their place. The consensus amongst a large number of leading designers was to be challenged and English architecture was to embark on an entirely different course.

10— War, Inventions and Introspection

—1760-1830

The long and hard war that Britain fought with France from 1793 was a defining event with long-term effects. Britain emerged from it as the only industrialised nation in the world.

Introduction

Between 1760 and 1830 England underwent profound changes. The American War of Independence (1775–83), the French Revolution (1789), twenty-two years of war with France (1793–1815), and a fundamental and irreversible restructuring of the economy saw England emerge as the world's great power. Whilst there was a British element to this it was a fundamentally English phenomenon directed, largely, from London.[1] War was an important driver but so were demographic factors. In 1801 the government commissioned the first official census; it found that 8.3 million people lived in England, an increase of about 25 per cent since 1750. By 1831 the population grew to 13.1 million. England's population was increasing 50 per cent faster than any other European country and a third of its people lived in towns.

Impressively, England managed to feed this expanding urban population. By 1800 each farm worker produced enough to support two in manufacturing and services. Agricultural productivity per head was rising and by 1851 agriculture employed a mere 22 per cent of the population – the lowest proportion in Europe. London and the northern manufacturing towns sucked in excess rural labour, creating new jobs in handicraft and retail, traditional employments with independent masters and only a small waged workforce. In these businesses an imperative developed to introduce machines, not because there was a shortage of people but because employing them was expensive. English wages were amongst the highest in the world; a London labourer earned fourteen grams of silver a day, whilst his equivalent in Amsterdam earned nine and in Vienna only two.[2]

Between 1760 and 1800 the British – and this time it was the British – invented inventing. A series of technological advances introduced new machines and manufacturing processes. The machines that replaced men were at first powered by beasts, wind and water, the impact of steam power being limited before 1830. The goods that were produced were traded internally to a huge market hungry for textiles, ceramics, cutlery and building materials; domestic demand expanded by 42 per cent between 1750 and 1800. At the same time the state had created an environment in which there was an enormous foreign market, and to this exports increased by 200 per cent. Yet these economic changes did not immediately transform society; the impacts were at first highly regionalised and localised.[3]

In 1760 France was still the great threat – bigger, richer and in some respects more powerful than Britain, and most importantly, Catholic. This is a defining characteristic of the age and one that led to a popular English view of France, in particular, but also much of Catholic Europe, as downtrodden and oppressed. The flip side of this view saw the English as a chosen race entrusted with an trading federation that would bring peace, prosperity and, importantly, Protestantism to millions of subjects. Belief in the innate superiority of English attitudes, institutions and behaviour was a foundation upon which Victorian and Edwardian society was to be built.

In 1793 France declared war on Britain. The wars of the 18th century had been fought by ruling oligarchies pursuing materialist policies; the wars against France after the revolution were an ideological crusade. This was war on a scale not seen in Europe since the barbarian invasions, the twenty-three years of nearly uninterrupted conflict constituting the most complex and prolonged military struggle ever undertaken by Britain. In terms of sustained effort it was if the First World War had continued until 1937. The numbers killed were small compared with the slaughter of the Great War but the wars affected everyone, not least in terms of persistent and heavy taxation to pay for the £1 billion they cost Britain, a colossal sum, yet one that was invested in the country's future. Although the war brought short-term economic hardship, when seen in a longer perspective, Napoleon destroyed France, leaving Britain to dominate world trade and manufacture. By 1850 a quarter of the world's population was governed from London and Britain was the undisputed superpower.[4]

The effects of war on English building were far-reaching and diverse, but one of its most important outcomes was enforced cultural introversion. Travel on the continent, previously a mainstay of architectural education, was drastically curtailed. Those who were lucky or brave enough to travel went to Greece and Asia Minor, thus stimulating a huge interest in Greek styles that reached its zenith in the 1820s. As if by way of recompense, fascination with domestic antiquities ballooned, as did membership of antiquarian clubs and societies.

Economic fluctuations had a big impact on building, too. Through the 1740s and into the 50s building activity was at a low ebb as war and the Jacobite rebellion caused credit to contract; in the countryside there was agricultural depression, and even trade at the Port of London declined. The Peace of Paris in 1763 marked the end of a low period after which building construction boomed, particularly in London; although there were periodic hiccoughs, development remained strong until the American war sucked money out of the economy after 1778. From the 1780s until the 1840s English building started on a period of cyclical booms, with peaks in 1792, 1810–11 and 1825.[5]

People who had designed buildings had previously either been talented gentlemen or aspiring craftsmen, but after 1750 the size and complexity of buildings grew, the spectrum of materials and techniques diversified, and the people who designed buildings changed, too. Three distinct types began to emerge: architect, engineer and contractor. Engineers had been the first to turn their discipline into a profession, forming an institution in 1818. The expansion of the canal network and the building of the docks had created a whole new discipline, and in 1763 the term 'civil engineer', as distinct from the long-standing 'military engineer', first appeared in a London directory. Their public reputation was high and, after 1793, war with France further glamorised their achievements. It is not surprising that of their number John Rennie was buried in St Paul's Cathedral and Thomas Telford in Westminster Abbey.

It took longer for an architectural profession to develop. In the 18th century the notion of an architect as design genius mediating between builder and client was, for most practitioners, a long way off. Many prominent architects, such as John Nash (p. 383), Robert Adam (pp 377–8) and Henry Holland, were still speculators who designed, built and sold buildings. Many other, less successful architects searched for a role in the increasingly pluralistic world of late Georgian building. Various attempts had been made since the 1770s to create a club for architects but it was only in 1834 that the Institute of British Architects was formed to give a distinct definition to the profession of architecture as opposed to that of engineer or surveyor.[6]

Whilst various types of contract had existed in the building trades since the Middle Ages, from 1800 it became increasingly common to agree a fixed-price contract with a single builder for the entire construction. This method had been used by the Barrack Department and the Navy Office during the Napoleonic Wars (p. 348) and, although not taken up so enthusiastically by the Office of Works, was increasingly used by the private sector. The new Theatre Royal, Drury Lane, designed by Benjamin Wyatt and built in 1811, was perhaps the first major private building to be built by gross contract. The churches built under the 1818 Act were also contracted for in this manner, whilst between 1828 and 1830 Henry Lee and Sons, together with Samuel Baker and Sons, won the contracts to build Covent Garden Market (p. 374). The largest building contractors, such as the Cubitt family, employed their own architects and could offer clients a design-and-build service as they did for Queen Victoria at Osborne House, Isle of Wight.[7]

The rise of the building contractor and the fixed-price contract was symptomatic of an increased commercialisation of architecture noted with dismay by architects such as John Soane. Domestic building speculation, which had started in earnest after 1666, now dominated the building world. In the decade 1811 to 1821, 309,000 houses were built in England and Wales; the following decade saw 443,000. Very large military and manufacturing complexes created buildings larger and more prominent than the cathedrals. The Church, royal family and aristocracy, the traditional patrons of architecture, were now minor clients in an economically and socially broader and more commercialised market. English architecture had become a commodity.[8]

Building Styles

English architecture after 1760 entered a phase of stylistic diversity and complexity after the more ordered standards of the early 18th century. This was the result of a number of powerful forces, the first of which was the rapid development of technology in building materials and techniques. Added to this were changing demands – new sorts of building were required for new activities: offices, markets, factories and warehouses, amongst others. The third factor was a more intense and scientific engagement with the past, seen in the rise of history and archaeology as matters of professional diligence and public interest. Lastly, there was the increasing breadth of associations issuing from Britain's dominating position in world commerce. These changes were mutually dependent and together led to fundamental shifts in the language of English architecture.

The 1760s saw the passing of a generation of architects, including Matthew Brettingham, Henry Flitcroft and John Vardy, who worked in classical styles based on printed precedents. But the architectural consensus had already begun to break up in three ways: first was the idea of architecture as scenery – buildings being part of landscape composition, seen, almost, as a picture; second was the increased value put on associational aesthetics, the power of buildings to evoke ideas and emotions, to be symbolic of something other than the building's function; third was the rise of archaeology, the close study of old buildings providing a stream of new ideas and forms to inspire designers. These impulses were not distinct or sequential but part of a more general change in aesthetic outlook.

The assembly rooms of 18th-century England provided an important but socially exclusive means of mixing and meeting outside the home. From the

Fig. 312 (right) The Chinese pavilion, Vauxhall Gardens, London, 1749; not remotely Chinese, nor a pavilion, but an exotic canopy containing supper boxes and a walk.

1730s another more egalitarian meeting place became all the rage: the pleasure garden. These outdoor venues, normally on the edge of towns, charged a fee for evening promenades with music, singing and refreshments. They were open to all who could pay and it was perfectly possible for a duke and an apprentice to enjoy the same entertainment together. In London alone there were sixty-four such venues built between 1661 and 1871; none was a garden in a horticultural sense – they were nocturnal pleasure grounds dotted with pavilions. The first commercial pleasure garden was at Vauxhall on the south side of the Thames; it was in many ways the most successful and welcomed some ten million visitors in the century after 1740.

At first the structures in Vauxhall Gardens were built in a classical style. The best was the Orchestra, which opened in 1735, an octagonal bandstand with a pyramidal roof raised on rusticated columns. But in the 1740s this rather austere look gave way to something increasingly frivolous, transforming a classical forum into an exotic fairyland. The Turkish Tent, erected in 1742 to provide more indoor space, was of no known style but combined classical and Gothic features with elements from court pageantry. In 1748 the Grand Assembly Room was built with an exotic interior designed by an engraver and enameller. Then in 1749 three 'piazzas' of supper boxes were built in which people could dine under cover and watch the passagata. One was known as the Chinese Pavilion (fig. 312), another the Handel Piazza and a third the Gothic Piazza.

At Vauxhall the commercial imperative of the owner, Jonathan Tyres, who needed the publicity generated by exotic new structures, combined with the ambitions of young avant-garde artists, actors and writers all intent on breaking the suffocating strictures of Good Taste. The temporary structures at Vauxhall were vehicles for equally avant-garde designers, and the garden became increasingly theatrical and its architectural elements more and more scenic. None of the buildings was taken seriously by architectural commentators but they were a Trojan horse infiltrating new styles into the mainstream.[9]

Whilst commercial urban pleasure gardens helped bring exotic architecture into fashion, more serious-minded exercises did the same in private landscapes. We have already considered the gardens at Chiswick and Stowe, where buildings were introduced not only for aesthetic effect but for their associational value (pp 321–2). Novelty was just as important in these gilded settings as in public pleasure gardens. At Stowe James Gibbs designed the Temple of Liberty in 1741 (fig. 313). It represented the democratic liberties of the Goths over the tyranny of the Romans and was designed in a celebratory Gothic style. At Hagley Hall, Worcestershire, in 1758, was the first Doric Temple in a Greek style designed by James Stuart, recently returned from Greece and preparing his great book on the antiquities of Athens.[10] Not far from Hagley was Shugborough Hall, Staffordshire, where a Chinese summer house was built in 1747 for George and Thomas Anson based on drawings of a Chinese building in Canton. After 1762 came a Chinese pagoda and bridges, a Palladian bridge, a Greek temple, a Grecian tower of the winds, a Hadrianic arch, a shepherd's house, a Gothic pigeon house and assorted ruins – an image of the entire world.[11]

Fig. 313 (above) The Temple of Liberty, Stowe House gardens, 1741–2; hardly just a folly, this is a big stone building with fine interiors originally lit by reclaimed medieval stained glass windows. Its Gothic appearance was enhanced in the 1750s by cupolas and pinnacles.

The effect of such exotic structures was to erode the notion of an objective standard of beauty; architects and patrons were now less inclined to aspire to a single classical ideal measured against printed standards. These fantasy landscapes were deemed to be beautiful and inspirational, bringing a new world of associations and emotions, and comfortably mixing buildings from every architectural style. Access to these new styles was hugely boosted by developments in archaeology.

Archaeology had started at home with an increased interest from around 1700 in the ruins of medieval England. In 1711 Samuel and Nathaniel Buck started producing prints of ruined castles and abbeys, and of historic English towns, which were eventually to amount to more than 400 views. In 1717 the Society of Antiquaries of London was founded, providing a focus for scholarly enquiry into the relics of old England.[12]

Improved road travel and increased leisure time for the well-off led to an enormous rise in domestic tourism. The great ruins of the Reformation and Civil War were particularly popular; so, increasingly, were prehistoric sites. We don't know how many people visited Stonehenge, for instance, but nearby Wilton House received 2,324 visitors in 1774. At Duncombe Park, Yorkshire, Thomas Duncombe incorporated the ruins of Rievaulx Abbey into his landscape (fig. 65); the abbey could be viewed from an artificial terrace walk adorned with classical temples. If landowners were not blessed with real medieval ruins new ones could be built. Sanderson Miller specialised in such follies, designing the entrancing ruins at Wimpole Hall, Cambridgeshire, which were eventually built to a variant design by James Essex between 1767 and 1770, providing the centrepiece of the view from the house (fig. 314).

English cathedrals also became objects of increased interest and admiration as repositories of ancestry and national history. Whilst one school of thought held that they ought to be made more perfectly Gothic by removing later accretions, others believed that such 'improvements' were an attack

Fig. 314 (right) Wimpole Hall, Cambridgeshire; the incredibly effective fictive ruins of 1767–70, designed to be seen from the principal rooms of the house on a slight hill.

on the architecture of their ancestors. All these monuments spawned guidebooks, which joined histories of counties, towns, families and great buildings in an avalanche of antiquarian print. At the same time John Britton's *Architectural Antiquities of Great Britain* (1807–14) followed by his *Cathedral Antiquities* made illustrations of Gothic architecture readily available, and these and the hugely successful *Gentleman's Magazine* radically changed attitudes to Gothic.[13] In 1817 Thomas Rickman took the next step by creating a stylistic taxonomy for Gothic architecture and publishing it as A*n Attempt to Discriminate the Styles of English Architecture from the Conquest to the Reformation*.

Antiquarian interest at home was matched by a more serious enquiry into the history and archaeology – as we would today call it – of other countries. Between 1740 and 1804 over fifty English architects studied in Rome though, between 1798 and 1815, war with France put much of Europe out of bounds. Unlike aristocratic Grand Tourists young architects were bent on acquiring technical skills and knowledge to further their careers, and William Chambers, Robert Adam, George Dance the Younger, James Wyatt and John Soane (to name a few) engaged in systematic and serious-minded study. What distinguished them from previous generations was their determination to minutely and accurately record what they saw, and to expand their scope of interest beyond religious and civic structures to domestic remains and tombs. This had become possible with the discovery of Pompeii in 1748 and a series of excavations in Rome itself. Excursions into Asia Minor became part of the Tour and resulted in lavish publications such as Robert Wood's *Ruins of Palmyra* (1753) and *The Ruins of Baalbec* (1757), and James Stuart and Nicholas Revett's *Antiquities of Athens* (vol. I, 1762).[14] In 1757 William Chambers brought out Designs of Chinese Buildings, based on drawings he had made in China when he was a member of the Swedish East India Company.

French archaeologists, commissioned and supported by Napoleon, added a further dimension to available information. In 1799 Napoleon set up two commissions of scholars to record the monuments of ancient Egypt. Their findings were published in the massive twenty-volume Description de l'Égypte between 1809 and 1822. This was a sensation and a fashion for Egyptian design swept Europe.[15] Collecting also formed an important source of inspiration. At its most extreme it was pillage – Napoleon received a huge convoy containing the best ancient sculpture from Rome in Paris in 1799. Meanwhile Lord Elgin, Ambassador to Constantinople, negotiated the acquisition of the Parthenon marbles, which began to arrive in London in 1803 and did much to establish a fascination with Greek architecture. Private collections, such as the vast assemblage of classical sculpture amassed by Henry Blundell, also played a role in refining people's tastes and deepening the understanding of ancient civilisations (fig. 315).

Fig. 315 (above) Ince Blundell Hall, Lancashire; the collection of Henry Blundell in the rotunda before it was dispersed. The rotunda was built in 1802–10 to show off his collection and designed in imitation of the Pantheon in Rome.

England's trading links across the globe brought another ingredient to the architectural melting pot. Between 1785 and 1788 the painter William Hodges, with the encouragement of Warren Hastings, the first Governor-General of Bengal, published a series of views of Indian buildings, and from

Fig. 316 (right) The Guildhall, City of London; the porch designed by George Dance the Younger in 1788–9. Parts of the original 15th-century porch remain in the lower levels but the windows and the lozenges derive from William Hodges' *Select Views of India* published in 1786. Other motifs are Greek and Gothic.

1795 Thomas Daniell and his nephew William published Oriental Scenery, one hundred and forty-four aquatints of Mughal, Hindu and medieval monuments based on their extensive travels in India. In 1803 the British finally occupied Delhi, the capital of the collapsing Mughal empire, giving tourists access to the great monuments in its vicinity, including Agra, which the Daniells and others had not been able to see. Appropriately, the first major English building in the Indian style was George Dance's new porch for the Guildhall in the City of London in 1788, a vote of confidence in the city's trade with the sub-continent (fig. 316).[16]

These developments meant that not only was there a desire to build exotic structures but the information as to how to build them was available. They also helped in distinguishing for the first time the differences between Greek and Roman architecture, early and late Gothic, and Indian and Chinese styles, allowing architects to see the original evidence for the architecture of ancient civilisations. By 1800 archaeology and travel had begun to have a significant effect on new styles, from the ephemera of garden ornament to the solidity of purposeful building. The practical effects of this can be illustrated by three broadly contemporary buildings: Fonthill Abbey

(1795–1812) (fig. 318) by James Wyatt in megalomaniac Gothic; Brighton Pavilion (1815–21) by John Nash (fig. 377) in European Hindu; and the British Museum (1823–47) by Robert Smirke (fig. 395) in academic Greek. The architects who designed these buildings were equally at home in other styles. Nash also designed the now demolished Ravensworth Castle, County Durham, begun in 1807–46 in a medieval castellated style (fig. 317), Smirke built the County Court in Lincoln Castle between 1823 and 1830 in a military style to blend in with the architecture of the castle, and Wyatt constructed the Darnley Mausoleum at Cobham Hall, Kent, which was crowned by a pyramid. From 1760 until around 1850 successful architects needed to be able to work in a multitude of styles.

Architecture after 1760 was not only changed by the broadening palette of styles available to patrons; it was also transformed by technology, most importantly the increasing use of iron and steel. The Middle Ages had been characterized by sensational feats of engineering but, other than the engineering advances that enabled the construction of domes in the late 17th century, the period from 1530 until the 1760s saw no advances in engineering. Buildings were constructed within entirely traditional structural capabilities. Iron and then steel, however, began to shift the boundaries. The introduction of iron as an everyday building material was not primarily promoted by architects but by manufacturers and craftsmen. The first and most important of these was Abraham Darby, who in 1709 developed a commercially viable application for coke-smelted iron. His invention was a way of casting iron with sand moulds, a technology initially used to make lightweight domestic utensils. Coke-smelted iron remained a product of Coalbrookdale, Shropshire, until after 1760, when it was sufficiently perfected to overtake charcoal smelting and begin the transformation of national iron production. As a result, over the period 1709 to 1850 the cost of pig iron fell by 63 per cent, making it a viable material for mass use.

In the mid 18th century iron was not new as a structural material. In 1692 Sir Christopher Wren had used it in the House of Commons, where, encouraged by the Royal Smith, Jean Tijou, he inserted columns to support new galleries, thus combining structural integrity, practical necessity and aesthetic effect. But designers remained to be convinced by its properties. This is why the new bridge thrown across the river Severn in 1781 was so important. Ironbridge, as it became known, was an advertisement for the structural properties of Coalbrookdale's coke-smelted cast iron (fig. 319). Three hundred and seventy-nine tonnes were used to span the 100ft gorge, 60ft above the water. The design was based on timber structures; even the joints in the bridge were mortises, tenons and dovetails, as the pattern makers for the iron components were joiners. Just over ten years later a much more ambitious iron bridge was built in Sunderland, spanning 250ft over the river Wear, high enough to allow tall-masted ships to pass beneath (fig. 320). Whereas Ironbridge had been a showpiece, the Wearmouth Bridge performed a structural feat impossible for stone or timber. It was a decisive engineering advance.[17]

Fig. 317 (above) Ravensworth Castle, County Durham; a vast rambling pile of battlements and turrets begun in 1807 and eventually completed in 1846.

Fig. 318 (above) Fonthill Abbey, Wiltshire, James Wyatt, 1795–1812. This was unquestionably the most spectacular and famous Gothic private house of its age shown here in a promotional engraving in 1823 by J Rutter; the jerry-built great tower collapsed in 1825.

Fig. 319 (above) The first iron bridge at Ironbridge, Shropshire, 1781; a demonstration piece for the skills of the Coalbrookdale ironworkers and the capabilities of their iron.

Fig. 320 (above) Sunderland iron bridge under construction in 1793. Special scaffolding designed by Thomas Wilson allowed river traffic to continue to operate. The centre of the arch was 100ft above the water at low tide. It was opened in 1796 and demolished in 1929.

Cast iron has a crystalline structure that derives from its having cooled from a liquid, and it is strong in compression but weak in tension. It is thus ideal for columns, struts and arched ribs; it is also good for beams, being stronger than timber, but as it is very brittle it can fail without warning. Wrought iron has a fibrous structure more like timber, and performs well in tension and compression; moreover, it is not brittle and deforms rather than shatters when overloaded. As a result, when technical advances made it possible to manufacture wrought iron on an industrial scale it took its place next to cast iron in mass engineering.

The House of Commons became typical of the earliest use of exposed iron in interiors, as it was recognised as a way of building slender supports in auditoria, creating good sightlines. In ironworking districts iron columns began to be used to support church galleries; between 1792 and 1794 at St Chad's Church, Shrewsbury, the architect George Steuart built iron columns that supported the gallery and ran through it to support the wide span roof above. But the most influential early building was in London – the Theatre Royal, Drury Lane, as remodelled by Henry Holland between 1791 and 1794. Here iron held up tiers of boxes but also provided fireproofing between floors. This concern with fireproofing was very important in the diffusion of iron technology, leading to a determined research programme to devise a structure without combustible materials and culminating in the construction of the world's first iron-framed building at Ditherington, just outside Shrewsbury, in 1797. But architects also began to adopt iron because of the decorative effects it could achieve. At the Royal Pavilion in Brighton (fig. 377), John Nash used iron decoratively to make 'bamboo' staircases, the hugely tall columns supporting the kitchen roof, decorated with copper leaves, and the structure of the great dome itself.[18]

The successful use of iron beams had a huge impact on architectural design. The plans of upper floors no longer needed to reflect those beneath. The bedroom floors of country houses could have a maze of small rooms built in brick over large state spaces below, and shops could be built with large floor plates and rooms on a tighter plan above.

Another important advance was in concrete. This is an agglomerate of gravel, sand and a binding agent that hardens to form a sort of artificial stone when mixed with water. From early times the binder used was lime, forming a concrete that set slowly but was strong and durable. As the material relied on evaporation to set, however, it was impossible to use it underwater. This is why the engineer John Smeaton invented a way of using hydraulic lime as a binder in 1756–7, as it sets by chemical action and so could be used in water. James Parker patented his version of a hydraulic lime mortar in 1796 as 'Roman Cement', and this was extensively used by engineers in bridges, tunnels and canals, and later by architects as stucco.[19]

Sailing the Seven Seas

The Royal Navy grew hugely between 1760 and 1820. Much of this was stimulated by the Napoleonic Wars; but the navy also grew in peacetime, illustrating the government's commitment to it. Key to this was the rise of the Admiralty, to which all other branches of the navy now reported. The First Lord of the Admiralty was a member of the Cabinet and as such combined strategic, financial and political control. The seniority of the First Lord was symbolic of the fact that the navy formed a central component in national identity. Rule Britannia was first performed in 1740, epitomising the beguiling effects of heroism, sacrifice and plunder that came with naval success, but most of all embodying the conviction that the protection of English Protestant liberty and national trade was secured by sea power. Fear of popish slavery lay behind British naval investment by parliament. That investment was huge, the navy being the single largest consumer of state finance of a government that had an unequalled capacity to raise revenue. This explains the magnificence and scale of naval building in England.[20] The hub was the Admiralty headquarters in Whitehall, rebuilt by Thomas Ripley between 1723 and 1726 in a worthy contemporary style but made exciting in 1760–1 by Robert Adam, who adopted the French idea of screening its forecourt with a colonnade of Doric columns, his first work in London (fig. 321). From the roof of this building, after 1796, a telegraph system communicated with Sheerness, Chatham, Portsmouth and – eventually – Plymouth via a series of hilltop relays. A message could be sent from London to Portsmouth in fifteen minutes. This system was made permanent in 1815 using Admiral Popham's system, which involved a 30ft pole with two moveable 8ft arms. The stations were robustly built brick towers, one of which stands complete with its mechanism on Chatley Heath, Surrey (fig. 322), part of the London to Portsmouth line.

Fig. 321 (above) The Admiralty buildings, Whitehall. In the background is the building erected by Thomas Ripley in 1723–6, the oldest surviving government office in England. It contained apartments for the Lords of the Admiralty and a shared board room. In front is Robert Adam's handsome screen, erected in 1760–1 when the street was widened.

By the time Adam's screen was up on Whitehall, the Navy Office, the Navy Pay Office, the Victualling Office, and the Sick and Hurt Board were petitioning the Admiralty for a new combined centre of naval operations closer to Whitehall. This desire coincided with the broader idea to build government

Fig. 322 (above) Chatley Heath Semaphore Tower, Surrey, built in 1822. It was in use until 1848 and was restored in 1989.

Fig. 323 (below right) Somerset House, river front, designed by Sir William Chambers. The huge rusticated arcade now at pavement level was on the water's edge; the large central arch gave access to a dock for the barges of the Lords of the Admiralty. Above, the long façade is broken up by dramatic semi-circular arches with porticos resting on their heads.

offices to house a number of departments that were poorly accommodated. The location was to be the dilapidated royal palace of Somerset House.

The old palace was replaced between 1776 and 1801 by a colossal office block in the single largest government building operation of the 18th century, costing £462,323. Its designer was the 52-year-old Comptroller of the Office of Works, William Chambers, who had spent his career waiting to build a great royal palace. When it became clear that new Somerset House was to proceed he made a research trip to Paris, which, unlike London, had a series of magnificent public buildings. This trip, on which he studied recent buildings such as the Paris Mint, helped re-enforce, if it were needed, the idea that Somerset House should be a magnificent monument to the king, the nation and the navy. Yet his eventual design was rooted in a more domestic vocabulary – the London square, the architecture of Inigo Jones, and the recently erected Horseguards and Treasury. What was novel was the lavish use of external sculpture, enlivening the otherwise cerebral classicism of the façades. This was stylistic preference but also political intention. The sculpture was designed to be easily read and was highly jingoistic: the Strand front, for instance, contains images of the royal family and is crowned by figures representing dominion and the arms of empire borne by the fame and genius of England (the keystones represent Ocean and the rivers of Britain). The most impressive elevation, on the river, is now marred by the Embankment but originally its 520ft length, raised up on a massive, rusticated arcade, was the most impressive structure on the Thames, brilliantly capturing the romance and awe of antiquity (fig. 323). Beneath the arcade was the barge dock that allowed the Lords of the Admiralty to land when they came downriver from Whitehall.[21]

Fig. 324 (above left) The Royal William Yard, Plymouth, John Rennie the Younger, 1822–34. It was built of local limestone with granite detailing but made extensive use of iron in the roofs and for internal columns. This was no utilitarian factory and distribution centre, it was a proud proclamation of the Royal Navy's success and power.

Fig. 325 (above) Royal William Yard, Portsmouth; entrance gateway. Large, powerful and impressive, it gave a foretaste of the monumental structures within.

It was not only naval governance that was clad in architectural triumphalism; so were operational sites. As well as strong central administration, the development that gave Britain unrivalled naval advantage was the revolution in victualling. The ability to supply the navy with food and drink was the key determining factor in keeping it at sea. In 1783 there were over 107,000 men on sea pay, a vast number to keep healthily fed, so the Victualling Board established a new yard, the Royal William in Plymouth.

This was commissioned in 1822 and designed by the 29-year-old engineer John Rennie the Younger, who was constructing a new breakwater in Plymouth Sound considered a marvel of its day. The yard was to be built on the Cremyll peninsula, a rocky outcrop that had to be blasted clear of thousands of tons of rock to create a fourteen-acre site on its sheltered northern side. Here, between 1822 and 1834, the most impressive planned industrial complex of its age was built (fig. 324). Two great blocks face the water, containing a brewery on one side, and a mill and bakery on the other. A basin lies between them, and behind lie more storehouses and workshops; to one side is a slaughterhouse. The rusticated yard gateway, topped by a 13ft-high statue of William IV, is adorned with bulls' heads and crossed anchors (fig. 325). The Royal William Yard is far beyond anything that the navy needed operationally and was an expression of pride after the defeat of the French. Like the buildings at Woolwich Arsenal, put up a century earlier, the yard uses an architectural language of military triumphalism to create a statement of the navy's power, scale and modernity.[22]

Not only did the numbers of ships in the navy increase between 1710 and 1810; the average size of a ship of the line doubled. This posed challenges for the principal royal dockyards at Portsmouth and Plymouth, and both were systematically reorganised and expanded from 1761. Workshops and dry docks had to be made larger, timber buildings were rebuilt in fireproof brick or stone and, in due course, steam engines replaced muscle power for many tasks. At Portsmouth collaboration between the sailor and inventor Samuel Bentham and engineer Marc Brunel introduced steam-powered sawmills, pumps and mechanised block-making machinery. The Portsmouth Block Mills were a revolutionary step forward. Just as the navy relied on rope, it also relied on about 100,000 new pulley blocks a year

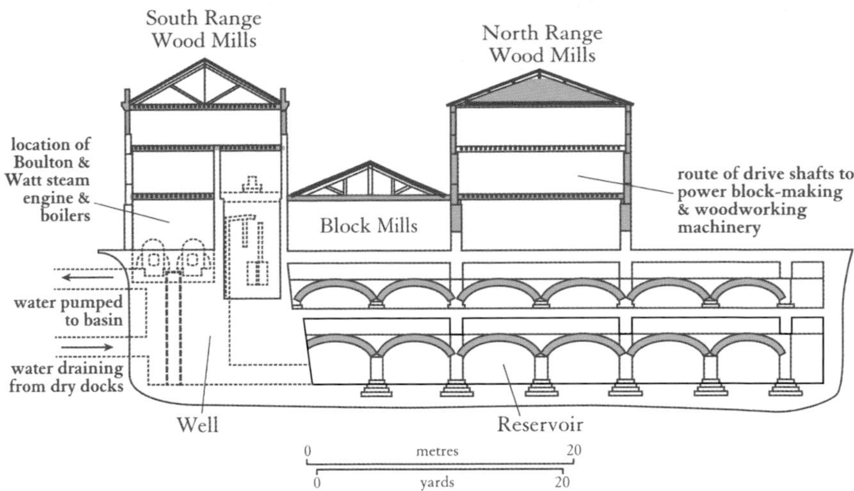

Fig. 326 (above and above right) The Block Mills, Portsmouth. Strangely unimpressive, this building was the most sophisticated factory of its age. Below was a reservoir for pumping out the dry docks. Left and right were the steam-powered wood mills, and between them the single-storey block mills.

to work the rigging and guns. These were made largely and laboriously by hand, but by 1808 Brunel's forty-five specialist machines were able to turn out 130,000 blocks a year with only ten unskilled men – a task previously undertaken by more than a hundred.

The Block Mills were built in two phases. First were the wood mills – two three-storey ranges with a wood yard between (fig. 326). The southern building contained a Boulton and Watt steam engine that could both pump out the dry docks into subterranean reservoirs and power the sawmills. These buildings were plainly functional and old-fashioned. Then, between 1803 and 1805, the space between the two buildings was filled in to create the block-making shop that was powered by overhead drives from the engines. This addition was more self-conscious, with a pediment, Diocletian windows and stone string courses. The roof was supported by turned Tuscan columns raised up on high bases. Brunel intended his new factory to be a showpiece and wanted the columns to be seen above the machinery. The Block Mills were the first mechanised mass-production factory and became one of the industrial wonders of Britain. They set the seal on the navy's position as the largest and most complex industrial operation in the world.[23]

There was a symbiotic relationship between the navy and national commerce. The navy created the stability for commerce to flourish, and commerce provided cash and the sailors for it to do so. The Americas offered huge opportunities for world trade and these were exploited by the English like nobody else. By 1815, after the destruction of France, England's trading supremacy was unchallenged. It was based on the import of tropical staples, especially tea, sugar, tobacco and, later, cotton, in exchange for manufactured goods and shipping services. The British Navigation Acts ensured that trade with Asia, Africa and America was directed through British ports regardless of its eventual destination – although the disgraceful business of human trafficking took place directly between Africa and the Americas, providing slave labour for the production of raw commodities.

Bristol and Liverpool were ideally positioned on the west coast at the head of excellent inland navigation to be the principal ports for transatlantic trade. But before the end of the 18th century Liverpool had pulled away as its hinterland became the industrial heart of England. In 1700 just over 100 vessels visited the port of Liverpool, by 1800 the number had risen to 4,000 and by 1871 19,000. The immensity of Liverpool's trade transformed a small town into England's second city, its population rising from 5,000 in 1700 to 311,000 in 1841. The river Mersey at Liverpool is a powerful stream, with a 30ft tidal range and shifting sandbanks, making it difficult to get suitable moorings. As a result in 1715 Thomas Steers designed the first commercial wet dock in the world to provide safe berths for ships taking on and unloading cargo.

At first private warehouses continued to be built adjacent to the houses of their owners, as they had been for centuries. The mansion and warehouse of the merchant-banker Thomas Parr, built in the 1790s, remain on Colquitt Street. But the scale of operations, and the necessity to be close to the docks, led to the separation of dwelling and warehouse. Soon warehouses were built by specialist operators who would rent space to merchants when they required it.[24] Meanwhile, a new type of warehouse was developed; this was the secure, regulated, bonded warehouse made possible by the Warehousing Act of 1803. These worked to the advantage of the port officials and the traders. Goods were delivered to regulated, walled stores in which officials could record the exact quantities landed. Merchants would pay duty only if the goods were removed for national sale. Goods left in storage or re-exported were not subject to duty.

West India Docks, built between 1799 and 1806 on the Isle of Dogs – a huge meander in the river Thames – were the first bonded docks. Intended to store sugar, rum and coffee – high-value, high-duty goods – their design was a combined effort led by the engineers William and Josias Jessop and the West India Company's architects, George Gwilt and Sons. The docks were entered from the river via the oval Blackwall Basin, which led via passages to the two big docks, one for import and the other export. The excavation of these involved the removal of 750,000 tonnes of soil. Steam engines drained the water, mixed mortar and hauled wagons up inclined planes. The dock walls were 6ft thick, with buttresses behind bound to the brick face by iron hoops, and were concave in section to accommodate ships' hulls. A series of ingenious moving bridges was invented to cross the water.

The docks were surrounded by a ditch with a low, railed wall just inside it and a cliff-like brick perimeter wall with massive gateways. Originally, on this side there was a total of six linked blocks of five-storey warehouses and three lower ones of over half a mile in length, designed by the Gwilts between 1800 and 1803. They were horribly bombed in 1940 and now only two originals survive; Number 2 is of five storeys, over a semi-basement topped with an attic. Its elevation is in three sections, separated by firewalls and loading doors that rise up to form dormers in the mansard roof. The walls are stock brick with Portland stone strings and cast iron windows, the columns of circular windows making a nice touch.[25]

It would have congested the text of the preceding paragraphs to point out each time a first was achieved at the West India Docks. The degree of innovation cannot be overestimated nor can their influence over dock and port construction. After 1805 the provisions of the Warehousing Act were extended to

Fig. 327 (above) Albert Dock Liverpool, 1843–7; not the first, nor the biggest, but the most perfect surviving docks of early 19th-century England. The genius of Jesse Hartley was to combine utility, monumentality and elegance.

other ports and it is in Liverpool that the most complete bonded warehouses now survive. Albert Dock, built between 1843 and 1847 by the greatest dock engineer of the day, Jesse Hartley, could house 250,000 tonnes of silk, cotton, tea, sugar and rice in a million square feet of space. The design of Albert Dock was not solely determined by utility. It was a civic venture, proclaiming the wealth and taste of the city corporation. The confidence that gave birth to the project still pervades the Herculean monumentality of the place. A 7.75-acre dock is surrounded by 40ft granite walls, around which stand five 60ft warehouses built on beech piles rammed into the subsoil (fig. 327). The warehouses marry warehouse planning with the fireproof technology of the textile mills, giving them an expression that is at once fashionable and utilitarian. A colonnade supported by squat, primitive Greek Doric columns of cast iron filled with masonry provided a transit area for unloading. Elliptical arches enabled cranes to swing goods from deck to dock with ease. Although superficially of brick, the warehouses have a cast-iron frame and roof trusses, and a roof laid with iron sheets. The idea of a colonnade – and much else – was copied from Thomas Telford and Philip Hardwick's St Katharine's Dock in London.[26]

Unquestionably, command of the oceans and the commercial advantages it brought boosted England's industrial economy, but for these to be properly exploited it was necessary to make advances in inland navigation, too.

Inland transport

We have seen that navigable waterways played a vital part in England's economic development from the earliest times. Some 700 miles of natural and improved river were navigable in 1700, but over the century from 1750 the inland network expanded to 4,250 miles, covering most of England, uniting markets nationally and linking the industrial heartlands with the ports (fig. 330).

Coal was the driver behind this. James Brindley, the first and most brilliant canal engineer, designed a canal from Duke of Bridgewater's mines at Worsley to Manchester. This was an ingenious and economically revolutionary solution as one horse with a barge could pull thirty tonnes of coal – ten times more than a single horse and cart. As a consequence of the canal the price of coal in Manchester halved. The first canals, such as the Bridgewater, were narrow, winding, contour-hugging watercourses. They were dug by farm labourers but by the 1790s there were gangs of navigators, or navvies, who worked only on canals. After the canals were threatened by the emerging railway network they became more ambitious and were often built by contracting firms, who would cut canals, excavate tunnels and build bridges.

Unlike rivers, canals were not natural watercourses and needed to be fed by streams, springs or, in upland areas, reservoirs. The first purpose-built reservoirs were created in the 1790s and from the same period many canals were fed by means of steam-powered pumps. Water was retained in the channels by puddled clay and, on one side, the spoil was hardened to serve as a towpath. In the 1760s a new craft was developed, around 70ft long and only 7ft wide, with a large, open hold suitable for grain, coal, stone or sand, with a small cabin at the back. These horse-towed narrow boats would have been lethal on rivers or estuaries, because they easily capsized, but were cheap to build and could move quickly in shallow canals.[27]

Changes in level and connections with other navigations were managed by means of pound locks. These had been used since the 16th century but technology rapidly developed in the 1760s, leading to the brick chambers closed off with timber lock gates and sluices familiar today. From the 1770s it became increasingly common to try to group locks together. A rise of immediately adjacent locks enabled boats to ascend or descend more rapidly and steeper gradients to be navigated. The Bingley Five Rise Locks on the Leeds and Liverpool Canal, Yorkshire, were completed in 1774 and could take a boat through a 59ft-level change in twenty-eight minutes (fig. 328). Bingley demonstrates both masterful engineering and the deliberate aesthetic impact achieved by the designers.

Huge numbers of brick and stone bridges were built, often to a standardised design, by canal-company contractors. On the Oxford Canal one company, Hollingsworth and Coates, built bridges at £50 a go with locally quarried stone. From the 1790s some began to be constructed of cast iron, such as the bridge over the Kennet and Avon Canal in Bath, cast in Coalbrookdale in 1800. The most spectacular bridges, however, carried canals themselves.

Fig. 328 (above) The Bingley Five Rise Locks, Leeds and Liverpool Canal, Yorkshire, 1774. Pound locks were not new technology, but they were now being used in a new and more effective way.

Fig. 329 (far right) Pontcysyllte Acquaduct, 1805; the engineering was not new, but the ambition was.

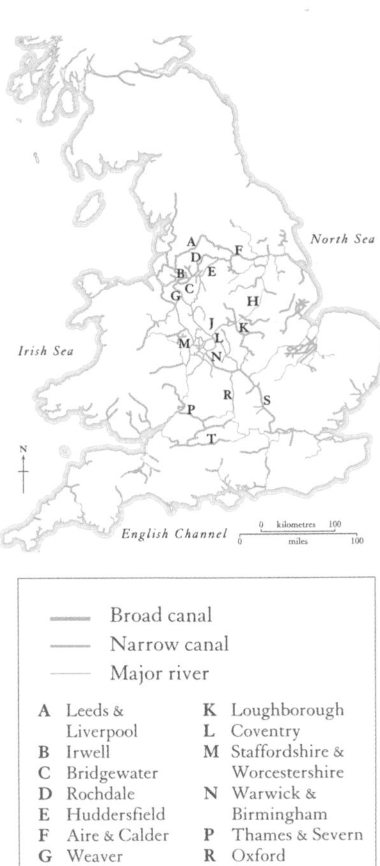

Fig. 330 (above) England's inland navigation system in 1830.

The first navigable aqueduct to be built in England, the Barton Aqueduct designed by James Brindley, was constructed on the Bridgewater Canal in 1761. The duke had seen both Roman and French 18th-century aqueducts, and was determined to build a successful one himself. The most ambitious was at Pontcysyllte, where the canal was carried in a cast-iron trough made of pre-cast sections bolted together. Designed by Thomas Telford and William Jessop, and completed in 1805, it is just over 1,000ft long raised up on tapering stone pylons with minimal tablet capitals (fig. 329).

Crucially, the canals joined up long-established river navigations and by 1790 the Thames, Severn, Trent and Mersey formed a single network, linking the principal ports of London, Bristol, Hull and Liverpool. At the intersections were transhipment points where goods could be moved from barge to river-going vessel. Stourport-on-Severn, Worcestershire, was a new town established by the Staffordshire and Worcestershire Canal Company. The canal linked the Trent and Mersey Canal with the river Severn, and the large basins enabled goods to be offloaded and transferred between vessels. Seven basins were excavated between 1771 and 1812. In the first phase a hotel was built that catered for merchants, tourists and the directors of the canal company. An elegant staircase led up to a ballroom and the bedrooms, and four houses were tucked into its wings. Later, warehouses and a whole town grew up around the basin.[28]

The docks at Gloucester are the most impressive assemblage of remaining early 19th-century warehouses. Gloucester became a major inland port trading in timber and grain after the completion of the Gloucester and Berkeley Canal, which allowed ocean-going ships to reach the city. Fifteen grain warehouses remain, of local brick, with Welsh slate roofs and timber floors carried on cast-iron columns. Large, hand-operated winches lifted up to 20,000 sacks of grain into each warehouse through external doors on every floor. The grain trade transformed Gloucester, and led to the construction of boat, timber and coal yards, rope walks, foundries and pubs.[29]

The canals were publicly authorised by Act of Parliament but privately financed by the creation of a joint stock company and the issuing of shares. The Trent and Mersey Canal, for instance, raised £130,000 by selling shares worth £200 each. Profits were made from tolls, and from leasing dock and warehouse space. Some toll houses remain; the one at Bratch Locks at Wombourne on the Staffordshire and Worcestershire Canal is an elegant brick hexagon with round-headed windows (fig. 331). The canal companies built themselves offices that expressed their aspirations; those of the Kennet and Avon Canal Company in Bath, built in about 1817 by Pinch the Elder, straddle the canal itself atop a rusticated bridge (fig. 332). They contained a 20ft-high boardroom, anterooms and secure storage, and are amongst the earliest purpose-built offices in England.

The rapid growth of the canal network was a radical moment in the history of English construction. It obviously transformed the ability to move goods around, particularly iron and coal, but it also introduced a whole new architectural taxonomy: locks, reservoirs, basins, offices, warehouses, hotels, new towns. Hundreds of villages acquired a canal wharf, transforming access to goods and markets. Many new structures were standardised in a way that had not previously been the case, the exact same buildings being replicated dozens of times along a canal length.[30]

Whilst the canal network developed, roads were also being improved. By the Restoration England was already covered by an effective system of road transport. Goods were delivered either by packhorses or by four-wheeled wagons, and people were conveyed to most provincial towns by carriages on a regular service. This required a substantial infrastructure of wagon and carriage construction, of horse breeding, inn-keeping and warehouse construction. Commercial operators dabbled in all these ventures and made their fortunes, especially in the major provincial capitals. But road transport was problematic. Packhorses continued to be popular because wagons and carriages were slow-moving on poor roads. Winter travel was difficult and slow, and towns such as Leeds were virtually inaccessible on wheeled transport.[31]

Before the 1750s parishes were responsible for the maintenance of roads, but their diabolical state inspired local businessmen and entrepreneurs to petition for Acts of Parliament to convert stretches into trusts (fig. 333). The trusts repaired and maintained the roads and funded their work through the power to charge tolls. By the mid 1830s 22,000 miles had been turnpiked by 4,000 trusts, perhaps 20 per cent of the whole network. From the 1750s and 60s these turnpike trusts, in addition to a new type of steel spring on carriages and better breeds of sturdier horses, made passenger transport infinitely more viable. New, more durable, road surfaces were developed, the most successful by John Loudon McAdam. His system involved ramming two layers of broken stone, in which no individual stone was more than six ounces in weight. Either side of the carriageway were ditches that collected water from the convex surface. This could be laid at a cost of £88 per mile for an 18ft width. The turnpikes were closed in the 1880s but, in their heyday, they relied on a network of gates and toll houses to collect fees. By 1840 there were over five thousand of these, with their distinctive bay fronts to give the pikeman a clear view of the road (fig. 334).[32]

Fig. 331 (top) Canal toll house at Bratch Locks, Wombourne on the Staffordshire and Worcestershire Canal.

Fig. 332 (above) Cleveland House, Bath designed by Pinch the Elder in 1817–20; this elegant purpose built office, amongst the first ever designed, was intended to impress shareholders and flatter company directors.

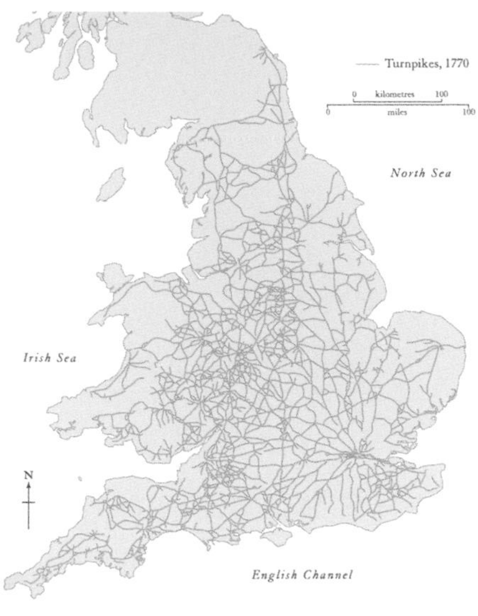

Fig. 333 (top) Turnpike roads in England and Wales in 1770.

Fig. 334 (above) Athelhampton Toll House, Dorset, *c.*1840. Typically, it has a canted front to provide a good view of the road and big eaves to shelter people paying their toll.

Fig. 335 (above right) The Angel, Guildford; rebuilt many times (it has a 13th-century wine cellar), it now appears as a Regency stucco coaching inn with fine contemporary lettering.

By the 1790s there was a national network of stagecoaches. In the 1740s it had taken four uncomfortable days to get from London to York. Now it would take just over a day. Before 1800 few roads were built and existing routes were turnpiked, but after that date new roads were laid up and down the country, many with bridges. London finally got new road bridges: Vauxhall Bridge in 1816, Southwark Bridge in 1819. The greatest of them all opened in 1833 – Thomas Harrison's Grosvenor Bridge, Chester, with a single-arched span of 200ft, still the widest span of any stone bridge in Britain.

The turnpikes transformed the towns through which they ran. Inns expanded, developed and multiplied because coaches had to change horses every ten to fifteen miles. The carriers struck deals with innkeepers, who were subcontracted to act as local agents as well as supplying stabling and provender. A big carrying firm such as Thomas Russell and Co., which operated between the West Country and London, owned two hundred horses and thirty wagons, and employed sixty to seventy staff. They had substantial premises in Exeter, including the proprietor's house, warehouses, stables, granary, wagon sheds, smiths' and wheelers' shops, an office and other structures. They used inns in twenty-eight settlements along their route and had a London terminus: the Bell and Saracens Head, near the Bank of England.[33]

None of Thomas Russell's inns survive and many coaching inns have been altered beyond recognition. Guildford had at least seven coaching inns vying for trade. The smallest, The Angel, survives, its handsome 1820s frontage concealing a medieval structure behind (fig. 335). Through the archway, leading to a paved yard, the crane to the hayloft above the stable can still be seen.

The Struggle Against France

Since at least the time of the Commonwealth the English had an overwhelming hostility to militarism and, despite the gravity of the threat from France after 1793, the ability to fortify the country or build a permanent military infrastructure was hampered by public and political suspicion. These attitudes were sufficiently strong to leave the country virtually defenceless despite invasion scares in 1797–8 and 1800–1. For twenty-seven months in 1803–4, however, Napoleon's Grande Armée camped at Boulogne and Calais with 93,000 men and over 2,000 barges, awaiting orders to invade. With a powerful telescope this mighty force could be observed from the English coast. The architectural response was staggering, in ambition, cost and scope far outdoing Henry VIII's fortifications of the 1540s and leaving a substantial legacy today.

Napoleon boasted that he would be in London within four days of an invasion and it was this that the land defences set out to prevent. It was assumed that any landing would be on the Kent or Sussex coast. The priority was therefore to protect naval and military bases surrounding London, and to fortify potential landing beaches on the south and east coasts. The commander-in-chief was George III's second son Frederick, (the Grand Old) Duke of York, and under him military construction was financed and devised by the Board of Ordnance.[34] At the start of the French wars English military engineering, in common with that of most of Europe, was based on the bastion system. Fort Cumberland, part of the defensive system for the protection of the naval base at Portsmouth, was started in 1794 and was the last self-contained English fort built on this system.[35]

The defence of Dover, the historic key to England, completely set aside the principles of the bastion system in favour of new French ideas on fortification published by Marc René, marquis de Montalembert. He argued that angled bastions restricted forward defensive firepower and proposed the construction of long flanks on which could be mounted mass artillery. His theory of fortification was based on achieving overwhelming firepower. He advocated the use of casemates for mounting guns, a return to a fashion abandoned centuries earlier partly because of the difficulty of ventilating them after guns had discharged. These ideas were put into practice on the Western Heights of Dover, the mass of high, cliff-top land that overlooked the castle (fig. 336). Here Lieutenant Thomas Hyde Page designed a fortress that was equal in power and size to the medieval castle to the east. Self-contained forts lay at either end. To the north was Drop Redoubt, designed to protect Dover from the landward side. It was a massive pentagon dug out of the rock and faced up with brick – utterly impenetrable, with bomb-proof casemated barracks on top. At the other end was the citadel, a larger fort, with gently zig-zagging ramparts. Between the two were deep-cut lines designed to be crammed with artillery. The defences on the Western Heights were never completed and never armed, though they were adapted and manned during the 1850s. They cost nearly £240,000, possibly the most expensive single piece of engineering during the wars.[36]

Fig. 336 (below) Dover, Western Heights, Board of Ordnance, built in stages between 1781 and 1859. Virtually unknown today, this great artillery fortress was larger and more ambitious than its much more famous medieval neighbour.

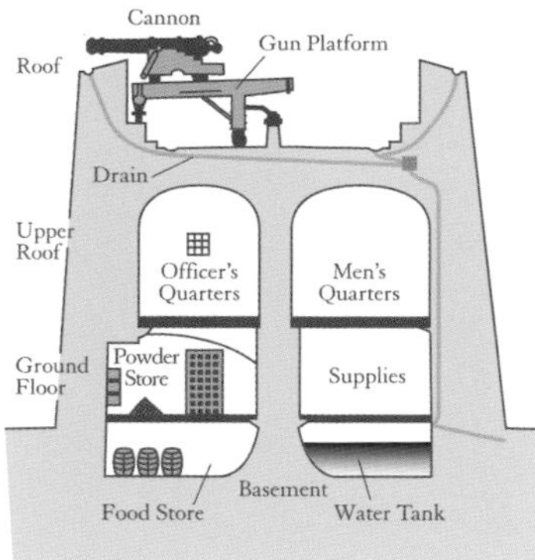

Fig. 337 (above) Cross section of a typical Martello Tower. The howitzer points out to sea and beneath the seaward walls are thicker.

Dover was the most important point on the south coast but it was realised that the entire coast, not just the crucial node, needed protection. After several years of disagreement a system of beach protection was devised and agreed, based on defences previously erected in the Channel Islands, and on a circular tower at Cape Mortella in Corsica that had been effective against the Royal Navy in 1794.

Martello Towers (after Mortella) were designed to enable a small number of men to hold their position against much larger forces (fig. 337). They look circular but were in fact elliptical, with their thickest walls facing the sea. Thirty-three feet high with a diameter of 26ft, they were built of brick and hot lime mortar – this mixture (lime ash and hot tallow) increased resistance to bombardment. The towers were entered by a ladder at first-floor level, where quarters for twenty-four men and an officer were located. The ground floor was for the magazine, food and water, and the flat roof on top – a bomb-proof platform –carried a 24-pounder and a 5.5in howitzer. The towers were lethal. Firing ten or twelve times a minute the two guns could discharge, between them, up to 3,300 balls a minute, the firepower of half a dozen companies of infantrymen. Seventy-four Martello Towers were completed by 1806. Spaced five to six hundred yards apart around the Kent and Sussex shore, no landing place could escape devastating fire. Between 1808 and 1812 a further twenty-seven towers were built on the east coast.[37]

Gunpowder was central to Britain's ability to prosecute war – a first-rate ship of the line would sail with nearly five hundred barrels of it. In 1759 the government had bought a leading commercial manufactory in Faversham to help secure supply and quality. Over the next twenty years, thanks to the efforts of the Royal Laboratory at Woolwich, English gunpowder became the finest in the world. Powder had traditionally been stored at the Tower of London and after the Great Fire at Upnor Castle on the Medway, but in 1760 a project was initiated to build five huge powder magazines at Purfleet, Essex, that would take 10,400 barrels each.[38] Perversely, during the Napoleonic Wars the Purfleet magazine exacerbated the Ordnance Board's problems. Because all of their depots and gunpowder factories were now in and around London, if the city fell to the French everything would be lost. So in 1802 a new site was chosen at Weedon Bec, Northamptonshire, deep in the Midlands but networked into the turnpikes and, crucially, close to the new Grand Junction Canal, which linked the depot to Birmingham, a centre of arms manufacture, as well as to London and the Royal Gunpowder Mills.

The 176-acre Weedon depot was the brainchild and design of the engineer Captain Robert Pilkington, and was arranged around two 12ft-high walled enclosures through which the canal branch ran. The largest enclosure was for the storehouses, of which there were four on each side of the canal. The upper floors of these were designed for 100,000 small arms, stored in racks and lit by patented sash windows faced with copper; the ground floors were designed for around three hundred and fifty pieces of field ordnance. Architecturally the blocks were very impressive, modulated by slightly projecting centre and end bays, and enlivened by stone plinths, string courses and cornices (fig. 338).

Fig. 338 (left) Weedon Depot, Northamptonshire, Robert Pilkington, from 1802. Behind the sturdy perimeter wall two of the brick storehouses are seen, only a lack of chimneys betrays their utilitarian purpose.

On each side there was a single 20ft-wide doorway framed by stone pilasters. The enclosure was entered at each end by guardhouses built over the canal and secured by double portcullises. Both of these were crowned by an ornamental cupola. The second walled enclosure contained four double magazines each storing 4,140 barrels of gunpowder, separated by traverses to prevent more than one magazine exploding at a time. There were barracks for the Horse Artillery to accommodate nine officers, one hundred and fifty gunners and drivers, and one hundred and sixty horses, in addition to the five fine houses for the civil officers responsible for the operation of the depot.[39]

Between 1789 and 1814 the army grew from 40,000 to 225,000 men, whilst the militia – the Georgian Home Guard – stood at 500,000 by 1804. Attempting to accommodate these numbers, even on a temporary or short-term basis, was impossible. The billeting system, which had supplemented the small number of barracks, collapsed: innkeepers and publicans refused to take more soldiers and petitioned parliament for urgent barrack construction. The first units to receive permanent new barracks were the marines, who, uniquely amongst British fighting forces, were barracked in the same town for long periods waiting to board ship. Their new barracks at Stonehouse, Plymouth, built in 1765, could be confused with a grand town square (fig. 339). Three blocks of noble buildings stood around the parade ground, with only the fencing and guard house at the front signalling its institutional use. But these 600-man barracks were dwarfed by the Royal Artillery Barracks at Woolwich, started in 1775.

By 1761 the Artillery Corps comprised 3,200 officers and men, sparking the need to urgently consider new accommodation. The solution was the construction of what were the largest single barracks in Britain to date (fig. 340). The design was a joint effort and built in stages, but it was unified and embellished by James Wyatt. The gargantuan façade at Woolwich, over 1,000ft

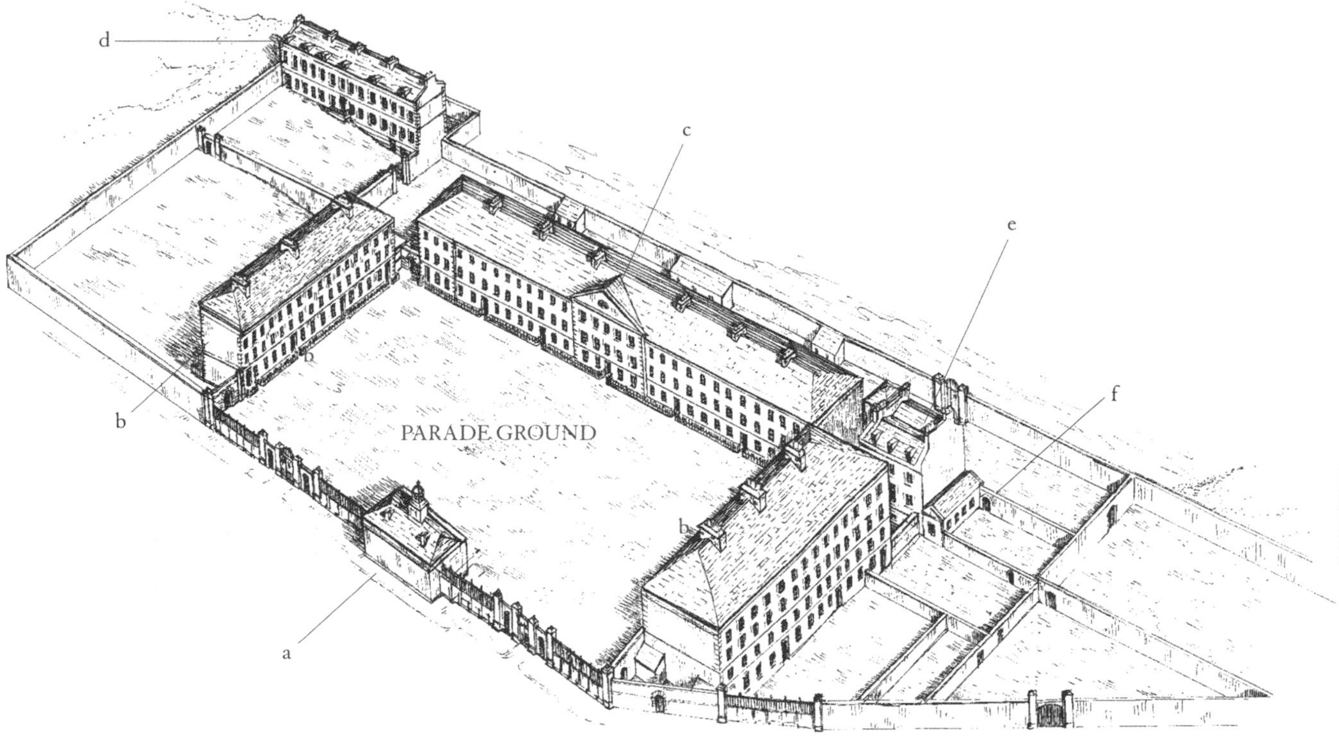

d

c

e

b

f

PARADE GROUND

b

a

Fig. 339 (top) Stonehouse Marine Barracks, Plymouth, 1765: a) guardhouse; b) officers' barracks; c) privates' barracks; d) infirmary and surgeons' quarters; e) canteen; f) kitchen.

Fig. 340 (above) The Royal Artillery Barracks, Woolwich, 1775–1802; vast, imposing, but not particularly threatening, as Britain's largest barracks were built in a domestic style.

long, is ruthlessly symmetrical on either side of Wyatt's triumphal arch, which leads through to washhouses, cookhouses, stables, hospital, magazine, riding schools, granaries, stores and workshops arranged like a Roman fort on Hadrian's Wall. The main residential blocks are linked with colonnades, and although the elements individually look back to a building such as the Grand Storehouse at the Tower, the massed effect is of an out-of-control city terrace. These buildings have an assertive militaristic presence directly challenging the long-held English antipathy to inland military barracks. There was no concealing the fact that here were stationed in some comfort and splendour, 3,492 men, 87 officers and 1,718 horses.[40]

In 1803 the Ordnance Board moved the Royal Military Academy up to Woolwich Common (fig. 341). The architect was again James Wyatt. This

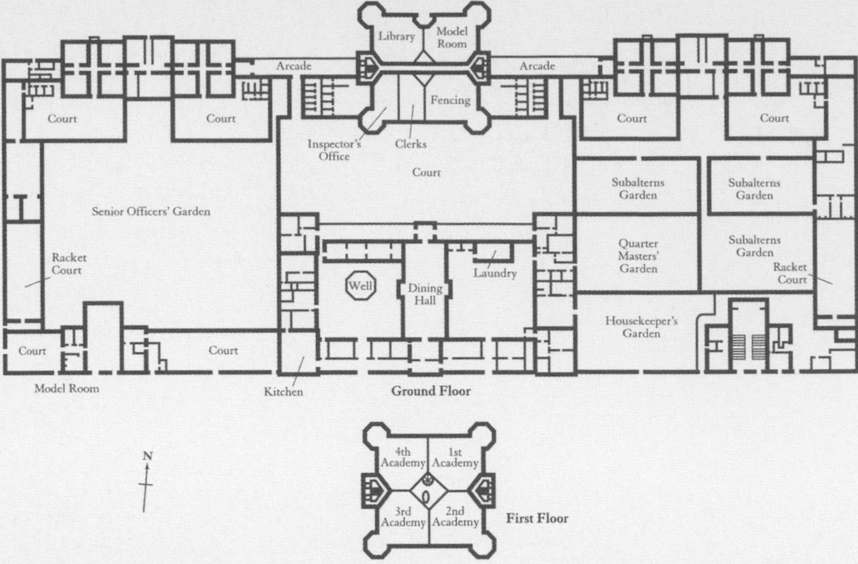

was a huge new college, and, as most educational establishments were Gothic or Tudor, so it was with the new academy. The central block also paid homage to the Tower of London, the birthplace of the Ordnance Board, complete with towers and onion-dome cupolas. The academy contained a lecture room, classrooms and library, as well as accommodation for the masters and professors. The cadets were housed in four divisions, and could enjoy racquets courts and a fencing room in which lessons were provided. In layout it drew on institutional buildings such as the Bethlem Hospital and the Royal Naval Hospital, Greenwich; ranges were long and narrow, and courts spacious, allowing for good ventilation and lots of outdoor space.[41]

Fig. 341 (above) The Royal Military Academy, Woolwich Common, designed by James Wyatt in 1805–8. As an educational establishment it was more festive than its near neighbour the Artillery barracks, yet it was no less carefully planned.

One of the most important developments during the Napoleonic Wars, born of the extraordinary efforts of the British state to defend itself, was the increasing elision between military and commercial engineering. The inventor and engineer Samuel Bentham's appointment as Inspector General of Naval Works in 1796 was an explicit acknowledgement by the Admiralty that the navy needed to benefit from the advances made in commercial engineering. Bentham sent his newly appointed Mechanical Engineer, Simon Goodrich, on a grand tour of industrial sites in the Midlands and the north. At dozens of mills and factories Goodrich made sketches and notes, bringing them back to the navy and breaking the introversion and conservatism of naval design for good.[42] Fireproof construction, as developed in the textile mills, was of concern to the navy, and it rapidly adopted the wrought-iron sheets fixed to the undersides of joists and boards first used at Drury Lane. It could also claim to have inspired the invention of machinery to mass produce wrought iron, a process stimulated by the need to make high-quality mooring chains. In 1806 under Edward Holl, their Civil Engineer, the navy used wrought iron to support the gallery of the Chatham dockyard church and then in 1812 used cast-iron beams, columns and trusses in the 1,200ft-long spinning house at Plymouth, in which even the window frames and shutters were of iron. Holl was also a pioneer in prefabricated construction, designing iron frames that were manufactured in England and shipped abroad for naval buildings in foreign bases. Indeed, he probably had greater experience of using structural ironwork than anyone else by the time of his death in 1823.[43]

Thus, during the Napoleonic Wars the navy entered the industrial age, matching commercial ventures in its output, engineering and technology. Henceforth, part of Britain's military might was the industrialisation of its military capability.

Working the Land

In 1806 Britain instituted a blockade of the continent to starve the French of imported goods and Napoleon retaliated with a total blockade of the British Isles. England now had to become self-sufficient in food. Agricultural production expanded rapidly, and by 1815 more land was in cultivation than at any time since the Black Death and before the Second World War. Grain prices soared, rental incomes rose and landowners had never had it so good. Some of the newly cultivated land was a result of enclosure (pp 320–1); around two thousand Enclosure Acts were passed during the war. Much, though, was marginal land that fell out of cultivation after the wartime crisis had passed, causing agricultural depression and distress. Landowners in parliament moved swiftly, passing a Corn Law in 1815 that protected domestic production from cheaper foreign imports. Although agriculture went through sustained depressions in the 1820s, rental income remained double what it had been before the war and landowners were cash rich.

Increased areas under cultivation, the intensification of production, and the greater integration of arable and livestock farming after around 1750 led to new and larger types of farm buildings, and new ways of organising farmyards. A steady stream of agricultural manuals, pattern books and surveys were printed from the late 1740s. Agriculture ceased to be a way of life – or for the rich, a pastime. It was now a business, an industry even. Large numbers of new farms were built, whilst many older ones were extended and altered. Many buildings were put up by their owners but the larger landowners also built for their tenants, who expected to be provided with everything they needed to stock and work their farms. Investments were substantial. A modest but elegant farm built by Lord Petre at Thorndon, Essex, cost £2,000 in 1777 (fig. 342). For the richest landowners show or model farms were constructed partly as a prestige investment, partly as a model for their tenants and others to follow. These commissions attracted contemporary big-name architects such as John Soane, James Wyatt, Robert Adam and Henry Holland.

Fig. 342 (above) Hatch Farm, Thorndon, Essex, 1777. Though a relatively isolated farm, the buildings betray a strong interest in primitive architecture and sport a Diocletian window, by this date a ubiquitous feature in agricultural and industrial buildings.

Before the 1760s farm buildings were generally located in villages at a remove from many fields. The new generation of farms in lowland areas were built in the heart of the lands they served. The intensification of agriculture put greater demands on farm buildings, and designers, like manufacturing

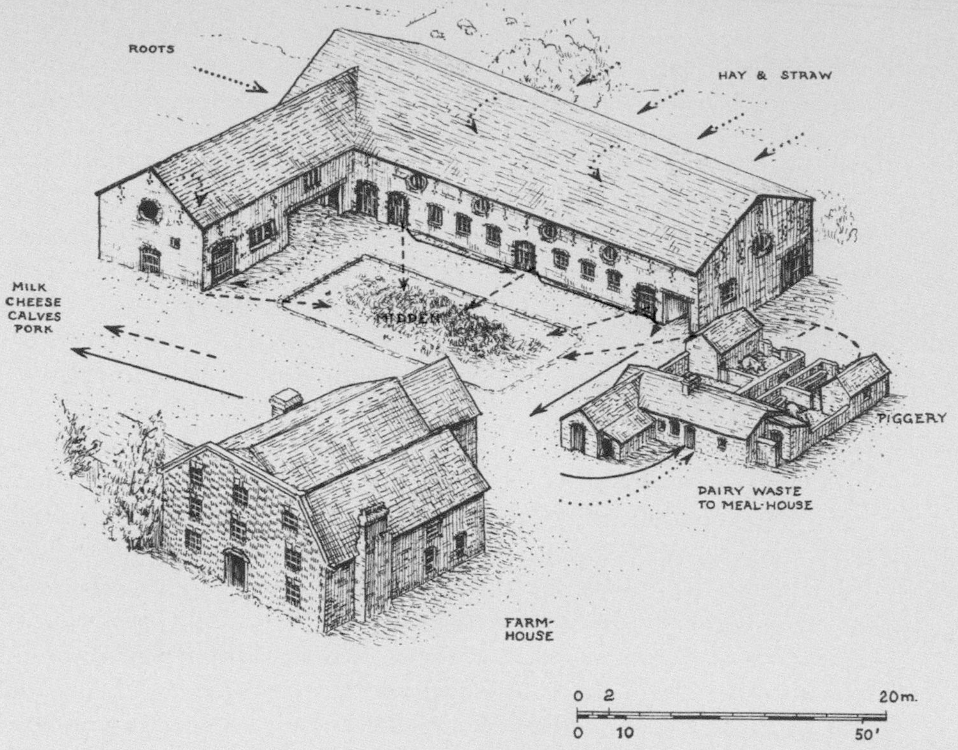

Fig. 343 (above left) Haycroft Farm, Spurstow, Cheshire. Hay and straw were stored on the first floor of the farm buildings and were passed down to cattle below. Roots were stored in the lower range at right-angles and passed to the cattle. Milk was taken to the dairy in the back of the farmhouse. The waste from cheese making was given to pigs. Manure from the cows and pigs was stored in the midden, then spread on the fields.

entrepreneurs, became more scientific in thinking about efficiently managing processes. In areas where animal and arable husbandry were equally important, efficient ways were devised for the production and distribution of manure, and the efficient handling of grains and animal feeds. Theorists were agreed that a quadrangular layout was the best, and most new farm buildings were arranged this way by 1800. The largest and most architecturally pretentious structure in the courtyard was the barn. These were smaller than their medieval predecessors, as the increasing mechanisation of threshing meant less room was required for flails and through draughts. Barns, normally sited on the north side of farmyards, stored foodstuffs and straw.

Either side of the quadrangle on east and west were often the livestock buildings, commonly a cattle shed and a stable. In both of these hay and straw were turned into manure, which was stored in the courtyard. In this way most farmsteads were essentially muck factories and, by the careful design of gutters, downpipes and gullies, great care was taken not to dilute the manure. Buildings were roofed in slate or tiles to preserve straw for the beasts. Pigsties were usually separate, as were poultry yards and dairies, both of which, in larger estates, were designed as ornamental features. In all a farm of six hundred acres could contain as many as fifty buildings. The farmhouse presided over all. Some were large, with perhaps six bedrooms; most were similar in style and plan to rectories of the period. Many had their own offices with a separate entrance to keep apart business and home life. Haycroft Farm, Spurstow, a dairy farm in Cheshire, nicely illustrates how processes were architecturally streamlined so that hay, straw and roots were taken into the farmyard, and milk, cheese, calves and pork were taken out (fig. 343).[44]

In much of England farm buildings displayed strong local characteristics. In Cornwall the bank barn – or chall barn – was ubiquitous. These barns were constructed on a slope so that cereals could be taken in on the first floor from the hill and cattle could enter on the ground floor. By the 1830s many of these had mechanised threshing machines upstairs, often powered by horse, as at Lynher, North Hill, Cornwall (fig. 344). Mechanisation in the countryside followed much the same pattern as in manufacturing trades. Threshing machines were available from 1786 but were first installed in areas in which labour was scarce and crops dense, such as Northumberland. Here fixed engines and machines were common before the 1830s, mostly powered by water, although some coastal ones were powered by steam as early as 1800.[45]

Stylistically, these buildings were free from polite architectural conventions and could be adventurous or quirky, often providing occasions for experimentation. What were believed to be primitive forms of architecture were popular, particularly Tuscan columns without bases and deep overhanging eaves. The language of the Diocletian window that had been developed in royal and aristocratic stables was widely extended to barns and steddings. At the top end fashions and processes were set by a small number of very well-known model farms.

Foremost amongst these was Holkham, Norfolk, where Samuel Wyatt (brother of James) put up over fifty buildings between 1780 and 1807. His patron was the great agricultural reformer Thomas William Coke, Earl of Leicester, who claimed to have spent £500,000 on agricultural buildings on the estate. Holkham was famous for its avant-garde farming practices and its annual sheep shearings were the precursor of the modern agricultural show. These were centred on Wyatt's Great Barn, one of the finest agricultural buildings of its age and one that was widely imitated (fig. 345).[46]

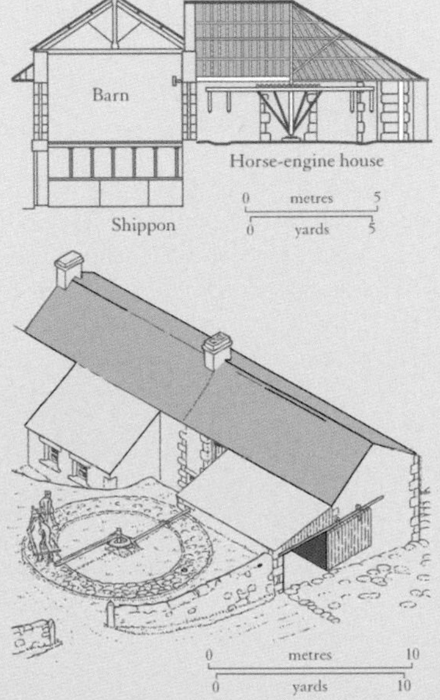

Fig. 344 (above and right) Lynher Farm, North Hill Cornwall; a horse-powered threshing machine in its own house was adjacent to the barn, with the cattle in the shippon below. At Toddy Park, St Neots, the horse walked round in the open, stepping over the drive shaft which took power to the barn. Cattle were, again, on the lower level.

Fig. 345 (left) The Great Barn, the Holkham Estate, Norfolk, by Samuel Wyatt *c.*1790. Two transepts expressed in pedimented points provided cross ventilation for the threshing floors. The detailing is sparse but perfectly placed.

Few new houses were built for the rural landless labourer in the late 18th century. Wages were low and so profits for speculators were thin, and many aristocratic and gentry landowners left it to their tenants to provide for labouring families. Most were disinclined to invest in new housing. The better houses were in the south-east of England and in the estates of big landowners sympathetic to the welfare of their workers. Conditions for the rural poor generally deteriorated northwards and westwards. The Earl of Leicester was happy to build cottages for his tenants at Holkham in the 1780s and 90s, each at a cost of around £110. They were of an ideal standard, with kitchen and front room, three bedrooms, a privy, wash house and pigsty. But such beneficence was unusual and over much of rural England high rents meant the subdivision of already inadequate houses. In 1864 the first study into rural labourers' dwellings found acute overcrowding; 41 per cent of cottages had only one bedroom and only 5 per cent had more than two. The average air space per person worked out at 156 cubic feet, whereas the minimum acceptable in union workhouses was 500 cubic feet.[47]

Manufacturing Buildings

Before 1830 the English economy was still an organic one. Energy was derived from muscle, from wind and water power, and from burning timber. Timber was the national staple, essential for building construction, shipping, industrial production, and domestic heating and cooking. It was this latter use that provided the most significant challenge. As London grew, seemingly out of control, it became essential to free it from its dependence on firewood, which is why coal production was so important from the 16th century. In 1700 England's coal production was five times that of the whole of the rest of the world and the furnace in which it was burnt was London.

We have already seen that in the 1620s coal-burning grates and chimneys were more widely used in the capital, but for coal to become London's sole domestic fuel it was necessary to perfect both grate and chimney for mass housing. The huge building boom stimulated by the Great Fire did this, creating effective coal-burning chimneys and fireplaces for everyone. By 1700 coal could be burned in every new building in London.[48] As well as ameliorating London's energy crisis this stimulated advances in mining technology as demand continued to soar. The most important spin-off was the invention in 1712 of the Newcomen steam engine for pumping water out of mines. By 1800 there were 2,500 of these steam engines in Britain; France had seventy. The Newcomen engines were set in brick houses 40ft tall, in which a massive iron or brass cylinder sat on a brick-cased boiler. The piston was linked to a large oak beam pivoted on the wall of the engine house and the see-saw action could be harnessed to pump mineshafts dry (fig. 346). Although only suitable to power relatively simple pumps in places where there was a ready supply of coal – the engines used vast amounts of coal themselves in operation – they opened up seams that were previously inaccessible. This represented a gigantic increase in available power; indeed, by 1760 the additional energy that coal production released into the English economy was equivalent to an additional 15 million acres of forestry.

The big advances of the late 18th century were, however, made using traditional sources of power. The most important advance was in the cotton industry, the rapid expansion of which was one of the economic wonder-stories of the world. Whilst in the mid 18th century both England and France made cotton, the centre of production was Bengal, where a manual industry with cheap labour was responsible for most of the world's output. But by 1830 the English cotton industry had exploded, employing 425,000 people, and cotton amounted to 51 per cent of national exports.[49] This was achieved by a revolution in production that began in 1733 with the invention of the flying shuttle,

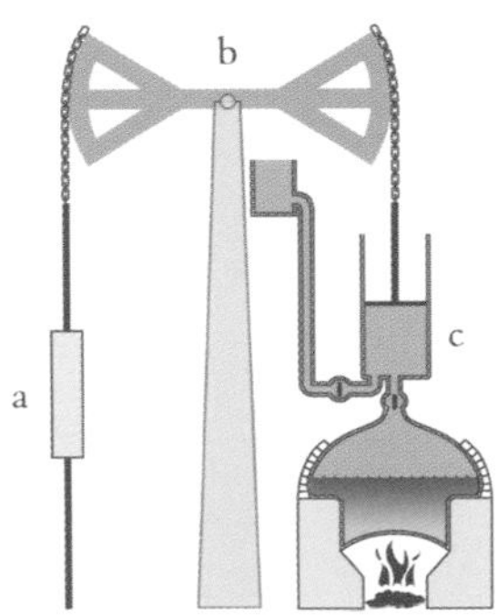

Fig. 346 (top and above) The Newcomen engine at Elsecar, Yorkshire, a rare survivor of the first common type of steam engine: a) mine pump rod; b) beam; c) cylinder.

Fig. 347 (right) Lombe's Derby Silk Mill on the river Derwent, Derbyshire, shown here in 1793. This was a manufacturing building of unprecedented size: five storeys high, 110ft long, with 300 workers. A single waterwheel operated 25,000 movements in the machinery.

which sped weaving up so much that the spinners could not keep the weavers in yarn. Richard Arkwright, an entrepreneur from Preston, solved this problem by reorganising production. He integrated in a single building the processes and machines that carded and spun cotton, turning it into a yarn for weaving. There was a precedent for this. To mass-produce yarn for silk stockings John and Thomas Lombe had set up a water-powered silk mill in Derby on the river Derwent. Their mill, built in 1721, was the first modern factory building (fig. 347), combining in one place the processes for producing silk yarn with spinning machines powered by a 23ft water wheel. Lombe showed how to stack the relatively light machines on several storeys in a long, narrow building that did not over-extend the timber-based power transmission. Arkwright followed this lead at Cromford on the river Derwent where, with his partners, he harnessed a new piece of cotton-spinning technology, the water frame, which was powered by water wheels. The first mill of 1771 was a five-storey stone building; a second mill was built between 1776 and 1777, and a third in 1785. By the end of the century there was a courtyard of buildings entered by a powerful-looking gate (fig. 348).

Fig. 348 (top) Cromford Mills, Derbyshire, Richard Arkwright, 1771–85.

Fig. 349 (above) Albion Mill, London, Samuel Wyatt 1783–6, sited on the Thames where barges could enter an internal dock. Unusually it adopted the style of polite domesticism.

The mills were 30ft wide so that two frames could sit side by side on floors built on unsupported single-span timber beams. Large sash windows on both sides provided good light for the fiddly business of handling threads. They were around 100ft long, creating a large, uninterrupted space for machinery. The first mill had a big, rusticated door case, a cupola with a bell to summon the workforce, and an internal staircase and privies. The second put these in an attached, full-height tower, also containing a hot-air heating system. This left more space within the main building for machinery. Arkwright's mills, which ran day and night with two twelve-hour shifts, were a new type of building and formed the model for a hundred years of factory design.[50]

Women and children worked in the Cromford mills whilst the men were at home weaving in the lofts above their cottages. Weaving was still literally a cottage industry until it was mechanised in the 1820s and 30s. So it was necessary for the big manufacturers operating in remote river valleys to provide housing. Arkwright's Cromford village had workers' cottages, a corn mill, an inn, a market place and a church; aristocratic estate villages were the only model for employer housing in existence.

By 1797 there were nine hundred cotton mills in England, around three hundred of which were of the Arkwright type. These early mills, almost all in rural surroundings, followed existing models for large structures built between 1660 and 1720, such as the storehouses in the Tower of London (fig. 260), Chelsea Hospital (fig. 251) and the Chatham Great Storehouse. They also had a close affinity to immensely long and sober London terraces, such as those in Gower Street of the 1780s (fig. 380). Some sported the odd flourish to relieve otherwise severe façades; the centrepiece of Arkwright's Masson Mill put on a show with its Diocletian windows, a feature already used in agricultural buildings and stables (fig. 350); Fiswick Mill, near Preston (1830), had a castellated centrepiece; Travis Brook Mill, Stockport (1834), featured thin pilasters at the corners. Many had bell cupolas to summon workers and tall

Fig. 350 (right) Masson Mill. Sir Richard Arkwright's new mill of 1783 had more architectural pretension, with its three bays with Venetian windows and small semi-circular windows topped with a cupola.

Fig. 351 (below) Stanley Mill, Stonehouse, Stroud, Gloucestershire; the all iron internal construction was not utilitarian but drew on both classical and Gothic elements to create a fine interior proudly dated 1813.

chimneys to power a steam engine that was used to recycle water to a nearby reservoir, ensuring the wheels would continue at full velocity. Engines did not power the machinery, something that had to await James Watt's improved steam engine, which allowed power to be converted into rotary motion. This led to the development of a different kind of mill, liberated from the fast-flowing waters of Derbyshire.

The Albion Corn Mill opened in London in March 1786. It contained only the third rotary steam engine made by Boulton and Watt to be installed in a commercial installation (fig. 349). The mill was designed by Samuel Wyatt and located in full view of Londoners on the south side of Blackfriars Bridge. It was an advertisement for new technology in every way; well proportioned, with a rusticated basement and elegant fenestration, it might be confused, in the twilight, for the town house of an aristocrat, although its façades were actually a skin on a heavy internal timber frame. It was a mighty thing with the capability to grind corn on a hitherto unimagined scale, potentially putting hundreds of small-scale millers out of business. When it was consumed by a wall of fire in 1791 it became a national advertisement for the problems of fireproofing. It took some time to find a way of creating a non-combustible mill, but the breakthrough came in 1797 at Ditherington Flax Mill, where Benjamin Bage carried floors on shallow brick arches that rested on iron crossbeams supported by iron columns. There was thus no exposed timber and a fireproof box had been constructed. An early mill that adopted fireproof construction and combined it with the fashionable use of decorative ironwork was Stanley Mill, Stonehouse, Gloucestershire. In west Wiltshire and south Somerset wool mills had prospered after 1800 but had mostly been small scale. Stanley Mill was very different. It was of brick with stone dressings, with Diocletian windows and Tuscan iron columns; the windows were of iron and inside were traceried Gothic arches on iron columns supporting iron beams (fig. 351).[51]

The other great challenge for mill owners was perfecting effective power transmission from the steam engines. The solution, as it had been with

Fig. 352 (left) A&G Murray's Mill, Manchester. In the foreground is the Decker Mill of 1801–2, and joined to it, behind, is the earlier Old Mill of 1798. Each is eleven bays and seven stories high, a cliff face of brick punctured by cast iron windows. The mills were designed to be fireproof, with cast iron columns and flagstone floors.

Fig. 353 (below) A&G Murray's Mill, Manchester; plan based on a survey of 1822. In the middle of the mill was the canal basin, linked to the Rochdale Canal by a tunnel. Dates of construction of the mills: Old Mill, 1798; Decker Mill 1801–2; New Mill, 1804–6.

fireproofing, was iron. Metal power transmission using wheels, cogs and shafts removed the size constriction placed on mill buildings by the unreliability of timber, opening the way for much larger factories.

In consequence, liberated from water power, safe from the risk of fire, powered by iron transmission, close to the coalfields of Lancashire and with easy access to the port of Liverpool, Manchester became the centre of the cotton industry. It had perhaps as many as sixty cotton mills by 1815: tall, close-packed, canal-side, urban and steam-powered. The first Manchester mill to be wholly powered by steam was the Piccadilly Mill in 1790; it was a five-storey job with the engine and boilers attached mid-way along one side. Ancoats, on the Ashton and Rochdale canals on the north-east edge of the city, became the most intense area of development, indeed the world's first industrial suburb. The mills were tall and narrow in proportion to their length, generally of an L or U shape, and built of hard, red, local brick roofed in Welsh slate, with full-height external stair and privy towers. Their casement windows were of a width. A large, arched entrance was provided for the workers, often with stone voussoirs; the offices, which were often less austere, were entered separately. Engine houses and chimneys were normally integrated.[52]

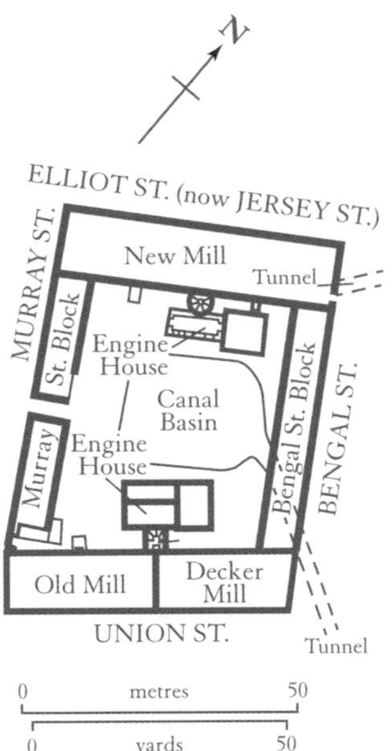

One of the first and largest mills in Ancoats, that of A&G Murray, largely survives today (figs 352 and 353). It was one of the first in which all processes were powered by steam and one of the largest of its day, employing around 1,500 people. The boilers and engine were in a detached building and provided power by a single upright, rotating shaft. Horizontal shafts were taken from this on each floor. The mill was unusually well planned around its own canal basin, allowing efficient transfer of goods.[53] Ancoats represents a decisive shift in British manufacturing. Large-scale enterprises needed to be in urban areas where the labour, materials and capital were available, and from 1800 a new type of dense, dirty and busy urban landscape developed. Places such as Leeds, Manchester and Birmingham were to be dominated by gigantic factories and surrounded by the grim housing of their employees.

In Ancoats, as the factories sucked in more workers, a housing crisis developed; the area had a population of 11,000 in 1801 and 31,000 by 1831. The urban mill owners did not build houses for ordinary employees and so it was left to building speculators to provide. Mill workers could only pay low rents so, on expensive land, housing had to be cheap to build and densely packed. The solution was the back-to-back house, a terrace of houses in which each house shared three walls with others. One room wide and deep, they had no through ventilation, no backyard and no privy. Normally built around yards that contained communal sanitary facilities, huge numbers of these houses were constructed across the north of England. In Leeds alone there were nearly 30,000 in 1910.[54]

In contrast to the cotton industry, woollen production remained an entirely domestic activity well into the 19th century. The clear, fast-running waters of the Pennines continued to provide both power for fulling mills and softness for the preparation of yarns. From the 17th century a specialised type of dwelling developed, with upper weaving and spinning lofts and ground-floor living, sleeping and cooking rooms. The loom shops were lit by long, low windows that let in plenty of light and avoided excessive window tax, as the mullions were less than half of the 12in that would have defined each light as a separate window. Technological advances, especially the flying shuttle, resulted in a gradual shift to the production of the wider broad cloth in place of the earlier narrower weaves. By 1780 most families were producing broad cloth and many were extending their houses to accommodate the larger looms. In the hamlet of New Tame, Delph, weaving took over from the local agrarian economy. Stout stone houses were built with loom houses capable of taking six looms, a spinning jenny and other equipment (fig. 354). By 1800 there were around 65,000 people working in houses like these in the Pennine cloth industry.[55]

By 1800 250,000 broad cloths a year went through the fulling mills of Yorkshire and were brought to market at £7 a piece. The pieces of woollen cloth were first sold in open-air markets but in 1755 Leeds, which had become England's largest cloth market, built itself a trading or 'piece' hall

Fig. 354 (right) New Tame, Delph, Oldham; weavers' houses with characteristic long light on the upper floor to light the loom house.

to which the pieces of woven cloth were brought and in which merchants could trade in security and comfort. Other towns followed: Huddersfield in 1766 and Halifax in 1774. The Halifax Piece Hall, the sole survivor, demonstrates the sense of civic ambition and commercial virility that underpinned provincial commercial architecture (fig. 355). It was probably designed by the young canal engineer and architect Thomas Bradley. His inspiration was drawn from Alberti's and Palladio's reconstructions of Roman piazzas, which were seen as a suitable model for the dignity of the town and the aspirations of its traders. But the building is no copy; it uses the language of classicism loosely, inventing a new rusticated order and deploying the elements in an invented proportional system. It provided over three hundred trading rooms and ample space in the vast central court for the poorer singleton traders who could not afford a room.[56]

Textiles had long been the backbone of the English economy but buildings for other types of manufacture developed from the 1760s. These varied from the self-conscious and pretentious, such as Matthew Boulton's Soho factory in Birmingham, built between 1765 and 1767, which was designed to promote the sophistication of his business as much as provide a home for it (fig. 356), to the sublime but functional casting hall of the British Plate Glass Company at Ravenhead, St Helens, of 1773. This latter cavern is vaulted with pointed brick arches carried on two rows of square brick pillars. Whilst the expense of the Soho Manufactory was an investment in Boulton's business, the ruggedness of the Ravenhead works was largely a response to technical requirements. These meant that the architecture of heavy industry, unlike that of textiles and light manufacture, was horizontal – long, low complexes of interlinked buildings.

The potteries provide a good example of an industry in which production was reorganised within a single industrial complex in exactly the same way as agricultural processes had been streamlined in the countryside. In 1769 Josiah Wedgwood built a new factory at Etruria, Stoke-on-Trent,

Fig. 355 (above) The Piece Hall, Halifax, Yorkshire, 1775; the most remarkable commercial monument to survive from the 18th century. It was entirely inward-looking; the outer walls present a prison-like blank façade to the town in order to secure the valuable cloths within. In the background is the 235ft spire of Square Congregational Church.

Fig. 356 (above left) The Soho manufactory, 1761–7 by William Wyatt, assisted by Benjamin Wyatt. Matthew Boulton wanted to raise standards of design and his manufactory expressed this ambition in being the most polite of all factories; not only did it mimic the architecture of a country house, but its landscape setting was deliberately domestic. The workers lived in the upper floors of the wings (like domestic servants); the forges were tucked away at the back.

Fig. 357 (above right) Wedgwood factory, Etruria, Stoke-on-Trent, 1767–73, by Josiah Wedgwood and his architect Joseph Pickford. The factory was planned round a courtyard; its principal canal-side elevation emphasised domesticity, while the inner faces were utilitarian.

Fig. 358 (above) Doncaster's Cementation Furnace, Sheffield, 1848; the only such furnace to survive. Iron bars and charcoal were packed in alternating layers into long stone pots. They were then fired for a week or so before being removed as steel. Up to sixteen tons of steel could be made at one time in such a furnace.

which divided the manufacturing process into stages within a single complex arranged to facilitate the flow of work from raw material to finished product (fig. 357). All the heavy work was done on the ground floor whilst the lighter decorative stages were undertaken upstairs. Its external elevations to the Trent and Mersey Canal were given an essentially domestic treatment, with polite features such as a pediment and rusticated key blocks above the windows. It also had the ubiquitous Diocletian window that became the defining architectural feature of the potteries. One of the few early surviving potteries is Gladstone Works, Stoke-on-Trent, bought as an ongoing concern by John Hendley Sheridan in 1818. It was typical of many of the medium-size potbanks, with two houses on the main road and a range of workshops to the rear. The kilns at Gladstone are representative of the thousands that once burned in Stoke. Each was enclosed in a bottle-shaped outer skin known as a hovel, creating the characteristic shape.[57]

The metal industries produced similar-shaped furnaces, 35ft to 60ft high, for the production of so-called blister steel, which was being made in Sheffield from around 1700. Doncaster's Cementation Furnace is the only one of hundreds of such furnaces that remain in the town (fig. 358). The impurities in blister steel made it unsuitable for high-performance applications and by the early 1750s a new process was devised that melted the iron in small pottery crucibles, skimmed off the slag and poured the steel into ingots. The crucible process required temperatures of 1,600°C, achieved by creating a powerful draught through a cellar and up wide, rectangular chimneys as tall as 40ft. The Abbeydale Crucible Furnace, Sheffield, built in around 1830, shows what was very typical of the buildings of the metal trades: low, utilitarian buildings given presence by the massive crucible stack (fig. 360).[58]

The chimneys of Sheffield, Stoke, Manchester and the mills of Ancoats made a huge impression; they were structures without relation to the human body, superhuman in scale and conception. Whilst medieval cathedrals emphasised human mortality in the face of God, new industrial landscapes

annihilated individualism in a different way by making workers cogs in Mammon's great experiment. The factory allowed owners to control, streamline, mechanise and concentrate manufacture for maximum profit. Although there were still advantages to dispersed production in some industries, the factory was the defining invention of the age.[59] Whilst these structures were not primarily designed to please, please they did, both as individual structures and as panorama. Indeed, this is how they were often comprehended by many tourists who set out to admire the new manufacturing areas. Painters captured the smoke stacks of cities such as Sheffield, and J. M. W. Turner painted panoramas of Leeds and Dudley (fig. 359).[60]

Going to Church

In 1760 the Anglican Church was unquestionably England's most powerful cultural and ideological institution. As the spiritual arm of the state it was at the height of its influence and power but from the 1770s this was increasingly challenged. First, there were structural problems because the geographical distribution of Church buildings and economic resources was ill-matched to new areas of population growth. Then there were social challenges; the 18th-century parson was often the JP and the social bedfellow of the local squire. His social exclusiveness and that of most of his congregation (who paid rents for the draught-proof box pews) tended to exclude labouring people. From without came further pressures from the growing strength of Roman Catholic and dissenting religion, whilst from within there were the forces of Methodism and the Evangelical Revival.

So disruptive were these forces to the status quo that by 1821 dissenting chapels outnumbered Anglican churches by seven to five. This revolution, and it was no less than that, was born of widespread disillusionment at Anglicanism's lack of emotional and social engagement, and with the authoritarianism and social exclusivity of its clergy.

Fig. 359 (left) Leeds, Yorkshire from Rope Hill *c.*1840. Up close the monuments of industry were impressive, but their power was only really felt in panoramas such as this. Leeds, amongst others, was an entirely new sort of landscape drawing gasps of amazement from those who first saw them.

Fig. 360 (below left) Abbeydale steelworks. In the foreground is the tilt forge of 1785, behind is the fitting shop and, with the big chimney, the crucible steel furnace built in 1829. Such early metalworking sites were semi-rural, requiring fast-flowing watercourses. Despite the Venetian window in the tilt forge, the complex was low, stone built and agricultural-looking.

Fig. 361 (bottom right) Walpole Old Chapel, Suffolk; cottages built in 1607 were adapted as a chapel by 1647 and then enlarged in 1698.

The birth of Methodism in 1739 had launched a flight from the established Church, closely followed by the Baptists and Congregationalists. These groups appealed particularly to the working class and the poor, who were attracted by the emphasis on equality before God, the personal nature of salvation, the opportunities for genuine participation in worship, and an absence of social stratification and exclusivity. Their greatest success came in areas in which the Anglican Church was weakest – Cornwall, the north Midlands, Yorkshire and Lincolnshire – and they attracted, in particular, skilled artisans.

The growth of new non-Anglican places of worship from the 1800s was truly remarkable; between 1810 and 1820 only 152 new Anglican churches were built against a staggering 15,601 non-Anglican ones. In the following twenty years a further 18,000 non-Anglican places of worship were built compared with only 943 in the Church of England. The established Church cannot take all the blame for losing the initiative to Nonconformity. It was still very difficult to create a new parish – it required an Act of Parliament – whilst non-Anglican churches could be erected anywhere. The main effect of this was that in the newly populous industrial areas Anglican parishes served vast populations; between 1816 and 1818 Manchester, with a population of nearly 80,000, had only enough pews to accommodate 11,000 people. There were only 2,000 parishes in the whole of the archdiocese of York covering the emerging industrial heartlands, whilst in the relatively rural province of Canterbury there were 10,000. Anglicanism, with the exception of London, had become a rural religion.[61]

Dissenting chapels had been built in England since the 17th century. Some, such as the remarkably well-preserved Walpole Old Chapel, Suffolk, were set up in houses or barns. At Walpole the chapel was carved out of two cottages in 1647 (fig. 361). Other early chapels were similarly built, such as the originally remote and isolated chapel in Toxteth of *c.*1604–18, now in the middle of Liverpool (fig. 362). Architecturally, these buildings began to become more distinct after the Toleration Act of 1689, and after 1700 it is possible to make some generalisations about them.

Nonconformist chapels were rarely cruciform but instead were usually rectangular, internally dominated by a pulpit in the centre of one wall. As preaching was the focus of worship there was normally a sounding board above the pulpit to promote audibility. Beneath there might be a pew for the clerk or precentor who led the singing. Larger chapels had galleries with panelled fronts. Walls below were also normally panelled to head height. The Chowbent Chapel, a Unitarian foundation in Atherton, Manchester, can be taken as fairly typical (fig. 363). Erected in 1722, it is a brick-built box with stone dressings and round-headed windows. Inside there are box pews both on the ground floor and in the gallery, which is supported by turned oak columns. A triple-decker pulpit in matching oak stands behind a small communion table.

Although the Baptists, Unitarians, Congregationalists, Quakers and others built some thousands of meeting houses, it was the Methodists who built the most – more than 1,500 by 1812, over 5,600 by 1851 and by 1932 a total of some 14,500, nearly as many as there were Anglican parishes. John and Charles Wesley formed the first Methodist Society in London in 1740, and their meetings were originally held in a converted foundry on City Road. John Wesley did not, it seems, have a particularly Puritan architectural aesthetic. He admired the octagonal Presbyterian chapel at Colgate, Norwich, built in 1754, mainly for its acoustic properties. This chapel inspired at least fourteen octagonal Methodist meeting houses, including Wesley's own favourite at Yarm, Yorkshire (fig. 364), where he preached to a full house at 5 a.m. on 24 April 1764.

In the end the octagon did not win over the traditional square or rectangular box and, indeed, Wesley's own chapel on City Road, built between 1776 and 1777, was typical in this respect (fig. 365). From the street it is five bays wide with a pediment and two tiers of big, round-headed windows, admired for bringing light and clean air. There were internal galleries and behind the three-decker pulpit was a shallow, railed apse for the Communion table. It was probably designed by George Dance the Younger and was regarded by Wesley as being 'perfectly neat, but not fine'. This domesticity is characteristic of Methodist chapels, which adopt an architectural style closely related to large private villas.[62]

Fig. 362 (above left) The ancient chapel of Toxteth, Liverpool, c.1604–18 but largely rebuilt 1774 when the walls were heightened. A simple box for Presbyterian worship.

Fig. 363 (top) Chowbent Unitarian Chapel, Atherton, Manchester, 1722.

Fig. 364 (above middle) Wesleyan Chapel, Yarm, Yorkshire, 1763. Wesley called this 'by far the most elegant in England'.

Fig. 365 (above) Wesley's Chapel, City Road, London, 1777. The large Greek Doric porch was a later addition of 1815.

Fig. 366 (right) Methodist Chapel, Bridport, Dorset, 1838; a fine building formally set in the streetscape, all stucco with an Ionic portico in antis and round-headed windows.

Fig. 367 (above) Methodist Chapel, Lelant, Cornwall, 1834; a simple building originally with a lime ash floor, pulpit and harmonium. Externally all the effort was concentrated on the street façade where there was a turret and clock. In 1839 there were 348 members of the congregation.

There was an opinion widely held by contemporary Methodists that the City Road Chapel should form the blueprint for chapels elsewhere. This was not slavishly followed but, before 1850, most Methodist chapels were in a similar classical style. They fell into three main groups: the big urban churches seating 1,000 or more, such as that at Redruth of 1826; market-town chapels, such as the elegant, Greek-influenced Wesleyan chapel in Bridport, Dorset (fig. 366); and the tiny village and country chapels, which, like Lelant, near Hayle, Cornwall, were scaled-down versions of the big ones (fig. 367).

Whilst these churches drew heavily on Anglican architectural forms as devised by Wren and his contemporaries, the need to accommodate large congregations who could hear and see the service meant that they also had much in common with the auditoria of theatres and other public gathering places. In this some Methodist chapels were very ambitious – horseshoe and oval auditoria were not uncommon in the slightly later larger chapels. A magnificent surviving chapel of 1843 at Ponsanooth, Cornwall, has an oval gallery with the area behind the pulpit reserved for the choir and organ.[63]

The failure of the Anglican Church to reach many, the growth – or at least public showing – of agnosticism, and the huge growth of Nonconformity were seen by many in the Establishment as a threat and a challenge, particularly against the backdrop of revolution and war in France. Pressure came from within the Anglican Church, and from within parliament, to address this by a programme of state-sponsored church building. The result was an Act of 1818 that set aside £1 million to build new churches. The 1818 commission, unlike its predecessor of 1711, did not specify a number of churches to be built, just an amount of money to be spent. Nor, despite suggestion to the contrary, were the churches intended to be national monuments; they were to be built as economically as possible with minimal ornament. Crucially, although enclosed and rented pews were allowed, part of the seating had to be open and free; a key objective was to attract and seat as many as possible.

When the commission met it decided that the new churches should be recognisably Anglican, in other words possessing a spire or tower, and that they should cost around £20,000 apiece; there was no preconception about the style in which churches should be built. There was, however, a certain amount of central control; a building committee was established to approve designs, and these were sent on to the three Crown architects – John Nash, John Soane and Robert Smirke – for scrutiny. The Crown architects took some dozen commissions themselves, but were too busy and grand to dirty themselves competing for small churches deep in the provinces.

In liturgical purpose and layout the commissioners' churches differed little from the model devised by Jones and Wren; they were essentially auditoria, with a font at the west end serving as one focus and at the east the altar, pulpit and reading desk providing another. The altar was in a shallow recess, rarely called a chancel and, at any rate, only 4ft to 5ft deep. Broadly speaking, classical styles were chosen for town churches and Gothic ones for those in the country.

Other than the Crown architects, other prominent designers included Thomas Hardwick, William Wilkins, C. R. Cockerell, George Basevi and Charles Barry. Less well-known and provincial men also gained commissions, the most prolific and successful being Thomas Rickman, who designed twenty-two churches. This entirely self-taught amateur, who had made his reputation through his analysis of the Gothic style, had his first church – the startling St George's, Chorley, Lancashire – built almost entirely out of iron between 1822 and 1825.

St Peter's (before 1972, Holy Trinity), Darwen, Lancashire, was typical of Rickman's work and typical of many these commissioned churches. The population of Darwen had increased from around 3,500 to 6,500 in twenty years, and the mechanisation of weaving had led to rising unemployment and economic distress. Holy Trinity was one of three churches designed by Rickman in the huge parish of Blackburn to directly address the risks of radicalisation and perceived atheism. Each was in a different period of Gothic, but all conformed to the general scheme of a rectangular box with galleries inside and a tower without.[64] St Thomas's, Stockport, is an example of one of the more impressive classical churches built by the commissioners (fig. 368). Designed by George Basevi, a pupil of Sir John Soane, and built at a cost of £15,611, it seated two thousand people. Here a portico was attached to the east end, providing an impressive elevation to the town's main road. At the west end was a tower.[65]

Thanks to the extension of the original scheme the commissioners managed to build two hundred and twenty-five new churches by 1838, and by the time the scheme was wound up in 1856 an outlay of over £3 million had provided six hundred and twelve churches. This expanded the capacity of Anglican churches by around 600,000, of which some 358,000 were free places. But the problem was that whilst the churches were being built the population of England had again increased by seven million, meaning that for every new place built there were twelve new inhabitants. But the new churches had unquestionably made a difference, especially in the industrial north, and contributed to securing the Church of England's position in both state and society.[66]

The seeds of a further problem for the established Church had been sown at the Reformation. By the late 18th century only 40 per cent of Church livings were in the gift of the Church. This situation encouraged plurality; indeed,

Fig. 368 (right) St Thomas's, Stockport, George Basevi, 1822–5. The Greek-style portico gave the church an impressive presence on the roadside – inside it has galleries on three sides carried on square fluted Corinthian columns.

in 1810 over half of all Anglican parishes had no resident priest. An Act of 1803 required incumbents to justify non-residence but it took until the Act of 1838 to curb the abuse. Part of the problem had been the lack of appropriate accommodation within the parish; even in 1833 nearly 3,000 parishes had no clergy house. A series of Acts allowed poor clergy to be lent money for parsonage houses from a fund known as Queen Anne's Bounty. In 1811 the governors of the Bounty set aside £50,000 a year for the purpose, triggering a huge upswing in the construction of parsonages. By 1825 the Bounty had lent more than £362,000 for the purpose.

New parsonage houses built under these provisions, like the commissioners' churches, were centrally approved, and employed architects or surveyors who drew plans and produced specifications. Typical of the sort of parsonage being built in the 1810s and 20s is Walkeringham, Nottinghamshire, built for Revd Joseph Miller by the builder and architect James Trubshaw in 1823. The house was of brick, two storeys and three bays, each separated by a tall, plain pilaster. The central bay was recessed and the windows above the door had a balcony. In plan there were three ground-floor reception rooms, a drawing room and dining room at the front, and a study behind the dining room. A kitchen projected out at the back. The staircase hall was adequately spacious and led to four family bedrooms and two for servants above. Its grounds were spacious enough to give a sense of isolation, although access to the church was possible across the garden.

Parsonages such as Walkeringham were little different in form from villas and farmhouses being built by other types of well-heeled people. House builders and designers could turn to a rash of books that suggested suitable designs. Robert Lugar's *Architectural Sketches for Cottages, Rural Dwellings, and Villas* came out in 1805, followed by his *The Country Gentleman's Architect* in 1806. These books, two of many, made a substantial contribution to the standardisation of plan and design in a period when thousands of such houses were being erected.

Town Building

Whilst the 17th century had been characterised by the enormous and rapid growth of London, urban growth in the 18th century was more widely spread. London continued to grow, but the number and size of provincial towns also increased, whilst, uniquely in European terms, there were numbers of new industrial towns full of new buildings. These provincial centres became more assertive and directly competed with the capital; they also began to shift the urban focus of England from the south-east to emerging urban zones in the north.

This book has stressed throughout the role of towns and their inhabitants in architectural innovation and change. Between 1770 and 1830 the architecture of provincial England was again transformed; market halls, hotels, baths, dispensaries, libraries, Sunday schools, chapels, asylums, workhouses, cemeteries, hospitals, bazaars, arcades, theatres and other new building types come to dominate the scene. The tastes of wealthy town dwellers were distinct and independent , and should not be seen as watered-down versions of aristocratic ones. Provincial merchants, financiers and professionals also had substantial disposable income, some of which was invested in the national debt but much of which was put into turnpikes, bridges and canals, and, after 1814, into public utilities, especially gas.

Although it had been known since the 1780s that it was possible to collect and burn the gases given off by burning coal, it took some years to usefully harness the technology. Gas lighting first appeared in mills as a substitute for dangerous, expensive and relatively ineffective oil lights. It was the mill owner, George Lee of Salford, who first applied the technology to his business in 1805 but not without first testing it in his house. Liking the strong, clear light with no smell or side-effects, he calculated that a pound of coal produced three cubic feet of gas. As only half a cubic foot cost the same as burning a candle, he worked out that gas was 70 per cent cheaper than burning wax and half the price of using oil. His mill became the first building in the world to be fitted for gas lighting. The same year the Prince Regent used gas lights on the walls of Carlton House on Pall Mall. They were supplied via an underground pipe almost 300 yards long from a furnace in a nearby house. In 1812 the first gas company was formed in Westminster by a German émigré Fredrick Winsor. He was empowered to lay pipes across the highway to provide street lighting. Only four years later companies were formed in Preston and Liverpool, and by the mid 1820s most major towns had a gas works lighting the streets.

Industrial buildings and streets were the first to be lit by gas, but shops and public buildings quickly realised the benefits. In 1817 the Theatre Royal, Drury Lane, became the first public building to be lit entirely by gas: stage, auditorium and front of house. In 1822 St Paul's Cathedral received its first gas lights and they were installed throughout the General Post Office building in 1828. Indeed, the London Gas Light and Coke Company's business grew from just four paying customers and annual revenues of £180 in 1814 to 122 miles of mains supplying 30,000 lamps turning over more than £100,000 six years later.

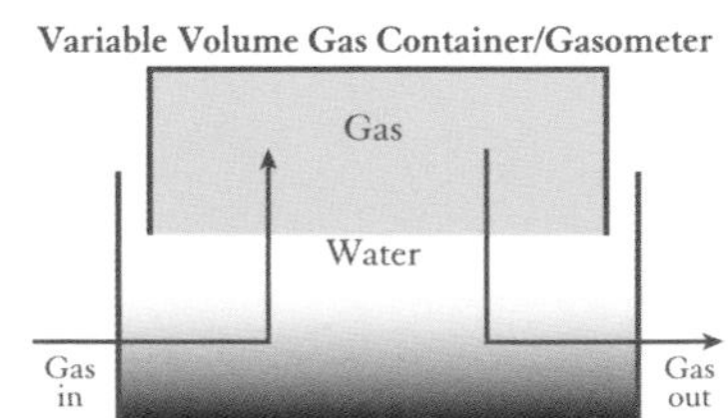

Fig. 369 (above) Diagram illustrating how a variable volume gasometer works.

Fig. 370 (top) Single gasholder No 8 King's Cross, London, 1880. Erected by the Imperial Gas Light and Coke company, the framework comprises a stack of Doric columns complete with entablature.

Fig. 371 (above) The Warwick gasworks, Saltisford, *c.*1822 were encased in brick to protect nearby residents from explosion and to give a reassuring, polite façade.

Gas was made in a retort that captured the mixture of hydrogen, methane and carbon monoxide produced by burning coal. There were two valuable by-products of this process: tar, which was washed out by a water-purifying process, and coke. Gas works were normally sited by canals or rivers for ease of coal delivery. Retort houses, coal stores and purifier houses were characterised by their chimneys. The Imperial Gas Light Company's works on the Regent's Canal in London was designed by Francis Edwards. Big blocks lit by round-headed windows in shallow brick recesses were linked by a central office building. The two main blocks were dominated by colossal Doric chimneys. But the structure that defined the gas works was the storage holder. These cylindrical, wrought-iron storage vessels were necessary to help match supply and demand. At first they were quite small but later in the century they could be enormous, some 120ft in diameter. Because of the fear that storage holders might explode, they were initially encased in brick. The gas holders at Warwick Gas Works of 1822 are reassuringly disguised as symmetrical parts of a domestic-looking composition (fig. 371). The earliest that survives today is the Number 2 Gasholder at the Fulham Gas Works, dating from the 1830s. A subterranean brick cylinder, sealed with water at its bottom, contained the bell-like iron holder that rose and fell, guided by delicately detailed cast-iron guides (fig. 369). Later cylinders were telescoped together to increase capacity and a towering iron frame was required to support these. The spectacular group of frames at King's Cross included a group of three built in 1861 around 52ft-deep pits. The superstructures of 1880 are of cast-iron, designed as three tiers of Doric columns braced with lattice girders (fig. 370). Gas holders were a prominent part of the landscape of at least seven hundred towns by 1850.[67]

Those who had money and promoted new technology and new buildings in the provinces were much less interested in their physical environment than their predecessors had been. The new and expanding towns of the north were introverted and private places where the wealthy lived in detached villas, not sweeping terraces and crescents. Workers' housing was built willy-nilly, with no thought of a larger plan. This aesthetic indifference was partly a result of the predominance of Evangelicalism amongst the wealthy; although some were interested in architecture, most thought spiritual things more important. What buildings looked like was a minor concern.[68]

The interests of this new provincial society were much less frivolous than in earlier periods; thus the assembly room and the theatre were replaced by the reading room, library and chapel. A new enthusiasm for learned societies swept the country; in 1749 there had been four hundred and fifty of these but by 1799 there were over a thousand. Palaeontology, geology, natural history, chemistry and political economy were just some of the subjects catered for. Many societies built premises for their meetings and collections. The Scarborough Philosophical Society commissioned a museum built between 1828 and 1829 to the designs of the Yorkshire architect and museum aficionado R. H. Sharp (fig. 372). Its upper part was a circular room that contained a revolutionary display of fossils. Literary and philosophical societies sprang up in large numbers after the end of the Napoleonic Wars. Many built impressive

Fig. 372 (left) The Scarborough Philosophical Society Museum, Yorkshire, 1828–9. The main exhibition room inside is reached by a spiral staircase that arrives in the middle of the room, leaving the walls free for a panoramic history of geology.

club houses or libraries, like the Newcastle 'Lit and Phil'; the successful local architect John Green designed them an immaculately constructed library in a Greek style in 1822 (fig. 373).[69]

Towns were, however, above all places of economic exchange, a role that became increasingly important with the development of agriculture and manufacturing in the countryside. Whilst agricultural produce was still sold in town-centre market places by retailers, the market for wholesale agricultural produce moved first into private rooms in inns and then into corn exchanges. Hundreds of exchanges were built from the 1820s right up to the end of the century. In an exchange grain was sold to wholesale dealers by means of a sample displayed by growers on tables in a large hall. In 1828 a consortium of businessmen in Bishop's Stortford, Hertfordshire, commissioned Lewis Vulliamy to design a corn exchange for the town. It has a portico of four giant Ionic columns facing the high street; above the entrance to the trading floor, designed for sixty-five dealers, stood a statue of Ceres, goddess of grain (fig. 374). Allegorical references were common on these buildings, whose elaboration expressed civic economic aspiration rather than simply meeting the needs of traders.

The retail trade also diversified and expanded. In the south of England, after the Napoleonic Wars, there was a shop for every thirty to forty people, perhaps double the density that exists now. Shops were increasingly outlets for finished goods and fewer were fronts for workshops at the rear. This was facilitated by improvements in glass manufacture after 1700 that meant that shops could afford to have large glass windows; by 1750 the shops on the City of London's principal thoroughfare, Cheapside, were all glazed. In 1762 hanging signs were banned in London so shops started to paint their names on a frieze or fascia above the windows. By 1800 this had been done by almost all shops; an example from 1770 is the confectioner Samuel Horton's shop in Cornhill, London.

Fig. 373 (above) Literary and Philosophical Society, Newcastle upon Tyne, John Green, 1822–5. A bold Greek façade leads to an internal stair with copies of the Parthenon Frieze sculptures.

Fig. 374 (above right) Corn exchange, Bishop's Stortford, Hertfordshire, Lewis Vulliamy, 1828. It is the oldest corn exchange in Hertfordshire and by far the most distinguished.

Much larger retail establishments began to be built in London and provincial centres, and it was these that led the way in fixed prices and an insistence on cash payments, demystifying shopping for a new generation of middle-class clients. Some were proprietor-owned and operated, such as James Lackington's giant bookshop, which opened in Finsbury Square in 1789–91. This, 'The Temple of the Muses', was designed by George Dance the Younger, who made use of cast-iron columns to support galleries stocked with books. Other establishments were speculatively built by developers and space was rented to traders. By 1830 most large towns had one of these bazaars, a large emporium, home to numbers of traders selling a variety of goods. Like Dance's bookshop they used new technology, particularly iron and glass, to create large, light halls. The most celebrated bazaar was perhaps the Pantheon on Oxford Street, London, converted by Sydney Smirke in 1834 from an earlier building by James Wyatt. It comprised a hall 116ft by 88ft, covered by a glazed barrel vault and, amongst other conveniences, there was a room in which ladies, burdened by bags of shopping, could await their carriage. An alternative model for the speculator was to build an arcade – a covered shopping street containing a number of individual shops, each with its own front door. Not the first, but the biggest, was the Burlington Arcade, Piccadilly, London, designed by Samuel Ware and opened in 1818 (fig. 375). It was 585ft long, containing seventy-two two-storey shops selling 'jewellery and fancy articles of fashionable demand'.[70]

Whilst shops for the wealthy were transformed into ordered and elegant emporia, an ornament to the streets in which they stood, the traditional town market was still a chaotic, open-cry exchange. After the Napoleonic Wars a more fastidious society looked askance at the petty crime, disorder, filth and pandemonium of town markets. The pragmatic solution was to re-house the market in a single large building under the control of the local authorities. As most towns wished to keep their historic market places, this involved compulsory purchase of areas of poor housing in town centres to create a site for a new building.[71]

The first of the new market halls was in Liverpool, designed by the city architect John Foster and built between 1820 and 1822. The interior covered 74,000 square feet and was lit by rows of gas lamps. But the best surviving Georgian example is Covent Garden Market, London, designed by Charles Fowler, master of market design and an expert in the use of cast iron (fig. 376). Fowler brilliantly created a building between 1828 and 1830 that rationalised the complex interactions of the market, giving growers, buyers, wholesalers and retailers defined zones. The structure is formed of three parallel ranges enclosed by a curtain of granite Tuscan columns. This arcade is interrupted at the corners by pyramid-roofed pavilions designed as pubs or coffee houses. Above, at each end, were terraces, where more exclusive goods were sold to superior customers.[72]

Shopping was not the only attraction towns had to offer. By the 1730s sea bathing was practised at a number of coastal towns for its supposed medical benefits. The leading centre was Scarborough, Yorkshire, which already had a spa, but soon Margate, Hastings, Brighton and Weymouth developed facilities for people wanting to bathe in the sea. After 1800 coastal resorts were amongst England's fastest-growing towns; Margate's population grew by 117 per cent and Brighton had become the twenty-second largest town in England by 1831. At the same time entrepreneurs set out to establish new towns on undeveloped stretches of coast; Bournemouth was founded by Lewis Tregonwell between 1811 and 1812, and his cluster of cottages and an inn developed into one of the country's leading resorts by the 1840s.[73]

Fig. 375 (left) The Burlington Arcade, Piccadilly, London, built by Samuel Ware in 1818 for Lord Cavendish as a speculation. This is much narrower than later arcades, with shops in groups of four divided by Ionic pilasters and cross arches.

Fig. 376 (right) Covent Garden, London, The Market House, Charles Fowler 1828–30. When first built, most of the market was open air, but in 1874–5 and then 1888–9 two new tall roofs were added by W. Cubit and Co. These give the buildings a bulky late-Victorian presence very different from their low-lying original form. See fig. 242 for the market before 1820.

The vogue for the seaside was given a huge boost by George, Prince of Wales, when he leased a farmhouse overlooking the Steine, Brighton's principal promenade, in 1786. The following year Henry Holland was commissioned to enlarge it; after travelling to France to gain inspiration, he designed a great domed bow with statues and French-inspired interiors. In 1803 William Porden designed the prince an adjacent domed stable block with exotic Indian detailing, but this was only the appetiser to the main course – the complete rebuilding and extension of the prince's house to create the Royal Pavilion (fig. 377). The Mughal style was chosen by the prince and his architect, John Nash, and ideas were plundered from contemporary prints. Those who knew about Mughal architecture, however, such as the Daniells, did not think much of the pavilion. This was because although the domes and the minarets were Mughal, inspiration elsewhere was distinctly Gothic and Chinese, and the proportions classical. Yet, the overall effect – the important thing – was extraordinarily exotic. The pavilion had a lasting influence on the architecture of the English seaside, which was henceforth fun, kitsch and fuelled by fantasy.

As people flocked to the sea, squares and crescents of handsome houses were built. These were not particularly distinctive, but the craze for balconies and bay or bow windows gave seaside terraces their own character from the 1820s. Brighton, perhaps, set the fashion; Regency Square, for instance, by the local architect Amon Wilds, is characterised by triple-height bows with canopied balconies, assuring a sea view for all (fig. 378). Developments such as this made Brighton the only town in England to continue the practice – started in Bath in the late 1720s – of large-scale planning, giving structure to a whole town (p. 311).

Seaside resorts were at first dominated by speculatively built houses such as those on Regency Square, which were rented weekly or monthly to visitors.

Fig. 377 (above) The Royal Pavilion, Brighton; the east front. Beneath the exoticism is Henry Holland's original classical marine pavilion, but neither John Nash nor the Prince Regent wanted people to know. Here Nash shows his brilliance in making an extended façade (over 400ft long) interesting and varied.

Inns were for single overnight stays only. Hotels, in the modern sense of the word, began to appear from the 1820s. The first was perhaps the Royal Hotel at Plymouth, a remarkable building combining an assembly room, theatre and hotel in a single courtyard complex. Its designer was John Foulston, who had won a competition started by the town corporation. The hotel had fifty suites, each containing a bed, dining room and sitting room; other facilities included coffee, dining and billiard rooms, and separate water-closets, as well as extensive stables. Hotels followed at Leamington, Worthing, Brighton and elsewhere in the 1820s. The best surviving example is the Queen's Hotel, Cheltenham Spa, of 1837–8, a monumental stuccoed palace with a six-column portico on a rusticated basement by the architect, builder and speculator R. W. Jearrad (fig. 379). There were suites for families and single rooms for single gentlemen. It was regarded by some at the time as the grandest hotel in Europe, although, unlike contemporary hotels in America, it had no en-suite bathrooms or lavatories.[74]

Polite Town Houses

From the 1760s a number of new factors began to influence house design. The first of these was legislation. Builders were no strangers to regulation; between 1605 and 1774 there had been no fewer than eighteen proclamations or Acts restricting what could be built, particularly in the capital. In 1774 came the

Fig. 378 (right) Regency Square, Brighton, built in 1817–30. The west side has large houses with bows and verandas, mainly stuccoed.

Fig. 379 (below) Queen's Hotel, Cheltenham, 1837–8 by R. W. Jearrad; a palatial building of thirteen bays framed by giant Corinthian columns.

first comprehensive Act covering central London. It was drafted by two leading architects, George Dance the Younger and Sir Robert Taylor, and aimed to improve construction and eliminate fire risk. The Act had the indirect effect of homogenising street elevations; window frames had to be rebated into the wall, only shop fronts were allowed to project by 10in and no other timber facework was allowed apart from a modest door case. Gower Street, built from the 1780s, epitomises the unrelenting austerity that the Building Act introduced (fig. 380). Dance lived at 91 Gower Street from 1790, demonstrating, perhaps, personal affection for the minimalism of its design.

There were ways around the austerity of elevation – the use of cast-iron balconies, railings and lamp holders was an obvious one. Made cheaply by mass production and sold in catalogues, these could add interest, variety and distinctiveness to individual houses or whole terraces. Another option that was to become hugely successful was Coade stone, a form of pale-coloured terracotta made by Mrs Eleanor Coade in her Lambeth factory. From 1774 thousands of houses, churches and public buildings were adorned with Coade architectural ornaments. For her own home, Belmont, Lyme Regis, Dorset, unique pieces were sculpted and cast: a head of Neptune over the door and sea creatures in plaques in the imposts.[75]

Just as the Building Act was being contemplated John, Robert, James and William Adam took a lease on the site of Durham House just off the Strand. Here they were to build an ambitious residential speculation – the Adelphi (adelphoi is Greek for brothers). Raised up on an arched substructure of warehouses were a series of terraces. This was probably the first time the word 'terrace' had been used to describe a row of houses. It was also the first time that Robert Adam applied his Roman ornament to London street architecture. Although the carcass of these houses differed little from their austere cousins in Gower Street, the façades were enlivened by delicately

Fig. 380 (above) Gower Street, London. The houses all have sub-basements with a railed area in front. The road in front was artificially built up to the level of the top of the area; the gardens at the back are at the original ground level. Thus where Gower Street joins Euston Road it has to slope down to meet it.

Fig. 381 (left) Adam House, Adam Street, Adelphi, faces down John Adam Street and is given special treatment. Giant pilasters with moulded anthemion motifs made of Liardet's patent cement support an attic and pediment with the Adams' arms. The cast iron balconies are amongst the earliest in London and were cast by the Carron Company of Falkirk

detailed pilasters, friezes, roundels, swags and door cases (fig. 381). The designs were promoted from 1773 in *The Works in Architecture of Robert and James Adam* and immediately picked up by the authors of pattern books. The influence of the Adam brothers can be seen in a development such as Bedford Square, London, of 1775–86.

But after the Napoleonic Wars stucco transformed the appearance of the most fashionable areas. This was largely as result of the Regent's Park and Regent's Street development masterminded by John Nash. Nash was invited to develop the old royal hunting park at Marylebone. His designs were very ambitious and set a royal palace, private villas, terraces, a church and public buildings in a picturesque rural landscape that included an ornamental lake. The development was to be connected to the Prince Regent's palace at Carlton House by a road lined with splendid new shops and houses (fig. 382). Work started in 1812 but the war held up progress, and it was only in the early 1820s that the main buildings were completed. Nash was in charge of what would now be called the master plan but other speculators, designers and architects were responsible for most of the individual structures. The buildings were all classical and most were stucco-faced brick. The first was Cornwall Terrace on the southern edge of the park, designed by Decimus Burton under the supervision of Nash. It set the scene – 560ft long with a central portico raised up on a rusticated basement and emphatic end pavilions (fig. 383).

The new street made the most of the convoluted property tenures through which it snaked. Its route was deliberately full of surprise and variety, modelled, Nash said, on the sublime curves of Oxford's High Street. Only the central curved section between Piccadilly Circus and Oxford Street contained shops; the rest was residential. In the central section were sweeps of cast-iron Tuscan colonnades to allow window-shoppers to stroll in comfort. Above were balconies for residents to watch the life of London's most fashionable street. The Regent's development set the tone, and the laying out of the Duke of Westminster's

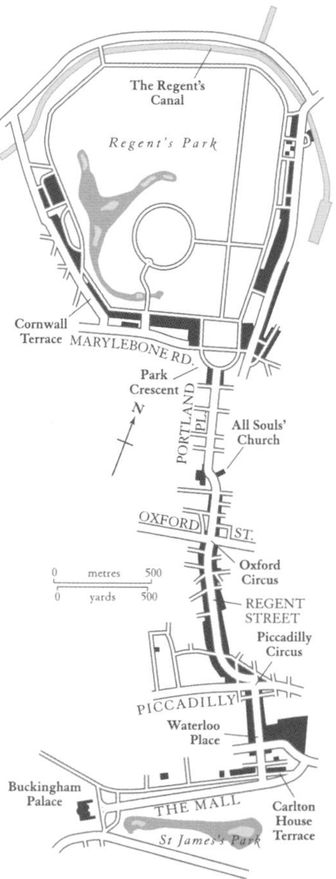

Fig. 382 (below) Regent's Park and Regent Street development from 1812, showing the principal buildings.

Belgravia by Thomas Cubitt after 1824 followed, with very long terraces given interest and accent by various porticoes, pilasters and projections. These mega-terraces were eventually copied in the richest provincial towns. Gambier Terrace, Liverpool, was started in the 1830s, a mixture of stucco and stone, and a fair match for any of the grandest terraces in the capital.[76]

Upper- and middle-class town housing was anonymous from the street. External façades gave no clue to the nature or even sometimes the number of houses behind the street elevation. Behind these discreet façades some important social changes were underway. Town dwellers' principal business was now more likely to be conducted outside the home and this led to a change in the balance of family life. As men left the house for a day's work the position of women became increasingly confined. Of course, many women had always had an interest in architecture, and a voice in the arrangement and furnishing of houses, but from the late 18th century there was a growing understanding that domestic economy and decoration were female spheres.

From the early 18th century the increasingly ritualised culture of visiting at home, which centred on the consumption of tea, had exposed private taste and discernment to friends and neighbours. Visiting was an overwhelmingly female pastime – Lady Mary Coke could easily make eighteen visits a day in town in 1767. The rooms in which visitors were received became the subject of almost obsessive attention. The principal social dividers in town housing were the possession of a dining room, so that you did not have to eat in the kitchen, and having a best room in which to receive guests. In houses of any pretension the dining room was on the ground floor and the drawing room was on the first. The drawing room was the place to which ladies retired after dinner, and in which the round of visiting and tea drinking would take place. The usage of rooms became much more rigidly defined after the Napoleonic Wars.[77]

Fig. 383 (above right) Cornwall Terrace, Regent's Park. The architect was Decimus Burton, but Nash refused his first design as too boring; holding the master plan for the project, he insisted on picturesqueness and theatricality.

Servants were still confined to the basement and the attics but in larger houses had their own staircases to give greater privacy to their masters. A number of times in the history of English architecture changing fuel technology made a decisive impact on how people built. One of these was the impact of coal on cooking from the 1770s. Cooking had already long removed from the central hearth to the fireplace where, in richer houses from the late 16th century, it had acquired a sophisticated technology of spits that were turned either by clockwork or hot air. Ranges developed in coal-burning areas from the 16th century; these were essentially iron baskets built into the brickwork of the chimney, some of which were adjustable and many of which had attachments for cooking pots. In 1780 Thomas Robinson patented a range that incorporated an iron oven and three years later another iron founder patented a version with an integral boiler. These were the ancestors of the all-iron kitchen ranges, the most successful manufacturer of which was William Flavel of Leamington Spa. His 'Leamingtons' enabled a single fire to roast, bake, simmer and warm food, as well as heat water. The invention of the saucepan in the 1680s, and the kettle and frying pan after 1700, completed a revolution in cooking and kitchens. By 1830 houses across the social spectrum had purpose-built kitchens containing iron ranges.[78]

Fig. 384 (below) Heaton Hall, Lancashire; the saloon or music room for Sir Thomas Egerton. Sir Thomas was very interested in the colour scheme for his house and worked closely with Wyatt. Scagliola columns are set off by pale colours (originally ungilded). Wyatt uses motifs and references from Rome, Venice and Egypt, creating his own archaeologically based language of architecture.

As room use became specialised so did the furniture required. An entirely new range of work tables, dressing tables, tea tables, reading and writing desks were available, and seat furniture became more comfortable. So-called easy-chairs were made possible by the invention of the coiled-spring seat; special wadding and padding for the back and seats came from the woollen mills, and brass castors were made for their legs. In 1721 duty on timbers grown in the North American colonies was abolished, opening the way for the import of mahogany, a hardwood that took a rich polish and grew more lustrous with age. Soon came satinwood and rosewood, both as veneers and in the solid. The new woods were sometimes used in doors and staircases, especially on hand rails; by 1760 mahogany had become the material of choice for middle-class furniture, replacing the previous fashion for walnut.[79]

The interiors of houses through the social spectrum were painted. Dark doors and coloured wall surfaces were set off in a white frame of windows and ceilings. After 1800 colour was used much more imaginatively. This was at first influenced by archaeological discoveries and involved the addition of painted motifs. The work of Adam and Wyatt showed what was possible with enough money (fig. 384). Soon this developed into a quest for a more correct application of colour, and marbling and bronzing were used. Sometimes archaeologically correct colours were used for a whole room; there were, for instance, short-lived fashions for Etruscan and Pompeian rooms.[80] Wallpaper began to be commonly used from 1700; in 1713 197,000 yards were bought in England and by 1785 this had risen to two million yards. It was possible to buy eleven yards of paper for the price of one yard of damask, and so for professional people, merchants and the provincial gentry, paper enabled a transformation of their interiors. Wallpaper started to be used fashionably in the houses of wealthy merchants in towns such as King's Lynn. Here, in the house of Andrew Taylor, head of a wealthy merchant dynasty, oak panelling was shorn of its mouldings, hessian stretched over the walls, and fashionable yellow, green and gold wallpaper hung.[81]

Aristocratic Houses in Town and Country

The huge profits made from agriculture, mineral wealth and industrial infrastructure transformed the aspirations of aristocrats and large landowners. Town houses remained a focus for most leading aristocrats. A trickle of London mega-houses continued to be built or remodelled that were trend-setting in their splendour and magnificence. Before 1800 Robert Adam succeeded in capturing many of the best commissions, including Wynne House, St James's Square (1771–4), Derby House, Grosvenor Square (1773–4), and Home House, Portman Square (1775–6). In these houses Adam effected a revolution in taste and design, vanquishing the ponderous fashion for cladding interiors with the exteriors of Roman public buildings. Adam's knowledge of the archaeological sources was, of course, superb, but he was no slave to them. The genius of his style lay in his ability to synthesise components of antique decoration and apply them to interiors in an original, harmonious and lively way.

Adam's great town houses were brilliantly and theatrically planned. Home House, whose interiors he transformed for the Dowager Countess of Home, displays Adam's mastery of planning a mixture of practicality and imitation of antique forms. Most brilliant, perhaps, is the staircase that rises up through a circular drum crowned with a skylight and adorned with niches, stucco trophies and trompe-l'oeil statues (fig. 385). There were others who followed in this mode, all rivals for patronage emphasising their individuality, including Adam's equally talented fellow Scot, James Stuart.[82]

After the Napoleonic Wars London palace building regained momentum. Charles Stewart, Marquess of Londonderry, bought Holderness House, Park Lane, for £33,000 in 1822 and commissioned Benjamin Dean Wyatt and Philip Wyatt to rebuild it in 1825 at a cost of £200,000. Stafford House (now Lancaster House) was begun as a residence for George IV's brother the Duke of York but sold after his death to the colossally wealthy George Leveson-Gower, Marquess of Stafford, who spent £200,000 on completing it. His architects were also the Wyatts. A ring of state rooms on the first floor approached by an imperial stair was supplemented in this exceptional building by further state rooms below. These houses remained the principal vehicles for aristocratic display, the possibilities of which were enormously enhanced by a flood of works of art coming on to the market after the French Revolution.[83]

Fig. 385 (above) Home House, Portman Square, London; the staircase. The house was begun by James Wyatt, who was sacked and replaced by Adam in 1775. His is the staircase – the most exciting in London. After the first flight it splits and rises to the first floor; its balustrade of iron, brass and lead is of open-work pilasters.

In the country, with more space, the extravagance of the aristocracy was given even greater rein. Huge sums were spent on enlarging existing houses such as Chatsworth, Derbyshire, which William Cavendish, Duke of Devonshire, spent twenty years extending and remodelling from 1820. At Belvoir Castle, for Lady Elizabeth Howard, Duchess of Rutland, work started in 1801 and was not finished until 1830 after an expenditure of £200,000. Lesser men with new money built big, too. Brancepeth Castle, County Durham, was bought for £70,000 by Matthew Russell of Sunderland, who had inherited his father's fortune made from coal. He hired John Patterson, a former assistant of Robert Adam, to transform the castle into a megalomaniac vision of Norman

Fig. 386 (left) Brancepeth Castle, County Durham. Whilst the towers to the left are medieval, those to the right, carefully modelled on them, date from 1818–21. The whole external effect is of a vast and utterly convincing medieval fortress.

England – the stairs and state rooms are a Brobdingnagian exercise in planning (fig. 386). The Jerningham's of Costessey, Norfolk, made their money from agriculture and in 1827 Sir George Stafford-Jerningham, Baron Stafford, commissioned John Buckler, an acknowledged expert in Tudor style, to redesign and extend the existing Tudor House. The project was grandiose in the extreme and the building was still incomplete after thirty years.[84]

The transformation of the road network had a big impact on the great country houses. In the mid 18th century the social radius of a house might be nine or ten miles, but after the roads were turnpiked the aristocracy and the gentry were suddenly more mobile, and people could travel long distances for a weekend or even a single evening. The age of the house party had dawned. At Belvoir Castle, the Duke of Rutland could easily contemplate a birthday party with three hundred dining at his table; some stayed, many were able to travel from many miles away for the evening. Owners rebuilt or remodelled their houses to cater for regular entertaining on a huge scale.[85] Easy access to the country no longer made a stay there seem like servitude. The landowning classes fell back in love with their estates, and shooting, hunting and riding now became a fundamental and enjoyable part of life, not a slightly irksome duty. Nature was something beautiful to be admired and enjoyed rather than avoided and abhorred. These changing attitudes to the natural world had a significant impact on the setting of country houses. The regulation of nature and the subjugation of landscape by a geometrical matrix centring on a great house were increasingly set aside for a much less structured approach. The essence of this was expansive lawns, normally bounded by tree belts and speckled with clumps of trees, through which serpentine carriage drives wound their way to the house. Views were contrived from the drives, revealing the house from a variety of angles. Wherever possible a naturalistic lake would be formed, ideally viewed in the middle distance from the house. Flower gardens, shrubberies or parterres were set to one side, concealed by carefully positioned planting.[86]

By the 1780s perhaps four thousand parks had been transformed in this way, and there were dozens of practitioners expert in conceptualising and executing the new type of landscape. The best-known and most successful landscape architect working in this vein was Lancelot 'Capability' Brown. He had started his career at Stowe (p. 322), where he was head gardener from 1741, but his career as a landscape architect started a decade later when he moved to London. Between then and his death in 1783 he had worked on one hundred and seventy major commissions. Brown's practice was big business and involved a network of craftsmen, engineers and plantsmen. After his death his mantle was inherited by Humphry Repton who, between 1789 and 1815, worked on over four hundred commissions.[87]

The landscape park was a return to the medieval aesthetic of setting great houses in landscapes that came right up to the castle gate. Indeed, at many houses Brown simply removed the 17th-century formal gardens from near the house to reconnect them with their deer parks. This certainly was the case at Longleat, Wiltshire, and Burghley, Cambridgeshire. Elsewhere, efforts were taken to incorporate as many mature trees as possible in newly created parkland to give the impression of a historic rather than a new setting (fig. 387). As in the Middle Ages, such open parkland required management. Grass was kept short by grazing, sometimes by herds of deer but more often by specialised breeds of sheep. Hay was grown in expressly segregated meadows and cut after the wild flowers had bloomed. Timber from the trees was, as always, commercially exploited.

Medieval hunting had been for stags and with hawks, but declining deer populations and the introduction of sporting firearms meant that other quar-

Fig. 387 (right) Heveningham Hall, Suffolk is a classic example of landscaping with lawns and a lake to give ideal views of the house.

ries rose in popularity. Fox hunting provided a sport that was fast, challenging and exciting. Its popularity increased concurrently with major changes in the landscape. In France, with highly fragmented land ownership, fox hunting was not possible, but in England landlords and tenant farmers owning big blocks of land facilitated wide-ranging hunts. By 1800 a shortage of foxes led to the concerted planting of coverts across parkland and farmland.[88] These doubled as breeding grounds for another quarry: pheasants. As guns got lighter and more manageable after 1800 shooting became more popular, and by the 1820s one of the principal gentlemanly recreations was the organised shooting of driven game birds, particularly pheasants, which, when disturbed, fly high and are exciting to shoot.[89]

The new landscape park and the wider arable landscape around it was thus a central amenity to the landowner, but it also was the thing that circumscribed his world because in some senses privacy lay at the heart of the whole enterprise. The effect of isolating a house in a vast sea of grass surrounded by game-stocked coverts was to create an inward-looking private world – one that could be regulated and controlled, and one that provided all the comforts a gentleman required. From the 1770s this world was increasingly guarded by gate lodges. These had been features of earlier houses, but the need to bar carriage drives to the unwanted and uninvited meant that they had to be manned day and night. Many early lodges were little more than two rooms, one on either side of the gate. These were later seen to be inconvenient, as well as providing substandard accommodation for the gatekeeper, so by the end of the 18th century gatehouses normally provided two residences either side of the gate, one for the porter and the other for a gamekeeper. In 1811 T. D. W. Dearn published *Designs for Lodges and Entrances*, a pattern book containing twenty examples of lodges in various styles, all with appropriate facilities for resident staff. These structures were not merely utilitarian; they heralded the main house, announcing the taste and wealth of the owner.

The gate lodges enabled parks to be opened to the public, who might drive through on a chaise; Stowe, for instance, was open on Sundays and visitors might approach through a colossal triumphal arch of 1767 that ingeniously concealed two houses in its flanks (fig. 388). The arch was suitable to the enormous house within. Lodges frequently announced not only the status of the house but also its style. The preposterous castellated gatehouse at Goodrich Court, Herefordshire, designed by Edward Blore and built between 1828 and 1831, was a deliberate foretaste of the great building beyond. It housed the owner's collection of medieval arms and armour (fig. 389).[90]

After 1800, as the taste for exotic architecture grew, the visual relationship between house and park underwent some important changes. The popularity of landscape parks did not wane but the setting of many houses was regarded as being too stark. A grassy landscape setting that had enhanced the tightly planned, austere boxes of the late 18th century did nothing for the more asymmetrical and florid buildings of the Regency. William Beckford's gardens at Fonthill Abbey, Wiltshire, were self-consciously more wild and exotic, but of course no less artificial than the gardens of Brown. A Chinese garden, a Swiss

Fig. 388 (top right) Stowe House, Buckinghamshire; the Corinthian Arch designed by Thomas Pitt in 1765–7. This was on the main axis to the south front of the house and contained, in its piers, two houses one room deep.

Fig. 389 (above right) Goodrich Court, Herefordshire; the Monmouth gatehouse, completed in 1837. The enormous tower-encrusted mansion that it introduced was demolished in 1950.

Fig. 390 (right) Hatchlands Park, Surrey, 1756–7; an ingeniously planned house in which the west front has three storeys and the south front has two. All the principal rooms were, however, on the ground floor, allowing direct access to the gardens.

garden and an American garden were planted, complete with species native to those countries. In 1813 Repton created fifteen separate gardens at Ashridge House, Hertfordshire, including a monks' garden, a mount garden and an American garden.

Just as the landscape setting of great houses became looser and less formal, so life within the houses themselves relaxed. The principal rooms began to be sited on the ground floor, frequently linked to the gardens by French windows. So whilst every major room of parade at Holkham was on the first floor (pp 317–8), at Hatchlands Park, Surrey (fig. 390), where Stiff Leadbetter built a house for Admiral Edward Boscawen between 1756 and 1758, the principal rooms led straight out into the garden. The elimination of a basement made it impossible to site the service quarters and kitchens below the main rooms. Increasingly, these were located in wings to the side of the main house. This was really only possible after the invention of the bell rope and, decisively, the bell pull in the 1760s and 70s, which allowed masters to summon servants who might be located some considerable distance away. From the 1790s servants' wings were not placed symmetrically; in most houses they lay to one side, normally the north.

Ashridge House, started by James Wyatt and completed by Sir Jeffry Wyatville between 1803 and 1817, is almost the sole surviving major new-built house of the early 19th century. Much larger, it was the product of about £300,000 of the Earl of Bridgewater's almost unlimited canal fortune. The house had around thirty guest bedrooms on the first floor and a separate ground-floor family wing, in which Lord and Lady Bridgewater could live when not entertaining (fig. 391). The entrance hall leads to a staircase hall, which is one of the greatest English interiors of its age. An imperial stair hugs the walls of a 92ft-high tower roofed by a moulded-plaster fan vault. The rest of the ground floor is given over to reception rooms in which a great party or ball could be held, but more often used for house parties (fig. 392). These were mixed-sex events over several days that revolved around the fixed points of breakfast and dinner. During the day the men would fox hunt or shoot, and the ladies would entertain themselves in the house and garden.

The plan at Ashridge retained some formality. The dining room and drawing room were balanced either side of an antechamber, but the disposition

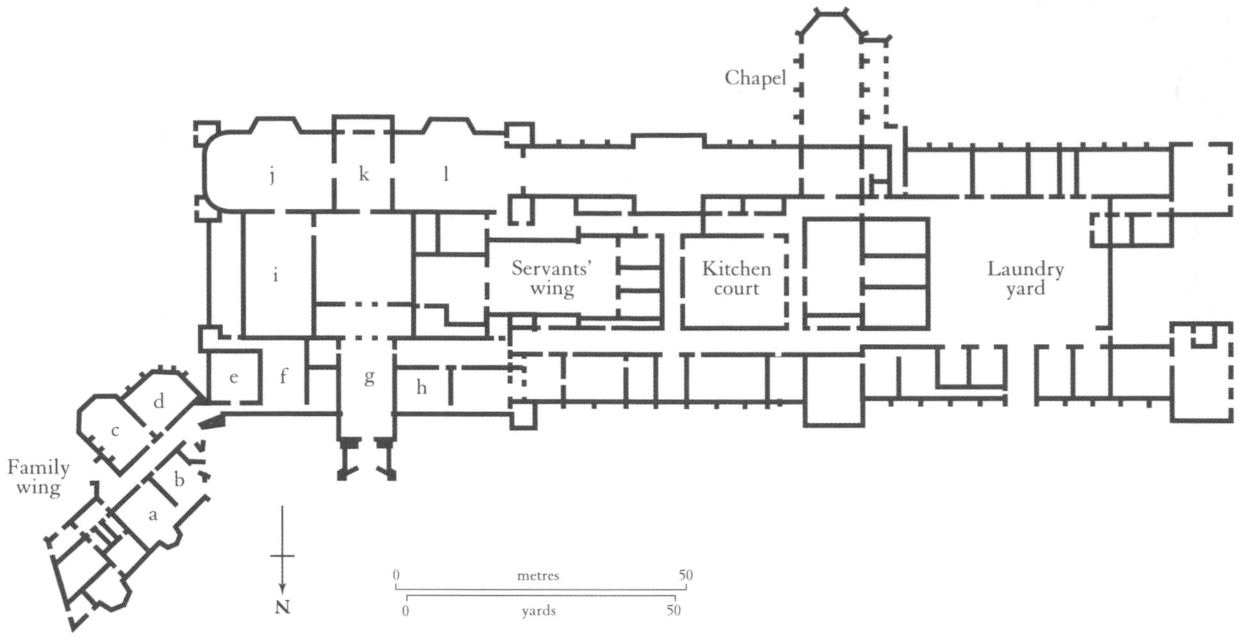

of rooms was otherwise designed to create an informal atmosphere. A large library, normally furnished as an informal sitting room, was a crucial component of any country house as in the early 19th century books were avidly read by country-house owners and guests. The house needed substantial domestic offices and these sprawled out to the west, screened from the gardens by a vast conservatory. At Ashridge, house and garden were designed to work together as a social and aesthetic unit.[91]

Public Buildings

By 1700 London was already the largest city in Europe, by 1750 it overtook Constantinople and by 1800 its population touched a million, putting it in the same league as the world's largest cities, Peking, Canton and Tokyo. But it didn't look like a great city; it had few public buildings and, with the exception of Somerset House, the machinery of government was housed in a ramshackle collection of historic buildings, whilst the monarch resided in various patched-up buildings of the 16th century and earlier. This situation was transformed after the Napoleonic Wars. The vast increase in state activity and the megalomania of the Prince Regent gave London an architectural presence it had lacked since the Great Fire. Windsor Castle and Buckingham Palace were transformed; the Palace of Westminster was extended and restored; new government offices were built on Whitehall; new buildings were erected for the Royal Mint, Post Office and Custom House; and two entirely new public cultural buildings, the British Museum and the National Gallery, were

Fig. 391 (above) Ashridge Park, Hertfordshire; the spectacular staircase hall that rises through three storeys. The hall is stone-lined with a staircase balustrade of polished brass; figures of medieval kings in niches sit below a ceiling with fan vaults and a gallery. It is the finest surviving Regency Gothic room in England.

Fig. 392 (left) Ashridge Park is the best preserved house of its age. The plan shows the scale and complexity of the house as a social organism: (a) Study; (b) Lord's dressing room; (c) Lady's room; (d) Family bedroom; (e) Lady's maid; (f) Billiard room; (g) Hall; (h) Breakfast room; (i) Library; (j) Drawing room; (k) Ante chamber; (l) Dining room.

started. In addition there was the Regent's Park and Regent's Street development, also under government sponsorship (p. 378). Between 1815 and 1832, when the old Office of Works was dissolved, the expenditure of the Office on public buildings in the capital was £2.5 million, as well as nearly £600,000 for Buckingham Palace, nearly £1 million for Windsor Castle and £1.5 million for Regent's Street.

For seventeen years between 1796 and 1813 James Wyatt held the post of Surveyor of Works. It was a troubled period, and in the last decade there were four investigations into ineptitude and malpractice. Wyatt's chaotic and lethargic administration, coupled with wildly fluctuating wartime building costs, left the Office of Works on its knees. His sudden and dramatic death in a coaching accident saved him from public disgrace but it didn't save the Office of Works from radical reform. The new man in charge, Benjamin Charles Stephenson, was a soldier and administrator, not an architect; under him he had three 'attached' architects who would undertake the work. John Nash, Sir John Soane and Sir Robert Smirke would each would be responsible for government offices in one of three districts.

The three were of fundamentally different character and enjoyed different power bases in the establishment. Nash was a scenic decorator who could conjure up a brilliant effect and was the Prince Regent's favourite architect, creator of the Royal Pavilion, Brighton, but a terrible administrator and a lazy workman. Soane was the opposite; an obsessive genius preoccupied with the minutiae of his work. In 1788 he had become Surveyor to the Bank of England, locking him into the metropolitan Establishment. Smirke was younger, and was a slick and efficient administrator. He was the first, for instance, to regularly use a quantity surveyor. He was often called in to sort out problems created by other less conscientious architects. His power base lay with the Tories, whose pet architect he was; his practice was one of the largest and most successful of the whole century, if perhaps one of the less inspired.[92]

Yet the first and, in many senses most important, public building of the age was not paid for by the government, but by a private corporation. Almost as soon as the Bank of England was completed in 1734 (p. 305) it was too small. Between them, the Wars of the Austrian Succession and the Seven Years' War added £88 million to the national debt, the majority of which was administered by the Bank. By 1790 over three hundred clerks worked there. The bank's architect between 1764 and 1788 was Robert Taylor, who quadrupled the size of the buildings, creating a massive, windowless, walled enclave in the centre of the City. Of all Taylor's extensions at the Bank, the Rotunda – the east wing with its great, domed Broker's Exchange – was the most important (fig. 393). This was effectively the world's first stock exchange, where British government paper securities were publically traded, in just the same way that tangible commodities had been traded over the road at the Royal Exchange (p. 305). Four identical transfer halls led from the Rotunda, where transactions were formally registered. Taylor's inspiration was the Pantheon, one of ancient Rome's most imitated buildings, particularly in this period; there was one at Vauxhall Gardens and another, built in 1810, at Ince Blundell Hall, Cheshire.

Externally, the Bank made a substantial impact on the commercial heart of the City, creating an impressive ensemble with the Mansion House (p. 306) and the Royal Exchange (p. 305). Its dominant architectural presence mirrored its institutional importance. It was widely recognised that its success as an exchange for government stocks had bankrolled the most expensive wars the world had yet seen, and to national benefit. As it gobbled up land in the City, demolishing the old taverns and drinking houses where business had traditionally been transacted, it began to create a new world of professionalised finance conducted in purpose-built offices with greater specialisation, segregation and control of

Fig. 393 (above) Interior view of the Broker's Exchange, Bank of England, Threadneedle Street, London, *c.*1790.

access. Across England, and at all levels, trade moved out of the open air, from alleys, churchyards and taverns to dedicated structures complete with vestibules, lobbies, corridors, anterooms, board rooms, clerical offices and the like.

Although Pitt the Younger instituted a so-called sinking fund to finance the French wars and introduced the first income tax, fighting France still managed to add £591 million to Britain's debt, trebling it to £834 million. To handle this the Bank's staff once more grew, doubling to over a thousand, so the Bank again needed to expand. This time the Bank's architect was Sir John Soane, and here he produced his best and most important work (fig. 394), although it was tragically demolished by Sir Herbert Baker in the 1920s. The Bank's complex operations were redesigned over a forty-five-year period and the whole site wrapped in a quarter-mile-long screen wall raised up on a plain podium, but elegantly grooved and capped with a crenelated skyline of Greek and Roman motifs. At the north-west corner was an elegant portico – the Tivoli Corner, designed to be a centrepiece in the re-planning of the City. The exterior certainly expressed strength and security, but it was curiously picturesque, a function of the synthesis of architectural styles. Inside the fusion was more complete. Soane used forms from both the ancient and medieval worlds to create an increasingly original and abstract style. Here was an architect not content with expressing Roman, Greek, Gothic, Egyptian or Hindu architecture, but creating his own curious hybrid of all these and more besides. At the Bank he experimented with top lighting, perfecting his genius for planning complex and dramatic spaces of varying sizes. It was also amongst the most technologically advanced structures of its age, making use of iron skylights, Coade stone, gas lighting, hypocaust heating systems and hollow clay-pot vaulting used to fireproof mills.[93]

The Bank of England, and indeed all the major post-war public metropolitan structures, apart from Windsor Castle (p. 263), were designed in classical styles that still resonated with the Establishment as reflective of their civic and national values. Two of them call for special mention as they were new building types expressive of the post-war age. Both were built in the prevailing fashion for Greek architecture; one was the General Letter Office (later the General Post Office), the other the British Museum.

A public postal service had existed in England since 1635. Letters were carried in relays between posts by mounted postboys and handed to local postmasters. The development of the turnpikes opened up the possibility of mail being carried directly from town to town by stagecoach, an innovation that was eventually accepted by Pitt the Younger in 1784. Within two years the network covered the most important towns as far north as Edinburgh. It was still, however, a complicated and bureaucratic system – letters were paid for by the recipient, and charged on distance and the number of sheets of paper. Many letters, such as those from MPs, went free, and various local systems had differing charges. War had increased both the cost and volume of post, and the old premises in Lombard Street from which the network had been run – originally a coaching inn – was an inadequate headquarters. A new site was proposed on St Martin's le Grand.

Fig. 394 (above) The Bank of England from the south east; aerial cut-away view by Joseph Michael Gandy, 1830. This drawing summarises forty years of Soane's work at the Bank, illustrating the main façade and the brilliance of Soane's planning and theatrical procession of interiors.

As with many contemporary metropolitan improvements a new premises was taken as an opportunity to remove slums and beautify a run-down quarter of the city. A competition was run for the design, but after all entries were judged to be inadequate, Robert Smirke, in whose district the GPO lay, was asked to furnish a design and building proceeded. Externally, the new building was a magnificent advertisement both for Smirke's confident handling of Greek architecture and for the world's first post office. Completed in 1828, it was expertly planned, with a clear separation of internal functions and efficient circulation. Technologically, it was the most advanced office structure in the world. In the basement a small railway connected various departments, machinery supplied each floor with coal, two steam engines provided ventilation and the whole building was constructed in fireproof materials, with fire hydrants provided just in case.

Just as a postal headquarters was a novel building exploiting new building technology so was a purpose-built museum. Many aristocratic houses effectively contained museums – rooms set aside purely for the enjoyment of collections – and some of these attracted considerable numbers of visitors. Dulwich Picture Gallery, designed by Sir John Soane and opened in 1817, was a development from this tradition. Although it was a single-storey building, it provided an elegant enfilade of top-lit spaces for hanging paintings.[94] The

British Museum, built between 1823 and 1852, was different in both concept and form (fig. 395). The museum had been established in Montagu House, Bloomsbury, by Act of Parliament in 1753. Initially, it contained a number of private collections purchased for the nation by the government. In this the novelty of the museum's position lay: princes in other countries still decided if, how and when to show their collections to their subjects. The British Museum was truly national. Further gifts and purchases were added, but it was the vast expansion of its collecting activities during and after the Napoleonic Wars that eventually caused it to outgrow its original home.

Across Europe new public museums were being conceived and all were built in the Greek style. This was inevitable. The idea of a museum itself was Greek, the *musea* being a Greek temple devoted to the muses. For the British Museum there was an additional factor; it now contained the greatest collection of classical sculpture in the world, with its star exhibit the Parthenon marbles. The architect chosen to design the building was again Robert Smirke. The building was planned as a massive quadrangle, the sides of which were to be built in phases. The interiors were spacious boxes, rational and austere in style, and dependent on massive iron beams

Fig. 395 (below) The British Museum; although this was a ruthlessly Grecian building inspired by Smirke's travels to Sicily and Greece, it was also intensely modern. Built on concrete foundations, the massive Portland stone slabs are fixed to a brick core by iron cramps.

and concrete foundations. Upper floors were of slate, bedded on iron plates, and roofs were of copper. The daring use of cast-iron beams over 50ft long in the King's Library was made possible with the help of John Rastrick, a leading railway engineer. The library reveals Smirke, and Greek architecture, at their best: expansive, noble but rich in colour and varied in rhythm (fig. 396). The entrance façade, too, is magnificent, but unusual and uncompromising in that it combines a forty-four-column Greek Ionic colonnade with a portico and makes no concessions to Roman design – the walls behind are smooth and austere. The whole thing is now topped-off with a tympanum sculpture by Sir Richard Westmacott showing the progress of civilisation. This was not part of Smirke's design but a yielding to demand for greater decoration added in the early 1850s.[95]

The long and hard war that Britain fought with France from 1793 was a defining event with long-term effects. Britain emerged from it as the only industrialised nation in the world, with rapidly increasing prominence in commerce, transport, insurance and finance, the largest colonial empire ever assembled and virtually unchallenged naval power. Supremacy of the seas had enabled the merchant marine to take most of the world's trade, stimulating industrial development, finance, commerce and shipping. This was a self-reinforcing economic, military and political cycle that, for a brief period in world history, propelled Britain to the fore. All this was bought for less than £1 a year per head of population or, to put it another way, 2 to 3 percent of national income.[96]

Advances in technology, within which architectural design was critical, was one of the decisive underpinning factors. The vitality of British innovation was buttressed by war, demography and an evangelical mindset. These drove innovations that for the first time in two hundred and fifty years challenged the capabilities of architects. The challenges were not only structural, – although these at face value were the most impressive – they were also organisational. Buildings such as the General Post Office, the Royal William Yard and the Albion Mill were an entirely new sort of commission, in which architectural design lubricated complex organisational processes.

Yet the background to this dynamic economy was a society that was, in fact, more serious-minded, sober, religious, book-loving and militaristic. Ordered, anonymous terraces, the detached private villas of the wealthy, the desire to order town centres and the urge to congregate in societies represent a less outward-looking society than that of the 18th century. The new towns that developed were entirely different sorts of place. The amalgam of buildings in Liverpool and Manchester, as in places such as Halifax, Bath and Cheltenham, was bewildering to outsiders. There was also a sense of social and political crisis, a fear that the whole order was in danger and that the poverty-stricken masses, excluded from the political process, would rise up in bloody revolution.

This, perhaps, makes the period sound conservative in terms of architectural style. It was not. It was, in fact, an era of great stylistic plurality coming after a period of greater consensus. The world was opened up to patrons and

Fig. 396 (above) The King's Library, British Museum, London, Robert Smirk, 1823–7, the noblest room of its age in London; rich but restrained, supremely confident and cavernous.

architects after the end of the French wars, heralding a creative, exotic and exciting period for architectural design. But, as every age is the prelude to the next, the seeds were being sown for an era, after 1830, when English architecture would, for the first time in history, break the bounds by which it had previously been constrained.

II— World Dominance

—1830-1870

Although the exponents of mid-Victorian architecture might not have felt that they adequately reflected their place in the world, their buildings express the confidence of a nation that had moved from being one of shopkeepers to being the workshop of the world.

By 1851 coal had begun to revolutionise the British economy. As we have seen (p. 357), demand for coal to produce heat energy had necessitated the invention of the steam engine to pump out deep mines. The steam engine transformed coal from a source of heat energy into a source of mechanical energy that powered manufacturing on a previously unimagined scale; mechanical energy also powered the railway, first needed to support coal production, but later to move goods, including coal, nationwide. Iron to make machines and railways was also dependent on coal. Whilst making 10,000 tonnes of iron required 100,000 acres of trees, relatively small amounts of coal enabled iron and steel to be made cheaply on a massive scale. Soon, goods were also being moved by coal-powered steam ships, allowing the products of British manufacturing to be sold worldwide. To facilitate all this, coal production, which had stood at 10 million tonnes a year in 1800, expanded to 64.7 million tonnes in 1854 and 181.6 million in 1890. Initially, it had been mined where it outcropped or at very shallow depths but the worldwide market for British coal meant that miners had to solve the problems of deep mining, including drainage, ventilation and underground transport. Large parts of the English landscape were transformed by coal mining as it diversified and moved from its traditional heartlands along the Tyne. Coal was found at Ashington, Northumberland, where a pit was sunk in 1846; four others followed. At first the village comprised two rows of stone houses; this increased to eight rows (335 houses) by 1880 and eleven rows (665 houses) by 1890. Another 1,300 were built in the next twenty-five years. Every house had a garden with an outside privy emptied by a tramway at the rear. There was a good water supply, sewers and gas lighting. It was not a bad place to live, but scarcely typical of the facilities of some pit villages (fig. 397).[1]

The labour of such villages ended up producing about two-thirds of the world's coal, powering Britain's mechanised manufacturing economy, raising national productivity and, because of railways and steam ships, enabling it to dominate world trade as no country has subsequently managed. In 1880 Britain was responsible for 41 per cent of manufactured goods entering world trade; it made half the world's iron, five sevenths of its steel, two-fifths of its hardware and around half of its commercial cotton cloth. Meanwhile, it became the centre of banking, financing new world markets; by 1875 over £1,000 million was invested abroad. Banking attracted other financial services – insurance, currency and commodity exchanges – establishing London as the world's financial capital. Added to this was Britain colossal domestic consumption, which grew and diversified.

Fig. 397 (above) Ashington Colliery, Northumberland, 1895–1900. Here the headgear and winding houses for the two shafts can be seen. Now a museum, originally such winding gear and headstocks were a common sight over parts of the midlands and the north.

The British government played only a small role in this. Victory in the wars against France had not led to political reform, as some hoped. War had, in many senses, entrenched a system in which membership of the established Church and land ownership were paramount. However, population growth, especially in the manufacturing towns, meant that large sections of the population now had no access to an MP. This was a serious disadvantage as most significant local developments had to be effected by private members' bills; without an MP this was difficult. The Tory administration of Lord Liverpool tried to accommodate new interests through administrative rather than political change, but the Tories had to concede political reform by the end of the decade. The Test and Corporation Acts were repealed in 1828 and the Roman Catholic Emancipation Act came in 1829. The following year the Tories were ousted by a Whig government that brought more fundamental reforms. The Great Reform Act of 1832 expanded the franchise and redistributed seats to give representation to new towns. Acts in 1867 and 1884–5 expanded the franchise further.

Reform did not satisfy everyone and, in the late 1830s and early 40s, there was an attempt to build an independent political party to represent labouring men – the Chartists. This, compounded by the great struggles of 1848 and 1849 on the continent between autocratic states and those championing the rights of individuals, disconcerted many in the Establishment, although Britain avoided violent revolution. Changes, many of which will be explored below, came piecemeal through the period and not in a single bloody rush, as some had feared they might.

Yet the changes that had begun to accelerate in the 18th century did cause a general loss of confidence in the structures of society. In particular, it was no longer possible from the 1840s onwards to regard the landscape of industry with optimism and confidence, as it signalled misery and personal hardship on a previously unknown scale. From different perspectives writers such as Thomas Carlyle, A.W.N. Pugin, Benjamin Disraeli, John Ruskin and William Morris criticised the dehumanising effects of Britain's global prosperity and expressed an intense nostalgia, a desire to rekindle the world of the Middle Ages both in terms of its social responsibility and its architecture. Each saw pre-industrial society, based on hierarchy and social deference but safeguarded by religious belief, as providing a model for the present. A historical sense became part of everyone's consciousness and history itself became a profession. The effects of this upon architectural design were profound and remained powerful, in various ways, until the Second World War.

In no sense were these effects confined to the adoption of a single historical style; now armed with detailed academic knowledge of every historical style known to man, British architects were able to create a series of architectural effects (the word 'styles' here is insufficient) that dazzled the world. Yet many of the men who designed were consumed with an anxiety as to whether they were working in a distinct, individual and palpable style for their century. Nothing of this crisis of confidence, however, can be seen in the conviction with which new materials and techniques were blended with a spectrum of architectural references to create buildings that – for the first time in British history – were the wonder of the entire world.

Icons of England's Olden Time

The Napoleonic Wars shook British society and, in the following decades, it became clear that much would never to be the same again, including the way people engaged with the national past. Symbolic of this was the publication in 1814 of *Waverley*, Sir Walter Scott's first novel, which marked a turning point in the way people perceived the past. Scott's realism was utterly engaging; his novels were rooted in historical events and set in existing historic places. Scott made the past tangible and realistic in a way it had never been before. Advances in printing soon led to illustrated editions of his work and magazines filled with a variety of historical prints. Joseph Nash's *Mansions of England in Olden Time*, the first volume of which came out in 1839, illustrated views of Tudor and early Stuart country houses, with groups of authentically dressed characters. Nash's books enabled people to see for the first time what life had really been like in the 'Olden Times' made familiar to them through novels and magazines.[2]

A major stimulus to this romantic view of England was the rebuilding of Windsor Castle by George IV between 1824 and 1828. In 1820 George had acceded to the throne of a nation still swelling with pride after the defeat of France. His response was to commission a triumphal rebuilding of his two principal residences, Buckingham Palace and Windsor. Buckingham Palace was completed neither for him nor his successor and left the reputation of its architect, John Nash, in tatters. The architect of Windsor was Jeffry Wyatt (later Sir Jeffry Wyatville), who acted on a brief prepared by the king's artistic advisor Sir Charles Long. Their achievement was to create a romantic masterpiece – a building that in close-up can be unforgiving and crude but at a distance is a brilliant, picturesque composition, the very epitome of the England of the Olden Times (fig. 398).[3]

It was exactly this old-English picturesque effect that was to be the defining characteristic of the new Palace of Westminster, started in 1840. The razing of the old palace by fire in October 1834 engendered varying emotions. For the antiquary and historian it was a catastrophe, the destruction of the spiritual home of English secular architecture. For the more politically minded it was either just retribution for what they saw as the sell-out of the Great Reform Act or the natural corollary to reform; an opportunity to express in a new building the principles established in 1832. Either way, it was decided by a select committee that the style of the new building was to be Gothic or Elizabethan.

We have seen that Tudor Gothic was one of the spectrums of styles that found favour from the 1760s (pp 332–4), but after 1800 there was an increasing interest in Henrician, Elizabethan and Jacobean architecture (referred to here as Tudor). The great advantage of Tudor was that its surviving examples were not primarily castles and abbeys; they were domestic, and right through the social scale from great country houses to the humblest cottage. Overlaid on these practical advantages was that Elizabethan England was seen as a

Fig. 398 (above) Windsor Castle from the Great Park. The long, low, romantic silhouette created for George IV by Sir Jeffry Wyatville from 1824 was part of Sir Charles Long's fashioning of the king's image. Long had been the mastermind behind the Coronation and it was he who set out a programme for the castle in 1824.

golden age of Protestantism, independence and prosperity. These were attractive notions for people building in the post-war years. Charles Barry, Edward Blore, Anthony Salvin and William Burn had all practised in the Tudor style, and pattern books, such as Robert Lugar's *Architectural Sketches for Cottages, Rural Dwellings, and Villas* (1805), made it available to the middle classes.

A competition was launched for the new Houses of Parliament in February 1836. The chairman of the selection committee was Charles Hanbury Tracy, an imaginative and capable amateur architect who had designed and built his own house, Toddington Manor, Gloucestershire, in an early Tudor style between 1819 and 1823. His committee reported on the ninety-seven entries received and Charles Barry's design was chosen. Barry was then forty years old and his co-designer Augustus Welby Northmore Pugin was twenty-three. The building we now have was a joint creation. Barry's plan efficiently accommodated the various functions of the palace, with separate entrances for the monarch, Lords and Commons, and a series of lobbies and galleries

that linked them. Its style was taken from the Henry VII Chapel less than a hundred yards away, a building that was seen to represent England's Tudor greatness. This was achieved by Pugin with meticulous archaeological correctitude and brilliant inventiveness (fig. 399).

Fig. 399 (above) The Palace of Westminster; famously a classically proportioned building with Gothic detailing, but nevertheless one that would help mould the medievalising taste, not only of the nation, but of an empire.

The new building was not only the seat of a democratic legislature; space given over to the royal apartments and the House of Lords exceeded, by far, that allocated to the Commons, and the vast Victoria Tower, the most prominent part of the new building, was the monarch's private entrance. Whilst the House of Lords provided a dazzling setting for royal ceremonial, the Commons chamber was too small to accommodate all of its members.[4] The Palace of Westminster ultimately represents a Tory moment of political and social reaction, but it also encapsulates some fundamental changes already underway in English architecture. First, it marked the moment when the picturesque Gothic of Wyatt and his contemporaries turned towards a more archaeological mode that sought to faithfully follow historical precedent; second, it marked the moment when nationalistic values became inextricably attached to the Gothic style; and third, it marked the point when a building designed with faithful reference to the past also lay at the technological cutting edge, incorporating iron technology and sophisticated heating, ventilation and fire-proofing. It is to technological advances that we must now turn.

Technology, Materials and Methods

Between 1850 and 1870 the Royal Navy underwent a revolution that led to the creation of a modern battle fleet, built and serviced in radically modernised dockyards. Whilst logistics to keep the fleet at sea for long periods had been perfected before the Napoleonic Wars (p. 340), the design of ships themselves had failed to keep up. The principal problem was the weakness of larger hulls that could not withstand prolonged sea service. This was rectified between 1800 and 1814 by innovations enabling the size of warships to double and, in due course, bear the weight and vibration of steam engines. The first iron warships were ordered in 1845 and the first to be designed solely for steam propulsion was built in 1849. With the launch of *HMS Devastation* in 1871 came the first recognisably modern warship without masts or rigging and equipped with gun turrets.

Steam power radically changed dockyard landscapes, with the construction of basins, dry docks and slips on a scale never before attempted. Particularly prominent were the new covered slips in which ships were built before being launched. From 1814 the navy had started to cover them with big timber roofs to prevent hulls rotting in the open air. At Chatham Dockyard, No. 3 Slip – dating from 1838 – still stands, its massive timber frame originally covered with zinc sheeting (fig. 402). Timber slip roofs were prone to rot and constituted a fire risk, so in 1842, on the advice of Captain Henry Brandreth, Director of Naval Works, the navy felt confident enough to decree that in future all covered slips were to be of iron. Corrugated-iron sheeting had been invented in 1829; it was light, strong, water and fireproof and, with an iron substructure, formed the basis of Brandreth's design for two slip sheds at Pembroke Dock, Wales, in 1842. They were built by the firm Fox, Henderson & Co. from 1844, but do not survive. However, an almost identical structure, erected by the same contractors, was built at Woolwich between 1844 and 1845. In 1880 this was moved to Chatham, where it still stands (fig. 401). These were the first wide-span iron roofs in the world.

Fig. 400 (above) 4–6 Slips Chatham Dockyard, Kent, 1847, are amongst the first widespan metal roof structures ever built.

Fig. 401 (below right) Cross section of the iron-framed number 6 slip at Woolwich, Fox, Henderson & Co., 1844–5. The slip cover spans 72ft but is 118ft feet wide including the aisles; it was 218ft long.

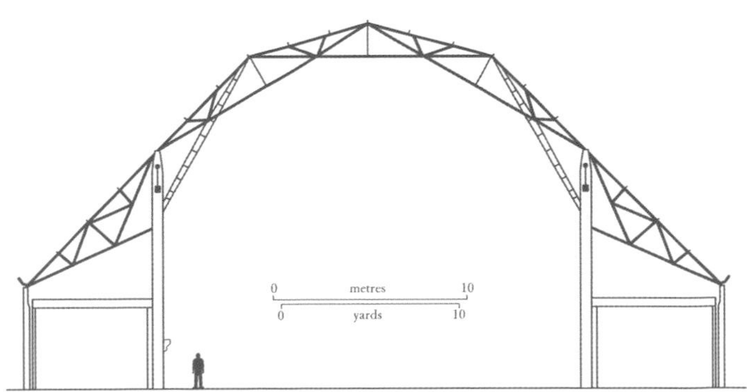

Fig. 402 (above left) Chatham Dockyard; timber-framed number 3 slip, by Sir Robert Seppings, 1837–8. This is colossal at 300ft long and 146ft wide. A mezzanine floor was inserted in 1904.

Fig. 403 (above) Crystal Palace built for the Great Exhibition, Joseph Paxton and others, 1852. The print shows the design masterstroke that led to the encapsulation of the great trees in Hyde Park as part of the exhibition, the great central nave containing their height.

Captain Thomas Mould of the Royal Engineers was transferred from Pembroke to Chatham, where in 1847 he designed three new slips with the aid of the contractor George Baker (who had built two further iron-roofed slips at Pembroke). Unlike the Pembroke and Woolwich sheds, where a timber structure had been rendered into iron, these slips made the most of the contrasting properties of wrought and cast iron, enabling the pillars to be spaced on a wide, 30ft grid. Eventually, the construction of iron ships made roofs unnecessary but not before the navy had built eighteen of them. These remarkable and innovative structures were sited, of course, within the high-security confines of naval dockyards, but they were designed and built by a partnership of contractors and military engineers. It was these contractors who transferred iron technology to the civil sphere.[5]

Had it not been for the naval dockyards, the Crystal Palace in Hyde Park in 1851 could not have been built. The Crystal Palace was created, like the dockyards and the railways, by a group of designers. The man who came up with the crucial problem-solving idea was Joseph Paxton, first a horticulturalist but also an engineer, railway director and promoter of newspapers. Paxton shares the credit for the building with Charles Fox (of Fox, Henderson & Co.), who had cut his teeth in the dockyards and worked under George Stephenson at Euston railway station (p. 409). Charles Barry was also part of the team; he had already used iron at the Houses of Parliament (p. 400) and at the Travellers Club. Others involved included Matthew Digby Wyatt and Owen Jones, designers responsible for embellishing the building's interior.

Paxton's initial expertise lay in the field of glasshouse design. Glasshouses had been common in England from the 1680s, most often in the form of orangeries but increasingly as greenhouses. After 1805 commercial glasshouse owners began to experiment, replacing timber members with iron for cheapness of construction and ease of maintenance. The decisive advance came in 1815 when George Mackenzie showed how curved glazed surfaces would better let in light.

Fig. 404 (above) The Palm House, Royal Botanic Gardens, Kew, 1846–8; 19th-century England's most beautiful surviving work of engineering. The frame is in fact wrought, not cast, iron: the use of I-section beams is the earliest substantial use outside shipbuilding.

A young agricultural improver, J. C. Loudon, and an ironmaster, William Bailey of W. & D. Bailey, then invented a curved wrought-iron bar that could be used in hothouses. Bailey started manufacturing large numbers of new curvilinear hothouses; an early surviving example, probably made using the Loudon and Bailey bar, is the wonderfully bulbous Palm House at Bicton Park, Devon, built in c. 1825. The greatest hothouse ever built, though, was the Palm House at the Royal Botanic Gardens, Kew, erected between 1846 and 1848 (fig. 404). The innovations in this remarkable building, concurrent with the buildings of the Newcastle Central Station train shed (pp 409–10), were again down to engineering manufacturers, principally Richard Turner of Dublin, who worked with the architect Decimus Burton on the design.

The Crystal Palace was the most important direct successor of these buildings (fig. 403). It was important both in terms of its engineering and its use of prefabrication materials, but also perhaps as the first building in history to enjoy instant world-wide fame – a structure that advertised to a global audience the uses to which iron could be put. It was 1,851ft long, covering eighteen acres, enclosing mature trees and constructed in a breathtaking nine months. The ridge-and-furrow roof sections channelled water into hollow uprights that acted as rainwater downpipes, and at the same time formed tracks for aerial trollies, enabling the glaziers access to the iron frame.

Advances in glass manufacture were as important as those in iron. Since the introduction of commercial glassmaking in England in the 1560s (p. 232), most glass was made by blowing and then spinning molten glass to create a disk of crown glass up to 5ft in diameter. Glass was thicker at the centre, where there was the crown or nipple, and only the outer parts of the disk were usable. As a result the size of sheet was very restricted, limiting, for instance, the size of sash panes. From 1696 windows were subjected to punitive taxes, first on the number of openings in houses, worth over £5 a year, and then from 1745 on glass itself. Glass tax, which had inhibited the English glass industry, was repealed in 1845 and window tax finally went in 1851. By then, however, techniques of glass manufacture, and thus its architectural possibilities, had been transformed. After 1832 a new technique was imported from France that involved swinging a bubble of glass to create a cylinder; this could be cut lengthwise and flattened to form a larger sheet without a nipple in it. Sheet glass was cheaper and thinner, making possible sashes with bigger panes, plate glass windows without glazing bars, conservatories, railway sheds and, of course, the Crystal Palace with its 900,000 square feet of glass.[6]

In the early 1840s the engineer Eaton Hodgkinson had brought mathematical and scientific method to iron construction, showing how to make stronger beams using less metal. His I-shaped girders, with flanges narrower at the top than the bottom, enabled engineers, at a stroke, to erect buildings with columns spaced at 20ft rather than 14ft intervals. His work was developed by others, including the navy, but the real leap forward came with the move from cast and wrought iron to steel. Steel, as we have seen (p. 363), could at first be made only in small crucibles and was therefore expensive, its use confined to small-scale, high-performance items. As a spin-off from his work on armaments during the Crimean War, Sir Henry Bessemer invented a process for making large quantities of high-quality steel. He announced his process in Sheffield in 1856 and within fifteen years steel had became the material of choice for railway rails, boiler plate, armaments, shipbuilding and bridges. Bessemer's process was improved upon after 1875, when the Siemens-Martin process produced steel of a more consistent quality.[7]

This development completed an extraordinary series of British innovations that set British heavy industry in a position of world supremacy. It also opened up a whole range of new architectural possibilities; steel beams could be thinner, lighter and stronger, and resisted fire better. Yet English designers essentially saw exposed glass-and-iron structures as a way of covering large spaces quickly and cheaply, and this was not a consideration for most commissions. Buildings such as the British Museum (fig. 395), the General Post Office, or the Houses of Parliament (fig. 399) were iron buildings clothed in stone, the completed structure giving no hint of the nature of its skeleton. This was at least in part a consequence of the vulnerability of exposed iron to the effects of fire but also the fact that, other than in limited circumstances, it was not capable of achieving the stylistic effects that patrons and architects desired.

Technological innovations were matched after the Napoleonic Wars by two trends in the building industry: the transfer of activities previously undertaken on site to the building yard, and the increasing use of mechanised plant on site. Off-site manufacture and prefabrication were rapidly mechanised in the thirty years after 1815. We have seen that machinery to work wood was introduced into the dockyards in the late 18th century (pp 340–1), but steam sawmills took a little time to be put into common use by contractors. The first commercial mill near London was established in 1810 and by 1850 there were seventy. By then they were not just cutting and planing wood; a machine for cutting tongue-and-groove boarding was invented in 1827, in the 1840s circular saws and mortice-and-tenon machines were perfected, and band saws were common from the 1850s. In country areas joiners were still working wood by hand but increasingly this was mixed with machine-made components in construction. An array of mouldings was available off-the-shelf; the General Wood-cutting Company in 1847 claimed to have more than a hundred different types in stock. So well developed was the industry by mid-century that manufacturers such as the High Orchard Saw Mills of Gloucester could produce 3,250 flat-pack timber huts in a mere three months between 1854 and 1855 for the government to ship out for use in the Crimean War.

Machines were invented to polish stone, in 1824 to saw it, in 1835 to plane it and finally in 1845 to carve it into irregular shapes. These allowed the mass production of stone components. In 1845 the Westminster Marble Company was offering one hundred different designs of marble chimney pieces. Many of these were made remotely in the quarries but most building contractors by the 1850s were furnished with such equipment in their yards. The most important development, however, was in brick production. Effective brick-making machines came into common use in the 1840s to plasticise brick earth, extrude it in the right shape, cut it into sections with wires and dry it. Meanwhile, kiln technology advanced and from 1858 the old brick clamp was replaced by the Hoffmann kiln. In such a furnace 40,000 bricks could burn at a time. Between 1830 and 1854 annual brick production doubled and by 1856 brick production in Britain topped 1,800 million bricks a year. But it was quality as well as quantity that mattered. The uniformity of size and colour achieved by mechanisation meant that more precise and colourful effects could be achieved with it as a face material, transforming the aesthetic opportunities brick offered. The result was that by 1866 brick had become the defining material of the age (pp 418–9).

Once on site, construction was increasingly reliant on new machines. There were more than four hundred portable steam engines in use by building contractors by 1850. Their first use was as pumps; John Rennie used them in the construction of the London docks, but by the 1850s steam power was used for mortar mills, concrete mixers, pile drivers, cranes, and earth-moving and excavation machines. There is a danger, however, in exaggerating the degree of mechanisation before 1900. The big metropolitan firms engaged in major contracts were highly mechanised but the degree of mechanisation rapidly reduced for smaller outfits, and in towns and villages. Yet all these technological advances began to have an impact on the design and construction process, particularly of houses. The architect was now, in the most extreme cases, disposing a kit of ready-made components for aesthetic effect, whilst builders focused on assembly and were much less concerned with manufacture.[8]

Railway Revolutions

The coming of the railways had a bigger impact on English building than perhaps any other single event.[9] In September 1830 the world's first inter-city passenger railway opened for business. Running between Manchester and Liverpool it already possessed the characteristics of all that was to come afterwards – the capacity to move high volumes of people and goods long distances on fixed routes at speed. Speed was a phenomenon that terrified early users; many believed that people would be brain-damaged and unborn babies deformed. They weren't, but what speed did was annihilate distance. By 1852 no town of any size in England was more than a day's travel from the capital.

The concept of moving goods in wheeled wagons that ran on rails was not new, nor – thanks to the canals and turnpikes – was a fixed transport network supported by a sophisticated business infrastructure. The big new idea was steam locomotion; harnessing the steam engine for propulsion. The engineering for this rapidly developed, dominated by the Northumbrian engineer, George Stephenson, designer of the first passenger railway in 1830. The Liverpool and Manchester Railway was built to move people and goods the thirty-six miles between the two cities – a pragmatic and economic resolution of a problem that was inhibiting business. Railways not only stole custom from stagecoaches and canals but rapidly expanded the market, putting rail travel within the reach of most people.[10]

During the forty years following 1830 the core of Britain's railway network was built. By 1871 it covered 15,736 miles, about 66 per cent of British Rail's operational reach a century later (fig. 407). Investment came in waves in 1837–40, 1845–7 and 1862–5. By 1870 the railway companies had invested £530 million in land, track, buildings and rolling stock. They operated a new business model; unlike the traditional family firms that still carried out most enterprises, they were public joint-stock companies with limited liability and dispersed ownership, and a large, separate managerial structure. Like the builders of canals before them they relied on individual Acts of Parliament to authorise land purchase and construction.

The canals that criss-crossed parts of the English countryside with cuttings, embankments, bridges and aqueducts (pp 344–346) had been accompanied by standardised toll houses, wharfs and warehouses made of mass-produced brick and ironwork. But canals were narrow, small-scale and sat lightly on the landscape. Locomotives were heavy – and became heavier – and the engineering required to convey them was massive and robust. Few railways were single-track; most were double and soon some were quadruple. In the early days locomotives were not sufficiently powerful to climb steep gradients, and keeping track as level as possible required savage cuttings, embankments, tunnels and bridges. Robert Stephenson's London and Birmingham Railway, completed in 1838 at a cost of £5.5 million, was one hundred and eleven miles long, with gradients nowhere exceeding 1:330. To achieve this, twelve million cubic yards of earth were moved for cuttings and eleven million cubic yards

Fig. 405 (top right) The High Level Bridge, Newcastle upon Tyne, Robert Stephenson, 1845–9; a combined road and rail bridge linking Gateshead and Newcastle.

Fig. 406 (above) The Tamar Bridge at Saltash under construction in 1858. This was Brunel's last and greatest railway project, completed, remarkably, on time and without loss of life. Hydraulic jacks were used to slowly raise the truss into position as the piers were built beneath it.

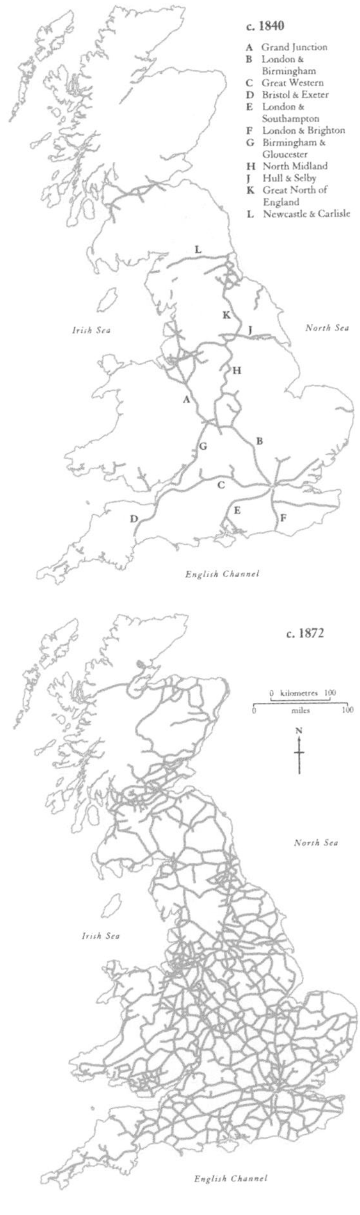

Fig. 407 (above) The British railway network in *c.*1840 and in *c.*1872.

for embankments, six viaducts and three hundred bridges were built, and three long tunnels were bored. The organisation and much of the engineering for such projects was based on the experience of canal building.[11]

Yet railway engineers faced challenges unknown to canal builders. Bridge building, in particular, developed rapidly in structural ambition, and between 1830 and 1860 some 25,000 bridges were erected. Most were of traditional materials – brick, stone and timber – but for the larger spans cast iron was increasingly used. At first, engineers had not fully understood the weakness of cast iron in tension and its lack of flexible strength. Flat girders were pushed wider and wider until one failed – with a train on it. This was Robert Stephenson's Dee Bridge outside Chester, which collapsed in 1847 with the loss of five lives. Learning from this disaster Stephenson embarked upon what was to be his aesthetic masterpiece, exploiting the contrasting load-bearing capacities of wrought and cast iron. The High Level Bridge at Newcastle upon Tyne, completed in 1849, was elevated 120ft above the river Tyne by elegant masonry piers. It has six breathtaking 125ft spans carried by arched cast-iron ribs. Beneath these, hung from wrought-iron rods, are a roadway and pedestrian walkways; above, resting on cast-iron struts and beams, is the railway (fig. 405).

Constructed at almost exactly the same time was his bridge over the Menai Strait. Less beautiful, but structurally more ambitious, the Britannia Bridge achieved its 1,512ft span by using giant box girders of rolled wrought-iron plate, through which the trains travelled. Isambard Kingdom Brunel was amongst the crowd that saw the colossal tubes raised into position. His solution to a similarly large span (455ft) over the river Tamar at Saltash led to a different solution in 1855–9 (fig. 406). Unable to use a suspension bridge, which was too light and flexible to cope with a heavy, moving train, he invented a new type of rigid suspension bridge that contained all the forces within its own structure. The tracks were hung on suspension chains carried by towers, but the towers were braced apart by giant, bowed tubes of wrought-iron plate rather than being anchored into the ground as in a normal suspension bridge.[12]

Fig. 408 (above) Brunel's engine shed at Bristol Temple Meads, 1839–41, depicted by J. C. Bourne, 1846. The Tudor hammerbeams are entirely decorative as are the transverse arches.

Riverbed foundations had generally been laid with the use of coffer dams but Stephenson's High Level Bridge had, for the first time, used steam hammers to drive piles into the bed of the river to support the bridge abutments. In the Tamar, with its 70ft tidal reach, Brunel used a new technique: pneumatic caissons. A 37ft-wide and 90ft-tall iron cylinder (weighing 300 tonnes) was dropped onto the river bed, and compressed air was forced into a compartment that allowed men to work underwater to lay a concrete foundation. Laying effective deep-water foundations was a fundamental step in advancing engineering.

Brunel won the job to build a new railway line from Bristol to London in 1833. He was twenty-seven years old and had only once travelled on a train. His genius was to design, in the space of nine months, the Great Western Railway, a trunk line linking all the major towns between Bristol and London. In Bristol he designed Temple Meads station, the first true railway terminus, in which trains and passengers mingled under a single roof without central supports. Designing a mainline station presented problems never faced before. Opened in 1840, the ticket office was on the ground floor, and from here passengers climbed staircases to the tracks on a viaduct 15ft above. The train shed had a purely decorative timber hammer-beam roof with a 72ft span and roof lights along the ridge, and was carried on octagonal iron columns joined by four-centred arches to make an internal arcade. Brunel designed Bristol Temple Meads in the Tudor style, as befitting one of the great medieval cities of England. It was also a style of familiarity and reassurance, one calculated to lull anxious first-time passengers into a sense of security (fig. 408).[13]

The Great Western Railway was unusual in that its engineer – Brunel – designed the stations. After the very early days of the railway, when many stations were domestic and ephemeral, companies tended to employ architects to

Fig. 409 (above) The station, Stoke-on-Trent, H. A. Hunt, 1847–8. Built for the North Staffordshire Railway Company, the station was located on a new square facing the North Stafford hotel. The whole forms an elegant and ordered gateway to the city.

Fig. 410 (below right) The Euston Arch, a giant portico or, more correctly, propylaeum by Philip Hardwick, opened in 1837 as the triumphant entrance to Euston station.

design them.[14] A number came to specialise in station design; William Tite designed all the stations on the Southampton line for the London and South Western Railway, Francis Thompson of Derby designed twenty-five stations for the North Midland Railway between 1839 and 1841, and G. T. Andrews built the magnificent railway hotels in York and Hull in the early 1850s. From the late 1830s railway architecture in towns became a matter of self-expression and companies vied with each other for attention. However, other than the first Liverpool Lime Street station (1836), where the corporation made a contribution to ensure a noble façade, and the fine Jacobean-style station at Stoke-on-Trent (1850) by H. A. Hunt, sited on a square facing the station hotel (fig. 409), there was no conscious attempt to integrate railway stations into the townscape. Yet many stations were monuments to civic pride as well as expressions of commercial ambition. The townspeople of Newcastle, Huddersfield, Chester or York would have considered their stations as ornaments to their dignity.

The London and Birmingham Railway's terminus at Euston was a case in point. Facing the Euston Road was a colossal and entirely decorative Doric portico flanked by handsome railings and pairs of lodges (fig. 410). This showpiece was designed by the finest industrial designer of the age, Philip Hardwick (p. 410), and completed in 1838; for many it must have seemed like a grand lodge to a palatial town house. The Central Station in Newcastle upon Tyne also disguised itself in the language of classical grandeur. It was designed and built between 1847 and 1851 by the talented Newcastle architect John Dobson, and presented a huge porte-cochère to the street (executed between 1862 and 1863 to a modified design). Behind this is one of the most beautiful of all train sheds; curved to a radius of 800ft, three bays of iron ribs cover an area of around three acres (fig. 411). This was the first time such a geometrical roof had been achieved in iron and it announced the great age of train-shed engineering.[15] London saw three of the greatest English train sheds: first, King's Cross (1851–2), like Newcastle, designed by an architect, Lewis

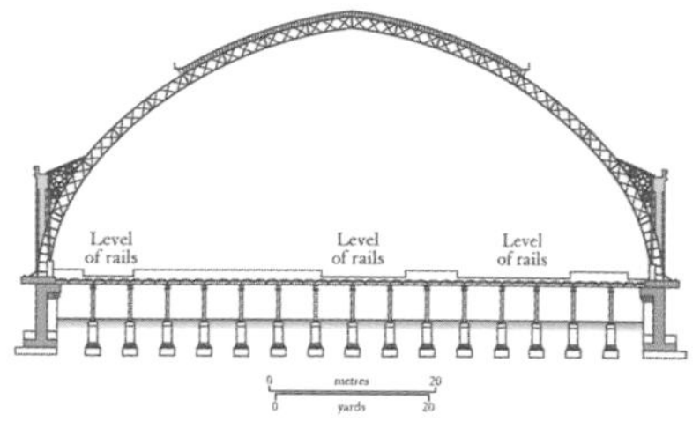

Fig. 411 (above left) Newcastle upon Tyne railway station; the engine shed, 1847–51. The whole covered area amounts to three acres. Its curved shape was made possible by the invention of curved wrought-iron sections made in a local rolling mill.

Fig. 412 (above) St Pancras station train shed; cross section showing a truss. Built in 1865–7, the tracks and platforms are suspended above a vast undercroft originally used for storing beer from Burton upon Trent. The trusses rested on deep foundations but were tensioned by a bottom chord below the tracks and above the beer cellars.

Cubitt; second, Paddington station (1850–4), the London terminus of Brunel's Great Western Railway. Brunel and his collaborator, the architect Matthew Digby Wyatt, were both involved in the Great Exhibition of 1851 and there is a sense in which Paddington was an attempt to reassemble the decorators and contractors who had achieved it. Paddington had three spans, four platforms, ten lines of track, and a massive office block and departure facilities along the side at Eastbourne Terrace. The collaboration between Brunel and Wyatt produced the richest and most enjoyable of all Victorian railway sheds, enriched by Wyatt's tracery and given spatial complexity by Brunel's transepts, installed to provide space for machinery that was quickly superseded.[16]

The third, largest and most spectacular shed was designed by the engineers William Henry Barlow and Rowland Mason Ordish at St Pancras in 1865. The shed, 689ft long, 240ft wide and 105ft high, covered four platforms, eleven lines and a cab stand. Its design sprang from the need to avoid a central spine wall as at King's Cross, for beneath the new station ran tunnels that would connect the Midland main line to south London. So the shed spanned the whole space with twenty-five magnificent 240ft arched trusses, the bottom chords of which lay beneath the tracks (fig. 412). The trusses themselves were slightly pointed at the top, giving the structure extra strength, and contributing to the overall Gothic effect of the place.[17]

Turnpikes had stimulated the construction of accommodation for the long-distance traveller, whilst seaside and spa resorts had led to the creation of a new type of place to stay for holidaymakers. But it was the railways that spurred the invention of the modern hotel. The first to be built was at Euston to a design by Philip Hardwick. The two blocks of accommodation were modest domestic-looking brick structures in the tradition of the canal and coaching inn, but the railways brought unprecedented volume and the next metropolitan railway hotel to be built anticipated this. The Great Western Hotel at Paddington, designed by P. C. Hardwick, was completed in 1854 (fig. 413). In the French Renaissance and baroque style, it had one hundred and fifteen bedrooms and fifteen sitting rooms above some splendid public rooms on the ground floor. This was the finest, and largest, hotel London had yet seen and

Fig. 413 (above) The Great Western Royal Hotel, Philip Charles Hardwick, 1851–4; this was a new sort of hotel for England, the first of a generation of ever larger and more magnificent establishments.

Fig. 414 (above right) The Grosvenor Hotel, Victoria Station, Westminster, 1860–2 by J. T. Knowles. This was the grandest hotel London has yet seen built, originally, as a speculation and only purchased by the railway in 1900. The entrance hall proclaimed palatial magnificence worthy of the townhouse of an aristocrat.

was a proud advertisement for the Great Western Railway. The Paddington hotel set the standard, scale and style for a generation of hotels that followed, aping the great town houses of the aristocracy. Lancaster House by Benjamin Dean Wyatt had a lavish imperial stair in the French style, completed in 1829 (p. 381). This helped set the image of a grand interior for much of the rest of the century, and it was directly echoed, for example, by the stair hall of James Knowles's Grosvenor Hotel (fig. 414).

The gold standard for comfort had been set by American hotels, and European hotels were keen to imitate them, with lifts, barber's shops, 'American' bars and more bathrooms. But in the 1880s many hotels still did not have en-suite bathrooms – the Savoy, built in 1889, had sixty-seven bathrooms for over four hundred rooms. At first, English hotels were relatively low as people were reluctant to climb stairs to the upper floors; the first passenger lift was installed in a department store in New York in 1857 and when the Grosvenor Hotel opened at Victoria Station in 1861 it had a steam-powered lift, one of the first in London. In due course railway companies came to be the largest hotel operators in the world, managing more than one hundred and forty in the British Isles. But railway hotel mania was over by 1880 and subsequent grand hotels were built by other types of operator.[18]

Amongst European cities London was unusual in that its main lines terminated at a number of different stations: when Marylebone station opened in 1899, it was the fifteenth London terminus. Paris was unusual, too, with eight, but almost every other European city had only one. A Royal Commission in 1846 had prevented stations from being built south of the Euston Road and north of the river, keeping termini outside the central districts. The eventual solution was to link the termini by underground railways (fig. 415). The Metropolitan Railway from Paddington to Farringdon, opened in 1863, started a transformation in urban travel. Although, at first, it stole custom from road carriers, it soon expanded the market and was carrying nine million passengers. The line of the railway followed Marylebone and Euston Road, enabling it to be constructed by cut and cover. The stations were of yellow stock brick with massive, blind-arcaded walls covered with elliptical, arched, wrought-iron roofs (fig. 416).[19]

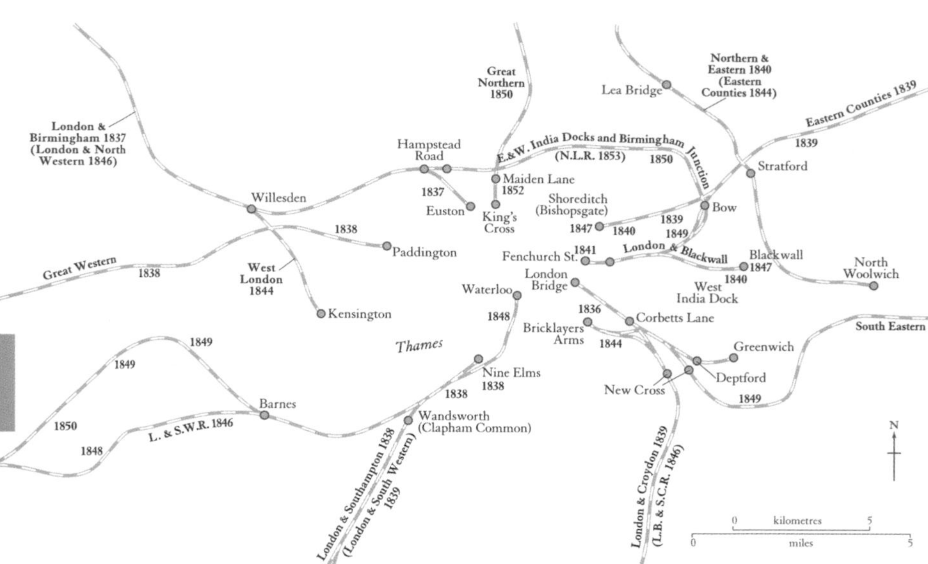

Fig. 415 (left) London railway termini in 1852. None of the main lines penetrated into the city centre, and none of the southern railways crossed the Thames.

Signals and junctions had at first been supervised by men sheltering in wayside huts but as mechanisms grew more complex, and particularly after the invention of the telegraph, the shelters became more elaborate. In the 1850s some control boxes began to be lifted up on stilts to give the signalmen a better view of the line. Thus was the signal box invented and by 1922 there were around 11,000 of them in Britain. They varied in design but increasingly the mainline railways developed standardised and prefabricated buildings that gave distinct identity to individual lines. Along the Midland Railway from St Pancras to Carlisle, signal boxes, waiting rooms, level-crossing gates, platform lamps and awnings were en suite (fig. 417).[20]

Railways had been originally been designed to transport coal rather than passengers. The early coal-carrying railways, such as the Stockton and Darlington of 1825, facilitated regional economic needs but once they started to form a national network the great prize was to supply London. London's appetite for coal had been one of the main stimuli to industrialisation and in 1840s three million tonnes were brought into the docks by coastal shipping. The railways took the docks head-on – by 1856 they were supplying nearly 30 per cent of the capital's needs and by 1867 more than 50 per cent. Most of this came via the Great Northern Railway into the King's Cross goods yard.

At fifty-nine acres King's Cross was one of the largest railway goods yards in England and, when it opened in 1852, it was the most impressive facility of its type in the world (fig. 418). The yard was essentially a transhipment point, transferring goods from rail to road and canal; like the dockyards it was secured by tall walls and gates. In 1865 almost 200,000 tonnes of coal were transferred from wagon to barge at King's Cross. In cases such as this the railway didn't destroy the canals, but complemented them. Coal wagons had opening bottoms and were able to discharge their 7.5-tonne load into hoppers below the tracks, where it could be bagged and transferred to canal or cart (fig. 419).[21]

Fig. 416 (top) London Underground station, Paddington, 1868. This is the best preserved of the Metropolitan Railway's standard stations with blind arcades on the flank walls and a wrought-iron roof. The tunnel mouth shows how shallow this first generation of cut-and-cover underground railways were.

Fig. 417 (above) Signal box, Bardon Hill, Leicestershire is an example of the Midland Railway style of signal box.

Fig. 418 (right) St Pancras and King's Cross stations, including, to the north of King's Cross, the vast area of the goods yard. This combined transport interchange was the largest in England.

Fig. 419 (below) King's Cross goods yard; section through the eastern coal drops. The wagons were on the upper level and dropped the coal through hoppers to the coalmen below, who bagged it and transferred it to cart or barge.

Fig. 420 (bottom) The granary and goods shed of the Great Northern Railway at King's Cross, Lewis Cubitt, completed in 1852, as depicted in the *Illustrated London News* in May 1853. In these buildings came together the ages of horse, canal and steam. The upper image shows the tunnels below the granary that admitted the barges. The lower image shows the internal docks and hoists.

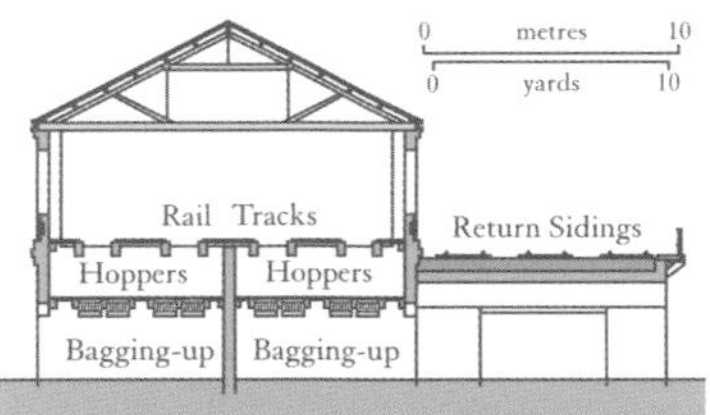

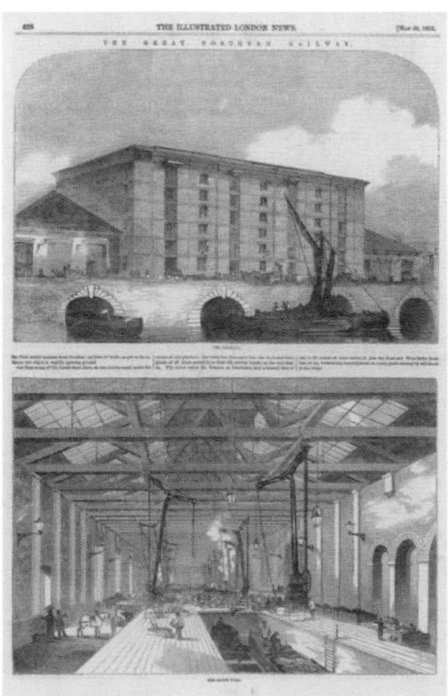
THE ILLUSTRATED LONDON NEWS.

THE GREAT NORTHERN RAILWAY.

At the heart of the King's Cross goods yard was the granary designed by Lewis Cubitt, a heroic composition flanked on either side by transit sheds (fig. 420). Six storeys high with a deep cornice and parapet, its façade has four shallow projecting bays like giant Doric pilasters, incorporating stacked hoist openings. In front of the granary was the canal basin from which barges entered the docks below. Wagons could come into the granary and be rotated on turntables, their goods deposited through holes in the floor to the barges waiting below.

All the mainline goods yards had to make substantial provision for stabling hundreds of horses, as both goods and people had to be moved onwards by road or canal, both of which relied on horse power. The railways and haulage carriers were pioneers of the industrial stable, a major feature of late 19th-century urban life. In 1893 the London railway companies alone stabled nearly 28,000 horses. In 1878 the Mint Stables in Paddington were designed for six hundred horses. Land was so valuable that the stables were built on four floors, with ramps serving the first and second floors. Such urban multi-storey stables with cast-iron stalls, mangers and racks, careful ventilation and ingenious drainage were common from the 1860s.[22]

In addition to the goods yards were the railway works. The Great Western Railway was serviced from a new site located more or less midway along its route, a mile north of Swindon, Wiltshire. This market town of 1,700 people grew into the largest in the county, with a population of over 40,000, of whom 14,000 worked for the GWR. To attract workers a new estate was built in Swindon, designed by Brunel and Matthew Digby Wyatt, comprising three hundred cottages in eight parallel streets. The houses were faced with stone, and had brick washhouses and privies. In 1842 a church was built, in 1844 shops and in 1855 the Mechanics' Institution for the education of the workers. Other similar settlements were designed for Derby and Crewe (fig. 421).[23]

The Swindon engineering works adjacent to the cottages grew to cover seventy-seven acres and were one of the largest anywhere in the world (fig. 422). The works buildings of local stone with brick dressings were disposed to allow rolling stock to move between the various workshops. As was customary, locomotives were at first stored and maintained in long,

Fig. 421 (above left) Derby Midland Railway Roundhouse, by Robert Stephenson, 1839–40 contained a large turntable to move locomotives into position for repair. It was the first such structure in the world.

Fig. 422 (above) GWR Works, Swindon. The Swindon engineering works covered 326 acres of which 77 acres were buildings. The workforce numbered 14,000 – this was one of the largest industrial concerns in the world.

rectangular buildings. The running-shed at Swindon was nearly 500ft long and could house forty-eight engines. A new type of shed was built between 1839 and 1840 in Derby for the North Midland Railway. Designed by Robert Stephenson, the shed was a sixteen-sided iron structure and roofed in slate, with a central turntable that allowed engines to be guided onto one of sixteen tracks, each one of which could take two engines (fig. 421).

By 1870 railways were no longer a wonder of the world but part of everyday life. Their growth slowed but didn't stop. Line mileage increased to 20,266 miles by 1913 (50,000 miles if all track and sidings are included). Constructing the network in such a short space of time was an economic miracle as building railways was expensive, costing on average £33,000 a mile in 1844. Some lines cost a lot more; the total cost of the Midland Main Line from Leicester to London was £10.7 million. The effects of such capital-intensive development on the economy were considerable, sucking investment from other parts. Manufacturing, though, enjoyed bouts of intensive stimulation. The huge growth in the metal industries was a direct result of railway construction. Perhaps 30 per cent of total pig-iron production went to the railways in the peak years around 1848. By the 1840s 25–30 per cent of the national brick-making capacity was swallowed up by the railways; a structure such as the mile-and-a-half-long Kilsby tunnel, Northamptonshire, designed by George Stephenson and built at a cost of £320,000 in 1838, contained 36 million bricks. Many were manufactured locally, but from the 1840s the hard, vitrified Staffordshire blues were used almost everywhere.

It has already been noted that early industrial design took its lead from military buildings and stables. Canal buildings had taken these as their starting point but railway buildings soon created an aesthetic effect of their own, breaking the relationship between human and architectural scale. The mills still related to the human form in their fenestration and portals; railway buildings didn't. These were the first structures that were designed in relation to a machine rather than a human form. Yet this does not mean that they were not designed to please. They were. They had to reassure passengers, to promote their services, and impress and attract investors. Building confidence was achieved through architectural design. So aesthetics played a central role and the engineers were as alive to the effects of their structures as the architects.[24]

Stylistic Developments

Charles Barry's new Palace of Westminster, although his most famous building, was not his most influential. In 1829 Barry won the competition to design the Travellers Club on Pall Mall, London. This was a club founded by gentlemen who, returning from the Grand Tour, wished to mix, meet and to entertain each other and their friends. Barry's model – Raphael's Palazzo Pandolfini in Florence – was entirely appropriate, but it was no slavish copy (fig. 423). It is plain, stuccoed and relies for effect on its finely balanced fenestration, with pedimented windows on the first floor and a deep cornice. This hugely important commission exercised, with its more mature and accomplished neighbour the Reform Club (also by Barry, 1838–41), a powerful influence over a generation of buildings.

The value placed on Renaissance architecture in the 18th century was quite different from that which caused its revival in the 1830s, 40s and 50s. The great palazzi of Florence, Genoa and Rome, built by newly rich merchant princes, provided a point of cultural reference for men whose extraordinary wealth had derived from industry and manufacturing. These modern-day Medici admired different things about their style, too: the 18th-century admiration of Italian Renaissance architecture focused on its representation of antique buildings and Palladio's use of proportion; from the 1830s what was admired was the warmth, colour and moneyed opulence of the cinquecento. The most brilliant exposition of this taste was Dorchester House, Park Lane, London, designed by Lewis Vulliamy and built for the millionaire art collec-

Fig. 423 (right) The Travellers Club, 1829–32 (left) and Reform Club, 1838–41 (right), Pall Mall, London by Charles Barry. Barry's palazzo, or Italianate, style was to be one of the most enduring of the century, flexible enough to be successfully used on a range of building types.

tor R. S. Holford between 1848 and 1849. Its central hall was the epitome of the Renaissance revival interior, rich with colour and interest, communicating both the opulence and the good taste that great wealth can bring (fig. 424).[25]

Fig. 424 (above) Dorchester House, Park Lane, London; the great staircase, Lewis Vulliamy, 1848–9. An extremely lavish show, this out-palaced any genuine Renaissance palazzo.

A renewed interest in Renaissance buildings came at the moment when large numbers of public and commercial buildings were being designed, often for new purposes. The regular fenestration, masculinity and hard-edged urban roots of the Renaissance suited commercial structures, and its associations reflected the aspirations of nouveau riche patrons and burgeoning businesses, particularly in the Midlands and the north. Manchester Free Trade Hall (1853) commemorates the success of the Anti-Corn Law League and the campaign for free trade of the 1830s and 40s, in which Manchester played a crucial role. It was designed by Edward Walters, who had studied under Vulliamy and who possessed outstanding first-hand knowledge of Italian Renaissance palazzi. It is one of the masterpieces of the age, unmatched in richness, elegance and harmony, its façades laden with sculpture celebrating the theme of free trade (fig. 425). But most buildings in this style were commercially rather than politically driven.

Offices, banks, insurance offices, warehouses, even factories and ironworks were influenced by the palazzo style. The richer architectural embellishment of commercial structures reflected the fact that they were increasingly being built in central districts rather than in ports or town peripheries. They were individualistic in that, from the street, they read as single buildings, not as terraces or blocks gaining from the enlarging presence of their neighbours. The effects of these new Italianate buildings were dramatic on cities such as Manchester, Liverpool and Bradford, the commercial centres of which were completely transformed.[26]

The palazzo style, made fashionable by Charles Barry, was a way of finding an architectural language acceptable to, and expressive of, the modern world. It was not one that Barry's collaborator at the Palace of Westminster, A. W. N. Pugin, was to accept. Pugin was young, angry and frustrated, and the most talented and single-minded of those who wanted to find a new model for society.[27] Almost uniquely for an architect his writings transformed the way people thought about architecture. In 1836, amidst the competition for the new Palace of Westminster, Pugin published *Contrasts: Or, a Parallel between the Noble Edifices of the Fourteenth and Fifteenth Centuries, and Corresponding Buildings of the Present Day, Shewing the Present Decay of Taste,* a journalistic polemic that juxtaposed images of medieval and modern buildings to illustrate the collapse of modern taste and morals. Pugin saw the decline of Gothic and the rise of classical styles as the consequence of the Reformation, an event which, as a fervent Roman Catholic, he despised. He was thus able to characterise Gothic architecture as morally superior to classical and to promote its virtues as a panacea for all that was wrong in society (fig. 426). Five years later Pugin followed his earlier work with *The True Principles of Pointed or Christian Architecture,* which took his ideas a step further. Here he argued that as pointed (i.e. Gothic) architecture was ordained by God, all deception or artificiality must be avoided. In other words Gothic

Fig. 425 (right) Manchester Free Trade Hall, Edward Walters, 1853. For sheer opulence its Italianate façades were never surpassed, and in communicating the economic doctrines and political views of its sponsors no contemporary building had a more legible message.

Fig. 426 (below and below left) A. W. N. Pugin, *Contrasts: or, A Parallel between the Noble Edifices of the Fourteenth and Fifteenth centuries, and Corresponding Buildings of the Present day; shewing the Present Decay of Taste*. 1836. This plate illustrates the contrast between a beautiful medieval conduit flowing with water and its Victorian equivalent, utilitarian and chained up.

must be a functional not a decorative style; plan must come first and decoration should be an enrichment of the essential structure. To morality and functionalism Pugin added nationalism, for it was through adopting English Gothic, he argued, that a national revival would come, a view that he put into practice in his designs for the Palace of Westminster.[28]

Pugin most brilliantly displayed his principles at St Giles, Cheadle, Staffordshire, from 1841. Here was a church that was true, Christian and English. Every part – nave, chancel, aisles and porch – crisply revealed its function (fig. 427). At first, Pugin advocated the use of what Rickman called Early English, but he later settled on Decorated as the culmination of the Gothic style. Pugin's rationalist principles and his advocacy of Decorated were to have a significant impact on church building – especially on Anglican churches – from 1850.[29] It was George Gilbert Scott who, inspired by Pugin's writings, first began to build Anglican churches in a new way. All Souls', Haley Hill, Halifax, built between 1855 and 1859, is perhaps his best, with a tremendous spire that dominates the town centre. Here the parts are clearly expressed and elegantly grouped; there is no gratuitous decoration, only sturdy buttresses emphasising the solidity of the whole (fig. 428).

The Italianate and the Gothic offered different symbolic and aesthetic values to architects. The commission to build new government offices in Whitehall, launched in 1856, threw these differences into stark relief. Gilbert Scott's Gothic entry was placed third in the designs presented to the Prime Minister, Lord Palmerston. Scott's position was rescued, however, by the incoming Tory government of Lord Derby, who responded to the barrage of support for a Gothic scheme by appointing Scott in 1858. Victory was to be short-lived as Palmerston returned to Downing Street in May 1859, insisting on a classical design. Scott tried to fudge the issue with an Italian–Byzantine compromise but was eventually forced to accept that the building was to be in an Italianate style. In the end it was a fine structure, formal in its front to Whitehall, informal and picturesque to St James's Park. Within, it was opulent in the extreme, an entirely suitable setting from which British foreign secretaries controlled relations with large parts of the world (fig. 429).

Victorian architects believed in progress and expected it in architecture as much as in engineering and science, but it was hard to see where the Italian and Gothic revivals were leading. What, they asked, was the style for the 19th century? How could it be that Britain, with all its wealth and innovation, its technology and its industry, a society that was changing how people lived, could only copy the styles of other, earlier civilisations? This was the architectural dilemma of the century; but it was not a dilemma of style, of classical versus Gothic, it was really about architecture versus engineering. For most architects during the 1830s, 40s and 50s, whether of classical or Gothic persuasion, architecture was in fact archaeology. Whilst architects minutely studied the proportions of buildings thousands of years old, engineers were creating a new world with new materials.

As we have seen, Crystal Palace was the extraordinary culmination of a run of superlative engineering and design that had started in the early 1840s. It was also the purest and most perfect architectural expression of plan and function, something for which Pugin and his followers had argued. It might thus have seemed to be the very model for Victorian architecture, the end of the apparent stylistic chaos that prevailed (fig. 403). Yet to most architects it wasn't architecture at all; 'Crystal Humbug' was how Pugin described it. Crystal Palace, therefore, did not unite technology and architecture but rather exposed the gulf between them. More recognisable to architects as an avant-garde structure was a building being constructed at the same time as Crystal Palace: All Saints', Margaret Street, London (fig. 430). Here for the first time the arts of industry and polite architecture fused to create a new sort of building for a new world.[30]

Brick, it has already been noted, was the building material of the age, but commercial brick architecture had not only led to mechanically repetitive mill facades (p. 360); it had also produced sublime geometrical structures. Freed from the necessity to only use locally fired bricks the railways were able to combine bricks of different size, strength, texture and colour in a single location (p. 406). The Eastern Counties Railway, established in 1836, had buildings of red, yellow and black brick, and the New Cross station engine house of around 1846 on the Croydon to Brighton line, had a tall, round chimney of yellow brick, decorated with a bold, spiralling coil of red and black bricks. Meanwhile, in 1840 at Christ Church, Streatham, the architect J. W. Wild used coloured brick in a daring and avant-garde way.[31]

Yet brick as a material for church building had not initially found favour; it was only with an increased admiration for the brick buildings of northern Italy that it became possible to champion the design of a new church in brick. William Butterfield's All Saints', Margaret Street, set out to change people's tastes. It was built on an awkward urban site that made for a cramped, if picturesque,

Fig. 427 (left top) St Giles Roman Catholic Church, Cheadle, Staffordshire, A. W. N. Pugin, 1841–6. Pugin called it 'a perfect revival of an English parish church of the time of Edward I'.

Fig. 428 (left middle) All Souls', Haley Hill, Halifax, George Gilbert Scott, 1855–9. The church was regarded by Scott as his best – paid for by Colonel Ackroyd as the church for his estate.

Fig. 429 (left bottom) Foreign Office, Whitehall, London; the State Stair, 1863–8. Gilbert Scott's slightly laboured Roman design, working with the decorators Clayton & Bell, was unquestionably grand and unquestionably classical.

Fig. 430 (above) All Saints', Margaret Street, London, William Butterfield, 1849–59. This building shares with Barry's Travellers Club (fig. 423), the distinction of being a model for thousands of buildings that were to follow. Its fusion of industrially produced materials, especially brick, with historical styles was a winning combination for many (but not all) building types.

composition. The overall effect is incredibly rich, as bands of darker brick and lighter stone contrast sharply with dusty-pink brick; the inspiration for this came not from Italy but from the brick churches of northern Germany. Inside, though, the inspiration is Italian, and there is an explosion of colour in brick, tile and polished stone. This building would not have been possible without the railways, the mechanisation of brick production, stone-polishing machines, precisely controlled tile kilns and ironworks. Yet it represented both the principles of liturgical arrangement championed by the ecclesiastical reformers and the over-riding principle of truth. For the polychromy was structural, not just skin deep; decoration constituted the structure itself.[32]

Ideas such as those expressed at All Saints' found a spokesman and champion in the brilliant but verbose art critic John Ruskin. For him architectural beauty lay in the beauty of decorative expression. In contrast to Pugin, symbolism in architecture for Ruskin was not directly religious. But it was Godly – it was decoration based on God's works of nature executed by earthly craftsmen. Ruskin argued for the liberation of the imagination and creativity of the individual craftsman from the mechanised and mass-produced products of industrialisation. His books, especially *The Seven Lamps of Architecture* (1849) and *The Stones of Venice* (1851–3), illustrated and disseminated this emerging taste; a taste that became an expression of artistic and national freedom when realised in the buildings of mid- and late-Victorian architects. Liberated from archaeology, Gothic emerged as a dynamic, individualistic and contemporary style. No longer a slavish exercise in imitation, it became confident and optimistic, whilst also being edgy and exciting.[33]

George Edmund Street was one of the architects in whose hands modern Gothic was most successfully deployed. In designing St James the Less, Westminster (1859–61), he deliberately turned away from English models and confidently melded ideas from north Italian, German and early French buildings. It is a copy of none of them, but is startlingly individualistic, robust and colourful, dominated by a massive campanile (fig. 431). George Gilbert Scott's Midland Grand Hotel at St Pancras station, London (1868–77), is the most famous surviving modern Gothic building (fig. 433). Scott's palette of architectural sources was extraordinarily wide and their combination extraordinarily rich. This was a building made possible by the railways, in every sense. Its materials came from far and wide – bricks from Nottingham, and stone from Ancaster, Mansfield and Ketton. This new generation of buildings dropped the nationalistic overtones of Gothic and looked abroad, producing a muscularity of design that strongly contrasted with the delicate filigree of Pugin's Decorated Gothic. Muscularity was masculine, and the values of society were increasingly tough and manly, which perhaps led to a greater acceptance of industrial buildings as architecture. The old hierarchy that saw buildings ranked by the nobility of their function was now overturned; a railway hotel, warehouse, factory or mill might now command the enthusiastic attention of the best architects.

Few commercial buildings advertised their presence in the manner of the Midland Grand, yet many commercial structures wanted to stand out. The Great Exhibition had shown architecture as advertisement, and the modern

Fig. 431 (left) St James the Less, Vauxhall Bridge Road, designed by George Edmund Street, 1859–6. This brilliant church draws for its inspiration on foreign Gothic models from Italy, Germany and France, yet the blend is beautiful and successful and rendered English by the use of brick and its setting with the en-suite school and later parish hall.

Fig. 432 (below) Royal Doulton Stoneware factory, Lambeth Walk London, Waring and Nicholson and R. Stark Wilkinson (1876–7). This palace of industry was an advertisement for the often florid stoneware goods manufactured within.

Gothic of the 1860s was a gift to the Victorian marketing guru. The palatial Doulton Pottery Works (1876–7) on the Albert Embankment, London, by Waring & Nicholson and R. Stark Wilkinson was in large part an advertisement for the wares that the company fired using the 233ft-tall version of the Palazzo Vecchio's campanile as a chimney. The chimney was a particular opportunity for architectural promotion. In 1877 Sir Robert Rawlinson, the engineer and sanitary reformer, published *Boiler and Factory Chimneys,* illustrating the potential for ornamenting a factory or mill with chimneys in a variety of styles (fig. 434). The flamboyant Welsh Back Granary in Bristol by Ponton and Gough of 1869–70 took a different route to self-promotion.

Fig. 433 (above right) The Midland Grand Hotel, St Pancras station, designed by George Gilbert Scott in 1865–7 and built in 1868–77. Once vilified, now universally admired, Scott threw at his hotel ideas from almost every country in Europe to create a unique synthesis of European Gothic architecture.

Fig. 434 (above) Robert Rawlinson, *Boiler and Factory Chimneys*, 1877. Two possible ways (out of many) of making your factory chimney into a campanile.

Heavily influenced by the fashion for brick polychromy and inspired by Venetian Gothic, their ten-storey grain warehouse is one of a number of modern Gothic buildings in Bristol built in the 1860s and 70s in a style sometimes dubbed as 'Bristol Byzantine' (fig. 438).[34]

Despite the robustness and fertility of modern Gothic, large-scale public buildings were generally still given a classical treatment. The culmination of this tradition was the single-most remarkable classical building of the whole 19th century: St George's Hall, Liverpool, opened in 1854 (fig. 437). Designed by Harvey Lonsdale Elmes and C. R. Cockerell, it was a response to the extraordinary wealth and expansion of Liverpool as a port. St George's Hall was megalomaniac civic ambition, Elmes's brief being to design the biggest civic building in England. It was stressed, in particular, that it had to be larger than Birmingham's town hall, and a plan of St Paul's Cathedral was superimposed over it just to show that St George's would be bigger. The guts of the design were Greek but many Roman details were also used. The interior of the hall had the logo SPQL stamped all over it, a variant on the Roman SPQR

– the senate and people of Rome. Elmes possessed deep archaeological knowledge and applied it with confidence; as with the Gothic of Street and Scott, the design was liberated from pure archaeology and became a style in its own right.

There were also a smaller number of important public buildings built in modern Gothic. Perhaps the most brilliant exponent of the mid-century free-style Gothic was the Mancunian architect Alfred Waterhouse, whose masterpiece is Manchester Town Hall (1867–77). As in Liverpool, the city wanted to spare no expense; the eventual bill was more than £850,000. There is much here from the English 14th century but the building is not an assemblage of architectural quotations; it is a synthesis based on a profound knowledge of architectural styles from 15th-century Belgian town halls to 16th-century French palaces. The richly articulated and picturesque façades overlay a straightforward steel skeleton, which, together with the machine-fashioned materials of its interiors, confirm it as an unashamedly modern building (fig. 435).[35]

The starting of the Royal Courts of Justice, the Strand, London, in 1874, marks the end of a period characterised by the fluid and accomplished blending of Gothic styles, which by the late 1860s included French Gothic (fig. 436). The project killed its architect, George Edmund Street, and so it was left to his son to complete the building. Something of Street's pain can be imagined on the Strand elevation, which is meticulously and skilfully modulated but very detailed; each element had to be minutely drawn, enough to break even a man of his energy and experience. It is an important building, possibly a great one, but by the time it was completed in 1882 it was out of fashion.

Churches

Fig. 435 (above) Manchester Town Hall, Alfred Waterhouse, 1867–77. His masterpiece and a masterpiece of its age. The hall was sited in the centre of the triangle, with civic rooms facing Albert Square (right), and committee rooms and offices on the other two sides. Above is the town hall extension and circular library by Vincent Harris.

Fig. 436 (above right) The Royal Courts of Justice, the Strand, London, designed by George Edmund Street, 1874–82. Built at a cost of £1,973,221, this was the last and most expensive of the great Gothic public buildings of London. Though impressive, both at a distance and close up, it fails to win affection – only admiration at the effort.

Fig. 437 (top left) St George's Hall, Liverpool, designed by Harvey Lonsdale Elmes and C. R. Cockerell in 1840–1: a *tour de force* and a tour of the classical sites of Europe. Here classical references are melded as confidently and effectively as G. G. Scott was later to do with Gothic details at St Pancras (fig. 433).

Fig. 438 (left) Welsh Back Granary, Bristol, Ponton and Gough, 1869–70. Exuberant brick polychromy transforms a utilitarian building into an architectural marvel.

Church building in the forty years after 1835 was more significant economically and architecturally than it had been at any time since before the Reformation (p. 208). Anglican structures were revitalised in the 1830s, these efforts being transformed by financial reform, Evangelicalism and an Anglo-Catholic revival. The first re-established the social and political credibility of the Church, the second rejuvenated its spirituality and the third transformed its building stock.

Reform came through the ecclesiastical commission skilfully steered by Charles Blomfield, Bishop of London, who put the affairs of the Church and its episcopacy on to a business footing. Evangelicalism, which had become an increasing force from 1800, was driven by the belief in the importance of conversion, biblical truth, the centrality of Christ's sacrifice and personal responsibility. Responsibility was the cause of Evangelical activism, one of the most powerful forces in Victorian Britain. But the Anglo-Catholic revival, of the three, had the greatest impact on church building.

This began in Oxford in the early 1830s and became known as the Oxford (or Tractarian) Movement. It emphasised Catholic continuity in Anglicanism, based on its unbroken apostolic succession, and a theology centred on a Catholic appreciation of the Eucharist. The founding of the Cambridge Camden Society (later known as the Ecclesiological Society) in 1839 and the establishment of its journal *The Ecclesiologist* in 1841 launched a parallel campaign for the construction of churches that would be suitable for a revived Anglican liturgy. For the ecclesiologists, church building was not a response to practical problems – it was a crusade. The preaching boxes that had prevailed in England since the 17th century, with their triple-decker pulpits and galleries (pp 364–8), were despised. New churches were once again to focus on the sacraments, with fully developed chancels and baptisteries. The unbroken catholicity of Anglicanism was to be stressed by a return to early 14th-century Gothic, the period advocated by Pugin as representing the high point of medieval Catholicism in England.[36]

Between 1835 and 1875 3,765 Anglican churches were consecrated, an average of ninety-six a year, or nearly two a week. In the same period some 7,000 medieval churches were restored, rebuilt or enlarged, around 80 per cent of the total. This was an extraordinary revival, both architectural and liturgical, for these churches were provided with clergy and non-residence was virtually eliminated. The total number of clergy rose from 14,613 to 24,968, the highest number since before the Reformation. Lay membership of the Church of England grew, too, and as a proportion of the population it was higher in 1914 than in 1831. The success of the revival lay not only in the energy and radicalism of the ecclesiologists, but also because their architectural and liturgical programme chimed with the wider medievalism of society, seen in the more general urge to recreate the behaviour and architecture of the past. In the 1840s new churches were built in a multitude of styles but almost all were elegant essays in cladding box-like preaching houses, such as St James the Great, Briercliffe, Lancashire, built between 1840 and 1841, and designed by Edmund Sharpe (fig. 439). It had a three-decker pulpit in front of a very shallow chancel and generous galleries around three sides.[37] But in 1841, the same year that Pugin's St Giles's was started (p. 417 and fig. 427), George Gilbert Scott designed St Giles's, Camberwell, London. Here was a church with a big chancel separated from the nave by a tower. This was a new sort of Anglican church, one in which Gothic was more than the decoration of a preaching box (fig. 440). Scott was responsible for building or restoring many hundreds of churches; in this he was not alone, as younger architects, such as Henry Woodyer, were building churches in the Puginesque mode approved of by the ecclesiologists. The single-minded focus on English models was dropped by the ecclesiologists after Butterfield's All Saints', Margaret Street, a church they had energetically promoted and that had been funded by their chairman. English church architecture then entered a phase of extreme originality, beauty and diversity, in which two of the most brilliant designers were William Burges and John Loughborough Pearson.

Funded by an extremely wealthy patron, the interior of Burges's church of St Mary, Studley Royal, Yorkshire (1870–8), transposes man into an earthly heaven (fig. 441). The chancel has windows with double tracery, filled with stained glass by Saunders & Co., the walls are lined with alabaster, the window reveals are richly carved, and the ceiling painted and heavily gilded. Nothing jars or is overdone; all is perfectly balanced and scaled. St Mary's illustrates perhaps better than any other church the central concern with craftsmanship, with fixtures and fittings. Following Ruskin, Burges and his contemporaries believed that decoration should be a principal concern of the architect and so, to a greater or lesser degree, churches up to the First World War were repositories of high-quality, architect-designed furnishings. Stained glass, a minute and immature industry, rapidly developed so that by the Great Exhibition no fewer than twenty-four firms could display their wares. The development of new types of glass in the late 1840s that more faithfully imitated medieval windows led to authentic and more brilliant effects. Large firms such as John Hardman's, Clayton & Bell and Lavers & Barraud provided high-quality stained glass windows for thousands of churches.[38]

Fig. 439 (below) St James the Great, Briercliffe, Lancashire, Edmund Sharpe, 1840–41. A typical pre-ecclesiological church; a box with galleries, an alcove for a chancel and a tower.

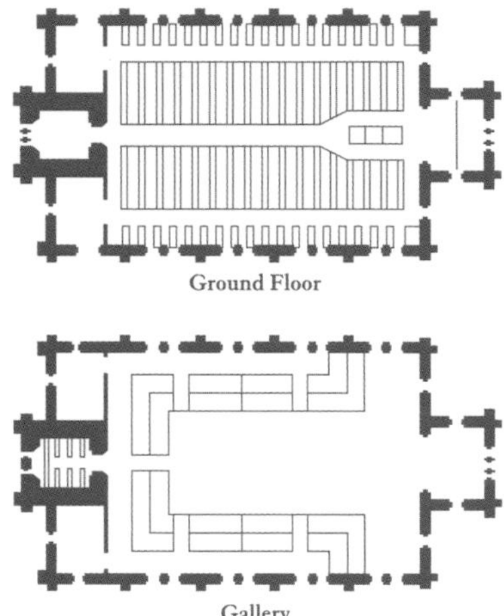

Fig. 440 (right) St Giles's, Camberwell, London, George Gilbert Scott, 1842–4. His first great church, with a massive crossing spire; but inside there were still galleries on iron columns.

Fig. 441 (bottom) St Mary's, Studley Royal, Yorkshire, William Burges, 1871–8. Under Burges's supervision a galaxy of brilliant craftsmen and designers collaborated to create this magical interior.

Fig. 442 (below) Sir George Gilbert Scott's Screen, Hereford Cathedral. Made by the Coventry metalworking firm, Francis Skidmore, in 1862, this eight-tonne choir screen was one of the great masterpieces of the Gothic revival.

In metalwork the most important firm was John Hardman of Birmingham, who entered into partnership with Pugin to make Gothic metalwork. The market they stimulated led to new firms springing up in Birmingham, London and Coventry; these not only made ecclesiastical fittings and furnishings but also a wide range of lighting, door furniture and architectural fittings (fig. 442). A similarly important partnership existed between Pugin, the ceramics manufacturer Herbert Minton, and a number of other architects and designers, such as Matthew Digby Wyatt and Alfred Waterhouse. Minton was an energetic and ambitious man, and under his leadership his family firm made technical advances in tile manufacture, eventually becoming a huge business that sold ceramic wall and floor coverings to churches, public buildings, commercial premises and private houses.[39]

One of the pressing concerns of the 1860s was for urban churches – buildings suitable for densely populated city centres. One of the architects particularly interested in creating a model for these was John Loughborough Pearson, who designed a large church, St Peter's, Vauxhall, built between 1863 and 1865 (fig. 443). The interior of St Peter's is a single vast vessel, vaulted in brick and stone, with an emphatic apse. It was intended to be lavishly decorated but this work was never completed. A series of such brick churches was built in the 1860s and 70s in the East End of London by James Brooks, funded by a City financier. Outside London other ark-like structures catered for the urban poor. A remarkable example, by the Brighton architect Edmund Scott, is St Bartholomew's, built between 1872 and 1874 in his home town (fig. 445). By the 1820s Brighton was growing faster than Bradford and had a population of 80,000. The 1851 census showed that the town churches could seat only 34.6 per cent of the population (Bath could seat 61 per cent) and a wealthy local clergyman decided to sponsor the construction of a series of large urban churches. St Bartholomew's is awe-inspiring in its size and severity. The nave is 135ft high and only 58ft wide, with no aisles. The nave walls are articulated by tall, pointed recesses, used as shallow side chapels. All is very plain, decoration provided only by polychromatic brick. Whilst some existing churches with 18th-century interiors survived, thousands of churches were internally remodelled after 1850. Galleries were removed, enclosed box pews taken out and replaced by open-ended benches, reading desks were eliminated or re-sited and pulpits reoriented. New churches – and the majority of existing ones – were thus significantly different places from St James the Great, Briercliffe (fig. 439). St Michael and All Angels', Woolwich, was commissioned by Revd H. R. Baker, a fervent Tractarian, who wanted to establish a High Church mission in a slum-ridden parish in the East End of London. The chancel was built by J. W. Walter between 1876 and 1877 and the nave, after Walter's death, between 1888 and 1889 by Butterfield (fig. 444). There is a formally designed setting for the font at the west end, densely packed pews and a deep chancel with a high altar, complete with a florid marble, alabaster and slate reredos. On the south of the chancel, which is richly coloured with mosaics tiles and painted decorations, is the Lady chapel. Despite the seeming comprehensiveness of these changes the Church of England did not adopt a theological or liturgical norm; indeed far from it. The Ecclesiological movement meant the destruction of the consensus of the 1662 liturgical settlement, and its replacement by a wide spectrum of worshipping styles from the simplest and most Evangelical Lord's Supper to a near-Catholic High Mass.[40]

These new churches, unlike those of 1711 and 1818, were paid for by private means. Some were funded by businessmen, such as All Souls', Halifax (fig. 428), which was financed by the industrialist Edward Ackroyd, together with a vicarage, houses for his workers and a house for himself. Others, such as St Mark's, Swindon (1843–5), were commissioned by the Great Western Railway as corporate venue for their workers. Housing speculators paid for some to lift the social standing of their estates; in Kensington, London, for instance, half a dozen churches were built by the estate for its wealthy residents.

Fig. 443 (below) St Peter's, Vauxhall, London, J. L. Pearson, 1863–5. This was the first major example of a new type of big town church built, here, together with school, orphanage and vicarage.

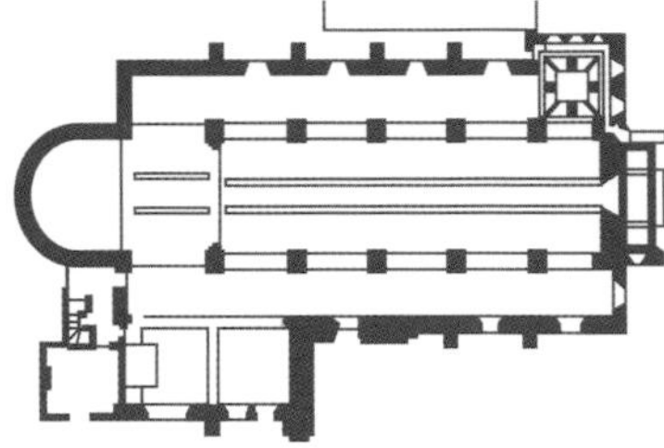

Fig. 444 (below) St Michael and All Angels', Woolwich, ground plan. The chancel was built by J. W. Walter between 1876 and 1877. The nave was built by Butterfield between 1888 and 1889, following Walter's death. This church was a fundamentally different sort of place to the generation of churches that preceeded it (for example fig. 439).

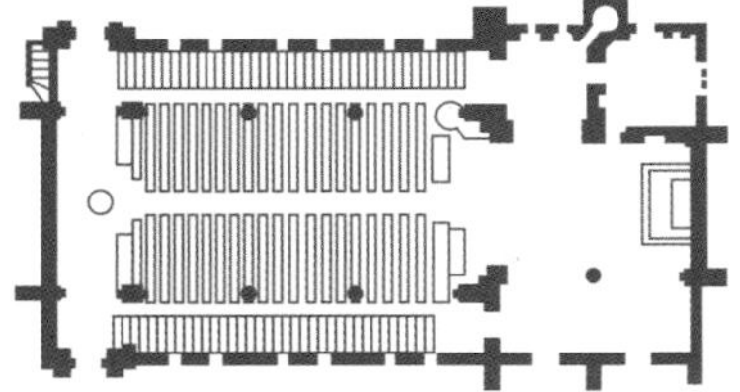

Fig. 445 (right) St Bartholomew's, Brighton, Edmund Scott, 1872–4. The crucifix above the altar is partly of encaustic tiles, an original fitting. The initial intended austerity was diluted with enrichments of 1895–1910 by Henry Wilson.

Others, such as St James the Less, Westminster (fig. 431), were paid for by religiously minded philanthropists, in this case the three daughters of the Bishop of Gloucester. Landowners in the countryside, their coffers swollen with the profits of agriculture, rebuilt their churches and enjoyed sitting in the front pews, their tenants in the rows behind them.

Country Estates

Until 1870 England was still a good place to be a landowner. The population continued to grow, from 16 million in 1841 to 26 million in 1881, and people were still principally fed from British farms. To meet growing demand production was increasingly industrialised, and farmers came to rely more on engineers, chemists and other specialists than on their own ingenuity. By the time of the Great Exhibition more than three hundred agricultural firms displayed their wares in Hyde Park. The industrialisation of agriculture led, for rich and forward-looking landowners, to the reconstruction of their farmyards, which became larger and more efficient. The underlying principles of farming, however, remained the same (pp 353–4). Stock was now often overwintered under cover, necessitating the construction of large sheds. This improved fattening and made manure production easier to control. In many farms feed was moved around the farmyard on trolleys running on rails, more effective drainage made the management of liquid manure more efficient and by 1870 the use of steam threshers was almost universal. The arrival of steam technology brought engines into the farmyard to grind corn, break oilcake and slice root vegetables, whilst their heat could steam potatoes, boil linseed and cook pig feed. Most machines were inserted into existing barns, transforming them from primary food-processing and storage buildings into machine sheds that processed animal feed.

At the top end a brand-new model farm such as Lord Bateman's at Shobdon, Herefordshire, built in 1861, incorporated a steam engine that powered the threshing machine and various pieces of cutting and grinding equipment. A mini tram that ran on gravity moved straw and grain, and there was enough space to fatten the herd under cover. For most other farms, such as the one at Beamish, County Durham (now a museum), an engine shed was simply added to existing buildings.[41] Agriculture was highly profitable and for a few brief decades the countryside was awash with cash. It was this that led to the 1860s and 70s being a boom time for new country houses (fig. 446) but, as we shall see, an agricultural crash in the early 1870s brought this to a rapid halt (p. 480).

The country houses of the mid century were driven by a vision of an English gentleman born of the national obsession with the Middle Ages. His house was to be substantial and serious, preferably in a suitable style for country living: grand but not ostentatious, comfortable but not luxurious, a place in which to bring up, protect and educate a family. Men who had made new fortunes wanted to buy into this vision as much as those who had been substantial landowners for generations.[42]

Landowners with new money, particularly in the 1840s and 50s, seem to have been much more conservative and preferred to build houses in classical or Renaissance styles. This was still the international language of wealth and authority, and the architectural style of the Establishment. It was given the royal seal of approval in 1844 when Victoria and Albert gave the commission for the Italianate Osborne House on the Isle of Wight to Thomas Cubitt, the builder and developer. Brodsworth Hall, Yorkshire, was built from 1861 in a

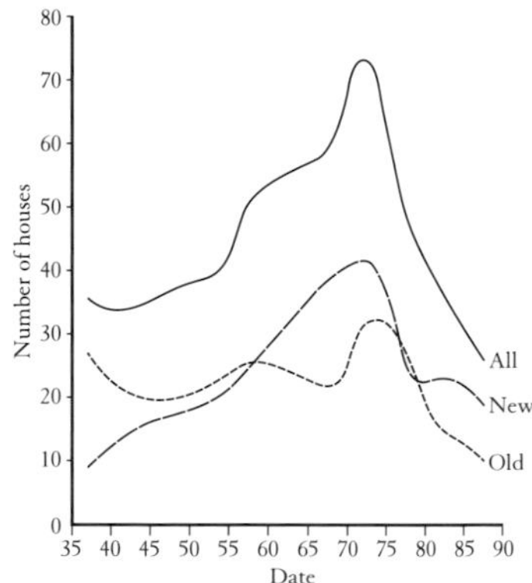

Fig. 446 (above) The 1860s and 70s saw an increase in country house building. An agricultural crash in the early 1870s however brought this to an end. The graph shows building activity in new houses and extensions to old ones.

Fig. 447 (above) Brodsworth Hall, Yorkshire, executing architect Philip Wilkinson, 1861–3. The entrance front has a porte-cochére and to the right is the long low servants' wing. The whole is quite austere and regular, urban even, especially in comparison to some of its contemporaries.

Fig. 448 (below) The daunting stone fortress of Peckforton Castle, Cheshire. In the top right was the circular dining room and in front the great hall. A gallery ran to a circular library (bottom).

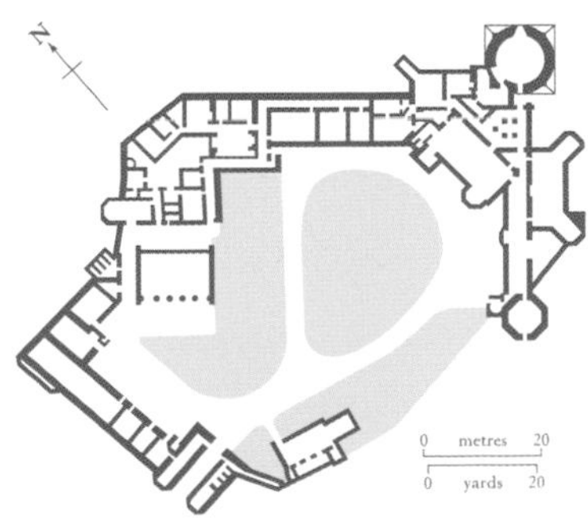

solid and regular Italianate style with a banking fortune inherited by Charles Thellusson (fig. 447), whilst Edward Bickerton Evans, the proprietor of the world's largest vinegar factory, built Whitbourne Hall, Herefordshire, designed by Edmund Elmslie in 1860 in a severe Greek idiom. Osborne, Brodsworth and Whitbourne were not designed by well-known – or, indeed, exceptionally capable – architects. This was common amongst the super-rich of the age, who wanted to keep their architects under control and normally employed one of the large contracting firms from London to undertake the work.[43]

Big-name architects tended to work for old families with whom they had contacts. For this group classical styles were increasingly seen as urban, un-English or even pagan. John Tollemache commissioned Anthony Salvin to build Peckforton Castle, Cheshire, in 1844. It is a daunting stone fortress, brilliant but bleak – and utterly feudal (fig. 448). Its owner was a landowner and MP before he went to the House of Lords in 1876; larger than life, with twenty-four children, he was a Tory and a fervent Evangelical. Tollemache lived his medieval principles of duty and responsibility only thirty miles from the urban industrial centres of Manchester, Salford and Macclesfield. He built more than fifty new Tudoresque farmhouses for his tenants, creating a feudal world over which he presided from an authentic stone castle.[44]

There were many exceptions to the generalisations about stylistic choice that have just been made, but what is clear is that for large country houses classical styles quickly lost out to Gothic and Tudor from the 1840s onwards. Between 1840 to 1844 41 per cent of new houses were classical, a figure that dropped to 16 per cent between 1860 and 1864.[45] For many who would be an English gentleman, Tudor became the style of choice. The German Jewish banker Nathan Mayer Rothschild came to England in 1798 and moved to

Buckinghamshire in 1833. His son set up as a country gentleman, building the colossal Mentmore Towers in 1852, designed by the man-of-the-moment, Joseph Paxton, fresh from the Great Exhibition (fig. 449). The house was closely modelled on Wollaton Hall, Nottinghamshire, and was set at the centre of what can only be regarded as a Tudor estate, largely designed by Paxton's son-in-law G. H. Stokes. Most of the houses were half-timbered; all were in Tudor styles. This was the recreation of Olden Times as depicted by Joseph Nash in *Come to the Maypole* in 1864 (fig. 452), a vision of the countryside in which the landowner paternalistically dispensed charity and presided over the rustic amusements of his tenants.

Fig. 449 (left) Mentmore Towers, Buckinghamshire, Sir Joseph Paxton and G. H. Stokes, 1850–5. The windows are very early in their use of large sheets of plate glass set in copper frames; Mentmore also has an early use of hot water heating and artificial ventilation.

We have seen how in the 1850s Gothic moved from the delicate and fussy to the robust and muscular. This larger, stronger, heavier architecture is also seen in the country houses of the late 1850s and 60s. John Pritchard's Ettington Park, Warwickshire (1858–63), with its clean, 13th-century Gothic lines, is constructed out of four different colours of stone, producing a monumental, polychromatic display (fig. 450). It expresses its plan elegantly, breaking an otherwise symmetrical entrance front with contrasting stair towers. This expression of plan in elevation was new in the 1850s. Before then houses were designed on what might be called picturesque principles. Various components were disposed for best visual effect, with towers, pinnacles and other features creating a

pleasing silhouette. Pugin's design principles had a fundamental impact on this. He designed from plan to elevation, creating a picturesque appearance but one in which every element expressed its function. Pugin's own home, The Grange, Ramsgate, Kent, begun in 1843 (fig. 453), was deliberately designed as a model for the 19th-century house. It had an impact across the social scale, from the suburban villa to the largest country house. In the right hands – as at Ettington Park – Puginian principles produced buildings of a coherence and legibility that made them beautiful; less accomplished architects merely created a skyline of confusion.[46] Country houses were complex organisms designed to facilitate an ordered, private and hierarchical existence for a large number of people. Families were big, and healthy couples had ten or so children, who were provided

Fig. 450 (left) Ettington Park, Warwickshire, John Pritchard, 1858–63. A very impressive essay in 13th-century Gothic revivalism; not just a picturesque jumble, but a house built from plan to elevation. The porte-cochére has structural rib-vaulting.

Fig. 451 (right) Prestwold Hall, Leicestershire, William Burn, 1842. Ground plan.

Fig. 452 (bottom) Joseph Nash, *Come to the Maypole*, an illustration for *Old English Ballads of 1864*. This captures the paternalistic image of the countryside, with villagers revelling in front of the Tudoresque manor house and church.

Fig. 453 (below) The Grange, Ramsgate, A. W. N. Pugin, 1843–4, seen here in a sketch by Pugin of *c.*1845. He died in the house in 1852 and was buried next door.

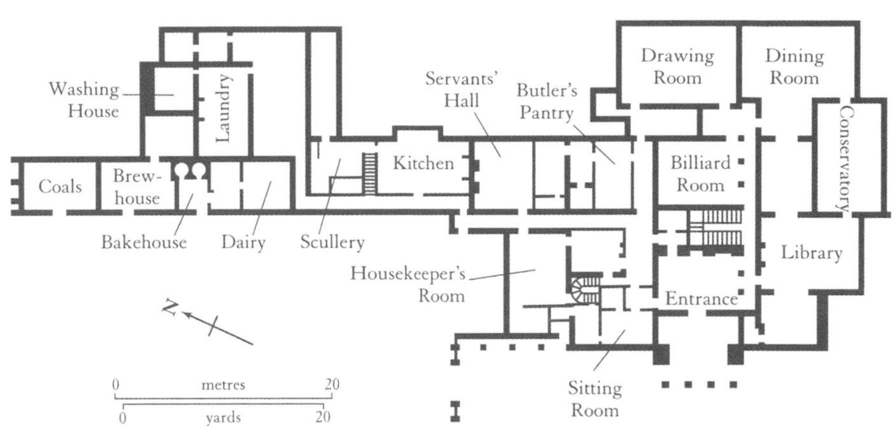

with nursery maids, nannies and tutors. In addition, a modest house would have perhaps eight other staff; the really big houses could have up to forty. House parties remained a major feature and weekend guests would bring a valet or a lady's maid. These groups – adults, children, servants, guests and their servants – all had their own defined zones. Generally, houses were arranged around a central hall. From this, corridors and staircases issued, enabling people to move about; servants invisibly, if possible. Most houses had a business room with a separate entrance, in which the master of the house could attend to estate papers. The service quarters were usually set at a remove from the main house in a wing. A particular concern was avoiding cooking smells, and tall, well-ventilated kitchens needed to be kept at a distance.

Prestwold Hall, Leicestershire, was remodelled in 1842 by William Burn, one of the busiest and most capable country-house architects and an expert in planning. For his client, Charles Packe, he opened up a large new hall as a central circulation space (using iron beams), built a new service wing and conservatory, reconstructed the main staircase, and built on a sitting room for his client and a boudoir for his wife (fig. 451). In such a house territorialism was most complex at mealtimes. Children would have eaten in the nursery, the upper servants in the housekeeper's room, the lower servants in the servants' hall, and the family and their guests in the dining room. When not at table, room use was divided according to sex: Mrs Packe in her boudoir, Mr Packe in his sitting room and breakfast room. The drawing room was for the ladies (and the men, on invitation); the opposite applied in the library. The billiard room – and smoking room, if there was one – were male preserves. Unmarried male and female guests were on separate corridors; male and female servants were on different staircases.

Living in Towns

Sometime around 1850 England became a predominantly urban country. That is to say that more people lived in towns of over 2,500 people than lived in the countryside. The 1820s and 30s were the most intense periods of urban growth; Bradford, for instance, grew by 60 per cent, Salford by 56 per cent, and both Leeds and Liverpool by 46 per cent. For many, such intense urbanisation was not to be admired and, from 1815, with increasing rapidity, wealthy families began to move out from town centres to the fringes, where there was cheaper land, more space, and less dirt and noise. A house such as that built in 1815 for the Hull merchant, George Adler, is typical of the Greek-revival villas that the rich favoured on urban fringes (fig. 454).

The Liverpool suburbs of Anfield and Breckfield began as home to large, detached villas belonging to city merchants. These were generally built in a single pre-existing field that provided extensive gardens. By the 1840s, however, houses were being built more systematically and intensively by speculative builders. Plots were smaller and the generous gardens of earlier times were redeveloped. Many new houses were semi-detached. Semis had occasionally been built in the 18th century but from 1800 they provided a way of combining some of the economies of a terrace with the prestige of a free-standing mansion. Crucially, they still gave a sense of life in the country, with façades set back from the road and gate piers bearing pretentious, gentrified

Fig. 454 (left) Sutton Grange, Salthouse Road, Hull, built for George Adler, 1815. A typical large but compact Regency suburban villa.

names. Their occupants were bankers, merchants, manufacturers, brokers and managers, who lived in some style and comfort. All had several servants and a gardener, as well as a coach and horses. These men, and the speculators who built their houses, were increasingly interested in issues of design and a market for pattern books and design manuals developed. J. C. Loudon's weighty *Encyclopaedia of Cottage Farm and Villa Architecture and Furniture* (1833) contained hundreds of elevations and perspectives in an array of styles. The new villas of Anfield and Breckfield show a strong awareness of these contemporary architectural fashions. Semi-detached houses in St Domingo Grove, a development begun before 1846, provided a choice of Italianate or Tudor styles. Mill Bank, a nearby development in Anfield Road (with an alluringly rural name), is in a more thoroughgoing Gothic, whilst the houses in the same road of the 1870s are of polychromatic brick (fig. 455).

These houses, even the semis, were big, some with six bedrooms. Over 40 per cent of families had between five and nine children; girls and boys had to sleep in separate rooms, maids might share an attic room, but a cook had a room of her own. A dining room and drawing room were basic essentials; a study and conservatory were common. The house was the woman's sphere; men commuted to work in city centres by foot, coach or later by horse tram. It was the final stage in the separation of home and work, and created a new type of suburban social life, regulated by invitations to tea, dinner and to parties. In between times the home was a private place, separate from its neighbours and far from the homes of social inferiors.

Fig. 455 (right) 21 and 23 Anfield Road, Liverpool. These handsome semi-detached houses of the 1870s have semi-circular sculleries at the front to keep the more prestigious garden front clear.

Whilst fashionable people escaped living in terraces from the 1840s, they remained the key house type for the poor. Pressure on suburban space was relentless and in the 1860s Breckfield, like many polite suburbs, succumbed to more modest terraces of houses. These were occupied by ship brokers, coal merchants, accountants, book keepers and other lesser merchants and professional people. Although they couldn't afford semi-detached or detached houses, they still aspired to a rural idea and the new streets were named after the lakes of the Lake District.[47] Breckfield illustrates the fact that suburbanisation was not an event; it was a process in which aspiring residents moved outwards from urban centres to occupy places that the wealthy were simultaneously vacating, a phenomenon that continued until 1939.

House building for the wealthy made a reasonable return for builders and landowners; building for the poorest sections of society did not. So few working-class houses were being built that the only solution for millions was subdivision. This would have been bad enough in solidly built middle-class housing, but in back-to-backs it led to appalling conditions. In Newcastle upon Tyne fewer than 35 per cent of families occupied self-contained houses and in 1866 9,639 families (43 per cent of the population) lived in a single room. The houses themselves were, in the main, unserviced; a survey by the Manchester Board of Health in 1831 showed that 55.4 per cent of the houses in Ancoats were without plumbing, and 56.1 per cent of the streets were not cleaned and were full of filth.[48]

The appalling human impact of these conditions became very apparent in the early 1830s. Whilst human life expectancy in Surrey was 45 years, in Manchester it was only 24. The 1832 outbreak of cholera killed 32,000 people and the 1848 outbreak wiped out 62,000. In 1840 a parliamentary select committee recommended an ambitious plan for reforming inner-city conditions, including the promotion of public parks and baths, and the banning of back-to-back housing. It was followed by a Royal Commission comprising powerful and influential individuals who looked into the issues in great detail. A series of measures was eventually passed, including the Public Health Act of 1848. This established a General Board of Health in London and local health boards where there was high mortality or local demand. Although the national board was disbanded in 1858, over 700 local boards were established by 1871. Some towns began to introduce local building regulations after 1858, but at first improvements were made to drainage and water supply rather than mass housing.

The greatest challenge for the new corporations was the pollution caused by intense urbanisation, most seriously the problems of sanitation. The disposal of human excrement had to rely, almost exclusively, on cesspools – collection pits beneath privies – which had to be regularly emptied. Manchester alone had to dispose of 70,000 tonnes of human excrement a year; the content of 200,000 cesspools in London was taken to around sixty local yards, where it was allowed to desiccate before being carted out to the countryside and sold to farmers as manure. The system just about worked in well-off areas, but in poorer parts cesspools were badly built and irregularly emptied, and they

Fig. 456 (above) Dalton Pumping Station in Cold Hesledon, County Durham (1866–80), where Hawksley designed the chimney as a Byzantine campanile.

overflowed into streets, yards and cellars, carrying disease as they went. Ironically, the invention of an effective, water-flushed privy or water-closet made matters worse. Instead of removing excrement from areas of habitation WCs flushed it into rivers, causing an increase in cases of typhoid and cholera.

In London it took the Great Stink of 1858, when the Thames clogged up with sewage, to stimulate decisive action. The Metropolitan Board of Works employed the brilliant engineer Sir Joseph Bazalgette to construct five great sewers of eighty-two miles in length. These carried out 52 million gallons of sewage a day fourteen miles east of Tower Bridge, from where the sewage was taken twenty-six miles out to sea by tidal action. It was an engineering marvel, costing £4.6 million and using 318 million bricks. Although the system worked by gravity there were four main pumping stations. The one at Abbey Mills, West Ham, laid out within formal gardens, was designed by Charles Driver and built between 1865 and 1868 in an indescribable style, of which the components were Gothic, Byzantine, Moorish and Russian. Inside, it contained eight huge beam engines pumping sewage eastwards.

Water-supply systems were not uncommon by 1800 in larger towns and wealthier districts, but they generally provided intermittent supplies at variable pressure. The needs of growing towns demanded something better, especially for fire-fighting, sewer-flushing and for public baths. As a result municipalities increasingly took responsibility for water supply, completely changing the scale and ambition of the industry. Like early railway and gas structures, water-pumping stations and storage towers were designed to inspire confidence amongst investors and customers. Pumping stations, for instance, were never grimy engine sheds but were set in hygienic-looking gardens with gravelled paths:; cleanliness, order and modernity were crucial to the image of the industry. The design of waterworks was dominated by a small circle of London-based engineers dominated by Thomas Hawksley, an engineer with architectural training who designed in Gothic, Tudor and Italianate styles. The building in which a pumping station is housed is determined by the layout of the boilers and pumps within. It was here that the technical expertise and expense lay; the external architectural shell was a relatively cheap window-dressing. One of the key stylistic challenges was the incorporation of the chimney; at Dalton Pumping Station in Cold Hesledon, County Durham (1866–80), Hawksley designed one as a Byzantine campanile (fig. 456).

The collective supply of water had a long history in England. Gas, however, had always been supplied by private enterprise. In London twenty-three gas-works and six gas-holder stations, owned by thirteen companies, with 1,750 miles of main, lit 37,728 street lights in the early 1860s. This was the high point of private enterprise and in the 1860s many companies merged, producing monopolies in many towns. The next step was municipalisation, as corporations purchased gas companies to guarantee standards and supply, as infrastructure of the water industry, gas structures became less functional and were designed in historical styles in the 1860s.

Commercial Buildings

The period from 1844 to 1870 following Robert Peel's Bank Charter Act, which gave the Bank of England sole power to issue currency, saw London established as the world's pre-eminent financial centre. The concentration of expertise, knowledge and money in London attracted merchants, bankers, brokers and agents from all over the world to transact their business. Other cities had control of single markets; Liverpool, for instance, cotton and Newcastle coal, but London was the centre for the money markets. In this way London engendered global financial confidence and its bills of exchange became the currency of international trade.

The first commercial telegraph system, developed by Sir William Fothergill Cooke and Charles Wheatstone, was installed in 1839 on the Great Western Railway from Paddington to West Drayton. Progress in the technology of underwater cables enabled the successful laying of the first transatlantic wire in 1866, and by 1872 the telegraph network could reach every continent, placing London at the centre of global communication. This is how London managed large percentages of trade in commodities such as coffee and rubber, of which it produced none and consumed little.

The architectural effects of the success of the City were huge. A place that had been largely made up of residential-scale Georgian buildings was transformed, and 80 per cent of buildings standing in the City in 1855 had been demolished and replaced by 1901. The new buildings were all commercial and so a population of 129,000 in 1850 fell to only 26,000 in 1900. In the 1840s, however, it was Manchester and Liverpool that set the pace for commercial architecture. Brunswick Buildings in Liverpool of 1842 by A. & G. Williams was one of the first and most sophisticated commercial buildings in the palazzo mode; this style went on to transform both cities, especially Manchester, where warehouses first became stylistically expressive structures equal in street weight to banks and offices. These buildings were not merely storehouses; they were showrooms, places for the reception of clients, and offices. Edward Walters became the most successful exponent of warehouses, 36 Charlotte Street of 1855–6 being a representative survivor of one of his palazzo buildings (fig. 457). In plan it is fairly typical of its type; steps led up to a raised main floor from which the principal internal feature was a stair ascending the whole height of the building. The ground floor had an office and showroom; above were more offices, sample rooms and waiting rooms for clients. Both the public floors were embellished architecturally but the upper storage floors – and the basement, generally used for packing – were not. Hydraulic hoists moved goods between floors, so boilers and steam engines were needed; light was provided by gas.

In London the charge to erect new buildings was led by the insurance companies, eager to use their offices to infuse their business with a sense of confidence, solidity and endurance. The earliest in the City is the old Atlas Insurance Office on Cheapside by Thomas Hopper of 1838 (fig. 458).

Fig. 457 (top) 36 Charlotte Street, Manchester, by Edward Walters, 1855–6. Such palazzo-style warehouses transformed the face of Manchester, sweeping away earlier cramped and dingy buildings.

Fig. 458 (above) Old Atlas Insurance Company Office, Cheapside, City of London, Thomas Hopper, 1838. Utterly reassuring, rooted in history, this early City office demonstrated the image big business aspired to in the 1840s.

This smooth essay in classicism, oozing poise and permanence, paid homage to the Banqueting House on Whitehall (fig. 229). Not strictly a commercial building, but one of the most important London Italianate buildings of the 1840s, was the Coal Exchange. As London became the world centre for trade in a wide range of commodities, exchange buildings were constructed by the City Corporation for agents to sample corn, coal, wool, metals – whatever the commodity was – and bid for them in noisy open auctions. The Coal Exchange stood on the corner of St Mary-at-Hill and Lower Thames Street; it was designed and built between 1846 and 1849 by the architect to the Corporation, James Bunstone Bunning. Two identical palazzo façades were linked by a quadrant portico, surmounted by what could be mistaken for a church tower (fig. 459). Whilst the palazzo façades presented a conventional scene, the interior was a spectacular demonstration of iron engineering. It comprised a circular hall 60ft in diameter and 74ft high, around which the offices were arranged (fig. 460). The decorative theme was industry and the iron castings resembled twined lengths of thick rope; ceramic panels and painted decoration represented fossil ferns and views of collieries. It is worth noting that exposed iron on street elevations was not acceptable in the 1840s.[49]

In the 1860s insurance companies started to look to their headquarters to convey different messages. The emphasis was less on the sober management of funds emphasised by the palazzi and much more on the advertisement of success and wealth generation. The Royal, an insurance company started in Liverpool, constructed a huge and flamboyant building in Lombard Street in 1857 designed by John Belcher (fig. 461). This was essentially an extension of their colossal annual advertising budget of some £20,000–£30,000 a year.

Fig. 459 (below right) Coal Exchange, City of London, James Bunstone Bunning (1846–9, demolished 1962). Two palace fronts were linked by an Italianate tower on the corner. The conventional façades hid a structure of advanced engineering.

Fig. 460 (below) Coal Exchange. There were many exchanges in the city and all required a large space for open cry trading. Until 1831 all coal had to be bought and sold at the exchange but even after free trade was established the exchange – the most important distributive organisation in the nation's economic life – dealt in more than eight million tons of coal a year.

Banks also started to move from sober and domestic premises to Italianate offices similar to those occupied by the insurance companies and, in the 1860s, like the insurance companies, they became much showier. The National Provincial Bank on Bishopsgate by John Gibson is the best of the lot (fig. 462). It was built between 1864 and 1865 to replace an 18th-century mansion by Sir Robert Taylor, built in 1750, that had been the bank's headquarters since 1840. The new building proclaimed the bank as a national rather than just a provincial success and, in presenting a single storey to the street with a giant order and a cornice topped with figures, seems to be aping the Bank of England itself. The bank was typical in that it contained an impressive ground-floor banking hall, handsome boardrooms on the first floor and, in the basement, strong rooms, boiler rooms and refreshment rooms for the clerks.

Drinking Responsibly

In the late 18th century inns were often the largest secular buildings in a town, functioning as multi-purpose centres for social and business life. As specialised buildings such as libraries, court houses and corn exchanges were built, inns morphed into hotels specialising in food and overnight accommodation. The alehouse, the inn's poor cousin, was also evolving. From the 1670s it began to be called the public house, reflecting the fact it was still a private house that served drinks.

Fig. 461 (far left) Royal Insurance Company Offices, Lombard Street, John Belcher, 1857 (demolished 1912). Depicted here in 1865, this was a much more florid and assertive approach to corporate architectural identity than had been seen in the City of London before.

Fig. 462 (left) Old National Provincial Bank, Bishopsgate, City of London, John Gibson, 1864–5; the best Victorian commercial premises to survive in the City. This building says all a Bank would wish. Behind rises its 20th-century successor, the National Westminster Bank Tower (now Tower 42) by Richard Seifert (1970–81), doing exactly the same job as Gibson's building but in a different language.

Fig. 463 (below) The Bass Maltings, Sleaford, H. A. Couchman 1901–5. This spectacular complex conveys better than any other the industrialisation of English agriculture. The total length of the complex shown here is over 1,000 ft.

Although beer was periodically challenged by gin as the nation's favourite alcoholic drink, it remained the national staple until well into the 20th century. Beer was at first produced on a local and small scale, and drunk in small public houses, but London's insatiable thirst for drink led to the development of the first industrial breweries and their chains of pubs. Beer is made from malted barley flavoured with hops, and the preparation of its raw ingredients requires maltings and oast houses, which are effectively elaborate drying kilns. Specialised malt houses were built from the 16th century; long and low, with good ventilation, there are still recognisable survivals. The arrival of industrial production, however, led to the construction of massive maltings, the greatest of which are at Sleaford, Lincolnshire (1901–5). These are the most impressive surviving group of Victorian industrial buildings in England (fig. 463). They were designed by H. A. Couchman for Bass, Ratcliffe & Greeton. Sited by an artesian well and adjacent to rich barley-growing lands, the malt was taken out to Bass's breweries by a branch rail line. The eight detached pavilions, centred on a massive water tower and chimney for the engine, cover thirteen acres and provided half a million square feet of floor space. The massive, red-brick blocks are enlivened by full-height buttresses framing windows with cast-iron glazing bars. The heavy industrialisation of malt production was not mirrored in hop preparation, which was undertaken rurally, close to hop fields in oast houses, rather than in town centres.

In 1815 the Anchor Brewery, Southwark, was the first to produce 300,000 barrels of beer a year. It was a giant. In 1834 only 134 breweries produced more than 10,000 barrels but this number doubled by the 1850s and trebled by the 1870s, reaching a peak of 627 in 1899, after which the numbers rapidly declined. Breweries were complex buildings requiring the movement of large quantities of raw materials and the temperature-controlled movement of liquid. Before the 1890s most adopted a gravity principle, hoisting or pumping materials to the top and letting the processes work downwards. They were thus tall, with even taller water towers and chimneys for their engines. The consequence of their technical sophistication was that they were designed by

specialist engineers not architects. Harveys Brewery in Lewes, Sussex, is a typical provincial brewery (fig. 464). Brewing started here in the 1820s and some of the early buildings survive; but between 1881 and 1882 it was enlarged and rebuilt to designs by William Bradford. Bradford specialised in breweries – his practice worked on over seventy – and he was fond of rich skylines and, as Harveys illustrates well, the use of ornamental ironwork, an increasing feature of breweries from the 1870s.[50] Although licensing regimes were devised during the 19th century, pubs and drinking places steadily increased in number. In 1830 just over 82,000 were licensed; by 1870 there were 112,000. From the mid 18th century brewers bought and leased pubs in which to sell their beers, and by 1816–17 they owned half of the pubs in London. By 1859 Harveys of Lewes, for example, owned seventeen pubs across Sussex, five in Eastbourne alone. Generally speaking, these pubs were purpose-built, whilst privately owned pubs – of which there were tens of thousands – were converted domestic dwellings. From the 1840s pubs began to be larger and more assertive in the street; most were Italianate in style – Gothic was associated with the Church – but from the 1860s they comfortably adopted the prevailing eclectic style, seen as suitably exotic for a place of entertainment and leisure.

Fig. 464 (above) Harveys Bridge Wharf Brewery, Lewes, Sussex, William Bradford, 1881–2. Typically for a brewery, it has a tower, here with a pyramid top and a louvered stage beneath.

All but the smallest one-room pubs were highly compartmentalised by screens or glazed panels and had a strong hierarchy of spaces and functions. The public bar was for the poorest and labourers, and the more regular customers amongst them would use the private bar. The Crown, St John's Wood, built between 1898 and 1899, was designed by C. H. Worley in an elaborate, eclectic style (fig. 465). It was in a rich part of London and no expense was spared in its fitting-out. Inside there were five drinking areas, including a ladies' zone, divided by glass screens. The saloon bar had a massive marble fireplace and a marble-topped bar. Typical of pubs of this date the largest room was for billiards; upstairs was a concert hall.

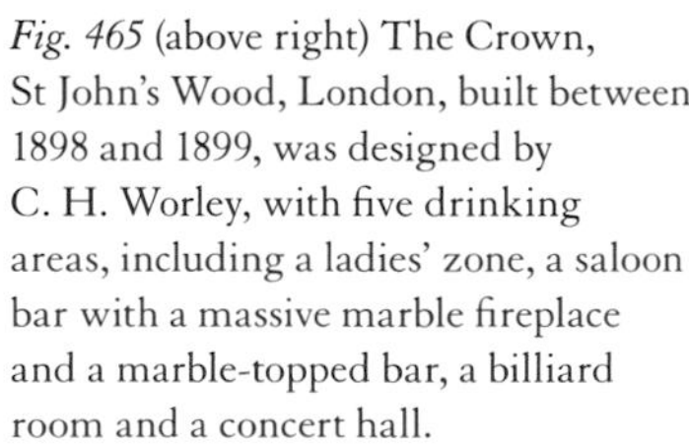

Fig. 465 (above right) The Crown, St John's Wood, London, built between 1898 and 1899, was designed by C. H. Worley, with five drinking areas, including a ladies' zone, a saloon bar with a massive marble fireplace and a marble-topped bar, a billiard room and a concert hall.

Fig. 466 (above) The Salisbury, Harringay, London, 1898–9. Hardy, easily cleaned materials that did not retain smoke smells were the staples of pub décor. The photograph shows the mosaic floor, ceramic wall tiles and glass panels.

It was, in fact, the gin shop not the public house that was the first architecturally pretentious drinking establishment. During London's gin craze of the 1820s a number of gin or 'dram' shops opened, influenced by gas-lit shops with the big glass windows of the day. Gin shops were both the first to have counters and the first to deliberately exploit vulgarity to attract attention. None survives, but the longevity of the term 'gin palace' suggests the extent of their over-the-top decoration. Such effects were possible on a mass scale in pubs after 1870, when the cost of glass and mirrors fell, and the incandescent mantle made gas lighting more congenial and brilliant. Hardy, easily cleaned materials that did not retain smoke smells were the staples of pub décor. Cut, etched, engraved and embossed glass, ceramic tiles and terracotta, and polished hardwood – or in poorer pubs, painted softwood – were everywhere. All these could take bright colours and highly ornamented shapes (fig. 466).[51]

Municipal Buildings

The Municipal Reform Act of 1835 did for the municipalities what the Great Reform Act had done for parliament – it attempted to bring into the democratic system people of wealth and influence who hitherto had been excluded. In the towns the dominant Anglican, Tory Establishment was joined by large numbers of Nonconformists and newly rich merchants and industrialists. One hundred and seventy-eight new corporations were established, each governed by an elected council that had the power to raise a local rate. In 1882 the number of corporations was increased by thirty-eight and in 1888 county boroughs were created; in all, by 1903, there were three hundred and thirteen municipal boroughs in England. This did not immediately result in a concentration of local power and influence, as it took many years to absorb the functions of independent boards of commissioners, previously established under Private Acts, who oversaw, for instance, paving, lighting, bridges and markets.

But the new corporations were rapidly empowered to undertake other activities, museums, public health, police and utilities amongst them. This expansion of municipal activity led to a boom in the construction of town halls. A conservative calculation gives thirty-nine in the 1840s, sixty in the 1850s and fifty-eight in the 1860s. Many were very expensive relative to the wealth of the town and were only made possible by cheap loans from central government.[52]

In the 18th century, in towns such as Worcester (p. 313 and fig. 292), assembly rooms had sometimes been added to town halls, augmenting their three traditional functions of meetings, markets and magistracy. But from the 1830s many more civic activities were given a home and town halls became increasingly complex organisms, often including police stations, fire stations, libraries, art galleries and museums. What all town halls had in common, however, was the expanding number of offices to house town clerks, treasurers, surveyors, inspectors and school boards. The expanding municipal-committee structures demanded committee rooms that could also double as entertainment suites and mayors increasingly wanted their own quarters or, at the very least, a parlour for receptions.

The story of rapidly increasing municipal functions is nicely illustrated by the case of Birmingham, which obtained an Act of Parliament in 1828 to allow it to make civic improvements, including the erection of a town hall. In 1830 a national competition was launched that was won by Joseph Hansom and Edward Welch. Their design was for a freestanding Roman temple modelled on the Temple of Castor and Pollux, built in the 2nd century BC as a meeting place for the Roman Senate (fig. 467). Inside was a public concert hall for three thousand people, which could double as a courtroom. Municipal business was conducted from a single committee room in the basement.[53] By 1853 the city had bought a site for a new building. This was only begun in 1874 but when

Fig. 467 (left) The Town Hall, Birmingham, 1832–4, Joseph Hansom and Edward Welch, extended 1837, 1849–51 by Charles Edge. This was the first major 19th-century Roman revival building in England, a stylistic choice reflecting an interest in Roman culture and government amongst the city's leading citizens.

Fig. 468 (above right) The Town Hall, Leeds Yorkshire, Cuthbert Brodrick, 1852–8. Brodrick was virtually unknown when he won the competition to design the hall. He drew on his detailed studies of contemporary continental buildings, especially French ones, made on a two-year study trip. The result was and is stunning.

Fig. 469 (above) Leeds Town Hall, Cuthbert Brodrick, 1852–8. The Victoria Hall lay at the centre of the building containing a colossal concert organ. The magnificence of this space reflected the ambitions of its patrons, the oligarchs of Leeds.

complete provided a huge amount of office accommodation, as well as a fine civic suite. In 1884 it became necessary to expand again, this time into an enormous new courtyard mainly of offices, but also containing a large art gallery. Another extension was planned in 1899 and was built between 1906 and 1919.[54]

Following Birmingham and Liverpool's town halls, a group of townsmen in Leeds started a campaign for the building of their own hall, which would beautify their town and raise the aesthetic aspirations of its inhabitants. The brief was the most ambitious yet: a hall for eight thousand people, refreshment rooms and kitchens, a mayor's suite, council chamber, extensive offices, four courtrooms and a police station. The competition was won by a young architect from Hull, Cuthbert Brodrick, who built a municipal palace between 1852 and 1858. Like the previous two halls it was in a Roman style, appropriate to the aspirations of the citizens. It was big, it was emphatic and it was very, very expensive (fig. 468). Civic patronage knew no bounds: Minton tiles, chandeliers by Osler of Birmingham, Walter Macfarlane for the ironwork, and the Victoria Hall decorated in the richest style by J. D. Crace (fig. 469). The completed building was opened by Queen Victoria herself in a celebration as over-the-top as the architecture of the hall. Leeds more or less defined the image of a new town hall and had direct stylistic progeny in Bolton, Portsmouth, Birkenhead and Morley.

Crime and Punishment

Combining law courts with town halls was expression of civic aspiration: justice, good government and personal improvement working in harmony. It was also an expression of status. The arrival of High Court judges for the assizes still involved processions, pomp and display, providing an opportunity for civic magnificence that most towns desired.

Fig. 470 (left) The Crown Court, Nottingham, T. C. Hine, 1876. A typical crown court of its age, with fine woodwork reminiscent of an 18th-century church. The seat of the judge was emphasised as if it were the altar.

Fig. 471 (below) Manchester Assize Courts, Great Ducie Street Manchester, Alfred Waterhouse 1859–65. Bombed in 1940–1, it was demolished after the abolition of the assizes in 1957.

In plan these courts reflected the increasing use of barristers in criminal trials rather than just in civil cases. Trials were now a carefully staged drama conducted by professional actors on behalf of defendants and jurors. Within the courtroom hierarchically disposed boxes, podia and benches conjured up the image of a compartmentalised 18th-century church interior with box pews, reading desk and pulpit (fig. 470). Yet the activities within had more in common with the ecclesiologists, for courtroom ritual and ceremonial became increasingly complicated and elaborate. Whilst the public performance was given a more formalised setting so too was the private consultation between professionals outside the court room, leading to an increase in back-of-house space.

The assize courts that represented a culmination of these developments, and also set the standard for those that followed, are the Manchester Assize Courts designed by Alfred Waterhouse between 1859 and 1865, and now demolished (fig. 471). The city spent £120,000 building these spectacular new courts to celebrate their grant of assizes. Aesthetically, the building was unquestionably one of the finest Gothic public structures of its age, but Waterhouse's genius also lay in the planning of complex institutions. He had been influenced by Street's Royal Courts of Justice on the Strand (fig. 436) and designed a central hall, around which clustered the courts. The offices and other parts were ranged around the outside, served by a ring of corridors. Accommodation for the barristers set new standards, with luncheon and robing rooms, and a library. In the court room, for the first time in a provincial court, the barristers faced the judge in a line rather than camping round a table at his feet.

The assizes dealt with a small minority of relatively serious crimes. JPs would either hear minor criminal cases in their own homes or would group cases together and hear them in petty sessions in the local inn. Civil actions, mainly for minor debt, were locally organised, too, but the system was slow,

Fig. 472 (right) The (former) County Court, Maddison Street, Southampton was built within the outer bailey or the former castle in 1851. Typical of Charles Reeves's courts, it is in brick and stone in a handsome Italianate style.

inefficient and expensive. Between 1846 and 1849 a group of Acts of Parliament reorganised local justice, giving power to counties and boroughs to provide proper accommodation for petty sessions and civil courts.

Police courts became the courts of summary justice for lesser crimes – the ancestors of the magistrates' courts. The model for many of these was the Clerkenwell Police Court (1841–2), a combined police station and courthouse. Here the magistrate had his own front door; centrally and to one side beneath a coat of arms, was the public entrance. A corridor led to the simple courtroom (with a WC) and then out to the cells. The building was probably designed by Charles Reeves, the Metropolitan Police Surveyor. Reeves was appointed to the job of supervising nationally the design of the new county courts; he designed sixty-four of these and set the standard for many more. Internally, they were less hierarchical and structured than the assize courts, although the judge presided on a throne-like chair. Externally, they are often recognisable by a prominent royal coat of arms over the door. Courtrooms were normally on the first floor, with large windows; offices and reception areas were below. One of Reeves's larger courthouses survives in Southampton; built in 1851 and characteristically Italianate with stucco quoins, it has entrances for the public and, separately, for the judge (fig. 472).

Thus the image and reality of criminal justice shifted away from a display of the state's power to publically humiliate delinquents to a structured system of professional trials conducted in efficiently designed modern courtrooms. This change was also reflected in the state's power to incarcerate malefactors.[55] By the end of the Middle Ages there were prisons in most major towns. New civic buildings, such as guildhalls or market halls, were often given a cell or two to serve as the local gaol, but by 1611 it had become compulsory for each county to have at least one prison or house of correction. Before the 1770s these had no common architectural form or deliberate civic presence, although there were a

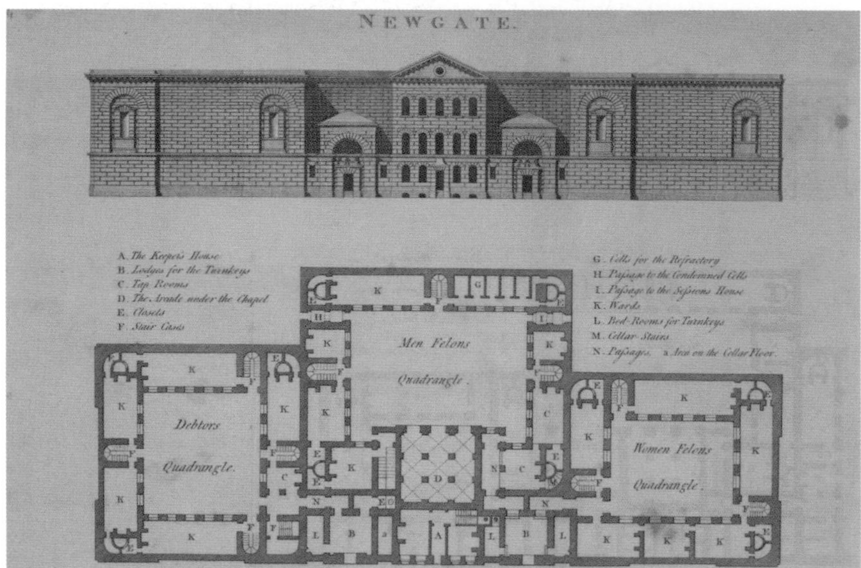

Fig. 473 (left) Newgate Gaol, City of London, George Dance the Younger, 1770–78 (demolished 1902). Constructed in a densely populated area, the plan was very compact and from the prison reformers' point of view this meant standards of lighting and ventilation were not adequate.

few exceptions. But in the last quarter of the 18th century a small number of new prisons were buildings of pretension. The last and most important of these was Newgate in the City of London. This gaol had grown out of the cells in the medieval city gate, and had been extended and rebuilt many times before 1768, when George Dance the Younger was asked to design a new building. The prison was his masterpiece. Its comprehensively rusticated exterior with menacing manacles over the doorways was utterly forbidding and chilled the blood of honest passers-by. In plan there were courtyards for men, women and for debtors. At the rear were cells for the condemned (fig. 473).

From the 1770s penal reformers turned against this deliberately oppressive type of architecture, believing that prisons could recondition criminals and rehabilitate at least some of them as good citizens. Various Acts of Parliament were passed that transformed prison buildings; individual cells were to be properly heated and ventilated, and connected to yards for exercise, although the regime remained harsh: solitary confinement at night, and labour and religious instruction by day. In 1775 the first purpose-built, fully cellular prison was built in Horsham.

The outbreak of war in America in 1775 was a turning point in the history of prisons in England, bringing an abrupt end to the practice of transporting malefactors to Maryland or Virginia. This led to severe overcrowding, so during the 1780s and 90s over sixty prisons were rebuilt. More than twenty architects and county engineers were involved but the man who made his name in prison design was William Blackburn, who designed seventeen. One of the few complete prisons surviving from this period is Littledean Gaol, Gloucestershire, built by Blackburn in the late 1780s (fig. 474). Surrounded by a tall wall, the prison lay in the centre of an enclosure divided into four exercise yards. There were two rectangular cell wings joined by a block containing the offices, chapel and gaoler's house. It was an elegant affair with deep eaves and finely cut stone, humane, business-like and functional.

Fig. 474 (right) Littledean Gaol, Gloucestershire, William Blackburn, 1789–91. This was one of four similar institutions in the county erected by Sir George Onesiphorous Paul. Great care was taken with every detail, most of which, miraculously, survive in its new use as an archive store.

The prison that set the tone for the future, though, was Millbank Penitentiary, Britain's first national prison and the first built to reform rather than merely incarcerate criminals. When it was completed in 1822 it was the largest prison in Europe, holding one thousand prisoners, covering sixteen acres and built at a cost of £458,000. Prison reformers had been obsessed with prison planning, and in the late 1770s the philosopher Jeremy Bentham was advocating the panopticon, the underlying principle of which was the ability of the warders to see all parts of the prison from a central vantage point. Millbank was designed by W. Williams on the panopticon principle in the form of a great wheel pivoting on a central, circular chapel that was surrounded by a hexagon of buildings. On the outside of this hexagon were six irregular pentagons, each with a courtyard in the middle (fig. 475). The building was functionally, structurally and politically a catastrophic failure, and was abandoned as a model prison in 1843. The experiments in architecture and penal reform carried out there, however, led directly to the new reform prison at Pentonville.

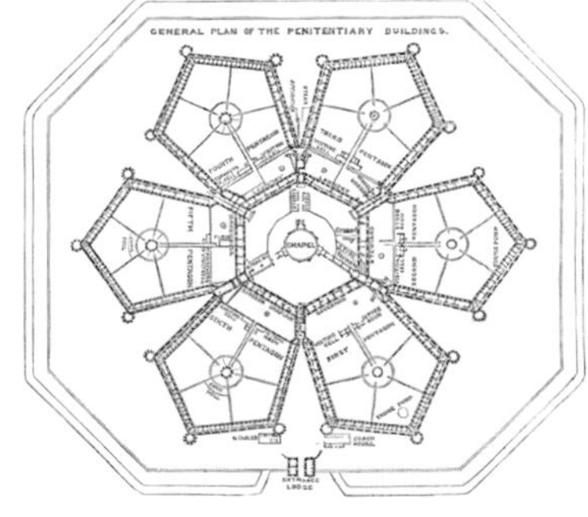

Fig. 475 (above) Millbank Penitentiary, London, various architects 1812–21. Built on the panopticon principle, the building was functionally, structurally and politically a catastrophic failure, and was abandoned as a model prison in 1843.

Pentonville was built between 1840 and 1842 as a model for the demonstration of the new system and to encourage county gaols to follow suit. It was designed by a Royal Engineer, Joshua Jebb, under the close supervision of Lord Russell, the Home Secretary. The main prison building centred on an entrance block with a full-height hall, off which ran four wings of three storeys and twenty-two bays. There were five hundred air-conditioned cells measuring 13ft x 7ft x 9ft, each containing a basin and lavatory. Communication with other cells was impossible. Inmates lived and worked in their cells and only left – wearing masks – to go to the chapel sited on the first floor of the entrance block. The exercise yards were wedge-shaped compounds grouped around the exterior. Twelve county and seven borough gaols were rebuilt on similar radial plans between 1842 and 1877, generally on greenfield sites on the edge of towns. They were large, impressive buildings, some of which were built in industrial styles, whilst others took more from polite architecture. Manchester, for instance, got a prison designed by Alfred Waterhouse in the suburb of Strangeways. He began work in 1861 after visiting Reading and Holloway gaols and consulting Jebb on the principles of radial design. It has an impressive gatehouse, and the buildings are in an eclectic mix of Romanesque and Venetian Gothic (fig. 476).[56]

The Poorer in Sickness and in Health

The sick, orphaned, destitute, crippled and mad could easily have been the principal victims of a rapidly industrialising and urbanised society in which traditional relationships and responsibilities were breaking up. In the event, welfare provision of all sorts, developed to such a degree that it promoted the free movement of labour and ameliorated the worst effects of downturns in the economic cycle. Indeed, the development of effective, if harsh, systems of relief was the principal reason why England, alone amongst the major European powers, succeeded in avoiding bloody revolution in the middle of the 19th century.[57]

The Act for the Relief of the Poor of 1601 had established a system whereby parishes took responsibility for their own poor through a vestry that had the power to raise a rate to provide for the destitute. Using powers conferred on them between 1722 and 1723, some parishes joined together to form a union and built a workhouse – a residential home for the able-bodied poor. Here, in uniform, they would earn their keep by performing mindless, unskilled jobs.

The Gressenhall Workhouse, Norfolk, was established in 1776 with a central H-shaped block and a single long wing built in a plain, domestic style (fig. 477). It was designed for six hundred paupers and sited on the top of a hill to encourage air circulation. By the 1770s there were nearly two thousand such workhouses with a capacity for ninety thousand of the poor. But the system was regarded as badly and corruptly run, as well as being a moral and social failure. By 1818 the charge of the poor rate nationally was £8 million, a fifth of national expenditure, and workhouses were seen not only as uneconomic and expensive but also as spreading physical and moral contagion. As the result of a Royal Commission the Poor Law Amendment Act of 1834 established a new network of union workhouses throughout the country under the supervision of a national Poor Law Commission. The principles behind the new arrangements were deterrence and segregation. The new workhouses were not places in which people would want to live; inmates would be strictly divided into seven classes, dependent on sex, age and infirmity. In 1839 there were two hundred and fifty-two new workhouses, one hundred and seventy-five old ones, sixty-seven under construction and nine in the course of alteration, all at a cost of £2 million, financed, as before, by a locally levied rate.

Central control of the provision of local services was a new phenomenon. Even more remarkable was the publication by the Poor Law Commission of model plans and elevations for unions to copy (fig. 478). Most were loosely

Fig. 476 (below) H. M. Prison, Manchester, Strangeways, Alfred Waterhouse with Joshua Webb 1862; opened 1868. It cost £170,000 and was designed for 1000 inmates. It was essentially planned on the Panopticon principle – here is the central core with Gothic arches giving onto cells on three levels.

Fig. 477 (right) Gressenhall Workhouse, Norfolk, 1776–7. A handsome classical building built at a cost of £15,000 and not instantly discernible as a union workhouse.

based on a panopticon principle, providing a supervisory hub or core at their heart. Guided by the models, competitions were held for new buildings. A number of architects quickly came to specialise in these; George Gilbert Scott's early career was founded on 'union-hunting', and he won a total of forty-four commissions nationwide.

The plans most often selected by unions were the square and hexagonal designs. Most were built in a severe and minimalist industrial style, a clear message about the lack of comforts within. A small number of architects, including Scott, built in stripped-down Tudor with gables and diapered brickwork, preserving an air of the traditional almshouse. The Epping Union Workhouse built in 1837 and designed on a square plan by Lewis Vulliamy illustrates life in a typical institution. New arrivals were seen in the receiving ward, where they would be cleaned and examined. The sick were sent to the infirmary, whilst the able-bodied were separated into their categories and sent to dormitories and their workrooms or schoolrooms. The unplastered, spartan dorms were heated either by a fire or, increasingly, by fashionable central heating. Stodgy food with a twice-weekly meat ration was served in the dining room; this normally doubled as a chapel on Sundays. Misbehaviour was punished by a spell in a tiny, windowless cell most often sited next to the dead house.

Fig. 478 (above) Perspective view of a 'square'-plan workhouse. Taken from the small-format editions of the 1st and 2nd Annual Reports of the Poor Law Commission.

Although the tough regime remained fairly constant, buildings from the 1840s to the 1870s increasingly abandoned the centralised plan and adopted a corridor plan, becoming long ranges of buildings with rooms facing out either way, whilst the master still occupied an increasingly elaborate location in the centre. Many were less severe, too, and reflected more closely the prevailing architectural fashions. The new Huddersfield Workhouse designed by John Kirk in 1870 was in a suitably masculine Gothic style, the master's house defined by central bay windows.[58]

Whilst the workhouse was increasingly a state-run service the provision of health care was the product of communal philanthropy. By paying for hospitals the rich showed that when they clubbed together they could balance the harsh impersonal regime of the workhouse with the individual compassion of the hospital. We have seen that from the 1660s hospitals developed buildings designed to promote health and healing, first in London, then in provincial towns. Although in 1730 there were none outside London, by 1800 there were thirty-eight, founded through the piety and prudence of local people and funded through their pockets. These cost money to build and money to run; involvement with a local hospital was thus not a one-off event – it was a life-long commitment, and one that principally fell to wealthy landowners and industrialists. So, for instance, Sir Richard Arkwright and the Duke of Portland both contributed to the Nottingham General Hospital.[59]

It was the navy that had led the way in hospital design in the late 18th century. The new hospital at Stonehouse, completed in 1762, had broken with the traditional long, narrow range and had disposed the wards in parallel blocks linked by colonnades. Individual ward blocks, ventilated from both sides, could be assigned to men with specific ailments. This was a plan that was much admired by hospital reformers and designers both at home and abroad. Whilst it was the navy that innovated in design it was the army that triggered a revolution in care. Florence Nightingale's experiences at the horrific Scutari hospital in Turkey during the Crimean War led to a revolution in nursing care and hospital practice. One of the first hospitals to be built on the principle of the Nightingale wards, and certainly the most prominent, was St Thomas's Hospital opposite the Palace of Westminster, built between 1868 and 1891 (fig. 479). It was designed by Henry Currey, an experienced hospital and asylum architect. To facilitate air flow the seven pavilions were 125ft apart, linked by arcades, and contained the latest ventilation technology, expressed in the busy skyline of chimneys and turrets. The wards were bright, light and built of impervious surfaces, easily cleaned. Beds were placed head to the wall between windows in the manner recommended by Nightingale. In style, like almost all hospitals, St Thomas's was Italianate. Smaller regional hospitals tended to be H-shaped, such as the impressive Netherlandish red-brick Norwich and Norfolk Hospital of 1879 by the prominent Norwich architect Edward Boardman, with the aid of T. H. Wyatt of London.[60]

The accession of Queen Victoria to the throne in 1837 coincided with the moment when Britain moved into a position of quite exceptional world dominance. Only a few years earlier the first railway had run, the Houses of Parliament had burnt down and the Great Reform Act had been passed. These events symbolised some of the changes that would sweep Britain. The railways changed the way people lived; they shrunk the size of England and, with the parallel and closely linked development of the penny post and the telegraph, affected a revolution in communication. Knowledge, opinions, resources and people could now be moved at speeds inconceivable before 1830. This was a revolution in the way people were able to think, as much as a revolution in transportation.

People did think differently about their world. Hidebound, torpid and oligarchic old institutions were swept away and replaced with new ones, blending state action and individual responsibility. The new Palace of Westminster

Fig. 479 (above) St Thomas's Hospital Lambeth, London, designed by Henry Currey. The foundation stone was laid by Queen Victoria in 1868. It was designed to accommodate 588 beds. The hospital was partially destroyed during World War II.

ushered in the great period of institutional renewal; first parliament itself, then the Church, the municipalities, public health, the law, the penal system, welfare and health care. As institutions were renewed so were the buildings in which they were housed. Again led by the Palace of Westminster, law courts, town halls, workhouses and hospitals were all recreated in modern, purpose-built structures, structures that represented, in their external form, the aspirations and values of the new oligarchies and, in their plan, the requirements of a very different society. Britain was the first country to require such new buildings, and the development of the police, the postal service, the underground railways and massive urban infrastructure were pioneering events in the creation of the modern world.

The architectural language in which these structures were clothed moved from one in which architects clung to the security of archaeological correctitude to one in which they felt confident to mix, meld and blend historical styles into new, individualistic forms. Although the exponents of mid-Victorian architecture might not have felt that they adequately reflected their place in the world, their buildings express the confidence due to a nation that had moved from being one of shopkeepers to being the workshop of the world.

12— 1870s to the Second World War

—1870-1939

The Modern movement, a way of designing that developed in Germany and France in the 1920s, was antagonistic to the idea of style and ornament, favouring abstract forms and new materials instead.

In the 1870s the rest of the world began to catch up with Britain. In 1880 Britain produced nearly 23 per cent of world manufacturing output; by 1913 the figure had fallen to 13.6 per cent. British output was growing and was still at an all-time high, but the economies of Germany and the United States had surged ahead. Yet although Britain's economy might not now be the world's largest, the country remained a big member of a small club. In 1890 Britain had greater registered merchant tonnage than the rest of the world put together and its navy was equal in power to the next two largest fleets. The merchant fleet was insured at Lloyd's of London, which had captured the global market in insurance, attracting financial services and entrenching London as the world's financial capital.

The First World War cost Britain £11.3 billion. The national debt grew from £620 million in 1914 to £8 billion in 1924, most of which was owed to the US. Britain tried to reconstruct its position during the 1920s but it took until 1927 for GDP to rise above its 1913 level, and foreign trade was already suffering before the worldwide slump of 1929 and the subsequent Depression. Yet the English economy was undergoing a fundamental restructuring. New manufacturing sectors in cars, radios and domestic appliances were developing, and the building industry was booming; four million new houses were built. Wealth was radically redistributed; the gross income of the top 1 per cent of earners declined from 30 per cent of the total in 1914 to 17 per cent in 1938. Vast numbers of people lived in better houses, had healthier lives, better education, more leisure time, increased political engagement and greater opportunities. Whilst average life expectancy in England was 43.8 years in 1891 it had risen to 51.3 in 1911 and 60.2 in 1931. Meanwhile, GDP per capita continued to increase – by 1950 it was double what it had been in 1900.[1] Much of this chapter is about how these rising standards of living were reflected in the way England's buildings developed.

This was not a bad picture, especially when contrasted with what took place in many other European countries where monarchies were overthrown, Church and state were separated, parliamentary democracy snuffed out, dictatorships established and bloody civil wars fought. The US and Germany both suffered more than Britain during the Depression. It could, of course, be argued that this showed that Britain had become fossilised; but, equally, many at the time thought it demonstrated that the country was uniquely blessed.

Well they might. Radio, newspapers, films, gramophones, electricity, telephones, cars, typewriters, motor mowers, aeroplanes and much more became part of people's lives. With these came new building types: the cinema, the garage, the airport terminal and aircraft hanger, the department store, the Tube station. Existing building types such as schools and libraries were also transformed. To deal with this fragmented architectural world architects began to adopt narrow specialisms: Archie Leitch in football stadia, Frank Matcham in theatres, Eugenius Birch in seaside piers, E. R. Robson in schools, Robert Sharpe in car parks, Sir Henry Tanner in post offices and H. Percy Adams in hospitals.

Too many historical narratives take decline as the principal theme of English history after 1870. This book sees the period between 1870 and 1930 as one of progress.[2] Unquestionably, some contemporary politicians and industrialists were concerned about Britain's declining relative position of power and prosperity in the world, but their concerns should be set against the confidence of its architects. This confidence came from the cultural assurance allied to national power and prosperity, together with architects' growing professional identity.

Before 1914 Britain was still the world's superpower, a position that brought global cultural influence. As well as exporting manufactured goods it exported architectural ideas; what was built in England was of international consequence, not just technologically but stylistically. The architect Hermann Muthesius, Cultural Attaché at the German embassy in London for six years, wrote a monumental report on English houses titled *Das Englische Haus*. His conclusion was that for the first time in its history England had discovered new artistic ground and 'was pointing the way to the world and the world was following'.[3] The work of Norman Shaw, for instance, was well known in the United States through magazines and exerted a strong influence on American domestic architecture.

Whilst English architecture gained a global reputation, English architects were gaining professional recognition. The Royal Institute of British Architects had been formed in 1834, giving a distinct identity and voice to an emerging profession. Routes into architectural design at first remained much as they had been; designers either came up through the building and craft trades or established practitioners took pupils into their offices, where they learnt drawing and measuring before branching out on their own. The building industry, however, was diversifying fast. Architectural competitions and the practice of tendering large construction projects meant that architects produced ever more detailed drawings and specifications – and became increasingly expert in contracts. Training therefore increased in importance, and from 1840 civil engineering and architecture was taught at King's College, London; the following year University College, London, appointed its first professor of architecture, T. L. Donaldson. Neither institutions taught design as such, but both prepared students for pupillage. In 1847 the first English school for architectural design – the Architectural Association – was founded.

Not everyone thought that these developments were healthy. Most architects practising in Gothic styles considered the best training to be drawing old buildings; writers such as John Ruskin thought that architects should study with painters and sculptors rather than receiving a technical education. In contrast, architects working in classical styles increasingly believed that there were rules to be mastered – and that here the new colleges and the RIBA could help. Their model was the École des Beaux-Arts in France, a centralised, state-run academy for architects with a system of examinations and accreditation. After a few tentative steps, in 1882 the RIBA inaugurated a compulsory membership examination and five years later instituted a three-stage examination system. As only 20 per cent of architects were members of the Institute at the time, many looked askance at what was being implemented, largely those who believed it vital to retain the links between design and craftsmanship.

After 1900 such views were increasingly outmoded. Liverpool University had founded a full-time architectural course in 1895 and within ten years had wholeheartedly adopted the Beaux-Arts formula, training architects who focused on design and coordination rather than craft, construction or engineering. In 1909 two hundred students were enrolled, some of whom were women. Women had been previously been admitted into pupillage, and Ethel Charles had become the first female member of the RIBA in 1898. But it took until the 1920s for it to be common for women to enter the profession, and until 1929 for Elizabeth Scott to be the first woman to design a public building.[4]

Technological Advances

As England entered the 20th century technology continued to stimulate architectural innovation but the lead that Britain had once enjoyed over the rest of the world was substantially eroded. The heroic innovations of the first half of

Fig. 480 (left) The Ritz Hotel, Piccadilly, London, Charles Mewès and Arthur Davis with Sven Bylander 1903–6. The photograph shows the hotel under construction in 1905. This was the capital's first substantial steel frame building.

the 19th century were not to be repeated, and French, German and American expertise became as important as native invention. Part of the problem was, ironically, Britain's head start. Rules introduced as a result of unregulated commercial innovation between 1830 and 1870 held English innovation back.

We have seen that steel became a common building material in the 1870s (p. 404) but it was not in Britain that the possibilities of mass-produced, prefabricated steel framing were fully developed. English architects looked to the US, in particular to Chicago, where regular steel frames were being introduced with standardised sections in the 1880s. In 1903 César Ritz commissioned the architects Charles Mewès and Arthur J. Davis to build him a hotel on Piccadilly. They turned to Sven Bylander, a Swedish engineer who had worked in New York, to design a regular steel frame that was clad by Mewès and Davis with elegant French-style stone façades (fig. 480). The foundations were piled rather than being on a concrete rafts – another first for London. Despite these structural innovations, the London Building Acts still applied and – unnecessarily – the walls at ground level had to be over three feet thick because of the Ritz's height. Soon Bylander was employed by the Chicago retailer Gordon Selfridge to build an entirely new sort of shop – Selfridges – on Oxford Street (fig. 538). This challenged the restrictive Building Acts head on. Selfridge wanted big glazed windows at street level and uninterrupted space inside, instead of compartmentalised rooms for fire-safety. Various waivers were obtained to allow the shop to be built; by 1909 the London County Council had changed the regulations. Selfridges went up in a year and soon both English architects and engineers were sold on steel framing with standardised sections and joints.

From the 1860s concrete had begun to play a larger role in the construction of big buildings (pp 390–2). Various types of reinforced concrete had been tried but it was the widespread adoption of the French-patented Hennebique system that transformed its capabilities. This used plain round rods to reinforce columns, beams and floors. Sir Henry Tanner, the chief architect in the Office of Works, had chaired a special committee to look into the use of reinforced concrete and between 1906 and 1909 he was to use it for the first time in a major public building in England. The new General Post Office, to replace the building by Smirke of 1829, was built on a reinforced concrete grid that had spans twice as wide as those achievable in steel or iron. As a Crown building it was exempt from the Building Acts and Tanner deliberately used this fact to demonstrate, in a hugely ambitious way, the capabilities of the new material.[5]

After the First World War Owen Williams became the leading practitioner in concrete construction systems and was appointed consultant engineer to the British Empire Exhibition at Wembley (p. 493). His Empire Pool Building contained the world's largest indoor swimming pool at the time, spanned by 236ft-span frames. Inside the building these were barely expressed; outside, the frames – spaced at 22ft intervals – were weighted down by vertical concrete fins, giving a striking and angular appearance (fig. 481). This commission helped Williams gain the confidence to branch out on his own. Built between 1932 and 1933, his Boots Wets Building in Beeston, Nottinghamshire, demonstrated,

Fig. 481 (above left) The Empire Pool, now Wembley Arena, Owen Williams, 1933–4. The fins that buttress the trusses can be seen along the left hand side. The pillars on each corner support water tanks.

Fig. 482 (above) The Boots Wets Building, Beeston, Nottingham, Owen Williams, 1932–3. This was for making and packaging creams and medicines. What was new about this building was that it was made of slabs of reinforced concrete that took the load evenly, making beams unnecessary. The columns have mushroom tops where the reinforcing spreads out into the slab above.

perhaps to the alarm of some architects, that an engineer could build something of sublime elegance and novelty with concrete and steel alone (fig. 482). That such a building could be built at all owed a great deal to the fact that, at the time, Boots was owned by the American United Drugs Company, which provided a very detailed brief to Williams. The building, arranged around two atria, was a four-storey structure built of concrete slabs, supported by regularly spaced mushroom-shaped columns and wrapped around with a glass curtain. It was completed in 1933 and opened by the chairman's wife who, as if launching a liner, broke a bottle of scent against it.

As steel and concrete construction was being perfected electricity was being developed as a commercial power source. Although Sir Humphry Davy had demonstrated the arc light as early as 1808 it took a long time for a commercially effective electric light to be made. Early advances came from France and it was only in the 1870s that British firms were making portable generators with lighting rigs. There was a breakthrough, however, in 1880, when Joseph Swan of Newcastle upon Tyne invented the light bulb. That year he installed his bulbs at Cragside, the house of the armaments manufacturer Sir William Armstrong, which had, ten years before, been the first in the world to have its own power station. Light bulbs were soon installed elsewhere, such as in theatres (p. 495) and public buildings. In 1881 the town council of Godalming, Surrey, decided to switch from gas to electricity for its street lighting, and the world's first public electricity supply was born. The adoption of electric light was not a smooth story, partly because it was feared that the new electricity companies would create local supply monopolies, just as the gas companies had done. For this reason electric lighting legislation encouraged a multitude of independent generation companies to ensure strong price competition.[6]

Despite electric trams and trains (p. 482), and the widespread use of electricity in the homes of the rich, in 1910 London's streets were still lit by gas, and power stations were privately run, small-scale and dispersed across the metropolis. In 1914 there were fifty-nine distributors of electricity supplying seventy-two different varieties of current. This was not the case elsewhere; in New York, a city that generated more electrical power than all the stations in Britain put together, there was a system of large, centralised power stations.

It took until 1926 to solve the problem of fragmentation. In that year the Central Electricity Board was set up to build a national supply grid, linking power stations in England and Wales. These would be obliged to sell power to the Board, which, in turn, would sell electricity to local suppliers. The creation of the National Grid had an enormous impact on the English countryside. Whilst canals and railways had cut lines through the landscape, and telegraph and telephone poles had carried wires across hills and fields, 70ft-high steel towers – soon to be called pylons in homage to the fascination with all things Egyptian after the discovery of Tutankhamun – were a different matter.

These pylons were designed by Central Electricity Board engineers based on a submission by the American firm Milliken Brothers, although they also consulted the distinguished architect Sir Reginald Blomfield. Between 1927 and 1933 26,265 pylons were erected and 4,000 miles of cable slung between them (fig. 483). The Grid selected one hundred and sixty-two power stations as its principal suppliers, and as a result hundreds of small stations closed over the following years. The selected stations supplied alternating current (AC) that could be transmitted at high voltage over long distances; local stations had previously supplied direct current (DC) that could be stored in accumulators but only transmitted a short way. To supply high-pressure AC a number of 'super-stations' were built by private companies. The model for these was the huge power station at Deptford designed by Sebastian Ziani de Ferranti, which supplied a pioneering 10,000-volt AC supply. With its massive turbine hall and two chimneys, the station ran at full power from 1891. The first, largest and most architecturally pretentious of the new stations was at Battersea, sited on the Thames to allow both for coal delivery and cooling. The engineers S. L. Pearce and H. N. Allot produced the design, based on a steel frame clad in brick and roofed with reinforced concrete; the chimneys were also cast in concrete. The station was to be built in two stages, the first stage being completed between 1929 and 1935. The external brickwork was designed by Theo Halliday but much of the detailing is down to Sir Giles Gilbert Scott, who was responsible, for instance, for the ornamentation of the upper levels and bases of the chimneys (fig. 484).

Fig. 483 (above) A standard 1928 design PL1 pylon to take 132KV.

Fig. 484 (right) Battersea Power Station, London in 1934, showing station A, built in 1929–35. Station B was built to the right in 1937–41 and a fourth chimney added in 1955. It closed in 1983.

Power stations that were on rivers, such as Battersea, beside the sea or that had cooling ponds had no need for special machinery to cool or recycle water. Urban power stations, however, developed timber cooling towers to do the job. These had a short life-span and in 1917 Dutch engineers invented a cooling tower in the shape of a hyperbolic curve and built in reinforced concrete. The design was taken up by the engineer L. G. Mouchel, who had been the British agent for the Hennebique system of reinforced concrete. Mouchel & Partners came to dominate the market in cooling towers, building one hundred and fifty-seven in Britain alone. The first were at Lister Drive Power Station in 1924. These were nearly 130ft tall and 100ft wide at the base, which was perforated to allow a natural draught to condense the water. Groups of such towers were soon to become a common and dominating sight in the English countryside.

Electricity had a huge impact on the geography of industry, the National Grid liberating factories from their proximity to coal fields. But the greatest impact of electricity was perhaps in the home. Consumption rose steeply in the 1930s, although despite the rapid construction of the Grid 30 per cent of British homes remained without electricity in 1935. Many people actively preferred to cook with gas. And by 1939 the only common electrical devices across social divides were lighting, the iron and the wireless. Middle-class households, however, took advantage of a much wider range of electrical goods, amongst which were vacuum cleaners, washing machines and, eventually, refrigerators.

The Languages of Polite Architecture

In around 1870 there was a revolution in architectural taste. The Gothic revival had run its course and an entirely new architectural expression was developed. The ideas that underpinned this were well established, but their expression was novel. The various languages of architecture fashionable between 1870 and 1939 were still inspired by a historical lexicon, but the range of styles from which they drew – and the reasons for admiring them – changed. The most important difference discernible is a new confidence. Skilled architects were able to create buildings of great originality, vigour and functional success, freed from the anxiety of how to correctly compose them.[7]

In these years we struggle, more than in most, with a plethora of art-historical terms attempting to categorise what was happening: Arts and Crafts, Queen Anne, Edwardian Baroque, Wrenaissance, Art Deco are amongst them. The reason so many buildings are hard to neatly categorise is because many architects sought to synthesise historical styles into blends that suited their purposes. Underlying that synthesis are perhaps four defining impulses. It is by considering these that we can begin to make better sense of what was happening.

The first impulse is nationalism. The strong nationalistic streak that had been so apparent in the architecture of Pugin and others in the mid 19th century re-emerged in the 1870s, becoming a powerful force from the 1890s. There were many reasons for this, but the patriotic content was now imperialistic, a tone reinforced by Queen Victoria's Diamond Jubilee, the coronations of Edward VII and George V, and the First World War. Architects returned to English sources for inspiration, to periods of perceived English greatness and architectural fertility. Fundamental to this was a revival of the study of English architectural history. In 1897 Reginald Blomfield published *A History of Renaissance Architecture in England 1500–1800*, in which the climax comes with the work of Sir Christopher Wren, whom he saw as the most English of English architects. In 1911 Thomas Garner and Arthur Stratton published *The Domestic Architecture of England during the Tudor Period*, in the Introduction to which they extolled Tudor architecture as indigenous, national and impossible to be imitated in other countries.

The second impulse was a desire to escape from the mechanisation that industrialisation had introduced into English design. John Ruskin had already thrown down a challenge to the machine age in his championing of a revival of individual craftsmanship. William Morris, inspired by Ruskin's *The Stones of Venice*, founded Morris & Co., specialising in all the arts and crafts involved in building and interior decoration. Like Pugin, Morris was as important to English architecture for what he believed as for what he designed. He set out to restore the broken links between art and workers, and thereby to transform people's everyday environment. This was not just about art for the well-off but good design for everyone, everywhere. Under the influence of these ideas architects looked to those periods in English architecture in which craftsmen still made a major contribution. The Tudor period and the 17th century were, rightly, seen as golden ages of craftsmanship, when architect and master craftsmen worked together hand in hand.[8]

Fig. 485 (below) Alliance Assurance Office, St James's, London, Richard Norman Shaw, 1881–3. As well as offices it housed shops and four floors of flats. The inspiration is Flemish 16th century with, perhaps, a pinch of France.

Propriety was the third impulse. Whilst the Gothic style had never been ubiquitous, and Italianate or neo-classical styles had always been used, the Gothic Revival had shown how absurd it was to attempt to build everything – from town halls to swimming baths, from railway stations to urinals – in a single style. After 1870 there was a return to a much stronger notion of propriety. As a result, whilst most domestic architecture settled into comfortable vernacular styles, public buildings were built either in heroic classical modes or, after the First World War, in Georgian; buildings associated with new technologies tended to be minimally classicist. Churches were the only buildings that were still built in a Gothic style.

The fourth notion was simply reaction. The anxieties that had wracked architects in the 19th century seemed to provide them with irreconcilable choices between individual and competing styles. The reaction to this for the new generation was not to choose but to synthesise. What Richard Norman Shaw did in his Alliance Assurance Office in St James's (1881–3) was to plump for neither Gothic nor classical. Like English and Flemish 17th-century architects he combined them (fig. 485). The new generation of buildings reacting against High Victorian Gothic defied categorisation. Architectural critics wanted to give the new look a name – oddly it became known as 'Queen Anne' – but others wanted to call it free-classic or even Re-Renaissance. Here I will refer to all its manifestations as classical freestyle.

The earliest two significant buildings in which all of these impulses can be discerned were both built in 1871. First was a house designed by the architect J. J. Stevenson for himself in Bayswater. Stevenson had worked in the office of George Gilbert Scott and was part of a circle of architects all of whom were thinking the same way about design. The formula at the Red House was in some ways simple; it was a building that arranged English 17th-century decorative details in brick on the framework of a traditional early 19th-century town house. It was instantly attractive and instantly imitated. The second building was by Richard Norman Shaw, the leading architect of his day, who inspired more than any other designer a return to English architectural forms. New Zealand Chambers was a commercial office block in the City of London that immediately commanded attention, presenting a Jacobean façade to the street, almost all glass, with rich, pre-Great Fire detailing (fig. 486).[9]

This comfortable, quirky English style perfectly suited upper-middle-class aspirations. Unlike the big, heavily detailed Gothic it replaced it was small-scale and pretty. Indeed, in a sense, it was a bourgeois style first patronised by people who had social, political and economic freedom, and only then taken up by others. An illustration of this was the growing fashion for mansion blocks in central London. In the 1870s the well-off middle classes were presented with a new opportunity. If they couldn't afford to buy a house centrally and disliked the idea of moving to the suburbs, a flat was an excellent alternative. The new blocks, of which there were scores, had to look impressive from the outside, even if rents were very reasonable. Richard Norman Shaw designed Albert Hall Mansions in 1879 after visiting Paris to study apartment plans (fig. 487). For the more discerning his classical freestyle became the language of choice for an apartment block. Thus, although the revolution in taste that took place in the 1870s was anti-modern, anti-industrial and anti-urban, it embraced modernity and technology as eagerly as had the previous generation.[10]

Fig. 486 (below) New Zealand Chambers, Leadenhall Street, City of London, Richard Norman Shaw 1871. A masterpiece, now sadly demolished.

Architects all over the world were searching for a mode of national architectural expression in the early 20th century and it seemed to many that the English had found it. The discovery was, in fact, a rediscovery of vernacular traditions, of cottages and farmhouses of the 16th century and of the small houses of the first half of the 17th century. Both these periods were seen as being homespun ones that were particularly English, in which individuality abounded and rules were broken. As we shall see, this style exercised a huge influence over domestic architecture across the social scale (fig. 497), but it was also used in commercial buildings (fig. 534), pubs (fig. 465), theatres (fig. 525) and shops (fig. 537). In skilful hands it led to delight; in less capable ones to decorative chaos.

This architectural language was, however, fundamentally unsuited to public buildings – it was deliberately domestic and vernacular. So a parallel route was adopted. This also drew on English 17th-century models, particularly the work of Wren, Hawksmoor and Vanbrugh. It was a classical language that deliberately broke the rules, combining and re-combining elements, and frequently including high-quality sculpture, a demonstration of the union of architecture and art. John Belcher's Institute of Chartered

Accountants of 1893 was a building that helped establish both the use of external sculpture and the fashion for monumental classical freestyle in public architecture. With the completion of the Victoria Memorial in Westminster (p. 468) it became the accepted style of government and corporations.

The First World War did nothing to persuade the English that they should turn from an admiration for England's past to a more hard-edged architecture of steel, concrete and industry; the war made people yearn for tradition and history. In this they were not alone, but architectural expression in England was more single-minded than in other European countries. What was different after the war was a move away from vernacular and rural models and a rediscovery of the urbanism of the Georgian era. The Georgians were perceived as being more cosmopolitan, more European and less xenophobic than the Victorians, inhabiting a refined world before the materialism and consumerism of the Victorian age. In the 1920s and 30s high society adopted Georgian as a way of decluttering and simplifying both architecture and interior decoration.

As we have seen, associations of classical architecture were different for every generation. The Edwardians admired the inventive classicism of Wren, Hawksmoor and Vanbrugh for its bombastic and nationalistic character and craftsmanship. In the inter-war years it was the Georgians to whom English architects turned. A minimalist sort of classicism associated with a world built after a long, hard and cruel European war: a world of political and social turmoil that managed to produce an ordered and elegant architectural expression. Thus when Hugh Grosvenor, 2nd Duke of Westminster, resolved to redevelop Grosvenor Square in 1932 he commissioned Fernand Billerey and Detmar Blow to design ranges of monumental flats in the Georgian style (fig. 488).[11]

Fig. 487 (top) Albert Hall Mansions, Kensington, London, Richard Norman Shaw, 1879. This vast mansion block towering over the Albert Hall set the tone for hundreds of imitators.

Fig. 488 (above) Grosvenor Square, Westminster, London, north side, built 1932–69. The grandiose centrepiece features giant Corinthian columns.

Like the Grosvenor Square flats all forms of architecture became gradually more minimalist during the 1930s. Details were stripped away, forms were reduced to their essentials. Sir Edwin Lutyens believed that what he called the essence of classicism was important; this allowed him to dispense with the decoration and produce a sort of abstraction of ancient architecture. His most remarkable English public building was the Midland Bank of 1924 on Poultry in the City of London (fig. 489). The use of massive steel frames enabled the façades of contemporary buildings such as this to be more playful and here he toyed with a rustication that fades in and out. The whole building gradually contracts as it rises, with each course of stone being an eighth of an inch less in height than the course below.

This type of abstraction was also practised by Charles Holden in his University of London Senate House, where he demonstrated again that he was brilliant at making a big building interesting and lively. Whilst clearly a building of the 20th century – it was built between 1932 and 1937 – its proportions make it look like piled-up sections of Georgian Bloomsbury, balconies and all. An almost exactly contemporary building by Sir Giles Gilbert Scott was the University Library in Cambridge, completed in 1934. Like Senate House, which of course contains a library, the great stack was in a tower (fig. 491). As befits Cambridge the library is in brick and is more abstracted than Holden's Senate House. More abstracted still is the monumental ventilation and control system of George's Dock at the Pier Head in Liverpool. This remarkable structure was designed by Herbert J. Rowse and built in 1932. The lower parts are anchored in the classical language but as the building rises it becomes increasingly abstract. As well as offices the buildings contained massive fans that ventilated the first Mersey road tunnel.

The designers of all of these buildings were working in a recognised traditional framework. But from the 1920s there were some, aware of developments in Germany and France, who wanted to work more closely in an international modernist style. They saw a counterpoint between traditionalism and modernism, or perhaps more acutely internationalism and indigenous culture. They possessed a belief in the rationalism of design, an engineering aesthetic and a socialist programme. Finsbury Health Centre was designed by the Russian architect, Berthold Lubetkin, and his practice Tecton between 1933 and 1935 (fig. 490). The scheme was intended to improve people's lives by centralising healthcare and medical services in a single place, whilst offering patients a bright and clean atmosphere. This was a design to transform the health of Finsbury's working class, who lived in cramped, dark, Victorian conditions. Lubetkin and his team argued that by creating a new architecture that rejected buildings of the past, society could be revitalised and made afresh. The belief in the ability of architecture to transform society was Puginian, although the design ideas and architectural clothing were modern and international.[12] But they were in a minority. Before the Second World War very little was built in England in a modernist style and – with only a very few exceptions – those who did build modern, such as Lubetkin, were not English.

Fig. 489 (above) Midland Bank, Headquarters, Poultry, City of London, Sir Edwin Lutyens, 1924–39. A steel frame liberated the façade from any structural duties. It is strongly classical but without any controlling order.

Fig. 490 (left) Finsbury Health Centre was a design which aimed to transform the health of Finsbury's working class by creating a new architecture that rejected buildings of the past, thus allowing society to be revitalised and made afresh.

The Hub of Empire

Although London in 1870 was easily the largest city in the world and the place from which a vast empire was ruled it was rarely a city en fête, unlike Napoleon III's Paris. Queen Victoria had withdrawn from public life in 1861 after the death of Prince Albert and royal spectacle on the capital's streets was virtually unknown. London did have some ceremonial routes but, other than Regent Street, they were serpentine medieval ways quite unlike the boulevards laid down by the rulers of Berlin, Vienna or Paris. In July 1867 London was shaken out of this torpor by the glittering state welcome given to the Sultan of Turkey and the Viceroy of Egypt. It was as if the city had suddenly realised its place at the centre of world power and influence.[13]

This realisation highlighted the distinctions between London the city and London the capital, and between local and national interests. From 1832 to 1885 representation in parliament was heavily weighted against London and rural MPs consistently opposed spending on the metropolis. However, the opening of the new Thames Embankment by the Prince of Wales in 1870 showed that government rather than ratepayers' money could be spent on embellishment and improvement, but the problem remained that there was no London-wide government to champion the city. The formation of the London County Council (LCC) in 1889 was a decisive moment, the LCC giving focus to the sprawling mass of disconnected places that London had become. As we shall see, it was to play a crucial role in improving housing (pp 471, 479), providing education and creating a unified transport system (p. 482).

The LCC was to make an important contribution to the public face of London but it was in Whitehall, under the control of central government, that changes first became apparent. The start was the construction of the Foreign Office between 1862 and 1865 (pp 417–8), followed by the erection of a series of huge new government ministries between 1870 and 1914. However desirable these might have been as expressions of national prestige, there were intensely practical reasons for them. In the 1850s there were 64,000 civil servants, By the mid 1890s there were 150,000, most of whom were employed within a five-minute walk of parliament. Their spacious new offices were built in the patriotic Portland stone classicism of Wren and Vanbrugh, although Inigo Jones's Banqueting House set some of the local tone.

Fig. 491 (below) Sir Giles Gilbert Scott Cambridge University Library, 1931–4, dominated by the 157ft-high tower containing a book stack.

The most impressive and influential were the New Government Offices – now the Treasury – designed by J. M. Brydon in 1898 and built in phases up to 1915 (the design was modified by Sir Henry Tanner). It is a measure of the skill of the architect, who was experienced at designing municipal buildings, that this Goliath of an office block was a pleasing success. An extraordinary reprise of the work of Wren's office, in some ways it was more successful than the work of the master in its boldness and lack of fussy detail (fig. 492). The new Whitehall that emerged in gleaming-white Portland stone became the backdrop for the royal jubilees of 1887 and 1897 and the coronations of 1902 and 1910. These events strengthened a popular sense of London as imperial capital and led, in turn, to the creation of a national memorial to Queen Victoria.

Fig. 492 (above) The Treasury (originally New Government Offices), Parliament Street, Westminster, J. M. Brydon (and others), 1898–1915.

Fig. 493 (left) Admiralty Arch, Trafalgar Square, Westminster, Sir Aston Webb, 1905–7, built 1908–11. The building was designed to be pompous but to fund it, it contained offices and other utilitarian functions. The geometry was complex as this picture shows – a fact brilliantly concealed on the ground.

Admiralty Arch, the Mall, the Victoria Memorial and the re-facing of Buckingham Palace were largely funded by private subscription in memory of the late queen. The architectural mastermind overseeing this was Sir Aston Webb, perhaps the most commercially successful architect of his age. It was a grand conception and quite unlike anything achieved in England before: a broad new avenue cut through St James's Park to Trafalgar Square centred on a colossal Carrara marble memorial to the queen by the sculptor Thomas Brock. At the Trafalgar Square end there was to be a triumphal arch (fig. 493) and, at the other, the façade of the palace was re-clad in Portland stone. This last element was added to the scheme as subscriptions flooded in. Arguments about who should pay for the arch demonstrate, however, that national pride in the project did not lead to generous backing either from government or the LCC.[14]

The LCC were primarily interested in improving the metropolis as a place to live rather than ornamenting it as the hub of empire. It was this motivation that led to the grandiose project to cut a new road through from the Strand to Holborn. Kingsway, as it was eventually known, was primarily a scheme of slum clearance and traffic-flow improvement (including a long tram tunnel), although it did have the effect of creating a magnificent, 100ft-wide new boule-

Fig. 494 (above) Gallaher House (originally Kodak House), Kingsway, London, Sir John Burnet, 1911. Refined modern classicism at its most minimal.

Fig. 495 (below right) County Hall, Lambeth, London, designed by Ralph Knott in 1908, started in 1912 but not completed until 1922 (other parts later). The river façade is 700ft long but never monotonous, only massive, imposing and melodramatic.

vard on Parisian lines. It was only partly funded by ratepayers; most of the necessary funds were raised through the sale of property on the twenty-eight-acre site. Architecturally, the LCC did want grandeur. They ran a competition and encouraged entries in monumental classicism. Although the intended single design was never executed, over a thirty-year period Kingsway and the great crescent at its southern end, Aldwych, now illustrate the whole gamut of imperial classical styles. These ran from the inventive and rich – but now demolished – Gaiety Theatre of 1902–3, whose elevations by Richard Norman Shaw brilliantly held the corner at the east end of the Strand, to Kodak House – now Gallaher House – on Kingsway by Sir John Burnet. Here, in 1911, Burnet stripped away almost all classical decoration whilst preserving the rules and proportions of classical design – Lutyens's 'essence' (fig. 494).[15]

There were other road improvement schemes, but the Mall and Kingsway were as close as London came to the boulevards of Paris. Meanwhile, central government did invest in fine public buildings – the Natural History Museum by Alfred Waterhouse (1872–86), the Victoria and Albert Museum by Aston Webb (1899–1909) and the extension to the British Museum by J. J. Burnet (1905–14) – whilst private enterprise rebuilt much of Trafalgar Square and Regent Street. It was, however, the LCC that created perhaps the most impressive monument: County Hall.[16]

County Hall was the product of a struggle within the LCC between proponents of efficiency of operation, architectural presence and economy. In choosing a design from the competition entries the last was stressed. But the design – by a brilliant young pupil of Sir Aston Webb, who had built nothing himself – made much of a little. Ralph Knott's building was started in 1912 but was interrupted by war, and the 700ft-long river façade was only completed in 1933 (fig. 495). Although the elevation could be characterised as plain, even austere, it succeeds in being very grand by the insertion of a pillared crescent in the central section and the construction of giant, rusticated pavilions at either end. The whole English 18th-century classical canon of Hawksmoor, Dance, Chambers and others was mined for inspiration. This building asserts London's presence as a political entity but also as a global one.[17]

Housing the Multitude

From the middle of the 19th century local authorities, armed with powers from central government began – slowly at first, then much more quickly from the 1880s – to raise the standard of housing by passing by-laws. Speculators who obeyed these usually did so to minimum standards, and streets of these so-called by-law houses are easily recognisable where they survive. They were built in terraces of varying length, cut by tunnels (known as ginnels in the north) that led to individual backyards with privies and sometimes a coal house. Front doors opened directly on to the pavements of long, treeless streets. The two-up, two-down houses in Albert Street, Bristol, were typical in having rooms of around 12ft by 9ft, but were larger than some due to a back extension with a scullery (fig. 496).

These houses were much more self-contained than those they replaced; instead of sharing privies, yards and even kitchens, they were built as individual units. Public space – the courts of the back-to-backs – disappeared, and houses were now built on roads where light and air could get in and people could create a private world of domesticity behind doors and walls. The effects of this can be seen at Nelson, more specifically Whitefield, the most complete Victorian townscape in Pennine Lancashire, with its mix of houses, mills, weaving sheds, church and school, all integrated with a canal. The majority of the buildings date from 1860 to 1890 and each house is a tight, self-contained unit with its own little backyard. Crucially, this contained the privy with its own little hatch to allow excrement, neutralised by ashes or soil, to be taken away each night.

As by-laws created opportunities for more individualistic domesticity, so, by the 1890s, technology began liberate families, and in particular women, from domestic drudgery. As we have seen, gas had been used for street lighting and in commercial and industrial buildings, but for domestic use it was less effective until the invention of the incandescent mantle in 1885. This made it possible to have bright, efficient lighting at home. Other gas appliances were rapidly adopted: the gas geyser – an instant water heater – was invented in 1865, and by the 1870s the gas cooking range and the gas ring were well established. Finally, in 1880, an effective gas fire was marketed. To begin with these benefited the upper and middle classes but the gas slot meter, pioneered in Liverpool and then introduced into London, was to transform domestic life for all. Pay-as-you-go brought gas into the houses of millions of working-class Britons. The system caught on quickly; the South Metropolitan Company in London had installed only 439 meters by 1892 but by the end of 1898 there were 80,115.

Gas in the kitchen, in particular, changed the way working-class people lived. Coal ranges were dirty and had to be lit the whole time, whilst gas could be used on demand. Cooking now moved out to the back scullery rather than the kitchen, and by 1900 the kitchen had become the everyday living and dining room. Many working-class sculleries by this date also had piped water, and 50 per cent of houses in Manchester and Birmingham had water closets.[18]

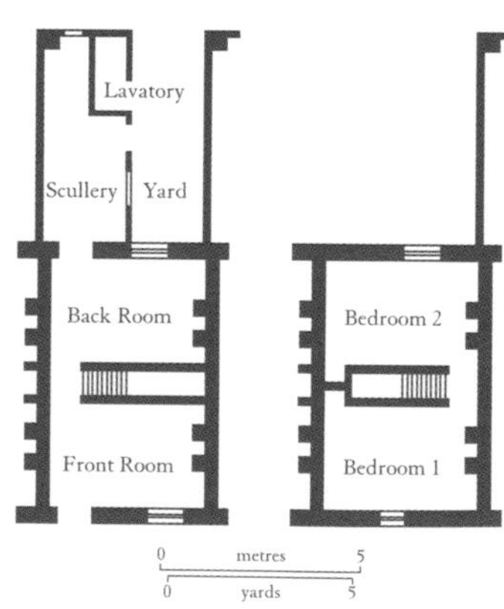

Fig. 496 (above) The two-up, two-down houses in Albert Street, Bristol, were built as individual units with their own privies and kitchens.

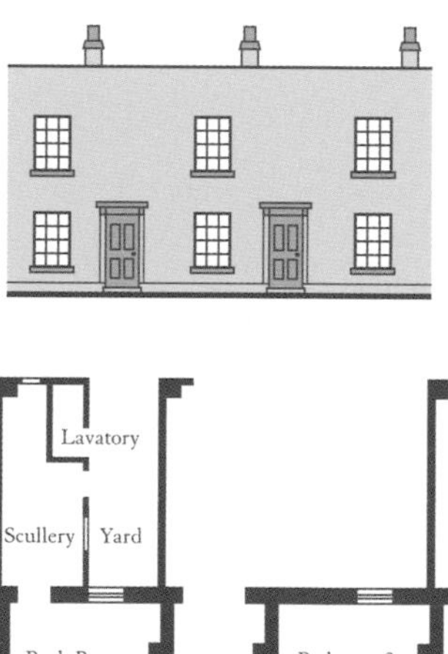

Fig. 497 (above) Boundary Street Estate, Bethnal Green, from 1893. The flats were innovative, elegant and well laid out but facilities were limited: many flats were not self-contained and some tenants had to share sculleries and lavatories.

There is a danger, however, in painting too rosy a picture. Many builders evaded the by-laws and, more importantly, the law could do nothing about the huge numbers of sub-standard houses in which people already lived in horrible poverty. Many realised that speculation would never solve this problem, and that collective action and, possibly, state subsidy would be needed. From the 1850s various charities had built blocks of apartments for working-class rent, limiting investment return to 5 per cent. Although numerically these buildings by so-called 5 per cent charities such as the Peabody Trust made little difference, they represented a break in English building practice. Apartment blocks, whilst the rule in Scotland and in some parts of the continent, were a novelty in England; but these new buildings demonstrated that high-density housing, to a good sanitary standard, could be built in inner cities. The early Peabody blocks were grim barracks in appearance, barely distinguishable from workhouses. It was the application of classical freestyle design principles that made these places into attractive dwellings for urban workers.

The breakthrough came in the East End of London in a desperate quarter of Bethnal Green, where one in four children died in infancy in 1883. Two developments meant that it was now possible to deal with the area's appalling problems. The first was the creation of London's first elected authority – the LCC – in 1889, which was dominated in its first years by progressive liberals. The second was a Royal Commission on the Housing of the Working Classes that reported in 1885, revealing in horrific, empirical detail the problems of overcrowding, disease and child mortality. This led to the Housing of the Working Classes Act in 1890 that empowered the LCC not only to clear the slums but to replace them. Their architects' department planned the new Boundary Street Estate in Bethnal Green in 1893, where, after some experimentation, they built between 1895 and 1900 a handsome series of brick blocks in classical freestyle laid out around a central circus and broad, tree-lined avenues (fig. 497).[19]

Council-built housing made few inroads before the First World War; more common was housing built by industrialists around their factories. The best-known practitioner was Titus Salt, who built Saltaire, West Yorkshire, for his workers as a model for the nation to follow. But the next generation of workers' villages was an attempt to get away from hard-edged urban environments and provide workers with the sort of amenities possessed by the suburban middle classes. W. H. Lever, George Cadbury and Joseph Rowntree all presented varying solutions to the problems of industrialised urban communities. Port Sunlight, on the Wirral, Merseyside, named after Lever's most successful product, Sunlight Soap, was begun in 1888 and set out to be anti-urban. It was a low-density village, with curving roads, open front gardens and half-timbered houses in clumps. A total of seven hundred and twenty houses were built, together with a hall, shop, church, school, social club, inn and more.[20]

Port Sunlight was much visited and discussed, capturing the imagination of Ebenezer Howard, a young and clever parliamentary reporter who was fascinated by urban social and economic problems. He proposed the idea of creating what he called garden cities – settlements built by a private com-

Fig. 498 (left) Letchworth Garden City; a view showing the town centre and the town hall in a Georgian style by Bennett and Bidwell, 1935. It overlooks Broadway Gardens.

pany that was limited to paying dividends of 5 per cent and that would hold the town in trust for its residents whilst reinvesting profits for the benefit of the community. These places were to meld town and country in a happy union. His ideas were published in 1902 as *Garden Cities of Tomorrow*. Letchworth Garden City, launched in 1903 as the first garden city, was planned by Barry Parker and Raymond Unwin. It was a careful and clever plan that fulfilled Howard's vision, with zones for residential, industrial, commercial and amenity areas. Roads with grass verges were tree-lined and houses had hedged front gardens. Open spaces were plentiful (fig. 498). The buildings were Georgian and classical freestyle.[21]

In due course millions would live in estates and suburbs based on garden-city principles. One of the first was developed by the LCC at Totterdown Fields, Tooting, where, between 1903 and 1911, 1,229 houses were built in low-rise vernacular styles in broad, leafy streets. Each had a living room, a kitchen with a sink, a copper for laundry, a coal bunker and, in most cases, a gas cooker. Many, but not all, had bathrooms. Vital to the LCC's strategy was the parallel development of electric trams that would convey workers from their suburban dwellings to their inner-city places of work.[22]

The First World War

When war broke out with Germany in 1914 the last major European conflict that Britain had experienced had taken place almost exactly a hundred years earlier. The defeat of Napoleon at Waterloo in 1815 had ended Britain's military engagement in Europe for a century. In fact since 1871 there had been no war between major European powers, with the result that nobody quite knew what this new war would be like. Those with responsibility for the preparations imagined troops marching to a series of great set-piece battles in which the outcome would be rapidly decided. They were, as we now know, completely wrong.

In August 1914 there was a rush to sign up and it was to Victorian and Edwardian drill halls that volunteers reported. During the Crimean War Britain had relied on the historic county and town militias to boost the numbers of regular troops in the field. This exposed a lack of military capacity and led to the fear that if Britain were sucked into the Second Italian War of Independence that had broken out between France and the Austrian Empire in 1858 it would not be able to cope. So, in 1859 a new Volunteer Rifle Corps was established as a home guard. After 1862 the corps became increasingly centralised and more closely aligned with the regular army until in 1907 they were reconstituted as the Territorial Army. From the 1860s these volunteer bands built themselves drill halls in which to train; in all, as many as 1,800 were built, paid for by voluntary subscription. Their most obvious characteristic was their large central halls, which were normally around 100ft long by perhaps 50–60ft wide and used for marching and weapons practice. Many were built in a quasi-military Tudor style, such as the large and showy hall in Lincoln built at a cost of £10,000, paid for by City industrialist and MP Joseph Ruston, and completed in 1890 to the design of Goddard & Son (fig. 499). As well as the main hall it had, amongst other facilities, a men's club, firing range, armoury and gymnasium.

Fig. 499 (above) Lincoln Drill Hall, Goddard & Son, 1890. This impressive hall adopted a Tudor military style suitable to its function.

In 1914 the network of drill halls was still usable but much military infrastructure was not. The extraordinary programme of coastal fortification undertaken in response to the Napoleonic threat was not repeated in 1914–18. It was generally felt that the Royal Navy would be effective at keeping any attempted invasion at bay. Major naval installations were therefore protected by new gun batteries and smaller ports were given lesser guns, but elsewhere defences were designed to slow down any invading force whilst gaining time for reinforcements to arrive. A network of reinforced-concrete gun emplacements – christened pill boxes for their resemblance to Edwardian pill containers – was built, and long stretches of the east coast were furnished with concrete obstacles and earthworks. Thus the impact of the First World War on the home front was not to be in massive coastal defence but in an entirely new sphere – aerial warfare.

The effective military use of aeroplanes was in its infancy at the start of the war; indeed, there was still an active debate as to whether the way forward would be with balloons or aeroplanes. In 1912 the Royal Flying Corps (RFC) had been founded and in 1914 a separate Naval Air Service was formed. Britain's first military airfield was at Larkhill near Stonehenge, where the first aircraft-storage sheds were built. At the outbreak of war more or less the whole RFC was moved to the front, leaving the defence of the mainland in the hands of the navy, who concentrated on airships to counter German Zeppelins. An airship factory was established at Cardington just outside Bedford between 1916 and 1917, and an enormous 180ft x 700ft x 110ft-high shed was constructed out of steel and corrugated iron to contain them. Although airships continued to be manufactured into the 1930s it became clear that aircraft would be necessary to protect both military and civilian targets against German Zeppelins and bombers. A programme of airfield construction was instituted, particularly on the east coast, which was within range of German airfields.[23]

Airfields on this scale were an entirely new development, requiring a range of novel building types. Most buildings were constructed at great speed out of brick, timber and corrugated iron; runways were grass squares not metalled surfaces. The most challenging structures were aircraft-storage sheds, vital to protect fragile aircraft from the weather. These structures, later to be called 'hangers' (a French term), gradually became more substantial and in 1916 a new type of flight shed was developed – the first in a long line of development. It was built with laminated-timber bow-string trusses 80ft wide with doors at one end, These early trusses were replaced in 1917 by a patented truss system developed in Belfast that was more economical and allowed sheds of multiple spans to be constructed (fig. 500).

In 1918 the Naval Air Service and the RFC were merged into a new service, the Royal Air Force (RAF), a body that consequently had a large number of bases – three hundred and one all told. Most of these were relatively ephemeral structures that were swept away once peace came, but in 1922 Lloyd George's government announced an expansion of the RAF to five hundred planes, resulting in the rehabilitation of many former sites and the establishment of some new ones. In 1934 Prime Minister Baldwin announced that in the face of German rearmament the RAF would be further developed. As a result of these initiatives much new building was undertaken. Few of the resulting structures were significant new building types, most being straightforward brick buildings used for operations; officers' messes and other prestige structures were built in the prevailing Georgian style. Hangers, however, did develop, becoming larger and more robust to cope with ever-larger aircraft. By the 1930s the Type C Aeroplane Shed had 150ft spans, and was 300ft long and 35ft high. These had steel trusses and, being very big and sited in rural areas, were at first clothed as sensitively as possible in brick or occasionally stone, although after 1936 their walls were often made from reinforced concrete.[24]

The war killed a million Britons, known throughout the 1920s as 'the million dead'. The vast majority of bodies were not repatriated, leaving a need for some physical memorial in the home towns and villages of the fallen. There was also a feeling that because many of those who had died, especially before 1916, were volunteers their sacrifice should be recorded. From the beginning of 1916 discussions began as to what sort of memorials might be suitable and various organisations put forward their views. Although there had been memorials for the Boer Wars they had tended to celebrate patriotic purpose with patriotic allegory. The memorials of the First World War were different. Perhaps 100,000 were put up, mainly during the 1920s, mainly by public subscription, and almost all organised on a local basis. They were generally a simple, dignified means of publically recording the names of the fallen; places of gravity and contemplation. Few were of high artistic merit

Fig. 500 (right) Hooton Hanger, Eilesmere Port, one of three completed in 1917 for the Royal Flying Corps. After the war they served as Liverpool Airport until the opening of Speke (fig. 513). The lattice trusses were developed in Belfast from 1866 and had achieved 80ft spans such as this by 1900.

Fig. 501 (below) Cross of Sacrifice, Memorial to the Missing, Thiepval, France. The design of the memorial cross was initiated at the cemetery at Forceville designed by Reginald Bromfield and completed in 1920. His cross, which featured a bronze sword attached to the octagonal shaft, became the standard memorial used by the Imperial War Graves Commission.

but most made a significant impact in the places in which they were erected. Locations were always prominent and created new points of focus, many with gardens or greens laid out with paths.

The most influential monument was the Cross of Sacrifice designed by Sir Reginald Bromfield in 1921 for the Imperial War Graves Commission at Forceville in France. It became a standard memorial to be erected in foreign cemeteries with forty or more burials (fig. 501). The monument had strong echoes of a medieval English country-village cross, raised up on an octagonal base. The cross itself had an inset bronze sword with its blade facing down. It was perhaps this English rural feel that made it such a popular form, copied in tens of thousands of places up and down the country. Crosses by no means had a monopoly; cenotaphs, obelisks and pillars were all popular, as were lych gates, village halls, chapels and even bus shelters. Of these more monumental expressions, the finest is unquestionably the Royal Artillery Monument of 1921–5 at Hyde Park Corner by the brilliant sculptor Charles Sargeant Jagger and Lionel Pearson. It epitomises the sensitivity and reticence found in the best memorials. Yet Jagger had served on the front, and close examination reveals an extraordinary intensity of expression and realism in the reliefs (fig. 502).

Fig. 502 (left) The Royal Artillery Memorial, Hyde Park Corner. The architect Lionel Pearson designed the monumental structure with its stone Howitzer and Charles Jagger was responsible for the sculptures and reliefs. Unlike most monuments, the Royal Artillery Memorial broke away from idealised ideas of a 'beautiful death' to depict the realism and force of war.

Industry and the First World War

War is incredibly expensive to wage, and the First World War was more expensive than any yet. One of the reasons for this was that in November 1914 the conflict settled into a war of attrition between two sides hurling shells and bullets at each other, the production of which was hugely costly. There were new types of weapon, too: mortars, machine guns and, above all, aeroplanes, all of which had to be manufactured. At first the government purchased munitions from private companies but these were unable to cope with the demand and, after the failure of the attack at Aubers Ridge in May 1915 (blame for which was placed on the shortage of high-explosive shells), a Ministry of Munitions was created under Lloyd George. This was one of the defining moments of the war and would, in due course, transform factory production in England. The National Factories, built under the supervision of the Office of Works, were a new type of industrial concern. Never before had such production targets been contemplated, let alone attempted, and to achieve this government took absolute control of machinery, plant, buildings and workforce. There was intense focus on the rapid development of more efficient and scientific methods of production-line manufacture. Almost all of the new National Factories were built on greenfield sites carefully located in relation to road and rail transport and in proximity to a large workforce. Some factories were built together with dormitory towns, complete with shops, schools and churches. The Royal Arsenal at Woolwich was extended by nearly 3.5 million square feet and to house the workers an estate was built at Well Hall, designed on garden-city principles. In all, the Ministry of Munitions spent £4.3 million on building 10,000 houses on 38 sites. The National Factories were mega-concerns; the National Filling Factory at Barnbow near Leeds, built on a greenfield site in 1915, for instance, covered 400 acres, employed 16,000 workers and produced 6,000 shells a day. In 1917 £1.5m was set aside to build three new aircraft factories in Croydon, Liverpool and Richmond, each intended to produce two hundred planes a month.

The ministry recruited 170,000 female workers – a small proportion of the total of 1.3 million women who worked in factories during the war. They were all unskilled and worked alongside trained technicians. This had a number of effects: production lines were more heavily mechanised to save women from heavy lifting, welfare facilities were much better than ever before, and factories were given canteens, washrooms and nurseries. The factories were commissioned from local architects and built by local firms. Almost all were built of brick, steel, timber and corrugated iron. The best surviving National Factory, and one of the finest built, is the National Machine Gun Factory at Burton upon Trent, begun in 1915 to a design by the Enfield Armament Company and intended to make four hundred machine guns a week. It was built by an established local building firm and provided with a rail connection to the main line. Behind the elegant Georgian front office were to be four vast, north-light sheds and various ancillary buildings (fig. 503). The construction of so many factories at such speed was an extraordinary achievement in itself. These drastic measures were hugely successful; shell production, for instance, soared from 500,000 a year in 1914 to a colossal 76.2 million in 1917.[25]

The wartime experience of the Ministry of Munitions had a major effect on the development of the British factory. It showed that factories could be efficiently built in out-of-town estates in which there was plenty of space and where transport facilities – or workers' housing – could be organised to deliver the workforce to the door. Welfare facilities on these estates could be shared, if necessary, amongst businesses. New factories, with large, uninterrupted floor spaces, could contain long, super-efficient production lines that could be easily modified and modernised when needed. As a result many established industries between the wars moved production to greenfield sites on which they built single-storey manufacturing sheds fronted by multi-storey administration blocks of some architectural presence.

We have seen that in 1769 Wedgwood's Etruria Works in Stoke-on-Trent had been amongst the first to bring together in a single complex the processes needed to make ceramics (fig. 363). The firm had traded on their precociousness ever since adopting the slogan 'A Living Tradition'. But that tradition was holding them back. By the 1930s it was clearly inefficient to make pottery in large volume in an antiquated maze of brick buildings. In 1936 a three hundred and eighty-two-acre estate was bought in the nearby village of Barlaston, Staffordshire, where an entirely new factory was built. Keith Murray, an architect and ceramics designer, was appointed to design it in partnership with the architect Charles White. The new factory was long, low and minimally classical, and built with a reinforced concrete frame and brick infill. It was efficiently planned around a vast kiln, with the raw materials entering at one end and finished goods exiting at the other. The factory was the first electrically powered pottery factory and this, as was the case in many new factories, meant the end of polluting black smoke.[26]

Fig. 503 (above) National Machine Gun Factory, Burton upon Trent, H. M. Office of Works, 1915–18. The Georgian-style front office conceals the massive single-storey factory floor behind.

Wallis, Gilbert and Partners were amongst the leading architects producing factories after the war. Their best known is the Firestone Factory in Brentford, commissioned by the American tyre company in 1927 (fig. 504). Here there was an imposing and original front to the two-storey block of offices executed in the Egyptian style. This choice allowed the architects to use eye-catching colour to draw attention to the business's new British HQ and perhaps to emphasise the fun that could be gained by buying its products. Behind was the large, single-storey manufacturing floor with the U-shaped production line and glazed north-roof lights. At the rear were higher buildings for taller machinery and at the back was the power plant with a tall chimney generating electricity for the whole enterprise. Great attention was given to the workers' welfare canteen, hospital, lavatories, cloakrooms, washrooms and personal lockers.[27]

Fig. 504 (above) The Firestone Factory, Brentford, Wallis, Gilbert and Partners 1927–29 (demolished 1980); used flashy American architectural ideas to advertise car tyres to passing motorists. The building mixed fantasy with production line technology.

Housing after the First World War

The First World War had a huge impact on the social policy of successive post-war governments. The scale and the intensity of the conflict involved more or less the whole population and, as the resources to wage all-out war required greater and greater sacrifices, the commitment of the government to make social reforms after the war had ended became part of a sort of unwritten social contract. In other words, as the war progressed it was only possible to continue to fight if there was the prospect of a better world for its survivors.

At the centre of this was housing policy. It had already been realised before the war that private enterprise alone was unlikely to bring about changes in the quality and quantity of the housing stock with sufficient speed. By 1918 it had become accepted that it would be necessary to use central government finance to subsidise local-authority house-building schemes. In 1918 there was already a shortage of around 600,000 houses in England and by 1921 this number was a little over 800,000. As a consequence, many returning servicemen found the situation to be worse than it was when they had gone off to fight, and were forced to move in with their parents or in-laws. Private investors were not building new rented accommodation as rents had been legally capped in 1915 at 1914 levels. There was simply no money in speculative rented housing for investors.

A plethora of committees, Acts of Parliament and regulations between 1918 and 1925 attempted to tackle the problem. These had the effect of specifying what was felt to be acceptable accommodation for working people in terms of size and layout, and then setting out what was believed to be the best way to plan new settlements. The influence of the garden cities and of classical freestyle was everywhere. Before the war it had been the middle classes who had moved out of city centres to create suburbia. After 1919 the decision to build new houses on the principle of the garden city meant that all new working-class housing would be far from city centres, where the crowded and discredited houses of the past had been.

Probably the most spectacular example of this is the work undertaken by the LCC, which built huge estates outside London. The largest of these was the Becontree Estate, begun in 1921 and designed as a cottage-garden estate, in which parks, gardens and green spaces were as important as houses. Over three hundred acres of former farmland were compulsorily purchased in Dagenham, Ilford and Barking, and a 500ft jetty was built on the Thames so that building materials could be brought in by barge. It took over ten years to construct and when finished was the largest estate in the world. Its 27,000 houses provided new homes for over 100,000 people. They were intended for the better-off working-class Londoner and most were large – two-thirds of interwar council houses had three bedrooms. All were fitted with gas and electricity, inside WCs, fitted baths, and front and back gardens.

The enormous expansion in housing after the First World War was not confined to state-subsidised estates for the working classes. In fact, of the four million houses built between 1918 and 1939, 2.5m were built by speculators and bought privately. This was a revolution in home ownership for middle-class people, one made possible by 95 per cent mortgages, mortgage tax relief and Building Societies brimming with deposits. Now any family with an annual income of £350–400 could afford to buy a home, and millions did; by 1939 nearly 60 per cent of middle-class families were owner occupiers.

This huge upsurge in house building coincided with a radical redistribution of land ownership brought about by deep-seated changes in agriculture. From the 1870s England was increasingly reliant on importing food; while British farmers had produced 80 per cent of the nation's foodstuffs in the 1860s, by 1913 they produced only 45 per cent, while the rest was imported. Wheat prices halved between the 1870s and the 1890s and the price of wool fell by 40 per cent. The landed aristocracy was heavily hit. Rents had to be reduced by up to 40 per cent in grain areas and, from the 1880s, many of the big estates began to dispose of land. These sales reached a peak after the War with half a million acres up for sale in 1919 alone. In fact, in the years around the First World War a quarter of the land in England changed hands.[28]

The dispersal of the great estates allowed landownership on a much broader basis in the countryside, but importantly it also released huge amounts of land for housing development. 860,000 houses were built in rural areas in 1918–1939, of these 700,000 were privately built and the majority were in the south of England. As there were virtually no planning restrictions houses were constructed in estates along existing roads forming what came to be known as ribbon development. This had a huge impact on the appearance of both towns and the countryside. Most houses were designed by the speculative building firms that constructed them, the majority were semi-detached and in the 1920s were built in neo-Georgian styles and in the 1930s in vernacular Tudor styles.

In 1851 Sidcup, Kent, had a population of 390. The arrival of the suburban railway meant that people could commute to London and by 1901 its population had grown to around 6,000. By 1939 40,000 lived there – most in brand-new houses, many built by the country's largest house builder New Ideal Homesteads Ltd. This firm, that advertised its houses in Sidcup as 'Designed by a Woman for Women', built 4,000 houses around London in 1933 alone.[29]

These developments were a radical and, in many parts of the country, stark change. By the eve of the Second World War 30 per cent of all English houses were new, and new with vastly more space and better facilities. This transformed the lives of millions. One of the new characteristics for men, in particular, was that they no longer lived close to where they worked. It now became necessary to commute. There was a massive explosion of tram and bus routes after the war, but the construction of new housing was also accompanied by the extension of the rail network, and in particular the London Underground. Indeed, some rail companies, such as the Metropolitan, also became property developers. They built ten estates along their new line to Uxbridge and Amersham. The Weller Estate at Amersham was one of the Met's investments of the 1930s (fig. 505). They had purchased the land in 1930 for £18,000 and by the outbreak of the Second World War five hundred and thirty-five semi-detached houses had been built to be sold, starting from £875.

Once again this rosy picture has to be tempered because for the working classes renting these commodious new houses was relatively expensive. Manchester council-house rents were 13s to 15s a week, at a time when slum tenants were paying only 7s to 9s. The new houses with all their mod cons were more expensive to run and commuting added to the weekly bills. Whilst mil-

Fig. 505 (below) Poster advertising houses on the Weller Estate, Amersham. Half-timbered semi-detached houses with early examples of integrated garages, these modern olde-worlde houses were, for many, dream homes.

Fig. 506 (above) Ebury Bridge Road Estate, 1936 by A. J. Thomas, Edwin Lutyens's former office manager who set up on his own in 1932. He achieved a striking elevation with minimal expense using contrasting brick colours.

lions had been given better homes the problems of the slums remained. In 1928 it was estimated that there were still one million unfit and two million overcrowded houses. The problem was finding a way of building new houses that were within the 9s-a-week rental bracket.

In 1930 the Labour government passed a Housing Act that, for the first time, made available a specific subsidy for slum clearance, one based not on the number of houses built but on the number of people to be re-housed. It also made a proper attempt to define what sort of houses constituted a slum. Costs were brought down in two ways: by reducing the specification and size of cottages built in garden estates, and by increasing the number of apartment blocks built in the big cities. Flat building in London in 1936 exceeded cottage building for the first time. A six-storey block built in the Ebury Bridge Road Estate in 1936 for Westminster City Council by A. J. Thomas is typical. Flats were either two- or three-beds, with a living room and a kitchen. Access was via a continuous balcony in the courtyard and the Georgian sash windows overlooked the road (fig. 506).

This burst of building before 1939 did not rid England of its slums but it made considerable inroads, eliminating half of all the officially identified ones and improving nearly half a million more slum dwellings.[30]

Getting About

The most important impact of electricity before the First World War was its transformation of urban transport. Tramways had become popular in America in the 1830s but it was not until a way of laying recessed rails in the street was devised in Liverpool in 1868 that they were introduced into England. The horse tram was a big step forward. Horse omnibuses might carry twenty-five people in a heavy vehicle over cobbled streets, but pulled on rails a vehicle could take double that. A horse-tram system rapidly developed; in London in 1896 it was conveying 280 million passengers a year and was by far the most important means of urban transport, linking the new suburbs with the central business districts. It took eleven horses working in shifts to service one tram and a large tram operator such as the London Omnibus Company owned ten thousand horses in 1893. These were kept in big depots with massive stables at the suburban ends of the tramlines.

Although the first English tram was electrified in 1883 on the Brighton sea front, it was not until the adoption of an American system transmitting power to trams from overhead wires via a pole that trams really took off. From 1891 electric trams began to appear in every big city; these were faster, could travel further and were cheaper to run. In London, in particular, they were exploited by the LCC to lay out estates for workers in the more distant suburbs (p. 480). In 1910 electric trams in the capital made 505 million journeys. The effects were mixed: on the one hand, London's streets were cleaned up, with the disappearance of thousands of horses; on the other, major routes were visually scarred with stanchions and wires.[31] New tram depots ringed most major cities; Bristol had seven depots, including the best-preserved surviving tram complex at Brislington. This was entered through an imposing gateway in a classical freestyle designed in 1899 by W. Curtis Green, with sheds in a similar style that were inspired by railway models.

The Bristol Tramways and Carriage Co. Ltd was founded in 1887, and in 1895 the decision was made to electrify the system. In 1898–99 the company needed to build a new generating station to cater for the massive expansion that was planned – by 1920 it was running two hundred and thirty-six electric tramcars. The company's new station at Counterslip was also designed by Curtis Green in a heroic classical freestyle that, like early gas and railway buildings, was intended to impress investors and reassure the public. Coal was delivered by barges and taken to four sets of boilers by conveyor-belt. The generators were American, based on units installed in Chicago in 1893.[32]

In London electric motors had another impact. The first underground trains had been run in relatively shallow cut-and-cover tunnels, with vents to allow smoke to escape (fig. 416). The invention of the electric train, drawing power from an electrified rail, opened up the possibility of an underground railway in deep-bored tunnels. The first such line, running between the City and Stockwell, opened in 1890. Bored tunnels were cheaper to build than cut-and-cover because they did not require expensive compensation to property owners. This

Fig. 507 (above) Morden Tube Station, Northern Line, London, Charles Holden 1926. At this point the terminus of the line, the tracks were in a cutting and steps led down from Holden's high ticket hall to the platforms. A parade of shops was integrated into the design.

Fig. 508 (right) Holland Park Central Line Underground station, H. B. Measures, 1900. The air space above this particular station was never commercially developed as originally intended.

fact made possible the Central Line, the first modern Tube line, which opened in 1900 and was sunk over 100ft below London's streets. Whilst the engineering of the tunnels was based on advances made in the previous century by Marc Brunel and Peter Barlow, the electrical technology was American and the project was funded by international finance.

The Central Line's thirteen stations were designed by an architect who had previously been a designer of middle-class housing in classical freestyle. Harry Bell Measures developed a standardised design with street façades of red brick and glazed beige terracotta (fig. 508). All were single storey, with flat roofs to enable subsequent commercial development above. The tunnels inside were tiled in white, and American lifts in banks of two or three took people down to platform level. This new, fast, clean railway posed a huge threat to the steam-powered underground companies who could not afford to electrify. They were saved by Charles Tyson Yerkes, a shady American financier who, with his associates, gradually bought out the existing lines, electrified them and built his own new deep-bored lines. In an extraordinary five years of takeovers, amalgamations and engineering Yerkes created the Underground Electric Railways Company of London (UERL), which owned all the lines except the Metropolitan. The only problem was that none of it made a profit. Yerkes died in debt and his company wobbled on the edge of bankruptcy.

Part of the problem was the intensity of competition. London's streets already had an efficient tram system, and after 1910 had reliable and profitable motor-bus services. The solution was to integrate the system, which is what UERL did in 1912, creating a near monopoly on London transport.[33]

Under A. H. Stanley (later Lord Ashfield) and Frank Pick, UERL became interested in improving the design quality of its assets. The entire transport system came under Pick's refined and educated eye, and the design of each part was carefully considered. Architecture was central to this and Charles Holden was appointed to improve the design of stations. Pick saw stations as shops that would be visited by customers and he wanted them to be filled with light. Holden's new stations on the Morden extension to what is now the Northern Line have double-height ticket halls faced in Portland stone, with a glazed screen above the canopy, similar to contemporary cinema and shop frontages (fig. 507). An extension to the Piccadilly Line was agreed in 1930, and Pick and Holden went on a European research trip to crystallise their ideas.

They were particularly struck by the simple brick stations in Holland, which successfully blended tradition with modern values. The influence of these can be seen in Holden's station designs: Sudbury Town Station was the prototype for what Holden called his 'brick boxes with concrete lids'. Here can be seen all the elements that were to appear in his later stations – extended vertical and horizontal lines built in red brick with smooth concrete, metal window frames and glazed tiles (fig. 509). Sometimes a tower was added or – as at Arnos Grove – a drum. The interiors were sleek and modern, although simple and less expensive than they looked, relying of standardised and mass-produced materials. Holden was conscious of how light should be used and aware that the stations had to be seen – and look good – at night.[34]

In 1933, after years of discussion, a bill amalgamated all of London's transport systems in a new public corporation as London Transport. Pick had the task of creating what would perhaps be described today as a unified brand for the new group, which was made up of five railway companies, seventeen tramways, sixty-six bus companies and sixty-nine other transport businesses. Everything came to his attention, right down to the bus-stop signs and shelters. London Transport was to give the capital city a continuous homogeneity of design, going a long way to making it feel like a single city.

As we have seen, in the 1920s people fell over each other to get out of the towns and into the country. Whilst suburbs tried hard to be villages, villages also tried harder to be villages. The first village-name signs were erected on the Sandringham estate by Edward VII, starting a rural tradition that quickly seemed like it belonged to time immemorial. Pubs lost their garish enamel signs and acquired 'traditional' hanging pub signs and names. Tea shops, cafés and petrol stations were designed to look like Olde World fixtures in the villages to which they had recently come. This countryside, which was re-made into a chocolate-box image of itself, was to be deluged by visitors coming by train, bus, car, bike and on foot.

During the First World War there were 331 stage bus operators, by 1930 there were 3,962 and by 1932 buses carried more passengers than the rail network. At the same time there was an explosion in car ownership. In 1918 there had been no more than 100,000 private motor cars but by 1939 there were two million. Cars were at first a leisure accessory rather than a means of business conveyance. Early motoring magazines focused not on cars but on where to drive them, as the car took people to places inaccessible by railway and even motor bus. The countryside was for the first time permeable to almost everyone.

The first car showrooms were set up in carriage repositories and, occasionally, in normal town-centre shops, but in the years immediately before the First World War interest was growing in the design of purpose-built motor showrooms; indeed, in the streets around Great Portland Street in London there were already twenty-nine showrooms by 1914. After the war London dealers trading in luxury marques congregated in clubland around St

Fig. 509 (below) Sudbury Town Tube Station, Piccadilly Line, Charles Holden, 1931. The tall, well-lit ticket office was flanked by lower ranges containing the station facilities.

Fig. 510 (above) Wolseley Car showroom, Piccadilly, London, Curtis Green, 1922. A prestige showroom for a new product deliberately built within walking distance of a wealthy clientele. The monumental columns and the bronze panels show a clear debt to the Selfridges store on Oxford Street (fig. 538).

Fig. 511 (above right) Carlyle garages for the Bluebird Motor Company, Robert Sharpe, 1924; of reinforced concrete and steel faced in white faience. Segregated waiting rooms were provided for chauffeurs and for female drivers. The building had space for 300 cars.

James's. The most splendid was the Wolseley HQ designed by Curtis Green in 1922, with giant Corinthian columns framing plain cast-iron panelling and wrought-iron grilles owing a considerable debt to Selfridges (fig. 510). Inside, the space was vaulted and supported by Doric columns. In these early showrooms cars were not being advertised and sold on technical specification but on their elegance and sophistication as leisure machines.

The car was fundamentally a forward-looking piece of technology and during the 1930s traditional structures started to give way to showrooms in a less ornamental style. In the exclusive shopping area of Bold Street in Liverpool there were a number of dealers housed in concrete showrooms with minimally classical details and big windows. People who bought cars tended at first to store them in existing stables or carriage houses if they had them, or purpose-built timber motor houses. It was only in the 1920s that integral domestic garages began to appear. Some of the earliest of these were built in the automotive manufacturing centre of Coventry.

Such domestic 'garages' – the French word first appears in England in 1900 – made only a minor impact on the appearance of English towns and villages before 1939. What did make a difference, however, was the need to park cars away from home. Londoners already owned more than 40,000 cars in 1910. Large car parks were built before the Second World War in seaside towns, in city centres, at railway stations and at entertainment venues. The model was the urban multi-storey stable, with the addition of lifts and turntables to move the vehicles. After 1918 the first ramps began to appear; these were free to run, faster to operate and reliable. Those in the Bluebird Garage on King's Road, London, designed in 1923–4 by the car-park specialist Robert Sharpe, were amongst the first; the Bluebird is also an early example of a commercial car park with pumps on the forecourt (fig. 511). Eventually, the staggered ramp system that is almost universally used for multi-storey car parks today was introduced from America in Poland Street, London, in 1922.

Fig. 512 (left) Tower Garage, Egham, Rix and Rix of Birmingham, 1935. Rounded corners, white render and a slender, streamlined tower proclaim modernity and speed, the pitch for selling motor cars.

By this date repair-and-maintenance garages were also a common sight; in rural areas many occupied converted or rudely built roadside structures but city-centre ones were more substantial. During the 1930s there began to be greater standardisation in car manufacture and fewer marques on the road. New models were less clumsy and more streamlined and for both of these reasons modern-style garages were increasingly favoured. The sleek styling of cars was thought to be set off better against a high-tech building than a neo-Georgian one. Mechanics were also keen to work on large, open-plan floors where cars could be serviced on a production-line basis. The Tower Garage (now Maranello Ferrari) on Egham Bypass, Surrey, was built in 1935 by Rix and Rix of Birmingham, a firm that specialised in such buildings. Long and low – it was later extended in length – it has a tower for visibility and a vertical accent, a common feature for transport and commercial structures (fig. 512).[35]

Although Britain had led the way in maritime, road, rail and canal travel during the 19th century it was much slower to take up the possibilities of air transport. After the war there was a drastic drop in the number of orders for new aeroplanes and aircraft manufacturers started to look for new markets. One of the most successful, Frederick Handley Page, established the world's first sustained commercial international air service in 1919. It flew between London and Paris using converted bombers with, at first, only two or four passengers each. By 1922 five companies were offering services between London and Paris, and soon routes were opened to Amsterdam and Berlin. In response to concerns over competition from state-subsidised airlines in France and Germany the government decided in 1924 to buy out the various operators and form a single international airline – Imperial Airways.

Fig. 513 (above right) Speke Airport Liverpool, Edward Bloomfield, 1937–9. This was deliberately based on the most advanced airports in the world, in particular the Fuhlsbüttel airport in Hamburg and American airports.

Fig. 514 (above) Imperial Airways headquarters, Victoria Street, London (now the National Audit Office), A. Lakeman, 1937–9; architecture in the service of the promotion of a new technology. The building looks skyward and its entrance trophy, by Eric Broadbent, is contemporary with the invention of the comic-strip character Superman in America in 1938.

Croydon was designated London's official airport, and the entry and departure point for all international flights. It was from there that Imperial Airways flew its first services in April 1924. The aerodrome was formed by joining two former wartime airfields together and during the 1920s it rapidly expanded, culminating in the completion of England's first purpose-built terminal building in 1928. This was designed by the Air Ministry's own architects in a minimalist classical style with a steel fame and concrete block work. As with the early railways a new hotel was built next to the terminal.

In the inter-war years the Port of Liverpool was at its zenith, carrying more tonnage than the next six largest ports put together. But it wasn't taking any chances. The success of Imperial Airways convinced the city that they should build an aerodrome to secure their place as the country's northern transport hub. A large estate to the south-east of the city was bought in 1928 and on this a makeshift airfield was established. Liverpool was in no mood to do anything in half-measures and from 1935 it commissioned a brand new airport from Edward Bloomfield, working with the city surveyor Albert D. Jenkins. The terminal, with its tiered observation decks, 200ft-long restaurant and flanking hangers, was closely based on German and American models (fig. 513). Like Holden's Tube stations, Speke Airport was influenced by contemporary brick Dutch architecture. Almost all references to the classical language of architecture are gone; the building expresses a deliberate modernity and, in its nine-storey control tower, an assertive monumentality. These, no doubt, were the qualities that Liverpool wanted to project to the world.[36]

As the 1920s turned into the 1930s the architecture of transport was at the forefront of the movement to at first minimise and then in some cases completely drop the decorative expressions of classical architecture, although most buildings retained classical proportions. The modernity, speed and elegance of travel increasingly ill-fitted the vernacular, Georgian and classical freestyle modes, and architects working on the Underground, airports and the car industry created a recognisable alternative means of expression. This reached their apogee in the 1930s on Buckingham Palace Road, London, where, facing each other, were Victoria Coach Station by Wallis, Gilbert and Partners (1931–2) and the Imperial Airways Empire Terminal by A. Lakeman (1937–9) (fig. 514). The latter – with a clock tower pointing to the heavens and a sculpture by Eric Broadbent, 'Speed Wings over the World', of super-humans flying across the globe – shows architecture promoting the new technologies.

Education

For the wealthy, schooling had always been an expensive business bought for sons from the public schools, universities and Inns of Court and provided for daughters by home tutors. For the sixth-sevenths of society that were not so lucky, gaining an education was a struggle. Most poor people did want to educate their children – access to the Bible and to cheap literature was thought important, and the economic benefits of literacy were widely appreciated. Equally, the Church, the authorities and reformers saw the spread of literacy as being a vital bastion against immorality, crime and disorder. As a result, in the 19th century there were schools everywhere of every sort and every quality; this led in the 1840s to half of all women and 60 per cent of all men being literate.

The state regarded education to be the responsibility of voluntary effort, in particular the churches that provided most of the elementary schools. The typical parish school had only one teacher, who normally lived on site and who might be assisted by an unqualified assistant. Many schools were only a single room but larger ones had separate rooms for boys and girls, some with smaller teaching rooms to one side. The school at Kibworth Beauchamp, Leicestershire, was typical of this sort, built in the Tudor style – the most common choice as it was thought appropriate for an educational establishment.

In 1870 the Elementary Education Act provided for the first time a national system of elementary schools in places where churches could not cope. The new schools were provided by locally elected school boards that could raise a rate to build a new school. In 1880 a further Act imposed universal compulsory schooling for children under the age of ten; this was raised to eleven in 1893 and twelve in 1899. As a consequence the number of board schools rose rapidly; there were over four hundred by 1895. The need for board schools was greatest in the cities, where the shortage of places was most severe: in Leeds sixty-one schools were built, in Manchester thirty-nine. But it was

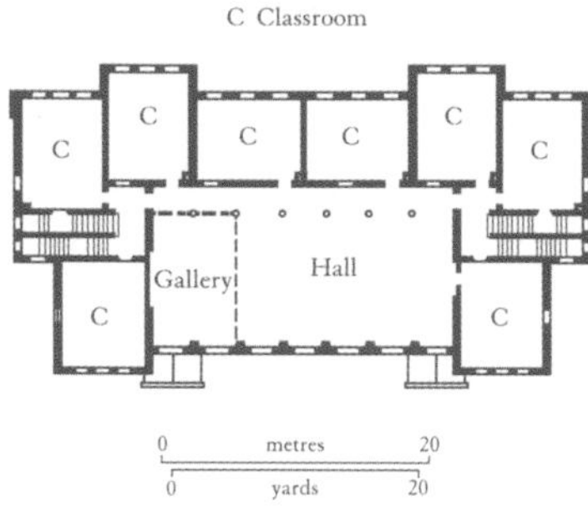

Fig. 515 (above) Jonson Street Board School, Stepney, T. Roger Smith 1873. Urban board schools, built on cramped sites, were normally tall and by 1880 had evolved a standard plan; as well as a large hall, there were numbers of smaller classrooms clustered around.

Fig. 516 (left) Kibworth Beauchamp Parochial School, 1842. The left three bays were the girls' school and the right three the boys' school; at the back was a house for the master.

Fig. 517 (above) Scarcroft Road School, York, Walter Brierley, from 1896. Brierley was a York architect who created his masterpiece in the educational Queen Anne idiom for the school.

Fig. 518 (right) High Storrs Grammar School; the building is recognisably Georgian.

London that led the way. Here, in 1871, E. R. Robson was appointed architect to the board; at first he contracted the design to private practices but after 1873 gained direct control. His partner was J. J. Stevenson and between them they created a model that was to be publicised and widely imitated through Robson's book, *School Architecture* (1874). Urban board schools, built on cramped sites, were normally tall and by 1880 had evolved a standard plan; as well as a large hall, there were numbers of smaller classrooms clustered around (fig. 515). They were spartan, with glazed brick and tile interiors; from the 1890s glazed wooden partitions were installed that separated areas. Gothic and Tudor styles were regarded as having ecclesiastical overtones and so Robson favoured classical freestyle, which was well suited to the big-windowed, tall brick structures that he designed. These schools became a very distinctive part of the late Victorian urban landscape.

In 1902 the Education Act abolished all 2,568 school boards and gave responsibility for these – and for church schools – to local authorities, who were also empowered to establish secondary and technical schools. Architecturally, the priority switched to the establishment of secondary schools, of which there were only two hundred and seventy-two in 1902. Within a decade there were a thousand, as England rapidly began to catch up with the higher educational standards in Germany and the US. These new schools were at first principally aimed at children from wealthier families and were prestige designs, enhancing the local authority and echoing the pretentious architecture of the great public schools. Gothic and Tudor styles were not favoured, nor was classical freestyle; most were neo-Georgian, and of some pretension. Like the board schools, most were organised around a central assembly hall. Many were girls schools – nine of the twelve built in Kent were for girls. The classicism became increasingly minimal in the 1920s and 30s, but even in a stripped-down form, as at High Storrs Grammar School, Sheffield (1933, by the city architect's department), the main building remains recognisably Georgian (fig. 518).[37]

Fig. 519 (left) Royal Holloway College, Egham, Surrey, H. Crossland, 1879–87. An astonishing building of vast proportions and unexpected style. Two huge courtyards accommodated the students in comfort and security and their tutors in some style.

Before the Dean and Chapter of Durham founded the University of Durham in 1832 there were no universities in the north of England. This geographical imbalance – and the imperative, in particular, to train more and better science teachers – led to the establishment in the 1860s and 70s of a number of new universities and colleges. Alfred Waterhouse was one of the leading architects to provide buildings in the north; his colleges in red brick and terracotta led to the term 'red-brick universities' being adopted for this rash of new late-Victorian foundations. Meanwhile, the older universities were considering admitting women. London led the way in 1848, with new colleges in Oxford and Cambridge being founded in 1871. The most remarkable university establishment of this first phase of women's education was paid for by the millionaire philanthropist Thomas Holloway, who had made his money selling spurious pills and ointments. Royal Holloway College, Egham, Surrey, was designed by W. H. Crossland, a brilliant but not well-known architect who was sent by Crossland to the Loire valley to study 16th-century French architecture for the new college. Stylistically, it is both extraordinary and brilliantly composed – a one-off display funded by a mildly eccentric patron. Each student had a study and bedroom, and there were common rooms for every six. Teaching staff were accommodated in larger suites in the corner pavilions. In this way students could be safely and securely lodged and taught in a single building (fig. 519).[38]

The Commercialisation of Leisure

Increased disposable income and more leisure time, particularly for urban populations, introduced two contrasting sets of aspiration. For pious reformers with a belief in self-improvement it meant opportunities to attract people to libraries, museums, public parks and to church. For entrepreneurs it opened up new ways of making money. The commercialisation of leisure after 1870 is a marked feature of English society, bringing a wide and important range of new building types and landscapes. It was a national phenomenon underpinned by the railways and intensive capital investment; some speculators became rich on the profits of leisure but the industry was a fickle one – many enterprises struggled to turn a profit and some went bust.

Like the railway stations and some factories new leisure buildings used architecture as advertisement to attract both punters and investors. But big, showy, recreational buildings were also frequently about fantasy; time off from work, especially for the less well-off, was escapism, and venues strove to make this a visual reality. Social distinctions remained important; some activities were undertaken exclusively by one class. Lawn tennis and golf, for instance, were exclusively upper-class or bourgeois activities. When people of different classes mixed at the theatre or the races, proprietors took care to provide segregated zones. Yet distinctions began to break down in the inter-war years and some sports – and cinema, in particular – became genuine shared national interests.

Sport had become a national obsession by the 1890s; in the 1840s only horse-racing, golf and cricket enjoyed any national organisation but by 1900 there were fifteen sports organised on a national scale. Public schools had made a major contribution to this surge of interest and the governing boards of most sports were composed of their former pupils. It was widely believed that sport was improving for both mind and body, keeping people from drunkenness and moral decay. It was therefore generally perceived to be a good thing.

The first substantial infrastructure for sporting events was built for horse-racing. Temporary grandstands had been built since the 17th century but more permanent structures were erected in the 18th century, such as the grandstand designed by John Carr at York Racecourse in 1755. York was a town racecourse but private courses were also developed by the Crown and the aristocracy. One of the finest was built by Charles Gordon-Lennox, 5th Duke of Richmond, at Goodwood House in East Sussex. His new grandstand, completed in 1830, held three thousand people. At the top was open-air raked seating and below, under cover, was a partially glazed arcade fronting an elegant saloon. Beneath this were refreshment rooms.[39]

Racing was transformed by the railways, which enabled horses to be easily transported to distant courses and spectators to arrive from far and wide. Although courses had always made money from betting and from expensive, well-appointed stands, most were open to everyone, making horse-racing a sport that transcended social distinctions. At one end of the scale was the future Edward VII, whose racehorses earned a colossal £415,840 between 1886 and 1910. At the other end were the tens of thousands of Cockneys who went by train to Epsom and watched the races for free. After 1870, however, courses increasingly began to charge for entry. The first to be enclosed and ticketed was Sandown Park in 1875; others soon followed and racing became more and more commercialised, with a big infrastructure.[40] The new grandstands at these courses lent themselves perfectly to iron construction; a fine surviving example designed by the versatile Lincolnshire architects William Mortimer and Son at Lincoln Racecourse was built in 1897 (fig. 520).

Cricket was another sport that acquired an early architectural presence. An accepted set of rules had been agreed in 1788 and soon there were work teams, church teams, county teams: in Bolton alone there were 110 cricket clubs in 1939. Gradually, as matches moved away from commons and village greens, and acquired privately owned pitches, pavilions and other buildings were put up. The quintessential English small-town pavilion was generally built in a vernacular style, often half-timbered and usually incorporating a veranda. A fine example, designed by a well-known architect, is T. G. Jackson's pavilion in The Parks in Oxford, finished in 1880 (fig. 521). By the 1890s it was possible for small clubs to buy off-the-peg prefabricated pavilions; these were not only sold in Britain but exported across the empire. Some English municipal pavilions funded by wealthy, cricket-mad locals could be very impressive, such as the one paid for by the furniture seller John Maple at St Albans. The largest were built at the county cricket grounds and were a development of grandstands long established at the smartest racecourses. The most important was at Lord's, London, built between 1889 and 1890 and designed by Thomas Verity, best known for his work on theatres. It incorporated fine terracotta and ornamental ironwork, and its festive air and careful planning allowing good sight lines for four thousand spectators had much in common with London theatres of the time.[41]

Fig. 520 (top) Grandstand at former Lincoln racecourse (closed 1964). Local architects William Mortimer and Son made good use of iron construction to ensure uninterrupted views of the course.

Fig. 521 (above) Cricket pavilion, The Parks, Oxford, T. G. Jackson, 1880. Quintessentially English architecture; the sort of pavilion Elizabeth I would have commissioned, had cricket been invented. Such buildings were exported across the globe.

Football was already a very old game by the time the Football Association (FA) finally acquired agreed rules in 1863 that enabled games to be played nationally without disagreement for the first time. In 1883 Blackburn Olympic, a team of working men from the north, defeated the Old Etonians in the FA Cup Final, symbolically ushering in the age of professional club football. By 1939 there were 18,000 clubs affiliated to the County Football Association. The FA's first matches, and its Cup Finals from 1872 to 1892, took place at the Oval Cricket Ground in south London, but in an increasingly commercialised sport money soon became available for purpose-built grounds.

Football, unlike many sports, was cheap to play. Other than a ball no equipment was needed and this, in part, accounts for its initial popularity, particularly amongst working-class people. Football matches were mostly attended by skilled working- and lower-middle-class fans, as poorer groups were excluded by ticket prices that supposedly kept out troublemakers. Women stayed at home. Crystal Palace FC (not to be confused with the club of the same name active today) was founded in 1861 by groundsmen who had worked at the Great Exhibition; they built a ground with the first permanent, purpose-built timber grandstands and it was here that FA Cup Finals were played between 1895 and 1914, the 1901 match attracting 100,000 fans.

After the collapse of a timber stand at Ibrox Park ground in Glasgow in 1902, killing twenty-five and injuring over five hundred, it became imperative to design a grandstand that could safely accommodate tens of thousands. The disgraced architect of Ibrox was Archie Leitch, a Glaswegian engineer who was to patent a system of crush bars to be installed on terraces that could safely take thousands of standing fans. Leitch was to go on to be the most prolific designer of football stadia, completing as many as fifty over the course of his career. Most combined solid terraces and covered grandstands, some of which were built in reinforced concrete.

Leitch worked for Tottenham Hotspur FC at White Hart Lane in north London between 1908 and 1934, and eventually constructed stands on all four sides of the pitch to hold a crowd of 75,000. Tottenham was a commercial venture, like all clubs, and developed the ground piecemeal; so, for instance, on winning the FA Cup in 1921 it used the prize money to build a roof over one of its terraces. The ground was illustrated in 1934 by Leitch's company artist and the drawing shows how the utilitarian steel and reinforced concrete grandstands were given an impressive street frontage, in scale if nothing else (fig. 522).

Fig. 522 (above) White Hart Lane Football Ground for Tottenham Hotspur football club, Archie Leitch, 1908–34. This sketch by the company artist shows Leitch's 40,000 capacity ground with the grandiose east stand in the foreground.

Fig. 523 (top) The Empire Stadium, Wembley, London, Sir John Simpson and Maxwell Ayrton with Sir Owen Williams, 1923 (demolished 2003). The stadium was entirely built of reinforced concrete down to its massive flagpoles – a fact that enabled it to be constructed in 300 days for £750,000.

Few new football grounds were constructed in the inter-war period but after 1900 two significant new stadia had been built for international events. The first was the Olympic stadium at White City in 1908, a great oval in which all 68,000 spectators were seated. Then in 1922, as part of the British Empire Exhibition of 1924, England's largest and most impressive stadium was erected. Wembley Stadium was designed by Sir John Simpson and Maxwell Ayrton with the help of Sir Owen Williams. Entirely built of reinforced concrete, right down to its massive flagpoles, it was also an oval but seated 120,000 (fig. 523). Designed as the centrepiece of a concrete landscape evoking the glories of ancient Rome and quoting directly from the Coliseum, it quickly became the icon of English football.[42]

Football had an overwhelmingly male audience but the same could not be said for music halls. By 1900 there were not only many women in the audience – some were also on stage. These places started up in the 1860s and were a commercialisation of forms of entertainment that previously took place in pubs and pleasure gardens. The predominantly working- and lower-middle-class audience would sit at tables, where they would eat, drink and smoke whilst a compère introduced a variety of acts.

The Canterbury Music Hall was the first, built by Charles Morton from the profits of his pub, the Canterbury Tavern. It was rebuilt in 1854 as a large hall with a stage and had a capacity of 1,500, but it was destroyed in an air raid in 1942. A surviving early hall is Wilton's of 1859, which, like the Canterbury, grew out of a pub. John Wilton, who had been manager at the Canterbury, employed Jacob Maggs of Bath to design a lavish hall complete with mirrors, chandeliers, richly painted papier mâché decoration, and state-of-the-art heating and ventilation (fig. 524). Music halls quickly became big business. By 1892 there were five hundred in London selling 25 million tickets a year, and in 1900 speculators invested over £5 million in London halls alone. In the provinces, meanwhile, Middlesbrough had ten halls and those in Birmingham, in total, could sit 16,500 a night. Music-hall architecture became increasingly exotic at the turn of the century; the Empire Palace in Nottingham, for instance, had pagoda domes with grinning statues of Krishna either side of the stage and vast, gilded elephant heads in the corners of the auditorium.

From the 1880s halls began to change in nature. Increasingly, patrons were seated, as in a theatre, and many were owned by syndicates of investors who formed national chains circulating touring artistes. Music halls were often seen by Victorian moralists as places of ill repute, disorder and drunkenness. This led to owners such as Charles Morton stressing their family nature and banning ribald jokes and banter; eventually, some did not sell alcohol.[43]

Music halls were not at first considered as theatre and were licensed by local magistrates in the same way as a pub. Since the Restoration only three London theatres had been officially licensed to stage spoken drama; the Theatre Royal, Drury Lane, the Theatre Royal, Covent Garden, and, after 1766, the Theatre Royal in Haymarket; there were also a number of these so-called patent theatres in the provinces. In 1843 the patent theatres lost their monopoly, and farce, tragedy and comedy could now be performed in any licensed venue.

This brought new commercial opportunities for investors, and between 1880 and 1914 English theatre boomed. Theatre audiences were generally wealthier than the original patrons of music halls but were still socially segregated. The stalls, boxes and circle were all entered through separate doors and provided with exclusive bars. In this way earls and bank clerks could enjoy the same play but did not have to rub shoulders. Hundreds of new theatres were built in London and in the big centres of population; in 1893 eighty-nine towns were listed as having at least one theatre and in London there were sixty-five with a combined annual attendance of 100 million. Touring companies, making full use of the railway network, took plays around the country.

Fig. 524 (below) Wilton's Music Hall, London, Jacob Maggs, 1859. Despite a serious fire in 1877 the hall still has the atmosphere of the first generation of music halls with space for supper tables, a gallery and a bar.

Fig. 525 (below) The Palace Theatre, formerly The Royal English Opera House, Cambridge Circus, London, T. E. Colcutt, 1888–91. Though Colcutt was architect, Richard D'Oyly Carte the patron, J. G. Buckle, expert on theatre interiors and the contractor G. H. Holloway all contributed to the design. As such the design process was more akin to a modern building.

Fig. 526 (bottom) The Hackney Empire, London, was a big suburban variety theatre typical of those designed by Frank Matcham.

In 1893 no fewer than seven of them were touring the hit farce *Charley's Aunt*. The distinction between music halls and theatres started to blur and many venues would stage what was known as variety, as well as spoken plays.

Theatres were inherently a fire risk and it was calculated in 1878 that the average life span of a theatre was only twenty-two years. In 1878 a new Act brought in stiff regulations for London theatres and by the early 1890s the capital's lead had been followed everywhere. The crucial developments were the erection of fire barriers between the stage and auditorium, and the provision of emergency lighting, fire exits and water hydrants. Most of the changes in theatres in the 19th century were driven by regulation and technology rather than theatrical performance. The adoption of steel and concrete engineering transformed what was possible in design. Richard D'Oyly Carte's new Royal English Opera House of 1891 on Cambridge Circus, London (now called the Palace Theatre), was the first to adopt cantilevered balconies, a breakthrough that allowed columns to be banished from auditoria. The introduction of the first gas light (1817) and then electricity (1881) enabled light to be controlled for dramatic effect for the first time.

Audiences wanted novelty – they wanted to be amazed and not just amused – and so theatre designers concocted ever more complex devices for raising and lowering scenery on to the stage. Deep basements, wide wings and tall fly towers were built to accommodate huge painted flats. At first these were worked manually by weights but after 1880 increasingly by hydraulics. Motor-driven turntables meant that whole sets could be moved on stage. These new capabilities supported an increasingly realistic style of performance pioneered in England by Sir Henry Irving. At the Lyceum Theatre he required eighty carpenters, fifty property men and thirty gas men to manage the stage effects for each performance.

The Royal English Opera House was designed by T. E. Colcutt, a well-known architect who made the most of an awkward site, creating a façade of great interest and richness that incorporated terracotta plaques (fig. 525). The contractor, G. H. Holloway, pioneered the cantilevered galleries and J. G. Buckle was consulted on the theatre's workings. A cavernous three-tier under-stage by the engineer Walter Dando housed D'Oyly Carte's unique stage machinery.

As this building illustrates, designing theatres was a highly complex business and a small group of specialised theatre architects emerged, such as C. J. Phipps, who built seventy-one, and the most successful, Frank Matcham, who built one hundred and fifty. Matcham created a new style of auditorium. No longer was it a space with rigid tiers of balconies facing a proscenium arch; the whole interior was now sculpted and moulded on a bewildering number of planes, and decoration was no longer applied to the gallery fronts but was an organic part of the conception. Matcham's style, which combined Moorish, Gothic and classical elements into a fantastic blend, can only be described as theatrical.

These interiors were only possible due to the invention of fibrous plaster, a means of moulding large decorative panels using hessian soaked in gypsum and supported by timber struts. The patent for this, taken out in 1856, quickly transformed the ability of designers to create large-scale sculptural effects. The

Hackney Empire, London, was a big suburban variety theatre typical of those designed by Matcham. It was built in 1901 as part of a chain of 'Empires' owned by Oswald Stoll (fig. 526). Like the Royal English Opera House it was terracotta clad externally and had two big cantilevered balconies within. The interior was lavishly and exotically moulded in fibrous plaster, a reassuring look for Stoll's investors, who bought £50,000 in ordinary shares in the venture at £5 each.[44]

Part of the stimulus for increasing theatrical realism had been photography but by the 1890s a new challenge was presented to the stage. In the United States Thomas Edison had invented moving film and soon entrepreneurs were touring short moving films around the country. At first they were shown in corn exchanges and in due course as part of a variety programme in theatres. Then, in around 1904, the first purpose-built cinemas were constructed. By 1914 there were 3,500 of these, including 497 in London and 90 in Manchester; as a consequence, by the early 1920s cinema had ousted theatre as the venue of choice for the masses, and between 1900 and 1920 theatres lost 90 per cent of their patrons.

The Gem in Great Yarmouth was built in 1908 and showed films on a continuous loop for those tired of the beach. Externally, it was not discernibly different from a hundred contemporary theatres but inside it was a single, long hall. If theatre was dangerous, cinema was lethal. Nitrate-based celluloid film could not only spontaneously combust but projectors had a naked carbon arc light source, ripe for igniting a jammed frame. The Cinematograph Act of 1909 insisted on fire-proof projection booths separately accessed from the auditorium, and the LCC demanded new 'push-bar' outward-opening fire exits.

After the First World War film-going began to change from a lowbrow activity in small, dingy, theatre-like venues to a mass cultural medium in smart, purpose-built cinemas. The Regent, Brighton, built in 1921, was the first of a new generation. It was designed by Robert Atkinson, who had been sent by the Royal Institute of British Architects to the US to study cinema design. His auditorium was built to an entirely new fan-shaped plan more suitable for projection, and the entrance façade contained a giant, three-storey, glazed proscenium arch, a feature to be much copied elsewhere (fig. 527).

The first talkie was shown in London in 1928 and many former theatres that were now showing films had to be quickly wired for sound. In the 1930s cinema became the most popular leasure activity with a weekly audience of 18–19 million; indeed English cinema goers became the world's single largest market for film. By this stage cinemas were starting to move away from the extravagant décor that had been expected by cinema goers in the early 1920s. The Sheen near Richmond upon Thames was opened in 1930; it was designed by the practice Leathart & Granger, who designed a number of west London cinemas in the late 20s. They broke away from the proscenium arch façade first adopted in Brighton to create a new model for cinemas. Their façade had a vertical emphasis, incorporating a glazed, back-lit tower topped by a stack of three urns. Inside, the lighting was all indirect, hidden in minimalist cornices or niches. Sheen was to become the template for thousands of medium-sized cinemas all over England, successful in blending with traditional brick high streets whilst still advertising the advanced entertainment within.[45]

Fig. 527 (above) The Regent Cinema, Brighton, Robert Atkinson, 1921, was the seminal cinema building. The great proscenium arch on the outside with bronze panels was widely imitated.

Fig. 528 (above) The Empress Ballroom, Blackpool Winter Gardens, Mangnall & Littlewoods of Manchester and decorated by J. M. Boekbinder, 1896. It was not only lavish, but huge, covering 12,500 square feet: in the First World War it was used for assembling airship balloons.

Fig. 529 (above) Hastings Pier, Sussex, Eugenius Birch, 1872. The first generation of piers were relatively modest, but they had already established themselves as an exotic art form.

Cheap rail travel and increasing amounts of holiday for working people transformed the English seaside. The 1871 Bank Holidays Act doubled the number of national holidays by adding four new days and by 1938 nearly eight million manual workers were entitled to some sort of paid holiday. Railways made it possible for these people to travel easily to the coast. In 1861 Blackpool, then still a modest-sized resort, received 135,000 rail passengers; in 1879 this had risen to a million and by 1914 four million arrived at the resort by train every year.

Investors fell over themselves to provide hotels and entertainment for seaside holidaymakers. Piers had originally been disembarkation points for visitors arriving by steamboat but the arrival of the railways transformed them into promenades. At first, piers had no superstructure, only a deck; but Hastings Pier, opened in 1872 and funded by local shareholders, incorporated a large domed pavilion at its far end for entertainments. This was in an exotic style, drawing inspiration from Brighton Pavilion (fig. 529), and became the prototype for a rash of ornamental piers around the English coast. The architect was the railway engineer-turned-pier expert, Eugenius Birch, who was to perfect screw piles driven into the sea bed as a substructure to support large buildings on piers.[46]

Blackpool's future position as England's busiest seaside resort was boosted by the completion of a new railway line to the town in 1863. At first its new piers, hotels and entertainment facilities were aimed at middle-class holidaymakers, but during the 1870s Blackpool underwent a significant change in the scale and nature of what it offered. In 1878 the Winter Gardens designed by Thomas Mitchell were opened, enabling Blackpool to entertain its visitors in all weathers. These were the most spectacular of many similar complexes built at coastal resorts and by the end of the century it was an astonishing fibrous plaster wonderland of exotic entertainment. The Empress Ballroom designed by Mangnall & Littlewoods (fig. 528) was cavernous, the adjacent Indian lounge by J. M. Bookbinder was exotic, and the Spanish Hall, Baronial Hall and Galleon Bar created by the film-set designer Andrew Mazzei were plaster wonderlands. All were conceived for the vast numbers of working-class holiday makers who came from nearby industrial conurbations wanting to experience the exoticism of foreign lands without leaving the shores of the north-west.

Blackpool's ambitions were crowned by the construction of its 581ft-high tower in 1894. This masterpiece of engineering, inspired by the Eiffel Tower, was designed by the Manchester practice Maxwell & Tuke (fig. 530). The tower was not just a steel pylon; it was a huge entertainment complex. For 6d holidaymakers could see an aquarium, menagerie, restaurant, billiard room, ballroom and circus, the floor of which was lowered at the end of each performance and flooded for an aquatic finale.[47]

After 1918 the seaside became home to buildings influenced by international modernism. Like Victorian piers and winter gardens they were built in what was seen as an exotic style emphasising the escapism of a summer holiday, transporting people, in their minds, to the fashionable French Riviera, or to luxury cruise ships. In Morecombe Bay the sleek, white Midland Hotel, designed by Oliver Hill and built in 1933, added to the conventional palette of exotica by bringing continental chic to a northern Victorian town (fig. 531). The hotel not only looked glamorous; it provided a novel sort of accommodation for the newly mobile rich arriving by motor car. In Hastings, Sussex, a development of service flats, Marine Court, was built between 1936 and 1938 to designs by Kenneth Dalgleish and Roger K. Pullen. It was modelled on the Queen Mary, a liner the architects had seen docked in Scotland, and comprises fourteen storeys of brick and concrete, with shops at the bottom and a promenade deck at the top. Every flat had a south-facing aspect and a view of the sea.

In a bid to outclass neighbouring resorts, Sidney Little, the Borough Engineer of Hastings, rebuilt the sea front with a double-decker promenade in reinforced concrete. In 1933 he added a fashionable lido, one of many constructed at seaside towns. This was no ordinary pool; it was no less than a water stadium, with tiered seating for 2,500, underground parking, a poolside café and a huge sundeck. Such developments in inter-war resorts were not funded by private investors as before the First World War, but were commissioned by town councils and paid for through the rates. Towns now competed with each other for visitors, believing that new facilities would tempt holidaymakers away from their competitors.[46]

Fig. 530 (top) Blackpool Tower and entertainment complex including ballroom, circus and menagerie, opened in 1894. James Maxwell and Charles Tuke were the architects and Heenan and Froude the engineers.

Fig. 531 (above) Midland Hotel, Morecombe Bay, Lancashire by Oliver Hill for the London, Midland and Scottish Railway Company, 1933. The railway wanted 'a building of international quality in the modern style'.

Communications

At first the only place in London where people could post a letter was at the General Post Office in the City (p. 459). From here, and to here, letters would travel from receiving houses – generally small shops, offices or inns – run by local postmasters in provincial towns and cities. The introduction of the Universal Penny Post in 1840 brought a vast increase in the volume of mail. In the late 1830s people on average sent three letters a year; by 1875 this had increased to thirty-one. In 1857 a government enquiry revealed that the existing and rather ad-hoc system of post offices was completely inadequate, so the following year responsibility for post offices in larger towns – the Class I offices – was transferred to the only government department that dealt with buildings: the Office of Works.

The architect put in charge of this new responsibility was James Williams, who set out to establish a standard layout for post offices. The new buildings had a large public hall at the front with a counter and on the floor above was accommodation for the postmaster. To the rear was a single-storey, top-lit sorting office. Clerk's rooms, retiring rooms and other offices were arranged around this basic framework. Williams also established a grand style of external design for his offices, both befitting the dignity of the state and fulfilling the civic aspirations. His favoured Roman style can perhaps be best seen in his post office in Newcastle upon Tyne of 1871–4 (fig. 532).

In 1884 Williams retired and was succeeded by Sir Henry Tanner, who was to be the architect of dozens of provincial Class I buildings whilst his assistants were the authors of scores more. The buildings they erected were increasingly complex because the range of services provided by post offices had expanded to include a savings bank, telegrams (from 1870), the sale of a variety of licences and a parcel post (from 1883). Tanner, as we have seen (p. 459), was keen on the use of reinforced concrete, a material that brought down the cost of the substantial building programme under his control. He was also concerned with the efficient planning of buildings to ensure their

Fig. 532 (below) Former post office, Newcastle upon Tyne, James Williams, 1871–4; an impressive building embodying civic pride.

Fig. 533 (below right) Walton-upon-Thames Post Office, John Rutherford, 1907. The Tudoresque appearance conceals a complex internal arrangement including a large sorting office, a telephone exchange and extensive technical stores and workshops.

smooth operation. There was great need for this as the Post Office was a giant operation, with 250,000 employees by 1914. Tanner exercised no control over the style in which new post offices were designed, and they thus enjoyed the full palette of architectural treatment employed by Edwardian architects. In semi-rural Walton-on-Thames the post office appeared a modest half-timbered structure from the street, but its plan reveals the complexities of a building that combined a telegraph office, telephone exchange and sorting office (fig. 533).

After 1910, however, the Office of Works was under an obligation to design post offices to a less lavish specification. Local authorities who wanted grand civic statements were encouraged to contribute to the building costs themselves; some, like Rochdale, which wanted a more elaborate façade, did so. This need to cut costs was more pressing after the First World War. Tanner retired in 1913 and Sir Richard Allison took his place. The number of post offices had grown from 4,028 (mostly privately owned) in 1840 to 25,354 (mostly state owned) in 1913. Tanner had not encouraged any house style and most Class I offices were more or less indistinguishable from neighbouring commercial buildings. Allison brought a different approach. Under his supervision the Post Office developed a highly distinctive architectural language sometimes known as Post Office Georgian. Allison was clear that his post offices were not to be assertive architectural expressions but instead should blend in with buildings in the towns and villages in which they were sited. Red brick and sash windows, in various combinations, were ubiquitous. This plain style had another advantage – it was relatively cheap.

From 1928 a campaign to rebuild old post offices was started; the new building at Hatfield, completed in 1936 to the Office of Works architect Frederick Llewellyn's design, is typical (fig. 535). This new generation of buildings deliberately tried to be more attractive, light and welcoming to customers rather than being grim government offices. As at Hatfield, ground-floor windows were made as large as possible to let light in. Standardised designs for counters topped in lino were produced and the old bronze grilles were replaced by glass screens.

Letters were overwhelmingly the most common means of communication, although we have seen that by the end of the 19th century the world was already criss-crossed with telegraph cables. Alexander Graham Bell patented his telephone in 1876 and three years later the world's first telephone exchange opened in Coleman Street, London, operated by the United Telephone Company. When it opened there were only eight subscribers but businesses in particular saw the opportunities provided by the telephone, and the service grew rapidly. By 1882 the company had opened fifteen exchanges in central London; all of these were within existing buildings, in which space was rented for the equipment. Operating the system was highly labour intensive but it offered jobs for politely spoken young women, one of the few acceptable forms of female employment.

In 1883 the largest telephone companies merged to form the National Telephone Company and many new exchanges were established, although the first purpose-built exchange was only constructed between 1904 and 1907. It was

Fig. 534 (above) National Telephone Company Exchange, Gerard Street, Leonard Stokes, 1905–7. From the outside it would be hard to tell this exchange from any other commercial building, yet it was one of the first purpose-built exchanges, a prestige structure for the company.

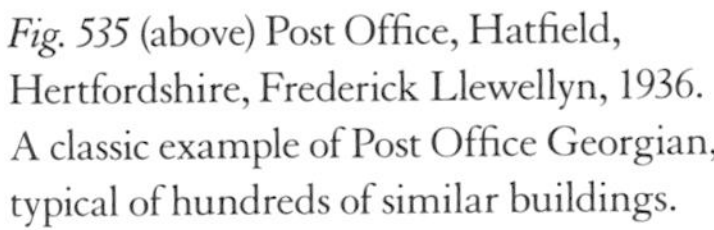

Fig. 535 (above) Post Office, Hatfield, Hertfordshire, Frederick Llewellyn, 1936. A classic example of Post Office Georgian, typical of hundreds of similar buildings.

Fig. 536 (above right) The vast derrick on the roof of the Lime Street Exchange, London, was octagonal and took 12,000 individual wires, which directly connected each building to the exchange.

designed by Leonard Stokes, who was conveniently married to the daughter of the company's general manager. A handsome classical freestyle building in brick and stone, its top-floor switch room was lit by big windows, with rest rooms and dining rooms below and the company offices on the ground floor (fig. 534). It had a 10,400-line capacity, with space for another 10,000. Stokes went on to design nineteen more exchanges.

The exchanges were connected to each other by wires that were stretched between steel gantries bolted to the roofs of the exchanges and intermediate buildings. As the network grew this system presented huge problems and created a visual blight. The vast derrick on the roof of the Lime Street Exchange, London, was octagonal and took 12,000 individual wires (fig. 536).

In 1905 the government agreed to purchase the National Telephone Company when its licence expired in 1911. As a result, in 1912 the General Post Office became responsible for the telephone system, inheriting 1.5 million miles of wire, 1,565 exchanges and 561,000 subscribers. Exchanges were now routinely combined with new post offices, which were consequently generally larger after 1912 to accommodate them.[49]

Until 1921 telephone coverage in rural areas was patchy and was often maintained only during working hours. That year small automatic rural exchanges were introduced and the first telephone kiosks were erected. The first model (Kiosk 1, or K1), made of concrete panels, was not particularly successful or loved, and a competition was held in 1925 to design a cheaper cast-iron model. The winner was Sir Giles Gilbert Scott, but his first attempts– and others by the Post Office – were considered either too expensive or too impractical. Scott's K6 design, however, in a minimalist Georgian style, proved satisfactory, and was installed in every town and village that had a post office. Phone boxes were painted red following the precedent set by post boxes that had been red since 1874. Together post boxes, and the 35,000 phone boxes installed by 1939, brought a standardised design to every corner of England, creating, in the way the Underground had for London, a unifying national image.

Shopping

Shopping is driven by levels of disposable income, and despite economic turmoil and the Depression of the 1930s the English had more to spend than ever before. The group that benefited most from rising levels of disposable income was the middle classes, which grew from a fifth to a quarter of the population by the start of the Second World War. But the 1930s saw a much more novel and important development; working-class incomes rose and, for the first time, a majority had risen above subsistence level. This possibly had an even greater impact on the world of shopping.

Since the early 19th century the shopping centre of London had been concentrated around Oxford Street and Regent Street. In 1906 the furnishing and interior-decorating store Waring & Gillow opened their new shop on Oxford Street (fig. 537). It was at the cutting-edge of English retail design and was designed by Robert Atkinson, who was later to make his name designing cinemas (p. 496). The classical freestyle street elevations were heavily decorated and the interior was planned around a dramatic central atrium topped with a glazed dome, off which the various showrooms opened. Shoppers would be invited to sit down and have goods brought to them and, in grand stores such as this, often be escorted from room to room; sales techniques relied on persuasion rather than seductive display. Shop assistants were often accommodated on site in the upper floors of the building.

Such shops, squeezed onto domestic-sized plots and full of small rooms, would have seemed old-fashioned when compared with those in Paris, where

Fig. 537 (below) Waring & Gillows shop, Oxford Street London, Robert Atkinson, 1906. In handsome classical freestyle, this shop was amongst the last of a retail generation – soon American influences would render its elegant showrooms old-fashioned.

Fig. 538 (below left) Selfridges, Oxford Street, London, begun in 1908, had a complex design history with a number of American and British architects and a Swedish engineer being involved. This was a revolutionary building, and a revolutionary concept in shopping. Its influence was huge.

Baron Haussmann had re-planned the streets allowing for big new units, or in New York, where undeveloped land facilitated the installation of huge floor plates. It is in this context that the revolutionary nature of Harry Gordon Selfridge's new store should be understood. With the building-control officers baulking at his proposals for big windows and uninterrupted spaces, Robert Atkinson was called in to negotiate. Particularly influential was the giant order facing the upper floors; decorative metal panels were fitted between columns, concealing the floor plates and framing the upper windows (fig. 538). When it was opened in 1909 shoppers were free to wander around the large open-plan spaces, where goods were enticingly displayed. Shoppers could eat, drink, have a haircut, smoke, borrow a book, buy tickets or post a letter – all of their comforts were taken into consideration. After 1911 there was even a bargain basement to attract poorer customers, keeping them away from the middle-class shoppers above (fig. 538). The other major London stores – Harrods, D. H. Evans and Dickins & Jones – fought back, but Selfridges had provided a model that was to be widely imitated.

Selfridges was a single shop but from the 1870s it had become common for successful businesses to open branch stores and a number of operations became chains. Grocers, in particular, invested in multiple retail; only a couple had more than a score of branches in 1880 yet by 1910 forty-four grocers had at least twenty-five. But grocers such as Liptons, who had a chain of two hundred and forty-five shops in 1898, had relatively small buildings stocked with a narrow range of goods. One of the first substantial English chains with a distinctive presence on the high street was the menswear retailer Burton. In the 1920s Montague Burton began to turn his tailoring business into a national brand. From 1923 he employed estate agents to find him high-street sites, particularly corner plots on which he built new shops. After 1932 these were designed by his own in-house architects. Burton's shops were relatively small scale and their interiors deliberately intimate – the same could not be said for the new store opened in Liverpool in 1909 by F. W. Woolworth.

Frank Woolworth had built up a successful chain of 'five-and-dime' stores in the US in the 1880s. In these shops factory-made goods at bargain prices were laid out for people to browse and examine before buying. After visiting England he saw a market into which he could expand, using his tried-and-tested techniques. His first shop fixed prices at either 3d or 6d and established its red fascia on the English high street. Highly profitable, his business expanded, and soon had its own architects' department and construction arm. A new Liverpool store opened in 1923, the large bronze panel in the centre of the façade showing the influence of Selfridges. The Liverpool shop, however, was not typical of Woolworth's stores in the later 1920s and 30s. Most were red brick in neo-Georgian or stripped-down classical styles. In all, Woolworth opened seven hundred and sixty-six branches before 1930.

In 1916 Marks & Spencer Ltd, one of the largest home-grown chains, decided to launch a counter-attack following the extraordinary success of Woolworth's. M&S was originally a bazaar in which everything cost a penny; by 1900 there were twenty-four branches, but Woolworth's was encroaching

on their business. In 1924 Simon Marks, the founder's son, visited the US to gain an insight into retailing techniques and returned convinced that the key was to build large, architecturally imposing, town-centre shops. Between 1926 and 1939 two hundred and eighteen M&S superstores were built and many others extended. By the outbreak of war the chain had two hundred and thirty-four prominent town-centre sites. They used three architectural firms, and Bovis as contractors. Most shops had recessed plate-glass windows facing the high street, above which – from 1924 – was a green-and-gold fascia to distinguish them from the red of Woolworth's. Most of the stores were faced with Portland stone on the first floor, with pilasters dividing the elevation into bays; there was also usually a stepped parapet bearing the company's name (fig. 540). Inside, however, there was little to distinguish M&S and Woolworth's. The sales floors were big, open and contained counters on which goods were relatively prosaically laid out. Assistants, with their tills, were stationed in the middle of these islands.[50]

Fig. 539 (above left) Broadcasting House, Langham Place, London, George Val Meyer, 1932. Rudely condemned by some, but a building that expresses its functions and aspirations perfectly. Concessions to its historic surroundings are just enough to make it a traditional London public building in Portland stone, but its resemblance to a wireless set makes it modern too.

Fig. 540 (top) Marks and Spencer's, Gallowtree Gate, Leicester, 1930. A typical inter-war M&S with big windows and the green and gold fascia.

Fig. 541 (above) Interior of a Marks and Spencer's shop, very similar to the interior of a Woolworth's shop at the time.

Last Words

In 1934 the writer J. B. Priestley identified three different Englands: the country of cathedrals and minsters, of country villages and inns, of winding lanes and quaint highways and byways; the heavy, hard England of industrialisation, of coal, iron, steel, cotton, railways and urbanisation; and then the England that wanted to be modern like the US. For him this latter England, the one on the rise, was symbolised by Woolworth's, a shop where things were cheap and accessible and mass-produced; a shop whose clients visited cinemas, dance halls and cocktail bars, and whose heroes and heroines were film stars, musicians and sportsmen.[51]

It was in leisure pursuits such as shopping that some – Priestley amongst them – saw the threat of creeping Americanisation. By the 1920s successful films – the ones people wanted to watch – were almost all American. So too was the music to which young people danced: hot jazz, ragtime and foxtrot. It was the BBC that acted as a bastion against this creeping Americanisation, championing British traditions in music and comedy, and instituting a calendar of national events, from the sound of the first nightingale to the choristers of King's College Chapel. In 1932, ten years after its foundation, the BBC commissioned the first purpose-built broadcasting building in Britain. Broadcasting House on Portland Place was designed by George Val Myer, a commercial architect who had built a number of city office blocks. The building was a great round keep, with the windowless studios in its core surrounded by offices (fig. 539). In the context of its neighbours the design could be seen as assertively modern, overwhelming the delicate All Souls', Langham Place, next door. But it was executed in Portland stone, the material of London's public buildings, had Georgian-shaped windows, and the sculptor Eric Gill spent months carving the figures of Prospero and Ariel on the entrance façade. This was a structure rooted in the traditions of London building.[52]

Stanley Baldwin's government set up the Empire Marketing Board in 1926 to promote imperial products worldwide. Its secretary was Sir Stephen Tallents, who invented the concept of national projection – the projection of images of Britain that married dynamic, forward-looking characteristics such as industry, tourism, universities and scientific research with a more established group of icons: the monarchy, London buses, the University Boat Race and the countryside. In 1937 Britain sported a pavilion at the Paris International Exhibition intended to convey exactly this. The structure, partly modern and partly traditional, was a white box with curvaceous lines but Georgian-shaped windows. Inside, it contained a traditional vision of England, with tennis, weekend cottages, shepherds in white smocks and a cardboard cut-out of Neville Chamberlain fishing. It was designed by the architect Oliver Hill but with significant input from Frank Pick, the brains behind the branding of London Underground.[53]

This remarkable display encapsulated the architectural mood of the 1930s. Whilst people were interested in what was happening on the continent and wanted to reflect this in Paris, English architecture was insular and traditional. Neither word is used in a pejorative sense. British architects – many were Scots – had developed from the 1870s a classical freestyle that, at its most successful, unified architecture and craftsmanship in a distinctively English way. Whether its roots were primarily vernacular, Tudor, from the office of Wren or drew on Georgian urban forms, it expressed the confidence in native traditions due to a nation that still enjoyed cultural dominance.

Also on Portland Place, and started the same year as Broadcasting House, was the new Royal Institute of British Architects (RIBA) headquarters, by Grey Wornam (fig. 542). Sixty-six Portland Place is a well-behaved building, in scale with the Georgian buildings on either side, with a rusticated basement, fenestration and balconies that draw from 18th-century street architecture. The year before their HQ was started the RIBA, growing in confidence and influence, had effectively gained control over anyone wanting to design buildings and call themselves an architect. Architects were now defined by law as having passed exams set for them by their governing body.[54]

Yet to many young architects their new HQ seemed old-fashioned. They were learning from developments in Germany and France, which were the diet of architectural schools and soon to be the criteria for passing their exams. The Modern movement, a way of designing that developed in those two countries in the 1920s, was antagonistic to the idea of style and ornament, favouring abstract forms and new materials instead. Problems were solved from first principles not by reference to precedent – and the skills of the builder were of little importance. Most of all, perhaps, this way of designing brought with it a strong desire to use architecture to change society.

Of course, this was not a new idea. Pugin wanted to change society, as did John Ruskin and William Morris. So the idea of architecture as an agent of social change was in no way revolutionary. But crucially, after 1945 the idea appealed incredibly strongly to both politicians and the architects in their pay. From the late 1950s modernism was to sweep aside the structures, both physical and legal, that had ensured continuity in English towns and cities, giving state-employed architects scope to redraw the architectural map of England. It was also to sweep aside the whole basis of architectural design and practice established in the inter-war period.

After the Second World War England's architecture entered a new phase, one that contains buildings of dazzling quality and interest; but it is a phase that is not yet over. Despite stylistic tags such as post-modernism and high-tech used to label recent buildings, today's architecture is still part of the architectural period that started after the war. How and when it will end we cannot tell; whether we will even notice its passing is not certain. But end it will; the pendulum will swing, and architects and patrons will start to want something different.

Fig. 542 (right) Royal Institute of British Architects, Portland Place, London, George Grey Wornam, 1934. This elegant structure, a homage to contemporary English craftsmanship, was commissioned by architects for architects. It perfectly captures the pre-war moment: a building rooted in tradition but confident and free in its use of classical proportions and elements. This was a building still rooted in history and tradition, commissioned by a profession that was soon to turn away from both.

Endnotes

The intention of these endnotes is to enable those who want to know more to follow up their interests. Much of what is covered in this book is contentious and I have only presented my own views, and not discussed alternative interpretations. Therefore I have tried to include in the notes books and articles that put contrasting views as well as those that support my own interpretation. In addition to the sources referenced in the endnotes three works of reference have been used extensively and have not been noted individually. Nicholas Pevsner's *Buildings of England* has been a constant guide to the buildings mentioned in this book, the *Oxford Dictionary of National Biography* has been my guide to the people who populate these pages and the third edition of Howard Colvin's *Dictionary of British Architects* provides definitive attributions to buildings designed between 1600 and 1840.

Introduction

1 See, for instance, the excellent multi-volume series, P. Langford (gen. ed.), *The Short Oxford History of the British Isles* (Oxford, 2000 onwards).

2 P. Robinson, 'Edinburgh – a tenement city', in B. Edwards and P. Jenkins (eds), *Edinburgh: The Making of a Capital City* (Edinburgh, 2005), p. 103.

3 H. Wölfflin, *Principles of Art History: The Problem of the Development of Style in Later Art* (New York, 1932). A perceptive analysis of the development of the discipline is D. Watkin, *The Rise of Architectural History* (London, 1980).

4 G. Worsley, *Classical Architecture in Britain: The Heroic Age* (Yale, 1995), p. 245.

5 E. Fernie, *The Architecture of Norman England* (Oxford, 2000), pp. 317–18; R. Hewlings, 'Does Palladian architecture exist?', *Society of Architectural Historians Newsletter* 88 (May 2006), pp. 1–5.

6 E. McKellar, 'Palladianism via postmodernism: constructing and deconstructing the "English Renaissance"', *Art History* 20 (1997), pp. 154–74.

7 D. Watkin, *Morality and Architecture Revisited* (London, 2001), pp. 79–127.

8 A. Saint, *Architect and Engineer: A Study in Sibling Rivalry* (Yale, 2008).

9 M. A. Saint, The Image of the Architect (Yale, 1983); M. Crinson and J. Lubbock, *Architecture, Art or Profession?: Three Hundred Years of Architectural Education in Britain* (Manchester, 1994).

10 Dummer has now been given proper attention in C. Fox, 'The ingenious Mr Dummer: rationalising the Royal Navy in late seventeenth-century England', *Electronic British Library Journal* (2007), pp. 1–58.

11 R. Scruton, *The Aesthetics of Architecture* (London, 1979), pp. 104–34.

12 For example, N. Cossons (gen. ed.), *England's Landscape* 7 vols (London, 2006).

13 T. Blanning, *The Culture of Power and the Power of Culture: Old Regime Europe 1660–1789* (Oxford, 2006), pp. 266–356; L. Colley, *Britons: Forging the Nation* (Yale, 1992).

14 A. Macfarlane, *The Origins of English Individualism* (Oxford, 1978). But see also, F. Pryor, *Britain BC: Life in Britain and Ireland before the Romans* (London, 2003), p. 439.

15 Deyan Sudjic, *The Edifice Complex: How the Rich and Powerful Shape the World* (Penguin, 2006).

16 Two recent books have argued this case strongly: P. Draper, *The Formation of English Gothic: Architecture and Identity* (Yale, 2006); M. Girouard, *Elizabethan Architecture: Its Rise and Fall*, 1540–1640 (Yale, 2009).

17 A. Pugin, *An Apology for the Revival of Christian Architecture* (London, 1843), p. 4.

18 Hansard, *The Official Report*, ser. 5, 393 (1943), col. 403.

Chapter One

1 A. S. Esmonde Cleary, *The Ending of Roman Britain* (London, 1989), pp. 188–205; Nicholas Higham, *Rome, Britain and the Anglo-Saxons* (London, 1992); Neil Faulkner, 'The debate about the end: a review of the evidence and methods', *Archaeological Journal* 159 (2002), pp. 59–76.

2 Bryan Ward-Perkins, 'Urban continuity', in N. Christie and S. T. Loseby (eds), *Towns in Transition: Urban Evolution in Late Antiquity and the Early Middle Ages* (Aldershot, 1996), pp. 4–17: S. T. Loseby, 'Power and towns in late Roman Britain and early Anglo-Saxon England', in G. Ripoll and J. M. Gurt (eds) *Sedes Regiae (ann. 400–800)* (Barcelona, 2000), pp. 319–70; A. S. Esmonde Cleary, *The Ending of Roman Britain*, op. cit., pp. 188–205; S. T. Loseby, 'Power and towns in late Roman Britain and early Anglo-Saxon England', op. cit., pp. 327–9.

3 J. C. Higgitt, 'The Roman background to medieval England', *Journal of the British Archaeological Association* 36 (1973), pp. 1–15; Ken Dark and Petra Dark, *The Landscape of Roman Britain* (Stroud, 1997), pp. 135–46; Barry Cunliffe, 'Earth's grip holds them', in B. Hartley and J. Wacher (eds), *Rome and Her Northern Provinces* (Oxford, 1983), pp. 67–83.

4 Nicholas Brooks, 'Church, state and access to resources in early

Anglo-Saxon England', *The Brixworth Lectures*, second series, 2 (2002), pp. 14–19; A. L. Poole, *From Domesday Book to Magna Carta* (Oxford, 1951), pp. 78–9; Hugh Davies, *Roman Roads in Britain* (Stroud, 2002), pp. 10, 20; Alan Cooper, *Bridges, Law and Power in Medieval England 700–1400* (Woodbridge, 2006).

5 Nicholas Howe, 'Rome as capital of Anglo-Saxon England', *Writing the Map of Anglo-Saxon England: Essays in Cultural Geography* (Yale, 2008), pp. 101–25; William Filmer-Sankey, 'The "Roman emperor" in the Sutton Hoo ship burial', *Journal of the British Archaeological Association* 149 (1996), pp. 1–9.

6 V. Ortenberg, *The English Church and the Continent in the Tenth and Eleventh Centuries* (Oxford, 1992), pp. 132–164.

7 Earl R. Anderson, 'The uncarpentered world of Old English poetry', *Anglo-Saxon England* 20 (1991), pp. 65–9; Jason R. Ali and Peter Cunich, 'The orientation of churches: some new evidence', *Antiquaries Journal* 81 (2001), pp. 155–93.

8 Julian Munby, 'Wood', in John Blair and Nigel Ramsay (eds), *English Medieval Industries: Craftsmen, Techniques, Products* (London, 1991), pp. 379–94; David M. Wilson, 'Craft and Industry', *The Archaeology of Anglo-Saxon England* (London, 1976), pp. 253–66.

9 E. M. Jope, 'The Saxon building-stone industry in southern and midland England', *Medieval Archaeology* 8 (1964), pp. 91–118; David Parsons, 'Stone', in John Blair and Nigel Ramsay (eds), *English Medieval Industries*, op. cit., pp. 1–17.

10 Cramp. 93.

11 *Beowulf*, trans. Michael Alexander (Harmondsworth, 1979), p.75.

12 Some think that the hall excavated at Northampton cited in Chapter 2, note 11 (below) was royal.

13 Barry Cunliffe, *The Danebury Environs Roman Programme: A Wessex Landscape During the Roman Era. I* (Oxford, 2008), pp. 126–9; W. J. Rodwell and K. A. Rodwell, Rivenhall: *Investigations of a Villa, Church and Village, 1950–1977* (CBA Research Report 55, 1985), pp. 56, 63–4, 74–5; S. James, A. Marshal and M. Millett, 'An early medieval building tradition', *Archaeological Journal* 141 (1984), pp. 182–215.

14 P. Rahtz, 'Buildings and rural settlement', in D. M. Wilson (ed.), *The Archaeology of Anglo-Saxon England* (London, 1976), pp. 49–98; Martin Welch, *Anglo-Saxon England* (London, 1992), pp. 43–53; Richard Bradley, 'Time regained: the creation of continuity', Journal of the British Archaeological Association 140 (1987), pp. 1–17.

15 S. E. West, 'The Anglo-Saxon village of West Stow: an interim report of the excavations 1965–8', *Medieval Archaeology* 13 (1969), pp. 1–11; S. E. West, *West Stow Revisited* (Bury St Edmunds, 2001), p. 9; Martin Welch, *The English Heritage Book of Anglo-Saxon England* (London, 1992), pp. 14–31; Helena Hamerow, *Early Medieval Settlements. The Archaeology of Rural Communities in Northwest Europe 400–900* (Oxford, 2002); R. Hodges, *The Anglo-Saxon Achievement* (Cornell, 1989), p. 36; J. Tipper, *The Grubenhaus in Anglo-Saxon England* (Yedingham 2004).

16 Richard Morris, *Churches in the Landscape* (London, 1989), pp. 19–25; T. Tatton-Brown, 'St Martin's Church in the 6th and 7th centuries', in M. Sparks (ed.), *The Parish of St. Martin and St. Paul Canterbury: Historical Essays in Memory of James Hobbs* (Canterbury, 1980), pp. 12–18.

17 Eric Fernie, *The Architecture of the Anglo-Saxons* (London, 1983), pp. 35–46.

18 Rosemary Cramp, *Wearmouth and Jarrow Monastic Sites 1* (English Heritage, 2005), pp. 348–61; C. H. Lawrence, *Medieval Monasticism* (London, 2001), pp. 58–61.

19 Jennifer O'Reilly, 'The art of authority', in Thomas Charles-Edwards (ed.), *After Rome* (Oxford, 2003), pp. 141–8.

20 H. Christie, O. Olsen and H. M. Taylor, 'The wooden church of St Andrew in Grenstead in Essex', *Antiquaries Journal* 59 (1979), pp. 92–112.

Chapter Two

1 J. Richards, *Viking Age England* (Stroud, 2007), pp. 109–25.

2 R. Krautheimer, 'The Carolingian revival of early Christian architecture', *Art Bulletin* 24 (March 1942), pp. 1–38.

3 D. Hamilton, *The Bridges of Medieval England: Transport and Society 400–1800* (Oxford, 2004), p. 37.

4 W. Rodwell, J. Hawkes, E. Howe and R. Cramp, 'The Lichfield Angel: a spectacular Anglo-Saxon painted sculpture', *Antiquaries Journal* 88 (2008), pp. 48–108.

5 H. M. Taylor, *All Saints' Church, Brixworth: How the Church Took Its Shape*, Vaughan Paper no. 32 (Leicester, 1984).

6 M. Brown and C. Farr, Mercia: *An Anglo-Saxon Kingdom in Europe* (London, 2001); D. S. Sutherland and D. Parsons, 'The petrological contribution to the survey of All Saints' Church, Brixworth, Northamptonshire: an interim study', *Journal of the British Archaeological Association* 137 (1984), pp. 45–64.

7 P. Geary, Furta Sacra: *Thefts of Relics in the Central Middle Ages* (Princeton, 1990), pp. 32–3, 41–2.

8 The term *Westwerk* (or *Westwerken*), which originates in German architectural history, has here been anglicised.

9 Richard Morris, *Cathedrals and Abbeys of England and Wales: The Building Church, 600–1540* (New York, 1979), pp. 130–43. For Anglo-Saxon taste, see C. R. Dodwell, *Anglo-Saxon Art: A New Perspective* (Manchester, 1982).

10 Dom David Knowles, *The Monastic Order in England* (Cambridge, 1963), pp. 31–56.

11 R. Gem and E. Howe, 'The ninth-century polychrome decoration at St Mary's Church, Deerhurst', *Antiquaries Journal* 88 (2008), pp. 109–64; C. R. Dodwell, *Anglo-Saxon Art: A New Perspective* (Manchester, 1982); P. Tudor-Craig, 'Nether Wallop reconsidered', in S. Cather, D. Park and P. Williamson (eds), *Early Medieval Wall Painting and Painted Sculpture in England*, BAR (BS) 216 (1990), pp. 89–104.

12 J. Blair, 'Palaces or minsters? Northampton and Cheddar reconsidered', *Anglo-Saxon England* 25 (1996), pp. 97–121.

13 B. Kjølbye-Biddle, 'Old Minster, St Swithun's Day 1093', in John Crook (ed.), *Winchester Cathedral: Nine Hundred Years 1093–1993* (Chichester, 1993), pp. 13–20; J. H. Gibb and R. Gem, 'The Anglo-Saxon cathedral at Sherborne', *Archaeological Journal* 132 (1975), pp. 71–110; 'Sherborne

Abbey: the early church', *RCHME Dorset* 1 (1952), Addendum (1974); Roger Stalley, *Early Medieval Architecture* (Oxford, 1999), pp. 46–53; T. Tatton Brown, *Great Cathedrals of Britain* (London, 1989), pp. 19–48.

14 Trans. and intro, S. Keynes and M. Lapidge, *Alfred the Great: Asser's Life of Alfred and other Contemporary Sources* (Harmondsworth, 1984), p. 101; P. Rahtz, *The Saxon and Medieval Palaces at Cheddar*, British Archaeological Report (BS) 65 (Oxford, 1979).

15 H. M. Colvin (ed.), *The History of the King's Works I* (London, 1963), p. 5; II (London, 1963), pp. 907–9.

16 D. Goodburn, 'Fragments of a 10th-century timber arcade from Vintner's Place on the London waterfront', *Medieval Archaeology* 37 (1993), pp. 78–92.

17 R. Hodges, *The Anglo-Saxon Achievement* (Cornell, 1989), pp. 80–92; G. Malcolm and D. Bowsher with R. Cowie, *Middle Saxon London: Excavations at the Royal Opera House 1989–99* (MoLAS Monograph 15, 2003), pp. 57–9, 150–8.

18 V. Horsman, C. Milne and G. Milne, *Aspects of Saxo-Norman London: 1. Building and Street Development* (London and Middlesex Archaeological Society paper 11, 1988).

19 R. Morris, *Churches in the Landscape* (London, 1989), pp. 168–226.

20 J. Blair, *Anglo-Saxon Oxfordshire* (Stroud, 1994).

21 W. Rodwell, *St Peter's, Barton-upon-Humber, Lincolnshire: A Parish Church and Its Community* 1 (Oxbow, 2010).

22 Christopher Dyer, *Making a Living in the Middle Ages: The People of Britain 850–1520* (Yale, 2002), pp. 58–70.

23 A. Oswald, *Wharram Percy Deserted Medieval Village, North Yorkshire: Archaeological Investigation and Survey* (English Heritage Archaeological Investigation Series AI/19, 2004); Stuart Wrathmell, *Wharram: A Study of Settlement on the Yorkshire Wolds, VI. Domestic Settlement 2: Medieval Peasant Farmsteads* (York University Archaeological Publications 8, 1989).

24 Christopher Dyer, *Making a Living in the Middle Ages*, op. cit., pp. 17–26.

25 C. Taylor, *Fields in the English Landscape* (London 1975, esp. chs 3–5); D. Hall, *The Open Fields of Northamptonshire* (Northamptonshire Record Society 38, 1995); D. Hall, *Turning the Plough: Midlands Open Fields* (Northampton, 2001). On the detail of the operation of 'open' or 'common' fields, see C. S. and C. S. Orwin, *The Open Fields* 3rd edn (Oxford, 1967).

26 H. Hamerow, *Early Medieval Settlements: The Archaeology of Rural Communities in Northwest Europe 400–900* (Oxford, 2002); E. Kerridge, *The Common Field of England* (Manchester, 1992).

27 J. Leary and D. Field, *The Story of Silbury Hill* (Swindon, 2010), pp. 165–70.

28 G. Beresford, *Goltho: The Development of an Early Medieval Manor c. 850–1150* (London, 1987); B. Cunliffe, *Excavations at Portchester Castle, II, Saxon* (Report of the Society of Antiquaries 33, 1976); P. Everson, 'What's in a name? "Goltho", Goltho and Bullington', *Lincolnshire History and Archaeology* 23 (1988), pp. 93–6; A. Williams, 'A bell-house and burgh-geat: lordly residences in England before the Norman Conquest', *Medieval Knighthood* 4 (1992), pp. 221–40.

29 R. Holt, *The Mills of Medieval England* (Oxford, 1988); D. Wilson and J. Hurst, 'Medieval Britain in 1957', *Medieval Archaeology* 2 (1958), pp. 184–5.

30 J. Blair, *The Church in Anglo-Saxon Society* (Oxford, 2005), pp. 58–65, 228–45, 463–71; D. Stocker and P. Everson, *Summoning St Michael: Early Romanesque Towers in Lincolnshire* (Oxford, 2006), pp. 81–91.

31 For drawings, see C. A. Hewett, *English Historic Carpentry* (Chichester, 1980), pp. 14–20; R. Gem, 'The early Romanesque tower of Sompting Church, Sussex', *Anglo-Norman Studies* 5 (1982), pp. 121–8.

32 E. M. Jope, 'The Saxon building-stone industry in southern and midland England', *Medieval Archaeology* 8 (1964), pp. 91–117; D. Parsons, *Stone Quarrying and Building in England AD 43–1525* (Chichester, 1990), pp. 1–16.

33 W. Rodwell, 'Anglo-Saxon church building: aspects of design and construction', in L. A. S. Butler and R. K. Morris (eds), *The Anglo-Saxon Church* (CBA Research Report 60, 1986), pp. 156–75.

34 R. Gem, 'England and the resistance to Romanesque architecture', *Studies in Medieval History Presented to R. Allen Brown* (Woodbridge, 1989), pp. 129–39; R. Gem, 'Architecture of the Anglo-Saxon Church, 735 to 870: from Archbishop Eqgherht to Archbisop Ceolnoth', *Journal of the British Archaeological Association* 146 (1993), pp. 29–66.

Chapter Three

1 J. Richards, *Viking Age England* (Stroud, 2007), pp. 109–25; E. Fernie, *The Architecture of Norman England* (Oxford, 2000), p. 218.

2 S. Inwood, *A History of London* (London, 1998), pp. 45–50; F. Sheppard, London: *A History* (Oxford, 1998), pp. 66–9.

3 K. Conant, *Carolingian and Romanesque Architecture 800 to 1200* (Harmondsworth, 1959), pp. 57–134; R. Stalley, *Early Medieval Architecture* (Oxford, 1999), pp. 191–213.

4 R. Mortimer, *Edward the Confessor: The Man and the Legend* (Woodbridge, 2009), chs 6–8; R. Gem, 'The Romanesque rebuilding of Westminster Abbey', *Proceedings of the Battle Conference* 3 (1980), pp. 33–60; E. Fernie, *The Architecture of Norman England* (Oxford, 2000), p. 195.

5 J. Blair, *The Church in Anglo-Saxon Society* (Oxford, 2005), pp. 433–51, 458.

6 George Zarnecki, 'General introduction', *English Romanesque Art, 1066–1200*, p. 15; E. Fernie, 'The effect of the conquest on Norman architectural patronage', *Anglo-Norman Studies* 9 (1987), pp. 71–85.

7 An old but good book is T. Atkinson, *Local Style in English Architecture* (London, 1947).

8 R. Higham and P. Barker, *Timber Castles* (London, 1992), p. 57; A. Williams, 'A bell-house and burgh-geat: lordly residences in England before the Norman Conquest', *Medieval*

Knighthood 4 (Woodbridge, 1992), pp. 221–40; D. Renn, 'Burhgeat and Gonfanon: two sidelights from the Bayeux Tapestry', *Anglo-Norman Studies* 16 (1993), pp. 177–86; D. Bates, *Normandy before 1066* (London, 1982), pp. 114–15, 156.

9 J. A. Green, *The Aristocracy of Norman England* (Cambridge, 1997), pp. 172–6; H. M. Colvin, *The History of the King's Works* I (London, 1963), pp. 19–27; R. Higham and P. Barker, *Timber Castles*, op. cit.

10 David Carpenter, *The Struggle for Mastery* (London, 2004), pp. 81–5.

11 P. Bennett et al., *Excavations at Canterbury Castle* I (Maidstone, 1982), pp. 70–2.

12 Edward Impey (ed.), *The White Tower* (Yale, 2008); Paul Drury, 'Aspects of the origin and development of Colchester Castle', *Archaeological Journal* 139 (1982), pp. 302–419.

13 J. Blair, *The Church in Anglo-Saxon Society* (Oxford, 2005), pp. 489–97.

14 A. W. Lukas, 'The architectural implications of the Decreta Lanfranci', *Anglo-Norman Studies* 6 (1983), pp. 136–71.

15 A. Klukas, 'The continuity of Anglo-Saxon liturgical tradition in post-Conquest England as evident in the architecture of Winchester, Ely, and Canterbury Cathedrals', *Les Mutations Socio-Culturelles* 2 (1984), pp. 111–23.

16 R. Gem, 'The Romanesque cathedral of Winchester: patron and design in the eleventh century', *Medieval Art and Architecture at Winchester Cathedral* (British Archaeological Association Transactions, 1983), pp. 1–12; John Crook, 'Bishop Walkelin's cathedral', in John Crook (ed.), *Winchester Cathedral: Nine Hundred Years 1093–1993* (Chichester, 1993), pp. 21–36.

17 F. Barlow, *The English Church 1066–1154* (London, 1979), p. 2; P. Drury and W. Rodwell, 'Investigations at Asheldham, Essex', Antiquaries Journal 58 (1978), pp. 133–51.

18 S. Heywood, *St. Margaret's Church Hales* (Churches Conservation Trust, 2004).

19 R. Rosewell, *Medieval Wall Paintings in English and Welsh Churches* (Woodbridge, 2008).

20 F. Barlow, *The English Church 1066–1154*, op. cit., pp. 133–5.

21 J. Le Patourel, *The Norman Empire* (Oxford, 1978), pp. 45–7; R. Fleming, *Kings and Lords in Conquest England* (Cambridge, 1991), pp. 194–200.

22 O. H. Creighton, *Castles in the Landscape* (London, 2002), pp. 156–7; R. Allen Brown, *Castles from the Air* (Cambridge, 1989), pp. 197–9.

23 B. Gauthiez, 'The planning of the town of Bury St. Edmunds', *Bury St. Edmunds: Medieval Art, Architecture, Archaeology and Economy*, British Archaeological Association Transaction 20 (1998), pp. 81–110.

24 An up-to-date bibliography for the hall is in C. Wilson, 'Rulers, artificers and shoppers: Richard II's remodelling of Westminster Hall, 1393–99', in D. Gordon, L. Monnas and C. Elam (eds), *The Regal Image of Richard II and the Wilton Diptych* (London, 1997), pp. 33–59.

25 *English Romanesque Art 1066–1200* (London, 1984), pp. 146 ff.

26 T. A. Heslop, *Norwich Castle Keep: Romanesque Architecture and Social Context* (Norwich, 1994); P. Drury, 'Norwich Castle Keep', *The Seigneurial Residence in Western Europe AD c. 800–1600*, G. Meirion-Jones, E. Impey, M. Jones, British Archaeological Report (IS) 1088 (Oxford 2002), pp. 211–34; P. Dixon and P. Marshall, 'Norwich Castle and its analogues', *The Seigneurial Residence in Western Europe AD c. 800–1600*, op. cit., pp. 235–44.

27 J. Goodall, *The English Castle* (Yale, 2011), pp. 98–103.

28 L. F. Salzman, *Building in England down to 1540* (Oxford, 1952), p. 119; David Parsons (ed.), *Stone Quarrying and Building in England AD 43–1525* (Chichester, 1990), pp. 1–12, 70–4; E. M. Jope, 'The Saxon building-stone industry in southern and midland England', *Medieval Archaeology* 7 (1964), pp. 93–5.

29 J. Blair (ed.), *Waterways and Canal Building in Medieval England* (Oxford, 2007), pp. 175ff.

30 E. Fernie, *The Architecture of Norman England* (Oxford, 2000), pp. 290–4; D. Knoop and G. P. Jones, *The Medieval Mason* 3rd ed. (Manchester, 1967), pp. 66–71.

31 B. Morley, 'The nave roof of the church of St Mary, Kempley, Gloucestershire', *Antiquaries Journal* 65(1) (1985), pp. 101–11.

32 Ibid, pp. 101–11; W. Rodwell, D. Miles, D. Hamilton and M. Bridge, 'The dating of the Pyx door', *English Heritage Historical Review* 1 (2006), pp. 24–7; *Victoria County History* Surrey III, p. 20.

33 Stuart Harrison and Paul Barker, 'Byland Abbey, North Yorkshire: the west front and rose window reconstructed', *Journal of the British Association of Archaeology* 140 (1987), pp. 134–51.

Chapter Four

1 A. Williams, *The English and the Norman Conquest* (Woodbridge, 1995), pp. 208–11.

2 Henry of Huntingdon, *The History of the English People 1000–1154*, trans. and ed. D. Greenway (Oxford, 2002); R. R. Davies, *The First English Empire: Power and Identities in the British Isles 1093–1343* (Oxford, 1999); J. Gillingham, *The English in the Twelfth Century: Imperialism, National Identity and Political Values* (Woodbridge, 2000); R. H. C. Davis, *The Normans and their Myth* (London, 1976).

3 F. Barlow, *The English Church 1066–1154* (London, 1979), p. 207.

4 N. Coldstream, *Medieval Architecture* (Oxford, 2002), pp. 23–30.

5 P. Draper, 'Canterbury Cathedral: classical columns in the Trinity Chapel?', *Architectural History* 44 (2001), pp. 172–8.

6 D. Robinson (ed.), *The Cistercian Abbeys of Britain* (London, 1998).

7 G. Coppack, *The White Monks: The Cistercians in Britain* (Stroud, 2000), pp. 23–39.

8 C. Wilson, *The Gothic Cathedral* (London, 1990), pp. 78–82; T. Tatton Brown, *Great Cathedrals of Britain* (London, 1989), pp. 91–4.

9 P. Draper, *The Formation of English Gothic: Architecture and*

Identity (Yale, 2006), pp. 233, 249; Paul Crossley, 'English Gothic architecture', in J. Alexander and P. Binski (eds), *Age of Chivalry: Art in Plantagenet England 1200–1400*, pp. 69–70.

10 E. Impey, *Castle Acre Priory and Castle* (English Heritage, 2008).

11 M. Aston, 'The expansion of the monastic and religious orders in Europe from the eleventh century', in G. Keevill, M. Aston and T. Hall (eds), *Monastic Archaeology* (Oxford, 2001), pp. 9–36.

12 P. Fergusson and S. Harrison, *Rievaulx Abbey: Community, Architecture, Memory* (Yale, 1999).

13 H. M. Colvin (ed.), *The History of the King's Works* II (London, 1963), pp. 910–22; T. B. James, *Clarendon Palace: The History and Archaeology of a Medieval Palace and Hunting Lodge near Salisbury, Wiltshire* (Society of Antiquaries of London, 1988).

14 P. A. Rahtz, *Excavations at King John's Hunting Lodge, Writtle, Essex, 1955–57* (Society for Medieval Archaeology Monograph 3, 1969).

15 H. M. Colvin (ed.), *The History of the King's Works* I (London, 1963), pp. 71–7; II, op. cit., pp. 629–32.

16 L. Cooper and S. Ripper, 'Medieval Trent bridges at Hemington Fields, Castle Donington', *Transactions of the Leicestershire Archaeological and Historical Society* 68 (1994), pp. 153–61; D. Harrison, *The Bridges of Medieval England: Transport and Society 400–1800* (Oxford, 2004); M. Roberts, *Durham* (London, 1994), pp. 64–5; Alan Cooper, *Bridges, Law and Power in Medieval England 700–1400* (Woodbridge, 2006).

17 F. M. Stenton, 'The road system of medieval England', *Economic History Review* 7(1) (1936), pp. 1–21.

18 D. F. Harrison, 'Bridges and economic development 1300–1800', *Economic History Review* 45(2) (1992), pp. 240–61.

19 C. Dyer, 'English peasant buildings in the later Middle Ages (1200–1500), *Medieval Archaeology* 30 (1986), pp. 19–45; J. Smith, 'The evolution of the English peasant house to the late seventeenth century: the evidence of the buildings', *Journal of the British Archaeological Association* 33 (1970), pp. 122–47.

20 C. Currie and J. Fletcher, 'Two early cruck houses in North Berkshire identified by radiocarbon', *Medieval Archaeology* 16 (1972), pp. 136–42; M. Nevell, 'Rediscovering Newton Hall', *Current Archaeology* 257 (August, 2011), pp. 32–9.

21 C. Dyer, 'English Peasant Buildings in the later Middle Ages (1200–1500)', op. cit., pp. 19–45.

22 R. Holt, *The Mills of Medieval England* (Oxford, 1988).

23 C. Hewett, 'The Barns at Cressing Temple, Essex, and their significance in the history of English carpentry', *Journal of the Society of Architectural Historians* 26 (1967), pp. 48–70; D. Stenning, 'The Cressing Barns and the early development of barns in south-east England', in D. Andrews (ed.), *Cressing Temple: A Templar and Hospitaller Manor in Essex* (Essex County Council, 1993), pp. 51–75.

24 A. Hutchinson, 'The origins of King's Lynn? Control of wealth on the Wash prior to the Norman Conquest', *Medieval Archaeology* 50 (2006), pp. 71–104; Vanessa Parker, *The Making of King's Lynn* (London, 1971).

25 G. Milne et al., *Timber Building Techniques in London c. 900–1400* (London and Middlesex Archaeological Society special paper 15, 1992).

26 D. Keene, 'Shops and shopping in medieval London', in L. Grant (ed.), *Medieval Art, Architecture and Archaeology* (British Archaeological Association, 1990), pp. 29–46.

27 D. Clark, 'The shop within?: an analysis of the architectural evidence for medieval shops', *Architectural History* 43 (2000), pp. 58–87.

28 M. Wood, *The English Medieval House* (London, 1965); S. Jones, K. Major and J. Varley, *The Survey of Ancient Houses in Lincoln* (Lincoln, 1990).

29 D. Stocker, *St Mary's Guildhall, Lincoln: The Survey and Excavation of a Medieval Building Complex* (Lincoln, 1991).

30 E. Prescott, *The English Medieval Hospital c. 1050–1640* (Melksham, 1992), pp. 8–10.

31 R. Morris, *Cathedrals and Abbeys of England and Wales: The Building Church 600–1540* (New York, 1979), pp. 177–208.

32 C. Wilson, *The Gothic Cathedral*, op. cit., p. 166.

33 P. Draper, *The Formation of English Gothic*, op. cit., p. 128.

Chapter Five

1 M. T. Clanchy, *England and Its Rulers 1066–1272* (London, 1983), pp. 241–62.

2 M. Prestwich, *Armies and Warfare in the Middle Ages* (Yale, 1996), pp. 219–31; J. Vale, *Edward III and Chivalry: Chivalric Society and Its Context 1270–1350* (Woodbridge, 1982).

3 M. Biddle, *King Arthur's Round Table* (Woodbridge, 2000); J. Mumby, R. Barber and R. Brown, *Edward III's Round Table at Windsor* (Woodbridge, 2007).

4 J. Goodall, *English Castles* (Yale, 2011), pp. 232–3; R. K. Morris, 'The architecture of Arthurian enthusiasm: castle symbolism in the reigns of Edward I and his successors', in M. Strickland (ed.), *Armies, Chivalry and Warfare in Medieval Britain and France* (Stamford, 1998), pp. 63–81.

5 Anne Payne, 'Medieval heraldry', in J. J. G. Alexander and Paul Binski (eds), *The Age of Chivalry* (Weidenfeld and Nicolson, 1987), pp. 55–9; T. Woodcock and J. Martin Robinson, *Heraldry in National Trust Houses* (London, 2000).

6 C. Platt, 'Revisionism in castle studies: a caution', *Medieval Archaeology* 51 (2007), pp. 83–102; C. Coulson, 'Structural symbolism in medieval castle architecture', *Journal of the British Association of Archaelology* 132 (1979), pp. 73–90; see also articles by Coulson and Platt in *The Castles Studies Group Journal* 21 (2007–8).

7 G. Beresford, 'Excavation of a moated house at Winteringham in Huntingdonshire', *Archaeological Journal* 134 (1977), pp. 194–286.

8 L. Cantor and J. Hatherly, 'The medieval parks of England', *Geography* 64 (1979), pp. 72–8.

9 T. James and C. Gerrard, *Clarendon: Landscape of Kings* (Macclesfield, 2007).

10 J. Clarke, *Helmsley Castle* (English Heritage, 2004).

11 M. Aston, *Monasteries in the Landscape* (Stroud, 2000); G. Coppack, *Abbeys and Priories* (London, 1990), pp. 100–28. G. Coppack, 'The water-driven corn mill at Fountains Abbey',

Studies in Cistercian Art and Architecture 5 (1998), pp. 271–96.

12 P. Binski, *Westminster and the Plantagenets* (Yale, 1995); C. Wilson, 'Calling the tune? The involvement of King Henry III in the design of the abbey church at Westminster', *Journal of the British Archaeological Association* 161 (2008), pp. 59–93.

13 N. Coldstream, *The Decorated Style* (London, 1994).

14 R. Marks, 'Stained glass, c. 1200–1400', in J. J. G. Alexander and Paul Binski (eds), *The Age of Chivalry*, op. cit., pp. 137–47; F. Eden, *Ancient Stained and Painted Glass* (Cambridge, 1933), pp. 64–90. M. Thurlby, 'The west front of Binham Priory, Norfolk, and the beginnings of bar tracery in England', in M. Ormrod (ed.), *England in the Thirteenth Century* (Stamford, 1991), pp. 155–65.

15 I am grateful to David Neave, who made available the draft of his Pevnser entry for this church.

16 C. Wilson, *The Gothic Cathedral* (London, 2002), pp. 191–6.

17 J. Moorman, *Church Life in England in the Thirteenth Century* (Cambridge, 1955); R. Morris, *Churches in the Landscape* (London, 1989), pp. 321–5.

18 C. Platt, *The Parish Churches of Medieval England* (London, 1995), pp. 25–30; D. Keene, A. Urns and A. Saint, *St Paul's: The Cathedral Church of London, 604–2004* (Yale, 2004), pp. 142–50.

19 *Victoria County History* Surrey III pp. 92–7.

20 R. Morris, *Churches in the Landscape*, op. cit., pp. 289–95.

21 H. A. Tummers, *Early Secular Effigies in England: The Thirteenth Century* (London, 1980).

22 T. D. Atkinson, *Local Style in English Architecture* (London, 1947), pp. 75–9, 87–94.

23 Not like for like, as it compares a monastic church with a secular cathedral, but it is still very informative.

24 P. Draper, *The Formation of English Gothic: Architecture and Identity* (Yale, 2006), pp. 197–215; G. Cobb, *English Cathedrals: The Forgotten Centuries* (London, 1980), pp. 108–23.

25 J. Cannon, *Cathedral: The Great English Cathedrals* (London, 2007), pp. 167–219.

26 C. Lawrence, *Medieval Monasticism: Forms of Religious Life in Western Europe in the Middle Ages* (London, 2001), pp. 238–41.

27 *Victoria County History* London I pp. 498–502.

28 M. Rubin, 'Development and change in English hospitals, 1100–1500', in L. Granshaw and R. Porter (eds), *The Hospital in History* (London, 1989), pp. 46–7.

29 C. Rawcliffe, *The Hospitals of Medieval Norwich* (Norwich, 1995), pp. 91–134.

30 C. Dyer, *Standards of Living in the Later Middle Ages* (Cambridge, 1990), pp. 27–85.

31 D. Webb, *Privacy and Solitude in the Middle Ages* (London, 2007), pp. 97–117; M. Girouard, *Social Life in the English Country House* (Yale, 1978), pp. 14–54.

32 J. Blair, 'Hall and chamber: English domestic planning 1000–1250', in G. Meirion-Jones and M. Jones (eds), *Manorial Domestic Buildings in England and Northern France* (Society of Antiquaries of London, 1993), pp. 1–21; D. Crouch, *The Image of Aristocracy in Britain 1000–1300* (London, 1992), pp. 252–79.

33 D. Oschinsky, *Walter of Henley and Other Treatises on Estate Management and Accounting* (Oxford, 1971), pp. 399–407.

34 K. Mertes, *The English Noble Household 1250–1600* (Oxford, 1988), pp. 14–15; C. Dyer, *Standards of Living in the Middle Ages* (Cambridge, 1989), pp. 50–1.

35 H. Summerson, *Stokesay Castle* (English Heritage, 2004); A. Emery, *Greater Medieval Houses of England and Wales* II (Cambridge, 2000), pp. 574–6; *Buildings of England, Shropshire*, pp. 608–14.

36 H. M. Colvin (ed.), *The History of the King's Works* I (London, 1982), pp. 491–510; P. Binski, *The Painted Chamber at Westminster* (Society of Antiquaries of London, 1986); J. Cherry and N. Stratford, *Westminster Kings and the Medieval Palace of Westminster* (British Museum, 1995).

37 J. Goodall, 'Dover Castle and the great siege of 1216', *Château Gaillard* 19 (2000), pp. 91–102.

38 D. M. Williams and J. R. Kenyon, *The Impact of the Edwardian Castles in Wales* (Oxford, 2009).

39 H. M. Colvin (ed.), *The History of the King's Works* I, op. cit., covers the castle building of this period, as does R. Allen Brown, *English Castles* (London, 1977).

40 J. Ashbee, 'The royal apartments in the inner ward at Conway Castle', *Archaeologia Cambrensis* 153 (2004), pp. 51–72.

41 C. Barron, 'London 1300–1540', in D. Palliser (ed.), *The Cambridge Urban History of Britain* I (Cambridge, 2000), pp. 395–440.

42 D. Keene, 'Wardrobes in the city: houses of consumption, finance and power', *Thirteenth-century England* (Woodbridge, 1999), pp. 61–79; C. Barron, 'Centres of conspicuous consumption: the aristocratic townhouse in London 1200–1550', *London Journal* 20 (1995), pp. 1–16; M. S. Giuseppi, 'The wardrobe accounts of Bogo de Clare 1284–5', *Archaeologia* 70 (1920), pp. 1–56.

43 J. Schofield, *Medieval London Houses* (Yale, 1994), pp. 34–51; M. Carlin, 'The reconstruction of Winchester House, Southwark', *London Topographical Record* 25 (1985), pp. 33–57.

44 J. Bony, *The English Decorated Style: Gothic Architecture Transformed 1250–1350* (Oxford, 1979), pp. 57–70; N. Coldstream, *The Decorated Style: Architecture and Ornament* (London, 1994), pp. 7–15.

Chapter Six

1 P. Frankl, *The Gothic: Literary Sources and Interpretation through Eight Centuries* (Princeton, 1960).

2 N. Coldstream, *Medieval Architecture* (Oxford, 2002), pp. 23–54; Important texts, neither of which can be taken at face value, for different reasons, are J. Harvey, *The Gothic World 100–1600* (London, 1950), pp. 91–132; N. Pevsner, *An Outline of European Architecture* (London, 1970), pp. 131–72.

3 C. Dyer, *Making a Living in the Middle Ages* (Yale, 2002), pp. 228–97.

4 S. Gerrard, *Dartmoor: Landscapes through Time* (London, 1997).

5 R. Schofield, 'The geographical distribution of wealth in England 1334–1649', *Economic History Review* 18, pp. 483–510.

6 S. Brown, 'Our magnificent fabric: York Minster, an architectural history c. 1220–1500', (London, 2003), p. 138; P. G. Lindley, 'The Black Death and English art: a debate and some assumptions', in M. Ormrod and P. Lindley (eds), *The Black Death in England* (Stamford, 2003), pp. 125–46.

7 C. Dyer, *Making a Living in the Middle Ages*, op. cit., pp. 330–49.

8 J. T. Smith, 'The evolution of the English peasant house to the late seventeenth century: the evidence of the buildings', *Journal of the British Archaeological Association* 33 (1970), pp. 123–34; C. Platt, *King Death* (London, 1977), pp. 164–9.

9 J. M. Maddison, 'Master masons of the diocese of Lichfield: a study in 14th-century architecture at the time of the Black Death', *Transactions of the Lancashire and Cheshire Antiquarian Society* 85 (1988), pp. 107–72; P. G. Lindley, *Gothic to Renaissance: Essays on Sculpture in England* (Stamford, 1995), pp. 21–3; L. F. Salzman, *Building in England down to 1540* (Oxford, 1952), pp. 72–4; H. M. Colvin (ed.), *The History of the King's Works* I (London, 1963), pp. 183–4.

10 J. Harvey, *The Perpendicular Style 1330–1485* (London, 1978), pp. 216–17; C. Wilson, 'Excellent, new and uniform': Perpendicular architecture c. 1400–1547', in R. Marks and P. Williamson (eds), *Gothic: Art for England 1400–1547* (London, 2003), pp. 106–16.

11 All the master craftsmen, or architects, mentioned in this chapter have entries in John Harvey, *Medieval English Architects: A Biographical Dictionary down to 1550* (London, 1984).

12 H. M. Colvin (ed.), *The History of the King's Works* II (London, 1963), pp. 864–88; C. Wilson, 'The royal lodgings of Edward III at Windsor Castle: form, function, representation', *Windsor, Medieval Archaeology, Art and Architecture of the Thames Valley* (British Archaeological Association Transactions 25, 2002), pp. 15–94.

13 N. Saul, *Richard II* (Yale, 1997), pp. 327–65.

14 C. Wilson, 'Rulers, artificers and shoppers: Richard II's remodelling of Westminster Hall, 1393–99', in D. Gordon, L. Monnas and C. Elam (eds), *The Regal Image of Richard II and the Wilton Diptych* (London, 1997), pp. 33–59.

15 H. M. Colvin, *Essays in English Architectural History* (Yale, 1999), pp. 19–20.

16 H. M. Colvin (ed.), *The History of the King's Works* I, op. cit., pp. 161–89.

17 H. M. Colvin, 'The "court style" in medieval English architecture: a review', in V. J. Scattergood and J. W. Sherborne (eds), *English Court Culture in the Later Middle Ages* (London, 1983), pp. 129–39.

18 K. McFarlane, *The Nobility of Later Medieval England* (Oxford, 1973), pp. 22–3, 194–5.

19 A. Emery, *Greater Medieval Houses of England and Wales* III (Cambridge, 2006), pp. 274–93.

20 P. A. Faulkner, 'Castle planning in the fourteenth century', *Archaeological Journal* 120 (1963), pp. 215–35.

21 A. Emery, *Greater Medieval Houses of England and Wales* III, op. cit., pp. 391–3.

22 K. McFarlane, *The Nobility of Later Medieval England*, op. cit., pp. 96–9.

23 A. Emery, *Dartington Hall* (Oxford, 1970), pp. 203–20; A. Emery, *Greater Medieval Houses of England and Wales* III, op. cit., pp. 34–5.

24 R. Morris, *Churches in the Landscape* (London, 1989), pp. 350–73; G. Rosser, 'Communities of parish and guild in the late Middle Ages', in S. Wright, *Parish Church and People: Local Studies in Lay Religion 1350–1750* (London, 1988), pp. 29–55.

25 K. French, 'Parochial fund-raising in late medieval Somerset', in K. French, G. Gibbs and B. Kümin (eds), *The Parish in English Life 1400–1600* (Manchester, 1997), pp. 115–32; C. Burgess, '"A fond thing vainly invented": an essay on purgatory and pious motive in later medieval England', in S. Wright, *Parish Church and People*, op. cit., pp. 56–79.

26 T. Heslop, 'The construction and furnishing of the Parish church of Salle Norfolk', in B. Ford (ed.), *The Cambridge Cultural History of Britain* II (Cambridge, 1995), pp. 194–9; E. Duffy, 'Late medieval religion', in R. Marks and P. Williamson (eds), *Gothic: Art for England 1400–1547*, op. cit., pp. 62–5.

27 L. Stone, *Sculpture in Britain: The Middle Ages* (Harmondsworth, 1955), pp. 207–10.

28 R. Hutton, *The Rise and Fall of Merry England: The Ritual Year 1400–1700* (Oxford, 1994), pp. 61–3.

29 G. Coppack, *Abbeys and Priories* (London, 1990), pp. 104–8.

30 M. Rubin, 'Development and change in English hospitals, 1100–1500', in L. Granshaw and R. Porter (eds), *The Hospital in History* (London, 1989), pp. 51–7.

31 C. Rawcliffe, *The Hospitals of Medieval Norwich* (Norwich, 1995), pp. 91–134.

32 A. Emery, *Greater Medieval Houses of England and Wales* III, op. cit., pp. 425–8.

33 P. Clark, *The English Alehouse: A Social History 1200–1830* (London, 1983), pp. 5–15, 34; H. A. Monckton, *A History of the Public House* (London, 1969), pp. 18–40.

34 W. A. Pantin, 'Medieval inns', *Studies in Building History* (London, 1961), pp. 166–91.

35 C. Dyer, *Making a Living in the Middle Ages*, op. cit., pp. 298–329.

36 V. Parker, *The Making of King's Lynn* (Chichester, 1971), pp. 136–48; P. Richards, *A History of St. George's Guildhall* (National Trust, 1992).

37 C. Barron, *The Medieval Guildhall of London* (London, 1974).

38 J. Schofield and A. Vince, *Medieval Towns* (London, 2003), pp. 62–3.

39 O. Creighton and R. Higham, *Medieval Town Walls* (Stroud, 2005); H. Turner, *Town Defences in England and Wales* (London, 1971).

40 G. Harriss, *Shaping the Nation: England 1360–1461* (Oxford, 2005), pp. 271–6.

41 On markets see J. Schofield and A. Vince, *Medieval Towns*, op. cit., pp. 58–62; M. Girouard, *The English Town: A History*

of Urban Life (Yale, 1990); J. Schmiechen and K. Carls, *The British Market Hall: A Social and Architectural History* (Yale, 1999);
A. Hallett, *Markets and Marketplaces of Britain* (Oxford, 2009).

42 M. Samuel, 'The fifteenth-century garner at Leadenhall, London', *Antiquaries Journal* 69 (1989), pp. 117–53; M. Samuel and G. Milne, 'The "Ledene Hall" and medieval market', in G. Milne (ed.), *From Roman Basilica to Medieval Market* (London, 1992), pp. 39–50.

43 M. Kowaleski, 'Port towns: England and Wales 1300–1540', in D. M. Palliser (ed.), *Cambridge Urban History of Britain I (600–1540)* (Cambridge, 2000), pp. 467–504.

44 J. Schofield, 'Medieval waterfront buildings in the City of London', in G. Milne and B. Hobley (eds), *Waterfront Archaeology in Britain and Northern Europe* (CBA report 41, 1981), pp. 24–30; V. Parker, *The Making of King's Lynn*, op. cit., pp. 89–91.

45 N. Orme, *Medieval Schools: From Roman Britain to Renaissance England* (Yale, 2006), pp. 187–255; J. Goodall, *God's House at Ewelme: Life, Devotion and Architecture in a Fifteenth-Century Almshouse* (Aldershot, 2001), pp. 99–108.

46 J. Catto (ed.), *History of the University of Oxford: I, The Early Oxford Schools* (Oxford, 1984); W. Pantin, 'Chantry priests' houses and other medieval lodgings', *Medieval Archaeology* 3 (1959), pp. 243–7.

47 L. G. Wyckham Legg, 'Windsor Castle, New College, Oxford, and Winchester College: a study in the development of planning by William of Wykeham', *Journal of the British Archaeological Association* 3 (1938), pp. 84–95; John H. Harvey, 'Winchester College', *Journal of the British Archaeological Association* 28 (1965), pp. 107–23.

48 J. Catto (ed.), *History of the University of Oxford: 2, Late Medieval Oxford* (Oxford, 1992), pp. 747–68; S. Thurley, 'The cloister and the hearth: Wolsey, Henry VIII and the early Tudor palace plan', *Journal of the British Archaeological Association* 162 (2009), pp. 179–84.

49 M. Keen, *English Society in the Middle Ages 1348–1500* (London, 1990), pp. 217–24.

50 R. Griffiths (ed.), *The Fourteenth and Fifteenth Centuries* (Oxford, 2003), pp. 125–6; J. Harvey, *The Perpendicular Style 1330–1485*, op. cit., p. 238.

51 C. Woolgar, 'The great household in late medieval England' (Yale, 1999), pp. 46–8, 76–8; C. Given-Wilson, *The English Nobility in the Late Middle Ages* (London, 1987), pp. 96–7.

52 C. Dyer, *Making a Living in the Middle Ages*, op. cit., p. 338.

53 G. Harriss, *Shaping the Nation: England 1360–1461*, op. cit., pp. 93–9.

54 R. Cowie and J. Cloake, 'An archaeological survey of Richmond Palace', *Post-Medieval Archaeology* 35 (2001), p. 34.

55 C. Drage, 'Nottingham Castle', *Transactions of the Thoroton Society* 93 (1989), pp. 54–60.

56 A. Emery, 'Ralph Lord Cromwell's manor at Wingfield: its construction, design and influence', *Archaeological Journal* 142 (1985), pp. 276–339.

57 G. Coppack, *Fountains Abbey* (London, 1993).

58 D. Knowles, 'English monastic Life in the later Middle Ages', *History* 39 (1954); A. Emery, *Greater Medieval Houses of England and Wales 1300–1500* (Cambridge, 2000), pp. 589–93.

59 C. Platt, *The Architecture of Medieval Britain: A Social History* (Yale, 1990), pp. 210–14.

60 C. Dyer, *Making a Living in the Middle Ages*, op. cit., pp. 337–8.

61 H. M. Colvin (ed.), *The History of the King's Works* I, op. cit., pp. 265–92.

62 H. M. Colvin (ed.), *The History of the King's Works* II, op. cit., pp. 884–5; III (London, 1975), pp. 305–14; C. Richmond and E. Scarff (eds), 'St George's Chapel, Windsor, in the late Middle Ages', *Historical Monographs Relating to St George's Chapel, Windsor Castle* 17 (2001).

63 H. M. Colvin (ed.), *The History of the King's Works* III, op. cit., pp. 210–22; T. Tatton-Brown and R. Mortimer (eds), *Westminster Abbey. The Lady Chapel of Henry VII* (Woodbridge, 2003).

64 H. M. Colvin (ed.), *The History of the King's Works* II, op. cit., pp. 269–78; III, op. cit., pp. 187–95.

65 N. Moore, 'Brick', in J. Blair and N. Ramsey (eds), *English Medieval Industries: Craftsmen, Techniques, Products* (London, 1991), pp. 211–36; L. F. Salzman, *Building in England down to 1540*, op. cit., pp. 140–54.

66 A. Clifton-Taylor, *The Pattern of English Building* (London, 1972), pp. 210–64.

67 H. M. Colvin (ed.), *The History of the King's Works* I, op. cit., pp. 279–92; J. A. A. Goodall, 'Henry VI's court and the construction of Eton College', in L. Keen and E. Scarff (eds), *Windsor: Medieval Archaeology, Art and Architecture of the Thames Valley* (Leeds, 2002), pp. 247–63.

Chapter Seven

1 C. Clay, *Economic Expansion and Social Change: England 1500–1700* I (Cambridge, 1984), pp. 3, 15, 103; J. Thirsk, *Economic Policy and Projects: The Development of a Consumer Society in Early Modern Britain* (Oxford, 1978); L. Levy Peck, *Consuming Splendor: Society and Culture in Seventeenth-Century England* (Cambridge, 2005), pp. 73–111.

2 D. Baker Smith, 'Renaissance and Reformation', *The Cambridge Cultural History of Britain: Sixteenth-Century Britain* (Cambridge, 1995), pp. 2–41; J. B. Trapp, *Background to the English Renaissance* (London, 1974); R. Porter, *The Renaissance in National Context* (Cambridge, 1994); J. Huizinga, 'The Problem of the Renaissance', *Men and Ideas* (London, 1960), pp. 243–87.

3 D. Knowles, *Bare Ruined Choirs: The Dissolution of the English Monasteries* (Cambridge, 1976).

4 E. Duffy, *The Stripping of the Altars: Traditional Religion in England 1400–1580* (Yale, 1992), pp. 478–503; M. Aston, 'Public worship and iconoclasm', *The Archaeology of the Reformation* (Society for Post-medieval Archaeology monograph 1, 2003), pp. 9–28.

5 N. Whyte, *Inhabiting the Landscape: Place, Custom and Memory,*

1500–1800 (Oxford, 2009), pp. 18–90.

6 L. Stone, *Sculpture in the Britain: The Middle Ages* (Harmondsworth, 1955), pp. 195–6.

7 B. Arciszewska, 'Classicism: constructing the paradigm in Continental Europe and Britain', in B. Arciszewska and E. McKellar (eds), *Articulating British Classicism: New Approaches to Eighteenth-Century Architecture* (Aldershot, 2004), pp. 2–3.

8 P. Drury, *Hill Hall: A Singular House Devised by a Tudor Intellectual* (London, 2009), pp. 84–9, 266.

9 S. Thurley, 'Somerset House: The palace of England's queens 1551–1692', *London Topographical Society* 168 (2009).

10 E. Mercer, *English Art 1553–1625* (Oxford, 1962), pp. 60–84.

11 A. R. Wagner, *Heralds and Heraldry in the Middle Ages: An Inquiry into the Growth of the Armorial Function of Heralds* (Oxford, 1939).

12 V. Hart, 'A peece rather of good heraldry, than of architecture: heraldry and the orders of architecture as joint emblems of chivalry', *RES: Anthropology and Aesthetics* 23 (1993), pp. 52–66; C. Anderson, 'Learning to read architecture in the English Renaissance', in L. Gent (ed.), *Albion's Classicism: The Visual Arts in Britain 1550–1660* (Yale, 1995), pp. 257–68.

13 M. Girouard, *Elizabethan Architecture: Its Rise and Fall* (Yale, 2010), pp. 229–40; M. Bath, *Speaking Poctures: English Emblem Books and Renaissance Culture* (London, 1994).

14 S. Thurley, *Hampton Court: A Social and Architectural History* (Yale, 2003); S. Thurley, *The Royal Palaces of Tudor England* (Yale, 1993).

15 H. M. Colvin, *The History of the King's Works IV* (London, 1982), pp. 367–726; A. Saunders, *Fortress Britain: Artillery Fortification in the British Isles and Ireland* (Liphook, 1989), pp. 34–68.

16 C. Platt, *The English Medieval Town* (London, 1976), pp. 180–3.

17 C. King, 'Closure and the urban great rebuilding in early modern Norwich', *Post-Medieval Archaeology* 44 (2010) pp. 54–80; A. Dyer, 'Urban housing: a documentary study of four Midland towns 1530–1700', *Post-Medieval Archaeology* 15 (1981), pp. 207–18; P. Hughes, 'Property and prosperity: the relationship of the buildings and fortunes of Worcester, 1500 1660', *Midland History* 17 (1992), pp. 39–58.

18 R. Tittler, *Architecture and Power. The Town Hall and the English Urban Community c. 1500–1640* (Oxford, 1991); M. Howard, 'Classicism and civic architecture in Renaissance England', in L. Gent (ed.), *Albion's Classicism: The Visual Arts in Britain 1550–1660*, op. cit., pp. 29–50.

19 D. Landes, *Revolution in Time: Clocks and the Making of the Modern World* (Harvard, 1983).

20 A. Saunders (ed.), *The Royal Exchange* (London, 1997).

21 L. Levy Peck, *Consuming Splendour: Society and Culture in Seventeenth-Century England*, op. cit., pp. 25–72; L. Stone, 'Inigo Jones and the New Exchange', *Archaeological Journal* 114 (1957), pp. 106–21.

22 S. Thurley, 'Somerset House: The palace of England's queens 1551–1692', op. cit., pp. 9–11; J. Wood, 'The architectural patronage of Algernon Percy, 10th Earl of Northumberland', in J. Bold and E. Chaney (eds), *English Architecture Public and Private: Essays for Kerry Downes* (London, 1993), pp. 58–9.

23 L. Stone, *The Crisis of the Aristocracy* (Oxford, 1966), pp. 385–403.

24 J. Bowsher and P. Miller, *The Rose and The Globe Playhouses of Shakespeare's Bankside, Southwark* (London, 2009).

25 J. Orrell, *The Quest for Shakespeare's Globe* (Cambridge, 1983), pp. 108–26; J. Bowsher and P. Miller, *The Rose and The Globe Playhouses of Shakespeare's Bankside, Southwark*, op. cit., pp. 14–21, 108–30.

26 G. Worsley, *The British Stable* (Yale, 2004), pp. 102–9.

27 J. Crofts, *Packhorse, Waggon and Post. Land Carriage and Communications under the Tudors and Stuarts* (London, 1967), pp. 109–24; J. Mumby, 'Queen Elizabeth's coaches: the wardrobe on wheels', *Antiquaries Journal* 83 (2003), pp. 311–67; L. Stone, *The Crisis of the Aristocracy*, op. cit., p. 397.

28 V. Belcher, R. Bond, M. Gray and A. Wittrick, *Sutton House: A Courtier's House in Hackney* (London, 2004), pp. 34–9.

29 M. Howard, 'Recycling the monastic fabric: beyond the Act of Dissolution', D. Gaimster and R.Gilchrist, *The Archaeology of the Reformation* (Society for Post-Medieval Archaeology monograph 1, 2003), pp. 221–34.

30 M. Howard, *The Early Tudor Country House: Architecture and Politics 1490–1550* (London, 1987).

31 M. Airs, 'Pomp or glory: the influence of Theobalds', in P. Croft (ed.), *Patronage, Culture and Power: The Early Cecils* (Yale, 2002), pp. 3–19.

32 For what follows, see M. Girouard, *Elizabethan Architecture*, op. cit.; N. Cooper, *The Jacobean Country House* (London, 2006); E. Mercer, *English Art 1553–1625*, op. cit.

33 D. Kiernan, *The Derbyshire Lead Industry in the Sixteenth Century* (Derbyshire Record Society, 1989). I am grateful to Jon Humble for his advice on this matter.

34 E. S. Godfrey, *The Development of English Glassmaking 1560–1640* (Oxford, 1975), pp. 200–15.

35 J. Harvey, *Medieval Gardens* (London, 1981); H. M. Colvin, 'Royal gardens in medieval England', *Medieval Gardens* (Dumbarton Oaks, 1986), pp. 9–21.

36 'Tudor Gardens', *Garden History* 27 (1999).

37 M. Girouard, *Elizabethan Architecture*, op. cit., pp. 95–112.

38 R. Machin, 'The great rebuilding: a reassesment', *Past and Present* 77 (1977), pp. 33–56.

39 N. Cooper, *Houses of the Gentry 1480–1680* (Yale, 1999), pp. 195–225.

40 J. Hatcher, *The History for the British Coal Industry, I; Before 1700: Towards the Age of Coal* (Oxford, 1993); P. Temple, *The Charterhouse* (Survey of London 18, 2010), p. 136; M. Spufford, 'Chimneys, wood and coal', in P. Barnwell and M. Airs (eds), *Houses and Hearth Tax: The Later Stuart House and Society* (Council for British Archaeology 150, 2006), pp. 22–32; D. Hawes Richards, 'The chimney', *Journal of the British Archaeological Association* 24 (1961), pp. 75–7.

41 P. Slack, 'Great and good Towns 1540–1700', in P. Clark (ed.), *The Cambridge Urban History, II: 1540–1840* (Cambridge, 2000), pp. 367, 369; see also pp. 221–2; W. Bushell, *Hobson's Conduit* (Cambridge, 1938); D. Jørgensen, 'All good rule of the

citee: sanitation and civic government in England, 1400–1600', *Journal of Urban History* 36 (2010), pp. 300–15.

42 J. Schofield, *Medieval London Houses* (Yale, 1994), pp. 86–7; C. Platt, *The Medieval English Town*, op. cit., pp. 69–72.

43 S. Thurley, *The Royal Palaces of Tudor England*, op. cit., pp. 167–71.

44 L. Stone, 'The educational revolution in England, 1560–1640', *Past and Present* 28 (1964), pp. 41–80.

45 N. Orme, *Medieval Schools: From Roman Britain to Renaissance England* (Yale, 2006), pp. 288–335.

46 M. Seaborne, *The English School: Its Architecture and Organisation 1370–1870* (London, 1971) pp. 19–21.

47 L. Stone, 'The educational revolution in England, 1560–1640', op. cit., pp. 41–80.

48 J. Newman, 'The physical setting', *The History of the University of Oxford* III (Oxford, 1986), pp. 597–633.

49 N. Tyacke (ed.), *The History of the University of Oxford* IV (Oxford, 1997).

50 H. M. Colvin, *The Canterbury Quadrangle, St John's College, Oxford* (Oxford, 1988).

51 L. F. Salzman, *Building in England Down to 1540* (Oxford, 1952), pp. 1–29: M. Girouard, *Elizabethan Architecture*, op. cit., pp. 43–4, 53; M. Airs, *The Tudor and Jacobean Country House: A Building History* (Stroud, 1995), pp. 31–56.

52 M. Girouard, *Elizabethan Architecture*, op. cit., pp. 23–31; D. Knoop and G. Jones, *The Medieval Mason* (Manchester, 1967); David Parsons (ed.), *Stone: Quarrying and Building in England AD 43–1525* (Chichester, 1990); J. Blair and N. Ramsey (eds), *English Medieval Industries* (London, 1991), pp. 18–25.

53 G. Addleshaw and F. Etchells, *The Architectural Setting of Anglican Worship* (London, 1947).

54 K. Fincham, 'The restoration of the altars in the 1630s', *Historical Journal* 44 (2001), pp. 919–-40; G. Parry, *The Arts of the Anglican Counter-Reformation: Glory, Laud and Honour* (Woodbridge, 2006).

55 J. Merritt, 'Puritans, Laudians, and the phenomenon of church-building in Jacobean London', *Historical Journal* 41 (1998), pp. 935–60; J. Newman, 'Laudian literature and the interpretation of Caroline churches in London', in D. Howarth (ed.), *Art and Patronage in the Caroline Courts: Essays in Honour of Sir Oliver Miller* (Cambridge, 1993), pp. 168–88; P. Guillery, 'Suburban models, or Calvinism and continuity in London's seventeenth-century church architecture', *Architectural History* 48 (2005), pp. 69–106.

Chapter Eight

1 J. Black, *The British Abroad: The Grand Tour in the Eighteenth Century* (Stroud, 2003); C. Hornsby (ed.), *The Impact of Italy: The Grand Tour and Beyond* (London, 2000).

2 S. Porter, *Destruction in the English Civil Wars* (Stroud, 1994); J. Goodall, *The English Castle* (2011), pp. 468–91.

3 J. Spraggon, *Puritan Iconoclasm during the English Civil War* (Woodbridge, 2003), pp. 177–216.

4 M. Airs and G. Tyack (eds), *The Renaissance Villa in Britain 1500–1700* (Reading, 2007).

5 G. Worsley, *Classical Architecture in Britain: The Heroic Age* (London, 1995), pp. 1–19.

6 H. M. Colvin, *A Biographical Dictionary of British Architects 1600–1840* 4th ed. (Yale, 2008), p. 20.

7 G. Worsley, *Inigo Jones and the European Classicist Tradition* (Yale, 2007); J. Harris and G. Higgott, *Inigo Jones: Complete Architectural Drawings* (London, 1989).

8 J. Schofield, *St Paul's Cathedral before Wren* (London, 2011), pp. 195–211.

9 H. M. Colvin (ed.), *The History of the King's Works* III (London, 1975), pp. 129-–59.

10 T. Mowl and B. Earnshaw, *Architecture Without Kings: The Rise of Puritan Classicism under Cromwell* (Manchester, 1995); but see E. McKellar, 'Palladianism via postmodernism: constructing and deconstructing the English Renaissance', *Art History* 20 (1997), pp. 154–6.

11 R. Gunther, *The Architecture of Sir Roger Pratt* (Oxford, 1928), pp. 135–66, 301–4; N. Silcox-Crowe, 'Sir Roger Pratt 1620–1685: the ingenious gentleman architect', *The Architectural Outsiders* (London, 1985), pp. 1–20.

12 G. Worsley, *Classical Architecture in Britain: The Heroic Age*, op. cit., pp. 21–43; Nicholas Cooper, *Houses of the Gentry 1480–1680* (Yale, 1999), pp. 240–9.

13 H. M. Colvin (ed.), *The History of the King's Works* V (London, 1976), pp. 433–6.

14 G. Tyack, *Oxford: An Architectural Guide* (Oxford, 1998), pp. 123–71.

15 Ibid.

16 N. Brett-James, *The Growth of Stuart London* (London, 1935), pp. 67–104; H. M. Colvin (ed.), *The History of the King's Works* III, op. cit., pp. 139–47.

17 D. Duggan, 'London the Ring, Covent Garden the Jewell of that Ring': new light on Covent Garden', *Architectural History* 43 (2000), pp. 140–61; R. Malcolm Smutts, 'The court and its neighbourhood: royal policy and urban growth in the early Stuart West End', *Journal of British Studies* 30 (1991), pp. 117–49; J. Summerson, *Georgian London* (Harmondsworth, 1962), pp. 28–32; J. Summerson, *The Romantic Castle and Other Essays* (London, 1990), pp. 41–53.

18 R. Leech, 'The prospect from Rugman's Row: the row house in late sixteenth- and early seventeenth-century London', *Archaeological Journal* 153 (1996), pp. 201–42.

19 P. Earle, *The Making of the English Middle Class: Business, Society and Family Life in London, 1660–1730* (London, 1989).

20 H. M. Colvin, *A Biographical Dictionary of British Architects 1600–1840*, op. cit., pp. 377–9.

21 H. J. Louw and R. Crayford, 'The constructional history of the sash window c. 1670 –1725', *Architectural History* 42 (1999), pp. 173–239.

22 E. McKellar, *The Birth of Modern London. The Development and Design of the City 1660–1720* (Manchester, 1999), pp. 155–84.

23 T. Longstaffe-Gowan, *The London Square: Gardens in the Midst of Town* (Yale, 2012).

24 C. Stevenson, *Medicine and Magnificence: British Hospital and Asylum Architecture 1660–1815* (Yale, 2000), pp. 11–85.
25 Ibid, pp. 125–44.
26 K. Downes, *The Architecture of Wren* (London, 1988), pp. 83–7.
27 A. Geraghty, *The Architectural Drawings of Sir Christopher Wren at All Souls College, Oxford: The Complete Catalogue* (Aldershot, 2007), pp. 8–13.
28 A. Saint, *Architect and Engineer: A Study in Sibling Rivalry* (Yale, 2007), pp. 37–40.
29 S. Thurley, *Hampton Court: A Social and Architectural History* (Yale, 2003), pp. 127–209.
30 S. Thurley, 'The King in the Queen's lodgings. The rise of the drawing room at the English court', in M. Chatenet (ed.), *Le Prince, La Princesse et Leurs Logis* (Paris, in press).
31 C. Rowell (ed.), *Ham House: 400 Years of Collecting and Patronage* (Yale, 2013).
32 P. Thornton, *Seventeenth-Century Interior Decoration in England, France and Holland* (Yale, 1978); J. Cornforth, *Early Georgian Interiors* (Yale, 2004).
33 D. Jacques and A. Jan van der Horst, *The Gardens of William and Mary* (London, 1988), pp. 17–34.
34 S. Thurley, *Hampton Court: A Social and Architectural History*, op. cit., pp. 223–42.
35 Ibid, pp. 232–3.
36 D. Jacques, 'The formal garden', in C. Ridgeway and R. Williams (eds), *Sir John Vanbrugh and Landscape Architecture in Baroque England 1690–1730* (Stroud, 2000), pp. 31–48; A. Hann and S. Garland, *Wrest Park* (English Heritage, 2011).
37 G. Keevill and S. Kelly, *The Tower of London New Armouries Project* (Oxford Archaeology Occasional Paper 12, 2006).
38 A. Saunders, *Fortress Builder: Bernard de Gomme, Charles II's Military Engineer* (Exeter, 2004).
39 E. Impey and G. Parnell, *The Tower of London: The Official Illustrated History* (London, 2000), pp. 61–5.
40 N. Barker, 'The building practice of the English Board of Ordnance 1680–1720', in J. Bold and E. Chaney (eds), *English Architecture Public and Private* (London, 1993), pp. 199–214.
41 C. Barnett, *Britain and Her Army 1509–1970* (London, 1970), pp. 111–25.
42 J. Douet, *English Barracks 1600–1914* (London, 1998), pp. 7–27.
43 R. Hewlings, 'Hawksmoor's "Brave Designs for the Police"', in J. Bold, and E. Chaney (eds), *English Architecture Public and Private*, op. cit., pp. 215–29.
44 Peter Guillery (ed.), *Survey of London 48: Woolwich* (Yale, 2012), pp. 128–45.
45 N. Roger, *The Command of the Ocean: A Naval History of Britain 1649–1815* (London, 2004); J. Coad, *Historic Architecture of the Royal Navy: An Introduction* (London, 1983).
46 J. Coad, 'Historic architecture of H.M. Naval Base Devonport 1689–1850', *The Mariner's Mirror* 69 (1983), pp. 341–52; C. Fox, *The Arts of Industry in the Age of Enlightenment* (Yale, 2009), pp. 48–69.
47 J. Coad, *Support for the Fleet: Architecture and Engineering of the Royal Navy's Bases 1700–1914* (English Heritage, 2013).

Chapter Nine

1 L. Mitchell, *The Whig World* (London, 2007).
2 J. Parry Lewis, *Building Cycles and Economic Growth* (London, 1965); C. W. Chalklin, *The Provincial Towns of Georgian England: A Study of the Building Process 1740–1820* (London, 1974), pp. 256–63; R. Wilson and A. Mackley, *Creating Paradise: The Building of the English Country House 1660–1880* (London, 2000), pp. 199–232.
3 F. O' Gorman, *The Long Eighteenth Century: British Political and Social History 1688–1832* (London, 2002), pp. 96–124.
4 E. Harris, *British Architectural Books and Writers 1556–1785* (Cambridge, 1990).
5 D. Cruikshank and P. Wyld, *London: The Art of Georgian Building* (London, 1975), pp. 90–5, 110–23, 154–9.
6 C. Sicca, 'The architecture of the wall: astylism in the architecture of Lord Burlington', *Architectural History* 33 (1990), pp. 83–101; R. Hewlings, 'Chiswick House and gardens: appearance and meaning', in T. Barnard and J. Clark (eds), *Lord Burlington: Architecture, Art and Life* (London, 1995), pp. 1–150.
7 M. Draper, *Marble Hill House and Its Owners* (London, 1970).
8 T. Mowl, 'Henry Keene 1726–1776', in R. Brown (ed.), *The Architectural Outsiders* (London, 1985), pp. 82–97.
9 S. Thurley, *Hampton Court: A Social and Architectural History* (Yale, 2003), pp. 275–7.
10 I. M. Green, *The Re-establishment of the Church of England 1660–1662* (Oxford, 1978).
11 D. Gardiner, *The Story of Lambeth Palace* (London, 1930), pp. 144–76; M. Roberts, *The English Heritage Book of Durham* (London, 1994); P. Hembry, 'Episcopal palaces, 1535–1660', in E. W. Ives, R. J. Knecht and J. J. Scarisbrick (eds), *Wealth and Power in Tudor England* (London, 1978), pp. 146–66.
12 S. Bradley and N. Pevsner, *London I: The City of London* (Yale, 1997), pp. 73–82; P. Jeffery, *The City Churches of Sir Christopher Wren* (London, 1996).
13 M. H. Port, 'The Commissions for Building Fifty New Churches: the minute books 1711–27 – a calendar', *London Record Society* (1986); H. M. Colvin, 'Fifty new churches', *Architectural Review* 107 (March 1950), pp. 189–96.
14 F. O'Gorman, *The Long Eighteenth Century: British Political and Social History 1688–1832* (London, 2002); J. Brewer, *The Pleasures of the Imagination: English Culture in the Eighteenth Century* (London, 1997), pp. 171–2; T. C. W. Blanning, *The Culture of Power and the Power of Culture: Old Regime Europe 1660–1789* (Oxford, 2002), pp. 288–90.
15 For these and this whole section, see T. Friedman, *The Eighteenth Century Church in Britain* (Yale, 2011).
16 H. Collins, *Edward Jerman 1605–1668: The Metamorphosis of a Master-craftsman* (Cambridge, 2004), pp. 115–44.
17 S. Jeffery, *The Mansion House* (London, 1993).
18 H. M. Colvin (ed.), *The History of the King's Works* V (London, 1976), pp. 431–3; J. C. Sainty, *Office Holders in Modern Britain I: Treasury Officials 1660–1870* (London, 1972).
19 H. M. Colvin (ed.), *The History of the King's Works* V, op. cit., pp. 433–43.

20 Ibid, pp. 207–13.

21 M. Girouard, *The English Town: A History of Urban Life* (Yale, 1990), pp. 127–44.

22 S. Thurley, *Lost Buildings of Britain* (London, 2004), pp. 75–110.

23 M. Girouard, *The English Town: A History of Urban Life*, op. cit., pp. 145–54.

24 P. Gale, *Pride of Place: The Story of Abingdon's Town Hall* (Oxford, 2006).

25 H. M. Colvin and L. M. Wodehouse, 'Henry Bell of King's Lynn', *Architectural History* 4 (1961), pp. 41–62; D. Higgins, *The Ingenious Mr Henry Bell: His Life, His Work, His Legacy, His King's Lynn* (King's Lynn, 2005).

26 D. Pearce, *London's Mansions: The Palatial Houses of the Nobility* (London, 1986), pp. 61–7.

27 J. Friedman, *Spencer House: Chronicle of a Great London Mansion* (London, 1993); R. Wilson and A. Mackley, *Creating Paradise: The Building of the English Country House 1660–1880*, op. cit., pp. 100–8; J. M. Robinson, 'Resurrected ducal splendours', Country Life (25 August 2010), pp. 50–5.

28 J. Cannon, *Aristocratic Century: The Peerage of Eighteenth-Century England* (Cambridge, 1984), pp. 117–21.

29 R. Hewlings, 'The classical Leviathan', *Country Life* (17 February 2010), pp. 46–53.

30 R. Hewlings, 'Chiswick House and gardens: appearance and meaning', op. cit., pp. 1–150.

31 I. C. Bristow, *Architectural Colours in British Interiors 1615–1840* (Yale, 1996).

32 L. Schmidt, *Holkham* (Munich, 2005).

33 James Rothwell, 'Dedicated to books', *National Trust Historic Houses and Collections Annual* (Apollo, 2010), pp. 56–9.

34 M. Overton, *Agricultural Revolution in England: The Transformation of the Agrarian Economy 1500–1850* (Cambridge, 1996).

35 Ibid.

36 J. Brewer, *Pleasures of the Imagination: English Culture in the Eighteenth century*, op. cit., pp. 615–52.

37 J. Cannon, *Aristocratic Century: The Peerage of Eighteenth Century England*, op. cit., pp. 126–47.

38 R. Wilson and A. Mackley, *The Building of the English Country House 1660–1880*, op. cit.

39 J. Harris, *The Palladian Revival: Lord Burlington, His Villa and Garden at Chiswick* (Yale, 1994), pp. 191–211.

40 P. Willis, *Charles Bridgeman and the English Landscape Garden* (Newcastle upon Tyne, 2002), pp. 106–27; J. Dixon Hunt, *William Kent: Landscape Garden Designer* (London, 1987), pp. 50–5.

41 G. Worsley, *The British Stable* (Yale, 2004), pp. 124–59.

42 J. Brown, Kelmarsh (Kelmarsh, 2003); R. Hewlings, 'Kelmarsh Hall', *Country Life* (4 June 2008); A. Gomme and A. Maguire, *Design and Plan in the Country House* (Yale, 2008), pp. 289–92.

43 D. Whitehead, *A Survey of Parks and Gardens in Herefordshire* (Hereford and Worcester Gardens Trust, 2001), p. 112.

44 A. Oswald, 'Farm Hall, Godmanchester', *Country Life* 130 (1961), pp. 1134–7, 1194–7; M. Hall, 'Island Hall, Cambridgeshire', *Country Life* 192 (1998), pp. 62–7, L. Geddes-Brown, 'The isle of enchantment', *Country Life* 204 (2010), pp. 96–101.

45 M. W. Barley, *The English Farmhouse and Cottage* (London, 1961).

Chapter Ten

1 T. Blanning, *The Culture of Power and the Power of Culture: Old Regime Europe 1660–1789* (Oxford, 2002), pp. 266–356.

2 R. Allen, *The British Industrial Revolution in Global Perspective* (Cambridge, 2011), pp. 25–79.

3 J. Mokyr, *The Enlightened Economy: Britain and the Industrial Revolution 1700–1850* (London, 2011), pp. 84–7; E. Wrigley, *Poverty, Progress and Population* (Cambridge, 2004), pp. 87–128.

4 M. Howard, *War in European History* (Oxford, 2001), pp. 75–93; C. Barnett, *Britain and Her Army: A Military, Political and Social Survey* (London, 1970), pp. 187–273.

5 F. Sheppard, V. Belcher and P. Cottrell, 'The Middlesex and Yorkshire deeds registries and the study of building fluctuations', *London Journal* 5 (1979), pp. 183–95; A. Cairncross and B. Weber, 'Fluctuations in building in Great Britain 1785–1849', *Economic History Review* 9 (1956), pp. 283–97; J. Lewis, *Building Cycles and Britain's Growth* (London, 1965), pp. 25–39; C. Chalklin, *The Provincial Towns of Georgian England: A Study of the Building Process 1740–1820* (London, 1974), pp. 285–303.

6 A. Saint, *The Image of the Architect* (Yale, 1983), pp. 51–62.

7 A. Satoh, *Building in Britain: The Origins of a Modern Industry* (Aldershot, 1995), pp. 8–59.

8 D. Abramson, 'Commercialization and backlash in late Georgian architecture', in B. Arciszewska and E. McKellar (eds), *Articulating British Classicism: New Approaches to Eighteenth-century Architecture* (Aldershot, 2004), pp. 143–57; A. Cairncross and B. Weber, 'Fluctuations in building in Great Britain 1785–1849', op. cit., p. 294.

9 D. Coke and A. Borg, *Vauxhall Gardens: A History* (Yale, 2011).

10 J. Stuart and N. Revett, *The Antiquities of Athens* (London, 1762).

11 D. Watkin, *The English Vision: The Picturesque in Architecture, Landscape and Garden Design* (London, 1982), pp. 1–44.

12 R. Sweet, *Antiquaries: The Discovery of the Past in Eighteenth-Century Britain* (London, 2004).

13 P. Aspin, '"Our ancient architecture": contesting cathedrals in late Georgian England', *Architectural History* 54 (2011), pp. 213–32.

14 F. Salmon, *Building on Ruins: The Rediscovery of Rome and English Architecture* (Aldershot, 2000), pp. 19–112; S. Suros (ed.), *James 'Athenian' Stuart: The Rediscovery of Antiquity* (Yale, 2007).

15 P. Clayton, *The Rediscovery of Ancient Egypt: Artists and Travellers in the 19th Century* (London, 1982).

16 M. Archer, *Indian Architecture and the British* (Feltham, 1968); G. Tyack, 'The empire strikes back', *Country Life* (15 February 2012) pp. 50–3.

17 B. Trinder, 'The first iron bridges', *Industrial Archaeology Review* 3 (1979), pp. 112–21.

18 R. Sutherland (ed.), *Structural Iron, 1750–1850* (Aldershot, 1997).

19 F. Newby (ed.), *Early Reinforced Concrete* (Aldershot, 2001).

20 D. Baugh, 'The eighteenth-century navy as a national institution 1690–1815', in J. Hill (ed.), *The Oxford Illustrated History of the Royal Navy* (Oxford, 1995), pp. 120--60; N. Roger, *The Command of the Ocean: A Naval History of Britain 1649–1815* (London, 2004), pp. 577–83.

21 H. M. Colvin (ed.), *The History of the King's Works* V (London, 1976), pp. 363–80; T. Hunt, 'A palace for the empire', *Somerset House: The History* (London, 2009), pp. 103–15.

22 N. Roger, *The Command of the Ocean: A Naval History of Britain 1649–1815* (London, 2004), pp. 304–7; J. Coad, *Support for the Fleet: Architecture and Engineering of the Royal Navy's Bases 1700–1914* (English Heritage, 2013), pp. 305–9; C. Miele, 'Bold, well-defined masses: Sir John Rennie and the Royal William Yard', *Architectural History* 49 (2006), pp. 149–78.

23 J. Coad, *The Portsmouth Block Mills* (London, 2005).

24 C. Giles and B. Hawkins, *Storehouses of Empire: Liverpool's Historic Warehouses* (London, 2004).

25 E. Williamson and N. Pevsner, *London: Docklands* (Harmondsworth, 2004), pp. 101–13.

26 J. Sharples, *Liverpool* (Yale, 2004), pp. 103–12.

27 N. Cossons, *Industrial Archaeology* (London, 1993), pp. 253–70; N. Crowe, *The English Heritage Book of Canals* (London, 1994).

28 C. Giles, *Stourport-on-Severn* (Swindon, 2007).

29 N. Crowe, *The English Heritage Book of Canals*, op. cit., pp. 71–2.

30 B. Trinder, *The Making of the Industrial Landscape* (London, 1982), pp. 53–9, 116–19.

31 D. Gerhold, *Carriers and Coachmasters: Trade and Travel before the Turnpikes* (Chichester, 2005).

32 N. Cossons, *Industrial Archaeology* (London, 1993), pp. 235–44; B. Trinder, *The Making of the Industrial Landscape*, op. cit., pp. 60–2.

33 D. Gerhold, *Road Transport before the Railways* (Cambridge, 1993).

34 R. Glover, *Britain at Bay: Defence Against Bonaparte 1803–14* (London, 1973).

35 A. Saunders, *Fortress Britain: Artillery Fortification in the British Isles and Ireland* (Liphook, 1989), pp. 133–5.

36 J. Coade, *Dover Castle* (London, 1995), pp. 81–90.

37 R. Glover, *Britain at Bay: Defence Against Bonaparte 1803–14*, op. cit., pp. 103–24; A. Saunders, *Fortress Britain: Artillery Fortification in the British Isles and Ireland*, op. cit., pp. 141–4.

38 W. Cocroft, *Dangerous Energy: The Archaeology of Gunpowder and Military Explosioves Manufacture* (London, 2000), pp. 30–65; J. Coad, *Support for the Fleet: Architecture and Engineering of the Royal Navy's Bases 1700–1914* (London, 2013).

39 B. Williams, *The Great Works at Weedon 1804–1816* (Daventry, 2003); D. Evans, *Arming the Fleet: The Development of the Royal Ordnance Yards 1770–1945* (London, 2006), pp. 33–41.

40 J. Douet, *British Barracks 1600–1914* (London, 1998), pp. 43–66; P. Guillery (ed.), *Survey of London 48: Woolwich* (Yale, 2012), pp. 327–35.

41 P. Guillery (ed.), *Survey of London 48: Woolwich*, op. cit., pp. 421–5; J. Martin Robinson, *James Wyatt (1746–1813): Architect to George III* (Yale, 2012), pp. 249–54.

42 J. Coad, *Support for the Fleet: Architecture and Engineering of the Royal Navy's Bases 1700–1914* (English Heritage, 2013), pp. 74–6.

43 Ibid, pp. 77–9, 366–8.

44 N. Harvey, *A History of Farm Buildings in England and Wales* (London, 1984), pp. 64–120; J. M. Robinson, 'Model farm buildings of the Age of Improvement', *Architectural History* 19 (1976), pp. 17–31.

45 P. S. Barnwell and C. Giles, *English Farmsteads, 1750–1914* (Swindon, 1997).

46 J. M. Robinson, 'Estate buildings at Holkham', *Country Life* (21 and 28 November 1974), pp. 1554–7, 1642–5; J. M. Robinson, 'Remaking the Shugborough landscape', *Country Life* (10 March 1977), pp. 578–81.

47 Joan Thirsk (ed.), *The Agrarian History of England and Wales: VI, 1750–1850* (Cambridge, 1989), pp. 743–52.

48 R. Allen, *The British Industrial Revolution in Global Perspective* (Cambridge, 2009), pp. 88–91; M. Spufford, 'Chimneys, wood and coal', in P. Barnwell and M. Airs (eds), *Houses and the Hearth Tax: The Later Stuart House and Society* (CBA Research Report 150, 2006), pp. 22–32. I'm grateful to Peter Guillery for discussing this with me.

49 R. Allen, *The British Industrial Revolution in Global Perspective* (Cambridge, 2009), pp. 182–213.

50 J. Tann, *The Development of the Factory* (London, 1970).

51 N. Cossons, *Industrial Archaeology* (Newton Abbot, 1993), pp. 187–94; E. Jones, *Industrial Architecture in Britain 1750–1939* (London, 1985), pp. 23–35.

52 M. Williams and D. Farnie, *Cotton Mills in Greater Manchester* (Preston, 1992); M. Rose and K. Falconer, *Ancoats: Cradle of Industrialisation* (London, 2011).

53 I. Miller and C. Wild, *A&G Murray and the Cotton Mills of Ancoats* (Lancaster, 2007).

54 Ibid, pp. 30–1; M. Beresford, 'The back-to-back house in Leeds', in S. Chapman (ed.), *A History of Working-Class Housing* (Newton Abbot, 1971), pp. 95–132.

55 A. Quiney, *House and Home: A History of the Small English House* (London, 1986), pp. 56–78.

56 P. Smithies, *The Architecture of the Halifax Piece Hall 1775–1779* (Halifax, 1988).

57 N. Cossons, *Industrial Archaeology* (Newton Abbot, 1993), pp. 160–8; E. Jones, *Industrial Architecture in Britain 1750–1939* (London, 1985), pp. 37–40.

58 N. Wray, B. Hawkins and C. Giles, 'One Great Workshop': *The Buildings of the Sheffield Metal Trades* (Swindon, 2001).

59 R. Floud and P. Johnson (eds), *The Cambridge Economic History of Modern Britain* 1 (Cambridge, 2008), pp. 36–47.

60 C. Fox, *The Arts of Industry in the Age of Enlightenment* (Yale, 2009), pp. 357–493.

61 C. Brooks and A. Saint, *The Victorian Church: Architecture and Society* (Manchester, 1995) pp. 2–7; A. D. Gilbert, *Religion and Society in Industrial England* (London, 1976), pp. 51–124.

62 J. Vickers and L. Griffiths, *Wesley's Chapel* (London, 2001).

63 J. Lake, J. Cox and E. Berry, *Diversity and Vitality: The Methodist and Nonconformist Chapels of Cornwall* (London, 2001); M. Binney and P. Burman, *Chapels and Churches: Who Cares?* (London 1977), pp. 15–33.

64 J. Griffin, *Holy Trinity Church: Now the Parish Church of St Peter, Darwen – The Church in the Nineteenth Century* (Darwen, 2008).

65 C. Hartwell, M. Hyde, E. Hubbard and N. Pevsner, *Cheshire* (Yale, 2011), pp. 595–6.

66 M. H. Port, *600 New Churches: The Church Building Commission 1818–1856* (Reading, 2006).

67 H. Barty-King, *New Flame. The Illustrated History of Piped Gas and the Way It Changed the Lives of Those Who Lived and Worked in Britain 1783–1984* (Tavistock, 1984), pp. 13–84; M. E. Falkus, 'The British gas industry before 1850', *Economic History Review* 20 (1967), pp. 494–508; L. Tomory, 'Building the first gas network, 1812–1820', *Technology and Culture* 52 (2011), pp. 75–102.

68 D. Rosman, *Evangelicals and Culture* (London, 1984), pp. 119–26, 147–50.

69 B. Hilton, *A Mad, Bad and Dangerous People? England 1783–1846* (Oxford, 2006), pp. 166–74.

70 K. Morrison, *English Shops and Shopping: An Architectural History* (Yale, 2003).

71 J. Schmiechen and K. Carls, *The British Market Hall: A Social and Architectural History* (Yale, 1999).

72 R. Thorne, *Covent Garden Market: Its History and Restoration* (London, 1980).

73 A. Brodie, 'Liverpool and the origins of the seaside resort', *Georgian Group Journal* 20 (2012), pp. 63–76; A. Brodie and G. Winter, *England's Seaside Resorts* (Swindon, 2007).

74 N. Pevsner, *A History of Building Types* (London, 1976), pp. 173–9.

75 J. Summerson, *Georgian London* (Harmondsworth, 1962), pp. 128–32.

76 G. Tyack, "Reshaping the west end' in G. Tyack (ed.), John Nash, Architect of the Picturesque (English Heritage, 2013), pp. 101–24; J. Summerson, *John Nash* (London, 1935), pp. 102–38.

77 C. Saumarez Smith, *Eighteenth-Century Decoration: Design and the Domestic Interior in England* (London, 1993), pp. 233–6; A. Vickery, *Behind Closed Doors: At Home in Georgian England* (Yale, 2009), pp. 291–302.

78 N. Cox, '"A Flesh Pott, or a Brasse pott or a pott to boile in": changes in metal and fuel technology in the early modern period and the implications for cooking', in L. Hurcombe and M. Donald (eds), *Gender and Material Culture in Historical Perspective* (London, 2000), pp. 143–57: P. Brears, 'Kitchen fireplaces and stoves', in P. Sambrook and P. Brears (eds), *The Country House Kitchen 1650–1900* (Stroud, 2012), pp. 92–115.

79 G. Beard, *Upholsterers and Interior Furnishing in England 1530–1840* (Yale, 1997).

80 I. C. Bristow, *Architectural Colour in British Interiors 1615–1840* (Yale, 1996), pp. 157–87.

81 A. Vickery, *Behind Closed Doors: At Home in Georgian* England (Yale, 2009), pp. 166–83; G. Saunders, *Wallpaper in Interior Decoration* (London, 2002).

82 S. Suros (ed.), *James 'Athenian' Stuart: The Rediscovery of Antiquity*, op. cit.

83 D. Pearce, *London's Mansions. The Palatial Houses of the Nobility* (London, 1986), pp. 85–108, 195–202.

84 D. Cannadine, *Aspects of Aristocracy* (Yale, 1994), pp. 9–36; R. Wilson and A. Mackley, *Creating Paradise: Building of the English Country House 1660–1880* (London, 2000), pp. 361–4; L. Stone and J. C. Fawtier Stone, *An Open Elite? England 1540–1880* (Oxford, 1984), pp. 364–74, 384–5; J. Robinson, *The Regency Country House* (London, 2005).

85 C. Ridgway, 'Rethinking the picturesque', in C. Ridgeway and R. Williams (eds), *Sir John Vanbrugh and Landscape Architecture in Baroque England 1690–1730* (Stroud, 2000), pp. 172–91; A. Tinniswood, *The Polite Tourist: A History of Country House Visiting* (London, 1998).

86 For much of what follows, see T. Williamson, *Polite Landscapes: Gardens and Society in Eighteenth-Century England* (Stroud, 1998).

87 D. Stroud, *Capability Brown* (London, 1957); S. Daniels, *Humphrey Repton: Landscape Gardening and the Geography of Georgian England* (Yale, 1999).

88 R. Carr, *English Foxhunting* (London, 1986).

89 J. Phibbs, 'The truth about Mr. Brown', *Country Life* (20 April 2006), pp. 71–5.

90 T. Mowl and B. Earnshaw, *Trumpet at a Distant Gate: The Lodge as Prelude to the Country House* (London, 1985).

91 M. Girouard, *Life in the English Country House* (Yale, 1978), pp. 214–44.

92 H. M. Colvin (ed.), *The History of the King's Works* VI (London, 1973), pp. 77–178.

93 D. Abramson, *Building the Bank of England: Money. Architecture. Society. 1694–1942* (Yale, 2005), pp. 59–196.

94 F. Nevola, *Soane's Favourite Subject: The Story of Dulwich Picture Gallery* (Dulwich, 2000).

95 J. Mordaunt Crook, *The British Museum* (London, 1972).

96 P. Kennedy, *The Rise and Fall of British Naval Mastery* (London, 1983), pp. 175–7; E. Hobsbawm, *Industry and Empire* (Harmondsworth, 1969), pp. 48–54.

Chapter Eleven

1 B. Trinder, *The Making of the Industrial Landscape* (London, 1997), p. 220.

2 J. Raleigh, 'What Scott meant to the Victorians', *Victorian Studies* 7 (1963), pp. 7–34; P. Mandler, *History and National Life* (London, 2002); P. Anderson, *The Printed Image and the Transformation of Popular Culture 1790–1860* (Oxford, 1991); S. Thurley, *The Men from the Ministry: How Britain's Heritage was Saved* (Yale, 2013).

3 H. M. Colvin (ed.), *The History of the King's Works* VI (London, 1973), pp. 373–93.

4 M. H. Port (ed.), *The Houses of Parliament* (Yale, 1976); C. and J. Riding (eds), *The Houses of Parliament: History, Art, Architecture* (London, 2000), especially D. Cannadine's essay, 'The Palace of Westminster as a palace of varieties'.

5 D. Evans, *Building the Steam Navy: Dockyards, Technology and the Creation of the Victorian Battlefleet 1830–1906* (London, 2004), pp. 42–59; J. Coad, *Support for the Fleet: Architecture and Engineering of the Royal Navy's Bases 1700–1914* (London, 2013), pp. 185–93.

6 A. Clifton-Taylor, *The Pattern of English Building* (London, 1972), pp. 394–401; N. Cossons, *Industrial Archaeology* (London, 1993), pp. 171–4.

7 Ibid, pp. 129–30; W. H. G. Armytage, *A Social History of Engineering* (London, 1976), pp. 153–7.

8 A. Satoh, *Building in Britain: The Origins of a Modern Industry* (Cambridge, 1995), pp. 111–255.

9 The building of the railways have probably the largest literature of any single event in English history. I am grateful to Stephen Brindle for his helpful and perceptive comments on this section.

10 T. R. Gourvish, 'Railways 1830–70: the formative years', in M. J. Freeman and D. H. Aldcroft (eds), *Transport in Victorian Britain* (Manchester, 1988), pp. 57–91; C. Wolmar, *Fire and Steam: How the Railways Transformed Britain* (London 2007).

11 Mike Chrimes, 'London and Birmingham' and 'Building the London and Birmingham Railway', in M. R. Bailey (ed.), *Robert Stephenson: The Eminent Engineer* (Aldershot, 2003), pp. 39–62, 241–61.

12 J. Simmons, *The Victorian Railway* (London, 1995), pp. 25–31.

13 S. Brindle, 'The Great Western Railway', in A. and M. Kelly (eds), *Brunel: In Love with the Impossible* (Bristol, 2006), pp. 134–61.

14 A. A. Arschavir, 'The inception of the English railway station', *Architectural History* 4 (1961), pp. 63–76.

15 G. McCombie, *Newcastle and Gateshead* (Yale, 2009), pp. 82–7.

16 S. Brindle, *Paddington Station: Its History and Architecture* (London, 2004).

17 S. Bradley, *St Pancras Station* (London, 2007).

18 O. E. Denby, *Grand Hotels: Reality and Illusion* (London, 1998), pp. 45–73; O. Carter, *An Illustrated History of British Railway Hotels 1838–1983* (St. Michael's, 1990); N. Pevsner, *A History of Building Types* (London, 1976), pp. 179–91.

19 J. Simmons, 'The power of the railway', in H. J. Dyos and M. Wolff (eds), *The Victorian City: Images and Realities* 1 (London, 1973), pp. 277–310.

20 N. Cossons, *Industrial Archaeology* (London, 1993), p. 297.

21 R. Thorne, 'The Great Northern Railway and the London coal trade', in M. Hunter and R. Thorne (eds), *Change at King's Cross: From 1800 to the Present* (London, 1990), pp. 111–23.

22 G. Worsley, *The British Stable* (Yale, 2004), pp. 226–36.

23 J. Catell and K. Falconer, *Swindon: The Legacy of a Railway Town* (Swindon, 1995).

24 C. O'Mahony, 'The Function of ornament: the consolation of design in the Industrial Age', in A. and M. Kelly (eds), *Brunel: In Love with the Impossible* (Bristol, 2006), pp. 300–17.

25 R. Middleton and D. Watkin, *Neoclassical and 19th-Century Architecture* (New York, 1980), pp. 261–7.

26 E. Jones, *Industrial Architecture in Britain 1750–1939* (London, 1985), pp. 85–100.

27 R. Hill, *God's Architect: Pugin and the Building of Romantic Britain* (London, 2007).

28 These two books, edited by T. Brittain-Catlin, were published in a Pugin Society edition in 2003.

29 R. Hill, 'Pugin's churches', *Architectural History* 49 (2006), pp. 179–205.

30 J. Mordaunt Crook, *The Dilemma of Style* (London, 1987), pp. 98–132.

31 N. Jackson, 'Christ Church, Streatham, and the rise of constructional polychromy', *Architectural History* 43 (2000), pp. 219–46; J. Mordaunt Crook, *The Architect's Secret: Victorian Critics and the Image of Gravity* (London, 2003), p. 53.

32 Ibid, pp. 35–83; P. Thompson, *William Butterfield* (London, 1971).

33 M. W. Brooks, *John Ruskin and Victorian Architecture* (London, 1989).

34 E. Jones, *Industrial Architecture in Britain 1750–1939* (London, 1985), pp. 122–36.

35 S. Allen Smith, 'Alfred Waterhouse: civic grandeur', in J. Fawcett (ed.), *Seven Victorian Architects* (London, 1976), pp. 92–121.

36 C. Brooks and A. Saint (eds), *The Victorian Church: Architecture and Society* (Manchester, 1995), pp. 1–24; M. A. Smith, 'Religion', in C. Williams (ed.), *A Companion to Nineteenth-Century Britain* (London, 2007), pp. 337–50.

37 G. Brandwood, *The Architecture of Sharpe, Paley and Austin* (Swindon, 2012), pp. 24–7.

38 M. Harrison, *Victorian Stained Glass* (London, 1980).

39 See the essays in P. Atterbury and C. Wainwright (eds), *Pugin: A Gothic Passion* (Yale, 1994).

40 N. Yates, *Buildings, Faith and Worship: The Liturgical Arrangements of Anglican Churches 1600–1900* (Oxford, 1991).

41 N. Harvey, *A History of Farm Buildings in England and Wales* (London, 1984), pp. 120–63; see also see the excellent essays in G. Mingay (ed.), *The Victorian Countryside* (London, 1981), pp. 177–272.

42 M. Girouard, *The Return to Camelot: Chivalry and the English Gentleman* (Yale, 1981).

43 J. Mordaunt Crook, *The Rise of the Nouveaux Riches: Style and Status in Victorian and Edwardian Architecture* (London, 1999), pp. 37–78.

44 J. Allibone, *Anthony Salvin: Pioneer of Gothic Revival Architecture* (Cambridge, 1987), pp. 98–106.

45 For what follows see M. Girouard, *The Victorian Country House* (Yale, 1979).

46 R. Hill, *God's Architect: Pugin and the Building of Romantic Britain*, op. cit., pp. 291–6; R. Hill, 'Pugin's small houses', *Architectural History* 46 (2003), pp. 147–74; R. Middleton and D. Watkin, *Neoclassical and 19th-Century Architecture*, op. cit., pp. 320–3.

47 A. Menuge, *Ordinary Landscapes, Special Places: Anfield,*

Breckfield and the Growth of Liverpool's Suburbs (Swindon, 2008), pp. 14–23.

48 I. Miller and C. Wild, *A&G Murray and the Cotton Mills of Ancoats* (Lancaster, 2007), pp. 30–1; M. Beresford, 'The back-to-back house in Leeds', in S. Chapman (ed.), *A History of Working-Class Housing* (Newton Abbot, 1971), pp. 95–132; M. Daunton, *House and Home in the Victorian City* (London, 1983), pp. 15–19.

49 H. R. Hitchcock, *Early Victorian Architecture in Britain* 1 (Yale, 1954), pp. 319–24; J. Summerson, 'The Victorian rebuilding of the city of London, 1840–1870', in J. Summerson, *The Romantic Castle and other Essays* (London, 1990), pp. 193–216; F. Sheppard, *London 1808–1870: The Infernal Wen* (London, 1971), pp. 193–201.

50 L. Pearson, *British Breweries: An Architectural History* (London, 1999).

51 For the above paragraphs, see G. Brandwood, A. Davison and M. Slaughter, *Licensed to Sell: The History and Heritage of the Public House* (Swindon, 2011).

52 C. Cunningham, *Victorian and Edwardian Town Halls* (London, 1981).

53 F. Salmon, *Building on Ruins: The Rediscovery of Rome and English Architecture* (Aldershot, 2000), pp. 153–68.

54 A. Foster, *Birmingham* (Yale, 2007), pp. 57–68.

55 For the previous paragraphs, see C. Graham, *Ordering Law: The Architectural and Social History of the English Law Court to 1914* (Aldershot, 2003).

56 For the previous paragraphs, see A. Brodie, J. Croom and J. Davies, *English Prisons: An Architectural History* (London, 2002).

57 E. Wrigley, *Continuity and Change: The Character of the Industrial Revolution in England* (Cambridge, 1990), pp. 118–22.

58 For the above, see K. Morrison, *The Workhouse: A Study of Poor-Law Buildings in England* (London, 1999).

59 R. Porter, 'The gift relation: philanthropy and provincial hospitals in eighteenth-century England', in L. Granshaw and R. Porter (eds), *The Hospital in History* (London, 1990), pp. 149–78.

60 C. Stevenson, *Medicine and Magnificence: British Hospital and Asylum Architecture, 1660–1815* (Yale, 2000), pp. 176–94; N. Pevsner, *A History of Building Types*, op. cit., pp. 147–57.

Chapter Twelve

1 P. Kennedy, *The Rise and Fall of the Great Powers. Economic Change and Military Conflict from 1500 to 2000* (London, 1989), pp. 290–9.

2 K. Robbins, 'The British way and purpose', in K. Robbins (ed.), *The Short Oxford History of the British Isles: The British Isles 1901–1951* (Oxford, 2002), pp. 73–100; J. Black, *1851–2010 Britain: A Nation Transformed* (London, 2010), pp. 117–46; W. Rubinstein, *Capitalism Culture and Decline in Britain* (London, 1994).

3 H. Muthesius, *The English House* (London, 1979), p. 13.

4 M. Crinson and J. Lubbock, *Architecture: Art or Profession?* (Manchester, 1994); A. Saint, *The Image of the Architect* (Yale, 1985). Scott Chesterton and Shepherd designed the Shakespeare Memorial Theatre, Stratford-upon-Avon between 1929 and 1932.

5 R. Fellows, *Edwardian Architecture: Style and Technology* (London, 1995), pp. 49–68.

6 G. Weightman, *Children of Light: How Electricity Changed Britain Forever* (London, 2011).

7 J. Mourdaunt Crook, *The Dilemma of Style: Architectural Ideas from the Picturesque to the Post-Modern* (London, 1987), pp. 161–224.

8 P. Davy, *Arts and Crafts Architecture* (London, 1995), pp. 9–51.

9 M. Girouard, *Sweetness and Light: The 'Queen Anne' Movement 1860–1900* (Yale, 1984).

10 A. Service, *London 1900* (London, 1979), pp. 61–71; 'Buildings of the Domestic Revival and later', *Survey of London, 38: South Kensington Museums Area* (London, 1975), pp. 325–48.

11 'Grosvenor Square: the rebuilding of the square from 1926', *Survey of London, 40: The Grosvenor Estate in Mayfair, Part 2 (The Buildings)* (1980), pp. 166–70.

12 A. Powers, *Modern: The Modern Movement in Britain* (London, 2005); A. Powers, *Britain: Modern Architectures in History* (London 2007); J. Peto and D. Loveday, *Modern Britain 1929–1939* (Design Museum, 1999).

13 F. Harcourt, 'The Queen, the Sultan and the Viceroy: a Victorian state occasion', *London Journal* 5 (1979), pp. 35–56.

14 E. and M. Darby, 'The nation's memorial to Victoria', *Country Life* (16 November 1978), pp. 1647–50.

15 A. Service, *London 1900*, op. cit.

16 M. Port, *Imperial London: Civil Government Building in London 1850–1915* (Yale, 1995).

17 M. H. Port, 'Government and the metropolitan image: ministers, parliament and the concept of a capital city, 1840–1915', in D. Arnold (ed.), *The Metropolis and Its Image: Constructing Identities for London, c. 1750–1950* (Oxford, 1999), pp. 101–26.

18 M. Daunton, *House and Home in the Victorian City: Working Class Housing 1850–1914* (London, 1983).

19 J. Burnett, *A Social History of Housing 1815–1970* (London, 1978), pp. 138–83.

20 E. Hubbard and M. Shippobottom, *A Guide to Port Sunlight Village* (Liverpool, 1990).

21 M. Miller, *English Garden Cities: An Introduction* (Swindon, 2010).

22 S. Beattie, *A Revolution in London Housing: LCC Housing Architects and Their Work, 1893–1914* (London, 1980); T. Barker, 'Urban transport', in M. Freeman and D. Aldcroft (eds), *Transport in Victorian Britain* (Manchester, 1988), pp. 158–9.

23 M. Osborne, *Defending Britain: Twentieth-century Military Structures in the Landscape* (Stroud, 2004).

24 P. Francis, *British Military Airfield Architecture: From Airships to the Jet Age* (Sparkford, 1996).

25 I. Beckett, *The Making of the First World War* (Yale, 2012), pp.

68–86; D. Stevenson, *1914–1918: The History of the First World War* (London 2012). The definitive *History of the Ministry of Munitions* in eighteen volumes has recently been republished by the Imperial War Museum.

26 D. Taylor, 'Keith Murray, architect and designer for industry', *Journal of the Twentieth Century Society* 1 (1994), pp. 45–54.

27 J. Skinner, 'The Firestone factory 1928–1980', *Journal of the Twentieth Century Society* 1 (1994), pp. 45–54.

28 D. Cannadine, *The Decline and Fall of the British Aristocracy* (Yale, 1990), pp. 103–112; M. Winstanley, 'Agriculture and rural society', in C. Williams, *A Companion to Nineteenth Century Britain* (Oxford, 2007), pp. 205–220.

29 R. McKibbin, *Classes and Cultures: England 1918–1951* (Oxford, 1998), pp. 70–84; T. Rowley, *The English Landscape in the Twentieth Century* (London, 2006), pp. 195–216.

30 J. Burnett, *A Social History of Housing 1815–1970* (London, 1978), pp. 215–43.

31 T. Barker, 'Urban transport', in M. Freeman and D. Aldcroft (eds), *Transport in Victorian Britain*, op. cit., pp. 134–66; G. Worsley, *The British Stable* (Yale, 2004), pp. 228–33.

32 M. Palmén, 'Bristol Tramways power stations 1895–1941: The Story of Beaconsfield Road and the Counterslip power stations,' supplement to *Histelec News* 30 (August 2005); M. Palmén, 'Bristol Tramways power stations: part II', supplement to *Histelec News* 42 (August 2009).

33 T. Barker and M. Robbins, *A History of London Transport 2: The Twentieth Century to 1970* (London, 1974), pp. 54–84, 104–18; D. Croome and A. Jackson, *Rails Through the Clay: A History of London's Tube Railways* (Harrow, 1993), pp. 34–42.

34 J. Rewse-Davies, 'London Transport design', in J. Peto and D. Loveday, *Modern Britain 1929–1939*, op. cit., pp. 95–106; L. Menear, *London Underground Stations: A Social and Architectural Study* (Tunbridge Wells, 1983).

35 K. Morrison and J. Minnis, *Carscapes: The Motor Car, Architecture and Landscape in England* (Yale, 2012).

36 R. Bowdler, 'Liverpool-Speke', in P. Smith and B. Toulier (eds), *Berlin-Templehof, Liverpool-Speke, Paris-Le Bourget* (Tours, 2000), pp. 62–84.

37 M. Seaborne and R. Lowe, *The English School: Its Architecture and Organisation*, 2 vols (London, 1977); E. Harwood, *England's Schools: History, Architecture and Adaptation* (Swindon, 2010).

38 J. Elliot, *Palaces, Patronage and Pills: Thomas Holloway, His Sanatorium, College and Picture Gallery* (Egham, 1996).

39 R. Baird, *Goodwood: Art, Architecture, Sport and Family* (London, 1988), pp. 185–8, 198–9.

40 R. W. Tomlinson, 'A geography of flat-racing in Great Britain', *Geography* 71 (1986), pp. 228–39.

41 L. Pearson, 'From the pavilion end: cricket's architectural heritage', *Conservation Bulletin* 68 (English Heritage, Summer 2012), pp. 19–21.

42 S. Inglis, *Engineering Archie: Archibald Leitch – Football Ground Designer* (London, 2005); D. Russell, *Football and the English: A Social History of Association Football 1863–1995* (Lancaster, 1998); S. Inglis, *The Football Grounds of Great Britain* (London, 1996).

43 P. Hartnoll, *Oxford Companion to the Theatre* (Oxford, 1993); J. Golby and A. Purdue, *The Civilisation of the Crowd: Popular Culture in England 1750–1900* (London, 1984), pp. 172–7; P. Horn, *Pleasures and Pastimes in Victorian Britain* (Stroud, 1999), pp. 190–7.

44 B. Walker (ed), *Frank Matcham: Theatre Architect* (Belfast, 1980); G. Wickham, *A History of the Theatre* (London, 2002), pp. 181–214; P. Horn, *Pleasures and Pastimes in Victorian Britain*, op. cit., pp. 197–207.

45 R. Gray, *Cinemas in Britain: One Hundred Years of Cinema in Architecture* (London, 1996).

46 A. Brodie and G. Winter, *England's Seaside Resorts* (London, 2007).

47 A. Brodie and M. Whitfield, *Blackpool's Seaside Heritage* (Swindon, 2013); V. Toulmin, *Blackpool Tower* (Blackpool, 2011).

48 S. Braggs and D. Harris, *Sun, Fun and Crowds: Seaside Holidays between the Wars* (Stroud, 2000); J. Smith, *Liquid Assets: The Lidos and Open Air Swimming Pools of Britain* (London, 2005).

49 D. Occomore, *Number Please: A History of the Early London Telephone Exchanges from 1880–1912* (Leigh-on-Sea, 1995).

50 N. Pevsner, *A History of Building Types* (London, 1976), pp. 265–72; K. Morrison, *English Shops and Shopping: An Architectural History* (Yale, 2003).

51 J. B. Priestley, *English Journey* (London, 1934), pp. 401–6.

52 'Broadcasting House is savaged for its Georgian-shaped windows' in B. Cherry and N. Pevsner, *London 3: North West* (London, 1999), p. 650.

53 M. Crinson, 'Architecture and national projection between the wars', in D. Arnold (ed.), *Cultural Identities and the Aesthetics of Britishness* (Manchester, 2004), pp. 182–97.

54 M. Crinson and J. Lubbock, *Architecture: Art or Profession?*, op. cit., pp. 90–1.

Index

Page numbers in *italics* indicate images.

B

C

D

E

F

I

M

N

O

P

S

U

V

W

Y

Z

Picture credits

All images © Alamy except for: Fig. 5 © West Stow Anglo-Saxon Village/Moyse's Hall Museum. **Fig. 14** © David Rowan/Lichfield Cathedral. **Fig. 17** © Geoffrey Smith/Fotolibra. **Fig. 18** © Chris Talbot. **Figs 19, 44, 140, 218, 219** © Dr John Crook. **Figs 32, 76** © The British Library Board. All Rights Reserved 2013. **Fig. 35** © Lionel Wall. **Fig. 59** © Universal Images Group/Superstock. **Fig. 74** © Leeds Museums and Galleries (Leeds Art Gallery) U.K./The Bridgeman Art Library. **Fig. 77** © Tony Grist via Wikimedia Commons. **Figs 79, 217** © Paul Barker/Country Life Picture Library. **Fig. 94** © Kippa Matthews/Rex Features. **Fig. 95** © Marrianne Forbes. **Fig. 98** © Dean and Chapter of Westminster. **Fig. 103** © Rex Harris **Fig. 104** © Chiswick Chap via Wikimedia Commons. **Fig. 105** © George Redgrave. **Figs. 106, 107** © David Ross/Britain Express. **Fig. 112** © Will Pryce/Country Life Picture Library. **Fig. 119** © Steve Wake/Wakes World Photography. **Fig. 121** © Kent Barker. **Fig. 132** © Mick Sharp/Loop Images/Corbis. **Fig. 145** © Britain on View/Getty Images. **Fig. 159** © Fitzwilliam Museum, University of Cambridge, UK/The Bridgeman Art Library. **Fig. 172** © Eton College Photographic Archive. **Fig. 174** © Avril Pierssiene. **Fig. 175** © Nottingham City Museums and Galleries. **Fig. 176** © Private Collection/The Bridgeman Art Library. **Fig. 177** © A. Linsell (owner)/Colin Brooks (photographer) **Fig. 180** © Bristol Museums and Art Gallery. **Figs 181, 196** © National Trust Images/Nadia Mackenzie. **Fig. 184** © Skyscan.co.uk / M. Clark Fig. 187 © Leicester City Council. **Fig. 193** © Martyn Goddard/Country Life Picture Library. **Fig. 194** © The Burghley House Collection. **Fig. 197** © New Hall School. **Fig. 199** © National Trust Images/Horst Kolo. **Fig. 203** © Christopher Simon Sykes/The Interior Archive. **Fig. 208** © City of London/Heritage-Images. **Fig. 213** Reproduced with kind permission from The Headmaster, Uppingham School. **Fig. 221** © Ydigresse via Wikimedia Commons. **Fig. 226** © Country Life. **Fig. 231** © DEA / G. NIMATALLAH / Getty Images. **Fig. 232** © Christie's Images / The Bridgeman Art Library (1749, Canaletto, (Giovanni Antonio Canal) (1697–1768)) **Fig. 236** © Shutterstock.com. **Fig. 242** © Museum of London, UK / The Bridgeman Art Library (Collet, John (*c.*1725–80)). **Fig. 247** © London Metropolitan Archives, City of London / The Bridgeman Art Library (1754, Nicholls, Sutton) **Fig. 248** © Private Collection / The Stapleton Collection / The Bridgeman Art Library. **Fig. 250** © Wellcome Library, London. **Fig. 251** © Shutterstock.com. **Fig. 253** © Look and Learn / Peter Jackson Collection / The Bridgeman Art Library (Knyff, Leonard (1650–1721)). **Fig. 256** © National Trust Images/John Hammond **Fig. 258** © Private Collection / The Stapleton Collection / The Bridgeman Art Library. **Fig. 259** © Getty Images. **Fig. 264** © Mike Kirby. **Fig. 266** © Mary Evans Picture Library/Castle Howard Collection **Fig. 277** © Shutterstock. com. **Fig. 278** © Getty Images. **Fig. 279** © Look and Learn / Peter Jackson Collection / The Bridgeman Art Library (English School, 18th century). **Fig. 283** © Look and Learn / Peter Jackson Collection / The Bridgeman Art Library). **Fig. 290** © Getty Images. **Fig. 295** © Borough Council of King's Lynn & West Norfolk. **Fig. 301** © Historic Royal Palaces/ newsteam.co.uk. **Fig. 306** © Country Life. **Fig. 308** © Country Life. **Fig. 309** © Peter Salt **Fig. 311** © Supplied by the author. **Fig. 312** © Look and Learn / Peter Jackson Collection / The Bridgeman Art Library (English School, 18th century). **Fig. 315** © Country Life. **Fig. 318** © Private Collection / The Stapleton Collection / The Bridgeman Art Library (1812, Storer, James (1781–1852)). **Fig. 320** © English School / Private Collection / The Bridgeman Art Library. **Fig. 321** © DeAgostini / SuperStock **Fig. 323** © Shutterstock.com. **Fig. 324** © Shutterstock.com. **Fig. 326** © Photograph reproduced with the kind permission of Portsmouth Royal Dockyard Historical Trust. **Fig. 327** © Shutterstock.com. **Fig. 336** © Dover Library. **Fig. 342** © Robin Lucas. **Fig. 344** © Crown copyright. English Heritage. **Fig. 345** © Nigel Jones. **Fig. 346** © Barnsley Arts, Museums & Archives Service. **Fig. 347** © Anonymous / Private Collection / The Bridgeman Art Library. **Fig. 349** © City of London / Heritage-Images. **Fig. 351** © English Heritage. **Fig. 356** © SPL via Getty Images. **Fig. 357** © The Potteries Museums and Art Gallery. **Fig. 358** © Sheffield Industrial Museums Trust. **Fig. 359** © Alphonse Douseau / The Bridgeman Art Library / Getty Images. **Fig. 361** © The Friends of Walpole Old Chapel. **Fig. 362** © Sue Adair m. **Fig. 363** © By courtesy of Chowbent Unitarian Chapel **Fig. 367** © David Carvey - The Magic of Cornwall. **Fig. 371** © Jane Gammie. **Fig. 373** © Country Life. **Fig. 384** © Country Life. **Fig. 385** © Country Life. **Fig. 387** © Heveningham Hall, Suffolk, UK / The Bridgeman Art Library (Taylor, Robert (1714-88)). **Fig. 389** © Philip Halling. **Fig. 393** © City of London / HIP / TopFoto. **Fig. 394** © By courtesy of the Trustees of Sir John Soane's Museum. **Fig. 400** © Danny Robinson. **Fig. 403** © London Metropolitan Archives, City of London / The Bridgeman Art Library (Nash, Joseph (1809-78)). **Fig. 406** © Hulton Archive / Getty Images. **Fig. 408** © SSPL via Getty Images. **Fig. 409** © Noel Walley. **Fig. 410** © SSPL via Getty Images. **Fig. 414** © By courtesy of Thistle – Geoman Hotels. **Fig. 416** © Science and Society / SuperStock. **Fig. 417** © H. N. Twells OBE. **Fig. 420** © Look and Learn / Peter Jackson Collection / The Bridgeman Art Library (English School, 19th century). **Fig. 421** © National Railway Museum / Science & Society Picture. **Fig. 422** © English Heritage. Aerofilms collection. **Fig. 436** © Shutterstock.com. **Fig. 441** © English Heritage Photo Library / The Bridgeman Art Library **Fig. 447** © Shutterstock.com. **Fig. 450** © Nomad /SuperStock m. **Fig. 452** © Look and Learn / The Bridgeman Art Library **Fig. 453** © Victoria and Albert Museum, London / V&A Images – All rights reserved. **Fig. 454** © Bernard Sharp. **Fig. 455** © English Heritage. **Fig. 456** © By courtesy of David Angus – www.east-durham.co.uk. **Fig. 457** © Stephen Richards. **Fig. 459** © Look and Learn / Peter Jackson Collection / The Bridgeman Art Library (English School, 19th century). **Fig. 460** © Look and Learn / Peter Jackson Collection / The Bridgeman Art Library (English School, 19th century). **Fig. 461** © Look and Learn / Peter Jackson Collection / The Bridgeman Art Library (English School, 19th century). **Fig. 463** © J.Hannan-Briggs. **Fig. 466** © Michael Slaughter. **Fig. 472** © Nigel Cox. **Fig. 473** © British Library/Robana via Getty Images. **Fig. 475** © Mary Evans/Peter Higginbotham Collection. **Fig. 476** © Crown copyright. English Heritage. **Fig. 478** © Mary Evans / Peter Higginbotham Collection. **Fig. 479** © Florence Nightingale Museum, London, UK / The Bridgeman Art Library (1871, Sulman, John (1849–1934). **Fig. 480** © By courtesy of The Ritz London. **Fig. 481** © The Francis Frith Collection. **Fig. 484** © Hulton Archive / Getty Images. **Fig. 486** © RIBA Library Photographs Collection. **Fig. 489** © UIG via Getty Images. **Fig. 494** © By courtesy of The Courtauld Institute of Art. **Fig. 498** © Letchworth Garden City Heritage Foundation. **Fig. 500** © Photograph courtesy of Cheshire Life magazine. **Fig. 503** © The Magic Attic Archives. **Fig. 504** © Topfoto. **Figs 505, 507, 508** © Transport for London / Collection of London Transport Museum. **Fig. 506** © Helen McFarland. **Fig. 511** © Hulton Archive/Getty Images **Fig. 512** © Nick Dawe/Arcaid. **Fig. 513** © Paul Riddle/View Pictures. **Fig. 516** © Kevin Feltham , Kibworth Improvement Team. **Fig. 517** © Scarcroft Road School. **Fig. 518** © Andy Chubb. **Fig. 519** Reproduced by kind permission of Royal Holloway, University of London, Egham, Surrey. **Fig. 520** © Dave Brownlow. **Fig. 522** Reproduced by kind permission of Tottenham Hotspur Football Club. **Fig. 523** © Getty Images. **Fig. 527** © The Ronald Grant Archive. **Figs 529, 530** © Mary Evans Picture Library. **Figs 533, 535** © Julian Osley. **Fig. 543** © English Heritage. **Fig. 536** © Private Collection/Look and Learn/Peter Jackson Collection/The Bridgeman Art Library. **Fig. 537** © H Bedford Lemere/English Heritage/Arcaid/Corbis. **Figs 540, 541** © The Marks & Spencer Company Archive. **Fig. 542** © Herbert Felton/Getty Images.

Acknowledgements

This book has taken a long time to write. It owes its genesis to my editor at HarperCollins, Myles Archibald, who first suggested that I should do it. That I even contemplated taking his advice was due to what I have learnt over the last ten years from my colleagues at English Heritage. Every day I have had opportunities to discuss aspects of buildings, often in obscure and microscopic detail. I can't name everyone who has helped and inspired me but I must thank our brilliant listing inspectors who, over a period of nearly five years, elucidated and revealed England's buildings to me on a weekly basis. I must also thank the staff of the English Heritage library who were endlessly patient and helpful with my every obscure request.

I'm really grateful to Gresham College, a wonderful institution which invited me to be Visiting Professor of the Built Environment. My lectures there over the last three years have helped clarify my thoughts.

I am hugely grateful to those who read chapters or parts of chapters and made many helpful comments and corrections. I feel very privileged to have had their expert views: Malcolm Airs, Stephen Brindle, Jonathan Coad, Joe Mourdaunt Crook, Neil Cossons, Peter Draper, Peter Guillery, Edward Impey, Anna Keay, David Stocker and David Watkin. I took most of their advice, but, as usual, the imperfections that remain are mine. I'm also grateful to a number of people who discussed specific issues with me: Roger Bowdler, Wayne Cocroft, Glyn Coppack, Barry Cunliffe, Richard Hewlings, John Humble, Linda Monckton, David Robinson, Andrew Saint, Warwick Rodwell and Treve Rosoman. Karen Jones and Becky Clark were always there in moments of crisis.

In no way would I claim that this book is better written, more deeply researched, or presents a deeper understanding than the many minds, much more brilliant than my own, that have gone before. Like most historians my own personal area of primary research and expertise is relatively limited and so this book is almost entirely based on the researches of other people. Thus the dangers of either misunderstanding or misrepresenting their work or inadvertently plagiarising their words are legion. I beg forgiveness for the places where this has happened.

My wife, Anna Keay, and I, claim to dislike sentimental book dedications. Yet I want to dedicate this work, with all its imperfections, to her, someone who excels at all she does and to whose high standards in everything from scholarship to parenthood I can only aspire.

Acknowledgements

This book has taken a long time to write. It owes its genesis to my editor at HarperCollins, Myles Archibald, who first suggested that I should do it. That I even contemplated taking his advice was due to what I have learnt over the last ten years from my colleagues at English Heritage. Every day I have had opportunities to discuss aspects of buildings, often in obscure and microscopic detail. I can't name everyone who has helped and inspired me but I must thank our brilliant listing inspectors who, over a period of nearly five years, elucidated and revealed England's buildings to me on a weekly basis. I must also thank the staff of the English Heritage library who were endlessly patient and helpful with my every obscure request.

I'm really grateful to Gresham College, a wonderful institution which invited me to be Visiting Professor of the Built Environment. My lectures there over the last three years have helped clarify my thoughts.

I am hugely grateful to those who read chapters or parts of chapters and made many helpful comments and corrections. I feel very privileged to have had their expert views: Malcolm Airs, Stephen Brindle, Jonathan Coad, Joe Mourdaunt Crook, Neil Cossons, Peter Draper, Peter Guillery, Edward Impey, Anna Keay, David Stocker and David Watkin. I took most of their advice, but, as usual, the imperfections that remain are mine. I'm also grateful to a number of people who discussed specific issues with me: Roger Bowdler, Wayne Cocroft, Glyn Coppack, Barry Cunliffe, Richard Hewlings, John Humble, Linda Monckton, David Robinson, Andrew Saint, Warwick Rodwell and Treve Rosoman. Karen Jones and Becky Clark were always there in moments of crisis.

In no way would I claim that this book is better written, more deeply researched, or presents a deeper understanding than the many minds, much more brilliant than my own, that have gone before. Like most historians my own personal area of primary research and expertise is relatively limited and so this book is almost entirely based on the researches of other people. Thus the dangers of either misunderstanding or misrepresenting their work or inadvertently plagiarising their words are legion. I beg forgiveness for the places where this has happened.

My wife, Anna Keay, and I, claim to dislike sentimental book dedications. Yet I want to dedicate this work, with all its imperfections, to her, someone who excels at all she does and to whose high standards in everything from scholarship to parenthood I can only aspire.

of Walpole Old Chapel. **Fig. 362** © Sue Adair m. **Fig. 363** © By courtesy of Chowbent Unitarian Chapel **Fig. 367** © David Carvey - The Magic of Cornwall. **Fig. 371** © Jane Gammie. **Fig. 373** © Country Life. **Fig. 384** © Country Life. **Fig. 385** © Country Life. **Fig. 387** © Heveningham Hall, Suffolk, UK / The Bridgeman Art Library (Taylor, Robert (1714-88)). **Fig. 389** © Philip Halling. **Fig. 393** © City of London / HIP / TopFoto. **Fig. 394** © By courtesy of the Trustees of Sir John Soane's Museum. **Fig. 400** © Danny Robinson. **Fig. 403** © London Metropolitan Archives, City of London / The Bridgeman Art Library (Nash, Joseph (1809-78)). **Fig. 406** © Hulton Archive / Getty Images. **Fig. 408** © SSPL via Getty Images. **Fig. 409** © Noel Walley. **Fig. 410** © SSPL via Getty Images. **Fig. 414** © By courtesy of Thistle – Geoman Hotels. **Fig. 416** © Science and Society / SuperStock. **Fig. 417** © H. N. Twells OBE. **Fig. 420** © Look and Learn / Peter Jackson Collection / The Bridgeman Art Library (English School, 19th century). **Fig. 421** © National Railway Museum / Science & Society Picture. **Fig. 422** © English Heritage. Aerofilms collection. **Fig. 436** © Shutterstock.com. **Fig. 441** © English Heritage Photo Library / The Bridgeman Art Library **Fig. 447** © Shutterstock.com. **Fig. 450** © Nomad /SuperStock m. **Fig. 452** © Look and Learn / The Bridgeman Art Library **Fig. 453** © Victoria and Albert Museum, London / V&A Images – All rights reserved. **Fig. 454** © Bernard Sharp. **Fig. 455** © English Heritage. **Fig. 456** © By courtesy of David Angus – www.east-durham.co.uk. **Fig. 457** © Stephen Richards. **Fig. 459** © Look and Learn / Peter Jackson Collection / The Bridgeman Art Library (English School, 19th century). **Fig. 460** © Look and Learn / Peter Jackson Collection / The Bridgeman Art Library (English School, 19th century). **Fig. 461** © Look and Learn / Peter Jackson Collection / The Bridgeman Art Library (English School, 19th century). **Fig. 463** © J.Hannan-Briggs. **Fig. 466** © Michael Slaughter. **Fig. 472** © Nigel Cox. **Fig. 473** © British Library/Robana via Getty Images. **Fig. 475** © Mary Evans/Peter Higginbotham Collection. **Fig. 476** © Crown copyright. English Heritage. **Fig. 478** © Mary Evans / Peter Higginbotham Collection. **Fig. 479** © Florence Nightingale Museum, London, UK / The Bridgeman Art Library (1871, Sulman, John (1849–1934). **Fig. 480** © By courtesy of The Ritz London. **Fig. 481** © The Francis Frith Collection. **Fig. 484** © Hulton Archive / Getty Images. **Fig. 486** © RIBA Library Photographs Collection. **Fig. 489** © UIG via Getty Images. **Fig. 494** © By courtesy of The Courtauld Institute of Art. **Fig. 498** © Letchworth Garden City Heritage Foundation. **Fig. 500** © Photograph courtesy of Cheshire Life magazine. **Fig. 503** © The Magic Attic Archives. **Fig. 504** © Topfoto. **Figs 505, 507, 508** © Transport for London / Collection of London Transport Museum. **Fig. 506** © Helen McFarland. **Fig. 511** © Hulton Archive/Getty Images **Fig. 512** © Nick Dawe/Arcaid. **Fig. 513** © Paul Riddle/View Pictures. **Fig. 516** © Kevin Feltham , Kibworth Improvement Team. **Fig. 517** © Scarcroft Road School. **Fig. 518** © Andy Chubb. **Fig. 519** Reproduced by kind permission of Royal Holloway, University of London, Egham, Surrey. **Fig. 520** © Dave Brownlow. **Fig. 522** Reproduced by kind permission of Tottenham Hotspur Football Club. **Fig. 523** © Getty Images. **Fig. 527** © The Ronald Grant Archive. **Figs 529, 530** © Mary Evans Picture Library. **Figs 533, 535** © Julian Osley. **Fig. 543** © English Heritage. **Fig. 536** © Private Collection/Look and Learn/Peter Jackson Collection/The Bridgeman Art Library. **Fig. 537** © H Bedford Lemere/English Heritage/Arcaid/Corbis. **Figs 540, 541** © The Marks & Spencer Company Archive. **Fig. 542** © Herbert Felton/Getty Images.